The Human Dimension of Africa's Persistent Economic Crisis

The Human Dimension of Africa's Persistent Economic Crisis

Selected Papers from the United Nations International Conference on the Human Dimension of Africa's Economic Recovery and Development Khartoum, 5–8 March, 1988

Edited by

Adebayo Adedeji
Sadig Rasheed
and Melody Morrison

Published for the
United Nations Economic Commission for Africa

HANS ZELL PUBLISHERS
London • Melbourne • Munich • New York • 1990

Hans Zell Publishers
is an imprint of Bowker-Saur Ltd, a Reed International Books Company.
Borough Green, Sevenoaks, Kent, England TN15 8PH

British Library Cataloguing in Publication Data

United Nations International Conference on the human Dimension of Africa's Economic Recovery and Development (1988: Khartoum)
The human dimension of Africa's persistent economic crisis: selected papers from the United Nations International Conference on the Human Dimension of Africa's Economic Recovery and Development, Khartoum, 5–8 March, 1988.

1. Africa. Economic conditions – Sociological perspectives I. Title II. Adedeji, Adebayo III. Rasheed, Sadig IV. Morrison, Melody V. United Nations Economic Commission for Africa
306.3
ISBN 0–905450–14–0

Library of Congress Cataloging-in-Publication Data

United Nations International Conference on the Human Dimension of Africa's Economic Recovery and Development (1988: Khartoum)
The human dimension of Africa's persistent economic crisis: selected papers / from the United Nations International Conference on the Human Dimension of Africa's Economic Recovery and Development, Khartoum, 5–8, 1988: edited by Adebayo Adedeji, Sadig Rasheed, and Melody Morrison.
412p.
ISBN 0–905450–14–0

1. Africa–Economic policy–Congresses. 2. Human capital–Africa–Congresses. I. Adedeji, Adebayo. II. Rasheed, Sadig. III. Morrison, Melody. IV. United Nations. Economic Commission for Africa. V. Title.
HC800.U57 1988 90–15522
338.96–dc20 CIP

Cover design by Robin Caira

Printed on acid-free paper

Typesetting by
VAP Publishing Services, Kidlington, Oxon, England
Printed in Great Britain by
Antony Rowe Ltd, Chippenham, Wiltshire

Contents

Foreword

ADEBAYO ADEDEJI

One of the adverse consequences of the economic crisis which has ravaged Africa since the late 1970's has been a precipitous deterioration in the conditions of the well being of the majority of Africans and an unjustifiable neglect of the need to effectively develop and utilize human resources for greater productivity. As a consequence, there has emerged in Africa a human crisis as a fallout of the economic crisis.

The *Khartoum Declaration* underlines the dimension of the situation:

> Regretably, over the past decade the human condition of most Africans has deteriorated calamitously. Real incomes of almost all households and families declined sharply. Malnutrition has risen massively, food production has fallen relative to population, the quality and quantity of health and education services have made tens of millions of human beings refugees and displaced persons. In many cases, the slow decline of infant mortality and of death from preventable, epidemic diseases has been reversed. Meanwhile, the unemployment and underemployment situation has worsened markedly

It should not have to be emphasized that the human factor is the ultimate dialectic whereby people are necessarily and immutably both the ultimate beneficiaries and the inevitable mentors of the processes of change. Yet we are still far removed in according centrality to the human dimension and the human factor. In our effort to grapple with the challenge poised by the recovery process and in our anxiety to avert impending economic disasters we have seemed more concerned with the financial viability of an economy and with its balance of payments equilibrium. Worse still, we have shown almost total disregard of the plight of the poor and vulnerable members of our society – women, children and the aged. In fact, our behaviour pattern has been as if growth and development are intrinsically predicated on the prosperity of a few and the misery of many.

The situation has been severely aggravated by the structural adjustment measures that have been pursued, which emphasize short term financial and fiscal adjustment concerns rather than long term balanced development. In many instances such adjustment measures have been implemented at high human costs and sacrifices in terms of depressed levels of investment in human resources and in the satisfaction of human needs. Such neglect for the human dimension is not only counter productive from the point of view of well-being, but is also detrimental to the economic process, the achievement of the objectives of recovery and the establishment of self-sustained and self-reliant long term development.

In 1985, the African governments adopted *Africa's Priority Programme for Economic Recovery*, 1986–1990 (APPER) in which they resolved and committed themselves to reverse the downward trend of social and economic conditions in Africa and to lay a lasting foundation for the long term development of the continent. At their request, a special session of the United Nations General Assembly was convened from 27 May to 1 June 1986 to consider the critical economic situation in Africa. From this Special Session emerged an historic document – the *United Nations Programme of Action for African Economic Recovery and Development 1986–1990* (UN-PAAERD) in which African governments and the international community forged a unique partnership whereby Africa would undertake far-reaching reforms and the international community would support and complement these efforts.

The *Khartoum Conference on the Human Dimension of Africa's Economic Recovery and Development* was organized in March 1988 as a collective UN inter-agency effort, and as part of a planned series of three conferences that would deal with UN-PAAERD and its implementation. It followed the International Conference on *Africa: The Challenge of Economic Recovery and Accelerated Development* which was organized by the Economic Commission for Africa in June 1987 in Abuja Nigeria, in collaboration with the Government of the Federal Republic of Nigeria and with the support of the Organization of African Unity and the African Development Bank. That Conference, which dealt with macro and global issues related to Africa's recovery and development challenges and opportunities, was, in a way, the pace-setter for the other two conferences which have followed it. The Khartoum Conference, some of whose papers are published in this volume, was the second in the series. The third and final conference in the series, held in Arusha, Tanzania, in February 1990, was in a way a follow up for both Abuja and Khartoum, as it was an attempt to operationalise them. Its theme was Popular Participation in the Recovery and Development Process in Africa, and its battle cry was *Putting the People First*.

The UN Inter-Agency Task Force on the Follow-up to the implementation of the UN-PAAERD at the Regional Level assumed responsibility for the organization of the Khartoum Conference and appointed an Inter-Agency Preparatory Committee to have overall responsibility for all aspects related to the convening of the Conference. This Preparatory Committee, which was chaired by the Executive Secretary of ECA, was composed of FAO, IBRD, IFAD, ILO, UNFPA, UNIDO, IMF, UNESCO, UNICEF, UNDP, WHO and ADB. The ECA assumed direct responsibility for the organization of the Conference. The Government of the Republic of the Sudan generously hosted the Conference during the period 5–8 March 1988.

More specifically, the Conference sought to achieve the following objectives:

1. To critically assess the central role that the human dimension plays, both as a means to, and an objective of development, in Africa's efforts towards achieving economic recovery and accelerated self-sustained and self-reliant development.
2. To assess trends in a number of African countries as they relate to human resources development and to the conditions of human well-being and analyse the offsetting actions that are required for a broader and a more human focused approach to adjustment and development.
3. To identify positive examples of sectoral and national as well as regional and sub-regional initiatives taken in Africa in recent years which could serve as models of human development that are worthy of

being built upon.

4. To propose practical measures at the sectoral and national as well as sub-regional, regional and international levels through which the strengthening and further development of human capacities, and the enhancement of conditions of human well-being are made integral parts of national strategies, plans and programmes of socio-economic recovery and development.

The Conference was attended by African ministers and high ranking officials and senior experts from government, UN agencies, representatives of international and regional developmental and financial organizations, donor agencies and governmental and non-governmental organizations, representatives of higher education and research institutions, African and non-African scholars, and the mass media. Participants came from both African and non-African countries. They were over 200 in number.

To prepare the *Khartoum Declaration,* a Drafting Group of 39 prominent experts in the field of socio-economic development – comprising government ministers and high-ranking officials, representatives of agencies of the UN system and international and non-governmental organizations as well as African scholars – was instituted under the chairmanship of the ECA Executive Secretary to initiate the draft and submit it to the Conference for adoption. The Drafting Group drew on the findings, conclusions and recommendations of the plenary as well as the working group sessions to prepare the Khartoum Declaration which mirrors the range of concerns of the Conference and which was adopted by consensus at the concluding session of the Conference.

The Khartoum Conference was a turning point for Africa – and for all those concerned with the continent's development. Over fifty papers which were submitted to the conference, as well as numerous speeches, contributed a wealth of detailed information on the social dimensions of Africa's current crisis. The message which emerged from many of the papers presented was captured succinctly by a metaphor introduced by Professor Reginald Green: "The stark reality", he wrote, "is that the fabric of many African societies – national, regional and local – has been wrent. The cooking pots of millions have been broken." The United Nations publication, *Africa Recovery* accurately described the contributions at the Conferences as follows:

> Just how wide the cracks have become in recent years was a story told from various angles, in these documents prepared by UN agencies, African governments and academics; some told it from a continent wide perspective, others zeroed in on specific country-level problems. Despite the normal lag between the onset of social problems and the time they show up in social indicators – and despite the paucity of such indicators in the first place – some measurement of these cracks did emerge from the documents presented to the Conference. (*Africa Recovery,* June, 1988)

The present volume includes, of necessity only a selection from the more than fifty papers discussed in Khartoum. They are intended to highlight the themes of the conference and the individual sections in the volume follow closely on the thematic organization of the conference. The chapters represent a broad range of opinions, approaches and conclusions which serve to underline both the complexity of the issues and problems facing the African continent and the immense difficulties in tackling these problems. Still, certain common themes emerge from the various chapters. Many authors agree that the concern for the human dimension is not new for Africa: it is just a new name for something Africans believe in deeply. Almost every chapter also points out that Africa's "vulnerable" are not an especially disadvantaged minority, although they may have been considered as such by many structural adjustment programmes to date. The fact is when the vulnerable women, children, aged, disabled, displaced and refugees are added up, they constitute a solid majority of the continent's population. The implications of this reality are explored and analysed in detail by the authors and their message of urgency to deal with these implications is palpable.

Part I of the volume contains two chapters providing an overview of the theme of the Conference. Professor Green places the emphasis and responsibility of recovery programmes on Africans themselves and makes the essential point that the one basic test of all stabilization and structural economic development and recovery programmes is whether they will improve the human condition. Professor Akeredolu-Ale sets out in detail, indicator by indicator, the extent of the effects of the crisis for African people and postulates the reasons for the trends evident from the data he provides.

Part II of the volume contains seven chapters representing a cross section of in-depth studies of the human dimension in recovery programmes at the country level. For example, Professor Ali Abdel Gadir Ali writes passionately of the Sudanese economic difficulties of the period 1978–1985, a time in which he describes the Sudan economy as being for all intents and purposes managed by the IMF in collaboration with the World Bank. The end result of this leadership, he states, was a deepening economic crisis which in turn precipitated declining social welfare and increased human misery. He supports his argument with conventional indicators showing the worsening human situation with health, education, nutrition, per capita incomes, employment statistics and non-conventional indicators including levels of corruption and repression. Ali recommends an alternative adjustment strategy that would be deliberately inward-looking and start by putting the institutional house in order first, and then cleaning the economic landscape from various distortions inherited from the past. He believes that Sudan must rely on its own fundamental values and in mobilizing its own physical, moral and human reserves.

The chapter on Zambia outlines the incredible decline of the country's economy from being one of the most prosperous countries in Africa in the sixties and seventies to being recently reclassified by the World Bank as one of the low-income countries. Professor Tsatsu Tsikata's analysis of how Ghana is tackling its own economic recovery programme provides a more optimistic picture of what is possible and he argues strenuously that African countries must devise these programmes on their own terms and through ardent and coherent negotiating positions force flexibility on the part of the IMF and World Bank.

Part III of the volume focusses on the impact of the crisis on the vulnerable groups in African society. In the first chapter, the authors point out that in spite of the fact that 85 per cent of rural women in Africa are involved in agriculture – producing and processing as much as 80 per cent of family food consumption, they continue to be left out of agricultural strategies. A situation in which the productivity of women continues to be undermined is clearly unacceptable and their conclusions stress the need for fundamental changes in the way agricultural and other policies deal with women in Africa. The ILO notes in the chapter on youth that they remain one of the region's more vulnerable groups. They constitute the new labour force recruits and thus are the first to suffer from rising unemployment and poverty during the periods of recession. The chapter makes a plea for youth employment issues to move into the centre stage of economic policy-making in African countries.

In the chapter on the State of Africa's children, UNICEF minces no words in painting the grim picture of the threat of the economic crisis to the lives of millions of African children and makes the case for the critical need to include social indicators in the design and implementation of adjustment programmes. A final chapter in this section discusses refugees. Africa, with 5 million, is the continent with more refugees than any other. By ignoring their plight, Africa risks losing another crucial resource in the process of developing sustainable economic recovery programmes.

Part IV is devoted to a discussion of structural adjustment measures and the macro human dimension. In chapter fourteen, Professor Sawyerr argues that current IMF/World Bank structural adjustment programmes will not be successful for two reasons. First, they contain no credible strategy for industrialization on the basis of full development and use of local raw materials and skills. Nor do they create the political and social conditions for the effective motivation, mobilization and organization of the whole nation behind the development drive. Second, financial flows on the scale required are unlikely to materialize. He concludes that progress will only occur when there is true democratic discussion within African countries about the real options open to them. Only with the full emancipation of the people can there be effective confrontation with the IMF and the World Bank and the liberation of the productive capacity of the majority of Africans.

The next chapter presents the World Bank's perspective and while acknowledging the human dimension and describing Bank policies to protect the vulnerable argues that without adjustment the situation for the poor would be much worse. It describes specific actions which are being taken to address immediate transitional and long term issues of poverty alleviation in connection with structural adjustment programmes. Specifically, the World Bank, in conjunction with the UNDP and ADB, is working to strengthen the capability of governments to integrate the social dimension in the design of future adjustment programmes. The final chapter in this part is an account of how the IMF is approaching the crisis. Mr Enweze insists that the lack of success of SAPs has more to do with the on-again-off-again nature of African governments' commitments to the Programmes, drought, political upheaval and dwindling external assistance.

In the next part the contributions focus on special social sectors – the effects of structural adjustment in the areas of children's well being, health and nutrition and agriculture. UNICEF makes the case for the development and implementation of social indicators in the important task of monitoring structural adjustment programmes country by country. FAO points out that Africa's rural poor are far less able to cope with structural adjustment measures. Pro poor agricultural policies must include "improved agricultural technologies, adequate producer prices, marketing services and related infrastructure and human resource development that should be spread widely throughout the rural sector". The chapter on health and nutrition continues in the same vein by emphasizing that a healthy population is the essential condition for sustained economic recovery and development.

The chapters composing Part VI concentrate on aspects of manpower development and utilization and creating an enabling environment to stop the unprecedented "brain drain" occurring in Africa. Human resources in Africa today are denied the opportunity to make their full contribution to recovery and development. The economic crisis and stringency of structural adjustment programmes have meant that a growing number of Africa's labour force cannot be engaged in any productive activity and cutbacks in education and health are eroding the skills base in Africa.

The final part of the volume deals with the short, medium and long term support for the human dimension by international and regional organizations, NGO's and the private sector. The first chapter emphasizes the decline in human resources development in much of Africa during the 1980s and argues that this situation may well continue into the 1990s unless national governments and international organizations take special measures to reverse it. Besides keeping Human Resource Development firmly on the policy agenda, the author urges international agencies also to campaign for larger volumes of concessional aid designed to ease the transition crisis as more countries enter a period of structural transformation. In addition, they must be prepared to offer effective technical cooperation in the design, planning and implementation of HRD strategies as part and parcel of the reconstruction programme.

In tackling recommendations for the bilateral donor organizations, Messers Berg and Yu emphasize the importance of coordination but make the very crucial point that African countries must take the lead in the task of coordination themselves. The chapter dealing with non African NGO's provides little direct discussion on the human dimension but instead gives an interesting overview of both the importance of these actors in the development process and insights into the dramatic changes in thinking and approach which are taking place as these organizations struggle to increase their contribution and improve their methods of assistance to their African partners. In the final chapter in the volume, we gain insights into the historic and contemporary reasons for the dismal performance of the private sector in Africa. The author's own reluctance to posit concrete recommendations to improve the situation only serves to highlight the complexity of trying to deal with this particular sector's role in Africa's recovery and transformation process.

The common theme running through almost all chapters of this volume is just how to put people back on the agenda in Africa and indeed is the focus of the Khartoum Declaration itself. The level of agreement and consensus arrived at during the Conference concerning this conclusion is reflected in the recommendations of the *Declaration* itself.

First, the *Declaration* insists that these programmes must be designed, implemented and monitored as part of the long-term framework of Africa's development, and therefore must be compatible with the objectives and aspirations of the African people as outlined in the Lagos Plan of Action and the Final Act of Lagos. Secondly, the human dimension should be the fulcrum of adjustment programmes. Thirdly, structural adjustment policies must incorporate the relevant adjustments of the social sector. Fourthly, the elimination of absolute and relative poverty and of gender biases must become integral parts and factors of adjustment programmes. Finally, if the ultimate objective of economic development is human well being, the entire process of monitoring stabilization and structural adjustment programmes must incorporate social aspects and criteria.

There is no doubt that the Khartoum Conference proved to be a major turning point in the debate concerning structural adjustment programmes. The Declaration was submitted to the United Nations General Assembly during the Midterm Review of UN-PAAERD in September, 1988 and provided a sharp focus to the discussions of just how well the compact forged between Africa and its development partners was working to achieve the goals of recovery and transformation for the continent. Some of the major recommendations found in the Declaration are indeed being implemented. In this regard, one notes the adoption by the ECA Conference of Ministers of the ECA crafted African Alternative Framework to Structural Adjustment Programmes for Socio-Economic Recovery and Transformation (AAF-SAP) and the work of the Inter Agency Task Force on Human Resources Development and Utilization in Africa, the latter a direct result of recommendations in the Declaration.

It is one of the tragedies of our time that it is more often than not forgotten that the business of economic recovery and development must be for the people and by the people. In the African context, recovery and development must derive from the premise that the African peoples are not to be alienated from the processes of adjustment and transformation. Rather, that all the peoples – of whatever category – should benefit, in just measure, from the ongoing processes of change while at the same time contributing fully to the processes themselves. This approach must, as of necessity, take into account the political and cultural realities as well as the characteristics and changing nature of the needs and aspirations of the people.

People matter. As the Declaration states "since the human being is the centre of all development, the human condition is the only final measure of development". It is my hope that the advocacy of, argument for and commitment to this fundamental principle found in the contributions to this volume and the Khartoum conference itself will serve to enlighten, inform and ultimately persuade those involved in the exceptional challenges of making Africa's transformation a reality of the centrality of people in everything we do.

Notes on the Editors and Contributors

Editors

Adebayo Adedeji is Under-Secretary General of the United Nations and Executive Secretary of the Economic Commission for Africa (ECA)

Sadig Rasheed is Chief Public Administrator Human Resource and Social Development Division of ECA

Melody Morrison is Programme Officer, ECA

Contributors

E.O. Akerdolu-Ale is Research Professor of Social Policy at the Nigerian Institute for Social and Economic Research (NISER) Ibadan, Nigeria

Ali Abdel Gadir Ali is Professor of Economics, University of Gezira, Republic of the Sudan

Pepe Andriomanana is Professor of Economics University of Madagascar, Madagascar

Robert Berg is Senior Research Fellow, Overseas Research Council, Washington D.C., USA

Beverley A. Carson is Senior Project Officer, Food and Nutrition Surveillance, UNICEF

Cyril Enweze is Division Chief, North West African Division, International Monetary Fund, Washington D.C., USA

Fred Fluitman is Programme Development Officer, Training Department, ILO, Geneva, Switzerland

Oladapo Fafowora is Executive Director of Manufacturers Association of Nigeria, Lagos, Nigeria

Reginald Herbold Green is Professor of Economics at the Institute of Development Studies, University of Sussex, Brighton, United Kingdom

Crispin Grey-Johnson is Economic Affairs Officer at ECA

G.K. Ikiara is Senior Lecturer, Department of Economics, University of Nairobi, Kenya

Kenneth King is Director and Deputy Assistant Administrator, Policy Coordination and Programmes, UNDP, New York, USA

Anthony Kozlowski is Executive Director of International Council of Voluntary Agencies (ICVA), Geneva, Switzerland

Teshome Mulat is Professor of Economics and Director of the Institute of Development Studies, Addis Ababa University, Addis Ababa, Ethiopia

Lamine N'Diaye is Chief of the African Division, UNFPA, New York, USA

Akilagpa Sawyerr is Vice Chancellor of the University of Ghana, Legon, Ghana

Ismail Serageldin is Director, Occidental and Central Africa Department, World Bank, Washington D.C., USA

Venkatash Seshamani is Professor of Economics, University of Zambia, Zambia

Edward Tapsoba is Senior Economist with FAO, Rome, Italy

Tsatsu Tsikata is Senior Lecturer, University of Accra and Adviser to the Provisional National Defence Council, Accra, Ghana

Joe U. Umo is Professor of Economics, Lagos University, Lagos, Nigeria

Alan K.L. Yu is Professor, Graduate School of Public Policy, University of California, Berkeley, California, USA

List of Abbreviations

AAF-SAP	African Alternative Framework to Structural Adjustment Programmes for Socio-Economic Recovery and Transformation
ADB	African Development Bank
APPER	Africa's Priority Programme for Economic Recovery, 1986–1990
ATRCW	African Training and Research Centre for Women
CGs	Consultative Groups organized under the aegis of World Bank
DAC	Development Assistance Committee of the OECD
EEC	European Economic Community
ECA	UN Economic Commission for Africa
ECOWAS	Economic Community of West African States
FAO	Food and Agriculture Organization
FAL	Final Act of Lagos
GDP	Gross Domestic Product
GNP	Gross National Product
IBRD	International Bank for Reconstruction and Development (World Bank)
ICVA	International Council of Voluntary Agencies
IGOs	Inter-Governmental Organizations
ILO	International Labour Organization
IMF	International Monetary Fund (Fund)
LDCs	Least Developed Countries
LPA	Lagos Plan of Action
NICs	Newly Industrializing Countries
NGO	Non-Governmental Organization
OAU	Organization of African Unity
ODA	Official Development Assistance
OECD	Organization for Economic Co-operation and Development
RTs	Round Tables organized under the aegis of UNDP
SADCC	Southern Africa Development Co-ordination Conference
SAF	Structural Adjustment Facility
SAP	Structural Adjustment Programme
TNCs	Trans-National Corporations
UN	United Nations
UNCTAD	United Nations Conference on Trade and Development
UNDP	United Nations Development Programme
UNICEF	United Nations Children's Fund
UNFPA	United Nations Population Fund
UNIDO	United Nations Industrial Development Organization

UNHCR	United Nations High Commissioner for Refugees
UN-PAAERD	United Nations Programme of Action for Africa's Economic Recovery and Development, 1986–1990
USAID	United States Agency for International Development
WFP	World Food Programme
WHO	World Health Organization

Acknowledgements

The editors wish to express their gratitude to the many people who were involved in this project from the beginning. Those who organized and participated in the International Conference on the Human Dimension of Africa's Economic Recovery and Development (Khartoum, Sudan), the authors of the learned papers, a selection of which composes this volume and the people and Government of the Republic of Sudan who hosted the Conference all contributed their energies and commitment to its success. The preparation of this volume would not have been possible without the unstinting efforts on the part of Ms Yeshimebet Araya and Ms Asnaketch Megersa to type the many revisions of the manuscript. To them and other dedicated members of the ECA staff who assisted we extend a special thanks.

The Human Dimension as the Test of and a Means of Achieving Africa's Economic Recovery and Development: Reweaving the Social Fabric, Restoring the Broken Pot

REGINALD HERBOLD GREEN

The human condition – the social fabric of people's lives, the state of their cooking pots – is the ultimate test of development. It is also among the vital means to achieving it. The malnourished, the sick, the illiterate and those worn out carrying wood and water cannot work long, hard or very productively. To waste much of Africa's basic economic factor of production,the work of its women and men, by allowing them to remain locked in vulnerability and poverty is not just a human and social failure; it is also gross economic inefficiency.

The stark reality of what is happening today is summed up in a 1985 UNICEF poster of a young African girl. "What do you want to be when you grow up?" "Alive". For millions of our infants and young children over the past decade it is a plea which has gone unanswered. They are prematurely dead.

The average human condition of our fellow Africans is appalling and it is getting worse. These facts are statistically known: for infant mortality and life expectancy, for malnutrition and food supplies, for access to pure water and sanitation, for illiteracy and access to education, for income per household and environmental degradation. The fabric of many African societies, national, regional and local, has been wrent. The cooking pots of millions have been broken. To pretend otherwise is to deceive ourselves and to betray the poor and vulnerable people: the women, the children, the displaced victims of drought and war, the poor peasants and the equally poor urban slum dwellers.

Objectives and Means: People as Actors

No nation can be great and prosperous if the majority of its people are poor and miserable. Those words of Adam Smith set out a central truth which many of his disciples now preaching sermons in Africa and at Africans would do well to ponder and to use as a test of their own proposals.

The human condition of individual people, of families, of communities and of societies is, as Mwalimu Julius Nyerere put it, the only ultimate objective, justification and validation of development. Human beings are ends not objects, actors not things to be manipulated. Of course, increased command over material resources (gross domestic product, to use macro-economic terminology) matters for a nation as well as a household. Food and health, education and water sanitation and environmental protection all require real resources. Balancing income and expenditure - closing external and fiscal imbalances – matter nationally as well as individually. Crushing debt and demeaning begging damage the human condition. Choices and sacrifices need to be made by States and societies as well as families. The need to provide for tomorrow and the duty to the rising and future generations are central to African thought and society. But these things matter because of what they mean for human beings, especially for poor and vulnerable human beings, not in isolation from, or worse yet, instead of their impact on the human condition.

But if people are actors – participants – then they are also in a basic sense means – means to achieving improvements in their human condition through economic recovery and development. Labour and land are two of the three basic factors of economic production. From work applied to natural resources the third, capital, can be won – created and embodied in productive assets such as hospitals, health posts, factories, houses, shops, schools and mines. But the poverty, malnutrition and inadequate access to education of a majority of the people of Africa increasingly weakens their ability to work long, hard and productively. Their poverty forces them to abuse and destroy the land so the bone white of ruined, dead and dying land creeps wider across earth satellite pictures like a destroying cancer. By rending the fabric of society, growing immiserization is equally breaking the cycles of production, of reproduction and of surplus generation.

To regard nutrition, health services and education as the fruits of development to be deferred until after high production, is self-defeating. Only the well-nourished, healthy and literate can consistently and increasingly be efficient, productive workers. To see access to pure water, reduction of women's work-load and child survival as goals for after economic recovery is to ensure that there will be, at best, delayed and stunted recovery. Women worn out from carrying water for miles, tending sick children and bearing replacements for those prematurely dead are not merely denied their rights as human beings but drained of the time and energy to be more productive.

Similarly, to restore and to expand output requires the fuller participation in production of the poor, not their exclusion from it. To provide tractors and large irrigated farms for the few and to ignore matchets and jembes (cutlasses and hoes) and improved seeds for the many is economic madness. Not only will it not solve malnutrition (the poor will have no means to buy food); it will not even restore a viable trend rate of growth of agricultural output.

Of course there is a need for balance. Production matters. It requires exports as well as textbooks; lorries as well as basic drugs; efficient factories as well as (indeed to produce) jembes and matchets; and taxes as well as protected wells. The point is not to argue for basic services instead of production or production by the poor instead of by the not so poor. It is to point out that most present stabilization and adjustment plans do the reverse: they fail to recognize the vital role of basic services and of production by the poor without which recovery will be limited and development (even in narrowly economistic terms) virtually unattainable.

Stabilization, Adjustment and the Human Condition

Economic malaise, crisis and decline have weighed most heavily on poor and vulnerable people. There are several reasons for this, none of which is surprising, but, equally, none is inevitable.

When government resources are reduced, provision of basic services and maintenance of infrastructure are cut back. They are usually cut back from the periphery – the feeder roads first, the capital city highways last. When health services face resource crises usually rural health posts and clinics are hit first and central reference hospitals last. It is to the credit of some African States, medical services and communities (and their external co-operating partners) that there are exceptions to that pattern. In some cases the basic rural and low income urban health services have largely been sustained or even, in some respects, strengthened. In general, however, the greater the distance, (geographic, social, economic or political) from the centres of power, the greater are the cutbacks.

Similarly, when production falters it is the vulnerable who lose their employment, see the product of their self-employment fall, have their entitlement (income) to food torn away. They do not have the resources to ride out a crisis nor the flexibility to adjust to new ways of earning a decent livelihood. Most have indeed adapted but millions could not. The infants, children and victims of drought and war have died. For the poor and vulnerable people of Africa death is very close; their margins above survival are often very narrow. As the proverb says – give a rich man less food and he will grow thin; give a poor man less food and he will die.

The crisis of falling export earnings and import capacity, of eroding government revenues and inflationary deficits, of inefficient policies and under utilized capacity are very real. But they are not more real nor more important than the crisis of rising numbers living in absolute poverty, rising infant mortality, the re-emergence of killer diseases like yaws and yellow fever virtually eliminated by the end of the 1950s, school systems near collapse and peasants without tools or seeds. Indeed, they are part of the same human and economic crisis.

Therefore, one basic test of all stabilization and structural adjustment, of all economic recovery and development programmes is whether they will improve the human condition – make poor people less poor and vulnerable people less vulnerable by making it possible for them to produce more and by increasing their access to basic services. If a programme cannot pass that test in prospect or in operation, it is fatally flawed and itself in need of structural adjustment or total redesign.

This test is stronger than that sometimes proposed to determine whether stabilization and adjustment programmes are the basic cause of poverty (of course they are not) or whether they address the problems of poor and vulnerable people directly injured by some of their components (important but inadequate). It is also a test of present, short-term as well as future long-term results. Human condition recovery must go step by step with production recovery or neither is likely to be efficient or sustainable.

Because the plight of the poor and vulnerable is the most desperate and urgent, it is useful to indicate more specifically who these people are. Most fall into seven groups:

(a) victims of prolonged drought and/or ecological degradation whose previous sources of income have been wiped out;

(b) poor (often female-headed) households pushed by land shortages onto marginal or sub-marginal land – the pioneers and victims of the "rural sponge" effect which has, to date, limited the rise of open unemployment;

(c) households in isolated or peripheral (to main centres) areas who are physically and institutionally at the end of the line for all goods and services (whether public or private sector) and usually suffer first and most severely from decreased flows;

(d) small producers, primarily engaged in self-provisioning but also selling food (even when they have a nutritional deficit, because it is their basic cash income source) who are unable to increase or even sustain output in the face of declining access to inputs and static relevant technological knowledge;

(e) victims of war dislocated, like those of drought, with loss of access to health, education and water as well as land, herds, homes, tools, seeds and foodstocks and plunged into a context of physical insecurity as government resources and physical capabilities are debilitated by war bills and destruction;

(f) "informal" urban sector members whose numbers have risen even as the incomes of the formal sector they served and supplemented fell and whose slum or exurb areas have become ever more crowded and ever less well provided with basic services;

(g) urban wage earners, formerly above the absolute poverty line, whose real wages have plunged so sharply that they and other household members have had to add on "informal" sector economic activities to limit the vertiginous fall in their living standards, indeed, in many cases, to survive at all.

How Did we Get Here?

How the economies of most African States and the human condition of most African people came to be as debilitated as they are today matters. It matters not primarily to win debates or to apportion blame but to understand how to win clear,recognize our mistakes and avoid repeating them.

The radical, general worsening of the situation dates to 1980. After very low growth over the years 1970–1975, most African States made fairly rapid economic progress from 1976 to 1979 and human condition indicators showed some, even if limited and unequally distributed, advances. Since then most of Africa's economies have been on a declining path in terms of per capita output while poverty and vulnerability have been growing. Why?

One major reason, probably the dominant one so far as output per capita declines in the majority of African States are concerned, is the 1979–1987 evolution of the international economic environment confronting Africa. The 1979–1982 recession and slow 1983–1987 recovery in the industrial economies have had a disastrous impact on Africa's exports valued in terms of import capacity. Over 1976–1981 a World Bank study showed several African economies eg., Cote d'Ivoire and the United Republic of Tanzania among the worst affected. The real values of many primary products (import purchasing power per unit exported) are at 50-year lows and the recent slight recovery in metals and virtually all projections give little promise of significant change. At the same time, protectionism and industrial economy dumping have hampered export diversification.

The financial flow position has also worsened. Real net concessional finance per capita (grants and new soft loans less interest and repayment on old) declined sharply from the mid-1970s to early 1980s and, at best, have since been stagnant. Non-concessional flows are negative. Africa has a debt burden, relative to exports, greater than that of any other region. Debt payment on present terms is not possible and the attempt to sustain it is dramatically limiting imports, choking off recovery and worsening the human condition. That is not the view of African governments, the African Development Bank, the Economic Commission for Africa and the Organization of African Unity alone. Analyses by the World Bank and the British Chancellor of the Exchequer come to the same conclusion.

Drought, on virtually a continental basis, has exacerbated the already unsatisfactory food production trend. After good years in 1985–1986, 1987 has seen several localized droughts. Until food production levels in normal years, especially by poor peasants, are much higher and vulnerability of output to drought is reduced, this scourge will regularly derail recovery efforts or put them into reverse.

For many African economies the macro-economic and human costs of war are greater than those of any other exogenous shock. Nowhere is this as brutally clear as in southern Africa. Production in Angola and Mozambique (excluding oil) is about half what it would be had South Africa not waged war against them, directly and by proxy. UNICEF's *Children on the Front Line,* details the horror: one million souls are dead as a direct or indirect result of the war, up to 12 million people have been driven from their homes and up to 8 million are in danger of starvation.

Not all causes of the economic and human condition decline are exogenous. African governments have made policy mistakes and have been too slow in responding to the worsening external context. In all candour, however, it should be noted that many of these decisions were taken on external advice and are now being attacked by those who once pushed them. In any event, with the adoption of *Africa's Priority Programme for Economic Recovery,* 1986–1990 (APPER) and the national rehabilitation, recovery and renewed development programmes being undertaken by a majority of African States, there has been substantial improvement on the economic policy front. That again is not the judgement solely of the OAU or ECA; the World Bank and the United Nations General Assembly have said the same.

Nevertheless, these economic policies still do not give adequate attention to the human dimension nor enough priority to improving it; not simply to increase human welfare but also to sustain and accelerate economic growth. That is not a new weakness; it typified most development plans and programmes of the 1960s and 1970s. Then, however, with less constrained resources and a less hostile international economic environment, the old export led, dependent, central city and high-income group focused model was consistent with some improvement in human condition indicators in general and in basic services extension in particular. Today and tomorrow no such compatibility is likely to be within the grasp of most African States. Either the nature and priorities of development will be re-thought and acted upon on new premises or what economic growth there is will march hand-in-hand with rising levels of inequality and poverty, misery and instability.

One concrete example is health. Life expectancy is much lower and mortality much higher in Africa than in the industrial North. The largest single difference is in infant, and under-five mortality which accounts for 30 percent of all deaths in sub-Saharan Africa and 2 to 3 percent in most industrial economies. The main causes are neo-natal tetanus, five epidemic diseases (including measles, tuberculosis and polio), malaria, impure water-related morbidity (including diarrhoea), malnutrition-related diseases and loss of resistance to disease. For older children and adults, malnutrition and impure water-related diseases, malaria, a handful of epidemic diseases and accidents treatable by first aid are the dominant killers. Urban hospital care is largely irrelevant to reducing these death tolls in Africa, but it still accounts for 60 to 70 percent of the typical African health budget. Primary health care (including first aid), basic drug lists and supplies, extended immunization programmes, oral rehydration and simple health education (including sanitation) are of proven low-cost effectiveness. They receive, however, 10 to 15 percent of the majority of African health budgets. The case for rethinking and reallocation seems clear.

What is to be Done?

To will an end is to will a means or a set of means adequate to achieve that end. To make the human condition integral and central to Africa's economic recovery and development requires a comprehensive political and socio-economic strategy encompassing at least eight elements:

(a) recognizing that people matter and are both the subjects and ends of and the main means and actors for attaining stabilization, recovery and renewed development;

(b) understanding that throwing away much of Africa's most basic factor of production – the labour of its people – as many modernization and narrow stabilization strategies do by excluding the poor and vulnerable is economically wasteful and inefficient;

(c) acting on the reality that marginal rates of economic as well as social return from enabling poor people to produce more are often high. The real problem is making small, contextual, poor people-centred projects visible to central decision makers and credible to bureaucrats and analysts, and then altering regulations to be compatible with implementing them;

(d) comprehending that health, education and pure water are not merely human and social goods but are important to maintaining present and raising future economic productivity and to making possible fuller participation in production by women who are the chief victims of illiteracy and on whose backs fall the burden of fetching water and caring for the sick;

(e) focusing on employment and production, not subsidies and relief, eg., through public works programmes to relieve drought or seasonal income losses;

(f) articulating short-term priorities to lay the foundations for long-term sustained development, eg., in applied, field-tested, peasant user friendly, producer cost-effective, agricultural research begun now to make it possible to sustain 5 percent agricultural growth in the late 1990s. Until then input restoration, infrastructural rehabilitation and generalization of best-known farmer or (more rarely) off-the-shelf research techniques can restore 4 to 5 percent output growth, but not beyond;

(g) political as well as economic awareness that participation in production by poor people is crucial to their survival and the improvement of their human condition; and

(h) understanding that strikes and riots, go-slows and loss of morale, steadily growing grinding poverty and recurrent economic disasters without human rehabilitation are devastating in narrow economic as well as social, political and human terms.

The poor and the vulnerable are not amorphous masses; they are groups of human beings. To fail to see what their needs are as perceived by themselves is to exclude them; to suppose their needs and capabilities are uniform is to render many of them invisible. In no case have these errors and blindnesses been as common or as persistent as in regard to women. Most African women are excluded or invisible but also over-burdened and under-assisted. The basic barriers to economic as well as human development posed by the excessive workload most African women bear are rarely recognized. The implications of the gender division of labour in agriculture are yet to be taken account of by agricultural research and extension.

These are central elements in any serious effort to improve the human condition. After all, over half of our people are women and they care for our children and produce most of the food we eat. How to address them is not simple and varies from context to context, but three elements are crucial:

(a) universal access to literacy, basic education, primary health care, pure water, agriculture inputs, and fuel are disproportionately beneficial to women because when access is limited they are disproportionately deprived of them ;

(b) serious attention must be addressed to reducing women's work-load, e.g., by closer water and health facilities, by programmes (e.g., immunization) reducing child illness and by improving technologies relevant to female tasks (e.g., food processing, moving water and fuelwood); and

(c) women should be centrally involved in planning and decision making about projects and programmes which will primarily affect them, e.g., rural water supply and maintenance, sanitation, food crop research and extension.

To will a strategy must lead to addressing questions of method. To cross a river requires a bridge, a raft, a boat, a tunnel or a ford (or perhaps a very good swimmer!). The same is true of economic recovery and development strategies giving central priority to the human dimension. More production is crucial, but in addition more of it must be by poor people. Reduced external and fiscal imbalances are necessary, but priority should go to increasing supply and not cutting uses important to the poor and vulnerable. Bad policies and restrictions inhibiting production and especially poor people organizing to better their own human condition should be eliminated, but not with any false faith in the perfection of markets or universal goodwill of the powerful and rich.

These methods, however, are not enough. Priorities in government expenditure must shift toward universality, e.g., more primary and preventative health care relative to hospitals and more food availability to poor people (through their own production or earning incomes adequate to buy it). This, in turn, requires much more emphasis on increased productive employment. Universal access to basic services allows development of basic survival, disaster period support and rehabilitation mechanisms. Disasters will recur; the question is how to minimize their human damage and to speed the progress of rehabilitation, neither of which national nor (a fortiori) international disaster relief mechanisms have done very well to date. Also vital to the future human condition of poor Africans is action on environmental and ecological protection. Millions are being condemned to life sentences of poverty and to early death by the present pace of environmental degradation and destruction.

These priorities require both production and government spending. Budgetary balance should be restored and sustained primarily by increasing revenue. Domestically, more production can allow more tax revenue and more efficient and progressive tax systems. But in the short run, Africa needs additional external support: additional support that accepts the primacy of African goals, respects the knowledge and judgement of Africans and which can be used to meet African requirements for improving their human condition through their economic recovery and development.

Unless stabilization and structural adjustment as usually defined today are broadened to make the human condition, and especially the human condition of poor people, central and integral, African economic recovery will be stunted and African economic development unsustainable. The challenge of turning around the post 1979 (or earlier for some countries) decline is a heavy one, but it must be accepted. A proverb from the Mara region of the United Republic of Tanzania cited by Mwalimu Julius Nyerere in his opening address to the South Commission is appropriate:

> "Rabbit, where are you going?
> I am going to kill the elephant!
> Can you do it?
> Well, I'll try and try again!"

The Human Situation in Africa Today: A Review

E. O. AKEREDOLU-ALE

For at least three reasons, the subject of this paper is very slippery indeed. First, there can be no general agreement as to which specific concerns, e.g., health, education must be included or excluded when one defines "the human situation" or what relative weight must be attached to each particular concern in the definition. Second, except perhaps for education, the data on most human situation concerns is generally deficient in Africa and, in many cases, unavailable. Third, whichever reasonable definition one may adopt and however narrow that definition may be, even if one had much-improved statistical data, it would still not be possible to state precisely what, in Africa today, is the quality of the human situation and how satisfactory it is.

Be that as it may, however, in defining the scope of the human situation, I have borne in mind the need to adopt a "developmental" conception, i.e., one that captures in full both the quality-of-life (or well-being) and the dynamic instrumental (or human-capacity) dimensions of the human factor in development. I must state, however, that I separate these two dimensions only heuristically and that I do not mean to impose any rigid categorization along this line on any of the concerns that I will consider presently. Of course, any such rigid dichotomy must be misleading since experiences which enhance the quality of life of people, e.g., better housing, better health care or improved nutrition, etc., are most likely to also improve their capacity to function as effective instruments of development.

More specifically, the conception of the human situation adopted here covers the following main concerns;

(a) health,
(b) food and nutrition,
(c) housing and environment,
(d) incomes and individual/household economic status,
(e) social problems situation,
(f) political welfare, human rights and justice, and
(g) human resources development and mobilization.

Concerns (a) to (f) relate more directly to the human-welfare or quality-of-life dimension while (g) relates to the human-capacity dimension of the human situation and of investment in man. However, in reality, the two sets of concerns feed into and determine the human-motivation process as well as the character and level of actual human mobilization. The human situation in Africa today is reviewed in detail below in terms of these main dimensions and concerns. But, first, let us briefly review the general demographic and economic status of Africa which has also played an important part in determining the quality of the human situation on the continent.

Demographic and Economic Background

By most accounts, the principal demographic characteristics of Africa are low population density, high fertility, high but declining mortality rates and high rates of population growth. Africa probably has the fastest growing population of any region in the world increasing at a rate of over 3.0 per cent per year. As a result of high birth rates and relatively short life expectancies, some 45 per cent of the population is under 15 years of age, as compared to 40 per cent for Latin America and 37 per cent for Asia. This youthfulness of the population imposes a heavy burden of job creation and provision of social services as does a high rate of urbanization which is also a significant feature of Africa's contemporary demographic situation.

The circle of those who believe that Africa's present economic and social problems have been due to the continent's rapid population growth is influential and enlarging. But while one must admit that existing resources at any point in time will go round better with a smaller population, this will not necessarily justify the view that Africa's economic and social underdevelopment has been caused by over-population or by the fact that Africa has, in recent times, recorded a higher rate of population growth than other regions.[1]

The economic performance of each country strongly influences that country's human situation, although it would be naive to let this assertion degenerate into a one-way economic determinism. The particular aspects of Africa's economic performance which have a bearing upon the human situation include economic growth rate, level and growth rate of income per capita, external debt obligations, net resource flows and the rate of inflation, among others. All these affect the capacity of each country to implement programmes of human resource development as well as the opportunities available to the average individual for the pursuit of his own welfare and personal development.

GDP and GDP per capita

All available evidence shows that Africa's performance in respect of these two important variables has been poor over the last 10 years. Table 1 below shows that the growth rate of sub-Saharan Africa's GDP which stood at an impressive 6.4 per cent per year during 1965–1973 had declined sharply to 3.2 per cent during 1973–1980 and had dropped further and further to an all-time low of −1.7 per cent per annum in 1984, the year in which many developing countries of Asia and Latin America had resumed some growth. As for the growth of GDP per capita, Africa's performance was poorer still, reflecting the tendency of the region's GDP growth rate to lag behind its population growth rate. The substantial growth recorded during 1965–1973 had diminished drastically during 1973–1980 and become negative (−3.4 per cent per year) in the critical 1980–1986 period. In effect since 1980, GDP per capita in sub-Saharan Africa has fallen by about 16 per cent.

Table 1: GDP, 1980 and growth rate, 1965–1986

Country group	1980 GDP (in billion of $US)	Average annual growth of GDP (in percentage) 1965–1973	1973–1980	1982	1983	1984	1985[a]	1986[a]
Developing countries	2,116	6.5	5.4	2.1	2.1	5.1	4.8	4.2
Low-income countries	564	5.5	4.6	5.6	7.7	8.9	9.1	6.5
Middle-income countries	1,552	7.0	5.7	0.8	0.0	3.6	2.8	3.2
Oil exporters	522	6.9	6.0	0.4	−1.9	2.3	2.2	−1.1
Exporters of manufactures	958	7.4	6.0	4.2	4.9	7.8	7.8	7.0
Highly indebted countries	890	6.9	5.4	−0.5	−3.2	2.0	3.1	2.5
Sub-Saharan Africa[b]	187	6.4	3.2	−0.2	−1.5	−1.7	2.2	0.5
High-income oil exporters	216	8.3	7.9	−0.5	−6.9	1.2	−3.8	–
Industrial market economies	7,570	4.7	2.8	−0.5	2.2	4.6	2.8	2.5

Source: World Bank, *World Development Report 1987*, table A.3.

[a] Preliminary.
[b] Excludes South Africa.

Table 2: Growth of GDP per capita, 1965–1995 (average annual percentage change)

Country group	1965 1973	1973 1980	1980 1986	1986–1995 High	Low
Developing countries	3.9	3.2	1.5	3.9	2.0
Low-income countries	2.9	2.5	5.4	4.8	2.8
Middle-income countries	4.4	3.3	−0.3	3.2	1.4
Oil exporters	4.3	3.2	1.8	1.9	1.1
Exporters of manufactures	4.8	4.1	4.3	5.3	2.7
Highly indebted countries	4.2	2.9	−1.8	3.1	1.2
Sub-Saharan Africa[a]	3.6	0.3	−3.4	0.7	0.0
Industrial economies	3.7	2.1	1.6	3.9	2.0

Source: World Bank, *World Development Report 1987*, p.26

Note: All growth rates for developing countries are based on a sample of 90 countries.

[a] Excluding South Africa.

External debt obligations

At the end of 1984, Africa's total external debt (35 sub-Saharan countries) stood at $US 78.7 billion, $US 6.0 billion (just under 8 per cent) of which was owed to the International Monetary Fund. By the end of 1983, some 25 African countries, under pressures mounted by the creditors and at the urging of the World Bank/IMF coalition, had begun to respond to their economic problems by adopting various short-term economic adjustment and stabilization measures. And by 1986, practically all of them were implementing major programmes of structural reforms or were about to do so. On average, about 27 per cent of total export earnings of African countries concerned went into the servicing of external debt. This debt-service ratio ranged from 2.3 per cent for Djibouti, through 69.8 per cent for Zambia to 84 per cent for Equatorial Guinea and to an impossible 204.6 per cent for Mozambique.

The immediate consequence of economic adjustment measures is summed up in the following passage:

> "The common aim of these measures is to improve the balance of payments, repay debts and reduce inflation. Important national objectives – such as expanding and protecting employment, ensuring a minimum income for households and providing basic public services – have become secondary. Ironically, the result has often been an aggravation of the economic crisis and a parallel human crisis as unemployment rises, incomes of the most vulnerable groups fall, import-dependent industries cut production, public services are curtailed and public discontent and political instability grow."[2]

No one would dispute the decisive part which the structural adjustment programmes have played in creating the present hardships in most affected African countries. However, it is important that we avoid the grievous error of attributing Africa's prevailing economic and social predicament simply to the present rash of so-called adjustment programmes, as such an error could divert attention away from more fundamental causes of our problem.

Net resource flows

The substantial decline in the volume of resource flows (net) into Africa during the 1980–1984 period shows clearly in table 3 below. Significantly also, the terms of borrowing have become stiffer, especially as concessional loans have become harder and harder to obtain. (See table 4 below).

Table 3: Africa: Net resource flows, 1980–1984

	1980	1981	1982	1983	1984
Indian Ocean Countries	885.5	722.9	475.0	370.2	393.2
East Africa	3,374.2	3,485.0	2,934.0	2,608.8	2,906.2
Southern African States	2,510.6	3,093.3	2,876.0	1,697.8	1,657.0
Central Africa	1,175.8	1,290.1	985.6	1,246.6	89.2
Sahel	2,675.5	1,982.1	1,548.9	1,827.4	1,446.3
Non-Sahel West Africa	4,637.0	4,149.3	7,060.7	5,302.8	2,619.2
North Africa	4,262.5	4,128.6	3,729.6	4,733.2	4,013.3
Total	19,521.7	18,651.3	19,618.8	17,787.3	12,948.6

Source: Extracted from OAU/ECA *Africa's submission to the special session of the United Nations General Assembly on Africa's economic and social crisis*, 1986, pp.183–184.

Table 4: Africa: Structure of outstanding debt (disbursed only) 1970–1983 (in billions of $US)

	1970	1975	1977	1979	1981	1983
Total	9,143.7	25,844.6	42,948.2	68,974.0	81,647.0	96,917.8
%	(100.0)	(100.0)	(100.0)	(100.0)	(100.0)	(100.0)
Concessional	4,719.1	12,405.9	18,872.7	25,860.6	32,409.8	36,751.1
%	(51.6)	(48.0)	(43.9)	(37.5)	(39.7)	(37.9)
Non-concessional	4,424.6	13,438.7	24,075.5	42,113.4	49,237.2	60,166.7
%	(48.4)	(52.0)	(56.1)	(62.5)	(60.5)	(62.0)

Source: *World Bank Debt Tables*, 1984–1985 edition.

Rate of inflation

The average annual rate of inflation for sub-Saharan Africa has been estimated by the World Bank at 12.7 per cent for 1965–1980 and 16.7 per cent for 1980–1985. Some of the countries which have had particularly high inflation rates during 1980–1985 are Sierra Leone (25.0 per cent), Mozambique (25.8 per cent), the Sudan (31.7 per cent), Somalia (45.4 per cent), Zaire (55.3 per cent) and Ghana (57.0 per cent). (See World Development Report 1987). This rate of inflation has, no doubt, implied a substantial decline in the standard of living of the populations concerned generally but of the more vulnerable groups in particular.

What the foregoing brief review of the economic situation in the period since about 1980 suggests is that one long quarter century of formal political independence and of so-called development planning and, even more specifically, the last one decade has only brought most African countries into critical material shortages and deprivations (even of basic necessities, including food), into crippling foreign debts, into a rapid decline in the standard of living of the vast majority of the people and, overall, into a situation presaging real economic and social catastrophe. The period since 1977 has been a particularly difficult one for Africa as the effects of prevalent inefficiencies were compounded by those of inclement climatic conditions, most especially by prolonged drought which incapacitated large portions of the continent, especially in the Sahel, and gave rise to the famine which ravaged many countries and placed Africa at the mercy of the international community.

The Human Situation in Africa Today

The various human-situation problems which have been exacerbated by the recent heightening of Africa's economic problems (especially by Africa's economic crisis of the 1980s) are well known. The rest of this section, will further describe these conditions and identify any general trends which they may imply while, in the next two sections, respectively, possible explanations of the situation and of the trends will be explored and some ideas will be put forward towards improving the situation.

(a) Specific human-situation concerns

(i) *Health*

As a recent assessment under the World Health Organization's Health for All By the Year 2000 Programme found, the general health situation in Africa, especially real access to many health services, has not improved significantly. Table 5 below shows that, for the selected African countries concerned, the population: physician ratio improved only marginally between 1974 and 1981, by which latter date it still stood at about 23,000 persons per physician.

But even if a region or a particular country had attained the WHO 12,000 physician recommendation, that would not necessarily imply adequate health-care services unless corresponding improvements had also taken place in the supply of necessary equipment and drugs and in the deployment of available health personnel. And this is where the economic crisis comes in.

In practically all African countries, inadequate funding (due, in part, to

Table 5: Africa: Health and health-related indicators, selected countries, 1960–1986

		Life expectancy at birth			Population per physician			Population per nurse			Infant mortality rate (IMR)		
		1960	1975	1985	1965	1974	1981	1965	1974	1981	1960	1965	1985
I(A)	*Low income (general)*												
1.	Benin	35	41	45	32,390	36,060	17,000	2,540	3,220	1,660	185	166	115
2.	Burundi	42	39	48	56,320	45,990	–	7,310	7,090	990	152	142	119
3.	Kenya	42	50	54	12,820	5,800	10,140	1,860	1,300	–	124	112	76
4.	Mozambique	40	44	46	17,990	16,680	37,000	5,370	–	5,610	174	171	147
5.	Sierra Leone	30	44	35	17,700	–	19,300	4,700	–	2,110	225	220	175
6.	Somalia	36	40	41	33,900	15,560	17,500	3,630	–	2,550	175	165	152
7.	Tanzania	41	45	52	21,700	20,800	–	2,100	3,180	–	146	138	111
8.	Zaire	42	44	51	35,100	27,950	–	–	11,770	–	148	135	103
Total I (A)		39	43	46	28,490	28,140	20,188	3,930	5,312	2,584	166	156	125
I(B)	*Low income (specially disadvantaged)*												
9.	Burkina Faso	35	38	46	74,100	59,570	55,860	4,170	4,520	3,070	220	193	145
10.	Chad	35	39	46	72,440	44,370	–	13,620	6,990	–	195	183	138
11.	Ethiopia	36	38	41	70,190	69,340	88,120	5,920	–	5,000	175	165	152
12.	Mali	35	38	43	49,200	33,000	26,450	3,200	2,480	2,320	210	200	175
Total I(B)		35	38	44	66,482	51,570	56,810	6,740	4,663	3,463	200	185	152
Total I(A) + I(B)		37	40	45	47,486	39,855	38,499	5,335	4,987	3,023	183	171	139
II	*Middle income*												
13.	Cameroon	40	41	52	–	–	–	1,970	2,270	–	163	143	99
14.	Egypt	46	52	59	2,300	2,300	760	2,030	4,420	790	179	172	93
15.	Cote d'Ivoire	39	44	52	19,080	15,270	–	1,850	2,220	–	200	174	105
16.	Liberia	40	44	50	12,400	11,500	9,400	2,300	4,500	2,940	180	171	127
17.	Nigeria	40	41	50	44,230	25,440	12,000	5,780	6,230	2,420	190	177	110
18.	Zambia	42	45	52	11,400	8,110	7,800	5,820	2,430	1,660	135	121	84
19.	Zimbabwe	42	45	57	18,000	15,700	7,100	990	–	1,000	110	103	76
Total II		42	45	53	16,235	11,393	7,412	2,962	3,678	1,762	165	151	199
Total I + II		39	43	49	31,860	25,624	22,955	4,148	4,332	2,393	174	161	119

Source: Compiled from UNICEF, *The State of the World's Children 1987* and World Bank, *World Development Report*, (1978 and 1987).

economic adjustment measures) has become a critical factor impeding the implementation of national health-for-all strategies, the situation being far more serious in the more heavily indebted countries. The health needs of low-income groups, notably the rural and urban poor, which are barely touched by the health sector of most African countries even in normal times, have been further neglected under the present economic crisis. There has been a worsening of the access problem during the period since 1977 as a result of the all-round squeeze on the health budget (budget cutbacks, reintroduction of various kinds of cost-recovery charges, substantial increase in the prices of drugs, etc.). These developments have tended to place available health-care facilities beyond the reach of the most vulnerable groups in society (the poor in general, rural populations, children, women, refugees, etc.)

The poor health facility situation is also, at least to some extent, reflected in the unsatisfactory health status of the population and of particular groups, judging by a number of sensitive indicators, namely life expectancy at birth, infant mortality rate (IMR), and maternal mortality. Concerning life expectancy, WHO reports that this has risen to 60 years or more in 98 countries, representing 62 per cent of the world population. But in the African region, life expectancy at birth is still below 50 years in a majority of countries.[3]

With regard to infant mortality rate (IMR), available data (see table 6 below) shows clearly that IMR remains much higher in Africa than anywhere else. For instance, going by the data in table 6, most of the countries in the world with IMR greater than 100 per cent per 1,000 live births (in fact, 68 per cent of such countries) are in the African region. It also shows that 32 of the 44 African countries included in the survey (i.e., 73 per cent of the African countries concerned) fall in the category of countries with IMR of 100 or higher. The corresponding figures for the Americas, SouthEast Asia and Europe are 9, 36 and 0 per cent respectively. Maternal mortality rate, another sensitive indicator of the health status of a country/region, also remains unnecessarily high in the African region, being as high as 10 per 1,000 live births in many African countries. Table 7 presents a picture of the situation as at 1982 and confirms that the situation in Africa in this respect is much worse than that in the developing countries of Asia (even South Asia), Latin America and Oceania.

Table 6: Infant mortality rate per 1000 live births, by WHO region

Rate (per 100) live births	Number of countries						
	Africa	Americas	S.E.Asia	Europe	Eastern Mediterranean	Western Pacific	Total
Below 50	2	24	4	30	7	13	80
50.0–99.9	9	7	3	2	8	3	32
100 and more	32	3	4	–	7	1	47
Sub-total	43	34	11	32	22	17	159
No information	1	–	–	3	–	3	7
Total	44	34	11	35	22	20	166

Source: WHO, *Evaluation of the strategy for health for all by the year 2000: Seventh report on the world health situation*, Vol.1, Global review, 1987, table 20, p.73.

Table 7: Live births and maternity mortality rates by United Nations regions

Region	Live births (1982) (in '000s)	National maternal mortality (per 100,000 live births) Lowest	Highest
Africa	23,100	108	1,100
Asia (South)	51,700	5	1,000
(East)	23,200	8	100
North America	4,400	6	10
Latin America	12,500	8	470
Europe + USSR	12,000	2	140
Oceania	500	14	900
World	127,400	2	1,100

Source: WHO, 1987, table 22, p.75.

Finally, an uncomfortably high percentage of Africans continue to succumb to diseases which, in other places, especially in the materially more advanced countries, have been overcome through improvements in environmental and living conditions and specific preventive actions. Most notable among such diseases are infectious and parasitic ailments, including certain respiratory diseases such as influenza, pneumonia, bronchitis, emphysema and asthma. According to one assessment, there has been "a startling increase" in the incidence of vector-borne diseases (mainly "tropical diseases" such as malaria, trypanosomiasis, schistosomiasis and onchocerciasis) over the last decade.

As for the factors to which we can attribute the unsatisfactory developments regarding the health situation in the last 10 years, the resource problems associated with the various structural adjustment programmes stand out clearly, at least in the sense that they have seriously affected the efforts of many African countries to improve their health-care services during this period, i.e., those who were inclined to do so in the context of the WHO global strategy. The second half of the 1977–1986 period has been particularly difficult as, in many countries, the health sector has experienced substantial cuts in available resources and funding, as part of the general austerity programme whose primary purpose is to release resources for the servicing of external debts.

In addition, however, it is also necessary to consider the long-standing policy orientations towards the health sector in different countries as well as the important influence which many factors located outside the sector unavoidably have over the processes which determine the quality of the health situation. With particular reference to such inter-sectoral factors, it should be noted that health care, even where it is available at a reasonably adequate level, normally alleviates only the symptoms of any given situation of endemic poor health. In the final analysis and for a lasting and stable improvement, it is the roots of that situation, namely widespread poverty, malnutrition and unsanitary living conditions, that must be attacked. And that raises the social question of equity (versus efficiency?) in the way that African countries distribute available national resources among various groups, including the weaker groups in society; it also raises the more practical question of the integration of health and other socio-economic policies and programmes in the planning process of each country.

(ii) *Food and nutrition*

In 1975, food production in sub-Saharan Africa fell below 140 kg of cereals per capita per year, considered by FAO as the minimum for a healthy diet. Production was estimated to have fallen by about 25 per cent during the 1970s and, as a result of the disastrous crop failures of 1983 and 1984, production in 1984 stood below 100 kg per capita. As shown in table 8 food production per capita for the 19 countries covered fell by 9 per cent between 1976 and 1982/1984, even when Burundi, the United Republic of Tanzania, Ethiopia and Mali are reported to have maintained their 1976 level of food production in the 1982/1984 period. It should be noted that poor performance of the agricultural sector and declining food production had been features of many African countries even without the drought. In fact, according to some projections based on performance during the 1970s, production would

Table 8: Africa: Food production, daily calorie supply and child malnutrition, selected countries, early 1980s

	Child malnutrition		Average index of food prod. per capita 1976 = 100	Daily calorie supply per capita	
	% infants with low birth weight	% children suffering from moderate/severe malnutrition			
	1982–1983	1980–1984	1982–1984	1965	1985*
I(A) *Low income (general)*					
1. Benin	10	–	97	2,008	2,173
2. Burundi	14	30/5	106	2,391	2,116
3. Kenya	13	30/2	82	2,287	2,151
4. Mozambique	16	–	73	1,982	1,678
5. Sierra Leone	14	24/3	95	1,836	1,817
6. Somalia	–	16/–	69	2,145	2,072
7. Tanzania	14	43/7	100	1,970	2,335
8. Zaire	8	–	92	2,188	2,154
Total I (A)	13	27/4	89	2,100	2,062
I(B) *Low income (specially disadvantaged)*					
9. Burkina Faso	21	–	94	2,009	1,924
10. Chad	11	–	95	2,393	1,504
11. Ethiopia	13	60/10	100	1,832	1,681
12. Mali	13	–	101	1,860	1,788
Total I(B)	15	60/10	97	2,023	1,724
Total I(A) + I(B)	14	43/7	93	2,061	1,893
II *Middle income*					
13. Cameroon	13	–	83	2,043	2,089
14. Egypt	7	46/1	91	2,435	3,263
15. Cote d'Ivoire	14	–	110	2,357	2,505
16. Liberia	–	17/2	91	2,155	2,311
17. Nigeria	25	–	96	2,185	2,038
18. Zambia	2	–	74	2,073	2,137
19. Zimbabwe	15	–	69	2,089	2,054
Total II	13	32.2	88	2,191	2,342
Total I + II	14	38/5	91	2,126	2,117

Source: UNICEF, *The State of the World's Children 1987*. Data on calorie supply from *World Development Report*, 1987.

* Corresponding 1985 figures for all low-income, all middle-income, industrial market economic were 2,339; 2,731; 3,417 repectively. For China, the figure was 2,602.

probably have declined to the 100-kg level by 1988 anyway.[4]

The nutritional status of most African countries has worsened significantly, especially under the prevailing regime of economic adjustment and austerity. And the deficiencies have tended to be particularly serious among children under 5 and, curiously enough, among the rural populations who produce the domestic component of the national food supply. For the selected countries of this paper, for instance, as many as 14 per cent of the children born in 1982–1983 were below normal weight (2.5 kg) at birth, ranging from 13 per cent for the middle- and low-income categories to 15 per cent for the specially disadvantaged low-income countries (see table 8). And, on the average, some 38 per cent of under-5 children were estimated to be suffering from moderate malnutrition and 5 per cent from severe malnutrition being much worse in the specially disadvantaged countries.

Concerning the rural populations, seasonal malnutrition seems to be the main problem and remains quite severe in most agricultural communities in Africa. It is due principally to the almost total dependency of such communities on their own local food production, the lack of storage facilities, their low purchasing power and their need for cash. And here we have a vicious circle in which, as one account puts it, "the combination of seasonal fluctuations in local production and recurring poor harvests diminishes the capacity of the undernourished groups to acquire the resources and skills needed to transform local production possibilities"[5] a situation in which deficiencies in diet and recurrent food production short-falls mutually aggravate each other and limit opportunities for improving the people's living conditions.

Africa's 1985 food crisis was indeed a human tragedy because of the untold misery, suffering and unnecessary deaths to which hundreds of thousands of our people, most especially children, were exposed. But in our view, the real disaster was the fact that, for various reasons, African countries not directly affected by the drought nevertheless lacked the capacity to bail out the affected countries through food transfers or even to play a prominent role in the salvage exercise. Of course, the inability of other African countries to respond to this food-security challenge could be attributed to the timing of this particular emergency, i.e., to the general resource problems which most African countries faced about that time and which they still face today.

It would be even more realistic, however, to consider more deep-seated factors, e.g., the poor organization and chronically poor performance of the agricultural sector in most African countries; the absence of food-security policies at national and regional levels; the prevalence of economic orientations and policies which tend to undermine the struggle for self-reliance; the prevailing undemocratic structure of income distribution, etc. In fact, Africa's persistent food-supply and nutrition problems must be attributed more to prolonged bad government in many countries than to prolonged drought in the Sahel.

No doubt, short-term measures are necessary to ensure rapid improvement in the present food-supply and nutrition situation of the food-short countries in Africa and in the nutritional status of the most vulnerable groups in all African countries, notably, under-5 children, rural populations and the urban poor. But such short-term measures must be developed as part of a medium-/long-term package of measures addressed to the structural foundations of the situation.

(iii) *Housing and environment*

Africa's housing problems have become increasingly serious over the last two-and-a-half decades due to the following factors:

(a) Decline in public housing development programmes;
(b) Escalation of the cost of housing construction (due mainly to inflation and to continuing dependence on imported building materials);
(c) Sharp increase in the interest rates attached to mortgage loans;
(d) Drastic reduction in the volume of available building loans and the exclusion of the vast majority of households from such loans;
(e) Drastic reduction in the real purchasing power of most households, both urban and rural;
(f) Reduced surplus-for-investment at the household level, as most of the household budget goes to feeding, health care, children's education, etc.;
(g) The deepening of mass poverty and the continuing enlargement of the population at risk.

At the end of the 1970s, it was estimated that about 60 per cent of urban households in developing countries could not afford to purchase any form of standard accommodation at the prices then prevailing. At the prices prevailing in most African countries today, especially those implementing adjustment programmes, the proportion of those who do not as yet own any standard dwelling of their own and who now belong to this can't afford-a-house category must approach 95 per cent for urban households and 100 per cent for rural households. In effect, most of those who used to regard themselves as "middle income" have now, in reality, joined the low-income/poor category, at least as far as their housing status and, especially, their house-ownership prospects are concerned.

There would seem to be a most urgent case for treating housing as a high-priority sector in Africa's medium-/long-term regional development planning. A situation in which the vast majority of the population occupy substandard accommodation (or, as in many cases, have nothing to occupy) and in which the vast majority can never hope to ever own a home, regardless of how hard they work, is bound, sooner or later, to give rise to severe social discontent, to mass frustration and to a social-conflict situation that will not be easy to contain or to resolve.

(iv) *Income and individual/household economic status*

The considerations relevant to this dimension of the human situation include income per capita but, perhaps even more important, the structure of income distribution, the state of income adequacy, especially among the urban low-income earners and rural populations and the state (incidence and prevalence) of poverty.

As noted earlier, Africa's performance in respect of the growth of aggregate national income and of income per capita has been poor over the last 10 years. World Bank estimates suggest the GDP per capita for sub-Saharan Africa fell at an annual average of 3.4 per cent in the period 1980–1986 and that, even for the decade 1986–1995, the "high" that the region could hope to achieve is an annual growth of 0.7 per cent in per capita income. This is way below the growth rate of 3.9 per cent forecast for developing countries as a whole.

The fall in GDP per capita during the period under review (estimated at 16 per cent for 1980–1986) has, of course, depressed household income and the standard of living of the population, the situation being made worse by rapidly rising prices of essential goods and services, by rigid wage/salary structures and by the high level of unemployment. In particular, the very high level of unemployment among young people has imposed severe strain on the already lean resources of most households, as many members tend to remain dependent on their parents long after they ought to have become self-supporting.

The various adjustment programmes on which most African countries have embarked during this decade have exacerbated an already bad unemployment situation. The various measures intended to reform and strengthen public finances and enterprises entailed substantial reduction in public employment through so-called "re-organization". The same narrow logic used for determining what constitutes efficient utilization of labour in advanced capitalist economies has been applied uncritically in the conception of efficient labour utilization in the predominantly agrarian and labour-surplus economies of Africa, in utter disregard of the peculiar role and significance of public-sector employment in the African situation.

Of course, owing to the high level of inequality which characterizes income distribution in most African countries and to the prevalence of poverty, the hardships just described are unevenly distributed among the different socio-economic groups. Those groups which have continuously experienced the more severe level of income-deprivation include rural populations in general, farmers, the urban labour force, the millions who operate the so-called "informal sector", the unemployed and, the chronic poor who inhabit the slums and shanty-towns of the apparently affluent capital cities.

As for how we must explain the persistence of poverty and of mass deprivations in Africa today, I believe that too much emphasis has been placed on the fact of slow economic growth. When the poverty and deprivations of the vulnerable groups persist and worsen regardless of substantial and prolonged improvements in the aggregate growth performance of many of the countries (most especially the oil-exporting countries), then one must suspect that some other more fundamental factors are at work. In my view, these factors include: the basically undemocratic structure of political power in most; the inequitable structure of income distribution; and, the inegalitarian structure of private property distribution.

In most cases, the ruling group (now civilian, now military, etc.) has, through the callous abuse of state power, established an undemocratic, exploitative and oppressive private property system which determines more or less rigidly the access of particular socio-economic groups and of their members to income and wealth and to the opportunities for making both. Thus, as at the international level, the wealth and comfort of the few and the poverty and misery of the many are to be seen as mutually produced manifestations of the same historical process.

I believe that we should expose and examine critically the prevailing situation whereby most African leaders continue to profess commitment to egalitarianism and poverty eradication at international conferences while they brazenly pursue, in their respective countries, policies which aggravate both inequality and poverty. I believe also that, as far as the problem of excessive income concentration is concerned, while some marginal improvements may be achieved through selective reforms, what history seems to suggest is that, in Africa's particular situation, an ultimate and lasting solution probably lies only in a major restructuring of power in society and in the total dismantling of the existing iniquitous property system.

(v) *Social problems situation*

If available data on such indicators as income per capita and on the provision of and access to various social services is inadequate, data on the various social problems is practically non-existent. In any case, such problems are amenable to quantitative assessment only to a limited extent. Thus, one's evaluation here is, unavoidably, largely impressionistic and tentative.

The material shortages and deprivations implicit in a situation of severe inequality and poverty often give rise to serious human problems at the level of the family. One thing which past studies elsewhere have established is the strong connection between family economic situation and family problems. In particular, poverty-stricken families tend to be conflict-ridden and beset by other problems such as unemployment, irregular incomes, dependency upon other families and by both physical and mental illness. The ability of the family to perform its adult stabilization and child development functions is severely hampered.

This is not to deny, however, the importance of several other factors which also determine the quality of the family situation, especially the educational status of parents; the availability of learning facilities; and the status of the mother in the household (and hence the status of women in the society). It is important, therefore, that programmes for Africa's economic recovery and socio-economic development, in the medium/long term, should include definite measures to improve substantially the income status of the majority of households in each country, i.e., of lower-class and poorer households in both the rural and urban settings. Such programmes must also include provisions for the advancement of literacy and education among the general adult population and for the improvement of the status of women in society.

There is an obvious connection between the growing impotence of an ever-increasing percentage of African families in their role as child development institutions on the one hand and the rising incidence of juvenile delinquency and of youth disorientation on the other. Of course, the lack of suitable youth mobilization policies and defective educational systems have also contributed towards the escalation of these problems, especially in the context of the increased hardships and strains which have been imposed upon the family situation during the last one decade.

The rising incidence of crime in African countries is yet to be subjected to systematic empirical study. Nevertheless, not many who are familiar with the situation will deny that the incidence of crimes against the person, crimes against private property, crimes against public property, official corruption, drug trafficking, drug abuse and alcoholism, vandalism and violence has risen to an unprecedented level in many African countries over the last 10 years.

The worsening situation of crime and violence in many African countries must be seen, however, not as something resulting from personality disorders but as survival responses to pervasive economic, political and social frustration. In most cases, the criminals are only struggling to succeed in terms of the materialistic achievement standards set by society, using the only resources that they have and the only avenues really open to them. Thus, it seems again that a drastic restructuring of the distribution of power, of opportunities for personal development and of consumption in favour of the low-income and poor classes is the only promising solution to the crime-and-violence problem.

One particular kind of social conflict generally regarded as endemic to the African region, is social conflict generated around the competing economic and political interests of primordial ethno-cultural groups. More recently, religious differences have become significant as a potential source of serious social conflict in many African countries. However, it seems to me that the social segmentation and conflict processes which are fast crystallizing around the social questions of poverty and inequality are bound to play a more decisive role in the political future of most African countries. Incidentally, the hardships and deprivations arising from current adjustment programmes may, if they continue long enough, impoverish the present middle-income socio-economic groups, hasten the polarization process and compel the societies concerned to evolve a more viable basis for their consensus and integration.

In closing this somewhat speculative account of the social problems situation, let me stress that this particular dimension of human development in Africa is in need of and deserves most urgent research attention at national, sub-regional and regional levels, since what happens to this dimension must constitute a critical consideration in any continuous monitoring and evaluation of the social and human impact of Africa's development efforts in the years ahead.

(vi) *Political welfare, human rights and justice*

In my view, Africa's record, over the past 25 years with regard to this dimension of human development is dismal and the current economic crisis and the various "belt-tightening" adjustment programmes have simply provided further grounds for the maintenance and extension of social deprivations in this sphere. What has already been said of economic inequality and mass poverty constitutes adequate illustration of the extent to which African Governments have neglected and often violated the consideration of economic and social injustice.

As for political orientation, political participation and political freedom, the record has been equally grim. Perhaps the indicators which reflect the state of these political-welfare factors best are the frequency with which people are denied their right to freely choose their leaders, the incidence and prevalence of other human rights violations, and the refugee problem.

For most of the period under review and in almost all African countries, the struggle for political power has been conducted as a war against the people and in flagrant violation of people's political rights. Not surprisingly, once in power, most African leaders have displayed little interest in human rights observance in their strategy of consolidation or through the pursuit of substantive human welfare and development programmes.

One must also admit, however, that in the few cases where African Governments have been disposed to work for human development and human rights, the lack of resources has usually limited both their efforts and their achievements. Incidentally, it is significant that it is the resource poor countries which have featured more prominently in this category, not the more richly endowed. And, of course, the current economic crisis and adjustment measures have, in many ways, strengthened the obstacles in the way of human rights observance.

The wide occurrence of military governments in Africa, the excessively long periods for which many military regimes have insisted on remaining in power and the manoeuvres through which some military leaders have appropriated power on a permanent basis show the extent to which Africans have had their rights to choose their leader violated. However, even though all military regimes in Africa are dictatorships, it must be admitted that human rights, even certain civil and political rights, have fared better under some military regimes than under others. In fact, except for the basic violation implicit in their mode of accession to power, some military regimes in Africa have turned out to be more democratic in their temperament and procedures than many of the so-called democratically elected governments. Of course, the recognition of this dilemma must not be taken as implying a support for military rule; rather, it should serve as a strong case for intensifying programmes which will improve the political capacity of the people, so that they themselves can defend their political rights and freedoms against invidious violations, from whatever source.

Another indication of the general state of political welfare in the African context is the refugee problem. According to a recent estimate by the United Nations High Commissioner for Refugees, in early 1985, Africa had about 4 million refugees – the largest concentration in any one region and, relative to its population, more refugees than any other region in the world. When the people displaced within countries because of drought and armed conflicts are added, the total number of uprooted Africans is estimated to exceed 10 million. (See Stockholm International Peace Research Institute,1985).

(vii) *Human resources development and mobilization*

The main elements of human resources development are basic (primary and secondary) education, mass literacy and adult education, higher education and specialized manpower training while human resources mobilization concerns manpower utilization and motivation, community organization and motivation for and commitment to development action.

As far as human resources development is concerned, Africa's efforts throughout the 1970s have, for the most part, been impressive, judging by the considerable resources which most African countries committed to education, estimated at 15–25 per cent of the national budgets[6] but often exceeding this upper limit and judging also by the phenomenal growth which was achieved in enrolment, especially at primary and secondary levels. (See table 9 below regarding the situation in the 19 selected countries).

Still, even at these two levels, the problem of access remains serious. In many African countries governments have used the argument of "qualitative education" to justify policies which tend to restrict the access of children from poorer homes to education. One result of such restrictive policies was that, by 1980, less than 60 per cent of eligible children were enrolled at the primary school level.

It is also significant that by 1980 as many as 15 out of 53 African countries had not established compulsory schooling and that these African cases accounted for almost 50 per cent of the world total of countries in the category. In general, the enrolment ratio in tertiary education also improved

Table 9: Africa: Enrolment ratio, primary and secondary and adult literacy, 1960, 1970, 1982–1984 and 1984

Countries	Primary school enrolment ratio			Secondary school enrolment ratio		Adult literacy		
	1960	1982–1984	1984*	1982–1984	1984	1970 Male/Female	1980 (M + F)	1985 Male/Female
I(A) *Low income (general)*								
1. Benin	27	68	64	22	19	23/8	28	37/16
2. Burundi	18	46	49	4	4	29/10	25	43/26
3. Kenya	47	100	97	20	19	44/19	47	70/49
4. Mozambique	48	80	83	6	6	29/14	33	55/22
5. Sierra Leone	23	39	45	17	14	18/8	15	38/21
6. Somalia	9	22	25	15	17	5/1	6	18/6
7. Tanzania	26	88	81	3	3	48/18	79	90/80
8. Zaire	60	89	98	23	57	61/22	55	79/45
Total I (A)	32	67	67	14	17	32/13	36	54/33
I(B) *Low income (specially disadvantaged)*								
9. Burkina Faso	9	27	29	4	4	13/3	5	21/6
10. Chad	17	38	38	7	6	20/2	15	40/11
11. Ethiopia	7	46	32	13	12	8/1	15	–
12. Mali	10	24	–	7	–	11/4	10	23/11
Total I(B)	22	51	50	11	12	23/8	24	41/21
Total I(A) + I(B)	22	51	50	11	12	23/8	24	41/21
II *Middle income*								
13. Cameroon	65	107	1067	22	23	47/19	–	68/55
14. Egypt	66	89	84	56	58	50/20	44	59/30
15. Cote d'Ivoire	46	79	77	19	20	26/10	35	53/21
16. Liberia	32	76	76	23	23	27/8	25	47/23
17. Nigeria	37	–	92	–	29	35/14	34	54/31
18. Zambia	43	95	100	17	17	66/37	44	84/67
19. Zimbabwe	–	136	131	39	39	63/47	69	81/67
Total II	48	97	95	29	30	45/22	42	64/42
Total I + II	35	74	73	20	21	34/15	33	53/32

Source: Compiled mainly from UNICEF, *The State of the World's Children 1987* and World Bank, *World Development Report*, 1987.

* For all sub-Saharan Africa, the average is 77 per cent for primary and 21 per cent for secondary enrolment. Corresponding figures for all lower middle-income countries are, on the average, 103 per cent for primary enrolment and 40 per cent for secondary enrolment; and for industrial market economies, 102 per cent for primary enrolment and 90 per cent for secondary enrolment.

but, is still low in comparison with more developed countries or even with many other developing countries.

Furthermore, in most African countries, as in developing countries generally, millions of children who are enrolled in primary schools get an incomplete basic education, many dropping out before reaching the higher classes. The problem is particularly acute in the rural areas where a majority of the schools are substandard and manned by inadequately prepared and poorly paid teachers. In effect, the education of children of the rich gets subsidized at the expense of the education of the children of the poor just as the education of urban children generally gets subsidized at the expense of the education of children in rural areas. And the children of the rich have the additional advantage of being able to afford to attend better quality fee-paying private educational institutions.

At all levels, the enrolment ratio tends to be lower for girls than for boys. The under-enrolment of girls, especially at primary and secondary levels is often due more to long-standing culturally based irrationalities regarding the status of women in society than to any deliberate national policy of denying educational opportunities to women. More concerted effort will, therefore, be required if the educational status of women is to be improved.

Concerning illiteracy, though the literacy ratio is rising, the number of illiterates also continues to grow as youngsters who do not go to school and those who do not stay long enough to acquire permanent literacy add to the pool. Available evidence suggests that the incidence of adult illiteracy, as at 1980, was highest in Africa (with the ratio still as high as 60 per cent), even though, over the preceding decade, the sharpest reduction in the illiteracy ratio had also occurred in Africa. Of course, again, the ratio was higher for females than for males and probably remains so now, though the gap had decreased substantially between 1970 and 1980.

In general, the data on the 19 selected countries (table 9) confirms the general improvement in the overall literacy ratio and in the literacy ratio for women (as compared to that for men) in the entire 1970–1985 period. Important issues regarding adult illiteracy in contemporary Africa remain, however, and include entry of children into the pool (due mainly to non-enrolment, non-completion or to reversion to illiteracy), the right of the adult to literacy education, the rising economic and social cost of adult illiteracy and the modality of adult literacy programmes.

Not many serious economists will deny the crucial role of education and training in socio-economic development. Yet, in many African countries, the planners continue to impose unreasonable limits on public expenditure in this sector on the basis of so-called cost-benefit analysis, resulting in an undemocratic and counter-productive access structure at all levels.

In the last decade or so, as a way of adjusting to the present economic difficulties and under the general tutelage of the World Bank/IMF coalition, many African Governments have introduced measures to shift an increasing share of the cost of education to the individual household, precisely at a point when what is required is further democratization of primary and secondary education and intensification of adult literacy programmes. Admittedly, the problem of education financing is real but the present move towards increased "privatization" of the responsibility for the basic education of citizens seems historically inappropriate and most unreasonable.

The situation of human resources mobilization in Africa is, in most cases, even less satisfactory than that of human resources development. In fact, this is the particular aspect in which most African Governments have registered least progress. The continuously high level of unemployment is, perhaps, the most visible indicator of ineffective human resources utilization. But at the level of the individual, there are other less visible dimensions of the prevailing situation of human resources wastage, most notably, very low productivity of labour in most sectors of the economy, particularly in public-sector institutions.

Attempts to explain the unsatisfactory situation of the chronically low productivity of labour in African countries have tended to emphasize endemic cultural tendencies, technological know-how problems and even the fact of direct state participation in the economic production. I would not wish to deny the possible relevance of these factors but I believe that none of them is as important as the total ideological framework of the society, the overall character of state policy, the prevailing structure for the distribution of development benefits, including income, health, housing, recreation, cultural facilities, etc., and the particular institutional arrangements which have been put in place for ensuring that people are adequately organized and motivated and that their efforts are properly co-ordinated.

These, in my view, are the more critical factors which need to be re-examined and streamlined in most African countries in order to ensure the effective mobilization of human labour in general, of the local communities and of various other social groups on whose creative energy and contribution the present and future socio-economic progress of Africa unavoidably depends.

General Trends and Explaining the Trends

Overall, the last few years have witnessed a strengthening of the obstacles to effective mass mobilization and to socio-economic development. The loss of self-confidence on the part of the people of Africa, the prevailing sense of failure and shame, the experience of national and regional humiliation, the state of mass demoralization, confusion and anxiety regarding tomorrow – this is the essential predicament of Africa today. In the OAU/ECA submission to the United Nations Special Session a wide range of factors were identified as causes of "major economic and social distortions in Africa's development" including:

(a) insufficient structural transformation . . . away from inherited colonial economic structures;
(b) serious deficiencies in economic and social infrastructures, most especially physical capital, research capabilities, technological know-how and human resources development; and
(c) the widespread low level of productivity of the African economies.

There is no doubt that the report was more directly concerned with economic problems. In fact, it seemed to regard the deteriorating human situation in Africa as deriving primarily from the continent's depressed economic performance. I believe, however, that such a one dimensional view of the causal relationship greatly over-simplifies reality and is likely to mislead policy. What seems to be nearer the truth is that both the economic problems and the deteriorating human situation have resulted from Africa's failure at developing its human resources. In fact, if any one set of factors may be said to have priority as a cause of Africa's present total predicament (economic, political and social), it is probably the enduring human crisis and human underdevelopment.

One other analytical principle should be stressed at this point, namely, that even though Africa's predicament came to its present crisis in the last ten years, the major historical and structural forces which produced the crisis have been with Africa for much longer than a decade. To restrict the explanation of the present economic crisis or of the wider human crisis of which it is a part to factors which lie in the last one decade, we may simply be mistaking symptoms for causes.

Subject to those clarifications, the following more specific sets of factors can be identified as having contributed, to a greater or lesser degree, towards the making of the present unsatisfactory human situation in Africa:

(a) external/global economic conditions;
(b) inadequacies of economic development and economic management policies and programmes both domestic and external;
(c) inadequacies of domestic social development policies and programmes;
(d) internal economic, political and social conditions; and
(e) inappropriate ideological orientations.

Global economic conditions which are largely beyond the control of African countries have, no doubt, seriously affected their resource situation, especially their performance in the external trade and finance sector. For example, the sharp increases in oil prices in 1973 and again in 1978–1979 escalated the import bills of most African countries, the only exception in this case being the oil exporters among them. About the same time, the prices of manufactured imports also rose sharply while the prices of most of Africa's traditional exports plummeted, reaching by 1985 their lowest level since 1950. These developments, added in many cases to the effects of natural disasters, contributed significantly to the making of the current debt situation of most African countries.

There is no doubt that these factors and others which marked the recession in the industrial market economies created serious resource problems and and distortions in the African economies. But they lie and will continue to lie beyond the control of African countries and are, in fact, the "given" to which African economies must relate in terms of their own interest, through more appropriate domestic and external economic policies, more appropriate social development policies through the creation and sustenance of internal conditions conducive to economic and social development and through basing their entire economic and social development efforts on ideological orientations appropriate to the historical situation in which they must operate.

The most immediate real cause of Africa's present problems is, of course, to be found in the prevalence of inadequate economic development and economic management policies and programmes, in respect of both the domestic and external sectors. In particular, all such economic policies as have advanced or otherwise facilitated the further incorporation of African countries into the world capitalist system as satellites of the industrial economies of the west and thus deepened dependency relationships must accept the greatest responsibility for the region's present predicament. And, of course, also matching excessive external dependency as a cause of their past and current weakness is the failure of African countries to strengthen co-operation among themselves in the areas of both economic and social development.

The decisive role of economic imperialism and neo-imperialism in the underdevelopment of Africa and in the making of the kind of economic and social crisis in which the region is currently embroiled has been extensively discussed and documented. (See, particularly, Rodney 1972). A high level of dependency implies, *inter alia*, more immediate exposure to the destabilizing influence of whatever economic crises overtake the centre of the world capitalist system. The way the two recent global economic recessions (1974–1975 and 1980–1982) severely disturbed most African economies is a confirmation of the high level of Africa's dependence on Western Europe and America.

The developing countries of Africa, like other developing countries, are victims of a world capitalist economic system that was designed to benefit only the more powerful nations. Recent vicious pressures to enforce debt repayment, with little or no consideration for the serious human suffering which debt-servicing obligations were creating in most of the affected countries and recent trends in aid flow show clearly that the so-called donor countries give only to take more. The drying up of aid is difficult to reconcile with the great extent to which the industrialized countries of the West have taken over control of the economies of Africa. In fact, it seems to me that we have here a classic case of calling the tune even without paying the piper.

At the domestic level also, the following policy tendencies have contributed: the neglect of agriculture; incomes policies which have aggravated income inequalities; industrialization policies which, being highly dependent on imports and capital intensive, have contributed very little towards solving the problems of mass unemployment and mass poverty in most countries; and economic policies which fail to take into full account the particular social and cultural context of African countries and which also fail, therefore, to anticipate or reckon fully with the possible social consequences and implications of economic programmes.

In my view, such counter-productive policies and the historically irrelevant so-called development plans of which they are part have persisted in most African countries because of a number of factors, the foremost of which are the prolonged domination of development planning in most countries by economists and, worse still, by the econocratic vision; intellectual laziness and associated mental rigidity on the part of the planning bureaucracy; the natural tendency of bureaucracy to resist and subvert movements towards major change; and the powerlessness of the masses which guarantees that anti-people tendencies on the part of the policy class will not be promptly corrected or penalized. Certainly, any serious programme to redeem African economies and ensure their future development must include a provision for the re-education of African economists and for a drastic review of planning systems in African countries.

Political instability is also one of Africa's perennial problems. Counting from Africa's inaugural military intervention (Egypt, 1952), by 1986, there had been more than 60 successful coups d'Etat in the region. By that year also, over 30 out of the continent's 51 independent countries had experienced at least one coup and 14 had experienced more than one, including three which had recorded at least five coups each. Today, only 13 African countries can boast of never having witnessed a successful coup since they became independent. Our concern for now is not with the propriety of coups and military rule but with the seemingly endless interruption of economic and social development plans and programmes; with the fact that, in most cases, regimes have replaced regimes so frequently and so abruptly that is has become impossible for a culture of long-term planning to take root.

Both political instability and poor leadership are closely interdependent not only in their effects but also in their probable causation. And one factor which seems to have contributed significantly to both is ideological uncertainty. I cannot take up here the issue as to whether African humanism, socialism or something else is the appropriate ideological orientation for contemporary Africa. However, a few lessons on this question seem to stand out from Africa's experience up to now, namely:

(a) that most African countries are already paying dearly (in terms of failed mobilization) for the inability of their leaders to clarify to the masses the fundamental objectives (ends) and strategy (means) of the development action to which the masses are invited to commit their energies and loyalty;

(b) that the particular ideological tendencies (however they may be named) which have informed the thinking and actions of most African leaders and served as the real intellectual basis of past development policies in most African countries have only brought such countries close to economic and social catastrophe and are, therefore, probably inappropriate to Africa's present situation; and

(c) that an appropriate ideology must address the various questions already raised concerning mass participation in power, income and consumption, human rights and 'social justice; it must also address the question concerning Africa's place in the international economic and political order. And it must resolve these questions within the framework of the commitment of the African people to democratic development.

Which Way Forward

In diagnosing Africa's economic and social problems or prescribing possible solutions to them, there is hardly any room left for originality. This is in the sense that most of the relevant factors have indeed been identified and stressed by one analyst or the other and by both the Organization of African Unity and the Economic Commission for Africa, through their several separate and joint initiatives. Concrete efforts have been made by both OAU and ECA to find solutions to Africa's economic problem. These efforts include the 1980 Lagos Plan of Action and the Final Act of Lagos and in 1985, "Africa's Priority Programme for Economic Recovery, 1986–1990" (APPER) which is meant specifically to get the region over the current crisis and set it on the path of growth.

However,a tendency evident in all these important official documents and in the meetings which produced them is the concentration on the economic dimensions of the situation, leaving the social problems and human factor aspects of the situation largely unattended. In particular though some elements of the human welfare and human resources mobilization dimensions were noted in such proposals (e.g., the health situation, the quality of human resources, "participation of the people" and even "political, economic and social justice") the critical social questions relating to those dimensions (e.g., the structure of power, economic inequality, poverty, exploitation, human rights, political welfare, etc.) were not raised or discussed. Nor were any of the proposals addressed specifically to the possible resolution of such questions.

These omissions are definitely important. In fact, in a fundamental sense, one suspects that the concept of "human resource development", as it has featured in these documents and in the planning process in most African countries is not only narrower than but also, in several ways, in conflict with the broader concept of "investment in man" which should be the basis of Africa's new policies and initiatives regarding the human dimension of development. Furthermore, given this serious shortcoming in the prevailing conception of the critical dynamics of the human dimension of development, it is hardly surprising that we have neither carefully formulated nor attempted to implement any specific strategy for transforming that dimension. Let me now suggest an outline of such a strategy in the next few paragraphs.

To start with, we must recognize that the kind of transformation necessary would require two different levels of intervention, namely:

(a) A macro-national level, whose objective is to transform the institutional structural dynamics in each country and render them more conducive to the pursuit of democratic economic and social development in the medium/long term; and
(b) A micro-sectoral level of intervention whose objective is to produce visible change and amelioration of the present situation, in particular the human/social development sectors, in the short/medium term.

Admittedly, these two sets of interventions do not, in reality, belong in two separate compartments, especially in terms of their implications for the institutional conditions to which they are both addressed. Nevertheless, for purposes of working out an operational strategy, we must differentiate conceptually between these two levels of intervention. The distinction is necessary for establishing a national- international division of labour in the promotion and implementation of the full complement of necessary changes. The position taken in the paper is that the macro-national level of intervention is, primarily, the responsibility of national political authorities and that the responsibility and opportunity of the international community, regional organizations inclusive, lies primarily at the micro-sectoral level.

This operational demarcation is proposed in view of the fact that the social questions which need to be resolved as a basis for and in the process of the kind of transformation envisaged at the macro-national level (the form of economic organization, the role of the state in the economy, the structure of political power, economic inequality, etc.) are essentially political in nature and their resolution will emerge in time from the revolutionary processes already gathering momentum throughout the continent. In contrast, the kind of transformation envisaged at the micro-sectoral level is addressed mostly to questions concerning the quality of life of the people/communities and of their capacity to perform effectively and optimally and to contribute towards stable improvements in their own life and towards national socio-economic development within the framework of their particular political systems.

However, in ending this observation on a possible division of labour I must state my belief that, under certain circumstances, the international human community (especially the United Nations and the Organization of African Unity) must continue to accept and discharge a moral-political responsibility for the protection and advancement of respect for human rights, even behind the walls of oppression which particular delinquent political systems may erect and seek to defend in the name of national sovereignty.

Furthermore, it is an important condition of the strategy of transformation that the choice of interventions at each level should be guided by a valid understanding of the reality of Africa's chronic underdevelopment and of the fundamental causation of its present crisis. Even more specifically, it is essential to view in their true perspectives the probable causes of the former and to see to what extent even the present crisis is only a manifestation of certain long-standing and deeper distortions.

To reach a better understanding of the reality of Africa's present problems, some basic misconceptions deserve to be pointed out and corrected. For example, I think we must discard right away the very idea of "recovery" as an objective of Africa's current efforts at self-upliftment. It is misleading and potentially diversionary. For one thing, it seems to suggest that Africa was well before the present crisis and that, if Africa could be restored to the status quo ante, then that would mean that Africa has been restored to its previous healthy state. But the economic and human situation in Africa has been one prolonged emergency throughout the last 25 years. To restore Africa to the immediate pre-1977 situation is, therefore, not to restore Africa to a state of health; rather, it is to restore the region to its status as a dependency and as an object of callous exploitation.

I have no doubt in my mind that the fundamental objective that African countries and the African region must pursue at this point is change, not recovery. The critical challenge posed by the current crisis is not one of recovery but one of transcending the structural limitations imposed upon the continent by virtue of its dependent status.

Second, we must accept and be guided in our search for a strategy of transformation by the reality that there will be no "Marshall Plan" for Africa: African countries will have to depend upon themselves for their individual and collective redemption and for their long-term economic and social development. Third, African countries, individually and collectively, must appreciate the importance of adopting the long-term perspective. Even in the present circumstance, many of the fundamental factors already identified as the causes of their problem situation are unlikely to prove amenable to necessary change in the short term, though a start can always be made in the right direction. Most of the factors to which macro-national interventions must be addressed are of this type. For another, the piecemeal and short-term solutions which have been applied so far have been generally ineffective and have actually worsened the situation in most cases. A new approach is required which will consider both the financial and human problems of all African countries and which will address short-term problems in their long-term context. In short, Africa's emphasis must be on long-term goals and objectives and on long-term strategies formulated for the pursuit of those goals.

Having entered these observations, let me return to the task of developing a strategy of transformation by offering more specific suggestions regarding necessary interventions at both the macro-national and micro-sectoral levels, taking first the latter.

Micro-sectoral interventions: The following general principles can be suggested to guide programmes for change at this level:

(a) the strengthening of regional and sub-regional co-operation in the human development sector;
(b) the according of highest priority to the implementation of regional and sub-regional programmes in the context of their own domestic development programmes and budgets;
(c) the strengthening of the inter-agency approach in the conception, planning and implementation of regional and sub-regional programmes, to minimize duplication and the various diseconomies which it usually entails;
(d) the identification of highest priority concerns, using as the principal criterion the strategic value of each concern as instruments for the attainment of critical human situation transformation objectives;
(e) the ordering of highest priority concerns in a hierarchy based on their relative strategic values, to facilitate the phasing of interventions; and
(f) the fullest utilization of and reliance upon Africa's own strategic human resources (its experts, its youth, its local communities, its non-governmental organizations, etc.) in the identification, conceptualization, planning and implementation of human situation transformation objectives.

The purpose of principles (a) and (b) should be obvious. Better coordination of strategy and programmes would ensure a more judicious use of available resources, both those provided from the outside in support of Africa's development efforts and those which Africa itself provides. The particular instrument for such co-ordination could be regional/sub-regional inter-agency programme development and co-ordination committees, set up under the joint auspices of OAU and ECA for integrated initiatives for the various concerns. As for the identification and ordering of highest priority concerns, the following stand out as possibilities:

(a) health (with emphasis on preventive measures);
(b) literacy and adult education;
(c) other education and manpower development;
(d) child development and youth mobilization;
(e) community mobilization;
(f) employment; and
(g) housing development and environment.

Of course, each of these areas of human situation transformation should be tackled with deliberate emphasis on the situation in the rural areas.

Accordingly, it might be appropriate to set up regional inter-agency programme development and co-ordination committees immediately for all high-priority concerns identified, including those in which actual country-based programmes may not commence immediately.

The sixth principle proposed above reflects, in part, a concern with the processes and economics of implementing approved programmes and is intended to call attention, among other things, to the need to review the utilization of external technical assistance. The present situation in which foreign experts are imported at enormous cost to advise regarding the planning and implementation of projects even when suitable African personnel are available in the particular African country concerned or in some other African country entails considerable diseconomies in terms of both cost-effectiveness and regional self-reliance objectives.

Macro-national interventions: As indicated earlier, this level belongs primarily to the political authorities of individual countries, though it must not be regarded as exclusive to them. For one thing, some of the interventions at the micro-sectoral level could have a transformative effect on aspects of the macro-national situation. For example, the attainment of health objectives could enhance national economic capacity just as the attainment of higher literacy and improved adult education could improve the political capacity of the people. For another, there must be circumstances in which it would be desirable, in the interest of regional/sub-regional solidarity and progress, for regional/sub-regional agencies to pressurize defaulting individual countries to act in accordance with agreed broad principles even in their macro-national economic and social development policies. Perhaps the foremost of such broad principles should be the need for all African countries to emphasize those policies likely to ensure progress towards higher levels of regional self-reliance.

But also, since there is no way that African Governments can achieve the objective of liberating their people from the situation of dependency without the fullest support and participation of the masses, social mobilization becomes a strategic necessity and certain policy orientations towards human development and human welfare objectives become almost imperative. In particular, every African country would need to address more seriously than ever before the crucial social questions regarding the sharing of power, unemployment, inequality and the prevalence of poverty. And every African country would need to initiate or strengthen (where they already exist) major transformation programmes in these respects.

In ending my comments here, one point deserves to be emphasized, namely that exhortation and enlightenment programmes (government propaganda, radio and TV jingles, etc.) do not have the least chance of mobilizing people and committing their energies to development action on a stable basis unless such programmes are accompanied by significant changes in the dimensions noted above, changes which improve radically the quality of the people's participation in power and policy determination and the adequacy of the real benefits that they stand to derive from the national gains which they are called upon to make possible.

Conclusion

The professed aims of current adjustment policies and programmes usually include the reduction of huge balance-of-payments deficits; the generation and conservation of enough foreign exchange to honour debt-repayment obligations and finance vital imports; and the laying of foundations necessary for renewed economic growth. However, judging by the experiences of all African countries who have agreed to solve their present economic crisis through such programmes, the most outstanding consequences of these emergency measures have been:

(a) the drastic deterioration of health, educational and other human resources development services;
(b) the higher level of unemployment, especially among youth;
(c) the heightened frustration experienced by most social groups with respect to employment and to the sharp and sudden fall in their standard of living;
(d) the escalation of social discontent and social problems;
(e) the continuing avoidance of critical social questions; and
(f) the worsening of Africa's long-standing social mobilization problems.

Fortunately, these experiences seem to have convinced many African Governments anew that they must re-think their survival and development strategies. A few general points and suggestions need to be further stressed in these closing paragraphs.

The first of such general points concerns the importance of power relations. On every problem in the sphere of the economic and social development of nations, especially in the sphere of determining what the specific content of that "development" must be, the issue of power becomes one with that of social justice and other problems of development tend to be inextricably tied up with the issue of social justice and with the way it is posed and resolved in particular countries.

Unfortunately, in most African countries, the leadership has demonstrated and continues to demonstrate only a very shallow understanding of the nature of the situation of underdevelopment. This leadership problem is probably the most fundamental of Africa's contemporary difficulties, the basic problem of the human situation. For, while there is much validity to dependency theory as an explanation of Africa's current predicament and crisis, it is Africa itself which must accept ultimate responsibility for its apparently chronic underdevelopment. By this reasoning, sensitivity to history and the adoption of a long-term perspective are essential to Africa's survival in the present situation and to its future progress. Apart from the question of power and the problem of leadership, the other points that bear stressing are the critical importance of regional and sub-regional co-operation to whatever strategy of survival and development Africa will adopt as a way forward; the situation of human rights in Africa, especially the obstacle which the prevailing economic hardships may pose to the pursuit of human rights objectives at national and regional levels; and the problem posed by intellectual imperialism.

Concerning the human rights situation, African countries must ensure that they do not compromise their commitment to the total liberation of the continent, even as they struggle against crippling debts, poverty, ignorance and disease. All African countries generally and the richer ones among them in particular must step up their support to the liberation movements in Southern Africa, for that is where the human situation in Africa poses the severest challenge to our collective conscience and pride.

Will this be a definite turning point in Africa's march towards true economic and social development? Or is Africa determined to resign itself to those relationships and approaches which ensure this continued and perpetual economic and social underdevelopment and which urge it towards catastrophe? What have the Lagos Plan of Action, etc., been worth as far as concrete initiatives to transform and improve the human situation are concerned? What will these plans, targets, programmes and continental declarations be worth by the end of this decade and even by the end of this century in terms of concrete human situation development? Will Africa rise now to establish those new orientations, policies and relationships which will facilitate and most probably ensure its effective economic and social transformation in the direction of greater self-determination, higher productivity and self-reliance and a higher level of material abundance and security? From all indications, and judging by the records of inaction to date, when it comes to the implementation of agreed programmes of action which call for major change, Africa seems to have an intractable problem of political will. We must give serious attention to devising a strategy to overcome that inertia and the prolonged misery and suffering which it has entailed for the vast majority of our people.

Notes

1 *Africa's Submission to the Special Session of the United Nations General Assembly on Africa's Economic and Social crisis*, Addis Ababa, 1986 p.7. The position of the OAU/ECA submisssion to the Special Session of the United Nations General Assembly was that Africa is not overpopulated in absolute terms but only in the sense that population increase surpasses food production increase.

2 UNICEF, *Within Human Research: A Future for Africa's Children* (New York, 1985), p.21.

3 WHO, *Evaluation of the Strategy for Health for All By the Year 2000: Seventh Report on the World Health Situation*, vol.1, Global Review, (Geneva, 1987), p.69. Of course, this reflects, in part, the high infant-mortality situation prevalent in Africa and the difference between Africa and other regions may be much reduced in respect of life expectancy at ages beyond, say five years.

4 World Bank, *Toward Sustained Development in Sub-Saharan Africa* (Washington, D.C., 1984), p.14 and UNICEF, Op cit p.23.

5 United Nations, *Report on the World Social Situation*, Department of international Economic and Social Affairs, New York, 1982, p.65.

6 World Bank, *World Bank Development Report 1980*, (Washington, D.C., 1980), p.87.

References

(a) *Official Publications*

1 ACARTSOD, *Social Implications of the Lagos Plan of Action for the Economic Development of Africa, 1980–2000* (Addis Ababa, 1983).
2 African Development Bank, *Annual Report 1984* (Abidjan, 1985).
3 ECA, *Survey of Economic and Social Conditions in Africa, 1979–1980* (Addis Ababa, 1981).
4 International Food Policy Research Institute (IFPRI), *Food Policy Issues and Concerns in Sub-Saharan Africa*, preliminary paper (Ibadan, 1981).
5 OAU, *What Kind of Africa By the Year 2000?* (Addis Ababa, 1979).
6 OAU, *Lagos Plan of Action for the Economic Development of Africa, 1980–2000* (Addis Ababa, 1980).
7 OAU, *Africa's Priority Programme for Economic Recovery, 1986–1990* (Addis Ababa, 1985).
8 OAU/ECA, *Africa's submission to the special session of the United Nations General Assembly on Africa's Economic and Social Crisis* (Addis Ababa, 1986).
9 Stockholm International Peace Research Institute, *1985 Yearbook* (Stockholm 1985).
10 UNICEF, *The Impact of World Recession on Children* (New York, 1984).
11 UNICEF, *Within Human Research: A Future for Africa's Children* (New York, 1985).
12 UNICEF, *The State of the World's Children 1987* (New York, 1987).
13 United Nations, *United Nations Programme of Action for African Economic Recovery and Development, 1986–1990*, document A/RES/S-13/2 of 13 June 1986 (New York, 1986).

14 United Nations, *Report on the World Social Situation* (Department of International Economic and Social Affairs, New York, 1982).
15 WHO, *Evaluation of the Strategy for Health for All by the Year 2000: Seventh report on the World Health Situation*, volume 1, Global review (Geneva, 1987).
16 World Bank, *World Development Report* 1978 (Washington, D.C., 1978).
17 World Bank, *World Development Report* 1980 (Washington, D.C., 1980).
18 World Bank, *World Development Report* 1983 (Washington D.C., 1983).
19 World Bank, *Toward Sustained Development in Sub-Saharan Africa* (Washington, D.C., 1984).
20 World Bank, *World Bank Annual Report* 1985 (Washington D.C., 1985).
21 World Bank, *World Development Report* 1987 (Washington, D.C., 1987).

(b) *Other sources*
1 Aboyade, O., *Issues in the Development of Tropical Africa* (Ibadan, Ibadan University Press, 1976).
2 Adedeji, Adebayo, *After Lagos What?* (ACARTSOD, General Series No.1, 1983).
3 Adedeji, Adebayo, "Critical issues of theory, with special reference to economic growth and development.", paper presented to the National Seminar on Innovative Approaches to Development Theory, NISER, (Ibadan, 1984).
4 Davidson, Basil, *Which Way Africa?* (Harmondsworth, Penguin, 1964).
5 Eze, Osita, *Human Rightica: Some Selected Problems*, Nigerian Institute of International Affairs and Macmillan Publishers (Lagos, 1984).
6 Freire, Paolo, *Pedagogy of the Oppressed* (Harmondsworth, Penguin, 1972).
7 George, V.and Wilding, P., *Ideology and Social Welfare* (New York, Oxford University Press, 1972).
8 Horowitz, I.L., *Three Worlds of Development* (New York, Oxford University Press, 1972).
9 Khan, M.S., *Macro-economic Adjustment in Developing Countries: A Policy Perspective* (World Bank, Washington, D.C., 1986).
10 Myrdal, Gunnar, *Asian Drama* (abridged version) (Harmondsworth, Penguin, 1972).
11 Okigbo, Pius, "The distribution of national income in African countries" in *The Distribution of National Income* (London, St.Martins Press, 1986).
12 Ovam, P.A. *et al.*, "Investment and input requirements for accelerating food production in low-income countries by 1990." IFPRI report No. 10 (1979).
13 Reiffers, Jean Louis *et al.*, *Transnational Corporations and Endogenous Development* (UNESCO, Paris, 1982).
14 Rodney, Walter, *How Europe Underdeveloped Africa* (London/Dar-es-Salaam, Bogle- l'Ouverture Publications and Tanzania Publishing House, 1972).
15 Rweyemamu, J.F. (ed.), *Industrialization and Income Distribution in Africa* (CODESRIA, Dakar, 1980).
16 Self, Peter, *Econocrats and the Policy Process* (London, Macmillan Press Limited, 1975).

Kenya

G.K. IKIARA

Kenya, like many other sub-Saharan African countries, has been under the grip of an economic crisis for more than a decade now, with the severity of the crisis varying during that period. The country has used both domestic and external measures in its attempt to deal with the crisis. One of the most important measures taken was the adoption, in 1980, of the structural adjustment programme supported by the World Bank and the International Monetary Fund (IMF). This programme, largely aimed at influencing various macro-economic aggregates, had considerable impact on the human welfare of the Kenyan population.

This paper tries to analyze how the Kenyan economy was affected by the economic crisis partly triggered by the 1973 global oil crisis, its attempt to deal with the crisis through structural adjustment programmes and other measures, and how the implementation of the programme and the economic crisis affected the country's ability to provide various social services to the people.

An Overview of the Kenyan Economic Performance Before the Crisis

Since independence the population of Kenya has more than doubled from 8.4 million in the 1962 census to an estimated 21 million people in 1986. At the same time, the country has continued to record fairly respectable economic growth rates compared with other black African States. The real gross domestic product (1976 prices) increased by more than three times, from K£715 million in 1964 to about K£1900 million in 1984.[1]

In the first decade, Kenya took advantage of favourable and stable international and domestic conditions to lay a solid economic base. Except for a brief period of uncertainty, from 1963–1965, when there was considerable capital flight from the country, Kenya has generally enjoyed a stable economic environment. Government policies soon after independence gave confidence to both local and foreign investors which enabled the country's overall investment to increase quite rapidly. Total capital formation almost doubled in three years, from K£45.14 million in 1964 to K£81.3 million in 1967. By 1973, total capital formation had reached K£182.25 million. This favourable trend continued into the second decade of independence, so that between 1973 and 1984 total capital formation in the economy more than quadrupled to reach K£836.12 million in current prices.

The country's impressive economic growth could be partly attributed to the high savings and investment performance achieved for most of the post-independence period. Total fixed investment as a proportion of GDP has remained above 20 per cent for most of the period. A notable aspect of the country's investment is that most of it was financed from domestic savings, although this has been declining in recent years. For example, in the period 1970–1977 domestic savings accounted for an average of 80 per cent of the country's total investments while the corresponding figure for the period 1978–1982 was only 58.1 percent.

The existence of a relatively well-established capital and money market in the country also acted as a catalyst in the development process. Since independence, Kenya has enjoyed the services of a number of banking and non-banking financial institutions, including one of the first of few stock exchanges in the continent. There was a massive expansion of financial institutions and banks in the country in the period 1978–1985. This impressive growth of the Kenyan economy was also facilitated by the pragmatic approach adopted by Government in economic management and the political stability which prevailed during that period.

Nonetheless, the economic performance in the first and second decades differed markedly mainly due to changed circumstances and the overall economic environment in which the economy was operating. During the first decade, the country had one of the best economic records in black Africa. The real GDP growth rate for the period 1963–1973 averaged 6.5 per cent per annum, with the key sectors, agriculture and manufacturing attaining average annual growth rates of over 5 and 10 per cent respectively. The period was further characterized by high investment growth rates, high international credit worthiness, low inflation rates, around 5 per cent per annum, and considerable balance-of-payments stability.

Structural Changes and Related Constraints and Issues

Like many other former colonies, Kenya inherited an underdeveloped economy at the time of independence. The economy was characterized by the existence of a large traditional sector, dependence on primary exports, heavy dependence on international trade, and an underdeveloped industrial sector.

The post-colonial Government adopted economic planning as a way of facilitating rapid change towards the desired direction. The theme of the first Five-Year Development Plan covering the period 1966–1970, was restructuring of the economy and rapid economic growth. The second and third Five-Year Development Plans placed emphasis on development of rural areas where more than 80 per cent of the population continue to live, employment creation and improvement in income distribution. The provision of basic needs such as education, health, housing, water, food and nutrition was the focus of the fourth Five-Year Development Plan – while that of the fifth Five-Year Development Plan, 1984–1988, was the mobilization of domestic resources for development.

While the economic structure inherited at independence is not yet overhauled, it has undergone considerable changes. With the growth of crop production, education, infrastructure, banking facilities and government participation in the economy, there has been an increase in the degree of monetization of the economy in the last two decades. The share of the non-monetary sector to the GDP declined from 27.1 to 5.8 per cent between 1964 and 1984.[2]

Attempts to diversify the economy have had some limited success. While agriculture contributed about 41.8 per cent[3] of the GDP in 1964, its share had fallen to 35.3 per cent by 1984. The fall in the contribution of the agricultural sector was accompanied by increasing shares of some other sectors especially the manufacturing, banking, insurance and real estate sectors.

While the share of the manufacturing sector rose from 10.5 to 13.3 per cent between 1964 and 1985, the manufacturing real output rose by almost 10 times from K£42.03 million to K£405.84 million during the same period. The country's industrial development has largely relied on import-substitution strategy, as has been the case with many other developing countries. The industrial development in the last 20 years has enabled Kenyans to enjoy a wide range of goods manufactured in the country and also to increase the volume of manufactured exports, especially to neighbouring countries.

Between 1963 and 1981, medium- and large-scale manufacturing firms employing more than 50 people increased from 181 to 450 respectively. The manufacturing sector, however, continues to be dominated by small- and medium-sized light industries. The period witnessed a large increase in the number of small-scale manufacturing concerns with a labour force of less than 50 people. Some of these manufacturing firms were established with assistance from government institutions, especially the Kenya Industrial Estates (KIE) and Industrial and Commercial Development Corporation (ICDC). Development of heavy industries like iron, steel and chemical industries has been constrained by market size and capital limitations and absence of required raw materials especially iron ore, coal, oil, etc.

One of the weaknesses in Kenya's industrial development so far has been its concentration on production of final consumer goods, leading to relative neglect of intermediate and capital goods production. Although the country has become almost self-sufficient in manufactured consumer goods, domestic industries are still heavily dependent on imported inputs which explains why about 70 per cent of Kenya's imports today consist of inputs for the local industries. Thus, in spite of the substantial industrial development which has taken place, the country's foreign exchange position continues to be strained. The situation is further aggravated by the fact that many of Kenya's manufacturing firms are not export-oriented.[4]

Generally, therefore, the Kenyan economy has so far achieved only limited diversification. It continues to be uncomfortably dependent on agricultural exports for foreign exchange earnings. The combined contribution of coffee and tea to the total domestic exports was 42 per cent in 1963 and 52.1 per cent in 1984. Manufactured products have not yet featured significantly in Kenya's external trade except to neighbouring countries.

The main disadvantage for Kenya, like many other developing countries relying so heavily on primary exports, is the fluctuation of export prices of these commodities and the deteriorating terms of trade. Kenya faced declining terms of trade for most of the period between 1975 and 1983. The only exception was during the commodity boom of 1976–1978. The country's international trade dependency index, expressed as the ratio of the value of exports and imports to GDP, remained high for most of the period under consideration. This index has averaged over 60 per cent annually since independence; a comparative figure for many developed countries is between 20 and 30 per cent.

This structural feature leaves the economy vulnerable to external events beyond its control. The above-average performance of the economy in the first decade of independence could, to a considerable extent, be attributed to the relative stability in the international economic scene which prevailed. When this stability came to an abrupt end in the 1970s following the international energy crisis, Kenya's economic performance suffered a sudden and major deterioration. The impact of this crisis and the subsequent international recessionary conditions have continued to have negative influences on the country's economic fortunes. Positive events in the international economic scene have also tended to have a dramatically positive impact in the domestic scene of such open economies. For instance, the high commodity export prices of Kenya's main exports – coffee and tea – in the period 1976–1977 led to an immediate and dramatic improvement in the economy.[5] High coffee and tea prices in the international markets in 1984 helped to ameliorate the effects of one of the country's worst droughts in that year.

The country's large balance-of-trade deficits is partly explained by the stage of development where infrastructural requirements have necessitated importation of machinery and equipment of all types. Its industrialization strategy based on import-substitution has also produced an industrial base heavily dependent on imported inputs. Thus, despite the impressive growth of volume of industrial production and almost self-sufficiency in consumer goods requirements, the country has not managed to reduce its volume of imports.

Kenya's trade with other African countries has remained low, especially as far as its imports are concerned. In 1963, only 4.9 per cent of Kenya's imports came from African countries and in 1984 the figure had gone down to only 2.0 per cent. On the other hand, its exports have increasingly found their way to other African countries expanding in proportion from 11 per cent of total exports in 1963 to 26.1 per cent by 1984. This is attributable to the country's advanced industrial sector relative to many of its neighbouring African countries.

Recent events, namely the opening of Kenya-Tanzania border, the normalization of relations between the three former East African partners after the signing of an accord about the distribution of assets and liabilities of the defunct East African Community, and the signing of the Preferential Trade Area (PTA) treaty by fifteen Eastern and Southern African countries, are expected to boost the country's external trade within Africa. It is becoming clear that if Kenya is to receive co-operation from these countries, the trade imbalance in its favour needs to be reduced by a deliberate policy of looking for ways and means of increasing its imports from other African countries.

The Kenyan economy can be termed a "mixed economy". Although the overall dominance of the private sector in the economy has continued throughout the period under consideration, the public sector has also grown significantly. The public sector accounted for only 29.3 per cent of the total wage employment in 1963, but by 1984 the figure had risen to 48 per cent. In terms of total domestic output, the public sector share of GDP rose from 24.1 per cent in 1964 to 27.6 per cent in 1970, and it is currently estimated to be about 30 per cent of GDP.

The Economic Crisis

Kenya's economic crisis began in 1974 following the global oil crisis of 1973. Temporary relief caused by high coffee and tea prices in 1976–1977 in the international markets came to an end when these prices fell drastically in 1978. The country's economic woes were intensified by the collapse of the East African Community in October 1977.

The impact of the economic crisis which has faced the country since 1973 is shown in table 1 which reveals that the average growth rates of virtually all macro-economic aggregates fell in the periods 1972–1981 and 1982–1986, compared with the period before the crisis, 1964–1972.

Table 1: Average growth rates

	1964–1972	1972–1981	1982–1986
GDP at factor cost	6.2	4.3	3.8
GDP per capita	3.0	0.8	− 0.3
GDP agriculture	4.6	2.9	2.2
GDP manufacturing	7.9	7.0	4.9
Share of investment financed from domestic savings	80.5	63.0	
Current account deficit as percentage of GDP	2.7	9.1	
Average terms of trade (1976=100)	106.7	96.3	
End of period terms of trade (1976=100)	100.0	72.3	
Rate of inflation in consumer prices	2.8	12.7	12.0

Source: Compiled from Republic of Kenya, *Economic Survey* (various issues).

For most of the period after 1973, Kenya's level of merchandise imports rose faster than the volume of exports, putting heavy pressure on the balance-of-payments. The volume of imports increased from K£82.8 million to K£1094.8 million between 1963 and 1984, while exports rose from K£7O.8 million to K£776.9 million during the same period. The balance-of-trade deficit in this period rose sharply from K£12.08 million to K£517.9 million. Fears have been expressed that the import liberalization policy pursued by the Government may worsen the country's balance-of-trade deficits unless there is a dramatic increase in the country's exporting capacity which seems highly unlikely. Import liberalization policy has been recommended and supported by the IMF and the World Bank, as part of the wider structural adjustment programme.

While the growth of the public sector had been crucial in the provision of essential services like education, health, transport and communications, extension services, etc., it has led to a number of problems especially since the mid-197Os. One of the consequences of a large public sector at a time of economic crisis was growth of government expenditure often in excess of its revenues,leading to chronic budgetary deficits. The problem has been aggravated by the fact that the country's taxable capacity has not kept pace with the growth of government expenditure requirements. For instance, total tax revenue as a proportion of total government expenditure fell from 74.8 per cent in the 1962/1963 financial year to 61.4 per cent in the 1982/1983 financial year. This in turn made it necessary to increase the Government's reliance on both domestic and external borrowing.

By 1984, government borrowing from domestic sources had grown to an extent that the Government itself was expressing concern about the trend.

Public sector credit as a proportion of total domestic credit increased from 14.9 per cent in 1970 to 42.7 per cent in 1982. This rise in public sector credit tended to deprive the private sector of essential credit facilities. Heavy domestic government borrowing also fuelled inflationary tendencies in the economy. Since 1973 the country has been suffering from high inflation rates which had reached 22.3 per cent at the end of 1982. However, there have been some improvements since 1983 with inflation rates declining to 14.6, 10 and 5.7 per cent in 1983, 1984 and 1985 respectively.

Kenya's total foreign debt has risen rapidly since the early 1970s. In 1971, the central government's total external public debt was only K£94.88 million, but it had reached K£1542 million in 1984 and K£2039 million in 1986. The debt service charges as a proportion of Kenya's exports of goods and services more than tripled from 6.3 per cent in 1971 to 19.4 per cent in 1984.

Since the early 1980s, the Government has expressed its desire to reduce its direct participation in the economy especially in joint ventures. There are, however, fears that this policy may slow down the rate of indigenization of the economy, especially if foreign investors are to buy off government interests in those enterprises where the Government is withdrawing or reducing its participation.

Rapid urbanization coupled with a high population growth rate (4.1 per cent per annum) has introduced a major imbalance between population and available resources. A large proportion of the country's resources is now devoted to provision of the basic needs of the people, leaving less for savings and investment. This has reduced the rate at which the economy's productive capacity can increase and aggravated the problem of unemployment in both rural and urban areas. Unemployment and the related problems of poverty and inequality in the distribution of income have thus become the most serious challenges to Kenyan policy makers.

In addition, fast population growth and the country's inability to substantially increase the land area under irrigation has resulted in food shortages. The period 1980–1985 experienced major food shortages especially during 1980 and 1984 when the country faced severe droughts.

Implementation of the Structural Adjustment Programme in Kenya

Kenya was among the first group of countries to embark on a structural adjustment programme in early 1980. The main features of the programme included rectifying the existing imbalance in the government budget, improving the debt management system and minimizing domestic commercial borrowing for budgetary support, devaluation of the Kenyan shilling, liberalizing imports and increasing incentives for exporters, and maintaining an appropriate level of interest rates in order to give savers a positive real return on their money. The country actively pursued this programme during the period 1980–1987.

Despite the attempts to implement many aspects of the programme, the economy performed poorly during 1980–1985 compared to 1970–1979 (see table 2). Gross domestic product grew at a slow rate of 3.1 per cent and exports by 11.0 per cent in 1980–1985 compared to 5.1 and 15.9 per cent respectively during 1970–1979. The average rate of inflation was 9.8 per cent during 1970–1979 compared to 15.1 per cent in 1980–1985. The country's total debt and balance-of-payments also deteriorated during this period.

Table 2: Economic performance indicators (1970–1985)

	1970–1979	1980–1985
	Average percent	
Growth in GDP (constant prices)	5.1	3.1
Rate of inflation (consumer prices)	9.8	15.1
Proportion of GDP of investment	24.1	27.6
Growth of exports	15.9	11.0
Growth of imports	16.4	8.9
Debt service ratio (of exports)	4.1	23.7
Overall balance (% of GDP factor cost)	19.8	− 1.5

Source: Derived from Republic of Kenya, *Economic Survey* (various issues).

However, some improvement took place in the balance-of-payments position between 1983 and 1986, except in 1984 when the country suffered one of the worst droughts in its history. During 1963–1986, the overall balance was positive except for 1985 partly due to the continuing effects of the drought. The current account deficit was reduced while foreign exchange reserves rose to their normal levels of three to four months import cover. The improvements which were achieved between 1983 and 1986 were due to a combination of good weather, favourable commodity prices and lower crude oil prices. These factors must be taken into account when assessing the effects of the structural adjustment programme. The weak performance of non-traditional exports, which experienced a 17 per cent decline in 1985, the persistent current account deficits, and generally poor economic growth could be taken as indicators of the ineffectiveness of the structural adjustment programme in the country during that period.

One of the factors which tends to reduce the effectiveness of trade liberalization measures in developing countries is that many of these countries including Kenya have tried to carry out trade liberalization without seriously undertaking the other necessary macro-economic policy measures covering issues such as aggregate output, employment price level, balance-of-payments, etc.[6] One of the constraining macro-economic policy areas is the conduct of monetary policy in the least developed countries. The currencies of these countries are usually pegged to some of the major international currencies while they also depend heavily on borrowing from the domestic banking system to finance budget deficits. These factors make it difficult for these countries to operate an effective monetary policy. Their monetary policies are usually not co-ordinated with exchange rate and fiscal policies.[7]

Trade liberalization also makes it difficult for the least developed countries to reduce their budgetary deficits due to lower revenue from custom tariffs and export taxes, reduction of government revenue as a result of reduced profits of enterprises following exposure to competition from imports and the need for the Government to support exporters as well as some of the firms suffering from increased competition from imports. Some of these undesirable effects could, however, be removed in the long run when the positive effects of liberalized trade become evident.

Reduction of real wages, regarded as necessary if trade liberalization is to be effective causes difficulty especially for countries like Kenya with well-established trade union movements as well as a generally low standard of living of the average worker. The inability to implement the required wage adjustments is seen as one of the main causes of unemployment and business failure in sectors formerly enjoying high protection.

In order to increase the production of exports, it is necessary for the Government to ensure credit availability. This is also not easy in developing countries where money and capital markets are not developed and heavy government reliance on borrowing from the domestic banking system reduces resources for private investment.

It has also been observed that if the Government's commitment on trade liberalization policy is not clear, it discourages entrepreneurs from re-allocation of resources to export production. Too gradual a liberalization has a negative impact on such re-allocation of resources, since it creates doubts about the Government's seriousness and encourages those forces opposed to liberalization.[8]

Kenya's attempts to liberalize trade have met considerable opposition from some local manufacturers who argue that reduction of protection of local industries is killing them. The growing opposition to liberalization of imports is reflected in the following excerpt from an editorial in Kenya's leading daily newspaper:

> ". . . but the real world of today has shown that there is no such thing as perfect competition. It is utopia. It is useful only as an abstraction for theoretical purposes to be bandied about within the confines of the institutes of higher learning . . . we know today that the greatest problem facing poor nations involved in international trade are the protective bans slapped against their products by developed nations just because the rich countries want to develop further and create more jobs for their own nationals . . . We in Kenya have allowed the importation of unnecessary and sometimes shoddy goods which strangle our own industries. Many jobs are at stake and capital and other resources are going down the drain."[9]

Other aspects of the structural adjustment programme which have been criticized are the depreciation of the Kenyan shilling, raising interest rates, reduction of government expenditure, limiting wage increases, and reduction or removal of government subsidies due to their negative impact on the provision of social services.

Kenya's Experience in Sustaining Human Welfare

Trends in the provision of social services in Kenya since the mid-1970s show that the economic crisis which has faced the country since 1973, coupled with the requirements of the structural adjustment programme, have slowed down the rate of expansion of some of the social services. Analysis of the available data,[10] however, shows that Kenya has managed to maintain comparatively good levels of its essential social services despite the constraints caused by the economic crisis and implementation of the structural adjustment programme.

(a) Expansion of education and literacy

The expansion of primary, secondary, technical and university enrolment had been generally impressive since 1963. The number of primary schools doubled between 1963 and 1983 while their enrolment rose almost five times.

The primary school pupil/teacher ratio improved between 1963 and 1973 from 39.2 to 32.1. But between 1973 and 1983, the pupil/teacher ratio deteriorated from 32.1 to 36.7, as the country's ability to employ teachers fell behind the primary school expansion. The picture is even grimmer if the pupil/trained teacher ratio is considered which shows that primary school expansion and teacher/training facilities were not planned in an integrated manner and has led to declines in educational standards.

In secondary education, the number of schools expanded by almost 14 times between 1963 and 1983, while the number of students rose from 30,100 to 493,700 in the same period. The student/teacher ratio worsened over time, however, from 19.7 to 24.2 in 1963 and 1983 respectively, indicating that training of teachers for secondary schools also did not keep pace with the expansion of schools and pupils.

The graduation rate for primary schools dropped from 85.2 to 63.9 per cent, in spite of the fact that free primary education was introduced in 1974. While the causes of the decline are not fully understood, one possible contributing factor could have been the inability of the parents to provide necessities like uniforms, meals for the pupils and other common expenses charged by schools especially in the form of "harambee building funds".

A Rural Literacy Survey carried out in Kenya in 1980/81 showed that the country's overall literacy rate was about 48 per cent and that only 32 and 39 per cent of rural population was able to read in English and Swahili respectively. The government's efforts to eradicate illiteracy are being thwarted by the cost of books and other reading materials which escalated following the devaluation of the Kenyan shilling at the beginning of 1980s.

(b) Nutritional indicators

Kenya, like many other developing countries, suffers from high levels of nutritional deficiency. However, the available scanty data indicate that there has been considerable improvement in the last two decades. Kenya's daily per capita calories and proteins for various periods between 1965 and 1981 show that the country's averages were above the minimum levels recommended by FAO/WHO.

Still, official estimates show that aboaut 33 per cent of the Kenyan population is "exposed to the risk of deficient nutrition". The current Five-Year Development Plan identifies the causes of nutritional deficiency as being:

> "The problem of nutritional deficiency is . . . closely associated with the general problem of poverty although there are other contributory factors, including inefficiency in food production and food habits, marketing weaknesses; lack of environmental sanitation; and lack of adequate understanding of the nutritional values of different food items. It is estimated that about one-third of Kenya's population is exposed to the risk of deficient nutrition. This includes the five identified poverty groups, especially pregnant mothers and children among those groups."[11]

In order to alleviate the seriousness of nutritional deficiency among children, the Kenyan government introduced in 1979 a free milk programme for all primary school children in the country.

(c) Housing facilities

Large proportions of the Kenyan population in both rural and urban areas live in housing facilities which are below standards. According to an urban rent survey carried out in 1979, only 25 per cent of the urban dwelling units had piped water inside, the remaining 75 per cent had water available outside the dwelling units, but within 100 m. Housing facilities in the rural areas are even worse than those in urban areas. Most of the country's rural housing facilities consist of temporary dwelling units, using traditional techniques of grass thatching and other local materials like mud, etc.

(d) Provision of health services

The Kenya Government has always regarded provision of health services as one of its major responsibilities in the post-independence period. Consequently a lot of resources have been devoted towards improvement and expansion of medical facilities, with free medical services being introduced soon after independence. At the same time efforts were made to expand medical facilities in terms of hospital beds and medical personnel. Thus, while in 1963 there were only 148 hospitals with a total of 8,683 beds, the numbers of hospitals and hospital beds had reached 249 and 31,356 respectively by 1986. This expansion can be attributed largely to direct government financing and people's self-help efforts especially through the country's harambee spirit.

The number of doctors and nurses per 100,000 population has also expanded impressively since 1963, although there was some deterioration after 1973. Table 3 shows that the number of doctors and nurses rose from 77 per 100,000 population in 1963 to 125 in 1973 and then declined to 114 per 100,000 population in 1983. This fall can be attributed to the fact that the rate at which medical personnel was being trained was slower than the country's population growth rate, and the fact that the economic crisis was putting heavy pressure on the government budgets.

Table 3: Number of doctors and nurses per 100,000 population

	1963	1973	1983
Doctors and dentists	11	7	14
Nurses and midwives	67	118	100
Total	77	125	114

Source: Republic of Kenya, *Economic Survey*, 1984, p.3.

These trends have made it clear to the planners that unless the rate of population growth falls substantially, it will be difficult to improve the quality and quantity of medical and other social services that the government is currently providing, especially given the now chronic government budgetary deficits. This explains the substantial weight given to family planning programmes in the country in the last decade or so.

(e) Access to social amenities

Another important goal of the Kenyan Government has been to improve the accessibility to social amenities in order to raise the welfare of the people.

Table 4 shows the access to various basic needs – health, education, drinking water and transport – by province. There is no doubt that large proportions of the rural population still live far away from essential services, leading to lower levels of utilization of such services and therefore rendering them less effective in uplifting the people's standard of living.

Lower accessibility to social facilities is a factor which contributes significantly to other undesirable results. For example, it was found that communities located far away from water facilities have larger proportions of poor households.[12] It is also generally acknowledged that household members who travel long distances to fetch water spend a lot of time doing so, thus leaving them with less time to spend on productive activities on their farms.

Table 4 further shows that the provinces with higher proportions of smallholder households living in areas with a primary school within 2 miles or a government secondary school within 8 miles, had generally higher proportions of children aged 6–12 years and 13–15 years attending schools.

Table 4: Access to services by rural smallholder households, by province (% of households)

Basic needs indicator	Central	Coast	Eastern	Nyanza	Rift Valley	Western	Total
Health centres within 4 miles	61.31	48.80	30.53	58.15	51.00	49.39	
Health centres within 8 miles	91.35	64.08	60.59	88.52	81.34	74.69	78.54
Education							
(a) Primary							
School within 2 miles	85.59	70.07	81.62	85.84	68.23	86.87	83.14
% smallholder population 6–12 years at school	75.46	47.76	58.90	46.36	61.76	63.53	60.74
(b) Secondary							
Government school within 4 miles	42.14	14.04	42.94	31.25	18.43	43.09	36.95
Government school within 8 miles	83.73	32.50	59.38	58.82	40.38	75.28	64.95
% smallholder population 12–15 years at school	4.45	2.44	0.18	1.20	2.17	3.30	2.23
Water (drinking)							
Wet season supply within 2 miles	99.45	90.19	96.06	98.42	99.95	99.77	98.02
Dry season supply within 2 miles	98.02	65.69	79.30	95.48	95.30	99.52	91.56
Transport							
Bus route within 2 miles	64.95	68.12	34.98	20.93	26.75	58.86	55.30
Matatu route within 2 miles	73.88	66.57	64.92	28.93	46.50	67.02	69.88

Source: Republic of Kenya, *Economic Survey*, 20, p.59.

(f) Impact of structural adjustment on provision of social services

The implementation of the structural adjustment programme has affected the provision of social services in several ways. Since independence, the Government had expanded social services by providing some of them freely or through heavy subsidies. For instance, in 1967 free medical services in government hospitals and dispensaries had been introduced. In 1974, the country also introduced free and compulsory primary education, although parents are usually responsible for the construction of classrooms. University education was provided free until 1975 when the Government introduced a student loan scheme so that beneficiaries of university education would repay the loan after they are employed. Various agricultural and veterinary facilities such as extension services, artificial insemination to upgrade their livestock, veterinary drugs, etc. were all provided free or were heavily subsidized.

One of the main requirements for Kenya in the structural adjustment programme was to rationalize and reduce government expenditure. While this requirement makes sense given the country's rising budgetary deficits due to expenditures growing much more rapidly than revenue, it has been difficult to do so without worsening human misery and related social and political problems. The country has not found it easy to significantly reduce the level of government expenditure during the period it has been implementing the adjustment programme. Available data shows that government expenditures have continued to rise.

Various arguments have been advanced against drastic curtailing of government expenditure. It is often argued that some of the main beneficiaries of the services provided by the Government are the poor, the unemployed and the landless who usually have no means of acquiring such services through the market mechanism. Another argument is that at this early stage of development, the Government has the responsibility of laying both social and economic infrastructure which would in the long run facilitate efficient operation of market forces. The Government created parastatals such as the Industrial and Commercial Development Corporation (ICDC), Kenya Industrial Estates (KIE) to facilitate and hasten the process of indigenizing sectors of the economy such as manufacturing and commerce which are still dominated by non-citizens. There have been fears that curtailing government expenditure and participation in economic activities at this stage could slow down such essential programmes.

The Government has started to push the idea of cost-sharing so that beneficiaries of government services would have to pay part of the cost. While this move is perhaps inevitable, there is the question of its effect on the poor groups of Kenyans who may not be able to pay the required share of the cost. This could aggravate the problem of inequality which is already a major issue. Cost-sharing in areas such as education and health could easily make it difficult for the poor to uplift their standard of living, and could widen the existing gap between the poor and the rich.

Some of the other structural adjustment policies have also had an impact on the human welfare. For instance, raising interest rates in the country has pushed up the cost of mortgage loans for those aspiring to own houses, especially in the urban areas. The growth of tenant-purchase schemes is reported to have slowed down in recent years partly due to high mortgage costs and partly due to the general poor performance that the economy has been experiencing. This has reduced the supply of housing and pushed up rents, making many people live in overcrowded and sub-standard conditions in urban areas.

(g) National initiatives to sustain human welfare

Inspite of the above indications of a definite declining trend in some of the social services from the mid-1970s, it is clear that there were no drastic deteriorations in the provision of most. Indeed, compared with many other countries in the continent, the decline in the human welfare in Kenya during the period cannot be said to have reached a real "crisis stage".

A number of factors can be identified as having helped the country to maintain respectable levels in the provision of essential social services. First, the country had a fairly strong economic foundation which was laid in the first post-independence decade, 1963–1973, when the country experienced rapid growth in virtually all sectors, including agriculture and industry. This performance, coupled with a growing pool of entrepreneurial skills, enabled the country to become fairly dynamic and resilient and to adjust and recover some of the economic upsets which occurred after 1973.

Thus, for instance, most of the sectors were able to recover after just one year following the droughts of 1980 and 1984, or the attempted coup in 1982. Kenya's relatively efficient management of economic resources helped to limit the negative effects of the crisis. Rational use of scarce foreign exchange resources helped to sustain the importation of necessary raw material inputs for agriculture and industry and other essential imports in the early 1980s, when the foreign exchange crisis was quite acute. The Government also managed to maintain high levels of public expenditure on various services without unmanageable budgetary deficits, mainly because of efforts made to widen the tax base and to close some of the loopholes which existed in the taxation system.

Another crucial factor in Kenya's ability to provide social services has been the country's self-help movement, known as "harambee" which means pulling together. The harambee spirit was popularized by Kenya's first President Kenyatta immediately after independence, and it has since then grown from strength to strength.

A large proportion of the country's schools, dispensaries, village polytechnics, institutes of science and technology, churches and financing of private overseas scholarships have been constructed or supported through harambee activities. The ongoing restructuring of Kenya's whole educational system, towards an 8–4–4 format, has to a large extent been accomplished through harambee spirit. In other words, the movement has enabled various social services to be provided without putting too much pressure on government finances.

The country's private sector, which accounts for more than 70 per cent of its gross domestic product and about 52 per cent of all wage employment has played an important part in the provision of various services such as education, medical care, food, etc. There is no doubt that without the dynamism of the private sector, the economic crisis would have claimed a bigger toll in terms of loss of welfare of the people.

The relative political stability experienced in the country in the last 24 years helped the country to maintain good levels of social welfare in the period 1976–1987 in spite of the difficult economic environment in which the country operated. Political stability enabled the country to minimize expenditure of its scarce resources on armaments and to use more of it in programmes which helped improve the population's social and economic conditions.

Flows of bilateral and multilateral foreign resources into the country also helped to ameliorate the impact of the economic crisis facing the country. The country's relatively low indebtedness, especially before the 1980s, and a pragmatic approach in its economic management had made the country considerably creditworthy internationally. In addition, Kenya's open-door policy to private foreign investors facilitated a good and stable flow of private foreign resources into the country.

Conclusion: Lessons from the Kenyan Experience

The Kenyan experience during the economic crisis of the period 1976–1987 and with the implementation of the structural adjustment programme brings out the following lessons for those tackling Africa's economic crisis:

(a) The economic crisis facing Africa has been caused by both internal and external factors;

(b) The apparent ineffectiveness of the structural adjustment programme in Kenya so far may be interpreted in two ways: either the problems facing Kenya and other countries are more complex than what is assumed in the SAPS or the programmes require much longer periods for the impact to be felt;

(c) There is need for more attention to be given to the impact of the adjustment programmes on human welfare than has been the case in the past;

(d) While some of the structural adjustment programme requirements are useful in terms of removing the distortions found in many of the least developed countries' economies, the pace of implementation should be more carefully considered. Given the heavy responsibilitire of public sectors in many African countries, the reduction of government participation in their economies cannot be carried out in a short term without serious human, economic and political repercussions;

(e) Political stability is an important factor in Africa's economic recovery programme. The countries in the region which have been more stable politically suffered less severely from the economic crisis of the last decade; and

(f) While external assistance and resources are important in the recovery programme of African countries, mobilization of domestic resources is more crucial. This mobilization will be achieved by giving incentives to individuals, governmental and non-governmental organizations, public and private sectors, etc., to participate in various economic activities to provide goods and services.

Notes

1 J.Vandermoortele, "Kenya Data Compendium", Institute of Development Studies, University of Nairobi, 1985.

2 The Republic of Kenya, *Statistical Abstract* and *Economic Survey* (various issues).

3 Combining the non-monetary and monetary agricultural sector shares.

4 See P.N. Hopcraft, "Outward-looking industrializaion: The promotion of manufactured exports from Kenya," Discussion Paper No. 141, Institute of Development Studies, University of Nairobi, September 1972.

5 For instance, although the real GDP growth rate was only 1.2 per cent in 1975, it rose to over 7

per cent in 1977 as a result of the unusually high coffee and tea prices during 1976/1977.

[6] Michael Mussa, "Macro-economic Policy and Trade Liberalization: Some Guidelines," in the World Bank, *Research Observer*, vol,2, No. 1, January 1987, p.61.

[7] Lal Deepok, "The political economy of economic liberalization", World Bank, *Economic Review*, vol. 1, No.2, January 1987, pp.275–276.

[8] Ibid.

[9] *Daily Nation*, 22 January 1987.

[10] Republic of Kenya, *Economic Survey*, 1984, .

[11] Republic of Kenya, *Development Plan*, 1984–1988, p.32.

[12] See ILO, *Increasing the Efficiency of Planning in Kenya*, 1983, p.42.

References

1 Bigsten, A., *Regional Inequality and Development: A Case of Kenya*, Gotborg University, 1978.

2 Collier, Paul and Deepak, Lal, "Poverty and growth in Kenya", World Bank Staff Working Paper No. 289, 1980.

3 Ghai, D. et al., *Planning for Basic Needs in Kenya: Performance, Policies and prospects*, ILO, Geneva, 1979.

4 Ikiara, G.K. and Killick, T., "The performance of the Kenyan economy since independence" in Killick, T. (ed.), *Papers on the Kenyan Economy*, Heinemann, Nairobi, 1981

5 Ikiara, G.K., "Social indicators and integrated development planning: The case of Kenya" in *Socio-Economic Analysis and Planning: Critical Choice of Methodologies*, UNESCO, Socio-economic Studies No. 12, 1986.

6 ILO, *Employment, Income and Equality: A Strategy for Increasing Productive Employment in Kenya*, ILO, Geneva, 1972.

7 ILO, *Increasing the Efficiency of Planning in Kenya: Concepts, Methods and Guidelines for Reviewing Performance and Assessing Impact*, Report of a Government of Kenya/ILO Technical Co-operation Project submitted to the Ministry of Economic Planning and Development, Nairobi, Kenya in June 1983.

8 Kenya, *African Socialism and its Application to Planning in Kenya*, Sessional Paper No. 10, 1965.

9 Kenya, *Development Plans*, (various issues).

10 *Economic Survey*, (various issues).

11 "Literacy in rural Kenya", *Social Perspectives*, vol. No. 3, CBS, Nairobi, August 1977.

12 "Urban purchasing patterns", *Social Perspectives*.

13 "The handicapped issue", *Social Perspectives*.

14 "Women in Kenya", *Social Perspectives*, vol. 3, No. 3 CBS, Nairobi, April 1978.

15 "Major highlights of Kenya fertility survey", *Social Perspectives*, vol. 4, No.2, CBS, Nairobi, December 1979.

16 "Continuity and change in metropolitan and rural attitudes towards family size and family planning in Kenya between 1966–1967 and 1977–1978", *Social Perspectives*, vol. 5, No. 1, CBS, Nairobi, December 1980.

17 "Infant mortality in Kenya: Trends and levels", *Social Perspectives*, vol. 5, No. 2, CBS, Nairobi, January 1981.

18 "Infant mortality in Kenya: Past and present differentials", *Social Perspectives*, vol. 6, No. 1 CBS, Nairobi, April 1981.

19 "Statistics on education: Developments and prospects", *Social Perspectives*, vol. 8, No. 4, CBS, Nairobi, April 1981.

20 "Modernization, birth spacing and marital fertility in Kenya", *Social Perspetives*, vol. 6, No. 5, CBS, Nairobi, September 1981.

21 "Literacy in rural Kenya, 1980–1981", *Social Perspectives*, vol. 7, No. 1, CBS, Nairobi, December 1982.

22 "The post-census survey of schools", *Social Perspectives*, vol. 7, No. 2, CBS, Nairobi, December 1982.

23 "The prospects for fertility decline in rural Kenya", *Social Perspectives*, vol. 7, No. 4, CBS, Nairobi, December 1982.

24 Kenya, "Towards a social perspective: A statistical appraisal", *Statistical Digest*, vol. XIII, No. 3, CBS, Nairobi, September 1975.

25 *Integrated Rural Survey, 1974–1975*, Basic Report, CBS, Nairobi, 1977.

26 *Integrated Rural Survey, 1976–1979*, Basic Report, CBS, Nairobi, 1982.

27 Social Accounting Matrix, 1976, CBS, Nairobi, 1982.

28 *Statistical Abstract* (various issues), Government Printer, Nairobi.

29 Killick, T. (ed), *Papers on the Kenyan Economy*, Heinemann, Nairobi, 1981.
30 Vandemoortele, Jan and Hoeven, R.V., "Income distribution and consumption patterns in urban and rural Kenya by socio-economic groups", Working Paper No. 38, WFP 2–32/wp 38, ILO, 1982

Ethiopia

TESHOME MULAT

The Nature and Evolution of the Crisis

The growing misery of the Ethiopian people has its beginning in the distant past. The current crisis and its adverse social consequences can be traced back to developments since 1973/1974. At that time there occurred disastrous droughts in Wello and the ensuing famine claimed the lives of a quarter of a million people [61, pp.7–8]. Although the bold features were visible in Wello, the drought was actually widespread in the North covering some 23 weredas (subprovinces) in Wello, Tigray, Shewa and Gonder administrative regions and affecting variously some 2 million people [60, ch. 3, especially p.84]. The drought of 1973/1974 is a culmination point of an accumulation of crises and is taken as a factor that triggered the violent overthrow of the monarchy in 1974 [60, 61].

What followed was war, internal strife and a breakdown of law and order and the attendant economic dislocations and human tragedy of enormous proportions. The war of aggression by Somalia led to the demolition and destruction of roads, bridges, railway lines and some production centres and other economic and social infrastructure. The costs of war (including purchases and usage of weapons and supplies) was high on both sides. There were large numbers of displaced persons some of whom moved to centres of care and shelter in Harar, Dire Dawa, Goba, and in many locations in Sidamo and elsewhere in Ethiopia. Large numbers also fled to Djibouti and to Somalia. In the process, uncountable numbers of the young and infirm perished, family life was disrupted and many persons sustained varying degrees of physical damage or ill-health [23, p.11].

At the same time a war of secession was being fought in Ethiopia and the central administration had to cope with fratricidal local feuds among competing contenders for political control. Both tendencies still linger on but during the years between 1974–1980 they were at the height of their fury and the social and economic consequences were on a scale verging on the imaginary.

The human tragedy and social crisis emanating from these disruptive processes (i.e., drought, famine and wars) were at a level perhaps unparalleled anywhere else in modern African history. Countless numbers lost their lives or were dislocated. Many homes were destroyed, family life shaken and children who lost their parents were everywhere. The political turmoil and economic dislocation left, both in the towns and the rural areas, marks of chaos, disruption and destruction. The misery of the people found expression in their malnourished and curving bodies, down cast eyes and in their aimless and untiring movements in search of water, food and shelter. As is usually the case in such situations, women, children and the elderly may have suffered more than other groups.

Then, came the great famine of 1984. Unlike the droughts of earlier periods the drought of 1984 was widespread and constituted a culmination point of a prolonged drought period covering about 10 years. The small rains (belg) failed to come on time in 1984 in most places and the long rains (meher) in June-August did not produce the usual quantity of moisture needed for grain cultivation. In many places the drought and shortfalls in rains lasted three years or more. The result overall has been reduction in the volume of agricultural production and sometimes complete cessation of agricultural activities and widespread destruction of livestock [23, 60]. In the northern provinces, where the majority of Ethiopians live, all households were variously and adversely affected by the drought. An estimate provided by the Relief and Rehabilitation Commission is that some 8 million people "needed immediate assistance" and of these "16 per cent were children under the age of four, 26 per cent between five and fourteen years of age and the remaining 58 per cent above fourteen years" [61, p.10]. The human tragedy that is a direct result of the 1984 drought and famine drew the attention of the United Nations and the international community. The 'crisis' was greatly aggravated by local wars of insurgency, poor economic and social infrastructure and the disruptions in economic activities. Large numbers died in the process and of those that survived many were sick and in need of medical attention. These had often to leave their homes and farms in search of relief which at the critical moment was not there or available only in insufficient amounts. According to a government report food aid and other assistance has been provided to 4 million people and only in 21 relief camps located in 54 Awrajas (subprovinces). In addition, special nutrition and medical services were provided to some 334,000 children only, who suffered from famine-induced diseases and showed signs of extreme loss of weight [20].

A Trend of Declining Economic Activity

Between 1973–1974 and 1977–1978 the GDP was growing at less than one per cent per annum and per capita GDP must have had a negative growth rate since the population was growing at about 2.5 per cent annum. Between 1977 and 1985 there were ups and downs with a continuing declining trend in production due, in the main, to the drought-induced fall in agricultural production and the economic dislocations from continuing local insurgency [24, pp.20–21].

There has been a marked decline in agricultural productivity. Since agriculture is the backbone of the economy, the effects of the decline tend to be widespread in the economic system. Land reform transferred much of cash crop agriculture to the State which lacked organizational and managerial capabilities at the early stages of the nationalization programme. Other private lands were transferred to newly established peasant associations and agricultural co-operatives. Production in these lands was further constrained, however, by reduced applications of agricultural inputs, including fertilizers, improved seeds and agricultural machinery. As a result, agricultural raw material supplies were reduced and the level of exports including coffee, oilseeds and fruits and vegetables dropped significantly [2, ch. 1] and [24, ch. 4].

A significant indicator of the problems of agriculture has been the marked decline in food production. Food production activity is carried out essentially by peasants although, in recent years state farms have contributed some on emergency and temporary arrangements. The economic dislocations following land nationalization, war with Somalia, internal insurgency and the continuing drought adversely affected subsistence agriculture. Food production is estimated to have grown during 1971–1980 by only 1.7 per cent per annum and food demand by 2.4 per cent per annum. Attempt has been made to fill the food gap through imports and food imports which were about 5 per cent of total imports by value in 1975 were close to 10 per cent in 1982. However, the magnitude of the shortfalls in food requirements around 1983–1985 were so large that nothing short of massive international food aid could avert the impending human disaster. Accordingly, between January 1984 and May 1985, a total of about half a millions metric tons of food aid was received from international voluntary agencies and distributed to the starving millions by the Relief and Rehabilitation Commission [61, p.12].

The decline of agriculture has its repercussions in other economic sectors as well. Industry in Ethiopia is at a rudimentary stage of development with a fair share (45 per cent) of manufacturing output coming from small-scale and handicraft industries. In 1979–80 manufacturing was only about 10 per cent of GDP (at constant 1960–1961 factor cost). Heavy industry is virtually non-existent and many of the medium- and large-scale manufacturing industries are of relatively small size by international standards [65, pp.4, 12–14]. The share of manufacturing in total employment is even smaller than its share in GDP. Only about 5 per cent of total employment in the economy is in manufacturing and this share rises to 7 per cent for the wider definition of "industry" (including, that is, manufacturing, mining and quarrying, building, construction, electricity and water) [65, p.22]. Although manufacturing output showed positive growth rates per annum over the past couple of decades, the development of industry has been greatly constrained in recent years. To begin with, most of the medium to large-scale manufacturing enterprises were owned by foreigners who fled the country following sweeping nationalization around 1975–1977. Managerial capacities in the state enterprises take time to build and in the meanwhile poor performance was in evidence. Disorders following the collapse of the monarchy were marked by a clear lack of industrial discipline among the workforce and in some instances physical destruction of industrial facilities occurred. Decline in foreign exchange earnings from agricultural exports led to conspicuous reductions in imported inputs, spare parts and general supplies as well as a marked drop in investment funds. Raw material supplies from domestic agriculture were also inadequate and irregular at times. Combinations of these difficulties forced industrial development down by half. Similar to the situations prevailing in agriculture and in the economy generally, industrial performance has remained far below expectations.

Other economic performance indicators also show the crisis situation of the Ethiopian economy. The deterioration of the balance-of-payments, depressed savings and investment and unfavourable developments in the fiscal and monetary fields characterize the developments in the past 10 years or so. Ethiopia's current account deficit steadily increased during the decade ending in 1984/1985. Coffee exports, accounting for over 60 per cent of the total exports by value, were adversely affected by supply irregularities and the general deterioration of the terms of trade for primary goods. On the other hand, "since 1981–1982 the value of merchandise imports has been running at more than double the value of merchandise exports" [67, p.28], thus aggravating the balance-of-payments crisis.

The foreign exchange shortages and shortfalls implied in the above considerations have precipitated a savings and investment crisis. Domestic savings which were estimated at 6 per cent of GDP during the years 1975/1978 were down to 0.3 per cent of GDP for the period 1983/1985 [67, p.23]. This is reflected in the declining rate of capital accumulation. Low investment in the economy is in evidence and aggravated by a general and perceptible decline in the rate of inflow of investible foreign capital. The economy has also been experiencing a trend of worsening inflation. The Addis Ababa retail price index was growing at about 6 per cent per annum during the 1980–1985 period. During this same period the supply of money was increasing at about 11 per cent per annum and the rather slower rate of increase of inflation is, in fact, explained by the application of price controls, overvaluation of the exchange rate and a wage freeze [67, p.28].

Reform Measures and the Crisis

Since the overthrow of the monarchy in 1974, the Provisional Military Administrative Council (PMAC) of Ethiopia has introduced a number of far-reaching institutional (organizational) and policy reforms. Aspects of these reforms were introduced to change the status quo and to bring about rapid industrialization. Others were formulated as corrective measures against mistakes resulting from natural disasters (such as famine, drought, etc.) or wars (border wars and domestic insurgency).

The first of such reform measures taken by the Government includes the publication of the Programme of the National Democratic Revolution and the Declaration on Economic Policy of Socialist Ethiopia [58, 59]. These establish the ideological break with the past and unambiguously define the socialist road of industrialization to be pursued by the Government. The Declaration in particular, differentiates and defines the economic activities to be carried out by private individuals and by the socialist state. It also limits the scope for foreign capital participation in joint ventures with the Ethiopian Government.

To provide concrete foundations for the socialist state economy, rural lands were nationalized and urban land and extra houses were also made government property. Large agricultural estates producing cash crops, manufacturing enterprises in the medium large-scale category and many businesses especially in the wholesale trade, import and export sector were also nationalized. In the same fashion, social and economic services and infrastructure were either nationalized or were brought under effective government control In addition, a number of new ministries and institutions were established to permit a manageable division of responsibilities, streamline the state sector activities and enable the socialist state to perform wide-ranging tasks. Most of these relate to the economic spheres, but there are also a number of such institutions relating to the social side and to the manifestations of specific social problems. Rapid nationalization led to problems of compensation and provision of insurance, pensions, welfare schemes, etc., for the workers transferred to state-owned industries. The drought led to a large displacement of the peasantry in the afflicted areas and drought-caused and war-induced migrations of large numbers focused public attention on the problem of children. As a result of these developments, therefore, new institutions were established including Children's Commission, Relief and Rehabilitation Commission, Compensation Commission, etc.

Steps were also taken to sensitize the masses and mobilize them in mass organizations and institutions. The peasantry was organized in peasant associations which constitute the reference unit for the rural economy. As political groups, the peasants belong to the All-Ethiopia Peasant Association which is organized at local (kebele), regional and national levels. Residents of cities and towns are also organized in a similar fashion and there is a hierarchy of the Urban Dwellers Association which is established at the kebele, higher and municipality levels. Industrial workers are expected to benefit from a new (and improved) labour law and are also organized into trade unions. To ensure complete coverage of social groups, laws were also enacted to formalize the voluntary association of the youth and the women. These now have their respective associations also organized on kebele (local, regional and national) levels.

The organizational machinery to carry out central planning activities has also been established now that the environment conducive for its introduction is effected through the government control of the "commanding heights of the national economy". The central planning organ was modified or even changed radically to give central planning the comprehensiveness and pervasive stance it requires under socialism. To enhance its local level operations, regional planning offices were also set up as integral parts of the Office of the National Committee for Central Planning. To date, there are eight such offices in the country.

Some Indicators of Performance in the Socio-Economic Spheres

The combination of these institutional and policy reforms was expected to yield tangible economic results and raise the welfare index of the society significantly. However, results are mixed and a set of forces including geopolitical, environmental and local circumstances have made the attainment of goals difficult.

(a) The rural economy

The public ownership of land, the establishment of peasant associations as grass-root level organizations, and the introduction of an All-Ethiopia Peasant Association are basic and fundamental reforms expected to transform agriculture.

The Peasant Associations are grass-root level organizations each with jurisdictional power over an area of about 800 ha and 2.4 hundred families. They perform various tasks including land administration (distribution), law enforcement and political functions in the promotion of socialist principles and ideals. They also co-ordinate activities in the social spheres such as the construction of health clinics, schools and cultural centres and carry out economic programmes aimed at raising the productivity and welfare of the peasantry. By the end of 1985 there were a total of 20,157 Peasant Associations with a membership of about 6 million households covering about two-thirds of the country's rural population.

While the Peasant Associations provide the peasantry with an umbrella organization, the like of which did not exist in the past and while such associations can become connecting links with central administration and the Ministry of Agriculture, the economic performance of the peasantry thus far cannot be described as being satisfactory. The continued drought and internal insurgency in some areas have complicated matters. The introduction of new ideas in traditional societies takes time and may possess destabilizing influences unless the introduction of these ideas is properly couched. There are also considerations which were not entertained in establishing Peasant Associations as grass-root level organizations. These include the absence of security in land holding and the discouragement to private initiatives suffered by the peasantry and the difficulties to be faced, therefore, to adjust to market demand for agricultural produce. An individual peasant has access rights but not ownership rights to land and he/she cannot vary the size of holdings on the basis of individual preference. The Peasant Association framework also possesses design limitations adversely affecting its role in the economic sphere. With the Peasant Association membership increasing through time from population (natural) increase and immigration, the size of individual household holdings is bound to diminish. This, together with the increased frequency of land redistribution programmes, instill a sense, of insecurity among the peasantry and works against individual investment in agriculture. It has been a common occurrence, at any rate in the earlier years of the reform, for peasants to cut trees on their land allotments without caring to protect the soil and in general to behave apathetically and with disinterest to improve the productivity of land through some form of capitalization. A recent report observes, "declining arable land per head, declining forests, livestock number and soil erosion are indicators of instability in the overall economic system" [8, p.19].

The adverse consequences of these processes are not difficult to discern. Peasant agriculture accounts for about 93 per cent of total agricultural production and occupies close to 94 per cent of the cultivated land. Outmoded agricultural implements are in general use and very few fertilizers, improved seeds or modern land management techniques are applied. Between 1969 and 1979 the volume of agricultural production increased by 0.4 per cent per annum which is far lower than the average of 0.9 per cent per annum growth rate for the low-income African countries. With population growing at more than 2 per cent per annum during the same period, the rate of per capita production is thus negative and estimated at −1.7 per cent per annum. Total food production grew by 0.4 per cent per annum while the average annual growth rate for non-food agricultural products over the 10 year period had been 1.3 per cent [66, p.167]. Food aid imports which were estimated at 58.7 thousand metric tons (or 2 kg per capita) in 1975 increased to 1,577 thousand metric tons (or 5.1 kg per capita) in 1979, clearly indicating reduced sectoral capacity to meet the national food requirement [66, p.24]. An ECA estimate gives a "food-gap" rate (i.e., the difference between food production growth rate and the growth rate of food demand) of −0.7 per cent per annum for the years 1971/1980 [13, p.12]. With the share of food imports in total imports (which in 1965 was 8.64 per cent, and 5.01 per cent in 1975) rising to the 9.81 per cent mark in 1982 and large expansions in food aid intakes in recent years, the agricultural sector is clearly deficient and malfunctioning, and this is so in spite of the many reforms and policy changes.

The macro-economic policy adjustments suggested by the World Bank have not been implemented. The basic content of these proposals includes the devaluation of the Ethiopian birr and the raising of agricultural (especially food) prices to the levels of (at least) import parity prices. It is expected that these policies would improve export performance and raise the level of agricultural production. It is also suggested that steps should be taken to improve private capital formation in agriculture by improving the saving potentials of the peasantry through increased incomes, improved marketing and enhanced investment possibilities [16, 67]. Even if these policy measures were implemented, however, it is unlikely that positive results will be forthcoming in the short term. Besides going against the socialist management of the economy, these measures are piecemeal approaches and are not based on a comprehensive review of the economic, institutional and policy arrangements put in place by the socialist Government of Ethiopia. Thus, it is difficult to see the gains from food price hikes if the supply of land is constant. How is the peasantry expected to respond to increased demand for food in such a situation when at the same time modern inputs, improved seeds and fertilizers are not easily available?

It is obvious that peasant agriculture is in a state of economic decline and stagnation and the attempt, on the side of the Government, to change the situation appears to progress without secession but also without tangible results. Here again time is of the essence and co-operative development is at an embryonic stage. Although the law was promulgated in 1975, by 1982 there were just over 1,000 Producers' Co-operatives in the country with a membership of 60,000 peasants accounting for about 0.2 per cent of the rural population [7, p.61]. In fact, the development of the Producers' Co-operatives has been progressing very slowly and the contribution of the co-operative sector to total agricultural output remains insignificant. There is also a strategic problem connected with co-operative development. Co-operatives perform reasonably well when they are properly linked to a dynamic sector such as a growing urban economy or the export sector. The collectivization of the means of production and the construction of planned collective activity on common lands by themselves are insufficient to sustain and maintain growth. This perhaps explains the slow and haphazard development of the co-operative movement in the country today.

With regard to state farm development, their contributions to alleviate the serious food shortages during the crisis period have been remarkable. In the longer term, state farms are expected to play important and determinant roles in agriculture especially in the production of agricultural raw materials and exports, in the development and expansion of irrigated agriculture and in the introduction of modern agricultural technology and land management practice. The perspective Ten-Year Development Plan describes the future of state farms in these terms. However, in the interim period, many state farms are reported to have incurred considerable losses, to suffer from misplanning and mismanagement and as a result have had to scale down operations. In 1983/1984, only 223,200 ha were farmed by the state farm sector accounting for about 3.5 per cent of the total cultivated land (and a similar share in total agricultural production) in the country [24, ch. 43].

There are two other important measures affecting the rural economy introduced by the Ethiopian Government recently: land settlement and villagization. Planned settlement has a long history in Ethiopia. But the settlement as a response to the 1984–1985 emergency is unique in that it involved millions of persons, constituted a major government activity at the time and the plan was to be effected within a short span of time. The plan, which was put into action during the latter part of 1984, consisted of moving about 300,000 families (or 1.5 million persons) from the drought-afflicted areas in the north and settling them in the southern parts of the country. There are many objectives to the plan including: (i) relieving pressures on the land in northern areas; (ii) enabling settled peasants to be self-sufficient and contribute to improved agriculture and especially food production; (iii) putting new and unused arable lands under cultivation; and (iv) bringing about a more balanced population distribution and a more efficient land/labour ratio than obtain at present [60, pp.184–201].

The settlement programme is viewed by the Government as an ongoing activity and up until 1987 it has progressed, more or less as planned. Still there are dissenting voices heard, and since there is wide international participation in the scheme, it is perhaps to be expected.The critics doubt the voluntary nature of the activity, make too much out of the short-run difficulties encountered in the course of programme implementation and also make a political case out of the perceived conflict between the "settler and the native". The Government, on the other hand, views the programme as one without alternatives. Some level of population removal from the afflicted areas is necessary if life is to be saved, if the land is to be rehabilitated and the Government claims much of the resettlement is done on new virgin lands and without displacing people. Outside of these areas, some settlers are absorbed in existing but less densely populated peasant areas.

As regards the villagization programme, it too was carried out as a planned activity. The effective and efficient distribution of public services (including schooling, health services, water, electricity supplies, etc.) is highly constrained in situations where scattered homesteads are prevalent. In such situations it is also difficult to introduce effective land use planning. On the other hand, some critics of the government programme point to short-run problems such as the accentuation of the deforestation trend brought about by the need to relocate the huts, the increased distance between the residential area and the farms, the loss of privacy and adjustment costs associated with the changing lifestyle. The government did not waste time in implementing the villagization programme and appears to have taken full advantage of peasant receptiveness created by the drought and famine conditions prevailing in the country at the time. Between February 1986 and 1987, some 11,460 villages were started and of these 5,178 were completed. The number of villagized persons during the year is estimated at 5,725,530 or 15 per cent of the rural population. The villagization programme, like the resettlement programme, is viewed by the Government as an ongoing activity and one that promises all-round improvement in the rural economy.

(b) Industry

Industry (broadly defined to include manufacturing, mining and construction) accounts for about 15 per cent of GDP and employs less than 5 per cent of the labour force. Manufacturing is the most important activity in the group and accounts for about 10 per cent of the GDP and has been growing very slowly in recent years [65, p.22]. Employment in manufacturing is estimated at about 100,000 in state enterprises, 60,000 in private firms and just above 300,000 in handicrafts [18, p.126], Thus industry is relatively small and the Ethiopian economy remains basically agricultural.

Small-scale manufacturing enterprises and handicrafts are expected to perform well in the economy in view of their relatively lower import requirements, larger capacity to use domestic raw materials and waste products and greater flexibility to adjust to local market sizes than large-scale manufacturing. In addition, it is generally assumed that they can provide a very high rate of employment per unit of investment. There have also been important policy reforms by the Government with a view to improving the sectoral performance in the economy and bringing about a more equitable and efficient geographical spread of industry.

However, results are far from expectations and the sub-sector suffers at the moment from extreme under capitalization, environmental uncertainties and organizational complexities. To begin with, the sectoral development has been too slow. Over a 10 year period since the establishment of HASIDA in 1977, there have only been 290 new enterprises in the Small-scale Industries group, with a capital of about E.B. 319,054,000 and providing a total additional employment of 3,671 persons [4, pp.1–2]. It means an average of 400 persons were employed every year during the period, which is too low seen against the high level of unemployment in the cities and the presumed high employment potentials of small-scale industries. Some blame the "highly uncertain environment" for the under capitalization [18, p.138]. The sub-sector faces other problems and inadequacies as well. Thus while the rate of dependency on imports in small-scale industries is generally smaller than in large-scale manufacturing, certain small-scale industries, such as those in the rubber, plastic, chemicals, etc., group depend heavily on imports. About 41 per cent of small-scale industries surveyed depend on both domestic and imported raw materials, and only 53 per cent use only domestic raw materials, while 6 per cent depend totally on imports [64, p.142]. Foreign exchange shortages have created supply difficulties for these enterprises and most of them are forced at times to close or to frequently operate at less than capacity. Indeed, according to a recent HASIDA survey only 56 per cent of the available capacity in all surveyed small-scale industries is utilized, although this ratio varies between towns and industry groups [64, p.143]. For the handicraft sector what HASIDA has been attempting includes the organizing of such craftsmen into service and producers' Co-operatives [39]. So far its own capacity limitations have confined its role mainly to urban areas so that the large rural economy remains unaffected in its manufacturing activities. Some others see constraints to the development of the small-scale industries and handicraft sector in the existing "restrictive" practices and suggest further institutional and policy reforms are necessary.

Large-scale manufacturing is predominantly public or state-owned. Much has been done to rehabilitate the enterprises which were abandoned by their foreign owners or were nationalized by the new socialist government in the mid-1970s. At the time of nationalization most of the enterprises were in disrepair, lacking in inputs and spares, using obsolete technology, operating with excess capacity and had very poor labour management practices. The new labour law was beneficial to workers in industry and those employees in the newly nationalized enterprises enjoyed security of employment and entitlement to pension benefits. The government also organized the enterprises into corporations within the Ministry of Industry, provided financing for their rehabilitation and introduced a new working framework within which their continued and planned operations are made possible. New laws on ownership, joint ventures and industrial management were also introduced to give the sector an enhanced performance and a fitting place in a socialist economy.

Despite these efforts, however, the large-scale manufacturing sector faces wide-ranging problems and its growth, measured by employment and production levels, has been very slow. Foreign exchange shortages have continued to keep imported input supplies low and irregular, thus forcing many enterprises to operate frequently at less than capacity. Industrial expansion has been greatly constrained by inadequate investment finance. During 1979–1984 total investment in new projects amounted to only E.B. 493 million with 56 per cent government share and 38 per cent from foreign loans [19, p.31]. The major impediment to the growth of industry is the lack of adequate finance. The 1983 Proclamation on Joint Ventures does not appear to have stimulated growth in investment finance to any appreciable degree and the level of foreign capital participation in industry, however desirable and necessary it may be, remains insignificant.

It thus appears that the changes generally advocated by the World Bank and the IMF including raising the price level, devaluing the birr, concomittant alterations in tax and monetary regimes, etc. would remain cosmetic and may not by themselves yield significant improvements in the level of foreign private and public capital participation in Ethiopian industries.

Another important economic activity with strong social impact is housing. Scattered homesteads and the generally unplanned nature of rural settlements have given rise to unique housing problems in rural areas. Basic services such as education, medicare and utilities such as the provision of improved water systems and energy sources were not being provided in sufficient amounts or meeting acceptable standards. Among the important aims of the villagization programme is to bring about settlement patterns which make the rational organization and provision of such services possible and also to permit the application of suitable land use planning in agriculture. Many new villages established by the Ethiopian Government are reported to have benefitted by the improvement programmes with household members having access to schools and clinics and the newly established village stores which provide the community with household supplies and merchandise.

However, the housing problem today is felt more strongly in the towns and cities than in the rural settlements. In all urban settlements in the country the housing problem persists, inspite of the many improvement plans put forth by the Ethiopian Government. A major source of the housing problem emanates from the fast growth of the urban population. It is reported that the urban population is growing at 5 per cent per annum and is expected "to double within 11 to 15 years" [24, p.207]. New houses have therefore to be built to accommodate the growing urban population. There is also a commensurate need to expand the infrastructure and services that support urban housing development. Together with the need to maintain and improve existing housing, the "housing requirements" of urban centres in Ethiopia today is clearly beyond the country's financial means. According to a recent government report "annual urban housing requirements are 15 times actual capacity" [24, p.211]. Shortages of building materials, the poverty of the urban population and inadequate finance have also aggravated the housing problem in the cities and towns.

The Government is still taking the initiative to correct the housing anomaly in spite of the fact that the magnitude of shortfall in housing is clearly too large. Between 1975 and 1980, it is reported that "a total of 30,275 houses have been built at a cost of birr 225 million" [24, p.211] – a large investment outlay by Ethiopian standards. Other steps taken by the Ethiopian Government to improve the poor housing situation in the country, in the coming decade, include the drawing up of an urban development programme for 98 towns, improving the efficiency of the public housing authorities, developing appropriate housing policies and improving the material and financial foundations for an improved and expanded urban development effort [24, pp.207–213]. The Government believes that the private sector has an important role to play in this. However, concrete steps may yet have to be taken to ensure the active (and expanded) participation in housing construction activities by private capital.

(c) The social services

The Ethiopian revolution has made tangible and credible gains in the sphere of social services. Of particular interest here are the measures taken to improve the education, health and social organization of the mass of people.

(i) *Education*

Following the land nationalization programmes of 1975 and the establishment of new systems of administration for the peasantry it was found necessary to launch wide-ranging programmes to consolidate the many gains made on behalf of the masses and to make the attainment of developmental goals possible. Among the measures taken by the Government were the establishment of a National Literacy Campaign Co-ordinating Committee in May 1979 and the launching of the National Literacy Campaign in July of the same year. The Campaign was organized on a biennial basis with each campaign round lasting about six months. By August 1983, nine Campaign rounds were completed and about 10 million adults made literate. There were about 20,000 literacy centres and about 27 million booklets prepared in a total of 15 languages. Some one million instructors have participated in the nine rounds [15, pp.42–43]. The Literacy Campaign, which is carried out as a continuing programme, has attained its objective of liberating a large segment of the population from illiteracy and covers all major geographic regions of the country. Its success is also indicated by the awards and recognition received from diverse international institutions. Ethiopia received awards during the annual UNESCO Literacy Prize ceremonies and in 1980 was selected for the International Reading Association Literacy Award [15, p.43].

The literacy campaign is strengthened by post-literacy and adult literacy programmes. By 1983 the communities where literacy classes were being conducted had built some 660 reading rooms, with the campaign co-ordinating committee providing the reading materials for these facilities. With UNICEF support, over 200 basic education centres have been put up since 1977. These are aimed at providing the educational and training needs of rural communities to undertake developmental activity. There are also some 400 community skill training centres where the development ministries and agencies provide specific development programmes for the rural communities. Some 50,000 peasants have participated in such programmes since 1979 [15, p.44]. In addition it is heartening to note that many participants in literacy programmes develop the interest and continue training by joining the formal education programmes during off working hours or during periods of slack agricultural activities. These diverse post-literacy programmes give the literacy campaign effort the practical orientation and sense of permanency and continuity that it requires.

A measure of success has also been achieved in the formal or "regular schools system". Pre-schools (kindergarten, child care centres, etc.) receive the attention they deserve by public authorities. For some time now they have been confined to urban centres and the beneficiaries were the children of the well-to-do. Following the radical reforms in educational spheres, growth in pre-schools has been rapid. By 1982 there were some 630 pre-schools established throughout the country with 4,000 teachers, the majority of whom are graduates of the Ministry of Education Pre-school Teacher Training Institute [15, p.45].

As regards the pre-tertiary level of education (i.e., primary, junior secondary, senior secondary, technical and vocational schools), the reforms were essentially in three major areas. First, by nationalizing private schools the bulk of the students were to get their education in government schools and it was thought such an arrangement would make the planned development and distribution of schooling effective. Second, by involving parent committees and introducing administrative streamlining, the attempt was made to increase community participation in the management of schools. Third, an appreciable increase in the student enrolment ratio was obtained by efficiently utilizing classroom space (including use of "class rotation" schemes), expanding school building activity and recruiting additional teachers. In addition, many teacher training institutes are being established and the curricula in schools have been revised to give formal education a technical/vocational bias.

Student enrolment in all schools (primary and secondary level) increased by 12 per cent per annum during the period 1975–1984 (as against 11 per cent for the 1964–1975 period). The number of schools increased appreciably – by 8.6 and 9.07 per cent per annum during 1964–1975 and 1975–1984 respectively. Other indicators of performance in schooling activities, including the number of classrooms and the number of teachers, also indicate a heightened effort on the part of the Ethiopian Government to raise the educational level of its school-age population as well as that of the society at large. During the decade 1974–1984 the number of classrooms and teachers increased by an average 7.6 and 9.5 per cent per annum respectively. This impressive growth in schooling activities has been achieved both in primary and secondary schooling and with a more equitable geographical spread than in the past. Similar successes are also recorded in the tertiary system of education.

The above need not suggest the schooling system is without problems. Even with the observed rapid enrolment growth rate, only 7 per cent of the eligible age group population are actually enrolled in senior secondary grades (grades 9–12) and in the primary plus junior secondary level grades (grades 1–8) the enrolment ratio is 23 per cent. There are also financial problems which are in fact at the root of the schooling problem at the moment. The state financial means are too small and the sources of finance too few. There is a large aid component in the schooling expenditure structure and the organization and management of schools are being reformed at present. New syllabi for schools are at an experimental stage and it will be a while before they are fully implemented. The exceptionally high student enrolment ratios in schools are obtained, in part, by lowering the teacher to student ratio i.e. by a deterioration of the quality of education. Then there is the serious problem of school leaver unemployment to be faced. A recent estimate shows that over 40 per cent of the registered unemployed are young persons aged 15–24 and more than 60 per cent of them are female [21, p.96]. With the economic difficulties Ethiopia is facing at the moment and the low employment-generating potentials of the small-scale industry, public enterprises and the agricultural sector, educated unemployment and underemployment will continue to grow and trouble policy-makers in the country.

Quite significant strides have also been made with regard to the development of higher education (tertiary level education). The Commission for Higher Education (CHE) was established in 1981 with the responsibilities of co-ordinating, planning and managing higher education in the country. Prior to the establishment of the Commission for Higher Education there were only two universities in the country – the Addis Ababa University and the (less developed) Asmara University. A high percentage of foreign nationals were involved in teaching, research as well as in the management and administration of education. The higher education system also depended, to a large extent, on foreign grant finance and borrowing [24, p.240].

Among the changes introduced with the establishment of the Commission for Higher Education, were the consolidation and upward increase in the number of post-secondary institutions. The Addis Ababa University expanded its existing programmes, established a few new departments and institutes and introduced post-graduate training programmes. The Asmara University was brought under the auspices of the Commission for Higher Education and was considerably expanded and its programmes diversified to provide training services for pupils coming from all over the country. The Alemaya College of Agriculture of the Addis Ababa University became the new Alemaya Agricultural University in 1985, and with its status thus raised, diversified its training and research programmes and began to cater for larger numbers than before. Many new post-secondary training institutions and research institutes were also brought under the Commission for Higher Education or newly established by the Commission for Higher Education [1, pp.24–28].

The other index of change in higher education is the increased enrolment of students in the various institutions. The student population in the "regular programmes" in all institutions of higher learning, which was 8,200 at its peak prior to 1984, increased to 16,000 in 1983 [24, p.243]. All students enrolled in the regular and extension programmes of the tertiary level education system numbered 27,616 in 1985. In 1974, about 80 per cent of the capital budget of the higher education system was provided by external funding. This share was reduced to the 20 per cent level by 1983. National instructors are predominant in the universities and research institutes and unlike the practice of the pre-1974 period when there were none, many faculties of the Addis Ababa University today provide post-graduate level training in many fields of specialization.

In spite of the above developments, however, the system of higher education in Ethiopia today faces serious problems of finance. The secondary schools matriculate in the hundreds of thousands but tertiary level institutes can only accommodate a few thousand students every year. With the economic difficulties, already described as harsh and overpowering, the school leaver unemployment problem is becoming an increasingly important issue of priority policy concern of the government.

(ii) *Health*

Comprehensive population health status surveys have never been carried out in the country. Epidemiological surveys are rare and there are no comprehensive and reliable morbidity and mortality data at the moment. What is presently available is information based on scanty sample data and rough national estimates and these lead to a conclusion that a lot more needs to be done in the health field than obtains at the moment. It is, for example, estimated that 60 per cent of childhood morbidity is caused by preventable diseases. Malaria is endemic in 70 per cent of the country and there exists a high prevalence of vectorborne diseases [69, pp.17–18]. Poor sanitation and malnutrition-caused diseases account for about 75 per cent of the health problems in the country [10, p.5]. Clearly these are indications of underdevelopment and of the low health status of the population. As a result, the bulk of the health problems are intertwined with the underdevelopment of the economy and can be solved by improvements in the economic field.

Table 1: Some indications of health development

Health development indicators	Ethiopia	Low-income sub-Saharan Africa	Middle-income sub-Saharan Africa
Population per physician (thousand)	88.1[a]	39.2	11.3
Population per hospital bed (thousand)	3.8[a]	1.7	1.4
Access to safe water (% of population)	14.5	25.2	45.8
Infant mortality rate (per thousand)	172.0	128.5	103.2
Family planning users (% of married women)	2.0	4.5	7.1
Energy consumption per capita (kg of oil equivalent)	16.7	54.6	530.7

Note: The most recent estimates are reported here, and most recent estimate refer to any year between 1982 and 1985.

[a] Refers to the year 1980. [see 69, p 1–2]

As the above table shows, the low level of health development for Ethiopia is in evidence using a variety of health development indicators. The above indexes, in fact, make the country the least developed in terms of health in much the same way as we have already shown its relative position in economic terms.

The response of the Ethiopian Government has been the production of a health plan – Health Sector Ten-Year Perspective Plan (1985–1994). This plan, whose implementation is now underway, is favourably evaluated, among others, by the World Bank [68, pp.vii–xii] and is aimed at making significant changes to the health status of the population. The plan emphasizes the prevention and control of diseases, community participation in the delivery of suitable health programmes and the co-ordination and equitable distribution of health services. The Alma Ata Declaration, to which Ethiopia is signatory, and its primary health care objectives appear to be the foundations of this plan. The major aim of the plan includes the attainment of "full and meaningful life for the broad masses" and the plan strategy includes disease prevention and control, provision of rural health services and the promotion of self-reliance and community involvement in health activities [10, p.2].

The specific targets of the health plan include (i) reduction of infant mortality by 40 per cent; (ii) increase of life expectancy to 55 years (from the present 42 level); (iii) reduction of child mortality rate [i.e., death rate of children under 5] from its present level of 247/1000 to the level of 150/1000 by 1994; and (iv) provision of health services to 80 per cent of the population by 1994 (as against the present level of 15–20 per cent [10, p.1, 13] The strategy developed in the plan in order to reach the above-mentioned health targets includes: the building up of administrative and institutional infrastructure and health services; training and recruitment of additional health workers; bringing into play a co-ordinated activity of supportive institutions; the introduction of health education for the public and the implementation of specific health programmes [10, pp.13–20].

A principal attraction of the health plan is its emphasis on the delivery of health services directed to the population at large. The land reform, the organization of the peasantry into peasant associations, the massive resettlement and villagization programmes, the impressive results obtained in the literacy field, etc., all add up to a co-ordinated development effort and the health plan fits in the scheme rather well. But a mass-oriented health plan calls for heavy health infrastructure, adequate budgetary provisions, the deployment of large numbers of health personnel and the delivery of suitable health services. When account is taken of these implications of the health plan, one is forced to heed to its description as being on the ambitious side. In effect, what is aimed at is the achievement of health goals in the coming 10 years that have not been attainable during the past millennia. An investment of E.B 515.9 million for the ten-year plan period, although small seen against the plan requirement, is equivalent to twice the investment in the health field of the previous decade. It is also worth mentioning that the plan relies heavily (for up to 24 per cent of the level of capital budgets) on foreign assistance and the level of planned community participation (of 26 per cent of the capital budgets) does not necessarily convey fully the sense of self-reliance and community participation of a primary health care system.

Conclusion

In Ethiopia, the current economic, political and social crises have been extreme and have resulted in a large-scale destruction of lives and property, displacement of large populations and disruptions in the existing political, economic and social order of the society. Severe drought, border wars, secessionist activities and internal disorders have coexisted and reinforced internal disorders have coexisted and reinforced each other to make the "crisis" the "most extreme" yet to be faced by the Ethiopian people.

The Ethiopian government has introduced an array of policy reforms and measures aimed at combating the adverse consequences of this "crisis". Some of these are radical and are focused on changing the old economic and political order and laying the foundations for a new one. Obviously the effectiveness of these measures takes time to show and requires the continued and sustained application of concerted developmental efforts in many lines of activities including the education, economic, health, defense fields, etc. Thus the main policy goals of the Programme of The National Democratic Revolution and the Declaration on Economic Policy of socialist Ethiopia can only be realized in the long term, and that, only if the path so charted is taken with the appropriate programme packages and sustained effort. The main problem is that resources are greatly limited and the course being pursued is full of difficulties, uncertainties and setbacks. On the other hand, some of the policy reforms and measures taken have either solved a problem that is an element of the crisis, or could be credited with having slowed down the progress of the crisis or of having reduced its severity. The war effort against Somalia and the secessionists in the north has resulted in victory and the maintenance of the territorial integrity of the country. The positive aspects of the resettlement programme include the starting of new life by the settlers and the promise of rehabilitation of the drought-afflicted lands in the densely populated regions of the north. The mass literacy campaign has enabled millions to read and write and the primary health care based health plan promises to bring about drastic and permanent changes for the better in the health status of the population.

Yet the crisis persists. At the time these concluding lines are being written, the Ethiopian government is requesting the international community to provide food aid since the current drought is expected to result in a substantial drop in food production during the 1987/1988 crop year. Export earnings are likely to fall far short of import bills since export prices and supplies of coffee are greatly constrained.

The recent population census (1984) established the size of the Ethiopian population in 1987 at about 46 million – far higher than past estimates suggested – with a rate of population increase of about 2.5 per cent per annum. The Ten-Year Perspective Plan has set very ambitious goals in the social and economic spheres of national endeavour. At the same time there seems no end to the unfolding crisis. These factors suggest that the going will be very tough for the Ethiopian people. More bold steps and the application of more sustained developmental efforts than have been attempted in the past are required to bring about a measure of improvement in the life and well-being of the population.

References

1 Commission for Higher Education, Higher Education in Ethiopia, Addis Ababa, September 1985. (In Amharic)

2 Plan Follow-up and Evaluation Department of the ONCCP, Evaluation of the six annual plans 1980/81 1985/86, Addis Ababa, January 1985. (In Amharic)

3 Ministry of Education, Educational Administration – Study and Evaluation of Educational Developments in Ethiopia, Addis Ababa, 1985.

4 HASIDA, HASIDA Information (special publication), Addis Ababa, December 1986. (In Amharic)

5 Addis Zemen (an Ethiopian daily), (24 March 1987). (Report by the Secretary-General to the sixth Meeting of the Central Committee of the EWP). (In Amharic)
6 Abdella Basha, FAO/FIAC Regional Seminar on Fertilizer Pricing Policies for Africa: Country report on Ethiopia, Nairobi, 1986.
7 Ministry of Agriculture, Report of the Peasant Producers' and Service Co-operative Division, August, 1982. (In Amharic)
8 FAO/Ministry of Agricultur, Ethiopian Highlands Reclamation Study: Macro-economic Reiew (Based on the work of the Joint ECA/FAO Agriculture Division, Working Paper No. 9, UTF/ETH/037/ETH, Addis Ababa, May 1987).
9 Ahmed Mohammed and Hayalu Shiferaw, Small-scale and handicraft industries in Ethiopia, (a paper presented to the first national Symposium on Industrial Development in Ethiopia, Addis Ababa, August 1986).
10 Central Planning Supreme Council, Health Sector Ten-Year Perspective Plan (1985–1994) of Socialist Ethiopia – Part I: Main Body of the Plan, Addis Ababa, March, 1984.
11 Commission for Higher Education, Statistics on Higher Education 1985/86 academic year, Addis Ababa, April, 1987.
12 Dessalegn Rahmato, Agrarian Reform in Ethiopia, University of Uppsala, (Sweden), 1984.
13 ECA, Analysis of food production and imports 1965–1984 (E/ECA/PSD-4/54, 23 December 1985).
14 ECA, Analysis of food production and imports 1965–1984 A Statistical Analysis. (E/ECA/PSD-4/54, Addis Ababa, 3–12 March 1986).
15 Ministry of Education, Education in Socialist Ethiopia: Origin, Reorientation, Strategy for Development, Addis Ababa, 1984.
16 Joint Government of Ethiopia/World Bank Mission, Ethiopia: Review of Farmers Incentives and Agricultural Marketing and Distribution Efficiency, 17 March, 1983. (Confidential)
17 Hudes, C.C. and Hunter J.M., "Disease and development in tropical Africa", Social Science and Medicine, 3, 443–493, 1970.
18 ILO/JASPA, Socialism from the grass roots: Accumulation, employment and equity in Ethiopia. (A report prepared by an employment advisory mission organized by ILO/JASPA, Volume I report. Addis Ababa, September 1983. (Confidential Draft)
19 Ministry of Industry, Policy study and research division, investment pattern in manufacturing industry, (The first national Symposium on Industrial Development in Ethiopia, Addis Ababa, August 1986).
20 Ministry of Information and National guidance, Addis Zemen, an Ethiopian daily paper, Tekemt 17, 1977 E.C.
21 JASPA/ILO, Youth Employment and Youth Employment Programme in Africa – The case of Ethiopia, Addis Ababa, 1986.
22 Mengistu Haile Mariam, "The National Revolutionary War in the North", Addis Ababa, Ministry of Information and National Guidance, 7 June 1978.
23 Mengistu Haile-Mariam, "Imperialist Aggression from Vietnam to Ethiopia", Addis Ababa, Ministry of Information and National Guidance, 30 January 1978.
24 Office of the National Committee For Central Planning (ONCCP), Ten-Year Perspective Plan 1984/85–1993/94, Addis Ababa, August 1984.
25 Niggli, P., Ethiopia: Deportations and forced-labour camps, a study on behalf of the Berliner Missions Werk, Switzerland, Documentation 25/85 May 1985)
26 Proclamation 19/1975, Proclamation to Establish the Ministry of National Resource Development.
27 Proclamation 19/1975, Proclamation to provide for the Public Ownership of Rural Lands.
28 Proclamation 47/1975, Government Ownership of Urban Lands and Extra Houses Proclamation.
29 Proclamation 54/1975, Public Ownership of Private Schools Proclamation.
30 Proclamation 62/1975, Ethiopian Science and Technology Commission Establishement Proclamation.
31 Proclamation 64/1975, Labour Proclamation.
32 Proclamation 70/1975, Compensation Commission Establishment Proclamation.
33 Proclamation 71/1975, Peasant Association Organization and Consolidation Proclamation.
34 Proclamation 85/1976, Labour (Amendment) Proclamation.
35 Proclamation 99/1976, Monetary and Banking Proclamation.
36 Proclamation 103/1976, Administration and Control of Schools by the People proclamation.
37 Proclamation 104/1976, Urban Dwellers' Association Consolidation and Municipalities Proclamation.
38 Proclamation 109/1 977, Higher Educational Institutions administration Proclamation.

39 Proclamation 124/1977, The Handicraft and Small-Scale Industries Development Authority Establishment Proclamation.
40 Proclamation 128/1977, Central Planning Commission Establishment Proclamation.
41 Proclamation 130/1977, All-Ethiopia Peasant Association Proclamation Amendment.
42 Proclamation 138/1978, The Co-operative Societies Proclamation.
43 Proclamation 141/1978, All-Ethiopia Peasant Association Proclamation Amendment.
44 Proclamation 142/1978, State Farms Development Authority Proclamation.
46 Proclamation 173/1979,Relief and Rehabilitation Commission Establishment Proclamation.
47 Proclamation 182/1980, Ethiopian Tourism Commission Establishment Proclamation.
48 Proclamation 187/1980, Revolutionary Ethiopia Youth Association Establishment Proclamation.
49 Proclamation 188/1980, Revolutionary Ethiopia women's Association Establishment Proclamation.
50 Proclamation 189/1980, Ethiopia Transport Construction Authority Establishment Proclamation.
51 Proclamation 190/1980, Ethiopian Water Works Construction Authority Establishment.
52 Proclamation 191/1980, Ethiopian Building construction Authority Establishment.
53 Proclamation 208/1981, Establishment of National Children's Commission Proclamation.
54 Proclamation 222/1982, Trade Unions Organizations Proclamation.
55 Proclamation 223/1982, Peasant Associations Consolidation Proclamation.
56 Proclamation 235/1983, Joint Venture Establishment Proclamation.
57 Proclamation 262/1984, Office of the National Committee for Central Planning Establishment Proclamation.
58 Provisional Military Administrative Council, Programme of the National Democratic Revolution, undated.
59 Provisional Military Administrative Council, Declaration on Economic Policy of Socialist Ethiopia, Addis Ababa, 7 February 1975.
60 Relief and Rehabilitation Commission, The Ravages of Drought: Ethiopia's Decade of Struggle in Relief and Rehabilitation, Addis Ababa, 1985.
61 Relief and Rehabilitation Commission, Tackling the Ravages of Drought, Addis Ababa, August 1985.
62 Survival International, Ethiopia's Bitter Medicine: Settling for Disaster – An Evaluation of the Ethiopian Government's Resettlement Programme, London, Calvert's Press (TU), 1986.
63 Teshome Mulat, "Educational Policy and the Regional Distribution of Schools", The Ethiopian Journal of Education (forthcoming)
64 Teshome Mulat, "Employment in small-scale manufacturing and handicraft industries in Ethiopia", *Labour and Society*, vol. 9, No. 2, April-June 1984.
65 Teshome Mulat (with Eshetu Chole) in ILO/JASPA, Patterns of Industrialization and Impact on Employment and Incomes in African countries: The Case of Ethiopia, Addis Ababa, JASPA, 1983.
66 World Bank, Accelerated Development in sub-Saharan Africa: An Agenda for Action, Washington D.C., World Bank, 1981.
67 World Bank, Ethiopia: Recent Economic Developments and Prospects for Recovery and Growth, Report No. 5929-ET, 25 February 1987.
68 World Bank, Sector Review Ethiopia: Population, Health and Nutrition, Report No. 5299-ET, 30 September 1985.

Nigeria

JOE U. UMO

Introduction

The dual role that human beings play, as producers and consumers, in contemporary development thought has been forcefully underscored by two popular paradigms. On the one hand, the "human capital revolution"[1] focusing attention on human abilities, has led to the realization that human beings constitute the key development input, as producers. The "new" development perspective which defines economic development as a self-reliant growth process associated with significant reductions in unemployment, poverty and inequality,[2] on the other hand, highlights the human being as the key beneficiary (or end) of development.

Nigeria, with an estimated population of 100 million (1986), has had a checkered development experience in terms of the human dimension during the last 27 years of its nationhood. The most current phase of this experience is the one induced by the global recession which set in since 1980. Although most economies have recovered from the adverse impact of this recession, the country seems to be slipping deeper into it. The different recovery programmes which have been put in place seem to be generating counterproductive results thereby worsening and prolonging the crisis. Assuredly, the long-term development goals of the nation can only be realized if the economy recovers without undermining the creative viability of its people as development agents.

This paper is therefore an attempt to profile and analyze Nigerias's recent experience in the broad area of human resources development and welfare. This will provide a background perspective for examining the development impacts of various recovery measures which have been applied since the onset of the current recession. The structural adjustment programme, in particular, will be evaluated in a human-situational context. The paper ends with policy considerations for Nigeria's recovery and development from the national, regional, and international perspectives.

Trends in Human Resources Development and Welfare

The importance of human resources development, especially through education, has often been given pride of place since Nigeria's political independence in 1960. This arises from the recognition that manpower shortages, especially in critical technical and executive areas have posed a binding constraint on the realization of national planning goals. Efforts to remove this constraint have resulted in liberal provision of school places and in consequence, the exponential trend in enrolment in schools as shown in table 1:

Table 1: Growth in enrolment and schools in Nigeria: 1973–1984/1985

	Primary schools		Secondary schools		Tertiary sector (universities)	
Years	No. of schools	Enrolment	No. of schools	Enrolment	No. of universities	Enrolment
1973/1974	14,525	4,746,808	1,337	448,904	6	25,900
1983/1984	36,126	16,171,380	5,076	1,627,905	35+	160,000+
Percentage increase	(148.7)	(240.6)	(273.6)	(262.6)	(483.3)	(517.8)

Source: Calculated from various tables in Joe U. Umo, "Political economy of Nigerian education 1960–1985", in T.N. Tamuno *et al.* (eds.), Independent Nigeria: "The First 25 Years", Institute of African Studies, Ibadan, 1985 (forthcoming).

+ Figure includes the Military University started in 1985 in the Nigerian Defence Academy, Kaduna.

The main issues arising from the above table are as follows:

(a) The number of primary schools which stood at about 15,000 in 1973 increased to about 36,000 in 1983, representing about 149 per cent increase in 10 years. Correspondingly, primary school enrolment rose from 4.7 million in 1974 to 16.2 million in 1984 registering an increase of about 241 per cent;

(b) Enrolments in secondary schools which stood at about 45,000 in 1973 rose to 1.6 million in 1983. This represents a 263 per cent increase in 10 years;

(c) In the tertiary sector, the increases in the number of universities and enrolment were equally dramatic. In 1973–1974, there were only six universities with student enrolment of about 26,000. But 10 years later (1983–1984), the number of universities (including degree-awarding colleges of education) had shot to 35, with student enrolment of about 160,000. Thus the number of universities and student enrolment had increased by 480 and 500 per cent respectively within the period.

It must be noted that despite these explosive growths, the enrolment ratios, especially in the secondary and tertiary educational sectors, are still relatively low when compared to other middle-income countries or the developed countries. For example, Nigeria's current enrolment ratios at the secondary and tertiary levels are estimated to be 20 and 2 per cent respectively, whereas the averages for the industrial market economies in 1983 are 85 and 37 respectively. Furthermore, some of the progress made in human resources development and welfare is more apparent than real.

(a) Progress and problems of human welfare

To put the economic crisis in perspective, a background profile of human resources development problems and welfare is in order. The concern here will be focused on key issues like the structure and impact of educational financing, distributional inequality and unemployment.

(i) *Educational financing*

From independence up to 1973–1974, Nigeria spent less than 1 per cent of its GDP on education but between 1975 and 1980, it spent an average of 4 per cent of its GDP on education. Since 1981, this expenditure has dropped to an average of 1.6 per cent annually. The declining expenditure stands in stark contrast to the explosive enrolment trends observed earlier.

But perhaps what is more disturbing is the emerging phenomenon of an inverted pyramid in the structure of educational financing[3] which has created a situation where the tertiary educational sector receives the highest financial allocation (over 50 per cent) while the secondary and primary sectors receive about 35 and 21 per cent respectively. The implications of the above financing structure can be identified as follows:

1. Adverse effects on the quantum and quality of primary education

Although the primary school enrolment ratio is 98 per cent nationally, the ratios for most educationally disadvantaged States are far below this average. With the introduction of fees in recent years, parents are finding it extremely difficult to educate their children at the primary school level, hence pupils are dropping out. Those who stay in public schools (about 16 million in 1986) have substandard education because of rising pupil/teacher ratios, lack of equipment and poor and irregular remuneration for teachers. This situation has compelled many well-to-do parents to withdraw their children from government schools into private schools (where quality is higher) as well as supplement this with privately organized after-school "lessons" for such children. The results of the National Common Entrance Examination have consistently shown that pupils from the private schools outperform those from public schools in Nigeria.[4]

2. Declining quality in secondary education

Using examination performance as a quality index, one can infer that a drastic decline has taken place for the Nigerian secondary school system in recent years. For instance, while quality passes [i.e., a minimum of five credit passes at Ordinary ("O") Level General Certificate of Education (GCE) examination] averaged 32 per cent in the 1960s, it dipped to 16.5 per cent in the 1970s and showed only marginal improvements in the early part of the 1980s. In terms of specific core subjects, the failure rate reached an unprecedented level of 82 per cent in the English language in 1985 and had been averaging 67 per cent for mathematics and biology between 1983 and 1985.[5] The adverse impacts of the declining quality of secondary education for further (especially tertiary) education and employment hardly needs elaboration.

(b) Equity

Equity, whether measured in terms of access to educational opportunities or distribution of basic amenities, has been seriously undermined in recent years. At the primary school level, high fees have limited access to primary education hence many children may remain illiterate for life. Correspondingly, poor quality education has limited the career chances of many graduates. But perhaps more disturbingly, it has been shown that investment in university education explains about 72 per cent of income inequality in

Nigeria, mainly due to the indiscriminate application of subsidy.[6]

Given the paucity of statistics on income inequality in Nigeria, other indicators of equity to be discussed below can only be regarded as approximate suggesting the trends in equity rather than the accurate depiction of the situation.

(i) *Salary and wage differentials*

Since independence, several commissions have been set up to review wages in Nigeria in order to relate these to the cost of living operating at that time. Before the Udoji Commission in 1975, the wage gap between the lowest and the highest paid civil servant was 1:20. Since 1975, this ratio has gradually been reduced as shown in table 2:

Table 2: Minimum wage in Nigerian public services and ratio between the highest and lowest wages, 1975–1981

Wage	Regime	Proportion of highest to lowest	Average minimum level per annum in naira
1975	Williams & Williams	18.2:1	792
1979	Adjustment by Military Government	13.9:1	1038
1980	Adjustment by civilian regime	9.74:1	1512
1981	Industrial Arbitration Tribunal Award	9.50:1	1572

As table 2 clearly shows, successive increases over the years from the bottom scale have reduced the differentials from 1:18.2 in 1975 to 1:9.50 in 1981. Thus within a period of five years, the minimum wage had been increased by about 92 per cent. The apparent improvement implied by this increase should however be qualified by the fact that only nominal rather than real wages are considered. Indeed, with the inflation rate of 40 per cent in 1982, the N125 per month minimum wage had a real value of N75. This amount is hardly enough to pay the monthly rent of a single room in Lagos.

A study of the income distribution pattern in the Nigerian Federal Public Service between 1972 and 1977 produced a fringe benefit adjusted-Gini index of 0.52.[7] This also serves to confirm the worsening equity in income distribution in Nigeria in the 1970s.

(ii) *Some basic needs indicators of equity in Nigeria*

Given the well-known shortcomings of the Gini index as a measure of inequality,[8] the basic needs approach can be used as a supplementary measure. This is because it aims at solving the problem of absolute (abject) poverty while avoiding the problem of tackling the elusive goal of narrowing inequality between the rich and the poor.[9] Let us examine two measures of the basic needs approach, viz: food and health.

1. Food

Detailed estimates of per capita calorie supply as an index of nutrition is lacking in Nigeria. The United Nations' estimate puts Nigeria's daily per capita calorie supply at 2,443 for 1983. This is about 1,000 short of the average for industrialized market economies. From one's personal observation, it appears that the United Nations' estimate is on the high side because of the growing incidence of malnutrition in the country. Following the depressed state of agriculture, Nigeria's food import bill escalated. In 1974, for instance, the food import bill stood at N155 million but by 1982, it had risen to N2,048 million representing an astronomical increase of 1,321 per cent. What was even worse was the fact that the imported food and other "essential commodities" hardly reached the poor because of the flawed and corrupt system of distribution during the Second Republic (1979–1983). Efforts to get essential food supplies to the villages were often frustrated by corrupt officials in the headquarters who colluded with middlemen to preempt them before they reached their destinations and target beneficiaries.

2. Health

From the mid-1960s to the end of the 1970s there were some marked improvements in most health indicators in the country. For example, population per registered medical practitioner dropped from 31,810 in 1964 to 12,530 in 1979, and by 1983, it was 8,000. Nevertheless, Nigeria's population per physician is about 15 times that of the average for developed countries which in 1983 stood at 554. In general, there has been some considerable progress in the training of other health personnel like nurses, registered pharmacists, medical technologists, etc. These efforts have, however, not matched the needs of the growing population for medical services. The reasons include the following:

(a) Health facilities tend to be located mainly in the urban areas thereby making access by rural people extremely difficult. The health personnel show a definite preference for the urban areas and hence the majority of the rural citizens still depend on traditional healers for medical services;

(b) Even within the urban areas, the cost-effectiveness of modern health delivery system is low. Thus between 1980 and 1983, the incidence of diseases like measles, whooping cough, chicken-pox, schistosomiasis and tuberculosis were on the increase (see table 1 of the annex);

(c) Life expectancy, which is perhaps one of the most reliable composite basic needs indicators,[10] stood at 47 years for the Nigerian male and 50 years for the female in 1983. This is a far cry from 72 and 79 years for males and females respectively in many developed countries;

(d) In terms of vital statistics, Nigeria's infant mortality which stood at 120 per 1,000 is probably one of the world's highest (see table 1 of the annex). Death rate is estimated at about 2.5 per cent annually between 1984–1986.[11]

(c) Unemployment

During most of the decade of the 1960s, unemployment did not pose a serious developmental problem for the country. In the labour force sample survey conducted in 1966–1967, about 24 million Nigerians (40 per cent of the population) were in the labour force. The rate of unemployment was approximately 1.7 per cent comprising 7.6 per cent in the urban areas and 0.5 per cent in the rural areas.

The major feature of the unemployment problem then was that of the youth. The total unemployment rate among youth aged 15 to 29 years stood at 10.5 per cent and this constituted about 86.3 per cent of all the unemployed. The youths involved were those with primary school education and high-school certificate holders; hence the sense in labelling the unemployment of this era as the "school leaver problem".[12]

The aftermath of civil war disruptions mainly accounted for the huge number of unemployed workers – 2 million in 1970. The effects of post-war reconstruction efforts however reduced unemployment to 1.25 million.

The 1974 sample survey of the labour force showed a wide variation in unemployment among the major urban centres of the country. The distribution among major cities was as follows (in percentage):

Lagos	7
Jos	6
Ibadan	6
Kaduna	6
Maiduguri	5
Benin	13
Port Harcourt	13
Calabar	22

It is clear from the above that the unemployment problem was becoming quite serious in the 1970s. A tracer study reported in the fourth National Development Plan (1981–1985) noted that urban unemployment ranged between 8 and 15 per cent in the big cities. The oil boom as well as the explosion in school enrolment generated massive migration which swelled the ranks of the unemployed in the urban areas. The informal sector which is characterized by underemployment grew substantially in many urban areas.

Unemployment in the 1980s

Despite the apparent increase in the nation's oil wealth, Nigeria entered the decade of the 1980s with serious unemployment problems. As has been aptly admitted by the Fourth Development Plan (1981–1985), "the persistence of unemployment suggests that the employment opportunities created by previous plan implementation were not sustantial to mop up the backlog of the unemployed in addition to absorbing new entrants to the labour market" (p.423). This observation has been borne out by the unemployment statistics generated by the 1984 labour force sample survey (see table 2 in the annex).

The three interesting features emerging from the labour force sample survey report in table 2 are that:

(a) Urban unemployment has grown worse than what it was in the 1960s and 1970s. States with double digit urban unemployment included Anambra (15 per cent), Bendel (13 per cent), Cross River (14 per cent), Gongola (12 per cent), Imo (16 per cent) and Lagos (10 per cent);

(b) Rural unemployment, once regarded as a rare phenomenon in Nigeria has grown substantially in many areas like Bendel (15 per cent), Imo (12 per cent), Rivers State (8 per cent). This trend is indicative of the growing rural poverty:

(c) Unemployment among females surprisingly outnumbered that of males in both urban and rural areas. Female unemployment was about 10 per cent vis-à-vis male, registering 7 per cent in the urban areas; while the figures were 6.3 per cent vis-à-vis 3.5 per cent respectively in the rural areas.

An additional feature of the unemployment problem emerging in the 1980s which is worth noting is the growing graduate unemployment. Although a comprehensive study and quantification of the problem is yet to be done, it is being observed that; (a) of the 45,000–50,000 graduates produced yearly from the country's institutions of higher learning, only about 10 per cent have been successful in getting job placements. The rest roam the streets as job applicants and those who can afford it have returned to graduate school for higher degrees; and (b) the economy has been shown to exhibit an inherent incapacity to absorb labour at the rate thrown out by the school system.[13] Thus, given the economy's monocultural condition, the adverse impact of the global recession which started in the early 1980s has indeed worsened the fragile employment situation in the country.

The Journey to Economic Crisis in Nigeria and the Recovery Menu

A fuller appreciation of the impact of the economic recovery programme on the human dimension of development as well as the associated policy implications must be seen against the backdrop of events that characterized the post-oil boom era in the Nigerian economy. A snapshot sketch of the main events of the era can be highlighted as follows:

(a) Before the oil boom era which started in 1973, Nigeria's total export income during the previous seven years (1966–1972) amounted to about N8 billion. In the subsequent seven years (1974–1980), the country's export proceeds were about N8 billion annually. The amount of money the country made in seven years became its annual export income via the petroleum windfall. This naturally catapulted it into a high mass consumption/investment plane which could not be matched by equivalent domestic production;

(b) The country embarked upon huge investment projects some of which were of dubious economic viability and had long gestation periods. Some of the projects of the era include various highway constructions, the hosting of the World Black Arts festival (FESTAC '77), building of the new capital at Abuja, founding 13 traditional universities in 1976 and seven universities of technology in 1982, and sustaining an expensive presidential system of civilian government;

(c) Meanwhile, the country's agricultural sector suffered substantial neglect and between 1970 and 1982 different cash crops suffered an estimated production decline as follows:

	In percentage
Cocoa	43
Rubber	29
Cotton	65
Groundnuts	64

(d) With the decline in agriculture, hence food production and the attempt to accelerate the pace of import-substitution industrialization, the demand for imports shot up dramatically. Nigeria's import bill which stood at N756 million in 1970 had risen to N12,599 million in 1981, showing an increase of about 1667 per cent within just a decade. The pressure for imports was validated by the availability of foreign exchange generated mainly by crude oil sales;

(e) By 1981, the global recession had struck and the oil market collapsed. The price of petroleum which stood at $US 22.4 per barrel in 1980 had dropped to $US 12.8 per barrel by 1982 and, after picking up again to $US 20 per barrel in 1985, slumped to the lowest level of $US 9.9 per barrel in 1986. The loss in oil revenue threw the economy out of gear and revealed most of its structural deformities. These include the monocultural dependence on oil exports, administrative wastes, misguided domestic policies, distorted prices (especially that of foreign exchange), over-subsidized and corrupt government parastatals, etc.;

(f) Government's attempts to maintain the tempo of production in the face of unresolved gaps like the foreign exchange gap, the fiscal gap, the food gap, etc., led to the acceleration of external borrowing. Nigeria's external debts which stood at N82.4 million, N488.8 million and N2,178.4 million in 1960, 1970 and 1980 respectively jumped to N17,290.6 million by 1985 and in the following year, it was estimated at N57 billion (including short term trade arrears). It should be noted, those debts were obtained on stiff terms including relatively high and floating rate of interest (averaging 11 per cent), low maturity period (averaging seven years) and unfavourable maturity profile.[14] By this time, Nigeria's credit rating had fallen from 55.4 per cent in 1981 to 22.8 per cent in 1986.

From the above account, the two broad issues which featured prominently in Nigeria's economic crisis need to be stressed. These were:

(a) internal problems of economic mismanagement and policy inadequacies; and

(b) the exogenous influence arising from both the oil boom and the global recession. The former generated some kind of "wealth illusion" which encouraged large-scale economic distortions while the latter worsened and exposed the distortions without necessarily providing a fundamental solution. Indeed, we shall argue that some of the externally oriented solutions have become the problem themselves.

(a) The Recovery Menu and Its Impact on the Human Condition

The first attempt at economic recovery from Nigeria's current recession was made by President Shagari in April 1982 when it was clear that the balance-of-payments was in deficit and external reserves had been depleted to a highly dangerous level. Shagari passed the Economic Stabilization Act aimed at structural adjustment of the economy and export diversification. The features of the Act included:

(a) exchange control measures in which basic travel allowances were reduced from N800 to N500 per adult (non-business) traveller, and from N30,000 to N25,000 for business travels;

(b) registration of Form M whose life span was kept at six months with administrative centralization at Lagos;

(c) use of fiscal measures to ban a few commodities like frozen chicken and gaming machines and increase in tariffs on some 49 imports; and

(d) use of compulsory deposits for imports ranging from 25 per cent (for materials and spare parts) to 250 per cent (for import of motor cars).

(i) *Effects of the Economic Stabilization Act*

These measures were largely unsuccessful in turning the economy around and some policies did not seem to have made any difference at all. For instance, the exchange control hardly stopped the middle class from going on either business trips or religious pilgrimages. Despite the enhanced strength of the customs in fighting smuggling, the process continued unabated. The various administrative regulations like Form M. affecting imports, stiffled business initiatives and generated more corruption. The tariff increases and compulsory deposit requirement had a deflationary impact, hence worsening the recovery efforts. The solutions to the human dilemmas of poverty, inequality and unemployment therefore remained largely untouched by the Act.

1. The 1985 national economic emergency

In 1985, the Buhari regime declared 15 months of national economic emergency under which two important economic measures were taken, viz:

(a) deductions varying from 2 to 15 per cent from all incomes including dividends, salaries and wages of all workers in the economy were undertaken; and
(b) importation of rice and maize was banned.

2. Effects of the emergency

Although there was an element of progressivity in the imposition of the economic recovery fund, the overall impact was to depress the disposable incomes of workers. The situation got so bad, especially for the low income workers, that the Government had to order a refund of the contribution of workers earning below N3,000 annually early in 1987. At the time of writing, some States are yet to get back these refunds.[15]

In the higher echelons of the public sector, the negative real income effect of the economic recovery contribution was evaded by a more intensive use of official facilities like cars so as to offset the loss in nominal income. In the private sector, more fringe benefits were given to offset this loss. This must have undoubtedly led to a worsening in income inequalities, although this is yet to be quantified.

(ii) *The 1986 structural adjustment programme*

The structural adjustment programme which was officially put in place in June 1986 was a logical extension of the restructuring initiative contained in that year's "recovery budget". The key elements of the programme were the second-tier foreign exchange market, tackling the liquidity crisis through debt rescheduling, privatization and trade liberalization. Other elements incorporated in the budget included the monetary and banking policies, rural development, employment generation, local raw material sourcing and export promotion. Let us briefly examine the performance of some of these recovery measures, especially as they affect the human welfare.

1. Second-tier foreign exchange market

The second-tier foreign exchange market, which has now been rechristened foreign exchange market after the unification of the first and second tiers, came into existence in September 1986. Its main purpose was to find a realistic exchange rate for the naira which had been overvalued. But additionally, the second-tier foreign exchange market was expected to create enormous incentives for the production of non-oil exportables; attract foreign capital into the country; discourage illegal currency trafficking and minimize the administrative wastes and corruption which characterized foreign exchange allocations via the import licencing arrangements.

Although the second-tier foreign exchange market has introduced order and discipline into the foreign exchange allocation, as well as restored creditor confidence in the Nigerian economy, it has generated some serious problems which must be confronted. The two key problems in this connection are:

(a) The marginalization of the agricultural and small-scale industrial sector of the economy in foreign exchange allocation. A summary of foreign exchange allocation published after seven months of operation showed that out of $US 1,200 million allocated so far, less than one per cent (0.34 per cent) went to agriculture, while about 71 per cent of the allocation was made to big industrial concerns.[16] The small-scale industries were completely "crowded out" as they could not afford the high price of foreign exchange which has fluctuated between N3.00 and N5.00 per dollar. As there can be no meaningful economic recovery without revamping Nigeria's depressed agriculture, it is evident that the second-tier foreign exchange market may have worsened the fate of the rural farmers – except the few who engage in the production of primary commodities whose prices had increased substantially. Furthermore, the crowding out of small-scale industries which often accounts for about 90 per cent of modern sector employment has adversely affected the welfare of people who depend directly or indirectly on this sector for livelihood;

(b) The second-tier foreign exchange market has so far not been able to define what the "realistic" rate of the naira is, since the rates fluctuate at each bidding session. The volatile exchange rate behaviour has meant that business cannot undertake future investment planning. Indirectly, this has affected employment generation. To be sure, many industries have closed down and most of them are estimated to be operating below pre-second-tier foreign exchange market capacity. It would appear that the very purpose of the structural adjustment programme may be defeated if the foreign exchange market is not modified to allow some sensitive sectors of the economy access to foreign exchange. This issue will be taken up in the last section of this paper.

2. Trade liberalization

The main objective of trade liberalization is to rid the economy of existing price distortions and inefficiency in the industrial sector by creating an environment for healthy competition. While this is desirable by itself, an indiscriminate (doctrinaire) approach to the policy has created a curious paradox of abundant industrial output and low capacity utilization. Foreign products have therefore flooded the markets while the indigenous industries cannot increase their capacity output, hence employment. Apparently, it appears that some multinationals have resorted to importation of cheap final products since the local production cost has escalated because of the second-tier foreign exchange market. Continuation of a policy of indiscriminate trade liberalization in Nigeria's peculiar circumstance can lead to a situation where no meaningful indigenous industry and technology can grow in the foreseeable future.

3. Export promotion

The policy thrust here is to encourage the development of non-oil exports given the country's monocultural dependence on oil exports. However, the non-oil export trend has declined since 1960.

An aggressive promotion of non-oil exports via generous export incentives is expected to close the export revenue gap, estimated at between $US 10 billion to $US 35 billion annually. Although improved domestic prices for some primary products have improved their supply response, it may not add much to export revenue in the aggregate. For example, the total exports of Nigeria's agricultural commodities was 2.4 per cent in 1986; while the exports of manufactures was a mere 0.4 per cent. In effect, therefore, the emphasis on non-oil export drive may be problematic in several ways. The high cost of Nigeria's industrial environment, the collapse of the world primary commodity market, and the growing "new protectionism" in developed countries against exports from least developed countries, etc., are discouraging signals against programmes of export promotion. But the real dilemma posed by the growing foreign debt is that the growth of oil exports with its characteristic fluctuations, may not be sufficient for both debt service and development needs of the economy.

4. Monetary and banking policies

The monetary policy package under the structural adjustment programme is contractionary. Thus the policy was targeted at a moderate increase in the supply of money and bank credit. The rate of interest which was earlier adjusted in an upward direction was allowed to be determined by market forces as from August 1987. With the rediscount rate of 15 per cent fixed by the Central Bank of Nigeria, the market rate is hovering around 17.5 per cent (at the time of writing). These measures have worsened the credit crunch which the economy has been facing since the operation of the second-tier foreign exchange market in September 1986.

(iii) *Summary of the general impacts of the structural adjustment programme*

A comprehensive quantitative assessment of the programme after one year of operation is yet to be undertaken. Nevertheless, the evidence which can be pieced together from different sources reveals the following:

1. A worsening investment climate

A six-month survey of the impact of the programme on the manufacturing sector by the Manufacturing Association of Nigeria shows that:

(a) Capacity utilization has dropped from 30 per cent where it was in 1986 to 25 per cent in 1987;
(b) The level of factory employment has dropped by 14 per cent between 1986 and 1987;
(c) Small-scale firms and marginal operators have closed down on a large scale; and
(d) There has been a 20 per cent decline in the aggregate supply of public transport.

2. A deteriorating employment situation

Unemployment in Nigeria is now estimated at 2–3 million workers made up of recent graduates from the country's expanded educational system, people who have been laid off for economic reasons, and who have retired either voluntarily or involuntarily.

3. Incipient factor input flight

There is a growing suspicion that capital flight is accelerating in the economy although this is yet to be quantified. The indicators creating this fear include: the rising bid rate at the foreign exchange market; the sluggish growth in domiciliare account deposits; the fact that no significant new investments are taking place; and some reported cases of fraudulent transfer of foreign exchange bought at the foreign exchange market by some firms.

With the deflation of the real value of domestic salaries through the foreign exchange market effect, some skilled professionals are leaving the country.[17] At the same time, Nigerians who qualify abroad in many professional areas are not finding it attractive to come back home. The quantitative significance of this human factor input flight is yet to be made but the adverse implications for the economy's long-term development is worth noting.

4. Deteriorating equity

Since the marginal salary review undertaken in 1982 to maintain wage relativities following the 1981 minimum wage adjustment, wages and salaries have been frozen in the economy through annual income policy guidelines. Although efforts have been made to increase fringe benefits in the private sector, wages in the public sector have remained static. The downward trend in the wages and fringe benefits in the Nigerian public service has been officially acknowledged by the Pay Research Unit of the Office of the Head of Service of the Federation.[18] The ratio between the highest and the lowest paid workers in the three key sectors of the economy are presently as follows:

Public service	1:15
Private industries	1:13
Banks	1:45

The top executive in the Nigerian banking industry currently has a basic salary of N70,470, which is over four times that of the highest paid public servants – the permanent secretaries. These inequalities in earnings coupled with inequalities in educational opportunities and distribution of basic needs analyzed earlier have serious implications for the human dimension both as the input and the ultimate beneficiary of development.

5. Trends in national income aggregates

A review of the macro-economic effects as reflected in some macro aggregates for 1986 published recently by the Central Bank of Nigeria shows the growth rates of some key parameters as follows:

	In percentage
GDP	−3.3
Industrial production index	−3.4
Unemployment rate	+12
Inflation	+5.4

Thus, apart from the inflation rate which was tempered by improvement in rural food production due to good weather, most other indices point to the fact that on the aggregate, the structural adjustment package as presently pursued has failed to generate recovery signals. And given the deplorable human conditions described earlier and their inevitable deterioration during this recession, serious policy issues are raised concerning what should be done to alleviate this growing human suffering. Furthermore, alternative and/ or complementary policy actions need to be considered along with the structural adjustment programme in order to ensure its long-run ability to revamp the economy and generate a poverty-focused growth path. These issues are explored in the next section.

Some Policy Options

The analyses in the last two sections have revealed that Nigeria's economic and human crises have complex geopolitical linkages. Our policy proposals will therefore attempt to reflect these linkages by focusing attention on three levels: the domestic, regional and international perspectives.

(a) Domestic policies

The focus on domestic policies is informed by two considerations. First, available evidence consistently points to the fact that Nigeria's economy is more supply constrained than demand constrained. The policy challenge should therefore be on how to trigger and sustain the supply response of the macro-economy. Second, the national objective of using self-reliance as a key development strategy makes a focus on domestic policies a natural starting point. With these considerations in mind, the following key policy areas at the domestic front are worth considering.

(i) *Turning the foreign exchange market into a multiple foreign exchange rate market*

Given the overwhelming impact of the foreign exchange market in determining the cost-structure in the economy and the observed adverse impacts it has so far generated in this respect, it seems logical to modify its working into a multiple foreign exchange rate market. It would then be easy for a multiple foreign exchange rate market to allow for a selective allocation of foreign exchange to the sensitive sectors of the economy like the agriculture and small-scale industrial sectors which have so far been edged out in the foreign exchange market's operations. The importance of these two sectors for employment, growth and equity is incontrovertible. Furthermore, a multiple foreign exchange rate market will yield the much-needed exchange rate stability for industrial and investment planning. The Nigerian economy cannot recover without this. Opponents of the multiple foreign exchange rate market are often quick to point out the administrative problems it may create. The issue is not whether a particular policy like the foreign exchange market or the multiple foreign exchange rate market is problem-free since they are not. Rather, one needs to weigh the costs and benefits of choosing one over the other. It would appear that the costs of sustaining the foreign exchange market would far outweigh the advantages to be derived from a multiple foreign exchange rate market.

(ii) *Relaxing monetary controls*

Following the contractionary monetary policy which has been pursued along with the foreign exchange market, the economy has been very sluggish. Consumer resistance has been widespread. The recent deregulation of the interest rates may worsen matters in this direction as most potential investors may prefer saving at an attractive rate (of, say, 21 per cent) to undertaking risky investments whose profit rates are much below this. The monetary authorities should search for the optimal amount of money supply that can sustain the economy's supply response in high gear.

(iii) *Selective trade liberalization*

The existing regime of trade liberalization has brought about a paradoxical situation where goods flood the market while industries are operating below pre-second-tier foreign exchange market capacity. A situation where imported goods flood the market before domestic industries even have the chance to increase their capacity and employ labour cannot augur well for the recovery efforts as well as the long-term growth of industrialization in Nigeria. While the principle of open competition should be upheld because of its dynamic impacts on efficiency, deserving Nigerian industries need some time-bound protection. The criteria for selection should include the industry's potentials for a combination of the following: high local value-added, employment generation, foreign exchange earnings/savings, promotion of indigenous technology and financial viability. A time-phased and selective approach to perfection will avoid the problem of "perpetual infancy", as well as other well-known problems which plagued the earlier approach to import-substitution industrialization.

(iv) *Hierarchical growth centre approach to rural modernization*

As a component of the structural adjustment programme, a massive effort has been undertaken to modernize the rural areas. The Directorate of Food, Roads and Rural Infrastructure has been set up to oversee the implementation of all the programmes in this area. Experience has shown, however, that while this approach is necessary, it may not be sufficient to obtain a self-sustained momentum for growth and development of rural areas. This can be accomplished if the Directorate complements its programme with an hierarchical growth centre strategy. This requires that growth centres be identified and hierarchically structured in the economy space so that agglomeration economies can be exploited for agro-based industrialization.[19] This approach will not only deal realistically with the problems of rural-urban migration but would integrate the rural economy with the modern urban sector.

(v) *Promotion of invisible and visible experts*

A careful glance at Nigeria's balance-of-payments account has revealed that the invisible (service) trade account has consistently remained in deficit. For example, in 1984, 1985 and 1986, the deficits in the invisible accounts were N2.0 billion, N2.2 billion and N2.6 billion respectively. In the first seven months of the second-tier foreign exchange market, about 4 per cent of the foreign exchange allocation went to invisible account payments. Given Nigeria's rich human resource endowment in different areas of professional expertise, the invisible trade sector can be turned into a "gold mine". The major activities here should include the promotion of the sale of human expertise in areas like consultancy, hotels, tourism, shipping, banking, education, etc. Success in this area would not only contribute to the absorption of unemployed graduates in the labour markets but would generate and/or save the much-needed foreign exchange.

Current efforts in boosting non-oil exports, though desirable, may not yield substantial returns in the short term for reasons proffered earlier. Besides, it seems inappropriate to encourage the export of primary commodities at a time when their markets have collapsed and the indigenous firms are in dire need of local inputs, like cotton, groundnut, palm oil, etc. Attempts should therefore be made to satisfy the local demand for primary raw material inputs before the surpluses (if any) are exported.

(vi) *Local sourcing of machinery and equipment*

Although the importance of capital goods including transport equipment accounts for about 47 per cent of the import bill in the last five years, policy focus has been directed only on raw material sourcing which accounts for only 21 per cent of the import bill. Assuredly, the emphasis on raw material sourcing is commendable because of other spill-over effects like local value-added and employment generation. However, the seeming policy neglect of local sourcing of capital goods, especially of intermediate and small-scale categories, needs to be redressed. Positive incentives need to be drawn up to encourage private operators in this direction. Boosting this programme will have the added advantage of developing indigenous technological capability.

(vii) *Direct poverty, equity and employment programmes*

While the above measures will directly promote recovery and growth in the Nigerian economy within the medium and long terms, some programmes to alleviate the deteriorating condition in human welfare need to be pursued, especially in the short term. Although the focus here is on consumption, it should be looked upon in human capital terms "as investment consumption" since, without this, the growth of the economy would be undermined by the poor quality of human agents. Within this mixed bag, the following elements should be considered:

(a) Selective subsidy to educational investment. Such a subsidy programme should aim at making education at the primary level free and compulsory while appropriate cost recovery fees are charged for some areas of secondary and tertiary education. Loan schemes should be used to ensure access to tertiary education for those who want it;

(b) Boosting food production and nutrition education extension service, especially in the rural areas. This will stem the growing tide of nutrition-related human ailments;

(c) Selective subsidy for meeting other basic needs like health, housing, transportation. Indeed, such subsidy programmes targeted on the poor can obviate the need for a minimum wage as its impact on the economy has been found to be marginally positive in some respects and strongly negative in others;[20] and

(d) Giving employment tax rebates to private sector firms. This can be graduated according to the number of different categories of skilled labour employed by the firms each year.

(b) Regional policies

The rationale for seeking a regional approach to recovery and development policies is based on the necessity to exploit economies of scale – be it in production, investment or negotiation. The following are the issues to be considered from the regional perspective.

(i) *Collective approach to the problem of debt overhang*

Perhaps debt overhang is the single most important threat to Nigeria's (and/or other African countries') self-reliance initiatives. The loss of such initiatives can create a situation where creditors impose conditions that distort the internal development priorities of a country. In order to neutralize this possibility, it should be possible for Nigeria and other debtor countries to form a collective front for dealing with the debt problems.

Experience of past rescheduling has shown that bilateral approaches to the debt question often address the issue of burden sharing between the creditor and the debtor. In this setting, the debtor is likely to come out with a less than ideal distribution of the burden. Matters can be improved if the club of creditors[21] face the club of debtors. The need to form the latter club is sometimes discouraged by the negative image that such a tag may have but this need not be a deterrent. The club of debtors can be named anything neutral: from "African Club" to "Libreville Club". Despite the claim that each country's debt problems are different, there are enough common grounds and problems which can bring African debtor countries together. As the debt phenomenon is not going to be a transient experience in African development, the need for forming a "permanent club", to deal with it becomes more pressing. An in-depth study of such a club seems a worthwhile exercise before its actual formation.

(ii) *Regional development institutions*

In view of the necessity to put up a collective fight against the deteriorating economic crisis in Africa, there is need to muster appropriate political will to encourage and sustain the growth of Africa's development institutions. Economic integration arrangements need to be rationalized so as to avoid costly duplications. The commitment of member countries to such organizations should be respected so that the organizations can pursue their set objectives successfully. More development banks with specialized orientation or functions can be set up. For instance, something like an African agricultural development bank can be useful through focusing attention on the financing and development of the agricultural sector of African countries as well as dealing with its peculiar problems. Others should include an African technological research/information centre, etc. These institutions need not necessarily rely on Africans for their funding. Some external agencies can contribute to their growth, especially when their usefulness is well articulated.

(iii) *Collective approach to externality: relevant issues*

Externality relevant issues are problems whose negative externalities have a regional dimension. Such issues include: the problem of pests which affects crops along the northern belt of the West African region; the problem of smuggling; and refugee problems. Given the nature of their geographical spread, no one country can be very successful in handling these problems by itself. Some collaborative efforts are called for; and appropriate institutional arrangements can be initiated to handle them effectively.

(iv) *A new approach to African political crises by the OAU*

Political crises in many African countries have taken a tremendous economic toll both in material and human resources. If Africa were spared the trauma of political crises, it could focus its resources on improving the lot of the people through meaningful development. The OAU should be urged to intensify efforts in tackling various pockets of political crises in the continent so that member countries may focus attention and resources in dealing with the deep economic crises facing them.

(c) International policies

It is clear from earlier considerations that Nigeria's economic crises cannot be adequately explained only in terms of its domestic policy failures. Any complete explanation must take into account some exogenous global forces impinging on Nigeria (or any other African country). Examples of such influences include:

(a) The misalignment of macro-economic policies of some industrial powers. The United States budget deficits have on many occasions contributed to the increase in real interest rates while the accumulation of surplus (of over $US 130 billion in 1986) by Japan has created trade imbalances and other related problems;
(b) The floating rate of interest which has compounded the debt burden of many debtor countries is a relatively new phenomenon;
(c) The global recession which started in the 1980s and whose impacts are worsening for African countries constituted a windfall for some industrialized countries especially in respect of the fall in oil prices;
(d) The collapse of the world commodity market with the deterioration in the terms of trade of primary exports; and
(e) The emerging "new protectionism" which has effectively reduced the market penetration of export products from the less developed countries.

When it is considered that the above features have contributed in no small measure to making the global environment more hostile to development efforts of the least developed countries and that both the developed countries and the least developed countries stand to gain mutually if these global development externalities are minimized, a strong case seems to emerge for international co-operation. The following are some key areas for meaningful policy action.

(i) *An "African Marshall" Plan*

The debt-induced capital flight from African countries to the developed countries cannot augur well for recovery and development prospects of African nations. A massive injection of foreign capital, similar to the classic Marshall Plan for the development of post-war Europe is called for. Just as the development prospect of Europe could have been unduly delayed without this US-sponsored capital inflow, the development of Africa is bound to be seriously retarded without a similar effort. The United States will, on this occasion, not be the only contributor. All industrialized nations will and should contribute their quota based on some operational formulas; and all beneficiaries will undertake appropriate internal policy reforms to enable them to optimally absorb such external capital injection.

(ii) *A new approach to the debt problem*

For the reasons advanced in the above paragraph, the debt problem cannot be solved by the debtor nations alone nor will further lending yield a lasting solution.[22] The policies currently suggested include the use of debt-equity swaps or securitization of debts, increased direct investments in the least developed countries as well as indexation of export prices.[23] Anything to stem the "revenue flow" of investment resources from Africa to the developed countries would contribute to the enhancement of global welfare through making Africa an economically healthy partner.

(iii) *Dismantling of trade barriers*

It has been estimated that non-tariff barriers on imports to North American and European Community markets have risen by 20 per cent between 1981 and 1986.[24] This constitutes an ominous trend for African countries contemplating a full-scale outward-oriented development strategy. While this strategy has paid off for the newly industrializing countries, the prospects for contemporary least developed countries may be dim. This is mainly because when newly industrializing countries embarked on this strategy, the global environment was a lot less hostile and indeed positively supportive of their efforts.

The protectionist stance of the developed countries has inflicted severe costs and losses on the least developed countries and one hopes that positive initiatives to dismantle protectionism during the ongoing Uruguay round of GATT negotiations will be made. Such a bold effort is needed to convince Nigeria and other least developed countries that an outward development strategy is worth the risk.

In conclusion, there is need to stress the point that the prospects for African economic recovery and development depend crucially on human initiatives. Such initiatives must not only be reflected in good and feasible policy blueprints but also on the demonstrated political will for their successful implementation. It is only humans that can save humanity from itself!

Notes

1 For a comprehensive survey of earlier and contemporary contributions of human capital see M. Blaug, "Human capital theory: A slightly jaundiced survey", *Journal of Economic Literature*, September 1976, pp.827–855.

2 See elaboration in Dudley Seers, "The meaning of development", *International Development Review*, no. 4, 1969 and his "The new meaning of development", no. 3 where the issue of self-reliance is emphasized as a vital component of the contemporary meaning of development.

3 See the elaboration of this phenomenon in Joe U. Umo, "Financing human capital infrastructure in the Economic Community of West African States (ECOWAS): Some lessons from Nigeria's educational industry", paper presented in the fourth biennial Conference of the West African Economic Association held in Lome, Togo, 23–27 November 1986.

4 The University of Lagos Staff School, for instance, registers over 80 per cent success rate annually in the National Common Entrance Examination.

5 West African Examinations Council Record, 1986.

6 Joe U. Umo, "The pure human capital investment model: Some empirical tests and income distributional implications for an LDC", *Nigerian Journal of Economic and Social Studies*, vol. 19, no. 2, July 1977 pp.135–151.

7 E.O., Anusionwu, "The distribution of personal income in the Nigerian public sector " in R.E. Ubogu et al. (ed.), *Development Planning in the Economic Community of West African States* (ECOWAS), Ibadan: Heineman Educational Books (Nigeria) Ltd., 1983, p.331.

8 The Gini index is conceptually and operationally deficient since it is silent on the character and location of the deprived people it is expected to measure. Its concentration on percentile measure actually masks the fact that absolute poverty may be consistent with low Gini index.

9 Paul Streeten, *First Things First*, New York, 1981, p.81.

10 It is regarded as a reliable composite indicator because longevity is a function of the availability of other basic needs like water, preventive medicine, basic education, good nutrition, etc.

11 Joe U. Umo, *Key Issues in Nigeria's Development*, ch.2, Department of Economics, University of Lagos, mimeograph, 1986.

12 W.Q. Orimalade and V. P. Diejomaoh, "Unemployment in Nigeria: An economic analysis of scope, trends and policy issues", *Nigerian Journal of Economic and Social Studies*, vol. 13, no. 2, July 1971. pp.127–160.

13 Joe U. Umo, "Education-employment connection: The Nigerian experience", *The Manpower Journal*, vol. XVIII, no. 4 January-March 1983, Institute of Applied Manpower Reaseach, New Delhi.

14 *World Bank, World Debt Tables, External Debts of Developing Countries, 1984–1985*, Washington, p.90.

15 The Cross River State Public Service went on strike for some few weeks in August 1987 because of non-refund of the economic recovery contribution as well as nonpayment of salaries.

16 See *The Guardian*, 27 May 1987, p.11.

17 Some Nigerian medical doctors, especially those in the teaching hospitals, are known to be taking up jobs in Saudi Arabia where they are highly paid.

18 Daily Times, 19 August 1987, p.18.

19 See the elaboration of the hierarchical growth strategy for Nigeria in Joe U. Umo, "Urban and regional development in Nigeria: Some considerations for a planned disequilibrium strategy", *Geographical Review of India*, vol. 41, no. 1, March 1979, pp.39–49.

20 In an ongoing study of the "Impacts of minimum wages (MINWAGE) in the manufacturing sector of the Nigerian economy between 1980 and 1982", by the author, the following regression results have been found:

(i) Log employment = 2.1956 + 0.4 log MINWAGE; R2 = 0.14 (2.4)
(ii) Log productivity = 3.96 + 0.6 log MINWAGE; R2 = 0.2 (2.36)
(iii) Log fringe benefits = 1.36 + 0.88 log MINWAGE, R2 = 0.4 (3.88)

N = 25; figures in parentheses are t – ratios.

It is observed that the minimum wage employment elasticity, fringe benefit elasticity and productivity elasticity are all below unity thereby suggesting minimal gains in these respects. For an elaboration of economy-wide negative impacts, see Joe U. Umo, "Wage policies and human resource utilization in Nigeria" in *The Fifth National Development Plan and the Restructuring of the Nigerian Economy*, 1985 Proceedings of NES Conference (forthcoming).

[21] The more prominent ones now are the Club of Paris and the London Club.
[22] Stanley, Fischer, "Sharing the burden of international debt crisis", *American Economic Review*, May 1987, pp.165–170.
[23] Ibid.
[24] The World Bank, *World Development Report 1987*, Oxford University Press, New York, 1987, p.10.

Annex

Table 1: Nigeria: Health indicators (1980–1983)

	1980	1981	1982	1983
Availability of health facilities				
Number of hospitals	787	800	806	850 +
Population per hospital bed	1,510	1,433	1,469	1,496
Number of doctors	8,037	10,399	9,623	11,294
Population per doctor	10,543	8,356	9,260	8,059
Number of maternity centres	2,273	2,320	2,335	2,365
Women of child-bearing age per maternity centre	7,456	7,490	7,568	7,645 +
Women of child-bearing age per midwife	606	576	526	596 +
Number of dispensaries	3,355	3,448	3,447	3,648 +
Population per dispensary	25,255	25,202	26,406	26,980 +
Number of dentists	285	379	425	588
Key health indicators				
Major notifiable diseases (cases reported)				
Malaria	1,171,071	1,471,561	1,147,518	1,273,090
Dysentry	293,749	293,747	272,079	251,241
Measles	129,671	129,671	139,785	136,778
Pneumonia	114,692	114,692	96,364	99,070
Gonorrhoea	68,087	68,087	56,731	53,732
Whooping cough	56,913	56,913	77,830	70,024
Chicken-pox	26,384	26,384	34,573	41,203
Filariasis	27,521	27,521	14,640	14,970
Schistosmiasis	41,662	41,662	40,628	41,889
Tuberculosis	10,838	10,949	10,949	10,212
Vital statistics				
Infant mortality rate	120 per 1,000 population*			
Crude birth rate	45 per 1,000 population+			
Crude death rate	45 per 1,000 population*			

Source: Federal Ministry of Health; Federal Office of Statistics, Economic and Social Statistics Bulletin, Lagos, January 1985, p.36.

* According to 1966 Demographic Survey.
\+ Estimates by Federal Office of Statistics.

Table 2: Urban and rural employment rates among Nigerian States, 1984

State	Unemployment rates Urban	Rural
All Nigeria	7.9	4.4
All male	6.9	3.5
All female	9.9	6.3
Anambra	14.8	5.6
Bauchi	7.0	3.3
Bendel	12.8	14.6
Benue	8.0	1.2
Borno	5.7	0.0
Cross River	14.1	14.7
Gongola	12.3	0.0
Imo	15.7	11.6
Kaduna	5.7	0.9
Kano	3.6	2.2
Kwara	0.3	2.2
Lagos	9.7	1.3
Niger	2.7	6.4
Ogun	6.5	0.8
Ondo	4.5	0.0
Oyo	8.1	0.0
Plateau	2.3	5.1
Rivers	7.3	8.7
Sokoto	3.0	0.6

Source: Federal Office of Statistics, *1985 Sample Survey*.

Sudan

ALI ABDEL GADIR ALI

The purpose of this paper is to provide a review of the debate on the design and implementation of the so-called structural adjustment programmes in the Sudan over the period 1985–1987, and to indicate the general directions in which alternative economic policy packages could be found.

Adjustment Programmes: A Review

The active pursuit of the so-called adjustment policies in the Sudan dates back to June 1978. According to the IMF, "by about mid-1978 the country was faced with a severe shortage of foreign exchange and a build-up of external payments arrears". To redress the unsatisfactory domestic and external performance, the Sudanese authorities have since then pursued corrective policies within the context of adjustment programmes supported by the World Bank and the Fund. The initial thrust of the development effort was concentrated on structural and institutional reform of the agricultural sector to provide incentives for higher output and on the budget in order to reduce recourse to domestic bank borrowing" [IMF (1985) p.3]. The responsibility for the design and implementation of the structural adjustment policies, it should be noted, rests with the IMF and the World Bank. In the World Bank's own words, "The Bank has co-operated with the IMF in the design and implementation of the economic recovery programme" [IMF (1986) p.37].

The so-called adjustment programmes revolved around various arrangements with the IMF starting with a first credit tranche purchase in June 1978. This was followed by a three-year extended arrangement in May 1979 which was subsequently abandoned and replaced by a one-year stand-by arrangement which became effective in February 1982. Another stand-by arrangement which became effective on 25 June 1984 had to be declared inoperative 17 days later.

As usual the policy content of the so-called adjustment programmes revolved around the conventional IMF package with devaluation being the most important policy tool. Except for the 1978 arrangement which concentrated on devaluation, the policy actions under the remaining programmes were pervasive, touching on almost every aspect of economic activity in the country. [IMF (1984) p.34–39]. A summary of the salient features of these policy actions is as follows:

(a) Agricultural sector: exchange rate adjustment for exportables, elimination of export taxes, cost recovery and pricing systems, physical rehabilitation and input procurement programmes, and institutional reform of parastatals;

(b) Manufacturing sector: institutional reform of parastatals, physical rehabilitation, management contracts, and area expansion in the sugar sub-sector;
(c) Domestic financial policies: increasing taxes on imports, departmental fees and charges, excise taxes and duties on cigarettes, liquor and luxury imports, increasing the prices of sugar, petroleum products and cement products, raising charges for public utilities, and reducing credit ceilings and increasing interest rates; and
(d) External policies: liberalizing foreign trade transactions, creating a market for foreign exchange, devaluation, and rescheduling of arrears to Paris Club members.

Prior to April 1985, the IMF's own assessment of the performance of Sudan under the adjustment programmes was positive. The IMF representative in his statement to the Paris Club in May 1984, said, "While the authorities followed policies substantially in line with the programme, only some of the targets were realized. The most significant achievements were: (a) the continued expansion in the output in the irrigated agricultural sector, particularly cotton; (b) the elimination of budgetary subsidies ahead of the timing agreed under the programmes; (c) achievement of most of the budgetary targets; and (d) a relatively orderly servicing of the critical and rescheduled external debt obligations" [IMF (1984), p.3]. The disappointing aspects of the performance, according to the IMF representative, were a decline in GDP (because of drought),monetary expansion in excess of the programme target (due to security reasons) and an acceleration in the rate of inflation (due both to drought and security).

This positive assessment which is sometimes brought about by deliberately revising the programme targets appropriately [see IMF (1984), table 7, p.35] has for some strange reason changed rather dramatically in the post-April 1985 period. Thus, for example, in a very recent confidential paper, the IMF had this to say about the policies implemented under the programmes: "Sudan's current precarious economic situation can be better comprehended in an historical perspective of gradual, but steady deterioration experienced in the past 10–12 years. Rather than adopting and implementing on a consistent basis a medium-term development strategy to harness the productive potential of the country, the previous governments resorted to ad hoc economic measures and during the past several years, the economy was handled mainly along 'crisis management' lines. Policy actions were implemented only at times of crisis with little or no consistency and continuity in approach. As a result, the momentum of economic recovery could not be established or sustained" [IMF, "The Current Economic Situation in Sudan", 25 June, 1986, p.4].

Which IMF is one supposed to believe – the IMF which says, "policies followed were substantially in line with programmes" or the IMF which says, "previous governments resorted to ad hoc economic measures and the economy was handled along crisis management lines"? Similar contradictory postures vis-à-vis performance under the adjustment programmes can also be found in the World Bank literature [see e.g., World Bank (1985) and (1986)].

From the Sudan's point of view it is now almost generally agreed that the IMF-World Bank management of the economy during the period 1978–1985 resulted in the current chaotic economic situation. Empirical evidence in support of this general conclusion is to be found in the various contributions of Sudanese academics. [See Ali (1985), Ali (1986), Ali and Hussain (1986), Hussain and Thirlwall (1984) and (1986), and Hussain (19869]. Wohlmuth and Hansohm arrived at a similar conclusion to that of the Sudanese analysts:

> "It may be argued that the stabilization policy failed both in respect to its own targets and, more important, in respect to a solution of Sudan's economic problems in the long-term rerspective. Furthermore, it may be argued that this failure is due to an adjustment strategy which aims at improving the debt-servicing capacity of the country in the short term, but lacks any consideration of the basic structural deficiencies. During the stabilization period since 1978 the structural malformation of the Sudanese economy was reinforced rather than surmounted" [Wohlmuth and Hansohm, p.19].

Further evidence is to be found in an IMF confidential memo in which it was noted that "Sudan has found it necessary in recent years to effect several depreciations of the exchange rate of the Sudanese pound against the United States dollar. As these depreciations have taken place at long intervals, they have by necessity been quite large and have unavoidably become public knowledge prior to their implementation. Such significant adjustments have had several undesirable consequences, the most important of which have been attendant sharp increases in the prices of imports, including essential imports such as petroleum, wheat and sugar; speculation, which has imposed real costs on the economy; and some income redistribution effects which have favoured the trading community" [IMF manuscript, "Pegging the Sudanese Pound to a Currency Basket",p.1].

From the IMF's own point of view the above admission is both rare and serious; it confirms the views held, and the results established, by Sudanese economists. While we would argue that the Sudan was forced to "effect the several depreciations" rather than "has found it necessary to effect" them, in the above statement the IMF is conceding the following:

(a) that the several devaluations of the Sudanese pound over the period 1978–1985 were inflationary;
(b) that IMF management of the Sudan economy resulted in speculative behaviour which has imposed real costs on the economy i.e., economic disarray; and
(c) that the so-called adjustment programmes have resulted in a worsened distribution of income.

The Human Dimension

The analysis of the effects of structural adjustment policies on the human situation could, following convention, be conducted in terms of indicators such as health, education, nutrition, incomes, income distribution, and employment, among others. This type of analysis, we conjecture, may sometimes be helpful in the context of what we might call institutionally mature economies where each indicator taken separately may signify a definitive trend of progress or retrogress. For countries which are still involved in the national struggle of building post-independence government structures, conventional indicators may not be that helpful, notwithstanding the availability or reliability of the data on the basis of which they are calculated.

Be that as it may, a few such indicators are available for the Sudan. Our analysis, however, will adopt a broader perspective with or without the use of conventional indicators. At this point it may be helpful to note that education (various enrolment ratios) and health (per capita accessibility to doctors, etc.) reflected a time trend improvement ! In what follows we report the evidence on the share of education and health in government expenditure, it being understood that this is perhaps a better indicator in the context of evaluating structural adjustment programmes.

(a) Education and health

The shares of education and health in total government expenditure have declined respectively from 9.3 and 5.4 percent in 1972 to 6.1 and 1.3 percent in 1983 [World Bank, World Development Report (1986)]. According to the World Bank, central government comprises the expenditure by all government bodies that are agencies or instruments of the central authority of a country: it includes both current and capital (development) expenditure.

(b) Nutrition

According to UNICEF, daily per capita calorie intake as a percentage of requirements has declined from 101 percent in 1980 to 90 percent in 1983. [UNICEF, *The State of the World's Children*, 1984 and 1987].

(c) Income

According to the World Bank, "Sudan's economy has declined steadily over the past ten years. Although GDP showed little or no growth between 1975–1976 and 1985–1986, population grew at about 2.8 percent a year, with the result that real per capita GDP declined by 2.8 percent a year" [World Bank (1987),p.1].

(d) Income distribution

Harris notes that, "Although the data on income distribution are very weak, we have pieced together fragments that are consistent with the following generalizations:

(a) During the period of adjustment cotton producers were slight gainers;
(b) While natural disaster cannot be attributed to the stabilization programme, the net result is that the rainfed sector experienced a net decline in real incomes;
(c) Output in the industrial sector grew slowly and capacity utilization declined. While prices of industrial goods increased, it appears that the gains were not realized by industrial producers;
(d) Real wages were badly eroded in the public sector; and
(e) It appears that the largest gainers in the system were traders who maintained access to scarce supplies of imported and domestically produced goods. Using aggregative data where sectors are used as income brackets, Ali (1986) reports an increase in the Gini coefficient for the distribution of nominal income from 0.3726 in 1976/1977 to 0.4208 in 1982/1983".

(e) Employment

According to the Economic Research Directorate, prior to 1978 the Sudan did not have an unemployment problem [1986, p.82]. In the post-1978 period the unemployment rate at the margin (defined as those who registered at labour exchange offices but were not recruited as a percentage of registered workers) increased from 80, 88 and 89 percent for unskilled, skilled and white-collar workers respectively in 1983/1984 to 83, 99 and 93 percent in 1984/1985.

The above is the available fragmentary evidence on the impact of structural adjustment programmes on the human situation in the Sudan. However, to ordinary Sudanese citizens going about their daily lives of earning a living, the proposition that the adjustment programmes have resulted in declining social welfare is an obvious one that does not require empirical evidence. To them, sufficient evidence is proved by the almost daily worsening of their lot and the observed increasing affluence of the 'fat cats' of liberalization.

But judging the impact of structural adjustment programmes by the above conventional indicators will, in general, be incomplete. More fundamentally serious and damaging effects have to do with the then ruling regime's onslaught on the morals and pride of the Sudanese people. The deepening economic crisis, thanks largely to the management of the economy by the IMF and World Bank, elicited from the regime two major reactions which in essence can be taken as effects of the structural adjustment programmes on the human situation, viz. corruption and repression.

(f) Corruption

Under the persistent impression that there existed no other way to deal with the economic difficulties of the country except that of the IMF-World Bank adjustment programmes, the Government developed a greedy attitude of grabbing anything being offered irrespective of the costs involved. The justification usually offered for this behaviour was the necessity of closing the balance-of-payments gap. This greedy attitude culminated in following a 'marketing strategy' so to speak, under which the whole of the Sudan was offered for sale to any bidder. As a logical result of corruption at the higher government levels, corrupt patterns of behaviour quickly permeated the lower levels of government and became an accepted way of accumulating personal fortunes [see Kamier and Kursany (1985)]. Thus the observed declining standards of civil service performance in general could be explained in terms of structural adjustment programmes-induced behaviour.

(g) Repression

Corrupt behaviour by government officials coupled with a liberalized economy generated opportunities for the 'parasitic' trader groups, financed largely by the banking sector, to wreck havoc in the market place where shortages in basic commodities used to be created at will. Increasingly, ordinary citizens, especially producers and fixed income groups, became squeezed. This situation resulted in an open challenge to the regime where following every announcement or implementation of a structural adjustment price-hike measure, primary school kids (aged 7–13 years) took to the streets. Reacting to such youthful demonstrations, the regime intensified its repressive measures culminating in the introduction of the so-called Islamic Laws

(Sharia) in September 1983 [see Khalid (1986)]. As has been rightly pointed out, many Muslims in northern Sudan saw the harsh application of these laws "as an attempt to legitimize repression in an increasingly shaky regime . . . The revulsion finally spilled over with the public execution in January 1985 of the 76-year old Mahmoud Mohamed Taha, leader of the small but active Republican Brotherhood, on a charge of heresy". [(Woodward, p.960)]. Thus, increased repression was also induced by the so-called adjustment programmes' impingement on the lives of ordinary people.

In the Face of Adversity

The deepening economic crisis, thanks largely to the management of the economy by the IMF and the World Bank, and its impact on the human situation in the country elicited from ordinary people but one major initiative: hardened political opposition. Professional syndicates (doctors, judges, lawyers, university teachers, bank employees, university students' unions, etc.) began to articulate political grievances and back them with trade union action. Strikes, work stoppages and demonstrations began to emerge despite the national security organ. Ultimately this led to the April Popular Uprising during which people chanted that "WE SHALL NOT BE RULED BY THE WORLD BANK!"; and although the crowds meant the IMF but substituted for language convenience, they were nonetheless not far off the mark! On 6 April, 1985 the Numeiri regime which implemented, or was made to implement, the so-called structural adjustment policy measures was toppled by the masses. "Thus for the second time (the first time was in October 1964) the Sudanese has accomplished the unusual feat of overthrowing a military ruler by peaceful action, but on this occasion the army itself decided to take the side of the people" [Woodward (1985), p.958]. The April Uprising was the ultimate initiative taken by the Sudanese people to sustain the human situation despite the economic crisis.

On the road to the April Uprising the Sudanese invoked a number of mechanisms to sustain the human dimension in spite of the deepening economic crisis. Perhaps the most important among these was the more intensive exploitation of the extended family institution vis-à-vis family members working in the Gulf States.

The most recent and detailed study of Sudanese migrants working abroad established that 65 percent of the remittances of migrants is used for consumption purposes in the Sudan. The report notes that "on balance, we also find that, across all countries of destination, Sudanese nationals abroad that are more skilled and more professional, target greater dollar amounts toward liquid assets and investment uses, while those at the lower end of the skill spectrum use their remittance more for consumption . . . In cases where the earnings are lower, the tendency to divert remittances primarily for consumption, literally, to support families back home, is higher". [Choucri, (1985) p.5–16. The average remittance figure calculated by Choucri is US$9,000 per worker.

Thus, to the extended family institution and the fundamental values of the Sudanese society goes the credit of absorbing the very first shocks of the famine that struck the country during 1984–1985. It was ordinary Sudanese people, themselves the victims of structural adjustment measures, who came to the rescue of their fellow citizens months before the regime could admit the occurrence of the famine to the international community.

On Alternatives

The period following April 1985 witnessed a wide-ranging public debate on the state of the Sudanese economy. The central question in the debate has consistently been – does there exist an alternative to the IMF way of doing, or undoing, things? The general agreement arrived at within the context of the National Economic Conference has been ably summarized by Affan (1986). In what follows we present an attempt at identifying the parties to the debate and their proposed alternatives, if any.

Rather surprisingly the IMF was a participant in the debate, first through the then Minister of Finance, H.E. Awad Abdel Magid, and a number of other proxies including high-ranking Ministry of Finance officials and later through fact-finding missions! Not surprisingly the IMF answer to the question posed by the public debate was that indeed there exists no other way but the IMF so-called adjustment programmes. This position was stated in the following documents:

(a) Statement by the Sudanese Authorities on Economic Policies – dated 15 July 1985;
(b) Statement of the Government of the Sudan on its Economic and Financial Policies – dated 31 October 1985; and
(c) The Current Economic Situation in the Sudan – dated 25 June 1986.

Their proposed programme was, in fact, identical to the policy package included in the defunct 1984 stand-by arrangement. The Transitional Government rejected it and as a result the Sudan was subsequently declared ineligible to IMF facilities. The Managing Director of the IMF then had the audacity to say in a telex to the Prime Minister dated 4 December 1985, that "I was, therefore, dismayed to learn that your Council of Ministers had not adopted the package of policies and that the status of understanding reached between your Minister of Finance and the staff is now uncertain"! Indeed, the IMF fact-finding mission did not propose any alternative policies but rather presented two scenarios for the budget and the balance-of-payments for 1986/1987 the objective of which, we believe, was to impress on the then newly elected Government, the non-existence of alternatives other than the so-called adjustment programmes.

The World Bank was also a participant in the debate. Mr. E. Jaycox, Vice-President for Eastern and Southern Africa Region in the Bank, visited the Sudan with the expressed objective of improving the public image of the Bank. The reason that prompted this 'royal visit', so to speak, was the slogans chanted during the April 1985 Uprising.

Mr. Jaycox, who held meetings with professional syndicates and academics as well as trade union leaders, preached the IMF-World Bank gospel of structural adjustment.

On 19 May 1986 the World Bank issued its alternative strategy, in the form of directives, embodied in a document entitled "Sudan: A Comprehensive Approach to Sudan's Economic Problems". Identifying the objectives of economic policy as economic growth and improvement in the balance-of-payments, the World Bank summarized the thrust of its comprehensive strategy as follows:

> "Considering the failures of the past, an economic programme aiming at these objectives should, on the demand side, put emphasis on a steep reduction in the budget deficit and money creation in order to reduce inflation and, on the supply side, create a substantial and permanent shift in the effective exchange rate to improve the international competitiveness of Sudanese producers. In this approach, domestic prices should be flexible and be allowed to respond to market forces. Complementary action would be required in the institutional field such as market orientation in the economic policies, and a rapid relaxation of the controls to allow for private sector development" [World Bank, (1986-b), p.15].

Given the World Bank's own report assessing the so-called adjustment programmes, and given the policy content of past policy packages, we need only to note that the World Bank's proposed strategy must have been written with the premeditated aim of insulting the intelligence of the Sudanese people!

As far as the illiterate Sudanese are concerned it is perhaps important to note that a consensus is now emerging:

(a) that the IMF-World Bank reading of the empirical evidence on hand pertaining to the cause of the Sudanese economic crisis is faulty;
(b) that the IMF-World Bank management of the Sudanese economy through the so-called adjustment programmes precipitated the post-1980 economic crisis;
(c) that the economic crisis is basically institutional- cum-political-cum-structural in nature and as such requires an analytical framework completely different from that adopted by the IMF-World Bank instant economists;
(d) that to solve its economic problems the Sudan has to do it alone, at least temporarily, with the objective of restoring its internal balance as a prerequisite to the restoration of overall equilibrium;
(e) that conventional IMF-World Bank policies are irrelevant simply because of the irrelevance of the analytical framework on which they are based;
(f) that there exists a set of policies, all closely related to the institutional structures of the economy that could bring about the internal balance of the economy;
(g) that these policies have to do with reforming the corrupt economic structures established in the past by the active involvement of the IMF and the World Bank and that these alternative policies are directly contradictory to the concept of liberalization and the free-market economy.

A sample of the policies envisaged by the Sudanese was reported to the Minister of Finance and Economic Planning in August 1986 by a special committee constituted by the Minister to study the relationship between the Sudan, the IMF and the World Bank. (Report of the Technical Committee on the Evaluation of Sudan Relationship with the IMF and World Bank, 1986).

The sample of alternative policies presented to the Minister is based on the realization that the Sudan economy is currently suffering from a state of disorder, and therefore the objectives of economic policy should be the restoration of economic order. If this is an acceptable diagnosis, then the relevant economic reform measures in the short-to-medium term must be macro-institutional in nature. Reported empirical evidence indicates the following areas of reform:

(a) Institutional reform

The need to reform the institutional structure of the management of the economy is rather obvious given that the elected government inherited not only the laws of the defunct regime but also its institutions and personnel. This is the political-structural dimension of the Sudanese alternative. Admittedly, it requires not only political credibility but also political will and it is an open question whether the elected government possesses any. However, being an elected body theoretically qualifies the Government to having both!

(b) The Banking sector

As far as the need to reform the banking sector is concerned, there exists evidence of its complicity in bringing about and sustaining the economic disarray in the country [see Bank of Sudan (1983) and (1986) for empirical evidence, and Ali and Hussain (1986) for analytical evidence]. On the basis of available evidence the following reform measures have been proposed:

(i) delicensing of all foreign and joint-venture banks that are indicated on technical grounds of having contravened the original conditions of their licenses at a point in time during the disarray period;

(ii) national banks, which would be overhauled under the institutional reform, are to call for an immediate repayment of their outstanding debts to the private sector. This collection of outstanding debts shall be effected under a reformulated law governing public funds such that requests issued to debtors to repay their dues are treated as credible threats; and

(iii) the reformed banking system is to operate as a tax levying institution on the principle of pay-as-you-borrow (PAYB), by withholding estimated income or profit taxes using an opportunity income imputation formula.

(c) Foreign exchange

Regarding foreign exchange transactions there is evidence that the black market in foreign exchange, far from representing an embodiment of the text-book free competitive market, is perhaps one of the most important monuments of economic disarray. The depth of the market, estimated as varying between US$4.2 million to US$8.6 million per day, could not have been sustained without the complicity of the banking sector. Further, there is also evidence that the black market in foreign exchange is dynamically unstable [see Ali (1985), Ali and Hussain (1986)]. Further, the extremely damaging macro-economic effects of the market have been conceded by the IMF. On the basis of available evidence, the following reform measures have been proposed:

(i) reinstatement of a full-fledged foreign exchange control system with an immediate revaluation of the Sudanese pound. The revalued exchange rate is to be determined on the basis of the speculation margin that ruled during the disarray period;

(ii) intensification of controls on foreign exchange transactions and promulgation into law of severe penalties for those contravening the regulations; and
(iii) appropriate use of tax-subsidy schemes for foreign exchange transactions with the objective of maximizing social welfare.

(d) Internal balance

Restoring the internal balance of the economy is largely fiscal in nature and requires only the effective application of existing taxation laws appropriately administered by overhauled institutions. In particular the following is proposed:

(i) collecting income or profit taxes due on the private sector as a result of its using the banking facilities over the period 1978–1985; specifically incomes generated, or profits earned by making use of outstanding debts;
(ii) collecting profit tax due on those who practiced foreign exchange buying and selling as authorized dealers; and
(iii) estimating profit taxes on the basis of banking facilities extended to the private sector with automatic withholding in accordance with PAYB principle;

It should be noted that over the period 1978–1985 estimates of revenue forgone by the Government, based on (i), (ii) and (iii), ranged between SE 0.81 billion and SE 3.4 billion.

The above, we hasten to remind the reader, is but a sample of policies. Correctly reading and appropriately assessing the evidence of disarray, we are certain, would lead to the design of a comprehensive policy package which will restore the internal balance of the economy in the initial phase. Having restored order to the economy the external balance would be established as a corollary in the medium term.

Summary

The major conclusions of this paper could be summarized as follows:

(a) over the period 1978–1985 (April) the Sudan economy was managed for all intents and purposes by the IMF in collaboration with the World Bank, the two institutions experimenting with almost all kinds of structural adjustment measures;
(b) the end result of the IMF-World Bank management of the Sudan economy was a deepening economic crisis which in turn precipitated declining social welfare and increased human misery.
(c) the major initiative taken by the Sudanese people to sustain the human situation in spite of the economic crisis was the April Uprising which overthrew the regime;
(d) following a wide-ranging public debate on the state of the economy a consensus has emerged that the so-called structural adjustment programmes are irrelevant to the Sudan. The alternative approach is to be found in a deliberate inward-looking strategy which has to start by putting the institutional house in order first, and then cleaning the

economic landscape from the various distortions inherited from the past (black market in foreign exchange, corruption, speculation, etc.);

(e) in following the above strategy the Sudan would have to do it alone relying on its fundamental social values and mobilizing its own physical, human and moral reserves. This would require political will and political credibility.

Finally, we do not expect the IMF or the World Bank or the Western donor community to lend a sympathetic hearing to the above type of analysis. Indeed it will be foolhardy on the part of any serious-minded African to expect otherwise.

References

1 Affan, K., (1986), "The National Economic Conference", in DSRC, *Background papers to the ILO/JASPA mission to Sudan, Employment and Economic Reform.*

2 Ali, A.A.G., (1987) from *Dependence to dependence: The IMF and the Sudan Economy* (forthcoming in Arabic).

3 Ali, A.A.G., (1986),"Structural Adjustment Programmes in the Sudan" in DSRC, *Background Papers.*

4 Ali, A.A.G., (1985), (editor), *The Sudan Economy in Disarray*, printed by Biddles Ltd., England.

5 Ali, A.A.G., and M.H. Hussain, (1986), "The IMF and the economic chaos in the Sudan: The black market in foreign exchange experience", paper presented to the Conference on Macro-Economic Policies, DSRC, University of Khartoum (in Arabic).

6 Brown, R., (n.d.), "International response to Sudan's crisis: 1978 to the April 1985 coup d'etat", unpublished manuscript.

7 Choucri, N., (1985), *A Study of Sudanese Nationals Working Abroad: Final Report*, vol. I, MIT.

8 Economic Research Directorate (1985), *The Economic Review 1985/86*, Ministry of Finance and Economic Planning, Khartoum.

9 Harris, J.R., (1986), "Macroeconomic Adjustments in Sudan 1972–1985", African Studies Centre, Boston University.

10 Hawyter, T., and C. Watson, (1985), *Aid; Rhetoric and Reality*, Pluto Press, London.

11 Hussain, M.N., (1986), *An Evaluation of the IMF Programme and Policies*, Report of the Sub-Committee on the relationship between Sudan, the IMF and the World Bank.

12 Hussain, M.N., and A.P. Thirlwall, (1984), "The IMF supply – side approach to devaluation: An assessment with reference to Sudan", *Oxford Bulletin of Economics and Statistics*, vol. 46, No. 2.

13 ILO, *After the Famine*, Geneva, (1986).

14 IMF (1986-a), Sudan Staff Report for 1985 Article IV Consultation, SM/86/33.

15 IMF (1986-b), Sudan Recent Economic Development, SM/86/38.

16 IMF (1986-c), The Current Economic Situation in Sudan. (Confidential paper 25 June, 1986).

17 IMF (1985-a), Statement by the Sudanese Authorities on Economic Policies.

18 IMF (1985-b), Statement of the Government of Sudan on its Economic and Financial Policies.

19 IMF (1984), Sudan Staff Report for 1984 Article IV Consultation, SM/84/283.

20 IMF (1983), Sudan Staff Report for the 1983 Article IV consultation and Review Under the Stand-by Arrangement, EBS/83/174.

21 IMF (n.d.), Pegging the Sudanese Pound to a Currency Basket, manuscript.

22 Kameir, E. and I. Kursany, (1985), *Corruption as the First Factor of Production in the Sudan*, Research Report No. 72, Scandinavian Institute of African Studies, Uppsala, Sweden.

23 Khalid, M., (1986), *The False Down*, (in Arabic), Dar Elhilal.

24 Ministry of Finance and Economic Planning (1986), *Report of the Technical Committee on the Evaluation of Sudan's Relationship with the IMF and the World Bank.*

25 Riad, H., (1987), (ed.), *The Most Famous Political Trials in Sudan* (in Arabic), Dar Eljeel, Beirut.

26 UNICEF (1987), *The State of the World's Children 1987*, OUP, Oxford.

27 Wohlmuth, K., and D. Hansohm, (1986), "Sudan: A Case for Structural Adjustment Policies", Discussion Paper No. 8, Sudan Economy Research Group, University of Bremen, West Germany.

28 Woodward, P., (1985), "Sudan After Numeiri", *Third World Quarterly*, vol. 7, No. 4.

29 World Bank, (l987), Report No. 6491-SU, vol. I, Washington.

30 World Bank, (1986-a), *World Development Report, 1986*, Washington.
31 World Bank, (1986-b), *Sudan: A Comprehensive Approach to Sudan's Economic Problems.*
32 World Bank, (1985), *Sudan: Prospects for Rehabilitation of the Sudanese Economy*, Report No. 5496-SU, Washington.
33 World Bank, (1983), *Sudan Pricing Policies and Structural Balances*, Report No. 45284-SU, Washington.
34 World Bank, (1982), *Annual report 1982*, Washington.

Zambia

VENKATASH SESHAMANI

Introduction

It is by now well recognized that the crisis in most African countries today is not merely an economic crisis (as judged by various internal and external macro-economic imblances, increasing scarcity of foreign exchange reserves, adverse terms of trade, rising indebtedness, etc.) but a much larger human crisis (as seen from the rapidly growing levels of absolute poverty, worsening income distributions and performance on various social and quality-of-life indicators relating to nutrition, health, education, etc.).

The one common fundamental problem in all these countries has been the highly inflexible and static economic structures that have undergone little transformation even after more than two decades since independence. These structures have been characterized by varying degrees of mononuclearity. In several cases, a single commodity constitutes the backbone of the entire economy; for example, oil in Algeria, cocoa in Sao Tome and Principe and copper in Zambia. Such structures are marked by few internal production linkages, reliance on one or a few commodities to earn foreign exchange and heavy dependence on imports. As a result, they cannot easily adapt to external shocks which inevitably lead to disastrous results for the economy.

Due to lack of sufficient diversification, there is a pronounced dichotomy as between a small, modern enclave sector and a large traditional subsistence sector and as between the urban and rural areas. This dichotomy has been chiefly responsible for the high degree of income inequality in most African countries and the concentration of absolute poverty especially in the rural areas. For example according to a recent unpublished survey by a government agency, the share in Zambia's national income of the top 5 per cent of the population is estimated to have reached 50 per cent. Indeed, for nearly a decade now, Zambia has been faced with the reputation of having one of the most unequal income distributions in the world.

The percentages of urban and rural populations below the poverty line in Zambia were calculated by the author from estimates provided by a 1981 ILO-JASPA study that 50 per cent of the rural households, 26 per cent of the urban households and 60 per cent of the total households in Zambia were poor or very poor in 1980. Alternative estimates of the number of poor households in Zambia provided by Seshamani and Mwanza (1986) when translated in populational terms yield poverty levels of 59, 31 and 48 per cent respectively for the rural, urban and total populations. From either of two sets of estimates, even though they differ significantly from each other, it can be seen that the dimensions of the poverty phenomenon in Zambia have been very serious indeed. It will be our contention that the poverty levels in

Zambia have risen still further during the last six to seven years.

The problem in Africa has often been identified to be not so much the lack of resources. It has even been contended that Africa needs resources only "as much as the Sahara desert needs sand". The problem has been the appallingly high level of inefficiency with which the resources have been utilized. The inefficient use of resources is reflected by the fact that despite high rates of investment in some countries, the growth rate of per capita GDP has been negative. In Zambia, for instance, during the 1970s, the investment rate was 30 per cent of GDP but the annual average growth rate of per capita GDP was −2.7 per cent. Somalia had a net investment rate of 12.6 per cent during 1960–1984, but the annual average change in per capita GDP was −1.0 per cent during the same period. Such instances demonstrate that a significant proportion of investment had gone into non-viable projects.

The failure to invest wisely in productive enterprises stems from a serious dearth of technical and managerial skills. If there is any other commodity that is as scarce as foreign exchange in Africa, it is human capital. And the human crisis that has emerged in most African countries is due to the failure of these countries not only to augment their stocks of human capital but to prevent even the existing meagre stocks from wearing away by according low priority in the national budgets to those sectors such as health and education which provide the necessary inputs for the building up of human capital. The development of human capital has to be accorded a much higher priority than at present if economic management of African economies is to be significantly improved.

With a view to restructuring their economies, reducing poverty and raising the living standards of their populations, African countries, over the years, have been experimenting with alternative economic policy instruments and packages. Especially during the 1980s, a number of them, including Zambia, urged mainly by the IMF and the World Bank adopted and implemented radical policy changes but with little economic success and much heavier social and political costs. As Frances Stewart (1987) aptly summarized, "after undergoing tough programmes, many countries found themselves with reduced real incomes, increased poverty, deteriorating social conditions, reduced growth potential and often with no significant improvement in their external accounts".

Little more than casual empirical observation is required to know that Zambia has experienced these very consequences from its recent policy experiments. The World Development Report which had, until last year, classified Zambia as a low middle-income country, has, for the first time included it in the low-income category in its 1987 issue. From its thirty-ninth position in the list of countries in ascending order of per capita income, Zambia has been moved to the thirty-first place. Zambia's reclassification was done because of a decline in its per capita income from $US 470 in 1984 to $US 390 in 1985. But Zambia's per capita income is estimated to have declined from $US 630 in 1981 to less than $US 200 in 1987.[1]

In this paper, I shall review the developments that took place in Zambia since 1975 that have led to its present human crisis, what potential the future holds for the country and what needs to be done to realize the potential. For despite the dire economic straits the country is in today, this author still feels that one could see light at the end of the tunnel.

The year 1975 is an appropriate year to start with. With the quadrupling of oil prices in 1973 and the collapse of world copper prices after 1974, the prosperous face of the Zambian economy changed dramatically almost overnight. In 1975 Zambia's terms of trade fell to 54 per cent, foreign exchange earnings fell by more than 40 per cent, the balance-of-payments deficit became 30 per cent of GDP, government revenue from minerals fell to less than one-fifth of its previous level and the budget (which was in surplus in 1974) moved to a deficit equivalent to 24 per cent of GDP. The country has not recovered since then.

I would, however, like to emphasize two points here. First, the change in the oil and copper prices is not, contrary to what politicians and some analysts often claim, the fundamental cause of Zambia's economic problems. The fundamental cause, already there since 1964, is an economic structure highly vulnerable to external forces. The catastrophic repercussions of the oil shock and the decline in copper prices only served to expose the extreme fragility of the economic structure.

Second, Zambia, like most African countries, tends to experience a ratchet effect in regard to the operation of international factors. When global factors are adverse, Zambia suffers its impact immediately and significantly; but when these very factors improve, the benefits do not accrue to the country with equal speed and magnitude. Both the first oil shock of 1973 and the second one of 1979–1980 resulted in dire consequences. The share of the oil bill in the country's total import bill rose from 5 per cent in 1973 to 25 per cent in 1983. This entailed a drastic reduction in the imports of vital industrial inputs and the average capacity utilization in industry fell from 65 per cent in 1974 to 30 per cent in 1984. But in 1986 there was a dramatic fall in oil prices from $US 29 a barrel to less than $US 10 initially whereafter it stabilized at around $US 15 in the latter half of the year. But the benefits of this price reduction never reached the consumers. Due to the depreciation of the Kwacha, the growth of industrial output declined from K423.9 million in 1985 to K421.2 million in 1986 at 1977 constant prices. The country's overall balance-of-payments position also worsened in 1986 over the already poor positions of the previous years.[2]

Economic Crisis and Policy Development in Zambia Since 1975

What had, until 1975, been one of the most prosperous economies in sub-Saharan Africa, fell apart almost overnight. By 1980, the budget deficit had become K872.8 million or 29 per cent of GDP. Concommitantly, the country's long-term public debt also rose to K1475 million, 70 per cent of which was from external sources. Since then, the proportion of foreign debt has been increasing and thus causing a worsening of the balance-of-payments position. Indeed, after 1974, except for 1979, the country's balance-of-payments has always been in deficit.

There has been a steady deterioration in the terms of trade since 1970 which of course became severe after 1974. By 1977, the terms of trade index reached its lowest value until that time – 34 per cent of the 1970 figure. The situation in 1977 was described in the International Monetary Fund Survey of 8 May 1978 as follows:

> "After a short-lived improvement in 1976, following some recovery in copper prices and a 20 per cent depreciation of the Kwacha in July 1976, the economic

situation deteriorated again in 1977. The price of copper fell by about 5 per cent, compounding the effect of a decline in export volume, while domestic demand, in nominal terms continued to rise despite efforts to contain it by increasing taxation and limiting wage increases. Although imports fell in real terms by 5 per cent, the overall balance-of-payments deficit widened and Zambia was unable to meet fully its external obligations. As a result, short-term external payments arrears rose to an unprecedented level and, at the end of 1977, the country's gross foreign reserves were the equivalent of less than one month's imports."

Consequently, Zambia negotiated a Standby Arrangement with the IMF in 1978 for SDR 200 million over two years. The agreement required Zambia to implement many of the well-known IMF measures including a 10 per cent devaluation of the Kwacha, limiting deficit financing, reducing payment arrears and instituting wage freezes. These measures, it was hoped, would eliminate the balance-of- payments deficit, stem the decline in GDP and bring about diversification of the economy. But the situation did not improve.

Real GDP declined by 9 per cent in 1979. Debt servicing which had been only 7.3 per cent of exports and 10.5 per cent of government revenue in 1974 had increased to 18.7 per cent and 27.5 per cent in 1977. By 1979, the corresponding figures were 27.8 and 34.2 per cent. The drought which emerged at the close of the 1970s and continued until the mid-1980s compounded Zambia's problems.

In 1981, the country again turned to the IMF for help and the Fund once again prescribed its standard medicine. This included complete price decontrol and at least a 40 per cent devaluation of the Kwacha. The country was unable to accept these conditions. But by 1982, foreign debt servicing had increased to 47.6 per cent of export earnings and payment areas were piling up. It was impressed upon Zambia by the IMF and the World Bank, which during the 1980s had become "the International Monetary Fund's twin" in terms of its conditionality for assistance, that what Zambia needed was a major restructuring of its economy. Further, such restructuring could not be achieved through piecemeal and minor adjustments within the prevailing policy and institutional framework but only through wholesale reform of the framework itself.

The need for restructuring Zambia's economy cannot, and has never been, denied. The economic future of the country depends on the extent and speed with which it can break the mononuclear position of copper and diversify into other hitherto neglected but key sectors such as agriculture. Although Zambia's economic crisis emerged in 1975 due to the beginning of a dramatic declining trend in copper prices, the key issue is no longer copper prices. Copper prices, in recent years have not been too sluggish and during the first week of July 1987, the price of copper on the London Metal Exchange was quoted at 1055 pounds sterling per tonne – the highest in recent years. The fact is, however, that the copper mines are dying out. Copper ore grades are decreasing drastically and, as a result, copper production in recent years has been going down while costs of production have been going up. For example, from 1985 to 1986, ore grade fell from 2.29 to 2.15 per cent, a decline of 28.7 per cent. Trends in copper production are shown in table 1.

Despite the uneconomic nature of copper mining, the country is forced to carry on with this activity due to lack of other significant sources of foreign

Table 1. Copper production (in tonnes)

Year	Production
1973	638.4
1975	619.2
1978	629.0
1981	560.6
1982	584.5
1983	576.1
1984	523.3
1985	478.5
1986	474.8 (estimate)

Source: Ndulo and Norton (1986), Republic of Zambia (1987)

exchange which it badly needs. But all the same, estimates reveal that, under the existing technology, it will be feasible to continue with copper production for at most another 30 years. This makes it imperative that the economy diversify away from copper to alternative sources of foreign exchange.

The Zambian economy has also been characterized by high and unabating levels of import dependency and correspondingly by minimal domestic production linkages. Economic restructuring would, therefore, warrant the progressive substitution of locally available inputs for imported inputs which concomitantly would reduce the demand for foreign exchange and lead to the development of a self-reliant, highly interlinked internal production structure.

At the very least, the requisites for restructuring the Zambian economy are, in the words of President Kaunda, "continued diversion of an increasing share of resources from non-productive to production uses; increasing utilization of local materials; increased efficiency and competitiveness of the mining sector; development of a wide range of exports and import-substituting industries; improved performance of the agricultural sector and in particular, the adoption of measures to make the peasant farmer, who is the focal point of the Party's agricultural strategy, more productive."[3]

In order to bring about the above kind of restructuring, the IMF and the World Bank insisted on the need for radical reform of policy which, at the macro level, would enable resources to move into the net export sector, involve cuts in government spending and a reduction of government deficits through tight fiscal policy; and, at the micro level, liberalize trade, allow the price system to operate and improve the efficiency of public enterprises.

Taking the cue from such suggestions, the Government of Zambia since December 1982, implemented several major policy changes aimed at transforming the economic system from one based primarily on administrative controls to one that would rely more on free market forces and price mechanisms. Some of these important policy reforms and the rationale behind them are explained below.

(a) Exchange rate regime

Since independence, Zambia had a fixed exchange rate which was pegged to the pound sterling until December 1971 and thereafter to the United States dollar. In July 1976, the link with the dollar was broken and the Kwacha was tied to the Special Drawing Rights (SDRs) of the IMF.

After shortages of foreign exchange began to be experienced from 1974 onwards, allocations were made through stringent controls. An importer had first to obtain a license from the Ministry of Commerce and industry and thereafter obtain foreign exchange from the Bank of Zambia. However, in view of the growing scarcity of foreign exchange not all importers who produced licenses could obtain foreign exchange. The suppressed demand for foreign exchange coupled with the allied phenomenon of an overvalued Kwacha led to black markets for foreign exchange at rates far exceeding the official rate. At the official level, there were considerable delays and scope for corruption in processing applications for foreign exchange. The actual allocation was also biased in favour of essential consumer goods imports. The overvalued Kwacha made imports relatively cheaper thereby encouraging import intensity while Zambian goods were rendered uncompetitive in the world markets.

In order to correct for overvaluation, the Kwacha was devalued against the SDR by 20 per cent in January 1983. Later in July 1983, the link with the SDR was broken and the Kwacha was allowed to crawl against a basket of six currencies. Under this crawling peg, the Kwacha depreciated from KI.24 to the US dollar in July 1983 to K2.22 in September 1985.

It was, however, felt that these depreciations had proved inadequate to step up exports and bring about significant diversification and hence further depreciations were necessary. At this stage, the Government had two options to consider: to announce another major devaluation or to introduce an auction system for foreign exchange allocations. The Government opted for the latter.

In the Zambian context, one could think of at least two advantages of the auction system over devaluation. First, while there was a consensus that the Kwacha was overvalued, there seemed to be no agreement on the true extent of overvaluation. It could be left to the auction system, based on the free market, to provide the answer. Second, the auction system could virtually eliminate the subjectivity and possible corruption involved in foreign exchange allocations.

Thus, on 4 October 1985, the Government introduced the weekly system of foreign exchange auctioning. The initial system of allocating foreign exchange to successful bidders at the marginal rate was modified in August 1986 to the Dutch auction whereby every successful bidder was allocated at the rate at which he has bid. This, it was hoped would bring Zambia more Kwacha revenue while curbing the tendency to bid too high. In January 1987, the auction was suspended. In March it was re-introduced in the form of a two-tier system whereby the first-tier rate was fixed between K9.50 and Kl2.50 to one US dollar for government transactions and the second-tier rate was to be determined through public auction. This system too was abandoned in May 1987.

(b) Interest rate regime

Until September 1985, there were ceilings imposed by the Central Bank on interest rates applied by commercial banks. Given the inflation rate, deposit rates have been consistently negative in real terms since 1970 and thereby discouraged private saving and also possibly impeded the development of financial intermediation. Low lending rates which in the 1980s were even negative in real terms created excess demand for credit, necessitating credit rationing with the consequent additional administrative burdens on the Government.

In September 1985, the Government deregulated interest rates. The treasury bill rate went up from 9.5 to 23.5 per cent and, in its wake, the commercial banks' lending rates went up to 30–33 per cent. These high rates were expected to stimulate savings, discourage capital-intensive investments and in general contribute to a more efficient utilization of financial resources.

(c) Price decontrol

Until December 1982, wholesale and retail commodity prices were controlled by the Government, with the main objectives of protecting low income groups and curbing excess monopoly profits. In practice, however, the fixed prices established on a "cost-plus" approach led to inefficient allocation of resources. There were several consequences:

(a) Price control in conjunction with the prevailing tariff structure led to negative effective protection for some goods whose production was consequently discouraged;
(b) Many firms, especially parastatals, experienced reduced profitability at the low uneconomic prices leading to liquidity problems and low investments;
(c) Some parastatals could not even cover costs at the approved prices and the consequent losses had to be covered by subsidies from the Government;
(d) Unfulfilled demand at the artificially low prices led to the development of black markets for goods which, like foreign exchange, were sold at prices much higher than the official, controlled prices;
(e) Low prices coupled with high transport costs led to scarcity of many essential goods in provinces outside the rail line; and
(f) Trading activities became more profitable than production.

In view of the above, the Government decontrolled most wholesale and retail prices in December 1982; only the price of roller meal was controlled.

Price decontrol understandably sparked off a higher rate of inflation. Part of this was sought to be explained in terms of the latent inflation which already existed as manifested in black markets and long queues at state shops. With the decontrol of prices, firms were in a position to charge remunerative prices. While the danger of consumer exploitation was there, it was hoped that the fear of pricing themselves out of the market would curb the tendency of firms to charge excessive prices.

With the decontrol of prices and the introduction of the auctioning system for foreign exchange, parastatals were given a clear signal by the Government that they were on their own and it was up to them to sink or survive. Many Zambian parastatals had been established to promote not only economic but social objectives. But there had been a tendency for some parastatals to use these social objectives as a shield to defend their inefficient, low-profit performances. Now they were required, while not forgetting the social objectives, to operate on predominantly commercial lines.

(d) Tariff reform

Nominal tariffs in Zambia ranged from zero per cent on priority items such as agricultural goods and essential consumer goods through 5–20 per cent on intermediate and capital goods to 50–150 per cent on non-essential durable consumer goods. Indeed, a conspicuous feature of the Zambian tariff structure was the very large number of goods with zero duty rate. The result of this tariff structure was to create a disparate range of effective rates of protection which provided maximum incentives for import-substituting final goods, moderate incentives for heavy intermediate and capital goods (thereby encouraging capital intensity) and minimal incentives or even disincentives (through negative effective rates of protection) for agricultural and industrial machinery and some export goods.

In response to some specific suggestions made by the World Bank, the Government made some changes in the tariff structure. A minimum duty of 10 per cent was introduced on raw materials and intermediate goods in late 1984 and this rate was raised to 15 per cent in the 1986 budget. The basis for levying duty was changed from f.o.b. to c.i.f. in order to increase the revenue base. The sales tax rate on imports was raised to 15 per cent to bring it on par with that levied on domestic goods and services.

(e) Export promotion

The Government effected several measures to encourage exports. In May 1982 a foreign exchange retention scheme was introduced whereby exporters could retain 50 per cent of their foreign exchange receipts (300 per cent in the case of copper) for a period of 21 days for their use in importing more inputs or (as from early 1984) to clear pipeline arrears. In the 1985 budget, the period of retention was raised to 60 days. In the 1984 budget tax concessions were provided to exporters of non-traditional products. They were required to pay only 15 percent tax on profits from such exports. In June 1987, the Bank of Zambia announced the cancellation of the foreign exchange retention scheme. A Zambian Export Promotion Board has also been set up with the aim of promoting non-traditional exports.

The above is the list of major reforms, and the rationale for making them, that the Government undertook up to May 1987. While the list does not include all details, it nonetheless clearly indicates that the reforms were implemented along the directions suggested by the World Bank and the IMF.

These economic policy changes were based on the belief that the desired economic restructuring could be brought about only by a fundamental shift from a centralized system of control to a free market regime.

The various monetary, fiscal and institutional measures were to be viewed as an integrated package in the economic restructuring programme. Clearly, it would be inadequate, for instance, to institute a monetary reform if say a corresponding fiscal measure was inconsistent with it. For example, if aggregate savings were to be increased, then both private and public savings would need to be raised. While positive real interest rates could help to stimulate private saving, increasing the level of public saving would require reducing budget deficits, particularly the operating losses of parastatals. Again, realistic exchange rates have to go hand in hand with high positive real lending rates if capital-intensive investments were to be discouraged. A distorted pattern of incentives was created in the Zambian economy due to inappropriate exchange rates, large fiscal deficits and inflationary monetary policies. Removing the distortions therefore required rectification in all these areas. Piecemeal adjustments would fail to bring about the desired results.

It was stressed that no policy package could act as a quick fix. Restructuring would take time. A medium- to long-term time lapse was supposed to be required before the economy could feel the beneficial impact of the policy measures. The World Bank suggested a period of three to five years. Indeed, in the short term, the net benefits could be expected to be very small or even negative. The negative net benefits in the short term would constitute the price the economy would have to pay for enjoying a much larger volume of positive benefits in the long term.

The radical policy reforms described above remained in operation until 30 April 1987. On May Day 1987, President Kaunda announced Zambia's breakaway from the IMF programme and the launching of a new economic recovery programme. The following excerpts from the President's address explain why Zambia chose to discontinue the fund's policy prescriptions:

> The International Monetary Fund conditionality has meant that the restructuring programme, which was and still is imperative in order to lead the economy to recovery, could only be sustained through recourse to massive external borrowing. Clearly this was going to aggravate the country's external debt even if temporary relief could be obtained from time to time by way of rescheduling agreements with creditors. Rescheduling is itself at a cost. Besides, it merely postpones and increases the debt.
>
> Nevertheless, the Party and its Government decided to go ahead with the measures . . . in the hope that the country's economic performance would improve and the drastic fall in the people's standard of living would be arrested.
>
> We have observed, with growing alarm, a situation where escalating unemployment is becoming a permanent feature of our economy. Galloping inflation has set in which has pushed the prices of basic essential commodities beyond the reach of our people, especially the low income groups who are in the majority. Cases of malnutrition are on the increase every day.
>
> There has been a sharp rise in the mortality rate, especially among the infant population, because hospitals cannot afford to import the essential drugs and other requisites necessary to support life. We are witnessing a situation where our social fabric is slowly disintegrating, thereby sowing seeds of unrest and undermining the peace and unity of the nation. This situation cannot and will not be allowed to continue. It is patently clear that far from improving our condition, we are not succeeding, hence the need for a fresh look."[4]

The principal measures contained in the new economic recovery programme are as follows:

(a) The country's debt repayment has been limited to 10 per cent of net export earnings. After meeting the foreign exchange requirements of Zambia Consolidated Copper Mines, ZIMOIL, Zambia Airways and fertilizer imports, only 10 per cent of the remaining foreign exchange will go towards debt repayments;

(b) The auctioning of foreign exchange has been cancelled and the exchange rate has been fixed at K8.00 to the US dollar;

(c) Maximum wholesale and retail prices will be recommended by manufacturers, producers and importers in conjunction with the Prices and Incomes Commission;

(d) Lending interest rates have been fixed at 15 per cent with a margin of 5 to 20 per cent ceiling;
(e) "No funds involved" import permits have been restricted to imports of essential consumer goods, inputs and machinery;
(f) An Export-Import Bank is being established with an initial capital of K50 million to assist exporters of non-traditional goods;
(g) A revolving fund facility is being set up to support small-scale entrepreneurs;
(h) A more realistic tax structure and a tariff system are to be devised that will widen the economy's revenue base; and
(i) To arrest unemployment, there will be expansion of public works schemes, mostly in the rural areas, increased public expenditure on low-cost capital projects with short maturities and the establishment of a realistic wage policy with a minimum living wage to be recommended by the Prices and Incomes Commission.

The Emergence of the Human Crisis in Zambia

It is important to recognize that economic activities and phenomena are ensconced in a series of ends and means relationships and that the means have value only in so far as they contribute positively to the promotion of ends. For example, various policy instruments and institutions may be designed to achieve economic restructuring of a country in a certain desired fashion. Economic restructuring in turn may be required to promote efficiency which may be thwarted by the prevailing structure. The evolution of an efficient economic structure, however, has, as its objective, the promotion of indigenous development which will progressively reduce poverty and improve living standards of the local population. Poverty alleviation in turn will expectedly contribute to the economic welfare component of a country's social welfare function. The ultimate goal of all human activity then in any spatio-temporal context is the optimization of the social welfare function. In evaluating the efficacy of economic policy instruments, therefore, even on a purely economic basis, one has to examine their impact on ultimate economic welfare. Even if they lead to very salutary results for their immediate objectives but cause a deterioration in overall economic welfare, the instruments cannot be deemed to be useful. The ends – means or instruments – objectives relationship can be lost sight of even in intermediate stages. I will illustrate this with a story of two Zambian parastatals which, for anonymity, I shall call firms X and Y.

Firm X for many years was producing a basic needs commodity using predominantly as input a commodity supplied by firm Y. At one stage, in the early 1980s, a foreign company suggested to firm X that if it improved the quality of its product by using a more sophisticated and modern plant, it could even export its goods abroad. Firm X bought the idea and imported the required plant from the country of its foreign partner. It was then found that this plant could not use the input supplied by firm Y. Firm X began to import its input. Very soon firm X also began to export its output and earn foreign exchange. Firm X was hailed a success. Since firm Y could not sell all its output domestically, it also, in due course, managed somehow to export its surplus output and earn foreign exchange, Firm Y was also thus successful.

But, from the country's point of view, these events cannot be regarded as desirable occurrences, for although both firms earned the country foreign exchange, a vital domestic linkage that existed between them had been lost. Instead, both firms had become externally dependent and hence vulnerable to the buffetings of external forces. The point of this illustration is that earning foreign exchange, however scarce the commodity may be, is only a means. The end is the development of a self-reliant economic structure in which the establishment of domestic linkages is a key element.

When judged in the context of the ends-means relationship outlined above, the World Bank/IMF prescriptions for Zambia had categorically failed to deliver the goods. It may be argued of course that had Zambia not adopted these prescriptions and had continued to follow the old policy regime, things could have been far worse. While one may engage in such speculation, nonetheless, as the saying goes, nothing succeeds like success. And mere casual empirical evidence is sufficient to demonstrate that the IMF policy package in Zambia did not succeed by and large. While bringing about efficiency in a limited sense, the policy reforms showed no signs of restructuring the economy in a healthy manner. What is more, it systematically led to the further immiserization of an already impoverished society that held serious potential for political instability of the country. The violent upheaval that occurred on the Copperbelt in December 1986 following a 100 per cent increase in the price of mealie meal was a clear portent in this regard. Here, it is my personal view that Zambia's breakaway from the IMF/World Bank policy package was necessitated not so much by any illogic in the package itself but by the utterly inflexible attitude of the multilateral agencies in regard to its implementation.

Economic restructuring in the Zambian context required, among others, the following:

(a) the development of agriculture;
(b) improvement in the capacity utilization of the manufacturing industry. And since the industry was highly import-dependent, it was necessary to ensure a smoother flow of foreign exchange;
(c) the promotion of small-scale industries which by virtue of their relatively greater labour intensity, and greater adaptability to locally available resources and ability to act as ancillaries to large-scale industries could serve to promote linkages within the economy; and
(d) reduced dependence on copper to earn foreign exchange by developing nontraditional industrial and agricultural exports.

The radical policy reforms did not do much to fulfil any of the above requirements. Agriculture, which is deemed to be the highest priority sector in Zambia's structural adjustment programmes, ironically suffered the most on the following counts:

(a) The sector's capacity to borrow was severely restricted due to the commercial bank lending rates shooting up to nearly 40 per cent. As a result of the tremendous illiquidity, even though the World Bank had allocated a sizeable amount of auction funds specifically for agriculture, the funds were hardly used;
(b) The farmers' liquidity problem was aggravated by the three successive years of drought;

(c) Cost of production went up due to the removal of subsidy on fertilizers;
(d) Due to the tremendous depreciation of the Kwacha that occurred under the auction regime, imports of tractors and other machinery became prohibitively expensive. A tractor which was earlier priced around K28,000 began to cost K150,000 and even more.

Owing to the above factors it was small-scale farming that notably declined. The high cost of borrowing and the steadily increasing kwacha price of the dollar also severely restricted small-scale industrial development. According to the Government's latest economic review (Republic of Zambia, 1987), after October 1985, despite the very significant depreciation of the Kwacha, neither agricultural nor manufacturing exports increased significantly. In 1986, the value of industrial exports remained stagnant at 2 per cent of total exports.

While none of the requirements for restructuring were satisfactorily met, the impact of the policy changes on various macro-economic variables was highly adverse. This can be seen from Table 2. The growth rate of GDP has been negligible. While there has been a high growth rate of population and hence a growth in the labour force on the one hand, there has been a steady decline in formal employment on the other. In 1980, 23.8 per cent of the 1.6 million labour force was in formal sector employment. In 1984, only 20.3 per cent of the 1.8 million people in the labour force was formally employed. These statistics suggest an increase in unemployment and growth of the informal sector. According to crude estimates, 49.13 per cent of the labour force are currently unemployed. The size of the informal sector has also grown from 0.9 million in 1980 to 1.3 million in 1987.

Table 2: Some macro-economic indicators

	1984	1985	1986
Real GDP growth rate (%)	0.4	1.5	0.5
Formal sector employment	365,290	361,520	360,540
Net investment outflow (in millions of Kwacha)	371.4	594.5	1,239.9
Deficit in balance-of-payments current account (in millions of Kwacha)	317	429.2	1,670
Debt burden (in billions of $US)	3.92	4.48	5.1 (1987)
Ratio of debt to exports	403.2	529.3	
Ratio of debt to GNP	154.5	210.3	

Source: Republic of Zambia, 1987; World Bank, 1987 b.

Increasing capital flight and increasing outflows of freight and insurance have contributed greatly to the increasing balance-of-payments deficits. Most significantly, there has been a heavy increase in the country's debt burden.

The worst impact of the policy reforms has been on poverty and income distribution. Since the beginning of the policy reforms in December 1982 (when prices were decontrolled) and more especially after the introduction of the foreign exchange auctioning in October 1985, inflation rates have gone up tremendously while wage incomes have remained relatively frozen. Again, the burden of inflation has been more on the low income groups than on the high income groups. The downgrading of Zambia from a low middle-income country to a low-income country in international classification itself speaks for the sharp economic deterioration that has taken place in recent years. Not only in terms of income criteria but also in terms of various quality-of-life indicators Zambia's performance has been below that of the low income countries in general. This is shown in table 3.

Table 3: Quality of life indicator for Zambia and low-income economies, 1985

	Zambia	Low-income economies
Life expectancy	52	60
Crude death rate per 1000 population	15	10
Infant mortality rate	84	72
Child death rate	15	9
Daily calories supply per capita	2,137	2.339
Population per physician, 1981	7,800	5,770

Source: World Bank, 1987 a.

While more recent statistics on the non-income criteria are hard to come by, evidence from ad hoc studies and other sources suggests no improvement. It has been estimated that one-third of the under-fives in Zambia are malnourished and that 40 per cent of all children die before the age of 15.

Some international agencies working in Zambia corroborate that the quality of human life has deteriorated after the implementation of the IMF's structural adjustment programme. For instance, Oxfam has been working with several groups in Zambia – the urban poor in the shanty compounds and the rural poor comprising mostly female-headed households, farmers with small land holdings and the disabled. Reviewing Oxfam's experience, John Clark states:

> "our local representatives say without a shadow of doubt those we work with have suffered in the following ways:
>
> 1) Urban malnutrition has increased as food prices rose steeply . . . food prices have risen much faster than wages.
> 2) Rural inequalities have been magnified considerably . . . As rural inequalities grow, so do rural prices (everything from kerosene to soap powder). Hence relative poverty can be readily converted into absolute poverty.
> 3) . . . The privatization of the marketing system has clear advantages for many, but it is proving a handicap for farmers in the remoter areas. Merchants are simply not prepared to pay prices comparable with those in the productive regions, and so farmers are offered an uneconomic rate of return . . . In economic terms, . . . their incomes will diminish and, most worryingly, they will be unable to make the necessary investments in their land. This will trigger a very rapidly descending spiral of poverty, we suggest.
> 4) Overall, cuts in government social spending, especially in health, have been an added blow to the poor.
>
> In our view, the adjustment measures have brought immense hardship and have yielded almost no benefits to the two categories of people we work with."[5]

One can say that the Oxfam experience is not exceptional but typical of the general state of affairs in the country. The fundamental reason why the human dimension of the economic crisis in Zambia began to assume critical proportions is that the radical policy reforms contributed little to indigenous development. I shall explain this by analyzing the impact of what was considered to be the most important element of the policy package, namely the foreign exchange auctioning system.

After the introduction of the foreign exchange auctioning system, both the internal and external value of the Kwacha depreciated considerably. The external value of the Kwacha fell from K2.23413 to a US dollar to K5.01 to a US dollar in the very first auction. Thereafter there was an inexhorable slide in the external value of the Kwacha until it reached the rate of K21.05 to a US dollar in the last auction with clear signs of further possible depreciation had the system continued beyond April 1987. The Kwacha had thus depreciated by 942 per cent within the space of one and a half years! Such depreciation, by hiking the Kwacha price of imported inputs and in conjunction with the greatly increased cost of money, inevitably led to galloping inflation that eroded the Kwacha's internal purchasing power.

The fall in the internal and external value of the Kwacha created an anomalous situation in which goods and services within Zambia were unaffordably expensive in Kwacha terms but ridiculously cheap in terms of hard currency. Thus, while most of these goods had been priced beyond the reach of the bulk of the indigenous masses, for foreign tourists and residents whose earnings were predominantly or wholly in foreign exchange, the country had turned into a consumer's paradise.

Who were the major recipients of the scarce foreign exchange that was being put into the auction system week after week? Most Zambian companies especially parastatals have always had liquidity and cash flow problems. With the high price of money and increasing price of foreign exchange, small businesses and parastatals found it very difficult to make meaningful bids.

A perusal of the list of successful bidders revealed that foreign companies constituted a majority on the list and received a major share of the supply of foreign exchange at practically every auction. Even though multinational companies may have been making useful contributions to Zambia's industrial and economic development, their ultimate interests lie not in Zambia but in the home countries of their parent companies.

Multinational companies have never had liquidity problems. Even if they did, they could obtain easy redress from the transnational banks or from their parent companies. Under the foreign exchange auctioning system, there were trends towards a dangerous situation whereby indigenous companies would have been pushed out of the production system altogether. It is futile to speculate whether cut-throat competition was being deliberately practiced by the high-level bidders (multinational companies). The fact remains that the throats of the indigenous manufacturing units were surely and systematically being cut.

According to Central Bank Governor, Leonard Chivuno, under the auction 90 per cent of the foreign exchange was allotted to just 100 companies of which 99 per cent were foreign-owned. Even in agriculture, one of the factors causing the decline of small-scale farming was the emergence of large-scale, private foreign-owned farms.

If most of the parastatals had closed down, the Government would have had no choice but to sell them – in tune with IMF/World Bank policy ironically! But who could have afforded to buy them except the multinational companies? Some time ago, Anglo-American had already offered to buy Zambia's mines.

Thus although Zambia was evolving into a highly efficient and competitive economy that ensured the survival of the fittest, it was also transforming itself into a country of the foreigners, by the foreigners and for the foreigners. Surely, no sovereign government could permit such a thing to happen.

Other policy measures too failed to realize their intended objectives. Real savings did not increase after deregulation of interest rates. It is useful to remember that savings are a function of not only interest but also of incomes which were severely declining. In 1987 nominal interest rates would have had to be raised to 60 per cent to become positive in real terms. And even if that had been done, sooner or later, the consequent further cost-push inflation would have nullified the positive value of the interest rates. Naturally, the inducement to save can hardly be stimulated in such an environment.

Again, the objective of price decontrol was to enable producers to charge cost-recovering and remunerative prices. But prices were inflated completely out of line with production costs. Retail prices in particular became exploitative, not seldom reflecting profit margins of 100 per cent or even more.

It was suggested that after decontrol of prices the supply of various goods which earlier were highly scarce had improved considerably. But it must be recognized that earlier, when goods were hardly available, the large majority of the local population especially in the rural areas did not have the purchasing power to avail of the goods anyway. After the supply position improved, the prices had been hiked so high that this majority did not benefit at all. The beneficiaries were the small elite group who had always commanded great purchasing power and who could now buy more goods, especially imported ones.

In this way, hardly any objective of the IMF's stabilization programme was realized in Zambia. Its programmes converted single-digit inflation into double digit runaway inflation. Through bringing about disparate growth rates of wage incomes and inflation, it exacerbated the already inequitious income distribution and led to social tensions. Instead of reviving the economy, it in fact led to severe economic contraction.

Reflections on the Human Crisis in Zambia

The economic philosophy underlying the IMF/World Bank policy prescriptions is, as expressed by one writer, that efficient growth through getting the prices right is the best approach to poverty alleviation. This philosophy perhaps would have a considerable degree of validity in a country where poverty levels are not already glaring and the prevailing state of income distribution does not deviate too much from acceptable norms. But in the Zambian situation where the afore-mentioned assumptions on poverty and income distribution are seriously violated, policies aimed mainly at getting the prices right cannot improve efficiency without placing enormous burdens on the already vulnerable groups in the society, which burdens, even in the short run, could prove to be the last straw leading to social upheaval. In our view, no structural adjustment programme in a country like Zambia can succeed unless it is based on the recognition that equity is an equally important objective as efficient growth.

As already pointed out efficiency was greatly at stake in Zambia due to gross price distortions resulting from a highly controlled policy regime. There was, therefore, an indisputable need to relax controls and liberalize the economy. To the extent that the policy reforms originated from a perception of this need, they were indeed highly logical. But the error was in attempting to swing, in a very short period, from a highly controlled regime to an almost unfettered free market system. For the conditions for the successful operation of free market forces with a view to improving economic welfare do not exist in Zambia.

We have already referred to the extremely skewed income distribution. Another deviation from the required conditions for a successful free price system is the predominating presence of parastatals. And so, it is in consistency with the economic liberalization measures that the IMF and the World Bank were trying to prevail on the Zambian government to privatize the parastatals as much as possible on grounds of their inefficient performances.

However, parastatals in Zambia were set up with several social objectives which are as valid today as they were at the time when the parastatals were born. If parastatals are sold to private hands, most of these social objectives would be thrown to the winds. Necessarily, therefore, parastatals in Zambia are there to stay. The solution for their inefficient performance lies in the development and improvement of indigenous managerial skills.

Again, the coexistence of parastatals, multinational companies and large and small private Zambian firms marks a significant divergence from the assumption of a predominantly competitive market structure that would ensure fairness in free market operations. What exists in Zambia is a nominally monopolistic competitive set-up (in terms of the number of enterprises) and a de facto highly oligopolistic structure dominated by the multinationals in terms of economic power. This was clearly in evidence from the way the foreign exchange auction system worked, and the consequences it entailed.

In the course of monitoring the operation of the liberalized price regime, the government did attempt to make several meaningful interventions and modifications in the regime to ensure that efficiency was not being promoted at the cost of other arguments of national welfare. But these interventions were not favoured by the IMF which regarded them as undesirable interference with the free market mechanism. For instance, during the auction regime, the Bank of Zambia rejected a couple of bids for the import of shoes and tyres by firms which were manufacturing these goods in Zambia. Later, the Bank was reportedly admonished by the Fund over these rejections. Again, the Bank in August 1986 suspended the holiday allowance – a wasteful drain of scarce foreign exchange – but very soon restored the allowance at the insistence of the Fund. It was suspected that in several cases, whereas items like raw materials and machinery were indicated at the time of bidding, finished goods were being imported instead. It was reported, however, that the Fund was against the Government investigating such cases. Such instances demonstrated the highly rigid approach the Fund adopted in regard to the implementation of the adjustment programme. And this is what finally brought about an impasse in the dialogue between the Government and the Fund. In the new economic recovery programme, the auction system was abandoned in favour of, once again, a fixed exchange rate system. But in my view, the auction system in a modified from (which would surely not have been approved by the Fund) might have proved beneficial.

Consideration of allocative efficiency in Zambia warranted drastic reduction in social service expenditures. Reduction in these expenditures have a two-fold effect:

(a) In the immediate run, it reduces the quantum of public services, and, as a recent UNICEF report states, "absolute poverty is correlated with lack of adequate access to public services. This is largely because of the relative geographic isolation of many absolutely poor rural families, and because most absolutely poor urban households are in squatter or other per-urban areas which are ill-served, especially if they were established or grew rapidly during the post-1979 years (post-1975 in the case of Zambia) of constrained public budgets";

(b) By denuding the existing meagre stocks of human capital the country has, it acts as a long-term constraint on development.

It is, therefore, essential that the levels of real per capita social service expenditures be at least maintained, if not increased. With the high growth in population at 3.5 per cent per annum, this might appear difficult in the face of extremely limited resources.

But the severity of resource limitation in Zambia, to a significant extent, has been the result of debt servicing. In recent years, a considerable amount of Zambia's resources have been frittered away in debt servicing, leaving a relatively smaller proportion for internal economic development. Indeed, projections revealed that Zambia was going to be a net exporter of resources to the IMF for the next six years.

A few months ago, World Bank Vice-President Edward Jaycox expressed skepticism that some African countries including Zambia, despite vigorously pursuing very difficult adjustment programmes, would recover economically because of their tremendous debt overhang. In a similar vein, another Vice-President of the Bank, Wilfried Thalwitz, stated:

> "The international community has never been stingy with Africa – the per capita level of aid to the continent has been among the highest – perhaps the highest in the world. However, what is being done now is not enough, mainly because much of it leaves the countries in servicing debts that were acquired in earlier days. What is needed is new lending, or gift-giving, to replace the outflows for the existing debt burdens. The action programmes of many African countries remain unfunded, there is too little investment, too little import capacity, with the danger that the economy cannot respond to what are otherwise excellent new policies" (*African Recovery*, February/April 1987, No. 7, p.3).

It is precisely to stem such a danger in Zambia, that in its new economic recovery programme, the Government announced the extraordinary but economically pragmatic step of restricting debt servicing to 10 per cent of net export earnings. This measure should make available a significantly larger volume of the country's own resources for domestic use. But, with the discontinuation of the IMF measures, the country has also lost the international "seal of approval" and thereby could have much reduced access to funds from western donor agencies. It is up to these agencies, however, to ponder over President Kaunda's rhetorical question: "which is a better partner for you in the long run, a nation which devotes all of its resources to paying the debt and, therefore, grinds to an economic and political halt, or a stable nation capable of sustaining the repayment of its entire debt?"

During a period of declining incomes, given the skewed nature of income distribution, it is the incomes of the poor that decline real fast. And this occurs due to the retrenchment of mostly wage earners in the formal sector and the consequent rise in unemployment. In Zambia, nearly one million youth are estimated to be unemployed in the urban areas. In order to contain this potential social explosive, it is necessary that public expenditure composition be so determined as to emphasize expenditures that have a greater impact on employment promotion and are most likely to benefit the poor.

In its new economic recovery programme, the Government has given due attention to this need by assuming that resources will be injected into labour-intensive public work schemes and low-cost capital projects with short maturities. Investment in irrigation schemes in particular would serve to protect small farmers' incomes by insuring against drought and ensuring food security. Scope for irrigation in Zambia rests on the fact that in 1982 less than 0.3 per cent of the cropped land was under irrigation.

Having allowed this poverty situation to deteriorate to the level it already has, it is perhaps imperative that Zambia should now adopt a more poverty-focused approach to policy. One relevant measure in this regard is to increase the quantity of assets owned by the poor. In a situation of great inequality in the distribution of assets, it may be necessary to first redistribute the assets (e.g., through land reform) before undertaking policies designed to enhance the productivity of those assets. Adelman (1986) calls this sequence "redistribution before growth" and considers its advantages to be two-fold:

> First, a better distribution of the major asset whose productivity is about to be improved, together with more equal access to markets and to opportunities for improving the productivity of that major asset, will obviously diminish the adverse effects of unequal asset distribution on income distribution. Second, the redistributed asset is not as valuable before improvements in productivity as it is after. Redistribution with full compensation would, therefore, be possible, at least in principle.

Adelman's thesis of "redistribution before growth" provides a sound theoretical underpinning for the kind of land reform in Zambia suggested in a recent study by Levi and Mwanza (1986). The authors state that not more than 250,000 ha. of land would be required to provide food to all those in the urban areas who face the risk of food insecurity. They further state their case as follows: "Given that vastly more than that much land (i.e., more than 250,000 ha.) on large commercial farms (239 farms of over 2,000 ha. in 1976/1977) is left fallow, in pasture and not classified, the problem of urban poverty is solvable if even modest amounts of land could be transferred to poor settlers from urban areas. Probably too, relatively poor and 'emergent' rural households could use land more intensely than it is on large farms. There is, at least, a case for land reform of some sort, and given the deteriorating urban economy, it is perhaps quite a strong case."

With the phasing out of copper and increasing scarcity of foreign exchange, a lot of efforts are being made to earn foreign exchange through non-traditional exports. While these efforts are laudable and must continue, with low commodity prices and unabating levels of protectionism in the industrialized countries both of which are unlikely to change for a long time, it would be unpragmatic to hope for extraordinary results. A major hope in trade, if at all, lay only in regional co-operation.

But, on the other hand, scarcity of foreign exchange can be alleviated by reducing the demand for it. Zambia can, and must, reduce its present high level of import dependence. In the first place, a firm political will needs to be exercised to prevent the import of luxury consumption goods especially those for which local substitutes are available. If the new economic recovery programmes theme of "growth from our own resources" is to acquire substance, Zambia will have to earnestly begin to develop indigenous technology that can adapt to "our own resources" and, in the longer term, explore possibilities of developing basic goods like rubber and steel. If this is not done, Zambian firms producing tyres, cars and so on will be import-dependent for ever.

Unlike the IMF programme which proved to be highly contractionary, the Government's new economic recovery programme is expansionary in essence and purports to bring about economic adjustment with a human face. Its success will depend upon the resources the country is able to muster and the will to implement the programme to achieve its intent. In this regard, a Zambian has bluntly pointed out that: "the most critical is the human factor. Development will not take place without the will, ability and capability of the people, even if all leaves turn into dollars". (Lewanika, 1987).

Is there a light at the end of the dark tunnel? Given the will, the answer is most certainly yes. But it is up to the country – and the international community too – to determine how long it will continue to grope in the dark before it sees the light.

Notes

[1] K. D. Kaunda, *New Economic Recovery Programme*, Cabinet Office, Lusaka, 1987.

[2] Republic of Zambia, *Economic Review 1986 and Annual Plan 1987*, the Government Printer, Lusaka, 1987.

[3] Republic of Zambia, "Restructuring in the Midst of Crisis", Vol. 1, 1984, p.iv.

[4] Kaunda, op.cit.

[5] J. Clark, "Zambia – OXFAM Experience with Structural Adjustment", Mimeograph, 1986.

References

1 Adelman, J., "A poverty-focused approach to development policy.", in J.P. Lewis and V. Kallab (eds.), *Development Strategies Reconsidered*, ODC Policy Perspectives, no. 5, Transactions Books, USA, 1986.

2 *Africa Recovery*, no. 1, February/April 1987.

3 Chivuno, L., "Auctioning of foreign exchange – Recent experiences in third world countries: The Zambian experience.", paper read at the International Conference on Auctioning of Foreign Exchange, Lusaka, 29 June – July 1987.

4 Clark, J., "Zambia-Oxfam experience with structural adjustment", mimeograph, 1986.

5 Kaunda, K.D., "New Economic Recovery Programme", Cabinet Office, Lusaka, 1987.

6 Lewanika, A., "Economic recovery drive opens new chapter", *Sunday Times of Zambia*, 5 July 1987.

7 Levi, J. and Mwanza, A.M., "Zambia case study: Agricultural policy issues", draft report prepared for the Economic Development Institute, World Bank, 1986.

8 Ndulo, M. and Norton, D., "Zambia case study: Macro-economic issues", draft report prepared for the Economic Development Institute, World Bank 1986.

9 Republic of Zambia, "Restructuring in the midst of crisis", vol. 1, 1984.

10 Republic of Zambia, *Economic Review 1986 and Annual Plan 1987*, The Government Printer, Lusaka, 1987.

11 Seshamani, V. and Mwanza, A.M., "The poverty phenomenon: Its nature, extent and causes", in Government of the Republic of Zambia/UNICEF Programming Committee, Situation Analysis of Children and Women in Zambia, Lusaka, 1980.

12 Seshamani, V. and Dewer, S., "Zambia case study: Industrial policy issues", draft report prepared the for Economic Development Institute, World Bank, 1986.

13 Seshamani, V., "The rationale and scope of economic policy reforms in Zambia", paper presented to the World Bank Media Seminar on Zambia's Economic Adjustment and Reform Programme, Livingstone, 12–15 January 1987 a.

14 Seshamani, V., "Issue on poverty and industrialization in developing countries: Lessons for

Zambia", inaugural lecture, 13 February 1987, University of Zambia, 1987 b.
15 Seshamani, V., "The mechanism of foreign exchange auctioning in Zambia: A suggested alternative", paper presented at the International Conference on Foreign Exchange Auction, Lusaka, 29 June – 3 July 1987 c.
16 Seshamani, V., "Economic crisis and development policy in the African countries in the 1980s", Institute for Developing Economics, Tokyo (forthcoming), 1987 d.
17 Stewart, F., "The fragile foundations of the neoclassical approach to development", *The Journal of Development Studies*, vol. 21, no. 2, pp.282–292, 1985.
18 Stewart, F., "Should conditionality change?" paper presented at Seminar on International Monetary Fund and the World Bank in Africa: Conditionality and its Impact, Uppsala, 29 January 1987, Scandinvian Institute of African Studies, 1987.
19 UNICEF, *The State of the World's Children, 1987*, Oxford University Press, London, 1987 a.
20 UNICEF, "Children on the frontline", New York, 1987 b.
21 World Bank, *World Development Report, 1986*, Oxford University Press, New York, 1986.
22 World Bank, *World Development Report, 1987*, Oxford University Press, New York, 1987 a.
23 World Bank, "World debt tables", Washington, D.C., 1987 b.

Madagascar

PEPE ANDRIOMANANA

Madagascar's economic difficulties worsened in the 1970s following stagnation in production. But it was in the early 1980s that the real impact of the crisis was felt due to a balance-of-payments crisis, followed by an inflationary policy imposed by the International Monetary Fund and the World Bank. As in most developing countries, African countries included, stabilization of external deficits was achieved at unbearable costs from the human point of view. Efforts made by some organizations of the United Nations system like UNICEF, WFP, etc., to alleviate the human sufferings were frustrated by macro-economic constraints which practically precluded any strategic initiative to preserve the human dimension.

Evolution of Social and Welfare Indicators

(a) Food and nutrition

Systematic studies on nutritional requirements in Madagascar. covering the period 1976–1986, are not available.[1] The problem will be examined by presenting the evolution of rice supply and the available main results of ad hoc surveys.

Rice occupies an important place in the diet of the Malagasy people. According to FAO, rice accounted for 57 per cent of the daily per capita calorie intake in 1975–1977.[2] It represented 56 per cent of food expenditures of families of the low-income group in Antananarivo in 1982–1983.[3]

Table 1: Madagascar: Total rice supply, 1970–1985

		Production			Supply	
	Population (in '000s)	Paddy (1,000 tons)	Import (1,000 tons)	Export (1,000 tons)	Local rice Kg/inhabitant	Total Kg/inhabitant
1970	6,800	1865	20	68	149	142
1975	7,600	1972	64	5	141	149
1980	8,710	2109	177	1	131	151
1981	8,950	2100	193	0	127	148
1982	9,200	1995	351	0	118	147
1983	9,460	2147	179	0	123	147
1984	9,720	2131	115	0	119	131
1985	9,990	2100	140	0	114	128
1986	10,260	–	–	–	–	–

Source: MPARA: Agricultural Statistics Yearbook.

Note: Calculation of the percentage of local rice supply presupposes that seeds, cattle feed and losses account for 19 per cent of the production

Table 1 highlights a constant fall in the per capita local rice supply since the 1970s (12 per cent between 1970 and 1980 and 13 per cent from 1980 to 1985). This fall was due to stagnation in production, coupled with annual population growth rates ranging from 2.2 to 2.5 per cent in the 1970s, and 2.8 per cent during the first half of the 1980s. Until 1983, rice imports made it possible to maintain some degree of consistency in the overall per capita rice supply. From 1984, ceilings for rice imports have been set according to IMF requirements. Total rice supply fell by 13 per cent in two years (147 kg/inhabitant in 1983 and 128 kg/inhabitant in 1985). According to some estimates, it fell to 125 kg/inhabitant in 1986.

This drop had an adverse effect on prices, especially over the last three years. The price of local rice increased by 300 per cent between 1982 and 1985. This considerable rise, coupled with the fall in the purchasing power, led to a reduction in family budgets as far as other food expenses were concerned. The undeniable deterioration in the nutritional food values as revealed by the various surveys is consistent with this evolution and that of income. In 1985/1986 the deficiency, according to regions, ranged between 5 and 20 per cent with respect to calories, 6 and 44 per cent with respect to protein, 68 and 70 per cent with respect to lipids and 30 and 60 per cent with respect to calcium.

Children were most affected by this situation. According to a study undertaken by UNICEF,[4] the infant mortality rate (nutrition indicator) increased from 110 to 162 per cent between 1980 and 1986, i.e., an increase of 47 per cent. At the Befelatanana hospital, for example, the number of children suffering from serious malnutrition (less than 60 per cent of the standard weight) increased from 28.8 to 41.9 per cent.

A recent survey conducted by UNICEF[5] in connection with the above study provides other alarming indications on the food situation in Madagascar. Food reduction appears as one element of the "strategy of survival of the vulnerable families". Only 56.8 per cent of families in the "major urban centres", 55.6 per cent in the "secondary urban centres" and 26 per cent in the rural areas prepare three family meals a day; between 49.1 and 83.6 per cent of the families have experienced a quantitative deterioration in their food over the last five years; and 22.3 per cent of the rural families have changed their food habits, with some dropping rice cultivation in fruit crop and export crop areas.

(b) System of health and adjustment

Some health indicators have experienced a positive evolution over the last 10 years, as evidenced by the number of inhabitants per doctor and paramedical staff. The number of inhabitants per doctor dropped from 13,703 in 1975 to 6,333 in 1985 while the number of inhabitants per paramedical staff has dropped from 5,950 in 1975 to 1,310 in 1985. Similarly, the number of medical units has increased considerably: 1,204 in 1978 as against 2,082 in 1985, i.e., an increase of 875 in seven years, corresponding to an increase of: 847 primary health care centres (PHCC); 8 medical centres; 6 health posts; 21 dispensaries; and 11 maternity homes. This means that the number of "basic units" has been strengthened while that of hospitals has virtually remained unchanged. This considerable extension of the health network, however, was, from 1980, incompatible with the budget situation resulting from the crisis and the adjustment measures. The end result was a serious deterioration of Madagascar's health system. The budget allocation of the Ministry of Health was reduced from 12 per cent in 1976 to 8.5 per cent in 1980 and 7.5 per cent in 1986.

The deterioration affected the entire system. The following are some examples:

(a) The running expenses of the Transmissible Disease Control Department decreased in volume by 85 per cent between 1976 and 1986. This department is now almost completely neglected;
(b) Drug supply at all levels was seriously affected. In the "medical units", the drug allocation in 1986 hardly met 25 per cent of the basic requirements; the teaching of disease prevention in schools was abandoned in 1984;
(c) Most of the equipment is obsolete (e.g., the baby-weighing scales are over 20 years old);
(d) There is no maintenance of the premises and the equipment. The dilapidated state of the health buildings is visible everywhere.

Beyond the consequences of the decrease in the volume of public expenditure, the enormous health problems in Madagascar can be seen through other aspects. There is the problem of drug distribution. Prices of drugs have increased considerably as a result of repeated devaluations. The "essential drug policy" is officially adopted in the public health centres. However, it is not implemented consistently, and remains ridiculous compared with the expansion of the private sector. In June 1987, an antibiotic treatment cost between 10,000 and 35,000 Malagasy francs, whereas the minimum wage was 30,000 francs.

Housing conditions have rapidly deteriorated. According to a recent study,[6] the number of persons per room in Antananarivo is 3.14 on the average, but 4.8 for single room accommodations which represent 37 per cent of the total accommodations. The number of square meters per person is below 2.5 with respect to 40 per cent of the accommodations; only 20 per cent of the accommodations have drinking water and electricity; 4 per cent have only water and 24 per cent only electricity. At the national level, in 1986, 16.5 per cent of the population had access to drinking water in the urban areas as against 1.5 per cent in the rural areas.[7]

(c) Education: structural and financial handicaps

Government's efforts to democratize education have produced quite spectacular results. The school population has increased as follows:

Table 2: School population 1974/75 – 1984/1985

	1974/75	1980/81	1984/85	Increase in % 1974/75–1984/85
Level I	1,133,013	1,723,779	1,625,216	43.4
Level II	107,428	–	378,623	252.4
Level III	29,776	–	128,594	331.8
Level IV	9,354	22,260	2,170,179	69.6

Source: UNESCO, 1986

School population had increased considerably between 1974/1975 and 1980/1981. During that period it was 7.2 per cent per year on the average with respect to level I. It has slowed down since and was even negative as far as level I was concerned. In 1984/1985, the number of school-going children in level I was equivalent to gross percentages of school attendance (6–10 years age group) of 97.9 per cent for public schools and 14.9 per cent for private schools, i.e., a total of 112.8 per cent. The net percentage of children attending public schools (the only percentage calculated by UNESCO) was 59.1 per cent for the 1984/1985 school year.

This rise in the number of school-going children in level I had an effect on level II (junior secondary), level III (senior secondary) and level IV (university). The gross percentage of school attendance more than doubled at level II (11–14 year age group) in 10 years and tripled at level III (15–17 year age group) during the same period. The number of girls attending school increased concurrently. In 1984/1985, it represented 46, 45 and 43 per cent of levels I, II and III school populations respectively.

On the other hand, there has been a downward trend in enrolment rates with respect to technical schools. This trend is due first and foremost to the priority given to general education in the allocation of resources. It is also due to difficulties faced by the graduates of technical schools in trying to enter the labour market: the programmes are not adapted to the needs of potential employers (state, parastatal and private); the training received is inadequate on account of the low professional standard of the instructors and there is lack of adequate and working equipment.

The entire educational and training system in Madagascar is currently facing resource problems, particularly since the worsening of the financial constraints linked with the current adjustment exercise. First, the increase in the school population has necessitated the massive recruitment of teachers. These requirements are largely covered through the recruitment of National Service Volunteers (NSV) whose pedagogical training lasts between five weeks and three months. Ninety per cent of the teachers in level I and 50 per cent of the teachers in level II have no professional qualifications. In level III, only 40 per cent of the teachers have adequate training. Second, these teachers work under increasingly difficult conditions. In a large number of rural schools (level I), the cycle is incomplete. What is more, one teacher is responsible for several classes. Lack of books and teaching materials is experienced at all levels, resulting in low educational output as follows:

(a) Each pupil in level I spends on the average, 2 years and 4 months in each year of the cycle, e.g., 11 years and 8 months in the five-year cycle;
(b) For levels II and III, the corresponding figures are 1 year and 7 months/year/pupil, and 6 years and 4 months respectively.

The quality of output is even more alarming: the number of unemployed school-leavers is increasing rapidly due to the shrinking of the labour market on the one hand, and, on the other, the irrelevance between training and employment. The latter is particularly acute at the junior and intermediate levels of manpower, paradoxically where, despite the situation, a large number of needs are not met.

Finally, the fate of the university can be used to illustrate the dramatic effects of financial restrictions on education and training over the last few years. In the Antananarivo "Centre universitaire regional" (CUR), the pedagogical expenditure per student has increased in constant franc (1978 price) from 115,000 Malagasy francs in 1978 to 16,000 francs in 1986, i.e., a ratio of 7.2. Furthermore, the "travaux pratiques" (TP) and "travaux diriges" (TD) have virtually disappeared from the first cycle (first and second years), especially in the first year during which the number of students promoted ranged between 1,500 and 3,500. Duplicated lecture notes are not available, and courses are no longer organized for want of finance. Similarly, the living conditions of the students are very poor: during the period under review, the scholarships have lost 67.5 per cent of their purchasing power and the budget of the "Centres des oeuvres universitaries" (COUM) has decreased in real terms by over 30 per cent. As a result, over 50 per cent of the students drop out after repeating their class in the first year. In 1985, the university awarded about 1,400 degrees for 37,000 students.

According to a study undertaken by UNICEF in 1987,[8] 35 per cent of heads of family who passed out from institutes of higher learning are either unemployed or in the "informal sector" in the major urban centres. The corresponding percentage is 56.6 per cent in the rural areas.

(d) Employment and income

The "social costs" of the crisis and the adjustment are borne first and foremost by the wage earners. In a country like Madagascar, however, where there is neither social security nor unemployment benefits, statistics on employment and employment demand are very partial and cannot therefore be used. On the other hand, data on the fall in the income of wage earners do exist as in table 3 below. The fall did not start in 1980, the year the adjustment exercise began, but was precipitated by a deliberate salary freeze policy concluded with IMF. The fall in the non-agricultural minimum wage in constant franc was 36 per cent between 1978 and 1985. That of the civil service (as shown in category 1 of table 3) was still worse at 60.8 per cent. It could even be underestimated, using INSRE price index as deflator. This index is based on

Table 3: Madagascar: Income of urban salary workers

	Price index in traditional area (1970)	Non-agricultural minimum salary[a]		Salaries of civil servants	
		In current MF	In 1970 MF	In category 1[b] In current MF	1,000 MF/Month In 1970 MF
1975	156.0	8,839	5,666		
1976	164.5	8,839	5,374		
1977	168.0	8,839	5,237		
1978	179.9	9,625	5,349	33.4	18.4
1979	205.3	10,018	4,879	33.7	16.4
1980	242.6	10,877	4,484	34.2	14.2
1981	308.1	13,038	4,232	35.1	11.6
1982	406.3	14,742	3,628	36.2	9.0
1983	461.5	15,591	3,378	36.7	8.0
1984	503.6	17,369	3,449	38.9	7.8
1985	556.7	19,000	3,413	40.2	7.2
1986	638.2				

Source: World Bank and IMF, quoting Malagasy Authorities.

[a] Basic minimum monthly salary calculated on the basis of 173.33 hours.

[b] There are 10 categories in the civil service (ECD and ELD excluded).

the obsolete family budget structures which do not take into account the effects of the recent and high increases in the price of rice.

This rapid fall in income (inconceivable in the major creditor countries), coupled with the effects of rising unemployment, has led to a rapid increase in the rate of poverty. According to the survey conducted by UNICEF in 1987,[9] the "vulnerable families" are identified on the basis of the replies obtained from the question as to whether the income of the family head makes it possible to "meet normal food requirements of the family". According to the results of the survey, 70 per cent of the families in the "major urban centres" replied negatively. This is consistent with the evolution shown by previous surveys on income and its distribution.

In fact, the household surveys conducted within the context of the "Greater Antananarivo Urban Development" project[10] have revealed that 12 per cent of the population of Antananarivo in 1981, and 25 per cent in 1984 were living below the threshold of abject poverty, estimated successively at MF 13,000/ month and MF 28,000/month for a family of five. Using the same method of calculation, this threshold went up to MF 37,000 and MF 40,000 in 1987, and 46 per cent of the families have to date nominal incomes below this threshold.[11] The results of UNICEF surveys can be interpreted thus: 70 per cent of the families are "vulnerable", 46 per cent of which live below the threshold of abject poverty.

The situation is no better in the rural areas where 81 per cent of the families are "vulnerable". In the absence of recent surveys on rural family income and budget, one can only rely on the evolution of the producer price to explain this situation.

The real producer prices[12] of the major export goods have experienced a downward trend since the middle of the 1970s. This trend continued despite the increase in the nominal prices contained in the programmes required by IMF. For coffee it was 46.2 per cent between 1974 and 1984, followed by a 12.3 per cent recovery in 1985. With regard to cloves the fall was 58.9 per cent in 1985. There have also been very serious fluctuations in the prices of vanilla.

These falls are attributable to the evolution of the export prices on the one hand, and, on the other, to the reduction in the share of the producer. In the case of coffee for instance,the export income share of the producer was 45 percent in 1975 and only 18 per cent in 1985. The corresponding percentages were 21.2 and 7 per cent for cloves and 25.4 and 9 per cent for vanilla.

The real prices of paddy rice were relatively stable during the second half of the 1970s. They suffered a 19 per cent drop between 1980 and 1984. Following the introduction of trade and price liberalization policy, nominal price increases were very high in 1985, and especially in 1986, i.e., from 100 to 200 per cent according to the regions. The fall which followed in 1987 was in the same order, and this ruined many producers who had invested with the hope that they would benefit from the same prices as in 1986. It should be emphasized that only between 20 and 25 per cent of rice production is marketed and that apart from the four or five major producing areas, between 10 and 20 per cent of the farms have marketable surpluses. Thus, most of the "producers" have experienced successive increases in the consumer price of rice, particularly during the periods of crises, not forgetting of course the general rise in the cost of living.

Long-Term Economic Trends, Crisis and Adjustment

(a) Long-term trends of the Malagasy economy

Madagascar's GDP stagnated in the 1970s (table 4) after experiencing some growth in the 1960s. This stagnation was due to an 18 per cent fall in the per capita GDP between 1970 and 1978 . The hoped for growth of the 1970s was linked, to a large extent, to the launching of the industrialization process known as "import-substitution". The secondary sector represented less than 10 per cent of the GDP in 1960, and 18 per cent in 1970. The industrial growth continued at an annual growth rate of 3.5 per cent between 1970 and 1974, and was followed by stagnation until the end of the decade. This shows the limits, as observed in a number of developing countries, of the import-substitution strategy in the low domestic market economies characterized by a regressive income distribution.

This industrial blockade went *pari pasu* with low agricultural performances. Rice production increased at an annual rate of 1.4 per cent between 1970 and 1977, a rate far below that of the population increase (2.8 per cent per annum). Rice imports increased, exceeding for the first time 100,000 tons in 1978 (a bad agricultural year) to reach 150,000 tons, e.g., 11.9 per cent of the domestic production, and over 60 per cent of the marketed production. This slow growth was due to low productivity. Indeed, it was due exclusively to an annual 3.3 per cent expansion of the farmed areas, while output fell by 1.6 per cent per annum during the period under review.

"Experts" give a number of "technical" factors to explain this fall in output: decline in fertilizer and selected seeds supply, deterioration of hydraulic infrastructures, research and personnel management, as well as absence of remunerative producer price. In enumerating these factors, they often forget to mention the fundamental problems facing Madagascar's agriculture, namely: agrarian problems (excessive fragmentation, monopoly of the better lands by former settlers and red tapism), credit difficulties faced by millions of small and medium-scale producers as well as problems of relative prices. It is precisely because appropriate and lasting solutions were not found to these problems that the "major operations" of the 1960s and the beginning of the 1970s, particularly the "Operation Rice Production" have not had lasting positive results. It should be pointed out that these operations were financed by FAC (France) and EDF (EEC) with the aim, among others, of creating a market for fertilizers and other agricultural inputs (seeds, pesticides, tractors, etc.). Their failure has ben acknowledged not only in Madagascar but also in the whole of Africa "associated" with the Common Market.

Other agricultural production trends do not tally with that of rice farming. Maize production is below its level of the 1960s, while ground-nut production has been falling since 1976. With regard to the major export crops, coffee production experienced a 4.6 per cent growth until 1975 and then stagnated. The growth in vanilla production was short-lived (1974–1978). Banana and sisal production also slumped.

Apart from the above reasons put forward to explain the evolution of its components, the GDP stagnation in the 1970s should also be linked to the low investment rate (relationship between FBCF and GDP) and the consequences of excessive dependence vis-à-vis the international markets. A study of the investment rates shows Madagascar at the bottom of the scale among the

Table 4: Madagascar: Selected economic indicators: 1970–1986

	1970	1976	1978	1979	1980	1981	1982	1983	1984	1985
GDP (1970 price) billion MF	249.4	249.5	248.7	273.1	275.3	251.5	246.9	249.1	254.2	260.4
Per capita/GDP (1970 price) thousand MF	36.7	31.9	30.2	32.2	31.6	28.1	26.8	26.3	26.1	26.1
GNP (1970 price) billion MF				272.1	271.9	242.8	234.5	231.5	224.1	
Per capita/GNP (1970 price) thousand MF				32.1	31.2	27.1	25.3	24.4	23.0	
FBCF/GDP (in %)	14.6	12.4	14.6	24.3	22.8	18.8	12.7	13.6	13.7	14.4
Industrial production index (basis 100:1970)	100	111	115	117	115	98	85	88	91	
Major agricultural production (1,000 tons)										
Cereals										
Paddy	1,865	2,043	1,918	2,945	2,109	2,012	1,970	2,147	2,132	2,269
Maize	109	136	115	116	128	121	113	132	141	130
Industrial crops										
Sugarcane	1,239	1,267	1,375	1,444	1,395	1,420	1,409	1,621	1,660	1,766
Groundnuts	41	54	34	44	39	33	32	31	32	28
Cotton	19	35	33	30	23	28	26	26	34	43
Coffee	67	79	78	82	80	84	81	81	81	80
Green vanilla	1.8	1.6	5.0	2.0	3.0	4.3	4.8	5.2	5.4	2.0
Clove	13.4	12.9	13.0	4.0	12.3	10.8	9.9	4.2	13.0	5.0
Export volume index (basis 100:1970)	100	106		86	83	84	91	73	80	
Terms of trade (basis 100:1970)	100.0	75.7	68.8	58.8	54.1	55.2	54.0	59.4		

Source: IMF, World Bank and INSRE.

African countries: the rate of investment in Madagascar was on the average 11.7 per cent between 1960 and 1973, as against 22.1 per cent in Zambia, 16.9 per cent in Cote d'Ivoire and 15 per cent in the United Republic of Tanzania. Dependence, i.e., survival of the colonial and neo-colonial relations is not extraneous to this state of perennial under-investment, linked to massive transfers of income (repatriation of profit, deterioration of the terms of trade).

(b) "Excessive investments" and balance-of-payments crisis, 1979–1980

The years 1979 and 1980 are to be set aside in the evolution of GDP in Madagascar. They were years not only of massive investment, but also of good agricultural results. The GDP growth rate was 9.8 per cent in 1979 as against 0.8 per cent in 1980.

The massive flow of international capital to developing regions, Africa included, dates back to the beginning of the 1970s. We know that it took the form of loans rather than direct investment. In Madagascar, the borrowing policy of the successive regimes was a cautious policy., In 1978, however, following the persistent advice, among others, of the World Bank,[13] the "revolutionary" government dragged the country into the "debt cycle". The 1977 outstanding external public debt virtually doubled in 1978, and tripled in 1979 ($US 456.9 million in 1977, $US 818.6 million in 1978, and $US 1,304.7 million in 1979).

These massive borrowings gave rise to what is known in Madagascar as "excessive investments". The investment rate increased to 24.3 per cent in 1979, 22.8 per cent in 1980 and 18.8 per cent in 1981, as against an average of 14 per cent during the previous period. The borrowing also led to an increase in the GDP components, i.e., 7.1 per cent for the primary sector in 1979, 12.7 per cent for the secondary sector and 11.6 per cent for the tertiary. Since this growth was laid on an unsound and very hypothetical basis, it quickly collapsed under the weight of the external payments crisis and the resultant adjustment exercise.

This crisis broke out in a sudden manner (table 5). The global deficit increased from $US 4.9 million in 1978 to $US 41.4 million in 1979 and $US 171.8 million in 1980, which marked the beginning of accumulated outstanding payment. These global deficits were due exclusively to the fall in the trade balance. This trade balance stabilized in 1978 but recorded deficits of $US 244.9 in 1979, and $US 328 million in 1980, corresponding to margin rates of 62.8 and 57 per cent respectively. This fall was itself due to import explosion, consequent upon massive borrowing. Admittedly, the number of all the items imported increased, especially the "capital goods" (66.8 per cent in 1979) and the "intermediate goods" (45.7 per cent). During the same period, the terms of trade continued to fall: 68.8 per cent in 1978, 58.8 per cent in 1979 and 54.1 per cent in 1980, i.e., a fall of 21 per cent in two years.

(c) Adjustment impacts on the economic situation

The first agreement concluded with IMF dates back to June 1980. Consequently, these impacts will be assessed using the 1981 data and the subsequent ones.

Table 5: Madagascar: Major items of balance of payments – 1978–1985 (in millions of US dollars)

	1978	1979	1980	1981	1982	1983	1984	1985
Export (f.o.b.)	405.1	413.7	436.3	331.6	327.1	308.6	333.2	278.3
Import (f.o.b.)	−404.3	−658.7	−764.3	−510.9	−450.1	−378.2	−352.1	−396.4
Trade balance	0.9	−244.9	−328.0	−179.2	−123.0	− 68.5	− 18.9	−118.1
Non-input service balance	−135.6	−207.3	−229.1	−157.9	−147.3	125.7	− 95.0	− 82.0
Official transfers without counterpart	52.3	63.0	42.6	62.6	72.3	60.9	67.8	67.9
Net transfer[a]	69.1	340.9	338.8	110.2	− 11.6	−159.8	−110.3	−133.1
Global balance	− 4.9	− 41.4	−171.8	−160.5	−209.1	−294.3	−153.1	−166.0
For information								
Debt-servicing ratio								
– Before rescheduling (%)	3.5	6.5	16.2	47.8	78.3	84.5	65.5	80.7
– After rescheduling (%)	3.5	6.5	16.2	31.7	49.0	28.7	22.9	36.4
Funding								
Rescheduling of IMF debt	0.0	0.0	0.0	63.7	92.7	198.8	168.9	150.3
FMI	− 3.1	− 4.7	49.2	37.2	56.9	7.0	18.2	− 4.0
Amounts outstanding[b]	0.0	− 4.2	227.6	69.6	68.9	74.6	− 8.8	− 8.0
Variation of reserves[c]	8.0	50.3	−105.1	− 9.9	− 8.6	13.9	− 25.1	27.7

Source: World Bank and IMF.

[a] Withdrawals – payment of input services – net transfer.
[b] = Reduction.
[c] = Increase.

(i) *Impacts on the balance-of-payments*

Table 5 shows a net improvement of the trade balance up to 1984, as well as an improvement in the balance of non-input services, though in lesser percentage than that of the trade balance. It also shows the non-effect of these improvements up to the level of global balance.

The significant reduction in the trade deficit until 1984 was exclusively due to drastic import cuts. The import ratio was 2.17 between 198O and 1984,i.e. a drop of 54 percent. In constant dollar,[14] the drop was 60.8 per cent. An analysis of the evolution of the import structure shows that the fall mostly affected "intermediate goods" (other than oil), consumer goods (other than rice), and capital goods. Contrary to the "expectations" of the protagonists of devaluation, exports continued to experience a downward trend.

The non-input service balance deficit is a constant negative factor of Madagascar's balance-of-payments. It reflects, particularly, the heavy burden imposed on the Indian Ocean island by transportation costs and other related expenses. This also involves external variables which are insensitive to indirect adjustment measures such as devaluation.

The global deficit slightly diminished in 1981 but the overall balance deteriorated again until 1983, i.e., after three years of adjustment. Despite a subsequent improvement, the deficit in 1984 and 1985 remained at levels comparable to those of the early years of the crisis (1980–1981). There is therefore a solution to continuity between trade balance and global balance. The reason is simple and can be found at the level of stock accounts: net transfers dropped way back in 1981 (67.4 per cent) and were negative from 1982. Between 1980 and 1985, withdrawals (positive flows) dropped by 65.2 per cent, while debt servicing (negative flows) increased by 3.2 per cent. It is a fact that debt servicing is dependent upon the outstanding debt (which is a stock), interest rates and terms of payment, while new withdrawals are dependent on factors which regulate the movement of international capital (for reasons which cannot be discussed here, bank credits in favour of developing countries were exhausted as from 1982). It is obvious therefore that the capital balance is dependent on an entirely external stock and variables, which, by definition, are independent from economic policies, be they "adjustment" policies.

In the case of Madagascar, there is a perfect illustration of the situation known as debt autonomization, seen in most of the third world countries. It is analyzed thus: despite the reduction in the trade deficit, realized through import cuts, the balance-of-payments continues to be very unfavourable due mainly to the capital balance, particularly considerable negative transfers.[15] It can legitimately be asked whether the current "adjustment" policies are justified or justifiable. For the aim was to achieve favourable balance-of-payments. Now, this has not only been achieved, the economic and social structures have also been seriously undermined.

(ii) *Impacts on production and consumption*

The negative effects of the adjustment policy had resulted in a 10.3 per cent fall of the GDP between 1980 and 1983. According to the World Bank, growth had been positive since 1983 at an annual rate of 1.8 per cent between 1982 and 1985. On the whole, per capita GDP after the regression of the 1970s (see section on long-term trends of the Malagasy economy) suffered another drop of 17.4 per cent between 1980 and 1985.

The fall in national income has been even more dramatic. An approximation could be made by referring not to the GDP, but to the GNP, which takes into account the net revenue transferred abroad. Between 1980 and 1984 (last period for which estimation is available), the GNP fell by 17.6 per cent and per capita GNP by 26.3 per cent.

The industrial sector was the first to be affected by the import cuts. As a matter of fact, the "import-substitution" industrial system is based on over 90 per cent production of consumer goods (export mining industry excluded). It is a weak vertical integration system which is heavily dependent on the outside world. The rate of external dependence, measured here by the share of imported intermediate goods, is more than 45 per cent in respect of five branches, the highest being the "electric equipment branch" (72.8 per cent). It is high as far as the agricultural processing industries are concerned: 28.2 per cent for timber, 24 per cent for leather. The industrial sector was therefore directly affected as far as its supply was concerned. In two years (1980–1982), the fall was 26 per cent. In 1982, the capacity utilization rate was estimated at 10 per cent with respect to "metal works", 25 per cent with respect to non-metallic mineral products, and 30 per cent with respect to parachemistry. There seemed to be a real disindustrialization, the secondary sector accounting for only 15.1 per cent of the GDP in 1982, as against 19 per cent in 1979.

From 1983, conditions of supply with regard to the industrial sector improved somehow, thanks largely to the credit lines opened by Caisse Centrale de cooperation economique (CCCE) of France and the World Bank through "structural adjustment loans". INSRE new industrial production indexes (basis 100: 1982) are as follows: 110 in 1983, 100 in 1984 and 103 in 1985. In other words, the 1983 recovery did not last. By 1984, the demand and supply ratios had reversed. This was because the drastic cut in real income (see table 3 and evolution of GNP above) had led to an increase in food expenditure in relation to family budgets – hence reduction in the money to purchase industrial products.

In fact, the recent distortion between demand and supply concerned the economy as a whole. As has been repeatedly emphasized earlier on, consumption was reduced in considerable proportions while domestic savings increased at an annual rate of 28 per cent. However, investments did not follow savings: public investments were cut by IMF programmes, and were not supported by private investments. Between 1982 and 1985, the investment rate dropped to 13 per cent, i.e., a level lower than the average rate before the 1979–1980 "crisis".

It is obvious, therefore, that despite the statement by the IMF authorities in favour of savings and investment, the adjustment policy aims solely at the balance-of-payments through the reduction in global demand, to the detriment of investment, economic growth and, what is more, human capabilities.

(d) Adjustment: gradual measures

Between June 1980 and February 1988 (date of the expiration of the agreement in force), Madagascar will have signed six agreements with the IMF, i.e., one agreement every 15 months. These agreements relate to a series of very short-term programmes code-named "structural adjustment". The programmes were aimed at ensuring an effective demand control so that the balance-of-payments objectives could be achieved. After two years of implementation, this control policy was strengthened with a trade policy characterized by repeated devaluations, and from the third year, the World Bank actively intervened with the introduction of reforms known as "structural reforms". These reforms led to liberalization and chaos.

(i) *Demand control*

"Traditional" budgetary and monetary instruments, coupled with an unpopular salary freeze policy, were used to effect this control. Public deficit (global deficit of the Treasury) was brought from 18.4 per cent of the GDP in 1980 to 4.7 per cent in 1985. This was achieved by maintaining the relative level of public income (17.9 per cent of the GDP in 1980 and 15.7 per cent in 1985) and making a sharp reduction in the level of expenditure (from 36.3 to 20.4 per cent). Stabilization of the relative level of income (increase in income at the same rate as GDP) has been achieved mainly at the expense of consumers and small producers: increase in indirect tax, linked, of late, to successive devaluations, and in the revenue of the "Fonds national unique de perequation" (FNUP) (National Equalization Fund). In 1985, FNUP revenue accounted for 20 per cent of the total public revenue.

Measures to reduce public expenditure were aimed first and foremost at investment expenditure. At constant franc, these expenditures were reduced by 20 per cent between 1981 and 1985. All new public investment projects without foreign participation were either reduced or canceled, depending on the years. Besides, the reduction was, as in the case of the stabilization of the relative level of income, borne by the consumers: rice consumer price subsidies were canceled way back in 1982; all categories of expenditure experienced a fall in real terms (in volume) with dramatic consequences on basic services such as education and health; and recruitment of new civil servants was limited to 1,000 people in 1984, and 500 from 1985. On the other hand, payment of debt interests increased eightfold between 1980 and 1985.

The monetary measures taken consisted in "framing" the credit and fixing high interest rates. In this connection, limited growth rates of the domestic credit were imposed, with quarterly and other constraints on the credit of the public sector. However, estimations prepared on the basis of the monetarists equation of "money demand" did not always tally with reality. This led to serious disruptions in the use of credits, as well as in trade and production.

Besides, credit users had to bear the growing interest rates. With regard to short-term credits, the following are the various interest rates (in percentage):

	1981	1986
	Percentage	
Down payment on crops	9	15
Agricultural credits	12	16.5
Overdrafts	18	25

These rising costs were added to the prices by the enterprises and were later passed on to consumers. They discouraged investment and contradicted, more especially, the government policy for the promotion of small- and medium-scale industries and enterprises.

With regard to demand control, the agreements fixed authorized salary increases at rates far below the inflation rates. The resulting consequences have been mentioned earlier on.

(ii) *Trade policies*

Initially, the government was able to resist IMF pressures to devalue as an adjustment measure. For example, the first measures relating to trade were taken only in July 1982. These included 15 per cent devaluation of the Malagasy franc, abolition of the fixed parity with the French franc and affiliation to a basket of currencies (different from that of SDR).

Later, several devaluations were made with the rates ascending: e.g., 25 per cent in August 1986 and 56 per cent in June 1987. On the whole, between July 1982 and June 1987, the MF has been devalued by 440 per cent in relation to the French franc. Since 1985, devaluations and liberalization have become the adjustment criteria,[16] it being understood that the freeze on demand through budgetary and monetary means was maintained.

Experiences have amply shown that the success of a devaluation presupposes a stable trade market, in other words sufficient elasticities of import and export demand and supply. There is no denying the fact that these conditions are lacking in African economies, including that of Madagascar.

For structural reasons, it is virtually impossible in Madagascar to reduce in the short and medium terms the importation of essential commodities (energy, food commodities, industrial and agricultural inputs) which represent 85 per cent of the total imports (see table 5). Besides, the competitiveness, resulting from devaluation, of import substitution goods has lessened on account of the high importation costs involved.

On the other hand, 80 per cent of exports are realized on markets where the prices (fixed in foreign currencies) and the quantities (for example the quotas fixed by the International Agreement on Coffee) are mere figures. Similarly, the competitiveness of the manufactured goods that can be exported is also hampered by the importation cost involved.

However, the devaluation is bound to have an effect on prices, namely increases in import prices which ultimately affect the general price level and diminution of global domestic demand. In Madagascar, after some recession between 1982 and 1984 and despite the stabilization in demand, inflation quickly rose from 1985. This was clearly due to devaluation and high interest rates. Devaluation should be seen here as an additional measure to reduce demand, borne exclusively by people with fixed income and those in the low income category. In 1987, drugs, cooking oil and many other basic commodities were no longer within the reach of most Malagasy nationals.

(iii) *Structural reforms*

As mentioned earlier on, the reforms were mainly aimed at liberalizing both domestic and foreign trade.

1. Liberalization of domestic trade

The monopoly of SINPA (Societe d'intert pour la production agricole) in the buying of agricultural produce was abolished in 1983. The "reform" was pursued until the total dismantling of the "Systeme d'administration des prix de la collecte et de la commercialisation du paddy et du riz" (paddy and rice marketing and price control system). Buying of agricultural produce was opened to State trading companies as well as private individuals. With regard to price, as from 1985, only one ceiling price of paddy was fixed. Ceilings for rice consumer prices were abolished. The new system is based on two factors:

free marketing of local rice and sale of imported rice at prices reflecting the long-term trends of world prices converted at fixed exchange rates. It should be pointed out that importation of rice has been curtailed since 1984.[17]

This new measure gave rise to unabridged speculation and increase in prices. In the middle of 1986, the producer price for paddy rose to MF 300/kg in some regions (the fixed price being MF 85); the prices of rice on the open market during two periods of crisis (end of 1985 and end of 1986) ranged between MF 800 and 1,000/kg, i.e., over 160 to 230 per cent compared to the ceiling price fixed at the beginning of 1985 (MF 300/kg).

Low-income families suffered a lot from these situations. Prior to the price hike, rice already accounted for 60 per cent of the expenditures of the low-income families living in Antananarivo. One can hardly imagine what these families went through when the price of rice doubled and even tripled.

In the short term, producers benefited from the increase. However, as was said earlier on, a majority of the small producers were compelled to buy back rice at high prices during the period of crisis. Only a small minority of traders who had access to credit benefited from the situation. These traders became extraordinarily rich in less than two years. Since the beginning of 1987, a "buffer stock" has been set up, with the help of donations and imported rice. The objective was to maintain the prices of rice between MF 350 and 425/kg. However, at those prices, traders who bought more than MF 200/kg of the paddy ran the risk of losing. Stocks piled up and were estimated at 80,000 tons in June 1987. Supply seemed to exceed demand. Prices of rice fell below FM 350/kg, resulting in the fall in the producer price. At present, the major concern of the Government is to ensure that people comply with the ceiling price of MF 125/kg.

In these circumstances, "liberalization" is synonymous with anarchy, coupled with wide fluctuations in prices. Like the "major" operations of the 1960s and 1970s, liberalization does not seem to have resolved the fundamental problems of rice farming in Madagascar. It would be surprising that problems affecting production were resolved through limited actions in the area of trade.

The other components of domestic trade "liberalization" are as follows:

(a) liberalization of the producer prices of other agricultural products with the exception of four products (coffee, vanilla, clove, pepper);
(b) liberalization of the factory prices of most industrial products;
(c) abolition of transport tariff control;
(d) liberalization of trade margins with the exception of a dozen of the products.

Most of these components stem from recent decisions. Their effects cannot therefore be discussed in this paper. It can be said, however, that they will be determined by such other decisions as devaluation and freeze on demand. In our opinion, "vulnerable families" should not be expected to benefit from such decisions.

2. External trade liberalization

"RIL" (Regime d'importation liberalise), which entered into force in January 1987, is the last in a series of measures taken to relax import and export regulations. In the previous regime, a "general import programme" was drawn up every year. The import quotas were shared among the holders of an import license, on the basis of the following three criteria: cost of the license, specialization, and percentage of the previous quotas used. With regard to the "RIL" system, any resident can send in a tender for import. After processing all the tenders, trade authorization is given using a certain formula.

The available foreign exchange package is fixed every month (7 million SDR/months of January to June 1987). Every tender must be preceded by the payment of a 10 per cent fixed tax (5 per cent from July 1987) calculated on the amount of the tender and accompanied by a bank guarantee. There are however two exceptions to the rule:

(a) The first is implicit: beneficiaries of "specific funding" (external sources) are not concerned by the "liberalization". Since 1985, they represent over 50 per cent of Madagascar's total imports;
(b) The second is provided for by law: enterprises which have realized 50 per cent of their export turnover (coffee, vanilla, clove and sugar excluded) are exempted from the 10 per cent fixed tax and authorized to import the totality of their inputs.

"Liberalization" therefore implies issuance of licences after obtaining permission to trade. The licences are issued depending on the amount of foreign exchange available, the financial capacity of each applicant and the total monthly import demand. The "general import programmes" are not abolished. This is understandable because of the limited availability of foreign exchange. It can be said that the IMF is experimenting in Madagascar one of the variants of the formulae for foreign exchange shortage control which it imposes on many developing countries. This enables it, among other things, to control the use of domestic foreign exchange resources.

The 10 per cent fixed tax can be considered as disguised devaluation (28 per cent according to different estimations). Its effects are negative both for consumers (general rise in prices) and small producers (increase in the price of imported inputs). With regard to enterprises, "RIL", with its exceptions, favours a small fraction of Madagascar's industry. On the other hand, it penalizes he other categories of enterprises with inadequate capital. At present these include the majority of State enterprises, import-substitution industries as well as small-scale industries and small-scale enterprises. Lastly, by increasing the import cost, "RIL" runs the risk of favouring the importation of high-profit products to the detriment of low-profit products, some of which are indispensable (basic drugs, etc.)

In conclusion, a general observation on the "structural reforms" is called for: the liberal philosophy behind these reforms seems to indicate that the game of the market alone is enough to define an "optimal evolution" and implies that real markets are "perfect". Now, the national sphere is characterized by chronic shortages and rigid structures, and the international sphere by strong protectionism, powerful international monopolies, and controlled fluctuation" of the major currencies. The result is a "narrow view" of the market, with enormous consequences from the human point of view.

Some Positive Examples and Human Adjustment Conditions

(a) Some positive examples in favour of human potential

The economic constraints relating to the implementation of the adjustment policies in Madagascar today encompass production, distribution and income distribution. We have shown its negative consequences from the human point of view. This means that they are incompatible with any global initiative aimed at protecting the human factor. The deterioration of the situation has however prompted some ad hoc initiatives with the support of international organizations other than the IMF and the World Bank. Three of these initiatives are worth mentioning, and relate to health, nutrition and employment.

The "PEV" (Programme élargi de vaccination) was launched in 1976 and yielded modest results. In 1985, however, it was relaunched with the help of UNICEF which hopes to mobilize $US 10 million by 1991. This amount will be allocated as follows:

	Percentage
Vaccinese	58.7
Vaccination equipment and cold chain	21.0
Training	7.5
Transport	11.3
Evaluation	1.5
Total	100.0

This programme will have a strategic impact from the health point of view if its objectives are attained. The success of the programme will largely depend on the level of mass mobilization.

With regard to food, a WFP project in the primary schools (level I)was launched in 1983/1984. It is a five-year programme which is very beneficial to the school boys and girls from the nutritional point of view. It is related to food education and agricultural activities in the schools. Its cost is estimated at $US 6.8 million, 81.4 per cent of which is provided by WFP. The wheat supplied by WFP is sold in order to generate funds for the purchase of rice and vegetables on the local market. In addition, WFP is to provide tin fish and vegetable oil for three years. The government expenses are provided for in the MINESEB budget.

The mere existence of this project proves the need for food supplements for a large majority of the people of Madagascar. It is only an experimental programme and will concern 111 schools (one school in each of the 110 directorates of primary education). It should be extended without delay to all the schools, and other nutritional programmes should be envisaged in favour of the poor sections of the population, particularly the breast-feeding mothers.

Employment could benefit from the implementation of the High Intensive Labour (HIL) project. This project was initiated by the Ministry of Public Works and concerns the construction and rehabilitation of roads in the districts. Preliminary technical studies were undertaken by the Ministry to determine the duration, the quality of work and the manpower required. They will be followed by tenders open to small-scale industries and enterprises. Those which will be selected will have to comply with the specifications laid down including the daily minimum wage. In 1987, this project was implemented on an experimental basis in only one suburb prefecture of Antananarivo. It should be extended without any further delay to all programmes of public utility (rehabilitation of roads in the major cities, repair of irrigation canals, repair and maintenance of public buildings, etc.). These projects should be implemented preferably using local raw materials (in totality or 90 per cent).

(b) Human adjustment conditions

No doubt the projects as mentioned above have limited scope. Human progress can be made only through the modification of the macro-economic framework, after which immediate far-reaching actions relating to basic services could be undertaken.

(i) *Resolving the debt problem*

In their statements, IMF and World Bank authorities are re-emphasizing that "the debt problem should be resolved through growth". Now, analysis of the balance-of-payments trends and the consequences of adjustment, in the case of Madagascar for example, has revealed that it is rather the opposite argument which holds, namely that growth presupposes the resolution of the debt problem.

On the one hand, we have also dwelt on the "autonomization" of capital flows resulting from the debt vis-à-vis the adjustment policies. These policies are deflationist policies (incompatible with growth) and would no longer be necessary if the debt problem were resolved. Indeed, the movements of "autonomous" capital alone determine payments deficits and entail transfer of large incomes abroad.

On the other hand, to find positive net transfers, there are only two solutions: either increase considerably the positive flows or curb the negative flows (debt servicing). According to the World bank, the first solution would mean, in the case of Madagascar, doubling the debt by 1990, thus locking up the debitor and the creditor in a vicious circle.

These two remarks easily apply to all the developing countries which are in debt. It is not surprising therefore that the directly concerned protagonists (debtor countries, banks, etc.), at the international level are becoming aware of the fact that the only solution to the external payments of the third world, given the trade prospects and movement of capital, is to limit the debt burden. In this connection, many possibilities are envisaged or have already been realized:[18]

(a) unilateral moratorium (Sudan, Brazil);
(b) unilateral limitation of reimbursement (Peru);
(c) conversion into long-term bonds with fixed interest rates, and development of a second market for these bonds; and
(d) establishment of an "international debt management institute" which would buy the debts from the banks and transform them into negotiable grants on the international markets.

Indeed, everybody, so to speak, is preparing for the non-payment of the debt of the third world. Banks are considerably increasing their stocks with a view to granting dubious credits. The major ones among them are encouraging the indebted countries to follow the example of Peru in order to "take them out of the cage in which they have locked themselves"[19] or proposing solutions mentioned in (c) and (d) above.

(ii) *Growth programmes*

In the first place, growth programmes can only be long-term programmes. This would involve making real "structural" adjustment, aimed at a new method of solvency. In the short term, however, growth implies, in the present circumstances, the introduction of demand-boosting measures and alternative devaluation measures for import control, a well-planned quota system and import planning, taking into account the basic needs in terms of consumption and production.

(iii) *Other immediate measures to safeguard basic services*

Human progress will be better achieved within the context of a debt burden-free economy geared towards growth. However, the efforts of growth will be felt only gradually. It should also be realized that long-term development implies that the basic services should be sustained, that health and education are as essential for the present and the future as other economic variables. In this connection, the following immediate measures are proposed:

(a) With regard to health, the "basic drug" policy must be firmly and effectively implemented. In Madagascar, the "material guarantee" for adequate distribution exists due to the large extension of the public health network: Malagasy children can benefit from RSDE[20] and chemoprophylaxy (anti-malaria) treatment can be given free to 80 per cent of the families;

(b) In the field of education, there is the need to reform without delay the school curricula and strengthen, at a reasonable cost, the teaching apparatus and the training of teachers;

(c) Regarding housing, immediate and reasonable solutions can be worked out, by breaking the land and real estate speculation (particularly in the urban areas), controlling the prices of building materials and increasing the number of "plateaux d'habitat viabilises" and providing them with water and electricity.

Notes

1 The scarcity of studies on social indicators reflects the little interest shown by the donors in these indicators.

2 FAO: Food Balance Sheets and Per Capita Food Supplies.

3 Source: MPARA-Enuete sur les budgets des menages urbains 1982/1983.

4 UNICEF: Ongoing study on the impact of structural adjustment policy (SAP) in Madagascar – 1987.

5 UNICEF/MPJS survey on "Survival and Adaptation Strategies of Underprivileged Families", April 1987.

6 "Greater Antananarivo Urban Development". Study financed by UNDP and implemented by CNUEH, 1985.

7 Government estimates.

8 UNICEF/MPJS: Survival Strategy, op. cit.

9 UNICEF/MPJS: Survival strategy survey, op. cit.

10 Greater Antananarivo Urban Development, op. cit.

11 Calculation based on a minimum daily consumption of 400g of rice, 50g of cone meat and lOOg of vegetables per person, plus the family rent.

12 Deflator used: Consumer price index or commodities other than food commodities (traditional families).

13 This "advice" is contained in the report on Madagascar (Recent evolution and economic prospects) dated October 1980 and prepared by a mission which went to Madagascar in 1978.

14 The deflator being the wholesale price index in the United States of America.

15 In the case of Madagascar and according to World Bank projections (March 1986 memorandum), payments deficits will remain at their present level unless account is taken of the borrowing made before 1986. Other large borrowings were made since that date.

16 It seems the situation is also the same in other African countries like Zaire.

17 After the salary freeze, this constituted another important departure from "liberalism".

18 A great nineteenth century philosopher said that mankind creates only problems which it can solve.

19 See *Le Monde* of 11 April 1987, page 28.

20 RSDE: "Revolution pour la survie et le developpement de l'enfant", a UNICEF concept, implies the implementation of a series of measures at reasonable cost in favour of children (vaccinations, TRO).

Ghana

TSATSU TSIKATA

Historical Background to Economic Recovery

Nothing more vividly portrays the seriousness of Ghana's economic decline during the decade of the seventies than the fact that close to 2 million Ghanaians left the country seeking greener pastures. The opportunities offered by the boom that oil brought to the economy of nearby Nigeria provided one of the major attractions to the young men and women for whom the Ghanaian economy no longer had much to offer. But it was not only Nigeria; several other African and European countries, as well as North American countries experienced this commentary on the state of the Ghanaian economy in the seventies through to the early eighties. And the comprehensiveness of the commentary was perceptible from the fact that the exodus affected virtually all classes of the Ghanaian population with various consequences that we shall discuss in this paper.

However, some of the greener pastures which large numbers of Ghanaians swarmed to in the seventies themselves began to dry up by the early eighties, and when in the early months of 1983 Nigeria expelled more than a million Ghanaians, the Ghanaian economy, and indeed the very fabric of the country's nationhood were stretched to breaking point. That Ghana not only survived this situation at a time of severe drought and amidst a sharply deteriorating international environment but has, since then, seen a strong recovery of her economy may be attributed not only to the resilience of Ghana's human resources and the improvement in climatic conditions in 1984 but also to the economic recovery programme which was firmly operationalized by the Government of the Provisional National Defence Council in the midst of these powerful forces of disintegration. No serious review of Ghana's economic recovery can therefore fail to address the human dimension and the social and political context within which the recovery effort was launched and has been conducted. Nor can any appreciation of the prospects for Ghana's economic development fail to relate recent statistics of economic performance to the outlook for the nation's social and political development always bearing in mind the economic realities that Ghana like other developing countries is continuing to endure.

The decline in the production of cocoa which had been the mainstay of the Ghanaian economy during the seventies illustrates the interplay of exogenous factors and well as domestic policy failures. From a production level of 413,000 tons in the 1970/71 crop year, production declined steadily to 254,000 tons in the 1980/81 crop year – a 40 per cent decline.

The impact of the first oil 'shock' in 1973 followed closely by severe droughts in 1975–77 were compounded by the lack of producer incentives within a framework of economic management that paid scant attention to the productive sectors and in which rent-seeking activities flourished. The maintenance of a fixed and over-valued exchange rate in this period effectively deprived the Cocoa Marketing Board of the resources for more equitable remuneration to the cocoa farmer. In real terms, the producer price of cocoa in the 1980/81 crop year also showed a decline of over forty per cent from the 1970/71 crop year even though nominally the producer price amounted in 1980/81 to over 85.5 per cent of the f.o.b. price at the official exchange rate.[1]

When Ghana produced the peak cocoa crop of half a million tons in the mid-sixties the split between the producer price, marketing costs and export duty was 68:24:8 respectively. By 1978/79 the producers were receiving only 26 per cent.[2] Even with the devaluation of the cedi in that year and the resultant doubling of the producer price the relative share of the producer in the higher export proceeds in cedi terms declined. Worse perhaps than the inadequacy of the producer price itself was a system of payment through promissory notes ('chits') whose realization from corrupt and exploitative produce clerks was often a prolonged nightmare for the mostly illiterate cocoa farmers. That the ratio of marketing costs remained 24 per cent in 1978/79 at a time of such high world prices is also worth noting. At the time cocoa production peaked in the mid-sixties, the Marketing Board employed less than 50,000 employees whilst by 1978/79, through a proliferation of subsidiaries and extraneous activities, more than 100,000 people were employed by the Board. Road and other construction activities by the Board also became a known source of corruption and profiteering. Marketing costs were thus a substantial burden on the farmer's production even as he received little by way of technical support and extension services to improve the yield of his crop and avert the destructive onslaught of the swollen shoot virus and other diseases on his income.

Equally, in the mining sector, it was virtually impossible for companies to stay float amidst foreign exchange constraints and shortages of imported inputs as well as the collapse in infrastructure, notably railways. Ghana's export volumes thus declined steeply such that in 1981 they were 0.05 per cent of world exports compared to 0.15 per cent in 1970.[3] Ironically, the steepest decline in cocoa and gold production took place at a time of unprecedented high world prices between 1976 and 1979. By not maintaining the volume of cocoa exports it had attained in 1971 Ghana, in those three boom years, lost additional foreign exchange earnings of some $US 600 million annually which could have expanded the import capacity by about two-thirds of the levels actually attained in those years. Ghana's share in world cocoa exports declined from being 33 per cent in 1970 to about half that figure in 1980. Part of this export volume decline was due to the increased smuggling that was an inevitable consequence of the inadequate producer prices, particularly at a time when neighbouring Ivory Coast was offering increasing incentives to its farmers.

Smuggling in the cocoa and mineral sectors, as well as of price-controlled imports, such as petroleum products and of domestically produced consumer goods supported a flourishing parallel market in foreign exchange throughout the decade of deteriorating export performance. With external aid virtually drying up, Ghana faced a severe foreign exchange crisis that led to the rapid shrinkage of imports. Attempts to priorize imports through a system of import licensing were rendered ineffective by the vagaries of the central bank's cash flow and the impossibility of rational import programming at the beginning of each fiscal year in the midst of ever declining resources. The significance of imports for production, especially in the export sector, meant that the contraction of import volumes had a telling impact on the rate of growth, not least because the import substitution economic strategies of the immediate post-independence period (which owed their inspiration to the wisdom of Sir Arthur Lewis and others) turned out to have established a significant import-dependence in the structure of industrial production in Ghana. The decline in the level of imports created chronic shortages of raw materials, spare parts, investment and consumer goods in the economy. By the time of the December 31st Revolution as a recent summary expresses it, "credit lines with international banks were totally blocked. Ghana was illiquid, virtually bankrupt."[4] Inflation had reached three digit levels.

After 1979, Ghana was faced with very adverse terms of trade when the prices of Ghana's major exports (cocoa, gold and manganese) softened and the second oil shock increased petroleum prices. Import volumes for 1982 came to about a third of those in 1970. For the period 1979–82, Ghana's net barter terms of trade declined by 12 per cent annually, twice the average decline for sub-Saharan Africa, and following upon a decade of declining production, especially exports, a veritable descent into total economic chaos and national disintegration was imminent.

In the face of such decline it was remarkable that a succession of Governments failed to take the corrective steps that were desperately called for. As the Government's tax base dwindled from declining exports and imports budget deficits grew and the resort to money printing to finance government expenditure led to run-away inflation. The national consumer price index increased by the breathtaking figure of 12,358 per cent between 1973 and 1983. Instead of policy initiatives to correct this untenable situation, there was nothing but drift into an ever deepening crisis. The financial deterioration was especially acute during the eighteen months prior to December 1981 as the fiscal deficit increased sharply from about 5 per cent of GDP in 1978/79 to 10 per cent of GDP in 1980/81.

Human Dimensions of Decline

The portrait of Ghana's economic decline has outlined the way in which production and productivity were increasingly ill-rewarded in the Ghanaian economy whilst racketeering and rent-seeking (which became known as "Kalabule") became extremely profitable and provided a few with enormous benefits at the expense of the national economy and polity. The average Ghanaian's income dropped by over one-third during the decade of the seventies with the producers of goods and commodities, especially export commodities like cocoa, urban fixed salary and wage earners bearing the brunt of the decline. A detailed analysis by Hamid[5] has shown, first, that it was around the mid-70's that the pronounced decline in incomes really took hold and second that "for 1975–83 real wage income was declining at more than 20 per cent a year, real cocoa producer prices by some 12 per cent a year and real returns to trading services was improving by 6 per cent a year." These trends, he concludes, "imply a fantastic change in the functional distribution of income". Smuggling and a variety of illegal activities provided additional incomes but the rewards for the "risk-taking" of illegality were perhaps even more inequitably distributed than the official rewards.

The tremendous exodus of skilled and trained manpower – teachers, nurses, doctors – as well as a large pool of potential agricultural labour itself further deprived Ghana of not only badly needed managerial, administrative, and technical skills with which Ghana was traditionally well-endowed, but also of the labour power to reverse the production decline that persisted through the 1970's. Agriculture in particular, with its high labour intensity, suffered and the large contraction in acreage under cultivation for both food and cash crops provides testimony to the impact of a manpower drain which may, without exaggeration, be described as a neo-slave trade.

The shift that was also discernible in the productive sector away from production to the monetary economy and the withdrawal towards subsistence or production for self (and family) consumption was a reflection of increasing apathy to national economic goals and a political statement about social inequity, which must thus be seen as having great relevance for productivity. That the share of the retail and wholesale trade sector in GDP at current prices doubled from 14 per cent in 1980 to 30 per cent in 1981 again illustrates how much the rent-seekers had ascended the "commanding heights"[6] of the economy. The cheapening of imports by the under-pricing of foreign exchange resources provided windfall gains only to the few who succeeded in obtaining the ever-decreasing amount of foreign exchange available.

The attempt to manage scarcity through administrative regulation only increased the scarcity premia and deepened the distortion of relative incentives away from the producer – who was easier to identify and regulate – in favour of trade with goods moving through a long chain of intermediaries and prices escalating all along the chain. None of the revenues from rent-seekers were available to Government since the tax net concentrated only on visible wage-earners and producers.

The decline in Government revenues rendered impossible the maintenance of infrastructure and social services. The road network, for instance, so vital a link in the economy had deteriorated sharply without the resources for maintenance, much less expansion. Restraining expenditures usually meant cutting development expenditures, leading to many uncompleted projects scattered throughout the country, monuments to the lack of rational budgetary norms to cope with declining resources.

Recurrent expenditures were simply insufficient to cope with the maintenance of basic social services much less their expansion to cater for an increasing population and particularly for the needs of those having no privileged access. Declines in central government expenditures in education and health for instance, have been estimated as follows: from $20 per capita (1975 dollar) in 1972 to $10 in 1979 to $1 in 1983 in the case of education compared to an average of $29 per capita in middle-income sub-Saharan economies and from $6 in 1972 to $4 in 1979 and less than $1 in 1983 in the case of health whilst middle-income oil importing countries over that period increased expenditures from $9 to $14.[7] Let me, however, sound a note of caution about these figures. Statistics on social indicators are notoriously unreliable for a country like Ghana given the limited data collection capability which is itself a pointer to the policy priority outlook that has existed on these social indicators. Furthermore, a breakdown of such global expenditure figures often paints a different distributional picture than might at first appear; higher expenditures may in fact be almost exclusively benefiting a privileged few.

Despite the cautions, it will have been obvious from the steady decline through the seventies that the Government's capacity to sustain social services would be in jeopardy, and that the drift in economic management as well as the tendencies to favour trade instead of production and productivity posed special dangers to social services. This was especially true given the strong initial base of social infrastructure that was created in the immediate aftermath of Ghana's independence and the need for considerable resources to sustain and expand access to them. Certainly, the tens of thousands of both teachers and health workers who left these social services through the decade of the seventies also created a serious gap in the delivery capability.

In considering the human dimension of decline, it is necessary to highlight an important aspect of these issues often thrust aside as a matter of politics. The failure of leadership not only at the level of government but also at the level of enterprises, the failure to confront economic reality, and the rather self-serving 'helplessness' of political leadership as racketeers and rentiers come into their own whilst productive people get frustrated and lack incentives to persist, represent fundamental contributions to the state of economic decline which are not reflected sufficiently in the statistics themselves. As a corollary, the real helplessness of the exploited producers in such an economic environment, their tendency to withdraw from a system which offers little reward for their production and the resultant apathy and lethargy are not merely poignant political commentary but need to be factored into the perspectives of development economics.

In its extraordinary neo-colonial deformation, the State has contributed to under-development by allowing, even if "unofficially", the increasing dominance of trade in declining resources with the downward slide of national productivity and sovereignty which is the raison d'etre of the State. It was not a coincidence that in the midst of a capital state of economic decline in the Ghana of the middle to late seventies, the desultory attempt of a government that failed to lead the way out to install a mode of perpetuating itself woefully failed and that an attempt to conduct local government elections in 1978 also met with public disdain. Regrettably, these "political" dimensions of development economics have tended to be lost in simplistic perspectives which view structural adjustment as a removal of so-called "controls" in favour of the infallible "private sector". The reality surely has been that "controls" have been precisely what were lacking in the kind of run-away decline that Ghana has gone through; a government's ability to affect an economic situation dominated increasingly by parallel market activity is severely limited. "Controls" really did not exist except as a rhetorical and often contradictory mask of reality.

In much the same way as "controlled prices" are often discounted in real economic analysis of the actual market, it is important for theorists of structural adjustment and development to go behind the mask of "controls" requiring dismantling as being at the heart of adjustment policies to a recognition of the nature of what I have described as the self-serving "helplessness" of leadership in periods when bold reactions to exogenous shocks as well as firm internal policy corrections are called for. Equally, the liberation of private initiatives in the national economy will often require the damming of the channels for racketeering and corruption by the private sector and its associates in government, coupled with strong and consistent governmental efforts to establish the appropriate channels whereby national productivity, especially from small-scale producers with little voice in national politics, can be increasingly encouraged and enhanced, and not be at the mercy of other powerful social forces and their deformations of national progress. Some discernment about the productive "private sector" is clearly called for.

Adjustment policies have in fact required definitive interventions, on even a sustained basis, from governments and without assessing the substantive merits of interventions by the State in their own terms, and specifying the kinds of roles of the state that prevent progress, policy recommendations about removing supposed "controls" and "liberalization" involve a fetishism of the State, and are somewhat facile. I believe that the validity of these observations will be further borne out by my discussion below on the economic recovery policies that Ghana has pursued under the government of the PNDC to reverse the above described history of decline.

Stabilization

Realizing the acuteness of the economic situation, the government, from the outset, put economic recovery firmly at the top of the national agenda. A number of urgent actions were taken to arrest the situation. These included a cash programme that was launched to evacuate cocoa from the producing areas where some of the produce had been locked up in some cases for a few years. The highest currency denomination, the C50 note was demonetized as part of an immediate effort to curb excess liquidity. Expenditure controls were immediately instituted and a war on fraud, corruption and waste in the public services was launched. The ill-gotten wealth of rentiers and racketeers came under close scrutiny. These measures began to be taken even as a more detailed economic review was being undertaken, and set the tone of a new economic and social order in which productivity would be encouraged and graft, racketeering and corrupt dealing severely punished. By also directly leading the people's community spirit into productive activity such as cocoa farm rehabilitation and replanting, as well as oil palm rehabilitation, and environmental improvement by way of garbage disposal, cleaning up of choked drains, tree planting etc., the Government acknowledged the importance of mobilizing the nation's human resources especially as foreign resources were not readily available. Yet the major tasks of economic recovery could not be achieved without needed imports and these efforts of mobilizing labour alone could not provide all the resources required to rehabilitate production in a sustained way.

Soon enough, there followed other broader-ranging policy reforms notably the inauguration of a flexible exchange rate policy with the exchange rate adjustment in April 1983, rehabilitation programmes for key sectors of the economy and the establishment of realistic relative prices consequent upon the exchange rate adjustment. Indeed, prior to the devaluation, a re-pricing of food imports took place, the first signal that the government had definitively decided to rectify past policy failures whereby the foreign exchange used for imports had been under-valued, as well as a firm indication of the policy of making local production competitive and profitable.

The devaluation itself was first introduced by way of a multiple exchange rate system in which bonuses were provided for foreign exchange receipts and surcharges imposed on foreign exchange payments. Crude oil imports, essential raw materials, capital goods, and basic foodstuffs and transfers in respect of official commitments were at an effective exchange rate of C23.375 $US 1 instead of the rate of C2.75 $US 1 which had been fixed since mid-1978. All other payments were subject to a 900 per cent surcharge resulting in an effective exchange rate of C29.975 $US 1. In addition, purchases of foreign exchange for travel abroad, education and medical treatment abroad and for unrequited private transfers were subject to a 5 per cent tax. On the receipts side also there were two groups of transactions, the first consisting of cocoa and other traditional exports which came in on the first window of C23.375 $US 1 thus enjoying a bonus equivalent to 750 per cent of the official rate of C2.75 $US 1. All other receipts enjoyed a bonus of 900 per cent on the second window.

Despite a certain degree of complexity about administering such a multiple exchange rate system, a number of factors recommended it to the Government. First, there was considerable educational and hence political value in projecting exchange rate reforms in terms of the provision of bonuses for the exports which earned the foreign exchange; resources for these bonuses were obtained through surcharging the importers who spent foreign exchange. Second, the higher bonus for non-traditional exports clearly signalled an incentive for producers who would be contributing to a widening of the resource base. Finally, putting essential imports such as crude oil and essential raw materials on the first window was based on a recognition of the priority significance of those inputs for the economy for improving public transportation, which had deteriorated significantly, and for industrial rehabilitation which was also important for economic recovery. In the case of petroleum, a consumer subsidy was even retained initially; at the same time explicit attention was drawn to the size of the subsidy that was in effect being borne by the budget and the need over time to phase it out. It is worth dwelling further on this situation regarding petroleum product prices in order to appreciate the magnitude of the imbalances that past policies had created. Whilst crude oil and petroleum products had accounted for only 5 per cent of total imports in 1970, by 1982 their share had increased to 50 per cent and though in the period 1977–82 GDP had declined by 10 per cent and productive economic activity had slowed down, the volume of crude oil imports increased by 6 per cent, with local petroleum product prices below the 1972 price levels even though world oil prices had increased more than five times.

This heavy subsidy on petroleum products through the under pricing of the foreign exchange made smuggling to neighbouring countries in the convertible franc zone highly lucrative. Whatever the value of a subsidy on essential inputs, a large and disproportionate subsidy on petroleum products in effect deprived other critical areas of the economy of much-needed resources and thus contributed significantly to the decline and drift that was described earlier. Being such an undifferentiated subsidy it was also unresponsive to the needs of specific sectors or groups for whose benefit specific subsidies might be justified. Through the policy actions of April 1983 the stage was set for a phased removal of the subsidy on petroleum products pricing with a full pass-through of subsequent exchange rate adjustments. Indeed, the multiple exchange rate system necessitated some focus on subsidies within the economy and their costs, particularly as the bonuses and surcharges system was not meant to create losses for the Bank of Ghana in its exchange transactions. However, in October 1983, the multiple rates were unified at C30 $US 1 at which time also adjustments were made in the retail price of petroleum products on the basis of crude oil being imported at C20 $US 1.

An important consequence of the exchange rate adjustment was that unlike the situation in which the previous government tripled the cocoa price only to find the Cocoa Marketing Board having to resort massively to the banking system, the Board was able to resume profitable self-financing operations even though the cocoa producer price was again increased from C12,000 to C20,000. The government decided to assume the Board's debts amounting to some C7.4 billions as of the end of April 1983.

In addition to the increases in the producer price of cocoa, the Government substantially increased the minimum support price for maize, rice and palm oil. The facade of generalized price controls also began to be eliminated as importers and domestic producers were able officially to adjust their prices to reflect the increasing costs of imports as well as other costs such as wages. A small number of basic consumer goods remained under price control but with increasing recognition by the Prices and Incomes Board of the need for manufacturing to be profitable.

Wage and salary adjustments were also an important element of the policy package. The minimum wage was doubled and civil servants obtained increases averaging about 60 per cent as part of a policy to increase real wages and begin a process of restoring them to the levels they were prior to the trough of economic performance. This was clearly necessary for the rebuilding of morale and efficiency in the civil service.

The restoration of fiscal discipline, which was such a key element in the stabilization aspects of the programme of economic recovery, involved not only a determined effort of expenditure control to reduce budget deficits but also an increase in domestic resource mobilization through effective and broader-based efforts at collecting taxes. At the same time the need to relieve the budget of the inefficiencies of public enterprises began to be addressed. Stricter control was exercised over the provision of budgetary funds or government guarantees for these enterprises which were now encouraged to take advantage of the new macro-economic environment to put their house in order. In this way government recourse to the banking system was held in check.

The stabilization programme also placed strict limits on domestic bank lending with credit guidelines being provided to the commercial banks by the Central Bank. Administrative regulation remained in the initial stages the mode of addressing credit allocation and ensuring that priority sectors, particularly agriculture, were not starved of resources. Negative interest rates had been the order of the day in Ghana for a long time but changes in lending rates to mobilize savings for private investment would by themselves have been ineffective since the depressed interest in private investment was more fundamentally the result of the general condition of economic collapse and the constraints imposed by foreign exchange availability to purchase imported inputs. Initial corrections were made regarding interest rates, 3–5 percentage points increase in October 1983, and the government began a review of interest rates having regard to its medium-term domestic resource mobilization objectives and the inflation targets for the period of the economic recovery programme.

Tariff rates for the major utilities were adjusted upwards to reflect the impact on costs of the new exchange rate. This of course increased road transport, railway freight and passenger charges as well as electricity, water and telecommunications rates. Through the cost-recovery policies that were introduced the utilities would be assured of resources for maintenance as well as investments in rehabilitation of plant and machinery.

Rehabilitation and Restoration of Growth

With the stabilization measures that began to be taken as part of the effort to reverse a decade of decline, rehabilitation programmes for key sectors were also launched to ensure an adequate supply response. The road, port, railway and transport infrastructure of the country and the state of plant and equipment in the productive sectors had so deteriorated that considerable resources were needed in order to begin a turn-around. In determining the priorities for investments in these programmes, there was an inevitable focus on the export sector which was seen as being capable of turning the tide. The timber sector for instance was considered to have great potential for growth as the exchange rate made exports of logs and timber products quite attractive. Credits were obtained from the World Bank's Export Rehabilitation Credit and from other donors to obtain spare parts and materials in this sector as well as in the minerals sector – gold, diamond, bauxite and manganese – and of course the cocoa sector. In the agriculture sector, generally, the importance of timely provision of imports, particularly fertilizers, seeds and petroleum products became acknowledged in concrete practice.

For both exports and agriculture it was necessary to embark on a major rehabilitation of roads, particularly feeder roads and significant resource allocations were made from both domestic resources and again foreign credits. In order to sustain the domestic funding for road maintenance, a road fund was established out of a levy on petroleum products as petroleum products prices were adjusted upwards through 1984. Imports of vehicle spares and tyres were regarded as a matter of urgency to ease the transportation bottlenecks.

The three-year investment programme formulated for the period 1984–86 placed emphasis on the rehabilitation of existing capacity rather than completely new investments. Increased imports were an important part of the programme. The import programme for the period allocated about 30 per cent of resources to the directly productive sectors, with production targets being set at 40 per cent for petroleum and transportation, over 20 per cent for other sectors and less than 10 per cent for food imports.

As part of the rehabilitation effort, key export sectors were allowed to retain portions of their foreign exchange earnings to import essential raw materials, spares and equipment. Percentages varied from 10 per cent for the Cocoa board to 45 per cent in the mining sector.

Rehabilitation of health and education services also began to be addressed with provision of both foreign and domestic resources; but it is fair to say that these efforts were in a relatively minor key in the first instance though increasing concern soon began to be shown by government about these sectors.

Ironically, the year in which the recovery effort was comprehensively inaugurated was also the year in which not only over a million persons were added to the population from Nigeria, but the drought which had hit Ghana since 1981 reached a peak. In these especially arid conditions bush-fires raged through the countryside devastating agricultural production throughout the country. The drought also had a severe impact on energy availability and on foreign exchange earnings from the export of power to neighbouring countries as well as to the VALCO aluminium smelter. Foreign financing in the first year of the programme also failed to materialize on the scale and with the speed that was required to effect a rapid turn-around despite the resumption of meetings of the Consultative Group of western donor countries after almost a decade. The deterioration in the timber sector also proved intractable and the considerable resources invested did not provide the immediate returns anticipated.

It was clear that exogenous natural factors were responsible for delaying the expected impact of the recovery programme. Nonetheless, the government persisted with the reforms and the efforts to assure foreign support of the programme. The exchange rate continued to be adjusted upwards. Net domestic credit expansion was contained within the ceiling negotiated with the IMF.

By the second half of 1984, the tide turned as the near normal rainfall in 1984 resulted in a sharp recovery in agricultural production turning scarcity into surplus in food crops. Prices dropped, particularly for staples, and inflation was significantly held down. Fairly sizeable external financial support began to materialize. Normalization in petroleum imports enabled the road transport sector to cope with increased domestic and foreign trade-related traffic and thus contribute to the recovery of the productive sectors. Substantial increases in imports of consumer goods also resulted from the Special Unnumbered License system whereby importers were able to use their own foreign exchange resources to import these essentials. Overall, a restoration of confidence in the economy became evident. Real GDP increased by 9 per cent in 1984 with agriculture contributing a 10 per cent rise, thus setting the pace for the next few years in which an average 6.3 per cent increase in GDP was recorded annually.

These improvements enabled the government to begin moving away from short-term stabilization to more medium-term development objectives. In particular, the need to focus on the destruction of human and social infrastructure became evident since the implementation and management responsibilities of economic recovery were increasingly straining the existing resources of personnel.

Whilst developing a medium-term structural adjustment programme for the 1986–88 period, and negotiating supporting multi-year resources from both the World Bank and the IMF (including the especially favourable Adjustment Facility), the government served notice of its determination to formulate more comprehensive measures both to address social costs from the adjustment efforts, such as redeployment of labour from the public services, as well as social costs inherited by the adjustment effort from the previous decade of decline.[8] In this way the government has begun to turn the human dimension into a major key in the evolution of the recovery programme.

External Support, Conditionality and the Politics of Structural Adjustment

It is clear that measures of the sort outlined above were necessary to bring an anarchic economic situation under a control. Some controversy has surrounded the taking of these measures particularly on account of the relationships with the IMF and the World Bank which the Government established in order to obtain resources in support of these measures. Even within the ranks of government, there were those who contested the need for such measures and the need for IMF involvement. As publicly admitted by the Chairman of the PNDC, Flight Lft. Rawlings, these disagreements, even to some extent, threatened the very stability of the government.[9] But the clear upshot of the internal debates, and even the political fall-out over these issues, was a clarity and firmness of the political leadership about the inevitability of these measures for economic recovery; not because the IMF wanted them.

In reality, of course, the negotiations which led to the support of the IMF for the programme, initially through a Standby Facility as well as a Compensatory Financing Facility to compensate for the drop in export earnings from cocoa, and subsequently through two further standby arrangements and now an extended fund, have affected the shape of the programme particularly as periodic performance criteria that come with IMF, and indeed World Bank resources, were fashioned as part of the implementation of the programme. As is well known, these criteria are largely expressed in terms of quantifiable macro and monetary aggregates which do not express all the important goals and policies in a programme, but it is clearly the particular responsibility of governments and national agencies to relate these aggregates to their substantive objectives. It is also worth raising at this stage the significance of the IMF involvement in Ghana's economic recovery, particularly as many have wondered about the absence in Ghana's case of the extent of political upheaval that has become a trademark of Fund involvement.

It cannot be gainsaid that with the severely adverse terms of trade that Ghana experienced between 1979–82 to crown a decade of economic decline, a significant inflow of resources by way of quick-disbursing balance-of-payments support was desperately needed. Apart from the substantial oil credits provided interest-free by Libya in 1982/83 bilateral support was largely hesitant as traditional donors awaited a seal of approval from the Fund. Fund support would, therefore, be critical even for the inflows of bilateral resources as has been amply confirmed subsequently. To some extent, even support from the Fund for Ghana's programme was initially quite cautious and between April 1983 and October 1983, despite the very sweeping reforms that were being implemented, the government was obliged to obtain a bridging loan pending the release of the first tranche of Fund resources. Clearly, it was not the Government's attitude that resources from the Fund were needed whatever the terms of Fund participation in the programme. After initial brief contact with the Fund in July 1982, the programme was only discussed with the Fund staff again in September 1982 and then in February 1983 by which time Ghana had elaborated its own approach to economic salvation.

The need for a developing country to establish patiently but surely its outlook and programme which then become the subject matter of negotiation with the Fund can hardly be over-emphasized. If a developing country finds it useful and/or necessary to obtain Fund resources, it must regard it as important enough for to devote the time and manpower resources that it takes to evolve such an outlook prior to negotiating. Furthermore, while the respective bargaining strengths are by no means equal, there remains, as in any such negotiations of a developing country, some scope for getting at least some of what a country wants and conducting the negotiation on the basis of legitimate sovereign concerns.

Much ink has been written about the biases of Fund programmes and their tendency to express particular political positions. It is correct for national negotiators to recognize the paradigm within which the Fund staff and management operate in our preparations to negotiate. That way systematic effort can be made, where appropriate and in the most effective manner, to shake the Fund off such a paradigm where necessary. In a recent paper,[10] Reginald Green has noted the conversion of the Fund to "stabilization with growth". He observes that "present IMF programmes in sub-Saharan Africa do diverge from the classic 1950's – 1970's South European and South American programmes in one crucial and three secondary (at least to date) aspects. They do not posit real resource use contraction even in year one if either additional concessional finance flows, debt rescheduling or both mean that present domestic supply plus projected soft external flow expansion allow rapid progress toward balance without contraction. To that extent the IMF, at least in sub-Saharan Africa, is a convert to stabilization with growth. Greater attention to raising supply (of output as well as export levels) is also visible as are more detailed prescriptions notably in respect to agriculture." But, he goes on; "the IMF has not, in fact, developed a coherent, comprehensive, desegregated real output model linked to its monetary magnitude macro one so that the relationship of these additions to the macro monetary demand management core is at best common sense or intuitive."

Ghana's experience with the IMF confirms most of these observations, though given the historical role of the IMF one would expect that they go beyond not positing real resource use contraction if additional concessional finance flows and debt rescheduling are available to quite actively proselytizing in favour of countries for these flows and debt rescheduling. In addition, the Fund has to consider rescheduling repurchases in the light of developments on resource inflows for countries undertaking serious adjustment efforts. Further, however, I wonder whether it is not a blessing that the IMF has not developed a real output model linked to its macro one for this could only lead to more conditionality! For the dynamic real world situation of sub-Saharan Africa, any such model would more likely than not be wrong – even more so than the macro one is currently argued by many to be. These real output concerns must for us in Africa present challenges to evolve a concrete workable agenda whose validity can be judged in actual experiences of growth and which also embodies valid social priorities.

That agenda will not only involve economists and their models but also, for instance, agronomists who will understand agricultural production not only in terms of price incentives but in terms of high-yielding varieties becoming available. It will involve nutritionists and doctors, as well as sociologists and political scientists, with perceptions about both the health status significance of such varieties and the social and political dynamic of their implanation, as well as engineers, including social engineers – even lawyers, perhaps – and others, all interacting in the design and implementation of such a national and indeed continental agenda. Most vital of all, I would say, is the political leadership that is committed to these historic tasks of economic development and socio-political transformation. For it has to be admitted, albeit painfully, that quite often it has taken the IMF's monetary aggregates model to induce fiscal discipline and consistency as well as prudence in managing scarce resources in many of our countries. My point is that it is the responsibility of our political leadership rather than the Fund to induce and enforce such discipline and prudence not so much for the purpose of meeting macro monetary aggregates, but as a contribution towards effecting the real output growth that will lift our countries from the degradation and despair that has sadly been our lot but which Ghana's recent experience has begun to confront.

There is a final point made by Reginald Green which is also worth noting: "over the past two to three years and especially the past twelve months – the IMF has begun to say with some conviction that poverty and income distribution do matter; that macro monetary approaches can have harmful side effects in these areas; that programme results should be monitored and country proposals for alternative policy instruments or resource allocations within ceilings based on poverty, vulnerable group or income distribution criteria should be assessed carefully and, if practicable accepted. What this may mean in practice is unclear. Neither dismissive cynicism nor hosannaing a Damacus road conversion is appropriate at this point; a critical welcome and a testing via applied programme negotiation dialogue are desirable responses."[11] It is precisely the ardent and coherent negotiation of such national priorities that can force the needed flexibilities in current Fund modelling, and more appropriate design, especially of the time-path of the adjustment programmes.

Human Dimensions of Economic Recovery

The details of Ghana's medium-term structural adjustment programme are contained in two public documents, one published by the Government in July 1987,[12] and another[13] prepared for the fourth meeting of the Consultative Group of donor countries which took place in May 1987. I believe the recently inaugurated "Programme of Actions to Mitigate the Social Costs of Adjustment"[14] (PAMSCAD, unveiled at a meeting in Geneva in February 1988 chaired by the PNDC Secretary for Finance and Economic Planning) as well as some other elements of the human dimensions are worth special attention. But before elaborating on these features, some developments in the macroeconomic reform programme must be noted, bearing in mind their significance for the social dimensions.

Reform of the exchange rate system not only led to continued depreciation of the rate, but also involved the adoption of an auction system in September 1986. This was initially a second window from which was exempted, on the payments side, crude oil imports, transfers in respect of official commitments as well as a specified amount of essential drug imports, whilst on the receipts side cocoa exports also remained at the then first window of C90 $US. Eligible importers at the auction were initially importers of raw materials, spare parts, equipment, machinery and other priority requirements in the economy, but the scope of eligibility has been progressively widened as part of the associated trade liberalization policy. By March 1987 the auction rate had been extended also to the transactions that were retained at the first window in September 1986 though the Government's own import programme did not require the submission of bids by the government at the weekly auction.

Clearly, critical management issues arise, with a great significance for attaining the objective of social development. The pace of import liberalization especially bearing in mind the continuing foreign exchange constraints, aggravated by the current slump in the cocoa price could, if not properly managed, affect the priorities of the recovery effort. Taken together with current repurchase obligations to the Fund and arrears clearance targets set in the Fund Extended Facility that was successfully negotiated by the Government in September 1987, undue pressure could be exerted on the exchange rate unless expected increases in external inflows materialize. It must be noted that the auction system has improved the disbursement rate of external inflows considerably and removed many administrative bottlenecks for importers. The quickened pace of inflows and the improved foreign exchange earning capacity of the economy have prevented wild fluctuations in the exchange rate as has happened in other countries. The most recent development with regard to exchange rates is the authorization of commercial banks and other authorized dealers to buy foreign exchange arising from non-traditional exports and remittances directly at market rates and to sell foreign exchange to importers or other customers with bona fide requests. The scope for official mobilization of foreign exchange by this means is considerable, bearing in mind the continued operation of the parallel market in Ghana. However, dangers of capital flight will also need to be addressed through a vigilance on the part of the authorities about the whole exchange rate reform programme. Indeed, close monitoring of foreign exchange cash flows of the Bank of Ghana is called for particularly in the light of the slump in the world price of Ghana's main foreign exchange earner. Again, further efforts to improve the pace and level of disbursements of foreign financing will be critical to sustaining the exchange rate reforms and their underlying objectives.

Interest rate reforms have also been embarked upon not only by further rate increases but by the abolition since September 1987 of maximum lending rates and minimum deposit rates, with the exception of the minimum savings rate which was maintained at 21.5 per cent to establish a floor to the overall structure of deposit rates. The Bank of Ghana is also putting in place more effective systems for timely monitoring of cash and liquidity reserve developments of commercial banks to enable the Bank to affect lending policy more actively in the direction of national priorities. Given the importance of the banking sector, particularly the development finance institutions, in the financial intermediation process a wide-ranging financial sector review is being undertaken to confront the management and other problems of the banks. Among the problems already identified as having significance for the development banks in particular is the problem of having to make foreign loan repayments at the current strongly depreciated exchange rate. Loan recovery from enterprises, both public and private, to whom the foreign exchange loans were lent has sometimes been problematic because of factors that bear careful analysis with a view to the design of appropriate remedies that would both strengthen the banking system as well as productive enterprise. Indeed, the whole problem of enterprise reform and adjustment to the new macro-economic environment has begun to receive attention on several fronts. Recognizing especially the need to develop small-scale enterprise, more medium-term lending instruments are being considered as part of the reform of the development finance institutions including the rural banks. The strengthening of extension services not only in the agricultural sector, but also in industry through the National Board of Small-scale Industries, are key elements of such small-scale enterprise development. The PAMSCAD portfolio contains elements of this focus, but is obviously only a beginning in terms of policy formulation in this area.

State enterprise reforms have also been initiated to ensure that such enterprises are efficient and profitable. In addition to liquidating a number of enterprises which existed more in name than in economic reality, the Government is seeking joint ventures with both local and foreign investors in a number of enterprises, as well as shedding selected ones which have become a burden on the national budget.

Public sector management reforms, notably the establishment of an effective national planning system that will enable an effective assessment of national priorities through interactive processes involving all levels and sectors of the nation, will enable the state machinery to administer the reform programme more systematically, effectively and democratically.

PAMSCAD

Emerging from background work carried out by the Government and UNICEF and a dialogue between the Government and a multi-agency mission by a group of donor agencies[15] in July 1987, a short-term (two to three year) action programme especially designed to tackle the immediate problems of the poor and vulnerable has been formulated. There is the basic recognition that the most important assurance of human welfare in Ghana has to be the restoration of the growth path of the economy in a sustained manner. However, despite promising medium- to long-term growth prospects the economy will not be able to alleviate the economic hardships of many of the poor and vulnerable groups in the short run, and without targeted actions for the benefits of these groups, they may well be by-passed and their situation exacerbated. Indeed, some components of the recovery programme itself create specific economic problems for certain groups which may threaten the sustainability of the recovery programme unless these are specifically addressed.

The significant reductions in employment levels in the public sector at a time when the private sector itself has had to undergo adjustment to the new economic environment has made employment-generation initiatives of prime concern. Several projects in the PAMSCAD portfolio aim at providing such an initiative. A priority public works project for instance seeks to finance labour intensive priority urban sub-projects with high economic and social rates of return. This involves infrastructure rehabilitation and maintenance in the major cities as well as urban upgrading through the provision of roads, water supply and sanitation conveniences.

The use of labour intensive techniques for road construction is also envisaged in a project which involves extending the lessons of an existing pilot project on a wider scale, and reducing the import of machinery for road construction whilst strengthening local labour inputs. In view of the large network of feeder roads in urgent need of rehabilitation, the significant capacity for employment generation here, linked also directly to the macroeconomic objectives earlier outlined, cannot be disregarded. In this area of employment generation are included food for work programmes in the northern part of Ghana, acknowledged as a geographically vulnerable area. The object of providing employment to rural unemployed especially during the lean season is strengthened by the likely impact of the intended public works on agriculture, for instance through the desilting of dams etc.

As part of the employment generation initiative there is also an important small-scale mining project which offers opportunities especially for personnel being redeployed to receive training and technical assistance to undertake small-scale mining in a properly regularized and regulated framework. Ghana has had a long history of small-scale mining particularly of gold. It was not for nothing that we were given the colonial name "Gold Coast"! But with the introduction of larger scale mining technology, small-scale mining was declared illicit unless, as in the case of diamond mining, it was specifically permitted. However, the activities of small-scale miners continued, albeit illicitly, and were fed into the parallel market in foreign exchange. Considerable environmental damage often resulted from such activity having to be considered in secret, in a hurry and often under cover of night. Current government policy is to legalize and regulate, appropriately, such mining activity and the project in PAMSCAD seeks to provide, on a hire-purchase basis, implements for the use of miners as well as training especially in environmental protection measures. Support for small-scale agriculture with medium-term credit facilities etc. also features in PAMSCAD.

Important to the realization of PAMSCAD is the encouragement of, and support for, community initiatives. Under the present Government and with the upturn in the economy, local communities have become active in seeking to provide for themselves important social services – water, electricity, sanitation etc. In acknowledging the role of local communities the Government is seeking to facilitate this initiative through the provision of complementary financing and certain imports. The important role in this connection of non-governmental organizations, both local and foreign, is recognized. This strengthening of community initiatives is to be located firmly within a programme of political decentralization in which political power is effectively to be in the hands of district level authorities to plan and administer development. A programme for democratic development involving the establishment through district-level elections of district Assemblies was announced in July 1987;[16] and planning has begun towards these elections.

A third theme that features in PAMSCAD is that of improved shelter and human environment. Several projects of waste disposal and management, sanitation as well as improved local building materials development especially for rural shelter rehabilitation have been embodied under this theme in PAMSCAD.

Finally, there is the underlying theme of human capital sustenance and development which in a sense runs throughout the programme. In this connection, we may highlight the recognition of the need to strengthen the participation of women in development. In Ghana, as in other African countries, women have been active participants in agricultural production and in rural production generally. However, constraints on the productivity of labour in agriculture, and the combination of such roles in production with domestic responsibilities have had a significant negative impact on their income and hence their capabilities within the social and political environment. A project for credit provision to small farmers has a special focus on women including those in the vulnerable north whilst a specific project on enhancing opportunities for women in development also seeks to provide materials and simple implements to groups of women in rural and poor urban areas to improve their productivity and income. It will seek to encourage the formation of women into groups so as to improve their purchasing, producing and marketing abilities. The need to ensure functional literacy among rural farmers has been recognized as an important tool to improve their productivity and their capacity to confront exploitation.

Important initiatives in the health sector particularly to increase the availability of essential drugs throughout the country by a revolving fund for imports and a new system of distribution also feature in PAMSCAD. The important role that training or re-training plays in many of the PAMSCAD projects underscores the fact that the growth of Ghana's economy will require the development of new skills particularly for productive employment including self-employment.

Education Reform

As part of its recognition of the longer-term needs for manpower development, the Government has embarked in the last three years on major reform of the educational system, involving a shortening of the period of formal education, increasing access of children especially at the level of first-cycle institutions, and improving the educational content of schooling and relevance to economic development. In an effort to sustain the resources to support these education reforms, schemes of cost-recovery of expenditures for feeding are currently under serious consideration. Such cost recovery could involve the participation of students, particularly in the second and third cycle institutions in agricultural production to sustain their own welfare. Again, in this connection, mention must be made of the uncovering of networks of corruption which have in the period of decline deprived the educational institutions of significant resources in favour of private interests.

Conclusion

Without a doubt, even these attempts to address the human dimension of adjustment will be constrained by the continued adversity of the international economic environment. The current decline in cocoa prices is depriving Ghana of significant resources that structural adjustment efforts had anticipated when they were being embarked upon. Without an automatic compensatory financing device, the volatility of commodity prices poses severe danger to reform programmes, of the kind Ghana is undertaking, for just as the programmes get underway, adverse terms of trade wipe off the value of increased production. The very credibility and sustainability of reform can be undermined as has happened in the recent experiences of African countries. That is perhaps what has made the role of the IMF and the World Bank rather more poignant for developing countries. That role cannot be satisfactorily fulfilled unless the operational paradigm of these institutions is specifically oriented to the human crisis that Africa confronts and the urgencies of achieving real transformations, not more improvements in monetary aggregates and global macro-economic numbers.

But even as we recognize both technical and ideological limits of the Fund's outlook as well as even biases with political and ideological origins, attention must also be drawn to the internal dynamic of economic recovery programmes such as Ghana is undertaking. The redistributive impact on incomes, even in the stabilization phase as pointed out earlier, will strike at powerful vested interests – rentiers and patrons whose opportunities come under threat as these measures bite. That such interests fight back to regain their ascendancy is only to be expected, and the recovery efforts will only be sustained if their political patronage no longer provides the protection they enjoyed in the past. That is why the politics of stabilization is so often also the politics of destabilization, as a Government determined to effect these transformations will face attempts to overthrow it. Ghana has had its full share of such destabilization effects and perhaps the best testimony to the role of the vested interests in these attempts has been the extent of external financial resources as well as external political backing they have received even from quarters in which the economic reforms have been applauded. It is possible such 'reforms' could be carried out in a manner that restores the pre-eminence of the vested interests which would firmly sustain the neo-colonial order. But quite simply, in our view, unless the neo-colonial state is transformed or is transforming there can be little hope for sustained recovery for Africa's economies much less hopes of attaining development.

Notes

1 World Bank "Ghana, Policies and Programme for Adjustment", April 1984, p.8.
2 *Ibid.*, p.9 fn.2.
3 *Ibid.*, p.10.
4 Government of Ghana "National Programme for Economic Development", July, 1987, para.5.
5 Tabatabai Hamid, "Economic Decline – Access to Food and Structural Adjustment in Ghana", July, 1986. World Employment Programme Research Working Paper p.32. This study also provides an interesting and detailed analysis of the impact of labour shortage on agricultural production in the 1970s and the effect of the return of the over 1 million Ghanaians who were expelled from Nigeria in the agricultural sector.
6 This popular expression was taken from the policy statement of the Acheampong Government (1972–78) when it launched an ostensibly nationalistic Investment Policy Decree that sought to establish national control over strategic sectors of the economy but in reality again provided avenues for administrative corruption and the corrupt fronting for foreign business interests by a few Ghanaians.
7 World Bank, op. cit., pp.32–33.
8 Government of Ghana, op. cit.
9 Flight-Lieutenant J. Rawlings, National Broadcast of December 31st, 1986, Ministry of Information, Accra, Ghana.
10 Reginald H. Green: "Articulating IMF Stabilization Programmes with Structural Adjustment in Sub-Saharan African Agriculture" September, 1987, paper presented at ODI Conference, London, England.
11 *Ibid.*
12 Government of Ghana, "A Programme of Structural Adjustment", May, 1987.
13 Government of Ghana, "A programme of Actions to Mitigate the Social Costs of Adjustment", Government of Ghana, May, 1987.
14 UNICEF, World Bank, UNDP, IFAD, ILO, WHO, WFP, CIDA and the UK ODA participated in this multi-agency meeting.
15 Government of Ghana, "Modalities for District-level Elections", July, 1987.

The Impact of the Economic Crisis on Women

AFRICAN TRAINING AND RESEARCH CENTRE FOR WOMEN (ECA/ATRCW) AND THE INTERNATIONAL LABOUR ORGANIZATION (ILO)

In response to the persistent economic crisis in Africa, African governments have initiated actions aimed at long term structural transformation of their economies. These measures to overcome the current economic crisis and to which African countries have fully committed themselves are elaborated in the OAU's African Priority Programme for Economic Recovery (APPER) 1986–1990 which African Heads of State and Government adopted in July 1985. Within the framework of activities related to the implementation of APPER and the United Nations Programme of Action for African Economic Recovery and Development (UNPAAERD) 1986–1990, human resources development has been singled out as one of the four priority areas of development at the national, sub-regional and regional levels during the period 1986–1990. Both documents have also stressed the need for improvements in the management of the African economies and the role that human resources play therein.

It goes without saying that women are part of the human resources of Africa and their role in national development cannot be ignored. In this respect, there is need to ensure that women are included and integrated in all aspects of national development and that the current economic crisis in Africa does not continue to perpetuate the poor economic conditions of women.

Elements of the Economic Crisis and their Impact on Women

(a) Drought and Desertification

Drought and desertification have been Africa's greatest environmental problems affecting more than two-thirds of the continent for more than two decades and severely damaging not only the physical environment but also social and economic conditions.[1] The severest spell of drought was in the period 1982–1985, when as many as 24 African countries were so badly affected that they required emergency food aid at one time or another. Drought has therefore become one of the most important causes of the economic crisis and has led to slow economic growth.

In respect to women, the situation has and continues to affect women as food producers, fuelwood collectors and water fetchers. Women's workload has increased as they have to walk miles and miles to fetch water and more time is spent collecting firewood needed for cooking. These activities are done at the expense of other productive activities in order to meet the basic needs of the family.

Measures to control drought and desertification in Africa at the national, sub-regional and regional levels have been included in APPER and subsequently endorsed in UNPAAERD. The involvement of women and the incorporation of their concerns into these measures should be seriously considered in order to improve women's situation in productive sectors such as agriculture and to ease their workload.

(b) Food Crisis

Agricultural development efforts directed towards cash and export crops have diverted fertile land and family workers from food production, putting additional strain on already overburdened women. This diversion along with drought, inappropriate human policies and activities have greatly contributed to food shortage and crisis in Africa. According to FAO figures over the past 20 years, there has been a steady decline in the amount of food grown per person regardless of rainfall.

Women remain the providers of 60 to 80 per cent of the household food in many parts of sub-Saharan Africa. Women are the key actors in ensuring the survival and well-being of children, the youth and the aged. However, agricultural development programmes generally have failed to recognize that women traditionally have been responsible for growing most all of the family food. These programmes have often neglected or even undermined women's role in all aspects of agriculture, including growing food and cash crops.

The introduction of commercial crops and the commercialization of food staples have drawn women into labour-intensive, low-producing work. The net effect of this, food shortages and increased food prices has been an increase in women's work. These aspects have affected women in their roles as wives, mothers and household managers.

(c) Debt Crisis

Africa is faced with a debt situation the servicing of which is creating tremendous strains on economic recovery programmes. Governments are under pressure to improve their balance-of-payment situation and to reduce their budget deficit within very short periods of time. The external debt service burdens have put serious limits on the resources that can be internally mobilized to promote domestic reconstruction and rehabilitation. On the part of women, direct, negative impacts resulting from external debt include: (i) inequitable access for women to credit and services support and hence their ineffective participation in the development process and in the productive sector; and (ii) a low priority accorded to women's concerns in economic development has led to the allocation of meagre resources for women's programmes.

(d) Structural Adjustment

The debt and declining economic situation have forced many African Governments into structural adjustment programmes in order to reduce the demand

and to stimulate export earning so that more money could be earned to pay for debt. Both Africa's Priority Programme for Economic Recovery 1986–1990 (APPER) and the United Nations Programme of Action for African Economic Recovery and Development 1986–1990 (UN-PAAERD) adopted in 1985 and 1986 respectively underscore the importance of structural policy reforms in Africa. To date 25 African countries have adopted structural adjustment programmes with the support of the International Monetary Fund and or the World Bank.[2]

The main features of these structural adjustment programmes according to an ILO paper[3] include: currency devaluation, elimination of subsidies, cuts in public expenditures, liberalization of foreign trade, increases in domestic interest rates, restraint in monetary expansion, deregulation in internal markets and privatization of public enterprises and increases in producer prices for farmers. The introduction of these structural adjustment measures and their implementation have had severe consequences on women. A few examples of such consequences are as follows:

(i) Cuts in government expenditure have affected social services more adversely than other elements as far as women are concerned. Social aspects, particularly, as regards employment and social services such as education and health tend to be affected by the budgetary cuts that are often required more as regards special population groups particularly women and children.
(ii) Budget retrenchment has generally meant a freeze in the salaries of public employees and a freeze on public employment.[4] These measures have had greater effect on women than on men. For instance, when it comes to reducing the number of employees women are generally the first to go.
(iii) Deregulation in internal markets has lead to inflation. With limited resources on the part of women, this has reduced their purchasing power and has made it difficult for women to meet the ever demanding basic needs of the family.

(d) Employment

A major aspect of the current socio-economic crisis in Africa which has serious implications for women, is the critical unemployment and underemployment problem facing many African countries. In reference to women, in spite of the fact that in recent decades interest in policies to promote women's participation in economic development has increased, by and large, their chances of participating in the formal labour force and in remunerative activities are still very limited.[5]

Women in Africa have always played an important role in the production of goods and services. The nature and significance of their participation in economic activity have, however, undergone major qualitative and quantitative changes during the last decades. According to the latest ILO estimates and projections, nearly 75 million of Africa's 279 million women were registered as economically active in 1985. This number represented nearly 27 per cent of the continent's total female population and 35 per cent of the total economically active population. The proportion of the female labour force in 1980 was as follows: 46.6 per cent in industry; 40.3 per cent in agriculture; 30.5 per cent in the services sector. In comparison with 1970, there was a slight decrease in agriculture and a slight increase in the other two sectors.[6]

(i) *Women in agriculture*

Taking the continent as a whole, the proportion of the labour force in agriculture is higher in the case of women than that of men. This applies to all the countries of West Africa (except Ghana, Burkina Faso and Togo), of East Africa (except Rwanda) and of Central Africa (except Angola and Equatorial Guinea), as well as to three countries in southern Africa (Botswana, Lesotho and Swaziland). In North Africa, the low proportion of women working in agriculture is due to the underestimation of the number of women occupied as family workers in agricultural activities.

The proportion of women working on their own account varies greatly from country to country, from a negligible percentage to the majority. In some countries the majority of self-employed women are in the agricultural sector as is the case for men; in others, the majority of active women are recorded as being in "unpaid family work". The proportion of the female labour force in the latter category is greater than that of the male labour force everywhere. Unpaid family workers are mainly found labouring on farms.

Recent developments have resulted, however, in making women's agricultural work more and more difficult to accomplish. Changes in crop patterns, deforestation, desertification and population pressures are limiting women's access to land. While modern technology often enables African men to cultivate larger amounts of land, the workload of women usually increases as a consequence. They continue to weed the land, to harvest and to carry water without the benefits of technological innovations.

Consideration of these points should result in major changes in planning for agricultural production if the objective of food self-sufficiency is to be reached in the not too distant future. There is still, for example, insufficient information on the real extent and the exact nature of women's involvement in food production. Statistical data often exclude various aspects of women's agricultural labour and fail to provide concrete information about the tasks performed by them. This situation represents a formidable obstacle to the adjustment of related development planning. Another barrier is the low social status of women, which results in the devaluation of labour performed by them and leads to the assignment of inadequate development resources to women's sphere of activity, in spite of the fact that their labour is vital for the community.

Structural adjustment programmes in many countries of Africa have focused on agricultural development including agricultural research, extension services strategies, marketing and others. But despite the acknowledged predominance of women in agriculture in many parts of the world and in Africa in particular, women continue to be left out of agricultural strategies and experience severe problems. As identified in a recent study in Ghana,[7] these problems include inadequate resources for production, mainly land; limited access to credit; lack of appropriate technologies to reduce drudgery associated with household work; land ownership that is still, in many countries of Africa vested in the male members of the family; the low level of development of productive forces and farming methods that are still mostly traditional and backward.

In terms of credit, women have no access since the title of the land for collateral is in the man's name. Perchonock,[8] for example considers the question of women and land matters and concludes that while both men and women suffer from the same type of oppression (i.e. in class relations) in depriving them of land, peasant women suffer quantitatively more than peasant men. Stressing this situation further Philomena Steady, states that in view of the pattern in some societies of allocating land to males even when land rights are determined by rules of usufruct, women as a group are likely to be more deprived of access to land under new land tenure conditions.[9] Due to the above factors, the productivity of women is severely undermined, and they are becoming more and more marginalized.[10]

In order to alleviate the above mentioned problems and others and to improve women's participation in agriculture the following ought to be considered and where possible provided for:

(a) appropriate labour and time saving devices to cater for all agricultural activities such as ploughing, weeding, harvesting, transporting, preserving and processing of agricultural products;
(b) appropriate food processing technologies to be made widely available to rural women, along with storage and marketing facilities to reduce post harvest losses;
(c) provision of farm implements, fertilizers, high quality seeds and agricultural extension services in order to improve the input/output ratio; and
(d) access to land and training in agricultural extension work.

The key issues with regard to technology are whether the changes brought about by the technology are beneficial to women in the long run, whether women can afford to purchase the new technology and whether they have access to the technical skills required for maintaining it. Technological improvements such as tractors allow more land to be plowed on the family farm, but on the other hand, this usually means additional burdens for women because they have more weeding to do by hand unless devices for weeding are also made available. In short, women have very limited access to land, capital, skills and technology which are major factors to increase income and productivity.

(ii) *Women as industrial workers*

The proportion of women workers in the industrial and service sectors has risen slightly in recent years. There are, however, enormous differences between countries within the region and in some the proportion of active women in industry is higher than the proportion of active men, while in others less than 2 per cent of active women are employed in industry.

Women find jobs in industries such as food processing and packaging, tobacco manufacturing, and garment making. However, employment is often on a precarious basis (daily paid, temporary and seasonal work), and there is a tendency to prefer women workers who are mainly illiterate, unskilled and non-unionized. These industries in most cases provide low paid, insecure jobs which many women are forced to accept in order to obtain cash income to maintain themselves and their dependants.

Technological and scientific progress has already had a strong impact on employment patterns and affects education and training systems in existing African national institutions. Serious questions have arisen in terms of how best to ensure that workers can take advantage of up-to-date scientific knowledge and technological advances and, at the same time, to protect their employment from the negative effects of these developments.

(iii) *Women in the services sector*

While in industrialized countries the services sector is clearly dominated by women, in Africa the great movement of workers in general, and women in particular, into the services sector has just begun.

A recent global statistical survey (1950–2000) on Women in Economic Activity undertaken by the International Labour Organization (ILO) and the United Nations Research and Training Institute for the Advancement of Women (INSTRAW),[11] showed that, in almost all African countries, more and more women were employed in the services sector in countries for which data was available. The proportion of women has more than tripled in some countries and doubled in others. For example, the percentage of working women in this sector rose from 3 to 8.3 per cent in Senegal, 7 to 13.6 per cent in the Ivory Coast, 19.8 to 30.5 per cent in Nigeria and 31.6 to 51.9 per cent in Mauritius. However, despite this increase, the proportion of women of the total labour force in the services sector is still very low compared to men.

The number of women working in offices and commerce varies from country to country. In developing countries, secretaries and teachers fall under occupational categories still carried out by both men and women. There is, however, a trend for these occupations to become more feminized. This is true of secondary-level teachers in Africa, where the number of women occupying such posts rose from 25 to 33 per cent between 1975 and 1980.[12] Community, social and health services in many countries show a high concentration of women since welfare services are considered to be a female sphere of activity. But even in these occupations women hold jobs in the lower echelons, while the higher echelons are almost exclusively occupied by men. This is particularly true of the health sector where women are usually employed as nurses, etc., but not as hospital managers, surgeons, technicians or researchers. More often than not clearly perceivable occupational segregation between women and men is usually to the disadvantage of women.

(iv) *Women in the informal sector*

Although insufficient information is available, it is estimated that in some African cities 50–60 per cent of the labour force may be found in this sector, the majority of whom are women.[13] Informal labour is widespread in both urban and rural areas and extends to all economic sectors. Its real impact on development is not yet fully understood and the importance of informal labour for women's income opportunities is not adequately accounted for. It is clear that it represents both opportunities and dangers for workers. Much more work needs to be devoted to the establishment of an adequate data base on women and men in the informal sector including types of work performed, incomes, legal coverage, social security, work conditions, links with the formal sector, possibilities for the introduction of improved technologies, training and the formation of co-operatives and trade unions in order to foster the development of appropriate and effective policy measures to improve employment opportunities and conditions for women in the informal sector.

Several resolutions and reports have called inter-alia for action to improve upon the conditions of work of the women in the informal sector, not only with respect to increasing their access to improved technologies, storage facilities, credit and other productive resources but also in making their work environment and welfare more human. The "Nairobi Forward-Looking Strategies" have stressed that governments should assist the increasing number of working women in the informal sector (see also the Arusha Strategies). Furthermore, the Inter-Parliamentary Union Conference in Dakar in October 1985 adopted several recommendations on the African employment situation including women's work in the informal sector. It observed that women had poor work environments and lacked governmental investment and support and therefore proposed both national and international action to ameliorate their working conditions in the informal sector. Despite these resolutions and recommendations, environmental conditions in the informal sector remain poor.

The informal sector plays a significant economic role in the urban as well as rural areas of African countries by producing goods and services in conformity with the needs of the population. Since women play a significant role in this sector, it should be perceived that enhancing the productive capacity of this sector as well as improving its working conditions, could simultaneously improve the living standards of the women in the sector and also the larger number of urban workers and poor who consume the goods and services generated by the sector.

Several problems within the informal sector hampering productivity need to be pointed out. On the part of the government, the attitude of most African governments to the informal sector can best be described as ambivalent. Development plans put strong emphasis on employment creation and basic needs satisfaction, however, the day-to-day reality is harassment of the informal sector. In most cases, despite the pronouncements in the development plans, governments have been reluctant to implement laws to favour the informal sector or even put it at par with the modern sector.[14] This remains difficult because of governments' hostile attitudes, and practical difficulties such as the absence of legal status of most informal sector participants and the absence of records which make it difficult to plan for the improvement of facilities and to integrate the informal sector in to development plans.

If we perceive that women play a significant role in the informal sector, then it is fair to say that something ought to be done to improve women's productivity in the sector. The following are suggested to help improve the situation of women in the informal sector:

(a) more use of appropriate technology to improve quality and increase market opportunities for the sector;
(b) training programmes designed for women could help, although in keeping with the technology practiced in the informal sector special programmes are needed for the informal sector to take account of its special needs; and
(c) improvement programmes for women in the informal sector are needed emphasizing reconstruction of physical facilities which could inevitably lead to some improvement in the work environment and welfare of the women traders.

In general, training would help women in the introduction of more appropriate technology into the informal sector. Similarly, in the long run, it would increase the capital intensity of the sector. Some form of technical or financial assistance is also needed by the sector especially to meet the needs of women, to maintain its dynamic nature and make major improvements in its production, sales, training and other aspects.

Womens Access to Education and Training

Education and training are among the major factors that promote national development and thus bring about positive change in the lives of the population. Over the past two and a half decades, there have been many substantial improvements in levels and standards of education and training in Africa. However, as a consequence of policies associated with the debt crisis in Africa, there have been major setbacks in almost all countries in terms of declining quality of education and training being provided.[15]

As mentioned earlier, cuts in government expenditure have affected social services. Education as part of social services is the largest single expenditure. Cutting expenditure in education has led to reduced enrollment and lack of facilities (e.g. text books). The decline in enrolment rates is due partly to the inability of governments to provide the facilities to cope with rising populations and in other cases due to the introduction of increased fees which has led to withdrawals from the education and training systems by those unable to pay.

To what extent do these developments have an impact on girls/women? Traditionally in African society priority in education has always been given to boys. In the situation where the family is unable to pay the increased school fees, chances are given to the boys first. To further illustrate this point, Kenyan educators who met in March 1987 to discuss issues of women in education, noted that the culture has not yet fully accepted the premise of equal education and opportunity for girls, especially in rural areas.[16]

Educational problems, to a greater or lesser degree, confront many African countries. Inevitably, the problems of inadequate educational facilities and manpower are much greater in the rural areas, since development planners and policy makers have not in the past addressed the problems of structural inequalities and rural-urban differentials in educational development.[17] This neglect in educational development has added to women inequalities in the education process.

One of the major obstacles to the achievement of equal access of women to vocational, technical and managerial training is the prevailing assumption that programmes of assistance directed to the population in general do reach men and women on an equal basis. On the contrary, such programmes often exclude the participation of women by virtue of not planning for their inclusion. To further aggravate the problem of unequal access, most vocational training for women is not linked to national manpower planning and in fact takes place outside of mainstream training programmes.

Available evidence indicates that there is a general tendency to concentrate on home, family and traditional female fields in the provision of non-formal education and training programmes for young women. There may be no legal obstacles to the access of girls and young women to vocational and technical opportunities such as exist to prepare them for the job market, but in practice a number of discrepancies exist in the distribution of opportunities between girls and boys. Moreover, the so-called "female subjects" in which the girls predominate offer very limited economic possibilities and they are generally peripheral to the main development process. The segregation of training is often mirrored by the provision of separate training facilities for boys and girls. Even in some of the training institutions which are in theory co-educational, separate courses for boys and girls still exist. The options for girls are also restricted by the inadequate preparation they receive in the formal school system so that their access to the so-called "male trades" in non-formal education programmes and in the labour market becomes very limited from the very beginning. A typical division of training is that boys have access to courses in carpentry, masonry and blacksmithing and girls to home economics, which offers limited employment opportunities.

The enrolment of girls at all levels of education (primary, secondary and university) is declining in many countries in Africa, although in a few it has increased. According to the various country reports presented at the Fifth meeting of the Sub-regional Committee on the Integration of Women in Development (Lusaka MULPOC, February 1987), in the area of formal education, Zimbabwe reported to have achieved equal enrolment of boys and girls at primary school and an increase in the proportion of girls at secondary school level.[18] In Tanzania, there has been an increase in the number of girls at secondary school level which is at present recorded at 37 per cent at ordinary level and 29 per cent at advance level.[19] At the university level, women's enrollment rose from 9.7 per cent in 1977 to 25 per cent by 1984. Teacher training institutions have also observed higher rates of women.

In Kenya, there has been a rise in the total enrolment of females. In 1984, for example, out of 4.38 million children attending primary schools, 2.1 million were girls. At the university level, the increase in female enrollment has been more modest than at the other levels, rising from 15 per cent in 1973 to about 23 per cent in 1984.[20]

In respect to non-formal education several countries, including Ethiopia, Ghana, Kenya and the United Republic of Tanzania have all embarked upon strong programmes of adult education to redress illiteracy. Literacy classes have observed a higher number of women in many countries of Africa. Since most of the rural women are either illiterate or semiliterate, non-formal education has played a significant role to widen their skills and ability to use new knowledge and techniques so vital to the development process. Non-formal education should enable women to assume new roles and expose them to greater contact with the social, economic and political life of their respective countries which in turn may lead to the development of new ideas, values and attitudes to development. Hence, non-formal education programmes for rural and urban women must not be planned in isolation, but must be linked to the overall national development plans and efforts.

As part of human resources development, what then can be done to increase the participation of girls/women in education and training within the structural adjustment programmes? As many analysts have pointed out, education has the potential for being a major force for greater equality but too often this potential is obstructed by perverse effects of structure and fees.[21] Several measures to develop the human resources (women) needed in the development process are suggested as follows:

(a) there is need for action to build in programmes within the curriculum/ school syllabus to encourage female participation on a more equitable basis in the school system in terms of enrolment, motivation to learn and aspirations;

(b) to develop preventive services such as systematic guidance and counselling services to minimize female drop outs and early pregnancies;

(c) to make the curriculum more relevant for females and to develop programmes such as career guidance education to strengthen linkages between the education system with the world of work; and

(d) in the field of science and technology where women's enrolment is very low, strategies aimed at increasing women and girls for entry into scientific and technical fields should be developed. In the urban areas where new technologies are being introduced, awareness should be created and appropriate training planned for women.

Health and Nutrition

In the period since 1980, several African countries have experienced increasing infant mortality and crude death rates, while the level of malnutrition has increased and per capita food supplies have dropped. The International Safe Motherhood Conference on Preventing the Tragedy of Maternal Deaths noted that of the half million maternal deaths that take place every year, 99 per cent of these deaths occur in the developing world.[22] The question of women's health is a question that is intricately linked to women's role and status in the community and to the level of socio-cultural and economic development of the society.

In Africa, as in most developing countries, women's health has been given cursory attention with emphasis on women's reproductive roles and insufficient attention to women's other health needs. Within the structural adjustment programmes, budgetary cuts in public expenditure have had a negative impact on social services such as health. A severe, chronic undersupply of essential drugs and equipment to health services exists in a number of developing countries especially in rural areas. This undersupply results partly from the shortage of foreign exchange, which causes delays in making settlement for supplies from commercial sources, so that suppliers charge an additional fee to cover the credit risk and delays in payment.[23] The delay and undersupply of essential drugs along with high prices have affected women, especially pregnant and lactating women.

The health needs of female adolescents and pregnant and lactating women require special attention for various reasons. Due to inadequate nutrition of expectant mothers 15 per cent of babies are born with low birth weight. Similarly, women's nutritional status is affected by work load and seasonal peaks in labour demand. It is often overlooked that women suffer a particular labour constraint – seasonal work stress which can present various health problems as well as weaken any incentive to limit family size or send children to school.

Closely associated with the health status of countries is their level of nutrition. As a result of the debt crisis and structural adjustment programmes adopted to resolve the crisis, a large number of African countries have had to eliminate or reduce subsidies on food products. This has led to increased food prices and falling living standards. In this respect, it is observed that the general level of nutrition has declined in a number of African countries during the 1980s. With increased food prices coupled with limited resources, women as mothers and caretakers of the family have found it very difficult to afford to buy the required food to keep up to adequate nutritional standards.

Since healthy people constitute (in economic terms) the productive labour force and women play a dominant role in the labour force and yet are the most affected group in terms of health (maternal, mortality and fertility rates etc.), it is necessary that special attention be given to women's health. African governments have been making significant strides in implementing and strengthening programmes in areas such as immunization, primary health care (PHC), maternal child health (MCH) and family planning programmes, all of which are of particular relevance to the health of women, but these programmes have yet to reach the majority of women in the rural areas in particular.

Housing, Water and Sanitation

Shelter and water have been defined by the various United Nations agencies as basic needs. And yet, housing in most African countries, especially in the urban centres has reached crisis proportions. Today, a large proportion of urban dwellers live in unbearable crowded slums and shanty towns, while others have no shelter at all. The slums and shanty towns are without proper sanitation and the actual living structures constitute serious health and fire hazards.

With respect to water, about one quarter of the people in Africa have access to adequate supplies of water for drinking and washing and the number is even smaller in rural areas. As a result women and children who are most affected continue to walk miles and miles to fetch water. The women and children of Africa will be the chief beneficiaries of any improvement in water supply and sanitation. Access to water supplies will save time and reduce drudgery for women. It will also enhance standards of health and sanitation, paving the way for a better life.

Efforts to formulate plans of action for community water supply and sanitation as part of the implementation of the International Drinking Water Supply and Sanitation Decade (IDWSSD) have been made by African governments. Some of these activities include rural water supply systems using hand-pumps as well as piped gravity systems. These are being operated and maintained by communities in countries such as Burkina Faso, Benin, Burundi, Central African Republic, Ethiopia, Gambia, Kenya, Malawi, Mali, Rwanda, Sudan and Uganda.[24] Furthermore, some countries have made progress by increasing their budget allocation for the sector. Despite these positive signs, much remains to be done.

Funding limitations, operation and maintenance, lack of trained personnel at the professional and sub-professional levels and inadequate cost recovery policies seem to be among the serious constraints hampering the implementation of the Decade plans. Consequently, women and children continue to suffer.

It is recognized that women are involved and participating in the community water projects. Participation alone is not enough. There is need to: (i) train women not only as para-professionals but at the professional level; (ii) integrate water supply projects within other health activities such as PHC; (iii) provide guidance and counseling services in relation to proper use of water for health benefits; and (iv) undertake needs assessments to identify problems and specific needs of women as related to health and their effect on women's productivity so that such identified needs could be incorporated into other women's health activities. Governments need to make every effort to generate resources needed to reach their targets for the Decade. Accordingly, since governments have and continue to be committed to the activities and attainment of the IDWSSD goals, it is here proposed that more attention for water and sanitation activities be directed to the underserved and rural populations using low cost appropriate technologies and locally available resources.

Women at Decision-making Levels and Political Participation

Political participation is a key issue for women because it is an indicator of their status as well as a tool to improve their situation in society. In many African countries, women have the right to vote and they do vote. However, the mere act of voting cannot be regarded as a measure of political consciousness or participation. In many instances, poor rural and urban women are mobilized by political parties to vote. In such situations, women vote in high numbers but they do not participate in any other political activities. Though a few women in some countries of Africa are now actively involved in politics, the situation of women in political participation is still unsatisfactory.

Factors affecting women's participation in politics include: resources, time, skill, experience, patronage, contacts and information. Women are at a disadvantage with regard to all these factors that promote success in politics. Above all, cultural attitudes towards women is a major factor hampering women's participation in politics.

In senior public offices, women are under-represented. In some countries in Africa, a few women have been appointed to responsible positions such as ministers but are mostly assigned to social services sectors such as education, culture, social welfare and women and youth affairs. In the judiciary, the majority of women are at the lower levels. Few women head various parastatal organizations or government departments, and institutions.

More effective participation of women in politics and in decision-making would inevitably bring women to the centre of power, thereby enabling them to contribute to national plans and policies that have to do with structural transformation taking place in their respective countries. After all, it is the politicians who make decisions, policies and priorities for national development. Women's participation in politics and at the decision-making level would enable them to act as pressure groups for ensuring that national policies, plans and programmes address women's concerns as well as promote implementation of national, regional and international strategies.

In the context of Africa's economic crisis, economic recovery programmes such as structural adjustment programmes have not included women in the design and planning of programmes even though the Lagos Plan of Action, APPER, and UN-PAAERD recognize the role of women in national development. For instance, despite the acknowledged predominance of women in agriculture in many parts of the world and in Africa in particular women continue to be left out of agricultural strategies.[25] Though there have been serious attempts to introduce affirmative action, variously defined as "equality policies" or "positive action" to enhance the status and promote the full integration of women into political and economic systems, the situation is far from changing.[26] Governments should take into account that women are equal partners with men, that their participation in politics and at decision making levels is crucial in development and that women are an economic asset whose contribution should be sufficiently acknowledged and utilized. If we take the position that women are potential human resources, then that potential must be developed and appropriately utilized in line with the structural transformation, national plans and recovery programmes taking place in the respective countries in Africa.

Measures Being Taken to Overcome Africa's Economic Crisis in Relation to Women

At the end of the United Nations Decade for women (1975–1985) all governments approved the Forward Looking Strategies for the Advancement of Women (FLS), thus expressing their political will to continue and improve their policies and activities for the advancement of women.

During the last ten years there has been some progress in such areas as legislation, education and employment, health and family planning and to some extent, the participation of women in politics. In general, however, the status of poor women in particular cannot be said to have greatly improved. Most women still bear a double workload and have little if any access to land, credit and training in technological improvements. Women are still a long way behind in education, employment, health and representation on decision-making bodies. This having being said, the discussion in the following paragraphs notes some of the progress that has been made in implementing the strategies and which have a bearing on the socio-economic conditions of women.

In the context of the Nairobi Forward-Looking Strategies endorsed by the General Assembly in its resolution 40/108/of 13 December 1985, specialized agencies and bodies of the United Nations system were requested to establish, where they did not already exist, focal points on women's issues in all sectors of the work of the organizations of the United Nations system.[27] Since then, the World Bank, the United Nations Industrial Development Organization (UNIDO), the United Nations Educational, Scientific and Cultural Organization (UNESCO), the World Food Programme (WFP), the International Labour Organization (ILO), and other United Nations programmes and funds have taken measures to establish Women in Development Divisions and/or to strengthen their existing respective focal points for the advancement of women.

Non-governmental organizations have also played a great role in publicizing and helping to implement the Nairobi Forward-Looking Strategies. Their activities have included among others, conferences and meetings held at local, national and international levels to bring women's issues to public attention, identification of priority problems and seeking solutions, assisting in the collection of data, in research and the production of community guidebooks for action and training manuals.

Most African governments have drawn up plans of action to implement the FLS in all sectors of national development giving more attention to sectors such as agriculture, health, education, water and sanitation. For instance, extension services have been extended to cover women in agriculture in countries such as Kenya, Zimbabwe, Tanzania, Niger and others. To improve the input/output ratio, efforts are geared towards the provision of farm implements, fertilizers, high quality seeds and agricultural extension courses designed to educate women farmers on modern methods in order to ensure higher agricultural productivity.[28] Similar measures are observed in Guinea and Niger.[29] In general, it is perceived that African countries in areas such as better management of water resources, improvement of drainage in irrigated areas, encouragement of afforestation, the control of deforestation, rehabilitation and maintenance of existing modes of transport and communication, protection of the environment and reorientation of the education system to meet development needs are taking into consideration women's concerns and special needs. Still, in most of these plans, women and families are conceptualized as welfare "problems" rather than economic assets.[30]

Within the UN Economic Commission for Africa, the sub-regional Committees on Integration of Women in Development within the framework of the existing Multinational Programming and Operational Centres (MULPOCs) based at Lusaka, Yaounde, Niamey, Gisenyi and Tangiers as well as the African Training and Research Centre for Women have spearheaded and promoted the activities of the subregions according to priority areas set forth by each subregion and in line with the Arusha and Nairobi Forward-Looking Strategies. These activities have focussed on; the role of women in the distribution of foodstuffs, training and research activities in agriculture, food and appropriate food technologies, marketing and processing, health issues such as water and sanitation, development and management of small-scale enterprises, the legal status of women, strengthening national machineries for women in development, as well as training in project planning, implementation and evaluation.

Though we cannot claim that the above mentioned measures and activities being undertaken have had a dramatic impact on the economic conditions of women, nevertheless, if these measures continue to be vigorously pursued, some changes may occur in the long run.

In the context of the United nations Programme of Action for African Economic Recovery and Development (UN-PAAERD) 1986–1990, the Secretary General's initial report (October 1987)[31] on the progress made in the implementation of UN-PAAERD noted that African countries have paid particular attention to assistance programmes for small farmers and the need to strengthen the self-help efforts of rural populations through participatory organizations and co-operatives.

With respect to women in this connection, almost four-fifths of the African countries responding to a recent ECA survey indicated that they had taken measures in line with the Programme of Action on the enhancement of the role of women in agricultural production and other development processes. In the area of human resources development, planning and utilization, the role of women is accorded special emphasis in the Programme of Action. In support of the efforts of African countries and the international community, the United Nations system has devised a co-ordinated approach aimed at ensuring the full participation of women's organizations and agencies.

Conclusion

The improvement of the status of women, their full participation in economic, political, educational and cultural life and their effective access to responsibilities related to development and the advantages resulting therefrom should constitute a major area of concern for governments, organizations and international agencies.

In the employment sector, lack of knowledge with respect to women's actual, as well as potential participation in the labour force will always have a detrimental effect, not only on women themselves, but on national development processes in general. Awareness of the real extent to which women's economic activity, the importance of women's income and the contribution of women to national development is essential to the formulation of adequate policy measures and the adjustment strategies so as to benefit both women and men and enhance the development process as a whole.

Concern with women's participation in economic activities should not be limited only to the recognition of their contribution to gross national product. Recognition in itself is meaningless unless it is translated into definite action that would have a favourable impact on their status. To improve women's participation in employment both formal and informal as well as in the agricultural sector in relation to the current social and economic realities in most African countries, the following are proposed:

(a) technical assistance in terms of training and material support through better access to credit, land, support services and training opportunities should be extended to women to enhance productivity;
(b) the intensification of agricultural extension work aimed at rationalizing the organization of production, training women in modern methods of production, marketing and introduction of technologies in food processing, preservation and storage;
(c) improving access to and control over production factors (land, credit, capital, labour), services and infrastructural facilities (water, energy, health care, education, information etc.); and
(d) reducing the workload of women, e.g. by introducing labour saving technologies;

In respect to health, it has become increasingly apparent that women are the primary health workers in both rural and urban areas since they have the greatest influence on the health of their families. Women themselves do not enjoy good health, owing to frequent pregnancies, abortions, substandard nutrition and cultural factors (workload, diet, female circumcision etc.). Every year, half a million women die as a direct result of pregnancy. It is necessary, therefore, for women to play a more active part in planning and carrying out health work projects and for those values and customs that have an adverse effect on the health of girls and women to be changed by means of health education.

In regard to population policy, it has been demonstrated that a falling birth rate is primarily related to better education and better incomes, women's knowledge of family planning methods and services and their availability. Birth control education programmes should also be aimed at men in order to make them aware of their responsibilities. Guidance and counseling services on use of birth control devices as well as cultural attitudes and perceptions on abortions, early pregnancies and surgical contraception should be designed and provided to women, teenage girls and men.

The Arusha and Nairobi Forward-Looking Strategies present concrete measures to overcome the obstacles to the Decade's goals and objectives for the advancement of women. These measures include all sectors of development. If attention is given to the implementation of these strategies, the socio-economic conditions of women could be vastly improved.

Notes

1 ECA *Survey of Economic and Social Conditions in Africa*, 1985–1986 E/ECA/CM.13/3.

2 Barber Conable: "Remarks of Barber Conable to the African Group September 26, 1987". (The World Bank Washington D.C.).

3 ILO,"ILO Unemployment and other social consequences of the debt crisis in Africa" paper prepared for the Organization of African Trade Union Unity Conference on the Question of External Debt and Debt Servicing in the Continent, Dec. 1987, Addis Ababa.

4 UN, *World Survey on the Role of Women in Development*; Report of the Secretary General – A/CONF.116/4, December 1984 p.34.

5 ILO/JASPA, *The Challenge of Employment and Basic Needs in Africa*, Oxford University Press, Nairobi, 1986.

6 ILO, *Economically Active Population Estimates and Projections, 1950–2025*. Vol. V, third edition (Geneva), 1986.

7 M.A. Abrokwa, "Study on Participation of Women in Development both as Agents and Beneficiaries in Ghana", ECA/Niamey MULPOC, 1987.

8 M. Perchonock, "Double Oppression: Women and Land Matters in Kaduna State", in *Women in Nigeria Today* (Zed Press, London) p.19.

9 P.Steady, Research Methodology and Investigative Framework for Social Change in *Seminar on Research on African Women: What Type of Methodology?* (AAWORD, Dakar Senegal) 1983, p.15.

10 N. Makamure, and R. Chimedza, The question of Agrarian Reform in Zimbabwe and its Implication for Women: *Women and Rural Development in Africa*, Association of African Women for Research and Development – Occasional Paper Series No. 2 Dakar, Senegal p.51.

11 ILO/INSTRAW, *Women in Economic Activity: A Global Statistical Survey (1950–2000)*, A Joint Publication of the International Labour Organization and the United Nations Research and Training Institute for the Advancement of Women (INSTRAW) June 1985 p.47.

12 ILO, *Equal Opportunities and Equal Treatment for Men and Women in Employment*, Report VII, International Labour Conference, seventy-first session, Geneva 1985, p.14.

13 Kathleen Newland, "Women, men and the division of labour", World Watch Paper 37, May, 1980, p.14.

14 ILO, *The Challenge of Employment and Basic Needs in Africa*, chpt 21, op. cit.

15 ILO, "Unemployment and Other Social Consequences of the Debt Crisis in Africa", *Ibid.*

16 *The Women's Watch*, Vol. 1, No. 2 Summer 1987, p.5.

17 Wanbui Karanja, *Family Policies and Programmes in the Context of Socio-Economic Development in African Countries*. ECA/TP/SD/86/2.2/(ii).

18 Zimbabwe country paper presented by the Ministry of Community Development and Women Affairs to the Fifth Meeting of the Sub-regional Committee on the Integration of Women in Development. ECA/LUSAKA MULPOC – Harare, February 1987.

19 Tanzania country paper presented by the Ministry of Community Development, Culture Youth and Sports to the Fifth Meeting of the Sub-regional Committee on the Integration of Women in Development. ECA/LUSAKA MULPOC – Harare, February, 1987.

20 Kenya country paper presented by Women's Bureau, Ministry of Culture and Social Services to the Fifth Meeting of the Sub-regional Committee on the Integration of Women in Development. ECA/LUSAKA MULPOC – Harare, February, 1987.

21 G. Cornia, R. Jolly, and F. Steward, *Adjustment with a Human Face: Protecting the Vulnerable and Promoting Growth*. Oxford University Press, 1987.

22 WHO, *Preventing the Tragedy of Maternal Deaths*, A report on the International Safe Motherhood Conference – Nairobi, Kenya, February 1987 (sponsored by World Bank, WHO and UNFPA).

23 UNICEF, *Within Human Reach: A Future for Africa's Children*, UNICEF Report, 1985.

24 *Ibid.*

25 World Bank, *Annual Report*, 1987, p.79.

26 ILO/INSTRAW, op. cit.

[27] *Implementation of the Nairobi Forward Looking Strategies for the Advancement of Women*, Report of the Secretary-General A/42/528, 14 September, 1987.

[28] Tanzania country paper presented to the Fifth Meeting of the Subregional Committee on the Integration of Women, op. cit.

[29] ECA Report of the 5th Meeting of the West African Sub-regional Committee for the Integration of Women in Development – ECA/MULPOC/NIA/87/V/IWD, March, 1987.

[30] Karanja, op. cit.

[31] UN, *Report of the Secretary-General on the Critical Economic Situation in Africa: United Nations Programme of Action for African Economic Recovery and Development, 1986–1990*, A/42/560, 1 October, 1987.

Impact of Africa's Economic Crisis on Youth

INTERNATIONAL LABOUR ORGANIZATION (ILO)/JOBS AND SKILLS PROGRAMME FOR AFRICA (JASPA)

Africa is going through a very severe economic recession and the youth in particular seem to be the first victims of the crisis. In normal times, the human potentials of youth are expected to contribute to economic development and nation-building but given the social and economic disarray in the region, they are increasingly viewed as threats to harmonious social development because of massive unemployment, marginalization, delinquency, crime and drug abuse among this group.

According to the internationally accepted definition, youth constitute the population between 15 and 24 years of age. This working definition of youth attempts to cover the transition period in life between dependent childhood and self-reliant adulthood, the age range in which the majority of young people join the labour force and form separate households. Youth thus defined account for approximately 20 per cent of Africa's total population and 30 per cent of the regional labour force.[1] Hence, the African youth represent at present a non-negligible group of about 112.4 million people, of whom an estimated 65.0 million are economically active.

Demographic Picture

Africa is the region with the highest rate of population growth in the world. Whereas in the rest of the developing world, the 1970s witnessed a beginning of the process of demographic transition (i.e., a slow process whereby fertility rates decrease following an earlier decline in mortality rates), the population growth in Africa continues to accelerate and is expected to do so for the next couple of decades.

The causes of high fertility rates are multiple. Africa consists essentially of agrarian societies which are characterized by widespread illiteracy, relatively high rates of infant mortality, early ages of first child-bearing and where family labour constitutes the predominant mode of employment. In this context, there does not seem to exist any economic gain to the family from lowering fertility because children provide their parents over their lifetime with more economic resources than they receive, creating a kind of "inter-generational transfer"[2] in favour of the parents. Hence, high rates of fertility merely reflect an economically rational behaviour, as the control over a sufficient reserve of family labour is one of the key factors for economic prosperity in small-scale agriculture.

Table 1: Population and labour force in Africa

Variable	1970	1980	1985	1991	2000
Total population (million)	360.8	479.5	554.9	645.8	871.8
Child dependency ratio	85.9	86.8	87.1	87.5	85.6
Urban population (million)	81.2	129.3	164.7	210.8	340.8
Labour force (million)	147.6	189.2	213.8	242.8	318.3
Adult literacy rate (per cent)	28.9	39.7	46.0	52.6	64.8

Source: "World Population Prospects", United Nations, New York, 1986.
"Economically Active Population", ILO, Geneva, 1986.
"A Summary Statistical Review of Education in the World", UNESCO, Paris, 1984.

Table 2: Proportion of youth in total population

Region	1950	1975	Percentage 1985	2000	2025
Africa	18.8	18.9	19.1	19.3	20.7
Latin America	19.0	19.7	20.2	19.0	16.4
Asia	18.8	19.0	20.7	17.6	14.8
Industrialized countries	17.2	17.0	15.9	13.7	12.9

Source: Report V of the 1986 International Labour Conference on Youth, ILO, Geneva, 1986.

As table 1 indicates, the population in the region approximated 555 million in 1985 and is growing at a rate of 3.1 per cent per annum, which implies a doubling every 23 years. Of course, the record differs from country to country. Gabon, for example, has a moderate demographic growth rate of about 1 per cent while the population in Kenya and Zimbabwe grow at the phenomenal rate of 4 per cent per annum.

Prolonged high demographic rates of growth affect the age structure of the population, and today there is a very large proportion of children in the African population. Because of this demographic momentum, Africa is the only region in the world where the proportion of youth population in the future will be larger than it is at present. The child dependency ratio measures the number of dependents, aged between 0 and 14 years, that every 100 potential economically active persons, aged 15–64 years, have to support. For the purpose of comparison, it is interesting to notice that in 1985 the child dependency ratio equalled 66 for Latin America, 57 for Asia and 33 for the industrialized world.[3] A high and increasing dependency ratio means that an ever-increasing proportion of national income needs to be committed to subsistence consumption, reducing the savings propensity[4] and hence the future growth potentials of the economy. Indeed, simple demographic arithmetic suggests that unmet basic human needs in Africa, such as food, health, education and employment are very likely to increase over time.

Rural-Urban Migration

The demographic picture of the region is further characterized by massive emigration from the countryside. Although the region is the least urbanized in the world, it is becoming urban at an alarming rate. The growth rate of the urban population exceeds twice the growth rate of the rural population. The degree of urbanization has increased from 15.7 per cent in 1950 to 29.7 per cent in 1985 and is expected to reach the level of 50.0 per cent in the year 2017.

It is estimated that in 1950 some 0.6 million people migrated from rural areas to urban centres. In 1985, the rural exodus is estimated to have increased to 3.3 million people or 0.8 per cent of the rural population. The internal migration rate is expected to attain 1.0 per cent by the end of the century, representing some 5.5 million people.[5]

In addition, rural-urban migration is a selective phenomenon in the sense that migrants are predominantly young, unmarried and relatively well-educated males. Hence, urban sex ratios in the region (i.e., the number of males per 100 females) normally range between 120 and 140, and sometimes reach the level of 200 for the younger-age cohorts. Still, urban sex ratios show a tendency to decline over time, mainly because enhanced educational opportunities for girls induce more female migration so that the sex disequilibrium in urban centres will gradually be phased out during the next few decades.

Thus, the degree of urbanization is markedly higher for youth than for adults. The Department of International Economic and Social Affairs of the United Nations Secretariat estimates that 35.9 per cent of all African youth were urbanized in 1984, compared to an urbanization rate of 29.1 per cent for the entire population.[6] The same study estimates that the urban youth in the region is growing by 4.9 per cent per year, compared to an annual increase of 1.9 per cent for the rural youth. Consequently, 47.4 per cent of youth is expected to be urbanized by the year 2000, against a projected figure of 39.1 per cent for the total population.

A rural exodus of this magnitude is of course very detrimental for balanced development, in particular in economies where agriculture constitutes the predominant sector. Young farmers have indeed a very important role to play in the process of technological change in rural Africa since they are the most receptive to improved farming systems.

Youth Unemployment

The measurement of labour force participation rates in developing countries poses some conceptual problems. The age at which people enter and leave the labour force is subject to a series of cultural, social and economic factors like income levels, fertility rates, extent of schooling, degree of urbanization, employment opportunities, etc. In rural areas children often engage in economic activities from a very early age while urban children usually start later. The age of retirement is generally open-ended since very few people have access to a formal pension scheme. Hence, for practical reasons, the labour force estimates of ILO refer to the population aged 10 years and above.

Table 1 shows that the labour force in the region approximated 214 million in 1985 and is growing at a rate of 2.6 per cent per year. In absolute numbers, this means that at present some 5.8 million new jobs have to be created annually in order to stabilize the employment situation in Africa. By the end of the century, some 9.4 million additional jobs will be required to achieve this objective. Taking into account an annual replacement rate of 0.5 per cent of the labour force, it can be estimated that currently some 7 million young people join the African labour force every year and this figure will be up to almost 11 million by the year 2000. Urban labour markets in particular will be under severe pressure since they will have to absorb an ever-increasing proportion of the growing labour force because of the accelerating rural-urban migration.

The above figures confirm that the provision of productive employment for millions of young persons constitutes one of the most intractable problems facing African countries in the 1980s and beyond.

The unemployment situation in Africa is already reaching alarming levels and the youth appear to be bearing a disproportionate share of the burden. The measurement of unemployment is subject to serious data constraints, but it seems that a person under 25 years of age has about three times as many chances of being unemployed as a person over 25, which means that between one-half and two-thirds of the total number of unemployed in African countries belong to the age cohort of 15–24 years. In Mauritius, for example, youth accounted for 66.1 per cent of the country's unemployed in 1982, while in the Seychelles they accounted for 59.1 per cent in 1985.[7]

Furthermore, the general pattern is that unemployment among teenagers is more severe than among young adults. Sizeable variations also exist according to gender, and girls usually suffer from higher rates of unemployment than boys. This pattern is clearly illustrated by the Seychelles, which is among the best documented cases in Africa. Total employment in this country virtually stagnated between 1980 and 1985 so that the overall unemployment rate increased from 5.2 to 22.5 per cent of the labour force. Moreover, table 3 shows that the youth has borne the brunt of the problem. Indeed, the unemployment rate for teenagers increased by 31.4 percentage points between 1983 and 1985 while the unemployed became increasingly concentrated among the female labour force, young girls in particular, whose unemployment rate soared to 61 per cent in 1985.

Table 3: Seychelles: Unemployment rates by sex and age (in percentage)

Age group	Both sexes 1983	Both sexes 1985	Male 1983	Male 1985	Female 1983	Female 1985
15–19	17.4	48.8	17.6	35.4	17.2	61.0
20–24	16.6	19.5	13.4	18.5	20.4	20.7
25 +	13.7	13.6	11.1	9.8	18.4	19.6
Total	15.4	22.5	14.3	16.2	16.6	31.6

Source: Derived from "Yearbook of Labour Statistics 1986", ILO, Geneva, 1986.

Thus, the youth are the first to suffer from rising unemployment during periods of recession because they represent the new labour force recruits. They are therefore one of the most vulnerable groups in the society.

But statistics on unemployment show only the tip of the iceberg. The notion of unemployment in African countries is to a large extent invalid because of the absence of a system of unemployment benefits. Most able-bodied persons have engaged in income-earning activities of some kind or other because their very survival depends on it. Although open unemployment is a serious and growing phenomenon, the problem of employment in the African context is primarily that of the "working poor". The prevalence of underemployment is approximately three times as serious as that of open unemployment,[8] so that the root problem is low-productivity employment, not unemployment. The majority of the active population works hard and long hours but is underemployed and therefore earns less than a basic needs income.

Employment Promotion for Youth

Conceptually, there exist two different approaches to the problem of youth employment. The first one views youth unemployment as a transient phenomenon which sorts itself out once the higher age-group is entered. According to this "employability-gap" argument,[9] youth are unemployed because they are too young, too inexperienced and physically or socially too immature to be competitive on the labour markets. The thesis of the employability-gap is supported by sharp declines in unemployment rates through the successive age cohorts. According to the second approach, youth unemployment reveals a structural weakness in the economy and is part and parcel of the overall employment problem. Although the problems for youth are unique, in the sense that a first job is important in making social contacts and in gaining work experience – two factors that determine success in future employment – the second approach argues that the fight against youth unemployment cannot be disassociated from the fight against unemployment as a whole. Given the structural nature of Africa's economic crisis, the second view is likely to be closer to the truth than the first one.

Five different types of measures can be adopted for alleviating the problem of youth employment. The first one consists in absorbing the educated youth in the modern sector, whereby the government generally plays the role of employer of last resort. But such guaranteed employment schemes are bound to fail because of budgetary constraints, overstaffing and declining labour productivities, while their ultimate impact remains negligible compared to the number of new labour force recruits.

The second measure attempts to decrease the supply of labour through early retirement schemes or through an extension of the legal minimum working age. Because of the steepness of the demographic pyramid in most African countries, it would be necessary to bring the retirement age down to about 40 years to have any significant impact on youth employment. This hardly seems to be a financially and politically feasible solution. Extending compulsory education, on the other hand, does not seem feasible because of budgetary constraints facing most African countries.

A third set of measures gives financial incentives, in the form of wage subsidies or tax rebates, for enterprises that recruit youngsters. But formal wage employment in the region represents only 10 per cent of the total labour force, and private sector wage employment represents probably less than half of it. In addition, there exists already a strictly enforced policy of wage restraints in most countries, so that the possible impact of such measures will at best be very limited. Moreover, such incentives rarely create additional jobs, but merely substitute young for adult employees.

A fourth approach consists in special employment programmes for youth. Since the 1960s, numerous programmes have been launched to curb unemployment among young people. For example, there is the Workers' Brigade in Ghana, the Farm Settlements Schemes in Nigeria, the Young Pioneer Scheme in Malawi, the National Youth Service in Kenya, Farming Brigades in Botswana, Somalia's Agricultural Crash Programme, Zambia's Rural Reconstruction Centres, the Corps of Volunteers for Development in Cote d'Ivoire, the Young Pioneers in Benin, etc. Most of the programmes have attempted either to instill civil discipline, to impart skills, to provide temporary employment or combine these objectives.[10] Unfortunately, only a few of them have been successful because the majority of those schemes have often been hastily created without a clearly defined set of objectives and without adequate human and financial resources. In addition, there is still a tendency for governments to treat youth issues primarily as a social problem instead of an economic one, which is reflected by the institutional set-up of Youth Departments within the Ministries of Culture, Social Affairs or Sports.

The major causes of failure of special youth programmes seem to comprise: (i) the displacement of people into a very different environment by transferring, for instance, urban-born youth to rural areas in so-called "back-to-the-land" projects; (ii) the unnecessary capital intensity of the schemes like the uneconomic mechanization of agriculture; (iii) the "feather-bedding" of youth through food provision, free accommodation, and monthly allowances; (iv) the artificial separation of young agriculturalists from experienced farmers; (v) the focus on unmarried youth who cannot rely on family labour; and (vi) the operation of centralized systems with an excessive number of supervisory staff.

Moreover, the direct employment effects of such schemes have been small because young people are seldom able to start their own farm or business because they lack access to land, experience, credit and marketing services. In addition, special youth programmes, successful or not, remain embryonic and the number of jobs involved is insignificant when set against the annual number of school-leavers. They often involve less than one per cent of the target group, and it seems inefficient and inequitable to offer youth access to resources (e.g., tractorization, irrigation, credit, etc.) which are denied to the majority of farmers. Hence, a more direct approach to small-scale agricultural development is likely to yield higher social and economic returns on a sustainable basis. But the neglect of rural development has kept returns for agricultural labour low, has reduced its power to retain youngsters in rural areas and the sector is unlikely to be attractive to the growing segment of urban-born youth.

The fifth measure for alleviating youth unemployment consists in school curricula reform and job training programmes. Generally, there exists a mismatch between supply of and demand for labour. The education and training system is often too academic, fostering preferences for white-collar jobs and wrong attitudes towards agricultural and manual work. In fact, formal education of a general nature is often seen by parents and pupils alike as their best hope of getting out of agriculture and poverty. Table 4 gives the distribution of second-level enrolment by type of education in Africa for the period 1965–1980. It appears that the importance of general education has increased from 80.1 to 86.7 per cent while that of vocational education has dwindled from 14.0 to 8.7 per cent. The excess supply of general education has become very obvious since the onset of the 1980s, and a slowing down in the growth of the number of students enrolled in secondary and tertiary

Table 4: Structure of second-level enrolment by type of education in Africa (in percentage)

Type of education	1965	1970	1975	1980
General education	80.1	82.9	86.2	86.7
Teacher training	6.0	4.2	4.3	4.5
Vocational training	13.9	12.9	9.5	8.8
Total	100.0	100.0	100.0	100.0

Source: "A Summary Statistical Review of Education in the World", UNESCO, Paris, 1984.

education has generally been noted since 1980. Moreover, the absolute number of the school population has dropped in a few countries including Benin, Rwanda, Senegal and Togo.[11]

In response, vocational content and direct employable skills are being incorporated into school syllabi. Agriculture, forestry, technical drawing, woodwork, metalwork and home economics are made compulsory subjects in many countries. But there are still a number of major limitations. Such courses are generally scheduled too late in the educational cycle so that the drop-outs do not benefit; they occupy too little time and the teaching programme is being over-crowded; they are dispensed in a too theoretical manner and the practical implementation is usually ineffective due to the scarcity of qualified teachers and because of high costs in terms of equipment and materials.

An additional aspect of vocational training schools is their focus on a limited number of standard trades and skills (such as masonry and carpentry for boys and knitting and sewing for girls) that easily leads to a glut on the labour markets. Another aspect of vocational training institutions is that they initially cater for drop-outs and primary school-leavers. But over time the entry requirements invariably rise because of the "bumping effect" or the "diploma disease". The qualifications are raised, not because of the intrinsic job requirements, but as a screening or rationing device because private benefits from additional education, be it technical or academic, consists in enhancing the probability for the individual of securing a formal sector job. Thus, the vocationalization of the education and training system is still faced with the enormous challenge to temper the demand for academically oriented education in view of obtaining a white-collar job.

Synopsis of Country Case Studies

This section reviews some recent experiences in several African countries in the field of youth employment promotion. It is a synopsis of the country papers that have been presented during JASPA's recent regional workshop on Youth Employment Promotion in Africa (November, 1986).

(a) Burkina Faso

The demographic picture of Burkina Faso is characterized by the important flows of migrants, both internal (rural exodus) and external (emigration). It is estimated that the latter equals one-third of the natural increase of the population. School enrolment rates are relatively low compared to other Sahelian countries. Burkina Faso has initiated a number of programmes aimed at relieving the youth employment problem. The training of young farmers is one of the major aspects of the thorough reform of the country's education and training system. In addition, training centres for rural craftsmen have been set up throughout the country. They provide a seven-month training course after which the graduate settles in his or her village of origin and receives continued extension services, including tools, raw materials and credit. Burkina Faso is also implementing a series of development activities in the form of special public works programmes. More recently, a special Ministry of Farmers' Affairs have been created in an effort to promote effective and integrated rural development. Also, a Popular National Service has been introduced whereby youngsters are enrolled for one year in training and production activities after which they will be employed permanently through the National Employment Bureau. Wage employment in the modern sector remains very limited and public sector employment is stagnant because of budgetary constraints. New recruitment is being promoted through early retirement schemes and a policy of Burkanization of formal wage employment. Informal sector enterprises that recruit apprentices receive the services of a training centre for urban craftsmen and technicians.

(b) Cameroon

Cameroon, with a population of about 10 million people, is classified among the middle-income oil-exporting countries. Despite a high demographic growth rate, per capita incomes increased by approximately 3 per cent per annum over the past two decades. To a large extent, the industrial sector has been the engine of growth. As a consequence, the employment situation in Cameroon is markedly better than in the majority of African countries. For example, the civil service recruited some 2,000 university graduates in 1985, at a time when many countries had to retrench thousands of public sector workers. Nevertheless, the youth appear to be the worst affected group by the growing employment problem in the country. For urban youth, the efforts of the Government have focused on the Cameroonization of formal wage employment, on the promotion of small-scale enterprises and on the design of a more appropriate system of post-primary education and training. In rural areas, a civic service has been introduced which focuses on agricultural training and whereby graduates settle either in their village of origin, in pioneer villages or on settlement schemes. A novel feature of this civic service is that it offers training not only through rural centres but also through mobile units that provide extension services to self-employed youth.

(c) Côte d'Ivoire

Côte d'Ivoire is the country in Africa with the highest rate of population growth because the high natural demographic growth is complemented by important inflows of migrant workers from neighbouring countries. The country allocates a considerable share of its annual budgetary expenditure on education so that school enrolment rates have increased substantially during the past two decades. But the modern sector does not employ more than 10 per cent of the country's labour force so that unemployment among educated youth is on the rise. The informal sector, on the other hand, is absorbing large numbers of urban-born youth and rural-urban migrants. The degree of urbanization is very high and will soon reach the level of 50 per cent. Hence, the rural economy is losing its able bodied workers at an alarming rate. Therefore, past efforts to alleviate the problem of youth employment have focused on back-to-the land projects, either through the civic service or through settlement schemes. Such activities have absorbed enormous amounts of financial resources without producing a lasting effect on the employment situation of youth. In urban areas, employment promotion for youth has been very much oriented towards the modern sector, through easy access to credit and a policy of Ivoirization, while the employment potentials of the informal sector have been relatively neglected. Therefore, new measures envisaged in the Youth Decade put the emphasis on self-employment and include the set-up of Youth Production Centres in urban areas. In addition, a major reform of the education and training system is under way. But the major feature of the activities that have been programmed during the Youth Decade is the improvement of the living and working conditions for youth in rural areas.

(d) Mauritania

Mauritania has a relatively small population which is becoming urbanized at a rapid rate. The rural population consists of nomads on the one hand and settled farmers and fishermen on the other. The relative importance of the former has dwindled since the late 1960s when the long cycle of severe drought set in. A special effort has been undertaken to develop the country's human resources so that primary and secondary school enrolment rates are increasing rapidly. However, the size of the formal sector remains very small so that only a fraction of the school-leavers obtain a job as wage employees. In addition, the current Economic and Financial Recovery Plan 1985–1988 puts a stop on public sector recruitment so that increases in formal wage employment will result only from the policy of Mauritanization. Because of rapid urbanization, the informal sector is becoming the single most important employer of the country's youth. Self-employment for young entrepreneurs is being promoted through a special fund, called FIRVA, which gives priority access to credit and technical assistance for youngsters who intend to establish a micro-enterprise. In the rural economy, the focus for employment creation lies on the agricultural development of the Senegal river basin and on fisheries activities. Such efforts are being supported by special public works programmes and by food-for-work schemes.

Conclusions

Massive youth unemployment constitutes one of the most obvious symptoms of economic maldevelopment and social mal-distribution within African societies. The main thesis of this paper is that the problem of youth employment is part and parcel of the overall employment problem. Special initiatives targeted on youth are important but cannot compensate for serious shortcomings in social and economic policy-making. New patterns of development in the region are therefore of paramount importance. Demographic factors and educational systems are not the fundamental causes of the problem, although they tend to contribute significantly to the aggravation of it.

The absorptive capacity of the agricultural and informal sectors will be of critical importance in solving the colossal employment problem facing the region. Hence, two crucial questions arise, namely whether those sectors have the potential for income and employment growth of the magnitude required, and whether official measures of encouragement will be capable of giving the necessary impetus. These questions touch upon the complex nature of development and there is no quick and easy solution to the huge employment problem of youth. But the current state of knowledge and experience in African countries indicate a number of valuable contributions that can be initiated in order to alleviate youth unemployment and underemployment. Such measures include:

(a) facilitating access to land for youth in a gerontocratic society or a dualistic agrarian economy;
(b) vocationalizing further the contents of the education and training system, with constant monitoring through tracer studies of graduates;
(c) emphasizing non-formal training for farmers and informal entrepreneurs. Considering the heavy subsidies for formal education, it seems unjustified to make the informal and rural sectors bear all training costs. Hence, the targeting of expenditure on education and training needs to be improved;
(d) applying incomes policies geared towards the economic and social promotion of technical and manual jobs, either in wage or self-employment;
(e) instituting a system of integrated pricing (comprising wages, interest rates, foreign exchange, agricultural commodities, public goods and services) whereby labour absorption in the economy is maximized and the rural exodus minimized;
(f) focusing on the appropriate design and efficient management of special youth employment schemes before they are launched on a large scale. Such initiatives should be better targeted on clearly defined groups of youth and should make an explicit distinction between male and female youth because they often face very different situations on the labour market;
(g) undertaking more analytical work on employment patterns for inclusion into national planning endeavours;
(h) devising a different institutional set-up whereby matters of youth employment move from the periphery to the centre of economic policy-making in African countries.

Finally, it should be noted that the balance of evidence suggests that the fundamental causes of youth unemployment are not associated with the attitudes of youngsters. The mismatch between job aspirations of youth and the realities they face is not so much based on their incorrect understanding or lack of awareness of those realities, but is due to the extremely slow adjustment process of social preferences. It seems that attitudes are slowly beginning to change and school-leavers show more realism with respect to their professional aspirations if no suitable job opportunities are offered. Hence, measures that promote youth employment are likely to become more effective in the future, provided they are properly designed and well-targeted.

Notes

1 ILO, *Economically Active Population, Estimates and Projections 1950–2025*, Geneva, 1986.

2 J. Caldwell, *Theory of Fertility Decline*, Academic Press, London, 1982.

3 United Nations, *World Population Prospects*, Estimates and projections as assessed in 1984, New York, 1986.

4 A recent ECA/ADB study on "Domestic resource mobilization in Africa" concluded that in recent years the savings potential has generally deteriorated compared to the early 1960s. *Economic Report on Africa 1987*, ECA/ADB, Addis Ababa, 1987.

5 Those figures are derived from the United Nations *World Population Prospects*, ibid.

6 United Nations, *The Situation of Youth in the 1980s and Prospects and Challenges for the year 2000*, New York, 1986.

[7] ILO, *Yearbook of Labour Statistics 1986*, Geneva, 1986.

[8] J. Vandemoortele, "Youth and Employment in Sub-Saharan Africa: Some Facts and Figures," paper presented to JASPA's regional workshop on Youth Employment Promotion in African Countries, Buea, Cameroon, 24–28 November 1986.

[9] ILO/JASPA, *Youth Employment and Youth Employment Programmes in African Countries*. A comparative sub-regional study. Addis Ababa, 1986.

[10] D. Freedman, "Youth Employment Problems and Programmes in Africa", in: *The Challenge of Employment and Basic Needs in Africa*. ILO/JASPA, Oxford University Press, Nairobi, 1986.

[11] J.C. Eicher, "Education and Employment in French-speaking Africa", paper presented to JASPA's regional workshop on Youth Employment Promotion in African Countries, Buea, Cameroon, 24–28 November 1986.

The State of Africa's Children: Priorities for Action

UNICEF

The infant and child mortality rates in some African countries are now estimated to be some of the highest in the world. Worse still, Africa is the only continent in the world where, if past trends continue, the number of infants and children dying each year is expected to increase absolutely until the end of the century. In every other continent, they are expected to decline. The tragic consequence of decline in economic performance and adjustment in many African countries is that some of the eight small African children who die every minute today could have probably been saved through low cost health programmes if these and other setbacks had not occurred.

This paper briefly analyzes the impact of world economy and adjustment policies, particularly in terms of their effects on the living conditions of African children. The paper indicates that unless the human dimensions of the economic crisis are given a focus of attention the situation of African children in the years to come will worsen. Low-cost but effective opportunities exist today to save the lives of millions of children. If these opportunities are not properly used over 4.4 million African children will die in 1988 and will continue to die each year in the years to come.

Socio-Economic Trends

Socio-economic trends in the 1960's and early 1970's were generally positive, often sharply so, in many African countries. Per capita incomes rose, though often with biases against rural areas and urban slums. During the same period many African countries expanded health and educational services through deliberate health policies. Water and sanitation programmes expanded. This resulted in the improvement of child welfare over the two decades or so of independence; and infant and child mortality rates declined. (See Annex 1) However, these trends have not continued into the 1980's.

A number of internal and external factors are responsible for the deterioration of human condition in most African countries. Large numbers of the African population have been affected by recurrent drought, locust, chronic food shortages, a rapidly growing population, war and South Africa's acts of destabilization in the case of SADCC countries.

On top of the difficult climate and political conditions over the last 15 years Africa has witnessed an equally bad international economic and financial environment. In 1985 UNICEF issued a report which showed that as a result of world recession and economic set-backs, a very real deterioration was taking place in the lives of children. (UNICEF 1985)

In 1986/87 there was a slump in Africa's export trade unprecedented perhaps since the great depression resulting in a catastrophic drop in values of exports. This has resulted in the escalation in the deficits of the current account of many countries. Africa's foreign debt dramatically increased. Many countries have had to resort to rescheduling exercises with only temporary relief for debt problems which often got worse later as arrears accumulated.

Money has been flowing out of Africa due to deteriorating terms of trade and a steep rise in interest rates, while at the same time the flow of money into the continent has declined (commercial bank lending has virtually ceased and aid stagnated in real terms). According to ODC policy focus of 1987, net financial flows from Africa to the IMF was $400 million in 1986. (ODC 1987).

The asymmetric nature of international trade and financial relations is such that any changes in the performance in industrialized countries is amplified in its effect on African economies. Countries that have been most vulnerable include those that heavily rely on imports (oil, machinery, raw materials and food), and are also excessively dependent on single or few primary commodities (eg. copper in Zambia) and those that are highly indebted.

On top of the difficult climate and political conditions and deterioration of the international environment, domestic policy failures in many African countries have contributed to the economic crisis. The domestic policies of many countries neglected the agricultural sector and the small scale producer (including women producers), overvalued exchange rates, formulated weak fiscal and monetary policies (which generated high inflation rates and created imbalances between different sectors of the economy and between rural and urban areas), subsidized consumption to please the urban population and nationalized profit making enterprises and quickly converted them into loss making public institutions dependent on financially weak central governments.

As a result GNP per capita average annual growth rate declined in many African countries. As countries imported goods and services at higher and higher costs and exported goods and services at lower and lower prices, their balance-of-payments worsened. Fiscal deficit increased with declining tax base and increasing Government expenditure.

The resulting imbalances led to increased economic difficulties and the need for economic adjustments in many countries. The majority of African countries, therefore, implemented policies for economic adjustment designed to repay debt, improve their balance-of-payments and reduce inflation. The economic difficulties were reinforced on the human side by the neglect of the human dimension in adjustment policies, especially for the urban poor. Government services and rural infrastructure deteriorated. There is increasing evidence that following a period of protracted recession and economic decline in the 1970's, and the neglect of human needs in the implementation of many adjustment policies in the 1980's adverse effects have increased on African children, women and other vulnerable population groups. The human crisis has included the increasing incidence of malnutrition among the poor, increasing unemployment, decline in the real incomes of the poor, and decline of Government expenditure in social services.

In many African countries, the rural population has often been hit by recurrent droughts revealing a long-term problem different from that caused by climate conditions. A combination of natural causes and man-made factors have created a historically unprecedented situation in some countries. Emergency relief operations and rehabilitation are often hampered by man-made constraints.

Moreover, war, internal unrest and destabilization have put many countries under stress. According to a UNICEF Report "Within Human Reach – A future for Africa's Children," civil unrest has affected almost one third of the countries of sub-Saharan Africa during the first decade. Some of these conflicts have continued unabated and unresolved for years, even decades – uprooting over 10 million people, destroying the fabric of rural traditional society, disrupting food production and national economies, diverting scarce national resources (i.e. $14 billion in 1982) to non-productive purposes and weakening governments' capacity to fulfill unmet basic needs of children and pursue sustained development.

According to a UNICEF Report, *Children on the Front Line*, children in Southern Africa are paying a heavy price due to the continued impact of apartheid, destabilization and warfare. By 1987 there were over 140,000 Angolan and Mozambican children under the age of five whose lives were lost as a consequence of war and destabilization. The human costs have also included hundreds of thousands of Angolan peasants displaced by war and the over 3.8 million Mozambicans at risk of famine. The economic costs are equally severe. The estimated total of the nine SADCC countries economic losses from the war, measured in terms of lost GDP was $US 25–30 billion for 1980–86. This is equivalent to the regions total annual production!

Chart 1: AFRICA UNDER STRESS:
THE OVERLAP OF WAR, DROUGHT AND APARTHEID
1984

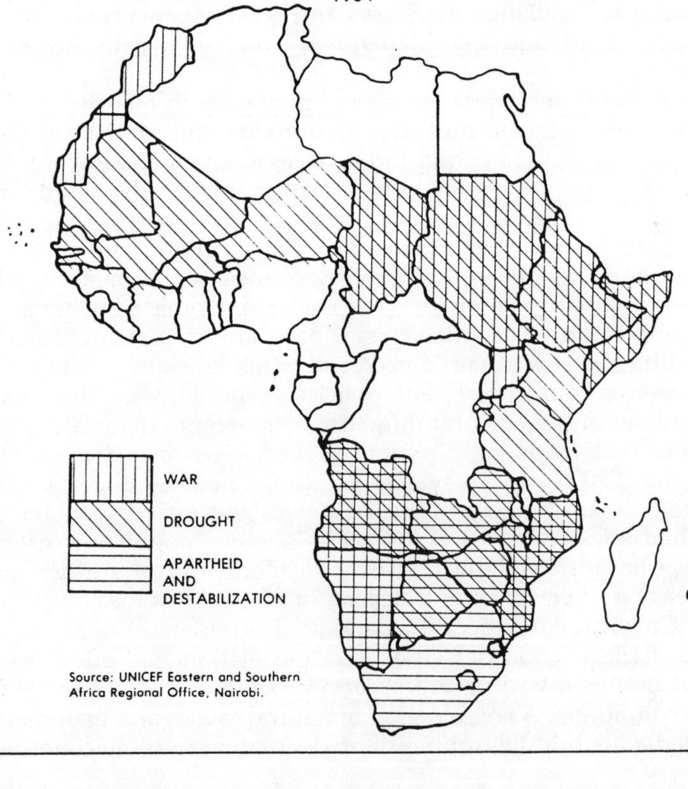

Source: UNICEF Eastern and Southern Africa Regional Office, Nairobi.

Situation of Children

Even though upward pressures have been selectively operating in many African countries (e.g. dramatic acceleration in child immunization in spite of the economic difficulties), the situation of children has in general been subject to very strong downward pressures due to the deteriorating socio-economic conditions discussed above.

Child Death

Magnitude of the Problem

The infant and child mortality rates in some African countries are now estimated to be among the highest in the world. Out of 33 countries with the highest Under Five Mortality Rate (U5MR) in 1986 (i.e., with U5MR of over 170), African countries accounted for 73%. It is believed that IMR has either gone up or remained static in many countries. According to UNICEF, *State of the World's Children Report, 1988*, about 4.4 million infants and children die per annum in Africa. Moreover, disturbing projections made by the UN Population Division indicate that if past trends continue, the number of under five children dying each year will increase to the point that Africa's share of all infant and child deaths in the world, without change, will increase from 30% to over 40% by the end of the century. (UNICEF, 1987).

Of these 4.4 million infant and child deaths – some 2.7 million were infants and 1.7 million child deaths. In Africa there is one child death for every one and one half infant death. About 168 of every 1000 children born in Africa die before reaching the age of five (compared to 18 in industrialized countries). About 104 of every 1000 children born in Africa die before reaching the age of one (compared to 14 in industrialized countries). The region with the highest infant and child mortality rates, Western Africa, has a mortality level that is about 20 times that of Northern Europe.

In 1950 Africa accounted for 15% of all infant and child deaths in the world. This percentage share has increased to 28% in 1980 and 31% in 1986. According to the estimates made by the UN Population Division, under five mortality rates in Africa have fallen from 332 in 1950 to 192 in 1980 and 168 in 1986. However, the decline is not keeping pace with the high birth rate. Therefore, despite the falling mortality rate the total number of infant and child deaths continued to rise from 3.8 million in 1950 to 4.3 million in 1980 and 4.4 million in 1986. Moreover, there are significant regional variations.

Regional Variations

In Eastern and Southern Africa, the mortality of children under five in 1986 ranges from less than 120 death per 1000 live births (Seychelles, Mauritius, Madagascar, Botswana, Kenya and Zimbabwe) to over 250 per 1000 live births (Ethiopia, Somalia, Malawi, Angola, Mozambique). (Annex 1)

The percentage annual reduction rates calculated over the periods 1960–80 and 1980–85 (see Table 1) indicates that these divergences between African countries has been growing. Mauritius, Botswana, Madagascar, and Zimbabwe have achieved higher and consistent reduction rates. It is interesting to note that after rapid progress during 1960–80, Comoros and Zambia have since slipped back.

Table 1: Under-Five Mortality Rate, Percentage Annual Reduction Rate* and GNP Per Capita Growth Rate in the East and Southern Africa Region 1960–1985

Country	Under-Five Mortality Rate 1960	1980	1985	Percentage Annual Reduction Rate 60–80	80–85	GNP Per Capita Growth Rate 65–80	80–85
Botswana	174	111	99	2.22	2.26	8.3	7.4
Burundi	258	214	200	0.93	1.34	1.4	−0.8
Comoros	261	150	135	2.73	2.09	−0.3	0.6
Ethiopia	294	262	257	0.57	0.38	0.2	−2.0
Kenya	208	136	121	2.10	2.31	1.9	−1.7
Lesotho	208	160	144	1.30	2.09	6.5	3.4
Madagascar	181	112	97	2.37	2.83	−1.9	−6.1
Malawi	362	298	275	0.97	1.59	1.5	−0.6
Mauritius	104	42	32	4.43	5.29	2.7	2.3
Mozambique	302	272	252	0.52	1.52	–	−13.6
Rwanda	248	230	214	0.38	1.43	1.8	−1.5
Somalia	294	262	257	0.57	0.38	−0.7	0.6
Swaziland	227	200	182	0.63	1.87	2.7	−1.1
Tanzania	248	201	183	1.05	1.86	–	−3.1
Uganda	224	188	178	0.87	1.09	−2.6	2.2
Zambia	228	148	135	2.14	1.82	−1.6	−4.1
Zimbabwe	180	134	121	1.46	2.02	1.6	0.0
E&S Region	255	208	195	1.01	1.34		

Source: UNICEF, 1988.
* Calculated using standard compound growth rates

It appears that countries that had relatively stable political systems without internal conflict or war, with limited adjustment problems seem to have achieved positive GNP per capita growth rate, strong health programmes and have managed to significantly and consistently reduce the mortality of children under five.

In Central and West Africa, in 1986, the under-five mortality rate varied from less than 120 deaths per 1000 live births (Sao Tome and Congo) to over 250 per 1000 live births (Mali, Sierra Leone, Gambia and Guinea). (Annex 1)

According to the percentage annual reduction rates, Cape Verde and Gabon have achieved consistent reductions. Countries such as Congo, Ghana, Cote d'Ivoire, Togo, Nigeria, Cameroon, Burkina Faso made significant progress and achieved higher annual reduction rates during 1960–80. However, their annual reduction rates have declined since then. (See Table 2)

Overall, during 1960–80 and 1980–85, Central and West African Countries seem to have achieved consistently higher annual reduction rates (1.85% and 1.77%) as compared to Eastern and Southern African countries (1.01% and 1.34%) respectively.

In brief, the differing experience in Africa shows that : (a) some countries have already managed to significantly reduce child death; (b) if the other African countries are also able to make similar effort, it is possible to make a major difference (i.e. about a million children could probably be saved annually); and (c) as this paper will later indicate low cost but effective actions exist for saving the lives of more children.

Table 2: Under-Five Mortality Rate, Percentage Annual Reduction Rate* and GNP Per Capita Growth Rate in the Central and West African Region 1960–1985

Country	Under-Five Mortality Rate 1960	1980	1985	Percentage Annual Reduction Rate 60–80	80–85	GNP Per Capita Growth Rate 65–80	80–85
Angola	346	261	242	1.40	1.50	–	0.1
Benin	310	211	193	1.91	1.77	0.2	0.1
Burkina Faso	388	260	245	1.98	1.18	1.3	−1.3
Cameroon	275	178	162	2.15	1.87	3.6	4.5
Cape Verde	213	114	95	3.08	3.58	5.0	−0.4
Central A. Republic	308	242	232	1.20	0.84	−0.2	−1.5
Chad	326	251	232	1.80	1.56	−2.3	1.8
Congo	241	133	122	2.93	1.71	3.8	4.9
Cote d'Ivoire	320	175	157	2.57	2.15	0.9	−5.2
Equatorial Guinea	315	242	223	1.31	1.62	–	–
Gabon	288	196	178	1.91	1.91	1.5	−1.2
Gambia	361	312	292	0.73	1.32	1.1	−2.8
Ghana	224	165	153	1.52	1.50	−2.2	−3.8
Guinea	346	279	259	1.07	1.48	0.8	−1.4
Guinea-Bissau	315	251	232	1.13	1.56	−1.5	1.9
Liberia	303	233	215	1.30	1.60	−1.4	−6.4
Mali	370	324	302	0.66	1.40	1.4	−3.0
Mauritania	310	242	223	1.23	1.62	0.1	−0.7
Niger	320	256	237	1.11	1.53	−2.1	−6.7
Nigeria	318	200	182	2.25	1.87	2.2	−7.3
Senegal	313	250	231	1.12	1.57	−0.6	0.0
Sierra Leone	357	324	302	1.01	1.40	1.1	−0.2
Togo	305	177	160	2.68	2.00	0.3	−5.6
Zaire	251	187	170	1.46	1.89	−2.1	−3.8
C&W Africa Region	309	213	195	1.85	1.77		

Source: UNICEF, 1988.
* Calculated using standard compound growth rates

Nutritional Status of Children

It is widely believed that the incidence of malnutrition among the urban and rural poor has increased. However, in many countries rising malnutrition has gone unnoticed due to lack of up-to-date and reliable data.

About 14% of infants in Africa are born each year weighing less than 2.5 Kgs., twice the proportion found in the industrialized countries. About 25% of children under five in Africa are suffering from protein energy malnutrition. Nearly one-third of the children between the ages of one and five in Africa have a low weight for their age.

In Africa nearly 60% of children under five suffer from nutritional anaemia compared to about 10% in the industrialized countries. About 44% of women of childbearing age in Africa suffer from nutritional anaemia, compared to about 10% in the industrialized countries. About 63% of pregnant women in Africa suffer from nutritional anaemia, compared to about 15% in the industrialized countries.

Table 3: The Nutritional Status of African Children (1985)

	Mils.	%
Prevalence of nutritional anaemia[a]		
Under fives	59	56
Women age 15–49	57	44
Pregnant women	18.4	63
Infants with low birth weight (1982)[b]	3.6	14
Protein energy malnutrition		
Under fives	26	25
Low weight-for-age children[c]		
Age in years		
1 year old		15
2 years old		35
3 years old		30
4 years old		24
5 years old		24

[a] Haemoglobin concentrate below WHO reference values for age, sex and pregnancy status.
[b] Weighing less than 2.5 Kgs at birth increases risk of difficulties in the first phase of a baby's life.
[c] The percentage of children falling two standard deviations below the United Nations Centre for Health Statistics reference standard.

Coverage of Health and Water Services

The percentage of rural populations with access to health services is very low. According to WHO estimates, in 1983 only about 34% of all births in Africa are attended by trained health personnel. There are about 650 maternal deaths per 100,000 births in Africa. Therefore, a large proportion of women die each year from causes related to pregnancy and childbirth, leaving a large number of infants without mothers.

According to WHO estimates in 1983 only 31% of under five children living in the rural areas have access to clean water – the lowest rate in the world. The corresponding figure for the urban areas is 83%. During the same period only 18% of children under five living in the rural areas have access to adequate sanitation.

Primary School Enrolment and Literacy

Although many African countries have made significant efforts in the 1960's and 1970's to achieve the goals of Universal Primary Education and Literacy, the problems of low enrolment and high female illiteracy continue to persist.

According to UNESCO estimates female children accounted for 44% of total enrolment in primary schools. Nearly 33% of children of primary school age, i.e., 38 million are not attending school. The corresponding figure for out of school youth (aged 12–17 years old) is 61%. In 1985 65% of the female population aged 15 and over were illiterate, i.e. 100 million illiterate adults. Therefore illiteracy has continued to be one of the major problems facing African children and women.

Education systems in Africa have experienced severe budgetary constraints in the 1980's due to the problems of adjustment. This has caused serious reversals to the positive gains of the 1960's and 1970's. Countries are, therefore, re-examining their educational policies and operations. Even though primary education and literacy has lost momentum in many countries in Africa, the potential exists for restoring momentum in spite of constrained resources.

In the first place more efforts could be made to save costs at the primary level. Second, it has been recognized that a small switch in resources from tertiary level to primary could greatly help to expand primary education and make possible the achievements of universal primary schooling in some countries. African countries need national political commitment to re-examine their educational policies and to establish effective administrative systems at national and sub-national levels to expand UPEL despite the current financial limitations. They also need to focus their priorities on the quality and relevance of education.

Children Living in Absolute Poverty

Under current projections, recovery from the commodity price collapse of the 1980's is expected to be slow and painful for many African countries. As a result, by 1995, per capita income in countries of Sub-Saharan Africa is forecast to be 20% below the 1980 level. Worse yet, in the year 2000, per capita income in the lower income non-fuel primary exporting countries is expected to be at least 10% below their levels in 1965. (North-South Institute 1987).

According to estimates by the World Bank and UN Population Division, nearly 60% of children under five in the rural areas of Africa are living in absolute poverty in 1985. The corresponding estimate for urban areas is 29%. These estimates of poverty and income are not expected to improve under current conditions in many African countries. Therefore, responding to the problems of critical poverty and its more visible manifestations in the form of high incidence of malnutrition is one of the major priorities in Africa.

In many African countries a decline in GDP per capita was accompanied by a decline in average real household income. Real resources at the household level have declined due to the low level of subsistence production, decline in money income (wages, self employment, transfers), and an increase in the rate of inflation (food and other basic items).

However, the relationship between income distribution and decline in GDP per capita is not known as there have been few studies conducted to investigate this issue. However, available data indicate that: the poor in the subsistence sector may not be affected; those at the bottom of the income distribution scale in the monetary sector of the economy are affected.

What happens when real resources decline at the household level? Experience shows that consumption needs in the area of food, clothing, and to an extent health, education, child care and water and sanitation decline. Poor households spending 60–80% of their income on food respond to decline in incomes by reducing expenditure on food. Therefore, for the vulnerable population groups trends in food prices are very important. In some countries food prices have dramatically increased due to reduction in food subsidies, increasing producers prices and decontrol of consumer prices.

Government Expenditure on Social Services

The decline in economic performance has affected government expenditure on health, education, supplementary feeding and food subsidies, child care services, water and environmental sanitation programmes. In many African countries the decline in Government expenditure on the social services resulted in the slow down of the coverage of health services including low levels of immunization coverage, and a general decline in the quality of health services because of low staff morale, lack of supervision and limited government capacity to mobilize communities. Lack of essential drugs in the rural areas has become a major constraint to the success of Primary Health Care in Africa.

Family and Community Circumstances

It is believed that the decline in economic performance has affected family and community characteristics, especially the mothers' level of health, skills and time.

The relationship between mother's health, her nutritional status and reproductive behaviour and the health of her child is quite obvious. It is also widely recognized that mother's level of education, her skills and knowledge affect child feeding and rearing practices, child care and clinic attendance for immunization and growth monitoring, etc. Mother's education might not have been affected in the short turn. However, the level of education and skills of future mothers has been affected. Young girls are the first to be withdrawn from school due to the inability of poor households to pay school fees, to help work in the field and to take care of the younger siblings.

During periods of economic decline many mothers will increase their labour to compensate for decline in income of the head of the household. Under normal circumstances many mothers are already overworked working in the fields and looking after their children and families at home. The problem of low frequency of child feeding due to lack of time for child care and high maternal workload has therefore been accentuated by economic decline in many African countries.

The Positive Upward Pressures and a Ray of Hope

At the same time, positive, upward pressures have been selectively operating in many African countries. This provides a ray of hope and solid experience upon which a much more promising future can be developed for African children.

(a) some countries have given clear and increased attention to social and human factors in their adjustment policies. e.g Zimbabwe, Botswana, recently Ghana, Guinea and Madagascar.

The Botswana adjustment experience during 1983–86 in response to the drought problem has shown that policies can be designed to protect the poor and at the same time promote growth. Programmes designed to protect the poor can be implemented on a wide scale, and be effective. Botswana belongs to this category with its relief measures and well established National

Nutritional Surveillance and Early Warning Systems.

In Zimbabwe, programmes designed to protect the vulnerable groups, i.e., health, nutrition, education, support for small farmers, drought relief programme, supplementary feeding programme for 250,000 children, immunization and DDC Programmes were sustained or expanded during the process of adjustment. Health expenditure continued to increase. As a result of these measures, the economic costs of recession, drought and adjustment process were not translated into substantial human costs in Zimbabwe. The Zimbabwean experience shows that the adjustment package adopted managed to secure continued improvements in the well-being of children (decline in IMR, malnutrition, increased coverage of immunization and use of ORT), while some of the long-term expansionary reforms initiated after independence contributed to resumption of growth.

(b) Many countries have undertaken a major expansion of low-cost, highly effective child survival and development actions focussed on reducing under 5 mortality and increasing child health protection and welfare.

In spite of the adverse consequences of the economic crisis many African countries are putting certain low-cost, but effective, child survival and protection actions into practice on a massive scale. As a result immunization coverage for children 12 months old increased in Eastern and southern Africa and Central and West Africa (See Table 4). The momentum towards achieving UCI by 1990 accelerated mainly during 1986 and 1987. By mid-1987 many African countries have achieved coverage of more than 50% for BCG, DPT and Polio.

Table 4: Immunization Coverage Rates: 1981–1986

Regions and Countries	12 months old children immunized against									
	BCG		DPT		POLIO		MEASLES		TETANUS*	
	81	86	81	86	81	86	81	86	81	86
Eastern and Southern Africa	40	55	30	43	25	43	33	43	17	26
Ethiopia	10	21	6	12	7	12	7	17	–	2
Rest of E&SA	51	66	39	54	32	54	42	53	17	34
Central and West Africa	31	42	21	21	20	21	40	26	12	19
Nigeria	23	30	24	14	24	14	55	16	11	11
Rest of C&WA	37	51	18	27	18	27	29	34	13	27

Source: UNICEF Statistical Review of the Situation of Children in the World, October 1987.

* Pregnant women immunized against tetanus.

The November 1987 review of UCI activities at UNICEF indicated that Egypt, Mauritius and Seychelles had already achieved UCI by 1987. Algeria, Morocco, Tunisia and Libya are close to achieving UCI targets. It is expected that Gambia, Rwanda, Swaziland, Gabon, Lesotho, Comoros, Congo, Kenya, and Cape Verde will achieve UCI by 1990. Another group of countries which has good possibilities to achieve the target of 75% coverage includes; Botswana, Sierra Leone, Malawi, Ivory Coast, Cameroon, Togo, Zambia, Zimbabwe and Madagascar. It is worthwhile to note that significant reductions in child deaths could take place in Africa through the universal application of immunizations and the use of ORT.(Oral Rehydration Technique)

(c) It is important to indicate that a number of significant developments to improve child welfare are taking place in Africa. For example, the OAU Summit meeting in July 1987 passed a landmark resolution on UCI in Africa. African Ministers of Health met in Bamako in September 1987 and made commitments for accelerating expansion of MCH through essential drugs for all. The first symposium of African artists, writers and intellectuals for CSD was held in Senegal on 20–23 March 1987. Excellent opportunities therefore exist today in Africa to build on the UCI infrastructure and to use the political priorities accorded in the regional meetings to improve child survival and development.

(d) Other areas of basic human needs have also been restructured and pushed ahead e.g. water and sanitation programmes, PHC and new initiatives for District Health Care, the Bamako initiative etc.

(e) Regional cooperation mechanisms such as the PTA, SADCC, etc. could provide good opportunities for discussing priority problems of African children and formulating sub-regional strategies to improve child welfare. In addition, there are a number of national, regional and continental plans and programmes designed to respond to the African economic crisis (see the Lagos Plan of Action, Accelerated Development in Sub-Saharan Africa, Agenda for Action and APPER) which could provide forums for responding to the human crisis.

Priorities for Action

The result for children is this war of conflicting general downward and selective upward pressures. Only country-by-country assessments can determine what the net result is on the situation of children. And only country-by-country action can help to deepen and extend the positive forces to protect children and to restore momentum in the expansion of basic services to meet the needs of all children and the provision of opportunity and some assistance to communities, to generate community actions and support.

UNICEF sees some reason for optimism. If many African countries press forward with certain low-cost but effective child survival and development actions, and if Bamako type initiatives are developed to strengthen PHC through the provision of essential drugs, it would be possible to reduce by half under five mortality rates by the year 2000 and to use this opportunity to strengthen basic services and to expand resources to meet basic human needs in general. Meeting essential human needs including household food security, health (PHC and MCH), primary education and literacy, etc., would in turn lay the foundation for restoring growth of household income and rural and urban and sustained economic growth.

Actions to Reduce Readily Avoidable Child Death

The lives of the majority of the 4.4 million African children who are dying each year could be saved. If the will exists African countries have the possibility of reducing Under Five Mortality Rate (U5MR) to achieve the goal of halving it by the year 2000. To achieve this goal, countries in the Eastern and Southern African Region have to reduce U5MR at an annual reduction rate of 5.86% over 1985–2000 (as compared to 1.01% achieved over 1960–80).

Table 5: The Expected Annual Reduction Rates Needed During 1985–2000 To Reduce Under-Five Mortality Rate (U5MR)*

Country	Under-Five Mortality Rate U5MR 1985	Target* 2000	Percentage Annual Reduction Rate 1985–2000
Botswana	99	56	3.78
Burundi	200	84	5.60
Comoros	135	75	3.84
Ethiopia	257	85	7.15
Kenya	121	68	3.77
Lesotho	144	68	4.84
Madagascar	97	56	3.60
Malawi	275	88	7.34
Mauritius	32	21	2.77
Mozambique	252	86	6.95
Rwanda	214	85	6.00
Somalia	257	85	7.15
Swaziland	182	75	5.77
Tanzania	183	84	5.08
Uganda	178	83	4.94
Zambia	135	74	3.93
Zimbabwe	121	67	3.86
E&S Region	195	79	5.86
Angola	242	85	6.77
Benin	193	84	5.40
Burkina Faso	245	84	6.85
Cameroon	162	82	4.45
Cape Verde	95	56	3.49
Central A. Republic	232	85	6.50
Chad	232	84	6.54
Congo	122	66	4.04
Côte d'Ivoire	157	75	4.83
Equatorial Guinea	223	84	6.27
Gabon	178	82	5.00
Gambia	292	86	7.80
Ghana	153	81	4.12
Guinea	259	85	7.18
Guinea-Bissau	232	84	6.54
Liberia	215	85	6.03
Mali	302	86	8.01
Mauritania	223	84	6.27
Niger	237	84	6.68
Nigeria	182	83	5.12
Senegal	231	84	6.50
Sierra Leone	302	86	8.01
Togo	160	82	4.39
Zaire	170	83	4.70
C&W Africa Region	195	83	5.55

Source: UNICEF, New York, 1988.

Based on the assumption of reaching the target of IMR of 50 or reducing IMR by half by the year 2000, which ever comes first; and using this target as a basis for estimating the U5MR target for the year 2000.

Some countries such as, Ethiopia, Malawi, Mozambique, Rwanda, Somalia and Angola have to redouble their efforts and accelerate at a much higher rate in order to achieve this goal. Similarly countries in Central and West Africa have to reduce U5MR at an annual reduction rate of 5.55% (as compared to 1.85% historically achieved). Some countries such as Burkina Faso, Central Africa Republic, Chad, Equatorial Guinea, Gambia, Guinea, Guinea-Bissau, Liberia, Mali, Mauritania, Niger, Senegal and Sierra Leone have to accelerate at a much higher rate (See Table 5).

Information exists about immunization, diarrhoeal diseases, promoting growth, breast-feeding, timing births, safe pregnancy, improved hygiene etc, which could be used to make rapid progress in reducing child deaths and malnutrition even in difficult times. However, this has not been done because of the gap between "knowledge" which exists in health services and what families know. However, through the "grand alliance" of health services, the school system, the political system, business and labour, religious bodies, the mass media, the voluntary agencies and members of the public, such knowledge and support could be put at the disposal of families (especially mothers).

Giving Greater Priority to Meeting Basic Human Needs

If effective child survival and development actions are widely implemented, and PHC is strengthened through Bamako type initiatives, then opportunities exist for the strengthening of basic services and the expansion of the resource base to meet basic human needs in general.

The policies and strategies needed to achieve this twin objective of meeting basic human needs in difficult times and also rebuilding the human foundation for sustained development have been presented in some detail in various UNICEF Reports. These broad strategies include:

- a broader approach to economic adjustment; strengthening monitoring systems at national and sub-national levels;
- achieving national/regional food self reliance and family food security, the expansion and improvement of basic services – particularly health care, water supply and basic education;
- recognizing the key role of women in development; and promoting greater local responsibility in development, meaningful popular participation and strong local organizations.

Opportunities exist to use the adjustment process to design compensatory programmes to protect the poor in the short-medium term. There are a number of successful compensatory programmes in Africa. Nutrition interventions could, for example, include supplementary feeding (targeted to malnourished children, lactating and pregnant mothers) and targeted food subsidies. Public works employment schemes should include cash-for-work and food-for-work programmes.

Promoting Growth and More Human Focused Development

Meeting basic human needs in Africa would in turn lay the foundation for improving productive activities restoring growth of household incomes and for sustained development in general.

However, no general strategy for promoting growth and protecting the poor will be appropriate for the entire region of 46 nations of sub-Saharan

Africa with differences in political systems, degrees of popular participation, policies and plans, resources and culture. Therefore, in advocating UNICEF's points of optimism for African children, and for guiding international support, there is need to distinguish between groups of sub-Saharan African countries.

First, we should consider those already undertaking human focused adjustment. (Botswana, Zimbabwe, Mauritius, Cameroon, Ghana and Guinea). Some of these countries especially Botswana and Zimbabwe adjusted in time, achieved sustained economic growth and at the same time protected their vulnerable groups. These countries should be supported to continue to broaden their adjustment programmes.

Second, over the last four years many African countries were preoccupied with far-reaching adjustments and policy reforms necessary for laying the foundations for economic recovery. Even though many Governments have committed themselves to policy changes and the necessary structural adjustments, they have not been properly funded and supported by the international community. The list of African countries with major structural reform programmes planned or underway as of March 1987 is given in Table 6.

Table 6: African Countries with Major Structural Reform Programmes Planned or Underway as of March 1987

Burundi	Mali
Central African Republic	Mauritania
Chad	Niger
Equatorial Guinea	Rwanda
The Gambia	Senegal
Ghana	Sierra Leone
Guinea Bissau	Somalia
Kenya	Tanzania
Madagascar	Togo
Malawi	Zaire
	(Zambia)

Source: The World Bank and US Treasury.

(a) Unfortunately, the flow of international funds currently available to these countries is nowhere near sufficient. In some countries any additional in flow of funds goes to pay previous debts. Moreover commodity prices have also collapsed. Therefore, international action and changes in international policy and practice are very important to assist these countries in the formulation and implementation of human focused adjustment programmes.

(b) The severe economic crisis in Africa today continues to underline the importance of "Adjustment with a Human Face" – protecting the poor and promoting growth. Much more effort should be made at national and international levels to promote a more concrete application of a broader, more humane and more efficient approach to adjustment. There is an urgent need for concrete applications of new programmes of income support for the poor, the genuine restructuring of expenditure on health and education, a much more efficient targeting of the poor and innovative forms of debt relief favouring children.

(c) The broader approach to adjustment should include the monitoring of the extent, nature and effects of the adjustment process on the welfare of children at national and subnational levels. The capacity of countries and communities to collect, analyze and use data on weight-for-age, low birth weights, school enrolment etc., should be strengthened. Monitoring of the "human dimension" should be given equal importance to monitoring economic and monetary variables.

(d) More efforts should be made to include social indicators and to involve the social sector ministries, local voluntary agencies, women and other vulnerable groups in the design and implementation of adjustment policies.

(e) As indicated earlier, due to severe cut-back in social expenditure, lack of funding has continued to be a major constraint in health and education sectors in many African countries. Peripheral health instructions are generally unsupervised and unsupported due to lack of operational expenses. As the problem of recurrent cost is unlikely to improve over the next 10–15 years, the international community should continue to provide long-term assistance to support the recurrent cost of priority child survival and development programmes.

(f) In the final analysis the decisive factors for Africa's economic recovery and development include the improvement in external commodity markets (both for demand and prices of African products), the vigorous pursuance of domestic reforms and sound economic management to protect the poor and promote growth and the response of the international community.

Third, the international community should consider the position of those war-torn countries such as Angola, Ethiopia, Mozambique, Sudan and Uganda. Some of these countries, by choice or force of circumstances have not joined those undertaking adjustment programmes. Most of these countries are at risk as they fail to effectively tackle grave economic problems. The persistent neglect of the need for adjustment has led and will continue to lead to high human and eonomic costs.

These countries should push ahead as much as they can with international support to counter the effects of war. More efforts should be made to focus national and international attention on the problems of children in especially difficult circumstances, in particular those affected by armed conflict. Assessing the magnitude of the problem, advocacy for "zones of peace", "days of tranquility", targeting of CSD initiatives in conflict affected zones, etc. are increasingly needed in war-torn countries. In particular, international support and solidarity is needed for people in Southern Africa.

Fourth, for those drought stricken countries there is an urgent human need to push ahead with moving from food emergency to food security (linking relief and development), protecting food entitlement (cash-for-work and food-for-work) for people in potentially critical and vulnerable situations, appropriate nutrition education and diversification of food sources, building efficient early warning systems (food and nutrition surveillance) at national and sub-national levels, and strengthening their emergency preparedness. There is need for the international community to change the perspective of aid from "emergency" assistance to long-term programmes of support.

Environmental concerns, the delicate balance between man and nature, and sustainable development are of primary importance to these countries. They should make much more concrete efforts to halt environmental degradation and promote sustainable development with more concern for the well-being of future generations of African children.

Annex 1: Trends in under-five mortality rates by country (1960–86)

	1960	1970	1980	1986
Eastern and Southern Africa				
Angola	346	302	261	300*
Botswana	174	148	111	96
Burundi	258	232	214	196
Comoros	261	184	150	132
Djibouti	–	–	–	–
Ethiopia	294	268	262	255
Kenya	208	170	136	118
Lesotho	208	187	160	140
Madagascar	181	144	112	94
Malawi	362	340	298	270
Mauritius	104	85	42	30
Mozambique	302	291	272	300*
Rwanda	248	237	230	210
Seychelles	–	–	24	21
Somalia	294	268	262	255
Swaziland	227	217	200	178
Tanzania	248	223	201	179
Uganda	224	196	188	174
Zambia	228	178	148	132
Zimbabwe	180	158	134	118
Sudan	293	254	209	182
Central and West Africa				
Benin	310	263	211	189
Burkina Faso	388	297	260	241
Cameroon	275	215	178	158
Central African Republic	308	260	242	228
Chad	326	291	251	228
Congo	241	166	133	119
Equatorial Guinea	315	281	242	219
Gabon	288	236	196	174
Gambia	361	344	312	287
Ghana	224	190	165	–
Guinea	346	313	279	255
Guinea-Bissau	315	284	251	228
Ivory Coast	320	250	175	153
Liberia	303	272	233	211
Mali	370	360	324	297
Mauritania	310	274	242	225
Niger	320	289	256	233
Nigeria	318	270	200	178
Sao Tome	–	–	–	91
Senegal	313	283	250	227
Sierra Leone	397	372	324	297
Togo	305	221	177	157
Zaire	251	223	187	166

Source: UNICEF, 1987, Statistical Review of the Situation of Children in the World. New York, 1987.

* Children on the Front Line: The Impact of Apartheid, Destabilization and Warfare on Children in Southern and South Africa, 1987.

References

UNICEF, *Review of Annual Reports and Country Situation Analysis, New York, 1987.*

UNICEF, 1987 *Children on the Front line: The Impact of Apartheid, Destabilization and Warfare on Children in Southern and South Africa: A Report for UNICEF*, New York, March 1987.

Overseas Development Council, *Should the IMF withdraw from Africa?* Policy Focus: 1981 No. 1 ODC, Washington D.C., 1987

UNICEF, *The State of the World's Children*, 1988, Oxford University Press, 1988.

UNICEF, *Adjustment With a Human Face: Protecting the Vulnerable and Promoting Growth*, October 1986.

UNICEF, *Impact of Recession on Children*, 1984.

UNICEF, *Within Human Reach: A future for African Children*, New York, 1985.

UNICEF, 1987 *Statistical Review of the Situation of Children in the World*, New York, 1987.

Culpepper, R., Forced Adjustment – The Export Collapse in Sub-Saharan Africa, the North-South Institute, Ottawa, Canada, 1987.

The Impact of the Economic Crisis on Vulnerable Groups in African Societies: Refugees

UNITED NATIONS HIGH COMMISSIONER FOR REFUGEES (UNHCR)

Introduction

This paper considers the impact of the economic crisis on refugees: persons who have been forced to flee their country either because of a well-founded fear of persecution or because of external aggression, occupation, foreign dominance or events seriously disturbing public order. In many cases, economic factors are likely to be contributory causes of flight. Once asylum is found, economic factors will determine to a great extent the prospects for refugee self-sufficiency and the impact on the hosts, and may also influence the prospects for voluntary repatriation after the political causes of flight have disappeared.

Eight of the ten countries of origin for the largest numbers of refugees on the continent of Africa are in the least developed category, as are all the main countries of asylum. The majority of refugees are located in the least developed areas within these countries. In these circumstances, it is evident that the economic crisis has compounded the problem of refugees. At the same time, the problem of refugees itself exacerbates the crisis. Vital human resources are lost to the country of origin. The pressures on the economy, infrastructure, natural environment and social framework of the country of asylum are increased just as a declining economy is making them less supportable.

Background and Prospects

Two related developments are of particular significance when considering refugees in the context of the economic crisis. First is the decline in food production by the subsistence farmer. Food shortages in areas affected by events seriously disturbing public order were the major contributory factors to the large-scale population displacements in the 1984–1986 African emergency. Drought was the immediate cause of these shortages, but the disaster was not primarily natural and unavoidable. Second is the rural exodus and consequent rapid growth of the urban centres, which has put great pressure on urban society.

As a result of the economic crisis, increasingly large numbers of African refugees are facing long-term dependence on outside assistance, without any real prospect of economic self-sufficiency and the concomitant start to regaining self-respect. Even some rural settlements that had been self supporting and integrated within national structures for several years have required renewed international assistance, particularly for the recurrent costs of services.

Many others among Africa's refugees are not directly assisted by the international community but have settled spontaneously in towns or villages, in some cases twenty or more years ago. In times of economic growth spontaneously settled refugees often made significant contributions to national economies. Now they are among the first to suffer from inflation, shortages, the breakdown of services and unemployment. As these pressures mount on urban populations, some governments have felt compelled to adopt measures that effectively limit the residence or employment rights of urban refugees, thereby accelerating their decline from self-sufficiency.

Within refugee communities, the effects of the economic crisis have been particularly severe on women and children. Some of the consequences are obvious and felt immediately. Others manifest themselves over time. Perhaps the single most important problem is the lack of proper educational opportunities for refugee children. This lack is evident in the great majority of refugee situations and reflects many factors. Some-such as the difficulties in reconciling conflicting considerations with regard to the preferred language of instruction – are unrelated to the economic crisis. But the crisis has increased the magnitude of the problem and thus the danger that still larger numbers of African children will be denied the opportunity to develop their individual potential. In turn, their potential contribution to continued African economic recovery and development will be irretrievably lost.

Political considerations apart, unless economic decline can be arrested and recovery begins, the prognosis is bleak. The well-being of existing refugees will be further threatened, both immediately and as a result of solutions becoming still more difficult to achieve, whether because self-sufficiency in the country of asylum becomes unattainable or because, even after voluntary repatriation, economic conditions inhibit reintegration. The burden on the countries of asylum, and particularly on the poorest of the poor among the hosts in the areas most affected by the presence of refugees, will increase. More persons will be uprooted or feel forced to uproot themselves and cross frontiers. Many will be refugees, others might more correctly be described as mass-distress migrants. Both groups would suffer greatly, and be part of and contribute to deepening the economic and social crisis in Africa. This cycle of despair can and must be prevented.

Action Towards Solutions

Discussion of measures that could help prevent refugee flows is outside the scope of this paper. However, it may be noted that the OAU's African Charter on Human and Peoples' Rights entered into force in October 1986. Its further ratification and respect for its provisions would make a major contribution, not only to the prevention of new refugee flows but also to the creation of conditions that would favour repatriation. Where economic factors are contributory causes of flight, it is equally evident that successful measures to promote economic recovery and development, particularly of the rural poor, will also help avert new flows and favourably influence repatriation. In this respect therefore, solving the economic crisis will contribute to both the prevention and solution of problems of refugees.

Whatever form measures to address the economic problems take, they can only be successful if they are able to build on an assured respect for the basic principles governing the treatment of refugees. These principles are embodied in the OAU Convention Governing the Specific Aspects of Refugee Problems in Africa, to which 33 of the 51 OAU member States have now acceded. The Convention affirms that the granting of asylum to refugees is a peaceful and humanitarian act and shall not be regarded as an unfriendly act, and stresses the importance of the principles of "non refoulement" and of voluntary repatriation. The 1979 Arusha Conference on the Situation of Refugees in Africa reaffirmed that respect for these principles should be considered as a fundamental right of refugees.

Once asylum has been granted, all concerned must respect the strictly humanitarian, civilian and non-political character that is inherent in the concept of refugee status and explicit in the provisions of the OAU Convention. A refugee has a right to security, and must in turn respect the laws and regulations of his or her country of asylum. But real solutions cannot be found, nor the potential benefits of refugees to their country of asylum be realized, unless the right to work, of movement in search of work, and of access to markets is also granted. Where refugee problems remain unresolved for many years, special consideration should be given to the full equation of refugees' rights and responsibilities with those of nationals by facilitating naturalization. Of particular concern is the fact that many Africans born refugees are now reaching adulthood "in limbo" in the countries where their parents were granted asylum a generation ago.

Before considering how the burdens on and of refugees might be lightened it may be noted that certain improvements will not be possible without major social change to correct underlying problems that are not refugee-specific, though they become more acute for refugees. In some societies the role of women places responsibilities on them that can become unsupportable in the context of life in a refugee camp. It is, for example, often not possible for a refugee woman alone to attend food distribution and fetch water and firewood as well as cook, keep house and care for children. Yet such may be expected of her even when she is not the head of family.

The economic policy reforms, structural adjustments and other measures that may be required to deal with the economic crisis must provide the framework for measures to address the needs of refugees and to ease the burden on their hosts. This requires that assistance to refugees and to the areas affected by their presence should be provided in a manner that is integrated within national development plans and thus allows best use of the resources available through national and international institutions.

In 1984, the second International Conference on Assistance to Refugees in Africa (ICARA II) set out the concept of development-oriented assistance to refugees and returnees. ICARA II also considered the impact of refugees on national economies and sought to mobilize assistance to strengthen social and economic infrastructure and thereby help alleviate the burden of refugees and returnees. The economic crisis and the African emergency limited the practical results, but have underlined the need for such an approach. Some momentum would already be regained by the redirection by donors to appropriate development projects of unused funds originally allocated to the emergency.

The presence of refugees and the direct assistance available through UNHCR, which already benefits certain of their immediate hosts, must be used as a catalyst for the mobilization of additional resources for the development of these areas, planned as a coherent whole and within the national and international development process. While the direct assistance available through UNHCR to returnees after repatriation is limited in scope and duration, the same approach is no less important for the reintegration of former refugees. It will help promote the most desirable solution for refugees and also lessen the likelihood that economic factors alone would precipitate a second flight.

For this approach to succeed, a number of actions must be taken or consolidated. First, the government of asylum must be convinced of its validity and take the necessary measures for its implementation. The OAU Council of Ministers has invited member States to take the necessary measures to incorporate refugee and returnee programmes into national plans. For many governments the critical question is "additionality": the funds required to implement integrated programmes should be additional to the resources that would have been available either through UNHCR's normal assistance or for non-refugee-related development assistance. The history of joint projects to date suggests that the donors will be prepared to make extra funds available. UNHCR has already demonstrated its ability to assist in initial fund-raising.

Host governments must also take practical measures to ensure the necessary co-ordination among the national entity responsible for refugees, the planning ministry and the technical ministries. An enhanced role for the latter is important even with respect to UNHCR's normal assistance. Without the proper involvement of the appropriate technical ministry, much of the potential benefits to local communities and infrastructure from the resources UNHCR can make directly available may be lost.

For their part, UNHCR and international development organizations must reinforce their own co-operation. Within the United Nations system, procedures to make the best use of available resources and expertise have been developed, as for example the co-operation between UNDP and UNHCR on refugees and development, and must be further refined. However, the key to success lies in the mobilization of development institutions that have not hitherto considered the problem of refugees as either a proper concern or a priority. Such mobilization should also include the non-governmental developmental sector at both the international and often neglected national level. The general public in some host countries is increasingly conscious of and concerned at the impact of refugees, and action is necessary to inform public opinion of the aims and benefits of this approach. The impact of the economic crisis would be greater were it not for the traditional hospitality of the African peoples, but the strains are real.

Some progress has been made, notably with the formulation of projects for areas affected by the presence of refugees by the European Economic Community under Lome III, in developing or extending World Bank projects to benefit refugees as well as nationals and in exploring possibilities for collaboration with the International Fund for Agricultural Development, whose target population – the poorest in rural areas – in many countries in Africa, themselves the immediate hosts of the refugees.

The necessary financial support from the international community for these and future initiatives is an obvious prerequisite. Mobilizing this support, and ensuring co-ordination at the international level, requires that whenever their numbers or importance so warrant, refugees and returnees are on the agenda in the various development fora such as round tables, consultative groups and consortia, as well as of the governing councils of the development agencies.

Conclusion

Refugees, and especially those who are spontaneously settled, are particularly vulnerable to the effects of the economic crisis. They are also inadvertent contributors to this crisis and its impact on the poorer of their hosts, whose hospitality has prevented worse suffering but has itself been sorely stretched by the crisis. In better times, refugees have made substantial contributions to economic development in Africa. They could do so again if concerted action is taken within the framework of an integrated national development programme to meet both their longer-term needs and those resulting from their presence. Even before the economic benefits are felt, human suffering will be reduced and hope rekindled for many refugees. However, it should not be forgotten that neither the underlying causes of refugees nor the measures necessary to solve their problems are at heart economic in nature.

The Politics of Adjustment Policy

AKILAGPA SAWYERR

Introduction

What is often described as "the African economic crisis" of the early 1980s has been engraved on the consciousness of the whole world by the glassy look in the eyes of emaciated and starving African children and the evident anguish of their equally emaciated and starving mothers in posters and pictures, on the television screens and in the newspapers the world over. Even as the international community was moved to provide emergency relief on an unprecedented scale, the virulence and scale of the disaster brought into sharp relief the question of underdevelopment and the long-term viability, not just of the countries of the Sahel belt, the hardest hit subregion, but also of all the countries of sub-Saharan Africa. This prompted a series of meetings, conferences and seminars, both within the African region and at the United Nations and other international fora, and the adoption of important resolutions and measures for dealing with the crisis.

For their part, almost all the countries of the subregion have had to institute programmes of economic reconstruction, generally described as "structural adjustment programmes" to remove what are perceived to be the causes of the crisis, and to put the economies of the subregion on a path of development that would prevent any recurrence of such a catastrophe.[1] This has been done usually under the auspices, or in accordance with the precepts, of the principal international financial institutions, namely the International Monetary Fund (IMF) and the International Bank for Reconstruction and Development (IBRD), otherwise known as the World Bank.

Since the crisis was seen as resulting from obvious failures in economic performance in all the countries of the subregion, the structural adjustment programmes have tended to focus on the strictly economic aspects of the corrective process. This left largely untreated the question of the political preconditions for the success of the structural adjustment programmes as well as the impact of the measures undertaken thereunder on internal social and political conditions in the short to medium term. This was perhaps understandable in the desperate years of the early 1980s. But in view of the devastating impact of the crisis on the living conditions of large sections of the populations in the sub-Saharan African countries, and the further deterioration of those conditions in the years immediately following the introduction of structural adjustment programmes, greater attention has more recently been directed at the non-economic dimensions of the crisis and attempts at its resolution.

It is now recognized, for instance, that the social and political conditions for the long-term maintenance of economic development programmes need to be properly appreciated and written into structural adjustment programmes. For, apart from the danger of a mis-prescription of corrective measures that results from a failure to do so, the unavoidable harshness of the austerity measures is liable to alienate important social groups and political interests, thereby jeopardizing the entire economic recovery process.

It is against this background that conferences such as this one are addressing the specifically "human dimension" of the crisis and measures for its resolutions.[2] This paper is intended as a contribution to the discussion of the political aspects of the adjustment process in Africa. The paper would attempt to situate the economic crisis and the resultant structural adjustment measures within the framework of the political economy of Africa; relate this to the economic development objectives explicitly set out at OAU summit meetings since 1980; and point out ways in which socio-political conditions pose serious problems for the entire recovery effort.

The Political Economy of Africa, the Economic Crisis and Structural Adjustment Measures – An Overview

In this section, we outline the principal features of the African economic crisis against the background of the political economy of Africa, then itemize the main elements of the structural adjustment measures undertaken by many African countries in response to the crisis.

(a) The African economic crisis in context

For the sake of convenience, the discussions will be focused on the economies of the countries of sub-Saharan Africa, excluding the Republic of South Africa. This focus, while difficult to justify scientifically, enables us to concentrate on a relatively monogenous category of countries and thereby simplify the argument and its presentation.[3] Set out below are the most critical manifestations of the African crisis as they show up in the economies of individual countries:

(a) Among the more obvious of the manifestations of the crisis has been a steep decline in the quality of life of an increasingly large proportion of the population in the affected countries. This shows up in the reduced availability and/or the increased cost of food and such social services as education and health. Technically, this decline in the quality of life can be demonstrated from the indices relating to health, sanitation, nutritional status, infant/child mortality, school enrolment, access to potable water, etc. Also easily observed is the rise in unemployment and underemployment, as new immigrants to the urban areas and school leavers find it increasingly difficult to secure remunerative employment;

(b) There has been a marked decline in the rate of growth in all sectors of the national economy. As observed by the World Bank, "The average annual GDP growth rate for low-income Africa declined by 2.7 percent during 1970–1980 to 0.7 percent in 1982 and reached a record low of 0.2 percent in 1983" (*World Development Report*, 1986,p.24). This was accompanied by decreases in the average income per capita (table 1), as well as the average per capita food production (Sutcliffe, 1986, 22). The result is that food self-sufficiency in sub-Saharan Africa has dropped from 98 percent in 1960 to 8 percent in 1986 (*South*, August 1986, 112), and "today one out of every five Africans depends for his/her survival on food imports, about 25 percent of which is provided by food aid" (*Submission*, 1986, para.16);

Table 1: Growth of GDP per capita for selected groups of developing countries, 1960–1984 (annual average rate of percentage increase)

Developing countries	1960–1969	1970–1974	1975–1979	1980–1984	1980	1981	1982	1983	1984
By region:									
Latin America	2.4	3.9	2.5	−2.7	2.5	−1.8	−3.5	−4.6	0.7
North Africa	3.1	2.9	6.1	−1.0	2.3	−3.0	−0.5	−1.2	0.7
Other Africa	1.6	2.9	−0.4	−4.1	0.4	−2.8	−2.7	−6.2	−4.3
West Asia	4.6	7.3	2.4	−4.7	−6.4	−5.6	−0.8	−8.4	−3.7
South Asia	1.3	−0.9	1.7	2.4	4.7	2.9	0.0	4.6	2.1
East Asia	4.0	6.2	6.6	3.3	3.6	4.6	1.5	3.9	3.8

Source: UNCTAD, *Trade and Development Report* 1986, p.151.

(c) Local manufacturing industry has been stagnant, when not in a state of collapse. The economy has become steadily "de-industrialized" as capacity utilization of industrial plants has fallen below economic levels, and the indices of the growth of industrial production read low or negative (table 2);

Table 2: Sector growth rates, 1965–1984

Country group		Industry	
	1965–1973	1973–1980	1980–1984
Developing countries	8.5	6.0	2.2
Low-income countries	8.7	7.3	7.7
Asia	8.8	7.6	8.0
India	3.7	5.0	4.2
China	12.1	8.6	9.3
Africa	8.1	1.3	− 1.2
Middle-income countries	8.4	5.6	0.3
Oil exporters	8.3	5.2	− 2.3
Oil importers	8.5	5.9	1.8
Major exporters of manufactures	9.2	6.4	2.1
High-income oil exporters	–	2.9	−16.4
Industrial market economies	5.1	2.3	1.6

Source: World Bank, *World Development Report*, 1986

(d) There has been a sharp deterioration in the foreign exchange position of the national economy. This is the result of the collapse of the export earnings of the region and the failure as well of financial inflows – grants, credits and investments – to make up the difference. Particularly noticeable has been the decline in export credits and private inflows, which combined, fell from a 1979 high of $US 6.9 billion to a low of $US 0.5 billion in 1984, and was provisionally estimated at $US 2.8 billion in 1986 (table 3). It has been estimated that for Africa, "net resources flows from all sources declined by 28 percent between 1980 and 1984, while . . . ODA flows declined by about 9 percent" (*Submission*, 1986, para. 32). The consequence of these movements has been the decline in the level of imports per capita, and the growing burden of external debt;

Table 3: Net Resource Flows to sub-Saharan Africa

	Current $ billion						Per cent total	
	1979	1981	1983	1984	1985	1986[p]	1980	1986[p]
I. Official Development Finance (ODF)	8.9	10.8	11.4	12.7	12.9	15.9	67.7	85.0
II. Total export credits	2.0	1.9	1.1	0.2	1.1	0.4	11.6	2.1
III. Private Flows	4.9	4.6	2.3	0.3	2.5	2.4	20.7	12.8
Direct investment	1.5	1.5	0.9	0.4	0.3	0.4	0.6	2.1
Int. baml sector (including short-term)	2.0	2.0	0.5	1.0	0.8	1.0	12.2	5.3
Other private[a]	1.4	1.1	0.9	0.9	1.4	0.9	7.9	4.8
Total Resource Flows (I + II + III)	15.8	17.3	14.8	13.2	16.5	18.7	100.0	100.0

Source: OECD, *Financing and External Debt of Developing Countries*, 1986 Survey.

[a] Including grants by Non-Governmental Organisations (NGOs).
[p] Provisional.

(e) Efforts to eke out a living from the land and the forests have led to the increasing degradation of the natural environment. The effect has been to reduce even further the capacity of the environment to sustain production and life;

(f) The deterioration in the political arrangements for the management of society is a further result of the crisis. This is reflected in a chronic instability in the national political infrastructure which therefore tends towards authoritarianism and repression, creating conditions for continued instability. Moreover, the deterioration of the political environment tends to exacerbate class splits and encourage ethnic politics.

The general effects of the factors described above, some of which will receive more extended treatment later, is a political economy within which investment levels are too low even to maintain or rehabilitate existing production capacity, let alone develop it, and in which political and governmental arrangements inhibit the full mobilization of the national human resources in the drive for survival and development. In consequence, the economy is left vulnerable to every natural calamity as well as to the vagaries of the international economic environment.

When one turns to the causes of the crisis, some very difficult problems of distinction between causes and effects emerge. To avoid the worst of these problems, we set out in simple terms what can be considered the principal causes, remote as well as immediate of the crisis.

The major causes of the crisis lie in the very structure of the economies of African countries. As it has been well put, "Lack of structural transformation and the low level productivity of the African economies are the fundamental causes of their continued underdevelopment and persisting economic crisis" (*Submission*, 1986, para. 20).

To enable us to grasp the full import of this observation, it is necessary to paint in the political/economic context – national, regional and international – within which the African economies operate. This context is defined by the colonial experience, the international relationships that were established thereby, and the relationship of both to the domestic and external economic structures.

In spite of the variety of historical experiences of the countries of sub-Saharan Africa they have a number of important characteristics in common. With the exception of Liberia and Ethiopia, all these countries were subjected to formal colonialism during the first half of the twentieth century. In the case of Liberia and Ethiopia, despite their formal independence, the subjection of their political economy to external political and economic domination was as thorough as that of the formal colonies, and they can for this purpose be considered in the same light.

As is well known, the objective effect of the colonial experience was to re-order the social, political and economic structures within each colony in such a way as to integrate the colony into the world capitalist system. This was done by aligning the dynamic sectors of each economy with the interests of the dominant classes in the metropolitan countries, and creating within the colony the political and social conditions necessary to sustain and reproduce the relationship established under the colonial system. So successful was this process that the termination of formal colonialism nowhere led to a radical change in the relationship between former colonies and metropolitan interests, at least at the level of the economy.[4]

The legacy of the colonial period can for present purposes be summed up as follows:

(a) political power is vested in an alliance of social classes with no fundamental interest in the transformation of the local political economy and a break from domination by metropolitan interests;
(b) given its untransformed structures, and because of its one-sided external orientation, the economy tends to work itself more closely into the international capitalist order, but in a position of subordination;
(c) the majority of people, the principal victims of the continuation of the colonial economic relations, are effectively disenfranchised and thus disabled from moving to effect the necessary transformations;
(d) the colonial economies are individually linked to the metropolitan economies in such a way as to preclude genuine regional or sub-regional integration – a situation which persists, in spite of the good intentions, the rhetoric, the many meetings and the formal institutions for co-operation set up throughout sub-Saharan Africa.

The picture presented by independent Africa is thus one of an unintegrated collection of non-industrialized, undemocratic, non-self-sustaining and dependent States, with little clout in international economic affairs. It is this situation that explains why Africa as a region has remained directly vulnerable to world capitalist recessions but in no position to affect policy or practice at that level.

This summary represents only a slight over-simplification of the brutal reality of the political economy of Africa. Failure to grasp this fully, at least as a starting point, will mean a failure to appreciate and begin to deal realistically with the current crisis. For the timing of the crisis is intimately connected to this subjection of African economies to one-sided determination by external events.

With the collapse of the generalized boom in the world economy following the Korean War, Western economies have been experiencing a succession of worsening economic shocks. These have stretched out into a long-run crisis, especially following the oil crises of 1973, 1974 and 1979. The consequence has been a severe reduction in the growth rates in all Western economies, especially in the 1980's (see table 2), creating a situation of very weak demand for commodities of export interest to sub-Saharan Africa economies. As a result, real prices of primary commodities other than oil, stand at their lowest level since the Great Depression (*Trade and Development*, 1986, 11), causing Africa foreign exchange losses amounting to some $US 13.8 billion over the period 1980–1983 (*Submission*, 1986, para.29).

Compounding these decreases in the export earnings of African countries, inflation in the Western industrialized economies has been passed on to Africa in the form of constantly increasing prices of items of import interest to African economies. Given the dependence of most of their industry on imported inputs and capital, this development would, by itself, have had disastrous consequences for production and consumption in the sub-Saharan African countries. To make matters worse, the difficulties experienced in the Western industrialized economies led to a sharp drop in private capital flows. The overall effect of all these movements in the export earnings and capital inflows has been a drastic reduction in the import capacity of African countries and therefore their capacity to extricate themselves from the current crisis.[5]

These structure-determined features were aggravated by specific policy measures adopted in the Western capitalist economies. These policies, often ill-defined and contradictory, contributed to the drastic slowing down of economic growth in some leading industrialized countries and hence the generally depressed conditions in the African countries (Westlake, 1987, 40–41). One could mention the impact of United States interest rate policy on the debts payable by African countries;[6] exchange rate fluctuations which led to serious instability and overall loss in the foreign exchange holdings of African countries; and the deteriorating terms of borrowing, with commercial banks imposing ever harsher terms and generally reducing credit to African countries. In the face of such evidence, it is difficult to escape the conclusion that these structural and policy movements in the leading Western industrialized countries are the principal causes of the problems in the economies of sub-Saharan African countries.

While these factors constitute the long-term causes, it is their conjuncture with other more immediate causes that often determined the timing and extent of the crisis in any particular country. Among such factors have been natural disasters like drought, floods and cyclones, and man-made disasters like civil wars and the destabilizing efforts of external powers. Though these have undoubtedly contributed, sometimes dramatically, to the current crisis, it needs to be emphasized that they were aggravating rather than fundamental causes, as can be seen from the fact that several countries affected by the crisis could claim no such excuses.

In addition to constituting the fundamental causes, external factors account to a large extent for the incidents of the crisis. Thus:

(a) Dependence on the export of a limited number of primary products and the importation of critical inputs, over whose prices Africa has no control, mean that the terms of trade between Africa and the Western industrialized countries lie totally beyond the control of African countries;

(b) The deterioration in the terms of trade, and the reduction in financial inflows, lead to a reduction in the capacity of African countries to import food and needed industrial inputs, which in turn contributes to the collapse of local production and employment generally – all of this in turn fueling inflation and balance-of-payments problems;

(c) These developments leave the African economies so little room to manoeuvre that they become prey to natural as well as man-made calamities, and create conditions of social and political instability which are neither conducive to the mobilization of local resources, human and material, nor to the productivity increases, which together provide the basis upon which alone Africa can work and earn its way out of the crisis.

In the light of these observations, it should be clear that no sustained resolution of the current African crisis is conceivable unless it addresses the roots of the crisis in the international capitalist order. The argument is not that the ending of recession in the Western industrialized countries would bring Africa's problems to an end. It could do no more than take Africa back to something like its conditions in the boom years of the 1960s and the early 1970s. The fundamental causes of crisis would remain, rendering Africa vulnerable to future bouts of crisis caused by external events. What is called for is a radical reshaping of African economies, which can only occur in the context of a fundamentally restructured international economic order, or the effective de-linking of African economies from the existing order.

The idea of a radically restructured international economic order has been under discussion, at least as far back as the end of the 1960s, reaching a climax in the resolutions of the United Nations General Assembly and UNCTAD in the 1973–1977 period. The failure of the proposals for the establishment of the New International Economic Order was not unpredictable (Sawyerr, 1984, pp.300–301). It is doubtful if the prospects for such a new order are any brighter now than they were a decade ago.

Turning to the notion of de-linking, it has received considerable attention, mainly among academic and political theorists not only in the third world, but also elsewhere. Somehow the notion has never been treated as a serious option because the political and economic pre-conditions for its realization have always been found too much for the existing order.

(b) The Lagos Plan of Action, APPER and UN-PAAERD

Africa has not been slow to acknowledge the crisis and take collective counsel on how to deal with it. In 1980, the OAU convened a summit meeting of African Heads of State and Government to consider exclusively the economic problems then gathering momentum. The meeting lamented the African condition, provided a diagnosis of the problems, and prescribed an action plan for dealing with them. This was set out in the "Lagos Plan of Action for the Economic Development of Africa, 1980–2000" and the "Final Act of Lagos", simply referred to as the "Lagos Plan of Action".

The Lagos Plan of Action included detailed analyses and prescriptions in respect of food, agriculture, technology and industry, etc., which it was intended should help African countries achieve self-sustaining development by the end of the century. The essence of the prescriptions can best be captured by reference to the basic principles which were to guide the implementation of the Plan. These, as set out in the Preamble, are as follows:

(i) Africa's huge resources must be applied principally to meet the needs and purposes of its people;
(ii) Africa's almost total reliance on the export of raw materials must change. Rather, Africa's development and growth must be based on a combination of Africa's considerable natural resources, her entrepreneurial, managerial and technical resources and her markets (restructured and expanded), to serve her people. Africa, therefore, must map out its own strategy for development and must vigorously pursue its implementation;
(iii) Africa must cultivate the virtue of self-reliance. This is not to say that the continent should totally cut itself off from outside contributions. However, these outside contributions should only supplement our own effort: they should not be the mainstay of our development;
(iv) As a consequence of the need for increased self-reliance, Africa must mobilize her entire human and material resources for her development;
(v) Each of our States must pursue all-embracing economic, social and cultural activities which will mobilize the strength of the country as a whole and ensure that both the efforts put into and the benefits derived from development are equitably shared; and
(vi) Efforts towards African economic integration must be pursued with renewed determination in order to create a continent-wide framework for the much needed economic co-operation for development based on collective self-reliance" (*Lagos Plan of Action* pp.8–9).

The promulgation of this Plan was followed by the Sahelian drought and famine, which struck with unimaginable virulence, peaking in 1983/1984. At the time there was a general feeling that the very physical survival of millions of Africans and, indeed, the very basis of several African countries, were in severe jeopardy. In addition to the emergency relief measures undertaken by the international community, an OAU summit, devoted primarily to the discussion of the African economic crisis, was convened in July 1985. The specific purpose this time was to prepare a position to be presented to a special session of the General Assembly of the United Nations, which was to consider and take action on Africa's economic and social problems.

The Addis Ababa summit produced a document, *Africa's Priority Programme for Economic Recovery, 1986–1990* (APPER), in which the African leaders noted that five years after the adoption of the Lagos Plan of Action little progress has been made in its implementation. They took note of the obstacles and constraints which were considered primarily responsible for this failure. Among these were:

(a) failure to restructure the inherited colonial economies;
(b) the deepening of dependency through the mis-allocation of domestic resources and over-reliance on external human and financial resources;
(c) the intervention of unforeseen factors such as drought, accelerated desertification, cyclones and South Africa destabilization, especially in the Front line States; and

(d) the "very slow" development of co-operation and integration in new sub-regional groupings.

"It is clear that some of these constraints and shortcomings can, and should be, remedied by African countries themselves, while others are beyond their control and may thus call for concerted international action. In any case, the implementation of the *Lagos Plan of Action* in the years ahead will remain a challenge which requires consistently conscious action and vigilance on the part of individual African countries and collectively." (APPER, 1985 pp.13–14)

The burden of the documents which emerged from this summit and which were submitted to the United Nations General Assembly for consideration in June 1986 was the acknowledgement by the African leaders of Africa's share of the blame for the parlous condition of the continent and the proposal of action programmes to deal with it; Africa's appreciation for the relief effort mounted by the international community to help alleviate the famine, etc.; and a call to the international community to go beyond emergency relief and to contribute to the long-term resolution of the African crisis. It was emphasized that international action was needed to ease the crushing burden of Africa's external debt and to improve the outlook for the export earnings of African countries by stabilizing and increasing the prices paid for their exports, as well as by allowing them greater access to the markets of the developed countries (*Submission,* para. 47).

The result of the United Nations session was a "compact" between Africa and the international community set out in the *United Nations Programme of Action for African Economic Recovery and Development,* 1986–1990 (UN-PAAERD).

The position thus taken by the African Heads of State in *Africa's Priority Programme for Economic Recovery* (APPER) and its submission to the United Nations General Assembly in 1986, while affirming the basic objectives of the *Lagos Plan of Action,* lacked the latter's confident insistence on collective self-reliance. No doubt in response to the deterioration of the situation since 1980, attention was more narrowly focussed on the priority areas, and the limitations of any action taken by the African countries on their own were frankly acknowledged. Hence, the appeal to the international community through a United Nations General Assembly discussion of Africa's problems, and the compact between Africa and the international community for joint action towards the resolution of the crisis.

(c) Adjustment measures

At the same time that they were making these formal pronouncements and proposals at regional and sub-regional meetings, individual African countries were instituting programmes for the rehabilitation/development of their national economies. The majority of these have taken the form of structural adjustment programmes, to which we now turn.

A distinction is sometimes drawn between structural adjustment programmes formulated under the aegis of the IMF/World Bank, and other adjustment programmes. This is a distinction we consider without much difference, except that in the case of the IMF/World Bank-sponsored programmes in sub-Saharan Africa, there is the added benefit of special access to financial flows from these institutions and other bilateral and multilateral sources.

It is undoubtedly the case that structural adjustment measures recently undertaken by sub-Saharan African countries are similar in all essentials. This is no mere coincidence. It stems primarily from the fact, already noted, that the economies of all these countries occupy objectively the same position in the world capitalist economic dispensation. So long as an underdeveloped country remains within that order, the basic choices open to it remain much the same. For instance, any attempt to raise bank credit during the crisis or secure investments from any part of the capitalist world is likely to be met by the demand that the country first conclude an arrangement with the IMF. Even if this were not the case, and a country attempted to proceed without recourse to the IMF, the structural location of the economy of the country within the international order would restrict its choices in responding to the crisis to measures of the same sort as would be imposed under an IMF/World Bank regime.

The claim is sometimes made by some sub-Saharan African countries that the particular adjustment measures they have adopted are "indigenous" either in the sense that they had been concluded independently of the IMF/World Bank, or that they were the outcome of hard bargaining on the part of the sub-Saharan African negotiators. While this may provide a psychological boost to sub-Saharan African leaders or salve their consciences, and while there may be short-term local variations, the claim is of very little consequence.[7] Our discussion will, therefore, make no distinction between IMF/World Bank and other structural adjustment programmes.

The essence of the structural adjustment programmes adopted by countries in the sub-Saharan Africa is the reduction/removal of direct State intervention in the productive and distributive sectors of the economy, restricting the State to the creation, mainly through the manipulation of fiscal and monetary instruments, of an institutional and policy framework conducive to the mobilization of private enterprise and initiative. This, it is believed, would give freer play to both internal and external market forces and provide the appropriate engine for a resumption of economic growth and development.

Within this very broad theme, adjustment measures adopted by sub-Saharan African countries include measures on some or all of the following:

(a) Public expenditure: steps are taken to reduce public borrowing and budget deficits by means of expenditure cuts and ceilings, as well as to shift the pattern of public investment towards the export sector. Moreover public service emolument expenditure is contained by the retrenchment of staff and a general restraint on wage increases, in some cases, actual salary and wage cuts. Finally, subsidies for the provision of public services are reduced or removed through the generalization of cost-recovery programmes;

(b) Domestic savings: a package of measures intended to increase domestic savings is introduced, among them the manipulation of interest rate policy and income tax reforms to put more money in the hands of those likely to save or invest their surpluses;

(c) "Rationalization" of the State-owned sector of the economy: the object here is to reduce State ownership and control of economic activities to the barest minimum, and to make surviving State-owned enterprises more profit-oriented and less protected and subsidized. To this end, profitable State enterprises are to be sold off, or private parties invited to buy in, the latter usually taking up management control as well. As to "unprofitable" enterprises, they are to be liquidated altogether, or, if of strategic importance, "rationalized" by retrenchment of employees, severe reduction in real wages and upgrading of the quality of management. In addition they are to charge economic rates for their services, thereby working themselves off State budgetary subventions; and

(d) Liberalization of the economy: in a sense the measures considered above are aspects of liberalization, which aim at allowing greater play to the forces of the market. Our concern here is with:
   (i) the removal of State controls on the determination of the value of the national currency (resulting almost invariably in its steep devaluation as against foreign currencies);
   (ii) the removal of exchange controls, thereby subjecting the external payments situation to market determination; and
   (iii) removal of curbs on imports, prices and distribution within the economy.

   The broad justification for this last set of measures is that market-determination will lead to the most efficient allocation of productive resources;

(e) Export promotion: to deal with the chronic shortage of foreign exchange, an export drive is vigorously undertaken. Thus in addition to the shifting of resources into the export sector, there is often a substantial real increase in the producer price of export products, as well as the strengthening of special arrangements to enable exporters to retain a proportion of their export earnings in off-shore "retention accounts". This is furthered by a liberalization of the uses to which such accounts may be put, e.g., the payment of dividends and trade bills, and the purchase of machinery and spare parts;

(f) Promotion of foreign private investment: this often involves the promulgation of investment codes setting out extensive concessions to foreign investors. In addition to these concessions, subsidies and protection for indigenous industry are often eroded in order to reduce its competitive edge over foreign investments. Finally, a general programme of wage restraint within the economy is more or less actively pursued in order to reduce the cost of doing business locally and thereby increase the returns to foreign investment.

It will be noted that there is no reference in all this to a specific push for industrialization, nor is there any indication of an industrialization strategy. In the typical adjustment programme this is either because the condition of the economy is considered too desperate even to think of industrialization, or because it is assumed that market forces and the investment concessions will lead to the setting up of "appropriate" industry. Such assumptions do not stand up to analysis, since the measures introduced tend to favour the old-style extractive industries and work against the establishment of locally sourced manufacturing industry. For instance, most of the heavy infrastructural development is focused on agriculture, mining and primary export production generally. Again, the focus on demand management and a low-wage regime deprive local industry of the effective demand without which it cannot survive, let alone thrive, even as the open-door policy exposes such local industry as survives to crippling competition from foreign imports, especially of finished consumer goods. The problems of local manufacturers are compounded by the general credit squeeze which deprives them of easy access to working capital. As the structural adjustment programme continues, therefore, many local manufacturers are forced to fold up or be absorbed by foreign "partners".

Similarly, there is no effort to fashion a coherent agrarian policy that will lead not only to increases in rural incomes, but also to the necessary complementarity between rural production and industrialization. Again, mere increases in the producer price of food products cannot substitute for reforms of rural ownership structures and technical supports that will be necessary to support a self-sustaining and industrializing domestic economy.

When it is recalled that a significant element, particularly in the *Lagos Plan of Action* was the insistence on an approach to the crisis which demands of the African States collective action, on the basis of self-reliance, with a view to self-sustaining, i.e., nondependent development, there emerges a major contradiction between the objectives of the *Lagos Plan of Action*, APPER, and UN-PAAERD, on the one hand, and, on the other, the nature of the structural adjustment programmes adopted by African countries in their attempt to resolve the crisis.

Political Implications of Current Structural Adjustment Policies

The degree to which external interests determine the particular policy measures adopted by a country depends obviously on the specific conditions under which the adjustment programme is adopted, including the strength and the political orientation of those in power in the country, the depth of the crisis affecting the local political economy, and the prevailing international environment. But in all cases the macro-economic framework is fundamentally conditioned by the external factors described above. This determination may take the form of the direct introduction of a package of policies into the sub-Saharan African country or, less directly, of "technical advice" insistently pressed. It sometimes comes under the guise of prerequisites for obtaining relief from other sources. This occurs where there is direct pressure by donors or where international private financial sources such as banks withhold loans until an appropriate arrangement with the IMF has been concluded by the country in question.

Whether the external influence takes the direct or indirect form, the result is a further constriction of the power of the African State to make fundamental policy choices. In this connection, particular attention needs to be paid to the political role played by aid and external debt trap circumstances. Indeed, in the contemporary world, aid and the debt trap constitute the carrot and the stick by which the industrialized countries seek to bend third world countries to their will.

Lest it be thought that resentment of this external determination of critical elements of the adjustment package within the sub-Saharan African countries is based solely on hurt national pride, it must be pointed out that, in spite of the pretence that the strategies and policies advocated by the IMF/World Bank are the most efficient means for the revival and sustenance of African economies in crisis, the specific strategies and policies are not as neutral as the rhetoric would suggest.[8] This arises from the very nature of the IMF/World Bank and their role in the world economy. The two institutions, as well as other multilateral financial institutions, are heavily dominated by the western industrialized States, in particular the United States of America. Indeed the IMF and the World Bank have been baldly described as "Western capitalist institutions" (Hayter and Watson, 1985, 150). As is only to be expected, those States pursue policies that advance their national interests, especially as those interests are interpreted by their transnational corporations and banks. In consequence, both the ideology that animates the IMF and the World Bank, and their specific policy prescriptions clearly reflect the interests of the principal actors, namely the transnational corporations based in the industrialized countries.[9]

This is not to deny that there are contradictions, sometimes of major proportions, between transnational corporations and between States in the Western industrialized world. The important issue is the fundamentally united position dictated by the objective interests of the principal economic actors in those countries in their relations with third world countries. Consequently, multilateral financial institutions, as agents of "multilateral imperialism", work to ensure that the economies of the third world are conditioned to "accommodate" i.e., serve, the basic interests of the Western industrialized economies. This accommodation takes the form of rendering their labour and resources open to exploitation in situ, supplying raw materials and other inputs needed by the industrialized economies, and providing markets for their products. For this purpose it is necessary to ensure unimpeded access to the raw materials and markets of third world countries, as well as the uninterrupted movement of capital into, and profits out of, third world economies.

To achieve this in the post-independence era, imperialism needs to control developments within third world countries, at least to the extent of putting in place, or keeping in being, mechanisms which reproduce the conditions of dependence. That way it is able to maintain conditions for indirect control through the manipulation of economic factors. In this regard, the situation of chronic shortage of foreign exchange, food deficits and the existence of a substantial external debt constitute an excellent basis for non-political, non-military manipulation of political and economic decision-making within third world polities, and the continued extraction of surplus value therefrom.

It has already been observed that the extent of external determination of the internal policies of any sub-Saharan African country depends on several factors. It is the case, however, that whatever the other conditions may be, the influence of external factors is perhaps greatest in times of crisis within the sub-Saharan African economies. It is, therefore, not surprising that even the most resistant African countries end up "suing for peace" with the IMF/World Bank.[10] Thus as a result of the desperation faced by most sub-Saharan African countries in the recent past, the leverage of the IMF and World Bank in Africa has become more pronounced and overt,[11] and the character of adjustment programmes adopted by these countries has been more decisively shaped by those institutions.

For instance, a critical focus of almost all adjustment programmes is the restoration of basic infrastructure allowed to collapse during the years of the crisis, with a very heavy bias in favour of infrastructure related to export production. Thus harbours, railways, trunk roads, etc., have tended to attract a disproportionate amount of the new public investment. A strong argument could be made that the restoration of such infrastructure is indispensable to economic recovery in any event. It just happens that this rebuilding of infrastructure tends to reinforce the commitment to, and dependence on, the production of primary commodities for export. The assured supply of such inputs certainly benefits the industrialized economies. The benefits to the sub-Saharan African countries of increased production of primary commodities for export are less clear in the long run, but even in the short run, the already low export prices should give cause for worry.

When one turns to the social sectors, it is noticeable that inspite of the lip service paid to the need to improve the social sectors of the economy, not much investment of new capital is made in those sectors. Such investment as gets made is of secondary importance, and the procurement methods adopted in connection therewith, as with the heavy infrastructural investments mentioned above invariably involve the importation of finished goods from the industrialized countries.

Another example relates to national policy on the use of foreign exchange. To contain the perennial problem of acute shortage of foreign exchange, almost all third world countries have introduced measures to control access to foreign exchange by their citizens. The argument for this set of controls is that it enables the State to allocate its limited foreign exchange resources to the most productive sectors of the economy. Much fault can be, and has undoubtedly been, found with the administration of such controls. This has provided a convenient basis for a wholesale attack on such controls. The leadership of this attack by the IMF/World Bank, which espouse an ideology totally opposed to exchange controls, has little to do with the well-being of individual third world economies. It has more to do with the manifest interest of the transnational corporations in the free mobility of their capital and the repatriation of their profits. For this reason, the Articles of Agreement of the IMF provide against the imposition by its members of any restrictions on international payments for "current transactions between members" [Art.1 (iv)]. It is, therefore, hardly surprising that among the principal features of adjustment programmes are the reduction/removal of exchange controls, the lifting of restrictions on imports and the free repatriation of profits by foreign investors.

What is the likely impact of the removal of such controls on the use of foreign exchange in a country suffering from a severe foreign exchange shortage? It does not leave much to the imagination. The flight of capital and the rampant importation of items with the readiest and most profitable markets would be the most obvious short-term effects. Were the country able to procure foreign exchange in sufficient quantity to meet all the demands on its foreign exchange resources, it would be possible to permit the market to determine access to foreign exchange. This would ensure the most efficient allocation of national resources in the medium to long term, without sacrificing essential but "unprofitable" imports. That is the ostensible argument for the push against exchange and import controls. Unfortunately, sub-Saharan African countries never have access to enough foreign exchange for long enough to achieve this effect. That indeed, is part of the essence of the crisis. What one finds, therefore, is the prolongation of the short-term capital flight and importation of profitable inessential goods into the medium and long term, and the continuing shortage of critical manufacturing inputs, leading to the contraction of the economy (Hansohm, 1986, p.154).

It can, therefore, be said that whatever the theoretical benefits of this liberalization of the foreign exchange position, in the specific conditions of third world economies in crisis, the negative effects tend to continue unrelieved by the expected benefits. Why, then, would anybody advocate liberalization of the foreign exchange position, in the specific conditions of third world economies in crisis, the negative effects tend to continue unrelieved by the expected benefits. Why, then, would anybody advocate liberalization in this form? The answer is that whilst the negative effects are felt by the majority in the sub-Saharan African countries, the benefits accrue to interests mainly outside. Not surprisingly, it is the representatives of those outside interests and their collaborators within who are the strongest advocates of liberalization.

The vulnerability of third world countries and the pressures exerted by the industrialized countries directly or through international financial institutions derives as we have seen from the dependent location of third world countries in the world economic order, and the extreme crisis affecting them. To reinforce this vulnerability, industrialized countries insist upon dealing with third world countries individually rather than in blocs. Thus, in spite of the obviously similar problems confronting, say, the sub-Saharan African countries, and their attempts to formulate common positions on any economic issues, the industrialized countries and their institutions invariably insist upon handling these matters on a case-by-country, basis.

This is particularly significant in the case of the international debt problem facing third world countries. It is recognized that African countries, for instance, are affected in broadly similar ways by external debt. They have, therefore, begun to take common positions on the approach to the debt crisis (APPER, 1985 para. 99–100; *Submission*, 1986 paras. 68–75). Yet the industrialized countries still insist that they are only prepared to consider and apply debt-relief measures country by country.[12]

Since it is easier in these bilateral discussions to treat different countries differently, often in response to non-economic factors, there is a strong temptation for African countries which expect to get special treatment to break rank and divide the front of Africa on this and other issues. The result is that in spite of the clear desire of African countries, acting through the OAU, ECA and sub-regional groups, to plan and act in concert in these matters (APPER, 1985 Para. 100), western industrialized countries are able to pressure them individually into adjustment programmes which lock them individually into western capitalist orbit. This weakens the drive by African countries to co-ordinate the attack on the crisis and to link up with other third world countries in a meaningful push for the reshaping of the international economic order.

We turn now to a consideration of the internal political conditions needed to push through and sustain the adjustment measures. We also consider the effects of these measures, in turn, on the social and political conditions of the country. The answers must be found not only in the character of the specific measures but also in their effect on the various social groups. For whatever the objectives and potential long-run prospects, a decisive political factor is the short-term acceptance of the austerity programme by people in the country, whether this "acceptance" be willing or coerced. This can be assessed in relation to the broad social groups as follows:

(a) The broad mass of working people, covering wage labourers as well as lower-level employees in both the public and private sectors, are very seriously hit by the retrenchment exercise which forms a critical part of any adjustment package. In addition to the large number of layoffs of this category of worker, the majority of those who remain in employment suffer from a widening gap between the bottom and the top of the wage/salary structure. This increasing differentiation is a deliberate policy measure aimed at increasing incentives to top executives and professionals, especially in the public service;
  (i) The effect of this reduced work force is to create a situation of fewer but, on the average, better-paid workers. It also leads to an expansion of the "petty services sector" – often no more than a thinly disguised addition to the pool of the unemployed. Unfortunately, of those who remain in employment, even the best-paid, particularly in the public service, are subject to a severe erosion of the real value of their earnings. This follows from the constantly escalating prices of essentials and the astronomic increases in the cost of public services resulting from the regime of cost recovery introduced as part of the adjustment process;
  (ii) In short, for the working people market determination of prices and cost recovery for public services lead to a further drop in the standard of living. Coupled with the constant threat of retrenchment, and without unemployment benefits, this puts workers in an extremely grim situation;

(b) We have noted the opening up of the domestic market to foreign competition through the removal of protective barriers for local industry and the liberalization of foreign exchange and import policy. We have also referred to credit policy and restrictions on money supply, and their effects on the liquidity position of local manufacturing industry by driving it increasingly into bankruptcy or partnership with foreign capital. These measures, therefore, constitute a severe attack on what we might describe as the national capitalist class. This would include indigenous entrepreneurs who would normally seek to bring under their exclusive control, and put to productive use, all national productive forces, thus becoming indigenous "captains of industry";

(c) When we turn to the loose category of the urban and rural poor, the condition is perhaps grimmest of all:
  (i) The urban poor we take to include town-dwellers with no access to farmland, and who, not being in wage employment, engage in small-scale buying and selling and the provision of petty services. The social and material conditions of this category are at all times no better than precarious. But this is made unbearable by the deterioration and high cost of public services. Since they do not dispose of significant money incomes and are not so placed as to benefit from the perquisites of public or private office, they sink deeper into poverty and degradation;
  (ii) Grinding rural poverty has always been a characteristic of the underdeveloped economy even at the height of commodity price booms. This is often obscured in the determination of aggregate or "average" rural incomes, which lump big landowners, commercial farmers and rural money lenders together with peasant farmers

> and landless agricultural workers for the purpose. One of the principal measures undertaken under the adjustment programmes is an increase in producer prices. But the benefits of this measure do not always spread evenly throughout the rural community, the bulk usually going to the better-placed large farmers, transport owners and money lenders. Thus, while they may not get the full benefit of increases in producer prices, the rural poor invariably feel the full rigour of the negative aspects of the adjustment process. The increasing cost of credit, inputs and services like transport weigh heavily on them, while social services such as education and medical facilities remain beyond their means.

The poor in society thus become poorer, both relatively and absolutely, under the austerity measures. As a recent UNICEF study concluded, "No adjustment policy is acceptable which allows children to be sacrificed for the sake of financial stability. Yet it has happened, and it need not happen" (UNICEF, 1987, p.4).

Clearly if these were the only groups in society there would be little possibility of such austerity measures being introduced or maintained. But there are social groups that benefit from the introduction of these measures. These would include:

(a) people in the higher echelons of the public service, who because of the technocratic thrust of the structural adjustment programmes, and big people in the party apparatus who through increased control over patronage, enjoy not only improved material conditions from the new order, but also increased political power and social prestige;
(b) top executives in private business, especially businesses to do with foreign capital, who therefore derive the most from the mini-boom conditions created by the injection of foreign exchange into the economy;
(c) the comprador class, embracing a wide variety of occupations – from local agents of foreign businesses, partners and consultants to such businesses, to institutions providing specialized services such as hotel accommodation and advertising to foreign interests;
(d) import and export merchants, especially those able to get foreign exchange at the official rate, usually through special connections;
(e) the beneficiaries of the privatization measures, who are able to buy up or buy into State-owned enterprises, usually at concessional prices and with credit easily obtained officially or through the appropriate connections; and
(f) large landowners and big-time commercial farmers who get the benefit of the higher producer prices, low-wage policy, as well as privileged access to State-provided inputs and services.

It thus becomes clear that, at least in the short run, austerity for the majority goes hand-in-hand with benefit, in some cases, windfall benefits, to a minority, who, not infrequently, indulge in the most conspicuous consumption.

What are the political implications of the developments sketched out above?

(a) The poor and deteriorating conditions of the majority of the people create a situation of more or less overt restiveness and opposition to the austerity measures. Whatever form such opposition takes, one of its effects is to isolate the alliance of minority groups who, in concert with foreign interests, support the programme;

(b) As the austerity measures tend to be opposed by the majority, usually spearheaded by organized labour and elements of the intelligentsia, it becomes necessary for the ruling alliance to: move to shut off public discussion of the measures and government policy generally; and put down such opposition by the suppression of the elements spearheading opposition, and by outlawing or restricting strikes and crushing mass demonstrations, if necessary, by the violent use of State power.[13] It is hardly surprising that military regimes and authoritarian civilian governments – whether of the one-party, no party or multi-party variety – provide the political conditions most conducive to the maintenance of the current crop of structural adjustment programmes in Africa;[13a]

(c) The resulting disenfranchisement of the majority and the shutting-off of public discussion tend to provide a smokescreen for mismanagement and corruption because there is no effective check on the activities of those in high office. Moreover, these developments lead to the demoralization and apathy of the mass of the people. Many governments are surprised by this, and complain bitterly about how unproductive and lazy the people are. They then resort to the most strident exhortations to people to produce, sacrifice, show discipline, loyalty to government or party or country, etc. In a few cases where the prevailing rhetoric favours "participation", it is noticeable that as soon as the mass of the people attempt to give meaning to the concept, the State quickly pulls it back in the supposed interest of discipline, productivity or whatever. The people promptly revert to the status of supportive, or at any rate silent and uncomplaining, producers. There is thus no serious attempt to mobilize and motivate the mass of the people, lest they start asking questions and making demands;

(d) Particularly as a means of counteracting the largely urban-based opposition to austerity, there is much play on a rural-urban dichtomy, usually in the form of the allegation that the people in town are "exploiting" the rural populace. This notion of an undifferentiated urban populace exploiting an equally undifferentiated rural populace clearly flies in the face of observable fact. Yet it has the merit of helping to divide the disenfranchised majority of urban and rural poor and therefore, at least for a time, to weaken the opposition to the austerity measures. This is particularly the case where the rhetoric is followed by an increase in investment and services in the rural areas. This divisive effect does not last too long, however, mainly because, whatever benefits come to the countryside usually accrue disproportionately to the rural rich and absentee owners. The rhetoric, nevertheless, tends to give legitimacy to rural chauvinism and ethnic politics.

It needs to be emphasized that not all effects of structural adjustment programmes are so negative, nor are all the negative outcomes the result exclusively of the adjustment programmes. Indeed, the location of most third world economies within the international economic order and their internal economic and class structures would alone predispose them in the directions indicated. The argument outlined above is simply that the nature of the adjustment process hastens them along the path and consolidates the process.

What is usually said in defence of the structural adjustment programmes is that without IMF/IBRD support and the financial flows it brings, adjustment would be too harsh on the people. On the other hand, if the strategy embodied in the structural adjustment programme succeeds, it will generate greater wealth all round, thereby making it possible to alleviate the sufferings even of the majority. The problem with this argument is that it is difficult to envisage a successful outcome of the programme. In the first place there is no credible strategy for industrialization on the basis of the full development and use of local raw materials and skills. Nor does it create the political and social conditions for the effective motivation, mobilization and organization of the whole nation behind the development drive – indeed, it can be argued that it does the precise opposite, at least in the short run.

Second, financial flows on the scale required are unlikely to be forthcoming even on the most optimistic assumptions. As estimated by African leaders, the total resource requirements needed to sustain APPER over the period 1986–1990 is $US 128.1 billion, of which $45.6 billion (or 35.6 percent) must come from outside. (*Submission* 1986, para. 100). Assuming that Africa is able to raise $US 82.5 billion out of its domestic resources – the record over the first two years gives no cause for optimism – what are the chances of it securing financial flows averaging $US 9.1 billion over and above debt service obligations conservatively estimated at $US 14.6 billion (Abuja Statement, 1987, para 12) each year for five years?

Even if these resources were mobilized, and the correct industrial policies followed, without substantial exportation of manufactures, the strategy is sure to founder. Where are the markets for these manufactured products, within the African region? In the underdeveloped countries? In the developed industrialized countries? Does anyone need to be reminded about the strong protectionist pressures in those countries against imports from the more "successful" third world countries? (Payer, *South*, Jan. 1987, 44).

Even if a few sub-Saharan African countries could overcome all these handicaps and make a break-through, can anyone expect this to be generalizable at the same time to other sub-Saharan African countries? Again, structural change of the sort needed to make such development occur and continue will take no less than 10–20 years to be fully established. What are the prospects of political stability in any sub-Saharan African country holding long enough for this to happen?

Given these circumstances, in particular the one-sided dependence on international capitalism, the stifling of productive national capital and the failure to develop industry which would productively absorb surplus labour and provide for national needs in the medium to long term, are we not faced with prospects of austerity without end?[14]

The future would appear to promise:

(a) The immiseration of increasing numbers or increasing proportions of the populace without exciting sustained, effective and militant resistance,[15] because of the absence of truly national capital and a developed and organized working class — the very classes needed to spearhead the resistance to domination by foreign capital.[16] But for the reasons given, the economy will not develop because the full development of the productive forces is not possible under the structural adjustment measures. The crisis will, therefore, persist. Continuing political instability will result in the replacement of one repressive fragment of the ruling group or military junta for another – a form of political musical chairs – with the mass of the people becoming essentially interested but demoralized observer-victims;

(b) As a decline in productive capacity occurs in one third world country after the other, the repercussions for the international capitalist economic order would become critical. Can the Western industrialized countries move out of deep recession under conditions of the near-collapse of the third world economies? Are we in for a 1930s-type depression, a development which has so far been successfully held back by the manipulation of monetary and fiscal measures, and the shifting of the burden of recovery into the third world countries? How can the many contradictions in contemporary capitalism be resolved? A third world war, perhaps?

Adjustment "With a Human Face"

The account given above of the African economic crisis and the attempts by the sub-Saharan African countries to resolve it, especially the impact of the adjustment measures on the poorer sections of society, make very sombre reading. In recognition of this, the question has been posed, both within Africa and by the international community: can the adjustment measures considered necessary to resolve the crisis be carried out in such a way as to remove, or at least minimize, the harshness of its effect on the people of the sub-Saharan African countries – in particular the most vulnerable groups?[17]

This concern to put a "human face" upon the various structural adjustment programmes has taken many forms:

(a) the introduction of special arrangements to cushion the impact of the adjustment measures on the most vulnerable groups in society – an example is the introduction of nutritional support programmes for special target groups such as children under five years old, and lactating and nursing mothers' with UNICEF playing a very active role;[18]

(b) the expansion of public services and an increase in resource flows into the social services – education, health, rural water and sanitation, etc., – specially directed at the poorer sections of society;

(c) "food-for-work" schemes aimed at putting unemployed and under-employed people, especially the youth, to work on projects of special community value, such as improved water supply, schools, clinics and feeder roads; and

(d) schemes aimed at increasing income-generation among lower-income households.

It is to be noted that the objective of these programmes is to alleviate the traumas that fall upon the vulnerable target groups as a result of the full implementation of the structural adjustment programmes. These schemes are, therefore, subject to the following considerations;

(a) They must be compatible with the ideological and theoretical basis of structural adjustment programmes in general, and specific measures in each country. This poses some serious problems. For instance, how do we reconcile the concern to extend the social services to the weaker elements in society with the insistence upon limiting public spending and ensuring cost recovery for public services? If the answer is that this is to be done by redirecting public spending away from the privileged and in favour of the underprivileged, given present political and social alignments, how promising are the prospects?[19] To take another example, the notion of providing special help to retrenched workers in a situation where the national economy is being effectively de-industrialized – at least kept industrially stagnant – will require considerable public expenditure to sustain them and help set them up in new occupations. How does this square with the drive to cut public spending and remove subsidies and handouts?

(b) The fact of the matter is that the proposals outlined above run counter to the basic thrust of structural adjustment programmes, namely the market-determination of prices and the allocation of resources and the reduced role of the State in the specific management of the economy. Consequently the measures aimed at ameliorating the harshness of the structural adjustment programmes must be seen as short term, to be removed as the economy "adjusts" and market forces smooth over the rough edges of the adjusted economy;

(c) The expectation that the fully "adjusted" economy will have no need for ameliorating measures of this sort rests on assumptions about the prospects of successful adjustment and the character of the "adjusted" economy. In particular, it presupposes real growth within the economy combined with equitable distribution of the benefits of such growth. Even if the correct policies were adopted and followed and the appropriate political and social conditions maintained within sub-Saharan African countries, it would take a great deal of optimism to anticipate the attainment and maintenance of an adequately supportive external environment to ensure the development of sub-Saharan African economies to the point of self-sustaining growth.[20] But were one to make that leap of faith as well, it would still not be realistic to expect sub-Saharan African countries to raise themselves from their present depressed and ill-structured condition on to anything like the plane of self-sustaining growth in less than 10, more likely 20 years.

Some crucial questions need to be answered. Is it possible to maintain the internal political and social stability required to give the programmes time to work? Put another way, what assurance is there that such growth as is generated will be accompanied by enough equity in the distribution of its benefits to create the conditions necessary for maintaining the required social cohesion and dynamism? What political conditions exist, or are in prospect, to enable the genuine mobilization of the full range of national talent and human resources needed to sustain a structural adjustment programme?

Without the development of a strong locally sustainable industrial base, what prospects are there in any sub-Saharan African country for true development of a self-reliant, self-sustaining economy, sufficiently flexible to withstand difficult economic conditions without going into reverse gear? In the absence of such prospects, is it conceivable that the harshness of the structural adjustment programme will ever abate?

(d) It should be clear from what has been said throughout the paper that it would not be enough to adopt the correct internal policies nor would it be possible to create and sustain the appropriate internal conditions, without radical adjustments of the international environment within which sub-Saharan African economies are so deeply embedded.

Conclusion

The burden of the above comments is not to counsel despair. It is to indicate that whatever policies are adopted should take full account of the very real limitations of the individual sub-Saharan African economies, and should form part of a realistic agenda for the effective transformation of the sub-Saharan African economies, no matter how difficult the path, or how distant the prospect of success. Unless the correct agenda is mapped out, the short-term steps could easily be seen as the unavoidable answer to the problem, rather than what they are, at best, steps necessary to create the conditions for addressing the fundamental issues.

Against this background, it may be noted that it is possible, even today, for sub-Saharan African countries to have greater influence on the terms of their relationship with international institutions than they do now. We have seen that the position of sub-Saharan African countries is weakened in part by the fact that they are compelled to deal individually with the international community. It is true that this weakness is recognized and steps are being taken to remedy it. It remains the case, however, that for several reasons, sub-Saharan African countries, like other third world countries, are unable to resist the temptation to reach out for individual advantage in their dealings with the Western industrialized countries, rather than hold out for collective action and collective benefit.

There are, clearly, major difficulties posed by the political reality of the present international economic order which stand in the way of collective action of the sort suggested above as distinct from collective pronouncement. But the argument here is that, as present arrangements fail in one country after the other, as conditions in individual countries and the region as a whole worsen, such collective action would come to be recognized as being no longer simply desirable, but indeed a condition sine qua non for true development. Fortunately, there are straws in the wind pointing to the increasing realization by many countries that this has to be the direction of movement.[21]

Even before we reach the stage of such collective action, however, individual sub-Saharan African countries could do much better in negotiations with the IMF/IBRD and the transnational corporations. Instead of pretending that structural adjustment programmes worked out with the IMF/IBRD are their own creation, the leadership in sub-Saharan African countries could be more honest about these programmes, acknowledging them as perhaps necessary evils by means of which they expect to be able to get needed international help. To be sure, this would mean that the regime in power would have to face vocal and active local opposition to the measures. But, could we not agree with President Nyerere that,

> "When they understand the problems, our people will response to these economic challenges as they have responded to other challenges in the past. I believe they will bear the further sacrifices, and further burdens, which pressing conditions impose upon us,just as long as they are assured that we are doing our best to share the burdens equitably, and continue to pursue our own policies." (Nyerere, 1980, p.9) (emphasis supplied)

In sum, where the leadership is able to take the people into its confidence because it is genuinely reflecting their wishes, there is greater assurance that the sacrifices required for adjustment will be forthcoming from the majority of the people.

Another consequence of such openess about negotiations with the IMF/IBRD and the investor community would be that both the third world leaders and the international community would be fully aware of the limits of tolerance of the people who will have to put up with the proposed measures. This would put third world negotiators in a position somewhat similar to that of those with whom they are negotiating. For neither the sub-Saharan African negotiators nor the representatives of the IMF/IBRD are ever in any doubt about the interests and the wishes of the industrialized countries and their transnational corporations. Similar clarity about true sub-Saharan African positions can only strengthen the bargaining hand of sub-Saharan African negotiators vis-à-vis the IMF/IBRD and the investor community.

The point here is that true democratic discussion within sub-Saharan African countries about the real options open to them is an indispensable condition for effective confrontation with the IMF/IBRD. [see *Abuja Statement* para. 33 (b) and (g)]. Not only will this help mobilize people for the necessary increases in production and productivity and predispose them to bear the sacrifices, but also it would bring more fully into the arena the disenfranchised majority of the people in most sub-Saharan African countries – the social groups best able to sustain a confrontation with the interests represented by the IMF/World Bank.

What all this means is that, in spite of well-meant palliatives, the present adjustment programmes will continue to work unconscionable hardship on the majority of the people, and still fail to achieve their long term development objectives, without political struggles within each country, and between the peoples of the underdeveloped world and the ruling interests in the industrialized capitalist world. It is only in the context of this two-level political struggle that one can contemplate the full emancipation of the peoples of sub-Saharan Africa, and the liberation of their productive capacity and genius, not just from the current crisis, but from domination by international capital and an unending cycle of such crises.

Notes

1 By the end of May 1987, 28 African countries were implementing structural adjustment programmes. (*Abuja Statement*, (1987), ECA/CERAD/87/75 para. 7.)

2 The latest at the time of writing were (a) "Africa: The challenge of Economic Recovery and

Accelerated Development", held at Abuja, Nigeria in June 1987 (see "The Abuja Statement", 1987); (b) "The impact of IMF and World Bank policies on people of Africa" organized by the Institute for African Alternatives, in London in September, 1987.

3 For a similar approach see Sutcliffe 1986, 18; and Szentes, 1978, 15–17 (Tropical Africa).

4 This is as true of those countries that have espoused scientific socialism and aligned themselves with the Socialist bloc as of the others.

5 This is succinctly set out in *Submission*, 1986, paras. 27–32, *Trade and Development*, 1986, 32; Sutcliffe, 1986, 19–20; OECD, 1987, 8–13.

6 It has been estimated that a 2½ percentage drop in United States interest rates implied a saving of US 13 billion on the debt-service burden of developing countries: *Trade and Development* 1986, II.

7 Moreover it is an open secret that in most cases the draft structural adjustment programme documents are worked out and approved by the staff and management of the IMF and/or World Bank before they are submitted to officials of the country to which the programme was to be applied for in-depth discussion. This does not, of course, mean that those officials make no contribution. But it does mean that the framework for the discussion is preset by the IMF/ World Bank.

8 See "The Arusha initiative", 1980, para.8; Girvan, 1980, 73.

9 For useful accounts see Abdalla 1980; Harris, 1986, 92–95; and Hayter and Watson, 1985, chap.7.

10 The cases of Jamaica after Prime Minister Manley and the United Republic of Tanzania after President Nyerere are well-known – see Manley, 1980, 5; Girvan *et al.*, 1980 113; Malima, 1986; and Biermann and Wagao 1986.

11 It is noteworthy that out of the total IMF credit committed worldwide under stand-by or extended facilities tied to conditionality, Africa accounted for 30 percent in 1979 and 1980 – the comparable figure for 1970–1978 was 3 percent (Harris, 1986, 83). Again, the World Bank is reported to be attempting to raise up to $US 2 billion per annum to be put into a special fund available only to sub-Saharan African countries pursuing acceptable adjustment programmes: Loxley, 1986, p.101; *Abuja Statement*, para. 13. On the general question of leverage, see Hayter and Watson, 1985, chap. 6.

12 A notable, perhaps pathbreaking, exception is the recent announcement by Canada that it was canceling debts owed it by francophone and Commonwealth African countries.

13 Examples of so-called "IMF/World Bank riots" (Hayter and Watson, 1985, 139) abound in the recent history of Africa: Egypt (1977), Tunisia, Morocco (1984) the Sudan and Zambia (1987), to name but a few.

13a Referring to the development of repressive regimes throughout Asia, Africa and Latin America in the course of the 1970's, Frank makes the following observation:
"This repressive political policy has very clear economic purposes and functions to increase the competitiveness of these economies on the world market by lowering wages and to suppress those elements of the local bourgeoisie who are tied to the internal market." (Frank, 1984, 64).

14 In its submission to the United Nations General Assembly in 1986, Africa's leaders could not avoid "the overall conclusion . . . that the adjustment packages so far adopted by African countries have not been particularly successful in realizing their overall objectives of restoring internal and external equilibrium and effecting a resumption of steady growth". (*Submission*, para. 109). OECD, speaking of financing prospects for the developing countries generally in 1986, observed that "The light at the end of the tunnel has yet to appear". (OECD, 1986, 8).

15 The periodic strikes and "bread riots", ferociously put down by the State, do not qualify as "effective militant resistance".

16 A panel of representatives of United States Government and business is reported to have said in 1971 about developments in the Philippines:
"As Filipino enterprises have grown and moved into new activities, Filipinos and American businessmen have become competitive and the former . . . have taken political action to minimize the threat of American competition. As the most influential political group motivated to limit access to Philippine resources and markets, they have provided a respectable nucleus around which diverse nationalist elements have coalesced . . ." (quoted in Bello, *et al*. 1982, 137).

17 In an address to UNCTAD M. Michel Camdessus, Managing Director of the IMF, had this to say: "Growth-oriented adjustment does not have to lower basic human standards. Indeed . . . the more programmes give proper weight to social realities – especially their implications for the poorest – the more successful they are likely to be." IMF Survey, 27, July 1987, p.234.

18 UNICEF reports on successful vaccination drives in Burkina Faso, the Sudan and Mozambi-

que. UNICEF, 1987, 22, 42 and 48.

[19] A noteable instance of exactly this redirection is Indonesia's success in increasing spending on immunization even while making cuts in overall health spending – mainly by postponing the building of new hospitals. UNICEF, 1987, p.4.

[20] UNCTAD reports that "The outlook for Africa is far from encouraging. Growth rates remain at relatively low levels throughout the period (1985–1995), and this was accompanied by a substantial worsening of all the external financial variables . . . The examination of regional situations . . . reveals the potential for the emergence of a debt situation in Africa that can only be described as alarming." *Trade and Development*, 1986, pp.121-122; see also *Abuja Statement*, para. 8.

[21] OAU is reported to be planning a summit meeting on the debt question for December 1987 to keep up the momentum towards an international conference on the whole issue of third world indebtedness.

References

1 Abdalla, I., "The inadequacy and loss of legitimacy of the International Monetary fund", *Development Dialogue*, 1980: 2, 25.

2 *Abuja Statement*, (1987), ECA/CERAD/87/75.

3 *Africa's Priority Programme for Economic Recovery 1986–1990*, OAU. (1985)

4 "Arusha Initiative: A call for a United Nations Conference on International Money and Finance", *Development Dialogue*, 1980: 2, 10.

5 Bello, W., Kinley, D., and Elinson, E., *The Development Debacle: The World Bank in the Philippines*, San Francisco: Institute for Food and Development Policy, (1982).

6 Biermann, W. and Wagao, J., "The IMF and Tanzania – a solution to the crisis?" in Peter Lawrence (ed.), *World Recession and the Food Crisis in Africa*, 140, London: James Currey. (1986).

7 Frank, A.G. "Economic crisis, export promotion and political repression in the third world", in Ngo Manh-Lam (ed). *Unreal Growth: Critical Studies in Asian Development*, vol. 1, 54, Delhi: Hindustan Publishing Corp, (1984).

8 Girvan, N, "Swallowing the IMF medicine in the seventies", *Development Dialogue*, 1980: 2, 55

9 Girvan, N., Bernal, R., and Hughes, W., "The IMF and the third world: the case of Jamaica 1974–1980", *Development Dialogue*, 1980: 2, 113.

10 Hansohm, D. (1986), "The success of IMF/World Bank policies in Sudan", in Lawrence, op.cit., 148.

11 Harris, L. (1986), "Conceptions of the IMF's role in Africa", in Lawrence, op. cit., 83.

12 Hayter, T., and Watson, C., *Aid: Rhetoric and reality*, London and Sydney: Pluto Press,(1985).

13 Loxley, J., "IMF and World Bank conditionality in sub-Saharan Africa", in Lawrence op. cit. 96.

14 Lagos Plan of Action for the Economic Development of Africa, 1980–2000, OAU. (1981)

15 Manley, N., "Message to South-North Conference on the International Monetary System and the New International Economic Order", *Development Dialogue*, 1980: 2, 5.

16 Nyerere J.K., "No to IMF meddling", *Development Dialogue*, 1980: 2, 7.

17 OECD, (1987), *Financing and External Debt of Developing Countries: 1986 survey*, Paris: OECD.

18 Payer C., *South*, January 1987, 43.

19 Sawyerr, A., (1984), "The New International Economic Order: What in it, for whom, and where is it going?" in A. Sawyerr (ed), *Economic Development and Trade in Papua New Guinea*, 292–303, University of Papua New Guinea Press.

20 *Africa's Submission to the Special Session of the United Nations General Assembly on Africa's Economic and Social Crisis*, OAU/ECM/2XV/Rev.2; E/ECA/ECM.1/1/Rev.2.

21 Sutcliffe, Bob, (1986), "Africa and the world economic crisis" in Lawrence op. cit., 18.

22 Szentes, T., "Tropical Africa", in J. Nyilas (ed.), *The Changing Face of the Third World: Regional and National Studies*, Pt. 1, Leyden and Budapest, A.W. Sijthoff and Akademiai Kiado.(1978).

23 UNCTAD, *Trade and Development Report*, 1986.

24 UNICEF, *The State of the World's Children, 1987*, (Report by J.P. Grant, Executive Director of UNICEF).

25 UN-PAAERD, (1986), *United Nations Programme of Action for African Economic Recovery and Development, 1986–1990*, United Nations General Assembly, A/RES/S13/2, 13 June 1986.

27 World Bank, *World Development Report*, 1986. Oxford University Press.

The Human Dimension of Structural Adjustment Programmes: The World Bank's Perspective

ISMAIL SERAGELDIN (WORLD BANK)

Introduction

The severity and depth of the African crisis have challenged the international development community as have few other problems. The World Bank responded to this challenge by a series of in-depth studies starting in 1981 and continuing to the present.[1] It also made assisting African Governments in redressing the decline in African economic performance an institutional priority.[2]

Currently, many governments in sub-Saharan Africa have adopted far-reaching stabilization and adjustment programs aimed at making the national economies more flexible and responsive to changing world conditions with a view to restoring real growth in the medium term. Throughout the design of these programmes, it has been very much a concern of both the governments and the Bank to ensure that the burdens of adjustment are equitably distributed across all population groups. Even more, that the fruits of the restored growth would benefit the poor as well as the more wealthy.

The integration of the concern for the poor in the design and implementation of development plans generally and of adjustment programs specifically has been a major objective of Bank action in the last few years. Fine tuning these actions and assessing their effectiveness, however, has been seriously hampered by the extreme paucity of the socio-economic data base in most African countries, particularly relating to income distribution and the pattern of consumption. As a result, it is only possible to make qualitative observations on the current socio-economic status of various segments of the populations in the countries and on the probable effects of different policies and programmes. The proper targeting of measures to protect vulnerable groups and/or to offset transitional costs is extremely difficult, and significant leakages may occur. It becomes essential, therefore, to make improvements in the socio-economic data bases needed to identify poor groups an integral part of the Bank's action plan to address poverty in sub-Saharan Africa.

Such country specific data bases are all the more needed given the wide diversity of country situations found in the region, which call for different focuses in the design of anti-poverty programs and make the transferability of programs and experiences from one country to another not obvious. Indeed, per capita GNP levels in sub-Saharan Africa cover a 10:1 range between the richest and poorest country. Likewise, average annual GDP growth rates in the current decade have varied from −10 percent to +12 percent. Population growth rates vary between 1.3 percent and 4.1 percent. Health and education indicators also show wide variations among the countries. Under such conditions, region-wide tendencies may provide a poor guideline for country-specific action. The rest of this paper, therefore has to be seen as a general statement with wide divergences in its applicability to country specific conditions.

Restoring Growth with Equity

The dire macro-economic plight of sub-Saharan African countries is well known. Among the 22 low-income countries in the region for which data are available, seven recorded a negative average annual growth rate of GDP over the period 1980–85.[3] Among those that experienced positive growth, only 3 succeeded in achieving a GDP growth rate in excess of the population growth rate. The performance of the middle income economies over the same period was only slightly better. Three countries recorded negative GDP growth, and in all but four GDP per capita growth was negative. Those four exceptions, however, are the countries with the highest absolute GDP per capita.

There is a basic consensus that restoring adequate rates of self-sustained growth is the primary objective of development in sub-Saharan Africa. No poverty alleviation strategy can be sustained without restoring economic growth. This is not to argue the old-fashioned "trickle down" theory, but to recognize that growth is a sine-qua-non for sustained poverty alleviation. Under any circumstances, growth is not an end in itself but must be widely distributed in its impacts if it is to be sustainable. This requires not only rising per capita income with reduction in income disparities but also the systematic development of human resources – a primary engine of long-term development.

Focus on the growth objective became particularly acute in the 1980s due to a series of unprecedented external shocks, the consequence of economic mismanagement in the second half of the 1970s and growing distortions in economic structures. In retrospect, the "euphoric" period of the 1970s which enabled economic excesses to be financed also masked the underlying weakness of African economies heavily dependent on a few primary export commodities which no longer held the prospect of being able to produce the growth rates of the past. As a consequence, in the 1980s country after country in Africa (25 at the latest count) adopted sweeping structural adjustment programmes. These programmes were launched in a period of fluctuating and often sharp further declines in the terms of trade, high real interest rates which exacerbated the crushing burden of excessive foreign debts, and droughts which wiped out the gains made by the poorer sub-Sharan countries. Nevertheless, the preliminary findings are quite encouraging. Countries with sustained adjustment programs succeeded in achieving 0.8 percent per annum real growth rates of GDP per capita over 1984–86, while those who had not adopted such programs registered a negative 2.5 percent per annum in GDP per capita. This should be compared to both groups registering declines in GDP per capita averaging −4.0 percent per annum over the 1980–84 period.

In some cases reforms could not be sustained because of the absence of adequate flows of external assistance. The adjustment programs were also associated with severe impacts on the most vulnerable groups and cuts in vital social spending. Yet the very sustainability of these programmes is a function of maintaining a political consensus for reform. It is an unhappy fact that the costs of adjustment will have to be borne by some groups before the benefits to all become fully apparent.

In this context, structural adjustment has three basic components. First, a reform of the system of economic incentives with the objective of changing the structure of incentives in favor of tradeable versus non-tradeable accompanied by measures to liberalize economies so that factors of production can seek their highest returns. Second, a retrenchment of the public sector by cutting the excessive size and costs of civil services,rationalizing the overextended public enterprises while directing scarce public financial resources towards the provision of basic infrastructure, the support of vital economic services and the development of human resources. An important feature of such programmes is the freeing of domestic resources for private sector investment and production. Third, the programmes also call for a comprehensive restructuring of the external debt with the objective of relieving the resource constraint as part of the effort to mobilize foreign assistance in support of a growth-oriented strategy.

Table 1. Per Capita GDP Growth Rates, 1960–86 (Annual average in percent)

Country Group	1960–70	1970–80	1980–86	1980–84	1984–86
Sub-Sahara: Low Income	0.9	−0.5	−2.1	−2.4	−0.6
Sub-Sahara: Other	1.4	1.7	−4.3	−5.0	−2.9
Sub-Sahara: Total	1.2	0.9	−3.4	−4.0	−1.8
Other Africa	2.8	4.1	0.8	1.3	−0.1
Total Africa	1.5	1.5	−1.9	−2.9	−1.5
Memo items:					
Sub-Sahara: Countries with adjustment programmes[1]	1.8	0.7	−2.5	−3.8	0.8
Sub-Sahara: Other	1.1	0.9	−3.6	−4.0	−2.5

[1] Countries with sustained and substantial adjustment programmes commencing before FY 1985: Cote d'Ivoire, Ghana, Kenya, Malawi, Mauritius, Senegal, Togo and Zambia.

The major challenge is to pursue a combination of macro-economic and sectoral policies aimed at achieving growth with equity, including programmes aimed at fostering the participation of the poor in the process of economic growth, in particular by improving their access to employment opportunities and income generating assets, and by increasing the productivity of their assets, both physical and human. An urgent first priority is the need to protect the most vulnerable groups through the adjustment process while growth gradually resumes.

This poverty alleviation strategy will need to be supported by an interrelated set of policy actions at three levels:

(i) macro-policy measures aimed at strengthening the foundation of self-sustained and balanced growth over the medium and long term;
(ii) sectoral policies, combined with a well organized programme of projects, aimed at fostering the participation of the poor in the process of growth; and
(iii) restructuring the public finances and mobilizing domestic and foreign resources for growth.

At the macro-level, sustaining the shift towards tradeables usually requires addressing the exchange rate issue. Further, expenditure reductions in non-tradeable sectors have to be combined with switching in favor of tradeable sectors. Measures to accomplish this include raising producer prices, focussing investment in support of tradeable activities (rural roads and markets) and economic services and inputs towards raising farmer productivity and output.

In the CFA zone, second best solutions for exchange rate changes have been introduced with varying degrees of success. In some countries, such as Gabon and Congo, inelastic supply responses in economies with substantial enclave sectors have required initial adjustment efforts to be focused on cutting domestic costs through expenditure reduction, particularly public sector wages. Other measures include harmonizing effective protection rates between agriculture and industry, and eliminating the bias in favor of urban consumers through reforms in pricing of basic food stuffs.

Sectoral policies include shifting new investment and maintenance expenditures towards the support of productive activities and employment generating projects, and modifying the composition of public expenditures to favor basic primary education and basic health services. In the key sectors, systematic efforts are usually required to remove distortions in markets by eliminating monopolies, price controls and uneconomic taxation. A particular feature of the many countries with Government-established producer prices system is to sustain the incentives of farmers to produce by a system of floor prices with flexibility above this level to reflect world market conditions.

In resource mobilization, major tax system reforms are underway to replace agricultural taxation and other taxes in production by taxes on consumption and value added. Improved direct tax collection is also called for in the areas of income taxes and real estate. In many countries, economic efficiency is adversely affected by banking system failures and lack of domestic intermediation and capital markets. This effects not only the capacity of the system to mobilize real domestic financial savings for development, but also hinders the development of credit schemes for small and medium scale enterprises and farmers.

In general, improvements in the urban/rural terms of trade will have favorable impacts on low income groups who are in large part rural based. Growth itself will inevitably alleviate the impact of adjustment on the most vulnerable groups – the urban poor and public servants who lose their jobs. In these areas structural adjustment should make provision for action programmes to avoid social distress in the short term, while sustainable economic growth and its corollary benefits are being secured for the medium term.

Poverty and Income Distribution

The evolution of private consumption per capita has generally followed that of GDP per capita, and confirms the conclusion of a falling average living standard in sub-Saharan Africa in the first half of the decade. The exceptions again are those countries where GNP per capita approaches or is above $1000. At the other side of the distribution, five of the countries with negative GDP growth over the period are among the poorest ten. The challenge of poverty alleviation is thus twofold: to raise living standards on the average, and to prevent the poorest countries from falling further behind (as is currently the case).

While the macro-economic performance figures make it plausible that the number of households in absolute poverty has increased in Africa, (particularly in the countries with the lowest GDP per capita) there is little direct statistical evidence. Likewise, there is virtually no empirical evidence on the overall evolution of the distribution of household incomes. The World Development Indicators list distribution data for only 4 sub-Saharan Africa countries: Kenya (1976), Zambia (1976), Cote d'Ivoire (1985–86), and Mauritania (1980–81). The only recent data, for Cote d'Ivoire, are derived from the Living Standards Survey undertaken there with Bank sponsorship, and while they provide a good estimate of the current situation there is no comparable survey in the past to provide a suitable bench mark to study progress.

However, the main data needs are not so much for poverty counts and for overall distribution figures. Especially the latter tend to change only slowly over time, particularly when the distribution is expressed in large units such as quintals. Such units are very heterogeneous indeed, and the economy at large can affect different groups within, say, the lowest quintal very differently, even though the total income share accruing to the quintal may not change much.

What is needed therefore, is a picture of the distribution of income by socio-economic groups, such as landless farmers, export crop farmers, governments workers, urban informal sector workers, etc. Such groups have as common characteristic the similar way in which they are linked to the production structure and hence in the way their income is generated. This makes it feasible to consider them as policy target groups and to estimate how macroeconomic trends will affect them. The approach requires, however, that social and economic data are available at the household level – and indeed for the individual members of the household – (e.g., their labor force participation). From such data the socio-economic categories can be aggregated and described in terms of their income and consumption levels and in terms of the fulfillment of their needs for housing, education, health and other social services.

This is the approach taken by the Bank in the Social Dimensions of Adjustment project which includes as one of its components the design and implementation of permanent household surveys in each participating country. The surveys are designed to cover a broad range of socio-economic indicators concerning employment, income, consumption, savings and credit, housing, education, health, and nutrition, and will be carried out annually. The data processing methodology of the surveys will make the data available about three months after the collection, so that a steady flow of socio-economic information becomes available as input into policy design.

Without waiting for the availability of these data bases, however, the Bank has attempted a twofold approach to raising the income level of the poor in the context of macro-economic adjustment programs. In the short run, the basic shift of incomes from urban to rural populations serves to redress the broadest income distribution aspects. In parallel, a number of measures can be taken that directly compensate for loss of income among the urban poor, such as severance pay for redundant civil servants, food or subsidies for fixed-income individuals in the wake of a devaluation, food-for-work programs, etc. More importantly, to ensure that such improvements in income distribution are sustained in the long run, measures are taken to enhance access of the poor to assets and/or to increase the return of those they already own. Examples are retraining and job counseling programmes for laid off workers and credit programmes to support the set up of small enterprises. In rural areas, land reforms, resettlement schemes, credit programmes, extension programmes as well as rises in administered producer prices all contribute to sustaining higher incomes for the farmers.

Such measures make it possible that improvements in income distribution become compatible with adjustment programmes and are sustained during the resumption of economic growth. For example, in Cote d'Ivoire, the ratio of urban to rural average per capita income declined significantly in the first half of the 1980s. At the same time the urban income distribution also became more equal as a result of reductions in high modern sector salaries (especially in parastatal enterprises), while earnings in the informal sector were more steady. The challenge is to design and integrate such measures in the adjustment programmes which the sub-Saharan countries must necessarily undergo, so that the (re)establishment of macro-economic growth coincides with reductions in incidence and/or depth of poverty.

Poverty and Hunger

The Problem

One of the most important dimensions of poverty in Africa is hunger. Inadequacy of food manifests itself both at a national level and at the household and individual level. Several African countries have periodic or chronic food security problems at a national level, affecting large numbers of people (Ethiopia, Sudan, the Sahel countries, Mozambique, Angola, Somalia are the most prone to this). Virtually every African country contains significant numbers of households whose members are chronically or periodically hungry. Average caloric intake for sub-Saharan Africa as a whole has declined to about 96 percent of requirements in the 1980s.[4]

The problem of hunger in Africa arises from four sources: (a) low income growth both at the national and household levels in most African countries which restricts ability to buy food; (b) for countries and households unable to buy food, food production not keeping up with population growth; (c) the transitory food problems of agriculture (caused by natural calamities such as drought, locusts, floods, and by wars); and (d) vulnerable groups of people, often living in rural areas and dependent on agriculture, which do not obtain sufficient food due to low incomes combined with inadequate food production. These vulnerable groups are often found in certain regions, urban slums, among women and young children.

In Africa, more than in any other continent, the agricultural sector is critical in providing food security (because incomes are higher on other continents, food can be bought). This is because agriculture not only produces food, but contributes a large portion of GDP in most African countries (20–60 percent depending on the country), provides an average of 71 percent of employment and 50–90 percent of exports.[5] Agro-industry, which is the predominating industrial sector in much of Africa of course depends on agriculture as its major source of inputs. Most of the structural adjustment programmes undertaken by African countries depend for their success on a rapid stimulus to economic growth generated largely by the agricultural sector. The reason for this is the general finding that the growth potential and comparative advantage of agricultural in most African countries is large, while that of other productive sectors is often relatively small, except for the oil producing countries. Stimulating agricultural growth is usually found to be the most important action which Governments can take to generate growth, to create employment, to provide more raw materials to industry, to reduce rural-urban migration (by reducing rural-urban income inequality); all of which contribute to food security. Most often, the majority of the poor live in rural areas, so that a focus on agricultural growth and growth of rural incomes relative to urban incomes also serves the purpose of poverty alleviation and assisting vulnerable groups. Solving the hunger problem in Africa is thus largely a question of stimulating agricultural development, and ensuring a wide distribution of the benefits of this development.

Unfortunately in Africa, agriculture has performed poorly, causing, to a large extent, the growing problem of hunger. Agricultural growth in sub-Saharan Africa, during 1973 to 1984 was 0.7 percent p.a. in real terms, or about −1.9 percent p.a. per capita. Comparing 1974–76 with 1981/1983, the index of food production shows a decline from 100 to 94.[6] This poor performance has led to a remarkable increase in food imports. Cereal imports by sub Saharan Africa have increased at 10.7 percent p.a. during 1973–84. The availability of food imports has greatly offset the impact of poor agricultural performance on food security. However, it was not enough in aggregate to ensure an adequate diet to even the average African. As indicated above, the average daily caloric intake was 96. percent of requirements in the 1980s (2205 calories). This compares to an average caloric intake of 105 percent of needs in all of the world's low income countries. In addition, problems in rural areas have contributed to a growth rate of urban population at 6.1 percent p.a.

Causes for the Problem

The first set of problems affecting agricultural performance and hunger are the cluster of often inappropriate agricultural price, tax, subsidy and exchange rates policies. In Africa, these policies have generally served in the last 20 years to depress farmers' incomes and incentives to produce. This has discouraged agricultural production for the market, encouraged rural-urban migration, reducing investable resources remaining in agriculture hence reducing agricultural investment.

Most African nations have emphasized Government-led growth, creating parastatal enterprises to manage agricultural marketing, processing, and regional agricultural project schemes. These Government enterprises tend to be inefficient and costly.

Government agricultural expenditures programmes often involve low allocations to agriculture, numerous white elephants, excessive Government expenditure allocations to salaries, and little to other operating costs. Governments often provide inadequate attention to agricultural research, extension, farm input supply, forestry services, and animal health services. Donors have contributed to this situation by dividing sub-Saharan African countries into a mosaic of expensive regional development projects which have caused the fragmentation of agricultural services.

The lack of adequate land tenure, land use and environmental policy has been a disruptive influence on agriculture. The absence of secure tenure by farmers in much of Africa has discouraged investment in the land and has not encouraged soil conservation measures. Lack of land titles makes eligibility for agricultural credit difficult. Women are often discriminated against in part because they have no security of tenure. Lack of environmental protection has permitted the widespread destruction of forests and animal life, and misuse of land, for example leading to desertification. These environmental factors may have contributed to an increase in transitory food problems (more frequent droughts, desertification, etc.).

A major non-policy constraint faced by agriculture in many African countries is the limit to good agricultural land and to areas having climatic conditions conducive to agricultural growth. Only 30 percent of Africa's land area (about 320 million ha) is capable of sustained production of rainfed crops. About ¼ of this is used (FAO estimates). Most of the unused cultivable area is presently under forest in central Africa, which for environmental reasons cannot be fully exploited agriculturally. Rainfall, soil and temperature patterns often conspire against African agriculture.[7]

There are limits to the speed at which traditional farmers can introduce improved technology, due to social and cultural barriers, level of knowledge and other factors. The most common technology used in African agriculture involves shifting cultivation. This is characterized by low input use, and is appropriate to low population density and abundant land situations. With rapid population growth, this technology is increasingly inappropriate, leading to low investment in the land, inadequate conservation efforts by farmers, and low output per unit area. The introduction of improved technology, appropriate to sedentary cultivation, must be accelerated.

A Development Strategy for African Agriculture

Addressing the problem of hunger in Africa involves primarily (but not exclusively) the development of agriculture. More rapid agricultural growth will generate more rapid GDP growth which is an essential element in food security since food can be bought as well as produced. Agricultural growth also implies more rapid growth of food production, and more rapid direct poverty alleviation since most of Africa's poor live in rural areas and are dependent on agriculture.

The strategy must include an appropriate policy package for each country involving the conventional growth orientation, which can be summarized briefly as follows:

(a) An agricultural price, tax, subsidy and exchange rate policy which provides incentives for agricultural investment and production;
(b) Improvement in public expenditure programs in agriculture, emphasizing national agricultural services rather than multi-component rural development projects. Donor support for the national programs should be promoted and their traditional support for multi-component regional projects or short-term projects discouraged. Institution building and human resource development projects in agriculture are essential. Projects should include those which address transitory food

problems, storage of agricultural surpluses, food distribution systems, and early warning systems for droughts;

(c) Privatization of agricultural marketing and processing: Governments should pursue parastatal divestiture and restructuring combined with measures to create financial markets serving the private sector so that private entrepreneurs can invest in agricultural marketing and processing;

(d) Policies need to be developed which promote security of land tenure, the tradeability of land (land cadastre, land titling, land documentation), and land reform where needed. This provides the basis for the creation of more effective land markets, land taxes, land investment, and credit; and

(e) Soil conservation is required in much of Africa to arrest desertification and erosion. This will involve:
- agricultural extension and research to encourage soil conservation;
- public works in soil conservation; and
- incentives to be established to encourage farmers to conserve the soil.

The Bank's Initiatives

Bank projects and programmes throughout Africa now emphasize both the policy changes and the project initiatives highlighted above. The central theme is that increased agricultural productivity in Africa will require both policy change and the development and introduction to farmers of improved and appropriate agricultural technologies. In many cases these technologies exist elsewhere in the world. To introduce new technology to African farmers requires its adaptation to their agricultural, economic and social environment. Extension services must introduce the technology once adapted, farm input and equipment must be made available, and markets and sources of finance need to be developed. Policy change alone is not enough to stimulate this productivity increase. Projects which increase agricultural productivity are needed. This increase can only come about by the introduction of improved agricultural technology as embodied in new and better crop varieties, improved agricultural practices, improved livestock breeds and management systems, better input supply and credit systems, improved storage, marketing and simple processing technologies, such as those cited by Paul Harrison in *The Greening of Africa*.

The approach that the Bank is following seeks to introduce technology through a massive effort to improve agricultural research, extension, credit, animal health, input supply, forestry, rural roads, and other agricultural and environmental services in a large number of African countries. These services will be developed through national programmes for which organization and management systems are carefully designed to assure effectiveness. Services will be designed to be low cost, simple, and sustainable over the long term. The initial focus will be on building national institutions and training local people to manage these institutions.

Current thinking in the Bank suggests that an agricultural growth rate of approximately 4 percent p.a. is needed to meet economic growth needs of Africa. This would constitute more than a doubling of the historical growth rate of agriculture in sub-Saharan agriculture. It is argued that the present generally poor condition of African agriculture leaves an extraordinarily large margin for improvement. Very low average crop yields in Africa make rapid growth possible. Even crop yield increases on the order of 4 to 5 percent p.a. will bring average yields to about the levels of those in other developing countries no earlier than the year 2000 to 2010. In addition, there are several African countries which have sustained agricultural growth rates above 3 percent p.a. for the last 20 years. If these good performers could be improved somewhat further and other countries brought to about the level of growth of the present good performers, the target would be achieved. There is, however, considerable skepticism that these targets can be achieved, based on past performance.

The strategy neglects to some extent the problems of vulnerable groups, neglects the transitory food problems of many African countries which occur due to drought, abundance (inability to store surpluses of food for use in bad years), other natural crises (locusts, army worms, floods), and man-made calamities such as are occurring in Uganda, Ethiopia, Angola, Mozambique, and the Moroccan Sahara. The Bank is therefore considering the addition of food security as a specific goal along with restoring sustainable growth. For some countries, this could imply the pursuit of food self-sufficiency as the most cost-effective means towards food security. This is to be achieved by a combination of agricultural policy reform and investment programmes. Of course, growth policies and investments which the Bank supports already do contribute to food security, by raising incomes which can be used to buy food for a large percentage of the population, and by increasing food production. Human resource projects supported by the Bank also contribute to food security. Population control reduces mouths to feed compared to no population control. Education and nutrition projects often help with food security.

A separate Task Force on "food security for Africa" is reporting in detail on these and related issues but will be developing suggestions and decisions and making rules for specific food interventions which might include one or more of the following:

(a) More serious targeting of agricultural projects on food production by vulnerable groups in rural areas is needed. This will be difficult to do in the context of existing projects because the Bank is undertaking a radical reduction in regional and rural development projects, which have proven to be remarkably difficult to implement and of limited economic benefit. This decision, however, means that special consideration must be given to extension messages delivered by national extension systems to resource poor farmers (minimum cash input recommendations). Much more agricultural research will have to be done by national agricultural research systems, to identify technological improvements for resource poor small farmers. Social infrastructure in rural areas should be targeted in part to assist the resource poor.

(b) Projects which address the transitory food insecurity problem are needed. These would include actions on early warning, drought recovery, as well as drought prevention projects. A drought prevention project might contain the widespread introduction of drought resistant crops and varieties of crops, combined with promotion of on-farm storage, water points, introduction of water harvesting techniques, etc. The Bank also intends to devote more attention to problems such as locust and pest control as well as environmental protection. The Bank might also assist in some cases to coordinate food aid.

(c) Policy based lending should estimate the impact of recommended policy changes on various groups of people in terms of income and food availability, and if necessary, incorporate specific measures to compensate for losses (employment programs, food for work, targeted subsidies). This type of analysis is being developed already in the Bank – supported "Social Dimensions of Adjustment" Project.

(d) Infrastructure development should be responsive to food security objectives, e.g., where to locate a road may be influenced not only by agricultural production potential, but by logistical needs in food distribution. Agricultural marketing systems need development, including more Bank attention to agricultural marketing projects to complement its promotion of private sector initiatives in this area (just "leaving it to be the private sector" may not be good enough).

(e) There needs to be a food security input into agricultural research: drought tolerant crop varieties, more serious attention to water harvesting techniques, irrigation and water development, with a food security as well as economic rationale.

(f) Attention to ways and means, including most importantly incentives, to get the private sector, both local and foreign, involved in food security: storage, food distribution, and crop production, all of which need to be profitable.

(g) Policy reforms in agriculture, especially when supported by policy based lending, should include a food security package of actions, which promotes food security such as food security plans, introduction of early warning systems, creation of early response systems, and various incentives for private involvement in storage and distribution.

(h) Land tenure and food security: Increased security of tenure is likely to contribute to food security at the household level.

(i) Women's issues and food security. Women are often responsible for most food production in Africa's rural areas. To promote food security means in part assisting women to produce food. This can be done by introducing labor saving technology to women, both agricultural (improved agricultural implements), as well as household (energy saving stoves which require less fuelwood for the same amount of energy), water supply (to reduce travel time to water). It will involve addressing women through extension, undertaking agricultural research on food crops cultivated by women, providing security of land tenure and ability to obtain credit by women heads of households.

(j) Rural development has become a bad word in the Bank's vocabulary, as well it should be, given the poor performance of rural development projects. But rural infrastructure continues to require development, in part for food security reasons. Now that the Bank does not finance rural infrastructure through rural development projects, free standing rural infrastructure projects or specific components in broader infrastructure projects will be needed.

Poverty and Basic Needs

The Existing Situation

Despite twenty five years of development programs and projects supported by multilateral and bilateral aid institutions, two thirds of the rural population and one-third of the urban population of sub-Saharan Africa remain below the absolute poverty level. Undoubtedly under the pressure of the present crisis, a number of governments have succumbed to the tendency to cut back on social spending at the basic and preventative levels in favor of sustained spending in some other areas whose political constituencies are more powerful. The results, in those cases, have been undoubtedly more hardship. In some cases, fragmentary data indicates a tendency for further deterioration of the already dismal indicators. Without arguing the issues of data and/or causality, it is undeniable that basic needs are inadequately satisfied in much of sub-Saharan Africa and that the situation is either precarious or deteriorating in most of the continent.

The Bank has tried to respond to this critical situation by:

(i) increasing its efforts in sector lending in education (e.g. Ghana and Senegal education sector loans both approved in 1987);
(ii) increasing its support for projects and project components which address basic needs (PHN, Water Supply, etc.);
(iii) focusing the attention of decision-makers on these issues through high-level seminars (sometimes sponsored by EDI) and in daily dialogue;
(iv) channeling aid away from high-profile, equipment-intensive projects (e.g., large urban hospitals, gold-plated universities) towards financing basic services through aid-coordination meetings;
(v) concentrating on protecting basic social services from the budget cuts during, and ensuring a reasonable balance between, salary and non-salary recurrent spending PIP and PEP reviews; and
(vi) ensuring that these issues are properly addressed at the time of designing Structural Adjustment Operations.

Poverty and Women

The Existing Situation

In many parts of sub-Saharan Africa (SSA), women represent about 50 percent of the population, as much as 60 percent of labor force in certain sectors, grow about 80 percent of the food and yet earn about 10 percent of the money income and own about 1 percent of the assets.

We have ample evidence that these economic facts translate in real hardships: incidence of extreme poverty is highest among women and children (since unlike the West, there is still substantial social concern with the elderly translated by children's support of their parents in their dotage). The statistical evidence (weak and inaccurate as it is) shows that malnutrition and poverty are gender biased with consequent increases in infant mortality and morbidity.

This seems to indicate that:

(i) Improving the condition of women would undoubtedly have major benefits in social terms, and will probably translate into considerable economic benefits to the country as a whole.

(ii) Improving the condition of women will have to be addressed through a two pronged approach:

(a) Providing opportunities to women to improve their economic position through; increasing their assets; increasing the productivity of their assets, (e.g. access to credit to agricultural extension services, etc.); ensuring more equitable treatment on the wage earning segments of the labor market; and

(b) improving the access of women to basic social services; e.g., education, health, nutrition support and population-related programmes.

The design of national programmes for Women in Development (WID) will doubtless have to focus on the policy front. But we must remember that there are fundamental differences between getting laws or policies enacted, and getting real change in the field. Social-cultural and political factors can transform macro-level national programmes into completely different micro-level realities.

We must also recall that communities within single national entities differ in their attitudes as well as their existing conditions. This is not just a matter of rural and urban environments, but also of ethnicity and religion. Thus as Professor Ali Mazrui has observed, one frequently finds that in Muslim communities of SSA women have more technical (legal) rights but are allowed a less active role in the economic scene. The situation is reversed in many non-muslim communities.

What the Bank is Doing

The structure of the Bank's intervention in support of a WID programme in a country could therefore include:

(i) agreement with the government on the outlines of a comprehensive national policy package and sectoral policies and programmes;

(ii) agreement with the government on whatever realignment of existing projects are required (especially Bank-financed projects);

(iii) agreement on public investment and expenditure patterns that reflect these concerns, especially for social services and basic rural infrastructure;

(iv) identification of additional specific Project interventions that could be financed by the Bank as well as other donors; and

(v) identification of whatever particular institutional reform programs may be needed to improve implementation of the program.

The structure of the ultimate financing of this operation could include some quick disbursing funds, or might even be solely composed of such funds. That question, however, should be addressed after the previous issues have been adequately addressed, and the "package" appropriately defined. The Bank is presently pursuing variants of the approach described in the two preceding paragraphs in Gambia, Guinea and Kenya as well as other countries. The finalization of these programs should be completed in CY 1988.

Poverty and the Environment

Environmental Degradation in Sub-Saharan Africa

Africa's environment is difficult. Rainfall occurs predominantly in erosive downpours. Stress on vegetation is greater than in temperate areas. The continent's soil resources are poor. According to an FAO study, only 19 percent of Africa's soils have no inherent fertility limitations, while 55 percent have severe or very severe constraints.[8] Outside the humid zones, rainfall is highly variable from year to year (by 20–40 percent up or down from the mean each year). The risk of prolonged droughts is high. Two-thirds of Africa's land area faces high or very high risk of drought. The Sahel faces the additional problem of unusually wet or dry periods persisting for one or two decades. To add to these difficulties, the tsetse fly predominates over central Africa preventing widespread introduction of cattle.

Africa's farmers developed traditional agricultural methods well adapted to the above problems. The most important adaptation is the system of shifting cultivation. This involves one to three years of cultivation on a plot, followed by leaving the plot to revert to bush and forest. However,in many areas fallow periods are no longer sufficient to allow fertility to be restored. And fallow areas are not large enough to provide adequate grazing and fuelwood. Pressure on the land is resulting in declines in crop yields, overgrazing of fallow and farmland. Fuelwood needs are met by attacking the forests. Vegetative cover is weakening and erosion accelerating.

The above has been known for some time at the micro level. Recently, information has been patched together showing environmental damage for the continent as a whole; and the picture which emerges is shocking. The first part of the problem is deforestation, related directly to the increase in population, and the consequent need to open up new farm land, and to find fuelwood. The FAO reports that Africa's 703 million hectares of undistributed forests in 1980 were being cleared at the rate of 3.7 million hectares a year – or 0.6 percent. Local rates ranged from 0.2 percent for the vast Cameroon-Congolese forest to up to 4 percent a year in West Africa. Deforestation outstripped the rate of new tree planting, which was only 126,000 hectares per year, by 29 to 1.[9] At the same time, 55 million Africans faced acute scarcity of fuelwood.[10]

The second aspect of the problem is desertification. Desertification affects primarily Africa's dry lands. An assessment for 1983 suggests that in these areas 80–90 percent of the rangelands, 80 percent of the rainfed croplands and 30 percent of the irrigated land may be affected at least moderately. Of the dry land population of 118.5 million, 92 million lived in areas affected by desertification, 52.5 million of them in severely affected areas.[11] The third aspect of the problem is soil erosion. Soil erosion is widespread in all areas of sub-Saharan Africa. It is perhaps most serious in Ethiopia, where top-soil losses of up to 296 metric tons per hectare have been reported on 16 percent slopes, but even moderate slopes can erode rapidly when unprotected by vegetation. In West Africa per hectare losses of 10–21 metric tons have been reported on slopes as gentle as 0.4–0.8 percent, and of 30–55 metric tons on 1–2 percent slopes.[12] Wind erosion is significant in drier areas. Even more serious in the medium term is the gradual decline in fertility of all types of land.

What is being done

In 1987 the World Bank created environmental divisions in its organization. The Bank has embarked on a vast series of studies on the above problems, and in the preparation of environmental protection projects. It has sought out and found partners among the environmental groups which have been its worst critics in recent times. Analysis undertaken in the Bank includes several studies on desertification, a study of the tropical forests, and several country studies.

Probably the most advanced country thinking has been undertaken for Cote d'Ivoire where the Government, assisted by the FAO and the Bank has prepared a sector program to deal with the country's major environmental problems. Cote d'Ivoire's tropical forest has virtually disappeared, largely due to farmer encroachment, and as the result of exploitation by logging companies. The measures foreseen to address the problem include:

(a) drastic reduction in the distribution of permits to obtain land in the forest areas both to farmers and to loggers;
(b) reduction in the number of logging companies;
(c) creation of incentives for logging companies to replant and protect their forest concessions by increasing the period of concession and entering into contracts with loggers which require minimum replanting and conservation;
(d) introduction of export duties and stumpage fees on timber production and export. This should discourage excessive cutting and exports, while not eliminating them, by setting the tax so as to permit environmentally sustainable cutting;
(e) creation of large conservation areas, to be protected by the forest service, which is to be assisted to improve their service;
(f) expansion of national parks, development of tourist infrastructure in these parks;
(g) research and extension on agro-forestry (farmers can plant and maintain trees); and
(h) development of industrial plantations as an alternative source of fulewood and lumber.

Finally, the combination of policy and project efforts to accelerate agricultural intensification and conservation will be critical. If successful, increased agricultural production can come from settled land, reducing the population pressure on the forest areas. Intensification will involve crop rotations, integration of livestock, measures to increase soil fertility, etc.

For the problems of environmental degradation to be resolved in Africa it will require a mammoth jump in the human and financial resources committed to it. The Cote d'Ivoire program for example will cost $US 200 million over five years. Given Africa's financial difficulties and many pressing problems, one can only hope that there shall be sufficient foresight, dedication and political will to ensure that the necessary resources will ge committed in time for this battle to be won.

Poverty and Debt[13]

The deterioration in economic growth experienced by the sub-Saharan African countries in the late seventies and eighties led to a deterioration of their debt situation as countries continued to borrow to finance their internal and external deficits. In spite of often heroic structural adjustment programs in many of these countries to restore macroeconomic equilibrium, the debt situation remains critical. Twenty-two sub-Saharan African countries are currently expected (in the absence of debt rescheduling) to face debt service ratios of 30 percent or more in the period 1988–90. All but two of these countries are in the low income group. A subgroup of seventeen countries[14] accounts for about 43 percent of total African indebtedness. Since 1975, medium and long term debt of these countries has almost quadrupled. Collectively, their debt is almost 80 percent of their GDP and 400 percent of their annual exports. The debt service ratio for the group was 50 percent in 1985 and over 45 percent in 1986 (excluding arrears).

It is not surprising that the macro-economic performance of these most debt-distressed countries was below average, even within the group of low income economies. During the first half of the 1980s, their growth rate was less than one-third the rate of other low income countries and GDP per capita declined by 2.3 percent per year. As a group, these countries did not share in the recovery of 1986. Their foreign exchange earnings capacity also appears to be below average, mainly because of a large and growing dependence on mineral exports. Given that a non-growth environment is already per se non-conducive to poverty reduction, one can expect that the below average performance of these debt-distressed countries has worsened the incidence and depth of poverty.

The undiversified export structure of the debt-distressed countries obviously does not bode well for their prospects of economic recovery. To that must be added the decline in investment ratios which they experienced in the 1980–85 period (in contrast to a rise in other IDA eligible countries). The lack of economic growth prospects translate in lack of prospects of poverty alleviation, without the design of special poverty-focused programs.

However, in spite of the adjustment efforts in many of the debt-distressed countries, they are receiving relatively less donor support. For example, between 1982–85, gross official development assistance flows to the debt-disressed countries with adjustment programs rose 3 percent per year; to other countries with adjustment programs, they increased by 9 percent per year. Clearly, measures to increase concessional debt relief and assistance are needed.

In that context, the World Bank is proposing a special program of assistance for 1988–90 to low income (IDA eligible), debt-distressed countries with adjustment programs. This program would require about $1.5 billion of external financing annually (after conventional rescheduling along the lines of the recent past-which in itself would already provide debt relief of about $1.4 billion per year). About half of that amount would constitute a minimum debt relief program, the other half being needed to support the resumption of import growth and to achieve modest per capita income growth. The programme is to be financed by concessional debt relief (retroactive terms adjustment, lower interest rates), increased IDA flows, and co-financing of adjustment operations.

At a meeting held in December, 1987 in Paris, the Bank was able to secure donor support for this program of the order of $US 6.4 billion, to be available over the next three years. These funds will be used under either formal co-financing or highly coordinated arrangements with the World Bank in support of overall and sectoral adjustment operations. Of this amount we estimate that $US 3.4 billion will represent additional commitments to the low-income heavily indebted African countries, over and above the level of quick disbursing assistance they now receive.

Beyond these efforts, the Bank is also considering special new initiatives for the middle-income heavily indebted countries of Africa, especially Nigeria and Cote d'Ivoire. At present, the Bank has deployed significant technical assistance efforts on financial engineering of packages of fresh money and rescheduling within the context of the Paris and London Club negotiations for both countries as well as a B-Loan for Cote d'Ivoire in 1986. The continued severity of the problem, however, clearly indicates the need for new thinking in this area if the heavy burden of debt is not to cripple efforts at growth promotion and poverty alleviation in these countries.

Poverty and Institutional Issues

Africa has never had a well developed set of institutions to deal with poverty or social problems, despite the large amount of resources devoted to health and education, the areas where Governments have attempted to play a primary role. It is therefore judicious to reflect on the difficulties encountered with many of the "modern" institutions created as a corollary to development and assess what has gone wrong and what should be done. Under the circumstances it is not surprising that traditional social institutions continue to perform a vital function as a social safety net in time of crisis and that Non-Governmental organizations (NGOs) have been the most effective providers of emergency relief as well as in many regions, longer-term health, educational and local development services.

A special dimension of the problem concerns the public sector incentive systems. While adjustment programs have stressed the role of incentives in promoting economic development little attention has been given to the impact on public servants of declining real purchasing power and cuts in vital spending for maintenance and supplies. The result is declining performance, increased corruption, moonlighting and absenteeism. Few governments have not as yet seriously faced this dilemma of increasingly ineffective public administrations at a time when adjustment requires exactly the reverse. Two examples provide some encouragement. Guinea, which is undergoing one of the most sweeping adjustment programs has just sharply raised civil service salaries after substantially cutting the numbers employed. This was made consistent with the financial requirements of the adjustment program by simultaneously raising petroleum product prices to the levels of neighboring countries. In Togo, the government reduced the public payroll over the past four years by 10 percent by not fully replacing retirees. Last year, with Bank encouragement, the civil service wage bill was raised by 14 percent to better compensate those still working.

Other answers to the problems may be found by privatizing certain Governmental functions such as data collection and work requiring superior technical skills. Semi autonomous agencies could be created with performance based pay scales.

NGOs, as pointed out earlier, constitute a vital complementary system for alleviating hardship among the most vulnerable groups, and for assisting to enhance their human and physical assets and improving the productivity of these assets. The NGOs are, however, a diverse group who work best when given autonomy but who often exist in a climate of mutual suspicion with the authorities. Much has been done to improve this situation by the Aga Khan Foundation's 1986 seminar in Nairobi on "the enabling environment", which was co-sponsored by a large array of institutions including the Bank. Further efforts at improving the climate of cooperation between Governments and NGOs can be a useful function of the Bank's multi-faceted work programs in member countries. A case in point is Togo where Bank support helped promote a stronger coordination amongst NGOs and helped establish better NGO liaison with Government so that NGO actions are more directly fitted in the Government's economic and social objectives. The proposal for a Togo/NGO/IDA project, being studied at present, would build on this experience and could specifically help fund NGO's activities in support of "the poorest of the poor". This would be one more variation in the array of instruments available to the Bank[15] and would help mount a focused and credible effort in those countries where circumstances call for an expanded NGO role.

In the past, development projects and macro operations have attempted to create new "modern" institutions based on Western models without sufficiently taking into account the positive aspects of traditional institutions. The Bank has moved significantly to correct this approach by stressing the use and strengthening of local institutions such as livestock herder associations, farmer cooperatives and community based programs in the social and economic projecst it finances.

More needs to be done to link the structures of the informal sector to those of the formal sector so as to produce better social services, and give the poorer groups access to credit, training and technical knowledge on behalf of economic development. Our programs with NGOs, credit at the local level, and community health and maternal child care are a beginning in this direction. We need to renew our efforts to improve our understanding of the urban and rural informal sectors. In particular, we need to gain a greater appreciation of the composition of productive activities in the informal sector, the way markets for goods and credit work and the social value systems in place in the different subregions. In this connection we do not have to reinvent the wheel or mount elaborate research programs. Instead, a first step should be closer working links with African intellectuals who come from these societies.

Structural Adjustment and Poverty Alleviation[16]

Contrary to some critics' impressions, it has been very much a concern of both the governments and the Bank to ensure that the burdens of adjustment are equitably distributed across all population groups. Even more, that the fruits of the restored growth would benefit the poor as well as the more wealthy.

Unfortunately, experience in some cases has seen significant hardships inflicted upon the poor. It is demonstrable, however, that the poor as a group, would probably have suffered considerably more if no adjustment programme had been in place. However, further improvements in the situation are possible and are being actively pursued. The Bank's recent work in Africa has increasingly addressed this with a comprehensive array of measures, which are described below.

The following paragraphs describe the comprehensive approach the Bank is now following in its support of Structural Adjustment. This approach is reflected under three broad headings: first, the general rationale of the basic design of Adjustment Programs which, we believe, gives due weight to the justified concern with the social effects of structural adjustment; second, specific actions that are being taken to address immediate, transitional and long-term issues of poverty alleviation in connection with adjustment programs in individual countries; and third, the specific initiative being undertaken by the World Bank in conjunction with the UNDP and the AFDB to strengthen the capability of governments to integrate the social dimension in the design of future adjustment programs.

The Basic Design of Adjustment Programs

The structural adjustment process as represented by specific Bank-supported operations and the associated Economic Recovery Programs (or comparable operations) drawn up by governments with our assistance should in the medium term contribute to broad based economic growth and allow increases in per capita income and consumption not possible without such interventions in the countries concerned. However, it is not expected that the costs and benefits of the programs will be evenly distributed. In general, the incentive structures are designed to encourage agriculture and increase real incomes in the rural areas relative to urban areas. Since the rural areas contain the majority of the population and a dis-proportionately high share of the poor, the interventions mentioned should contribute to absolute poverty alleviation in the medium term, although much will of course depend on individual country circumstances. In West Africa, unlike some other regions, most farming is done by relatively small farmers and increases in producer prices directly translate into increased incomes for small farmers. In countries such as Cote d'Ivoire and Senegal, reforms in the industrial incentive system should also lay the foundation for a resumption in industrial growth, which should, in turn, provide employment opportunities in the urban areas.

The second major policy thrust of the programs – improvement in the efficiency of the public sector – should translate eventually into more than a lower share of national income absorbed by the public sector. It should result in better social services as a consequence of explicit efforts to raise the productivity of government agencies. These effects would contribute to improved living conditions for all groups, and probably the urban population in particular, which is likely to remain the major beneficiary of education, health and other government services. Although the reform of public enterprises will usually involve some layoffs of redundant workers, demonopolization and the new incentive frameworks should permit, in many cases, the private sector to undertake some of these formerly solely public activities with positive impacts on urban employment.

In the short turn, however, all groups will feel some loss of consumer purchasing power associated with, for example, increases in water, electricity, public transport tariffs, and retail prices of petroleum products and basic consumer goods, most of which are imported. Often the first stages of structural adjustment have necessarly coincided with demand restraint policies which have led to reduced growth of GDP (and of sectors such as construction which relies heavily on public investment expenditures).

The severe lack of data on income distribution and consumption patterns makes both the design and analysis of the social impact side of economic policy reforms extremely difficult. To address this situation, there is a need for research projects designed to track some of the real income effects of adjustment and the pace of adjustment at the household level in representative segments of the population. Carefully designed surveys of household income and consumption patterns in selected urban and rural communities will be carried out and repeated in our countries at regular intervals, as part of the process described in the last part of this section.

At present, however, only qualitative observations on the probable effects of the adjustment process on various segments of the populations of our countries taken as a whole may reasonably be made. Those populations can be divided into groups according to the nature of their economic activity. In the rural areas, much depends on country specific factors, although the sharp nominal increases in producer prices clearly lead to a significant short-term increase in gross income in certain households, and depending on world prices for export crops and other factors, may provide a significant transfer to the rural population. On the other hand, the elimination of fertilizer subsidies will cause input prices to rise, as will prices of imported food items and other goods consumed by farm families. Provided that cash crop producer prices are maintained in real terms at their current levels and climatic conditions are favorable, real per capita incomes and consumption will still improve. In fact they have improved and most probably will continue to improve for farmers in many African countries.

Non-farm households (both herders and rural traders/craftsmen) are not expected to gain directly from the changed incentive structure, although increased farm incomes should spill over into increased demand for other products and services and the adjustment should promote a larger role for private traders in the countryside, as input suppliers, credit agents and marketers. Migrant farmers (usually from neighboring countries) who commonly provide farm labor for cash crops on a wage or share cropping basis should also experience increased incomes in countries where they play a significant role.

In the urban areas, somewhat less than half of employment (although a much higher percentage of income) is usually located in the formal sector. Formal sector income is primarily generated by the public sector, either through direct employment or government contracts, and in a few countries through tourism. Real incomes in the formal sector are expected to decrease in the short turn as a result of the adjustment programs and to decline relative to the incomes in the rural areas. Civil service reforms will result in some unemployment, as may the curtailment of public investment. In the medium term, improved incentives for the private sector, especially in resource-based industries such as agro and fish processing, should stimulate private sector employment, helping to mitigate the negative effects of the contraction in the public sector.

The effect of the adjustment process on urban informal sector incomes is less clear. The slowdown in urban formal sector production and income growth will hurt this sector, but may be partly compensated by growing demand for informal sector services/products from the rural areas. In addition, most informal sector products are import substitutes (soap, textiles, etc.), whose demand will be boosted by the adjustment process. Taxi drivers, artisans and others who service the tourist industry in those countries where there are prospects for this sector should experience less income compression. However, at least initially, all urban groups will experience a loss of purchasing power associated with increased prices for tradeable food items, fuel, and utility and transport tariffs, as these constitute a large proportion of the urban household budget.

The net effect of adjustment programs on poverty in the urban areas is difficult to assess. The link between production units and consumption units is weaker in urban areas. For example, a consumption unit may include formal and informal sector participants. While all available indicators (wages, health status, infant and child mortality, literacy, access to potable water, etc.) suggest a much higher living standard in the urban areas than in rural villages, it cannot be denied that the adjustment process will be difficult for the urban poor. Some reduction of the high rate of rural/urban migration of the past decade will most likely occur as employment opportunities shrink in urban areas. Extended family networks, the welfare system of low income countries, will have a major role to play in easing the transition. On the whole, however, adjustment programs in Africa will probably improve the relative position of the poor even if they coincide with a real (though temporary) decline in per capital incomes.

Specific Measures

Against this general background, the Bank is supporting specific actions. These actions may be part of a SAL or a SECAL, or have as their vehicle other projects and instruments. Sometimes, they are fully funded by other donors, but are an important part of the Bank country dialogue (e.g., food-for-work schemes). Together, these interventions complement the adjustment process in four essential, if slightly overlapping, areas:

- (a) protection of the most vulnerable groups;
- (b) compensatory actions/transitional arrangements;
- (c) measures to ensure that the poor effectively participate in the growth process; and
- (d) protection of the long-term interests of the population.

These interventions are not all used systematically in every case. Each country, however, has adopted one or more measures of this kind to accompany their adjustment programs. Examples of each of these types of intervention are given below.

(a) Protection of vulnerable groups: The most vulnerable groups in society are the poor generally, and women and children specifically. The key services that they benefit from need to be protected from the possible adverse impacts of budget cuts. This is done primarily through protecting public expenditure on key health, education, nutrition and other basic welfare services that benefit primarily the poor. Composition (quality) of expenditure is essential. For example, simply protecting "health" and "education" expenditures is inadequate if the bulk of these expenditures is going for a posh hospital or a lavish university at the expense of basic rural health programs and primary education. Such reviews are integral parts of the programs in the Gambia and Cote d'Ivoire and Senegal. Furthermore in Senegal, an education sector loan supports the reorientation of government expenditures and investments in the sector; and in Cote d'Ivoire the government is establishing an action plan improving basic health services for vulnerable groups.

(b) Compensatory actions/Transitional arrangements: Compensatory actions may be appropriate for some individuals who will face substantial costs in adjustment, e.g., redundant civil servants can receive a severance pay. Occasionally, special privileges (food, subsidies) may be required for fixed-income individuals in the wake of devaluation. Other transitional arrangements are justified to help change the possibilities of a disadvantaged group to enable it to compete more effectively in the environment created by adjustment. Under this heading, we can point to the case of Guinea which has a system of severance payments for laid-off public servants, and also has introduced bonuses for voluntary departures from the public sector. In Senegal, there is the example of the retraining and rural resettlement scheme for laid-off civil servants and extension workers, while a comparable fund is also being set up for laid-off workers in the manufacturing sector. In the Gambia, retraining and job counselling for laid-off civil servants is supplemented by a line of credit to fund new cooperative ventures. Mauritania has introduced Food-For-Work (FFW) programs with better targeting of food distribution to the neediest groups, and also has a system of temporary reassignment for banking sector employees to be laid off in the course of streamlining, while the Central African Republic (CAR) has a personnel bank for redundant civil servants. In Guinea-Bissau and Sao Tome and Principe, civil servants have access to subsidized food aid during the initial stages of adjustment, and obtain severance payment if laid off.

(c) Participation of the poor in the growth process: It is essential that opportunities be given to the poor to participate in the economic growth process by ensuring access to assets for the asset-less and increasing returns to those assets already in the possession of the poor. Land reforms, resettlement schemes, and special credit opportunities and training programmes are immediate types of interventions. Over the longer-term the investments in human resource development are key to both increasing returns to labor and promoting social mobility. These are the usual objectives of Bank-supported PHN and Education projects.

In terms of specific immediate interventions in African countries we can cite the example of Cote d'Ivoire which has a smallholder credit scheme in the rubber sector, an improved agricultural extension scheme for small farmers, increased water supply connections to poverty areas, a rural roads upgrading and rehabilitation program, and an informal sector micro-credit scheme. Senegal, on the other hand has taken steps to ensure access for the landless to the ownership of lands becoming available under irrigation projects. In the Gambia, a small and medium enterprise operation has a special component focussing on the role of women. In Mauritania, a similar SME project also provides a line of credit for artisans. Similar initiatives are underway in CAR and Equatorial Guinea. Guinea is considering informal sector micro-credit mechanisms (with NGOs) in Conakry, and emphasizes the local administration of the renovation and construction of educational facilities. Sao Tome and Principe is developing a credit scheme for small farmers, and a land distribution scheme as part of an incentive system for cocoa workers.

(d) Protecting the long-term interest of the population: namely by ensuring that the crisis atmosphere of stabilization and adjustment programming, debt rescheduling, etc., the long-term issues of Human Resource development and the environment are adequately addressed. Far from being a "luxury", appropriate attention to overarching environmental issues such as desertification and deforestation is essential for the socio-economic welfare of the population. The poor will be those most directly affected by this environmental degradation, and appropriate natural resource management is therefore an integral part of any sensible long-term development strategy.

Many of these measures are still in the early stages of implementation. They will undoubtedly raise difficult administrative and institutional problems during their execution. The effectiveness and efficiency of the programs, therefore, still remain to be seen, but they undoubtedly represent the most thoughtful designs that governments and outside experts can put together.

Further Actions being Considered

A project is being undertaken in conjunction with UNDP, the AFDB and other donors (the Social Dimensions of Adjustment Project SDA) with the objectives of improving our common understanding of the social aspects of adjustment programs; monitoring the shifts in socio-economic conditions experienced by particular population groups and strengthening the institutional capacity of governments to integrate the social dimension into the design of future structural adjustment programs.[17] The project is structured around three parallel streams of output: (i) development and maintenance of adequate statistical data bases on the social dimension of structural adjustment; (ii) studies on the socio-economic implications of structural adjustment; and (iii) monitoring of existing, and where appropriate identification and appraisal of new, poverty alleviation programs and projects to accompany structural adjustment programs. Project activities are being initiated for a core group of ten countries in sub-Saharan Africa. The country coverage of the project will be progressively extended in response to requests received from the countries. The project is funded by UNDP, AFDB and others, with the World Bank as executing Agency. There will be mechanisms of regular consultations with other Agencies, donors, and interested African Governments.

Conclusion

The preceding discussion has highlighted the multi-faced nature of the problem of poverty in Africa. Therefore, effective poverty-alleviation efforts will only bear fruit if consistent progress is made on many, if not all of these fronts simultaneously. Poverty alleviation in Africa, therefore requires a broad range of mutually reinforcing actions on such disparate issues as debt, the environment, the role of women, institutional development, food security and basic social services. It requires actions that will aim at inducing policy changes at the macro and sectoral levels as well as to support the effective implementation of programs and projects at the micro scale. Assisting the governments and peoples of Africa in this broad range of activities is a daunting task indeed. The most encouraging signs are the courage and vision of many African governments, the resilience and solidarity of the African peoples and the mounting awareness of the world community.

This is the ambitious agenda that the Bank is trying to pursue. The complexity of the problems, the vastness and fragmentation of the territories concerned, the weakness and turmoil besetting the existing socio-economic structures and the hostility of the international environment delineate a formidable challenge for the years ahead. It is an inescapable challenge and one which the Bank has decided to take on. The key to success will remain the extent to which poverty alleviation becomes a central concern of program design along with growth promotion, rather than an afterthought, and the systematic way with which this comprehensive vision of the problem and its solution is pursued.

Notes

1 "Accelerated Development in Sub-Saharan Africa: An Agenda for Action" (1981); "Sub-Saharan Africa: Progress Report on Development Prospects and Programmes" (1983); "Towards Sustained Development in Sub-Saharan Africa: A Joint Programme of Action" (1984); "Financing Adjustment with Growth in Sub-Saharan Africa, 1986–9O" (1986) supplemented by "Population Growth and Policies in Sub-Saharan Africa" (1986).

2 The "Joint Programme of Action" (1984) and the creation of the Special Facility for Africa (SFA) in 1985 marked the institutional commitment of the Bank to its Sub-Saharan Africa (SSA) initiative.

3 Source: 1985 World Development Indicators – countries with populations below 1 million people are not included.

4 The World Bank: "Financing Adjustment with Growth in Sub-Saharan Africa, 1986–9O", April 1986.

5 Ibid.

6 Data from The World Bank's Report: "Financing Adjustment with Growth in Sub-Saharan Africa, 1986–90", April 1986.

7 See Paul Harrison, *The Greening of Africa*, International Institute For Environment and Development, Earthscan, Penguin Books, 1987, pp.27–45.

8 FAO, *Crisis of Sustainability; Africa's Land Resource Base*, AGD/801/1, FAO, Rome, November 1985.

9 Jean-Paul Lanly, "Tropical Forest Resources", Forestry Paper 30; FAO, Rome 1982, pp.80–97.

10 FAO, *Fuelwood Supplies in Developing Countries*, FAO, Rome, 1983, pp.16–17.

11 Jack Mabbut "A New Global Assessment of the Status and Trends of Desertification" *Environmental Conservation*, Vol. 11, No. 2, 1984, pp.106–108.

12 Harrison, op. cit., p.114.

13 This section is drawn from "Proposals for Enhancing Assistance to Low-Income Countries Facing Exceptional Difficulties", paper prepared for the Development Committee Meeting of September 28, 1987.

14 Excluding four small countries (Comoros, Equatorial Guinea, Guinea-Bissau, and Sao Tome and Principe) and Mozambique (for lack of data reasons).

15 These are catalogued in a note dated November 17, 1987 by I. Serageldin entitled "Lending Instruments for Poverty Alleviation".

16 This section is taken from an April 8, 1987 paper by I. Serageldin entitled "The Social Dimensions of Structural Adjustment: Experiences from West Africa".

17 United Nations Development Programme Regional Programme for Africa: Fourth Cycle. Assessment of Social Dimensions of Structural Adjustment in Sub-Saharan Africa Project No. RAF/86/037/A/01/42.

Improving the Human Dimension in Africa's Economic Recovery and Development Through Structural Adjustment

CYRIL ENWEZE (INTERNATIONAL MONETARY FUND)

Recent and ongoing efforts in the Fund and elsewhere have underscored the many conceptual, analytical and empirical issues involved in trying to analyze the highly complex question of the distributional impact of adjustment policies among various income groups in an economy. Broadly speaking, these efforts show that the problem can be dealt with either by analyzing the macroeconomic effects of policies, with special emphasis on their distributional implications, or on a microeconomic, case by case approach which evaluates the specific distributional impact of selected policies (or programmes) in individual countries, or by some combinations of both. The approach of this paper is a modest one: at a qualitative and macroeconomic level it attempts to highlight the fact that two broad determinants will contribute to an amelioration of the costs of adjustment. One determinant is the amount of appropriate external financing which supports the adjustment effort. The other, at least equally important determinant, is the sustained implementation of appropriate economic and financial policies, while at the same time taking cognizance of the need to target the relatively disadvantaged and vulnerable groups for special treatment.

Factors Affecting the Human Dimension

A number of factors impact, in varying degrees, on the human dimensions of adjustment in the African countries. In this connection, perhaps one of the best summaries of these factors is contained in a recent Food and Agricultural Organization (FAO) report[1] which classifies these factors broadly into internal and external ones. In the words of the FAO report, the internal factors include: "disproportionate allocation of public investment and expenditure to industry and administration and institution building and social infrastructure, with relative neglect of the agricultural sector; inadequate pricing and other producer incentives for both domestic and export crops (leading to high food imports and low agricultural exports); high urban biased food subsidies in some cases, high production input subsidies; distorted exchange rate policies; low level of domestic resource mobilization; ineffective coordination and monitoring of foreign commitments; civil wars, political upheavals, and excessive military expenditures." Among the external causes the FAO report cites the various oil shocks, recessions, falling commodity export prices, high international interest rates, decrease in concessional development aid and intermittent droughts.

The Fund has attempted, in the context of Fund-supported adjustment programmes, to assist the African countries in addressing the non-political, nonmilitary factors within the control of the authorities (i.e., the bulk of the internal factors) while assisting these countries in coping with the problems caused by factors outside the control of the authorities.[2] This effort is consistent with the provisions of the Articles of Agreement of the Fund. Thus, although popular perceptions of the Fund tend to focus only on the role of the Fund in balance of payments adjustment, Article I (ii) of the Fund's Articles of Agreement specifies one of the purposes of the Fund as:

> "To facilitate the expansion and balanced growth of international trade, and *to contribute thereby to the promotion and maintenance of high levels of employment and real income and to the development of the productive resources of the members as primary objectives* of economic policy" (emphasis mine).

Similarly, Article I(v) charges the Fund:

> "To give confidence to members by making the Fund's resources temporarily available to them under adequate safeguards, thus *providing them with the opportunity to correct maladjustments without resorting to measures destructive of national or international prosperity*" (emphasis mine).

In the African countries, the Fund has continued to exercise its mandate in a number of ways, including the provision of various forms of financial resources as well as policy advice in the context of adjustment programmes designed to generate and accelerate economic growth while at the same time fostering and maintaining internal and external balance.

Provision of Financial Resources

The Fund's preoccupation with growth as well as the central need to assist countries implementing appropriate adjustment policies, was a major consideration in the design of the structural adjustment facility (SAF), which is now being supplemented by another new concessional facility. Thus, in the recent words of the Managing director of the Fund:[3]

> ". . . it has long been apparent that the limited assistance that the SAF can provide – somewhat less than SDR 3 billion in all – circumscribes the role that it can play in promoting and supporting growth-oriented adjustment over the longer period that is often needed for policies to begin to show results.
>
> Happily, efforts to bring larger resources to bear on this problem have . . . now met with success. Thanks to firm commitments of loans and grants from more than a dozen countries [the Fund has] been able to establish a new concessional lending facility, the Enhanced Structural Adjustment Facility (ESAF) which will have at its disposal new resources – additional to those of the SAF – totalling SDR 6 billion. This new facility is significant for two reasons. It attests to the urgency that the international community attaches to finding solutions to the problems of its poorest members. And it

affords a unique opportunity for those countries to adopt, and to hold to, the bold macroeconomic and structural reforms that are needed to strengthen their external accounts and regenerate the development process."

In addition to this new initiative, as noted earlier, the Fund has provided, and continues to provide, considerable financial support to countries implementing appropriate adjustment programmes. As of end-January 1988, the Fund had 18 stand-by arrangements with African countries (excluding South Africa), with total commitments amounting to SDR 807 million,while total CFF purchases from the Fund, by African countries, up to January 1988, amounted to SDR 1.0 billion. The provision of these financial resources has helped to sustain inflows and enable countries to focus on growth, at a time of dwindling external financial aid, low commodity export prices and worldwide recession. In the absence of these resources, the human dimension in Africa's economic recovery and development would have worsened considerably.

Furthermore, several multilateral and bilateral aid flows to the African countries are catalyzed in the context of the implementation of Fund-supported programmes, particularly as a number of multilateral and bilateral donors make a large part of their financial assistance to African (and other countries) contingent on the implementation by these countries of appropriate adjustment programmes. Similarly, in the context of debt relief provided under the auspices of the Paris Club alone, the debt of the African countries rescheduled during 1986–87 amounted to $US 19 billion.

However, apart from the beneficial effects of these financial flows on the human dimension in Africa's economic recovery and development, discussions also need to focus on the adequacy of the policy measures being implemented by the African countries, particularly in light of the continuing difficult economic and financial prospects of African countries.[4] Clearly, as indicated by the Deputy Managing Director of the Fund,[5] it is the interdependence between the availability of scarce external financial resources and the pursuit of appropriate domestic policies which will assist the African countries to further cushion the impact of an adverse external environment on their efforts to achieve sustainable economic growth. In this manner, the African countries can promote and maintain relatively higher levels of employment and real incomes, than would otherwise be possible in the absence of adequate external financing, underpinned by appropriate adjustment policies.

The Relevance of Appropriate Domestic Policies

The adjustment programmes implemented by the African countries in recent years have exhibited different combinations of demand-management and supply-inducing measures, in each case, tailored to the specific circumstance of the individual countries; in a number of instances, certain country-specific measures have been implemented, depending on the special problem being addressed in the countries in question. However, for purposes of discussing the implications of these policies, an attempt has been made to broadly group these measures under a few main categories, such as exchange rate policies, liberalization of trade and payments systems, decontrol of domestic prices, credit and monetary policies, fiscal policies (with special emphasis on public sector incomes policies, and on policies to reduce subsidies). Owing to the occurrence of a number of these policy measures in many of the African countries, albeit in different forms, degrees and combinations, an attempt is made below to outline, in fairly general and qualitative terms, the broad thrust and effects of the more common policy measures, as well as their potential to assist in improving the human dimension in Africa's economic recovery and development.

Prior to the implementation of appropriate exchange rate policies in a number of the relevant African countries, the existence of highly overvalued exchange rates for many national currencies created widespread distortions and parallel market activities which led to escalating rates of inflation, misallocation of resources, especially towards the non-tradeable goods sectors, thereby aggravating the foreign exchange crunch in these countries. For the most part, these highly misaligned exchange rates were artificially propped up by many unsustainable policies, including trade restrictions, excessive foreign borrowing, (often at unfavourable terms and for unproductive purposes), thereby aggravating the debt servicing problems of these countries. Under these conditions, unemployment was rampant and rising, the politically powerful groups reaped massive rents from the distortions and the restrictions in the economy, while some bureaucrats who sometimes reportedly dispensed favours to businesses under these conditions also prospered. Meanwhile, the poor and other vulnerable groups continued to bear a large part of the cost of the maladjustment of exchange regimes.

The implementation of appropriate exchange rate policies by a number of the African countries provided these countries opportunities for the rectification of many of these anomalies. The cancerous growth of parallel market activities were contained in many cases or curtailed, with beneficial medium to long run effects on the domestic inflation rate. Producers of tradeable goods, (mostly export commodities), many of whom are in the rural farming areas, enjoyed large increases in their incomes as a result of the boosts in producer prices made possible by the increase in the local currency counterpart of export earnings following exchange rate depreciations. In the process (after also taking into account the effects of the exchange realignments in reducing domestic absorption) the supply of foreign exchange resources to these economies generally increased, thereby obviating the need for reliance on excessive short-term foreign borrowing, the servicing of which had led, among other things, to rapid depletion of scarce resources. Budgetary resources were also relatively increased as a result of two broad effects: the reduced need to service high and growing debt service payments and, in many cases, the net positive budgetary impact of the exchange rate realignment, operating mostly through an increase in foreign trade related taxes. These developments permitted a relative easing of foreign exchange and budgetary resources which national Governments could target to benefit the poor and other vulnerable groups.

Frequently, the realignment of exchange rates was accompanied, where relevant, by a liberalization of the trade and payments systems, in many cases in a phased manner. As with the case of realignment of exchange rates, trade and payments liberalization contributed to an improved allocation of resources, a deceleration in inflation rates, a reduction of distortions and their associated rental premiums, rationalization of foreign exchange use, and an easing of artificially created scarcity situations in the goods markets. As a result, budgetary resources generally benefitted from increased import duty receipts, and this also provided an opportunity to the national authorities to use the increased resources to target, through the expenditure side of the budget, disadvantaged and vulnerable groups for more favourable treatment.

The decontrol of domestic prices, (sometimes also in a phased manner) was, in some cases, also another necessary accompaniment to exchange rate realignment, as this enhances the channels through which the effects of exchange depreciation are transmitted throughout the economy. Hitherto, not alone did widespread price controls artificially constrain the rates and levels of remuneration to producing economic agents in the economy, they also tended to channel less transactions through the official channels and more through the parallel markets, with two undesirable consequences. First, budgetary revenues suffered to the extent that transactions took place in the difficult-to-tax informal sector; second, many commodities were priced out of the range of the urban poor, who ordinarily do not have easy access to the network of bureaucrats, middlemen, and other agents through which the powerful and well-connected operated in securing controlled goods at official prices. The deleterious impact of informal activities on the budget limited the room for national authorities to target financial resources to the poor, while the scarcities generated by price controls aggravated inflation and reduced real incomes, especially for the poor. By contrast, indications are that traders, illicit operators and some of the bureaucrats who administered the price control systems prospered from the distortions created by controls. Generally, the dismantling of the price controls under adjustment programmes tended to benefit the poor by increasing incentives through an increase in the price of the goods supplied by the poor: in the rural sector, these goods usually included agricultural products; for the urban poor, the general experience has been that the price decontrol policies may not have involved additional cost, since, as noted above, owing to their disadvantaged position in society, they did not have access to commodities at the controlled prices, and were already paying escalated parallel market prices for these goods.

Typically, the adjustment programmes implemented by many of the African countries aimed at continuing the overall rate of credit expansion, within appropriate limits, consistent with the targets on growth and internal and external balance. These limits were set with a view to containing the adverse impact of excessive monetary expansion on the balance of payments and the rate of inflation; such monetary expansion when allowed to continue unabated for prolonged periods will typically aggravate the balance of payments situation, undermine the conditions for sustained growth, and, in the process, give rise to overvalued exchange rates, restrictive practices, price controls and inflation, all of which we noted earlier would impact more severely on the disadvantaged and vulnerable groups who are relatively less equipped to safeguard their own interests under these circumstances. Hence, the efforts of the African countries to curtail excessive monetary expansion have generally tended to work in the medium to long run interest of the poor. Furthermore, since the credit limits usually included ceilings on net credit expansion to the government, adequate care was generally taken to ensure that the credit requirements of the productive private sector were met. In addition, to the extent that, (as a number of studies have shown) flexible real interest rate policies are effective in encouraging domestic savings and capital inflows, the chances for sustained growth in the adjusting African countries, should be greatly enhanced, to the benefit also of the poor. By raising the cost of borrowing funds for capital purposes, such interest rate policies should also favour the adoption of relatively more labour-intensive production methods, to the benefit of the unskilled, usually poor, labour force. Finally, certain specific types of financial reform measures under the programmes,such as the establishment of credit guarantee schemes as well as the restructuring of agricultural development banks or the promotion of rural banks, have also benefitted the rural poor.

Efforts have also been make by the African countries to reduce the overall budgetary deficit, usually by implementing measures on both the revenue and the expenditure sides of the budget. With regard to tax measures, Bird[6] has noted that the transmission mechanism of the effects of taxes on the structure of industry, (and through that on the poor) may sometimes operate indirectly. Thus:

> "In countries with considerable unemployment, for example, . . . exemptions from customs duties for imported capital equipment, especially in countries with overvalued exchange rates, tend to maintain the cost of capital at artificially low levels and to encourage the relative expansion of capital-intensive lines of production, particularly by the large firms which have easier access to import licenses and foreign suppliers' credits which tend anyway to use less labour per unit of capital. Furthermore, tax and other incentive policies which induce more investment through lower capital prices will tend, simultaneously, to reduce the desired level of utilization of existing capital equipment (which depends in part on the relative prices of capital and labour) and hence will further reduce employment."

Broadly speaking, this would appear to describe the situation in many African (and other developing) countries. To the extent that these exemptions and incentives favour capital intensive production, the unemployment problem would be aggravated, with the poor being hardest hit. However, many of the programmes adopted by the African countries called for the substantial reduction of exemptions as well as urging a systematic reevaluation of the incentive system, in line with the objectives of the programme.

As far as the direct impact of tax measures are concerned, appropriate distributional objectives in favour of the poor can be pursued in the context of certain specific tax handles.[7] Thus, the attempts which were made under some programmes in the area of personal income taxes to make such taxes progressive, coupled with the delineation of appropriate exemption levels, and the lowering of marginal tax rates of income tax were factors which tended to work in favour of the poor. Similarly, higher international trade taxes, (especially import duties), on which significant parts of the budget of many African countries depend do not appear to have hurt the poor; in any event, these taxes could be targeted mostly on luxury goods and other items, which do not hurt the poor. By contrast, some of the excise taxes, which are generally regressive, impacted more on the disadvantaged and vulnerable groups; however, excises can also be targeted on the rich, through the selective taxation of goods and services. Finally, the undertakings in many of the African programmes for improved tax administration when implemented, usually impacted relatively on the more affluent members of the society who had established networks for tax evasion or avoidance, compared with the poor.

On the expenditure side, the typical pre-adjustment situation was characterized by major difficulties experienced by national authorities in implementing appropriate policies; typically, the room for manoeuvre had already been greatly circumscribed. Thus, with respect to current expenditures, long before adjustment policies were implemented, many governments found themselves confronted with the following broad scenario: wage and salary expenditures had grown to unsustainable proportions, sometimes with a few months' wage and salary arrears outstanding, and with the retrenchment of workers already commenced, (beginning with the relatively more vulnerable wage earners); debt servicing, although also contractual, had frequently fallen into substantial arrears, with adverse implications for the inflow of new foreign external resources; for countries with high levels of domestic arrears, often the provision of government goods and services by the private sector had increasingly ground to a halt; in some cases various budgetary subsidies had become unsustainably large, threatening the overall execution of the budget. All these factors had started impinging adversely on the capital budget, (which is usually one of the first causalities) with a number of government projects in some budgetary constraints. The adjustment programmes adopted by the African countries have attempted to tackle these problem areas directly, and discussions of the impact of adjustment measures have usually centred on the cost of the adjustment measures to the disadvantaged and vulnerable groups.

In general, budgetary restraint on public sector salaries has not directly hurt either the rural or urban poor, (except to the extent that these restraints may have reduced intra-family transfers), since such restraint usually affects government salaried employees who are considered among the middle-income class in the African countries. Public sector wage and salary restraints have provided room in some cases for expansion in the employment of wage earners, instead of the retrenchment which would have subsequently occurred in some cases, (often at the expense of the relatively more vulnerable daily paid wage earners), if the problem had not been contained. Furthermore, such restraint, while also helping to ameliorate (to the benefit of the poor) the adverse impact of the budget deficit on the economy, also releases resources in the budget which could be targeted on the spending programmes that directly benefit the relatively disadvantaged and vulnerable groups. However, a major constraint in the implementation of budgetary restraint in this area has been that, since this measure would, (in the short run at least), adversely affect the articulate urban middle-class in African economies, it has continued to pose major political problems for national governments, as distinct from any implications it may have for the poor.

A relatively more sensitive, and oftentimes politically more complicated issue pertains to the question of subsidies. These subsidies which usually benefit the urban population,[8] may cover not only some imported items, but sometimes some domestic agricultural products as well. In addition, as was noted earlier, the subsidies are usually financed by depressing the prices paid to the usually relatively poor producers of agricultural commodities, through the payment of low producer prices or the levy of agricultural export taxes, (or, more frequently, a combination of both), all of which impact adversely on the poor. The subsidies are also sometimes financed by the maintenance of highly overvalued exchange rates (with all of their restrictive accompaniments) which favour the politically well-connected and other strong vested interests, at the expense of the poor. The resulting low rate of return to the agricultural sector sometimes also aggravates the rural-urban migration, with adverse implications for agricultural output and for employment.

Overall, the distributional impact of government policies to phase out subsidies by appropriate pricing policies will depend on the precise calibration of the price increase for the commodities, taking into account the consumption patterns of various income groups. Thus experience has shown that in the case of petroleum product subsidies, for example, the burden of adjustment can be more progressively and equitably distributed by targeting relatively higher price increases on the petroleum products primarily consumed by the relatively more affluent (e.g., petrol and diesel fuel) and less for petroleum products (e.g., kerosene) which is primarily consumed by the relatively poorer segments of the population. The same distributional principle can be employed also in the case of food subsidies. However, as has been observed by virtually all writers on the subject of income distribution, the universal empirical fact has been that the decisions on the question of subsidies are expected to be made by the same people who enjoy considerable political power and who, along with their business-sector associates, reap large rents from the distortions caused by subsidies and the scarcities which they give rise to.

Policies with respect to debt service payments in the African countries were relatively less problematic, at least from a political standpoint. In the case of countries experiencing major external debt servicing problems, many of the governments have tended, in the context of adjustment programmes, to reschedule debt service payments, (with the assistance of the Fund) thereby releasing resources immediately which could be used by the national authorities to target disadvantaged and vulnerable groups, while at the same time opening up possible fresh lines of external financial resources. In countries where domestic areas have also been a major problem, policies have been articulated to bring about at least a phased reduction in such arrears, thereby benefitting the private sector. On capital expenditures, experience has shown that, to the extent that policies which have a bearing on the current budget permit, national authorities can at least maintain, and in some cases, increase productive capital expenditures. In cases where, because of the size of the budgetary problem, a temporary curtailment of capital expenditures[9] may have been warranted, a number of African governments have sought the assistance of multilateral institutions with some expertise in evaluating the productivity of various government expenditure projects. Nevertheless, even in these cases, the final decision regarding the sector targeting for the cuts is made by the national authorities.. They could therefore seize the opportunity to deploy the resources released on the process of effecting budgetary savings, to protect certain health and education expenditures which benefit primarily the poorer members of the community. However, the same conflicts of interest noted earlier may have arisen in practice in these cases, where politically powerful and vested interest are also being asked to take expenditure decisions which may jeopardize their own benefits.

Conclusion

The discussion above shows that, if sustained and appropriately targeted, the sum total of the impact of the adjustment policies being adopted by the African countries would be to improve the incomes of rural inhabitants compared to their urban counterparts. Although, in some countries, subsidies on farm inputs, such as fertilizers, may have been phased out in the context of adjustment programmes, the increase in the prices of agricultural products to more remunerative levels, the elimination of subsidies, price decontrol and the liberalization of marketing arrangements – coupled with the impact on export prices of more flexible exchange rates – resulted in relatively higher farm incomes, with favourable implications for output, employment and resource allocation. In addition, the increased availability of external resources to support the adjustment efforts of the African countries generally permitted a higher level of imports than would have been possible without such financing. In view of the rural population's relatively low consumption of imported goods, this segment of the population would generally have been relatively less affected by import price increases resulting from flexible exchange systems than the urban population. By contrast, a relatively small group (usually traders) who, hitherto the implementation of appropriate policies, exploited the distortions and scarcities in the market, reportedly in collusion with some bureaucrats, would stand to lose as the adjustment programmes whittled away the rents and premiums which they enjoy – hence the strong opposition to adjustment usually put forth by these vested interest groups. Even then, the entire population, including these traders and bureaucrats, would benefit in the long run from the higher growth of the economy. Although urban dwellers would appear to be hurt by increases in certain user prices, as well as the increase in prices of food or petroleum products as subsidies are removed, most of them would, in fact, have already been paying high scarcity prices in excess of the officially controlled prices – only the rich and powerful with well-established networks who could purchase at controlled prices would lose substantively.

That many of the favourable distributional effects of adjustment have not occurred to a large extent in many countries may be attributable to a number of factors. First, in some countries, the adjustment process has followed an on-again, off-again pattern, with all the costs but few of the benefits of adjustment. Second, the human dimension in Africa's economic recovery and development has continued to be bedeviled by the persistence of droughts, civil strifes, political upheavals, falling commodity export prices, high international interest rates and recession, as well as dwindling external assistance.[10] Third, some countries have still not yet made the socially critical choice to persevere with policies which will hurt the relatively more vocal and powerful vested interests but which will benefit the (usually politically more quiescent and harmless) disadvantaged and vulnerable groups; but this would be a self-imposed cost, albeit, perhaps unavoidable. While it is difficult for national authorities to do much about the external factors, there are strong reasons to believe that some of the changes needed at the domestic policy level will call for strong political will. Herein lies the dilemma, particularly as all Governments are wont to consider first the political dividends for them involved in any course of action. While cognizant that this is not a simple problem, the point should nevertheless be clearly articulated. Finally, for the same reasons, experience has shown that the social costs of adjustment would be relatively lower if countries embarked on comprehensive and sustained adjustment early, rather than delaying the implementation of appropriate economic and financial policies; again, for political reasons, countries generally exhibit a tendency to prevaricate, sometimes in the hope that some favourable (external) event might occur to obviate the need for adjustment. Unfortunately, the reverse has usually tended to occur, thereby aggravating the adjustment problem, and, with it, the costs as well.

Notes

1 FAO, *Impact of International Monetary Fund/World Bank Recommended Structural Adjustment Policies on Food Production and Consumption in Africa,* Government consultation on the Follow-up to World Conference on Agricultural Reform and Rural Development (WCARRD) in the Africa Region, Harare, Zimbabwe, 3–6 September 1985.

2 Specifically, the Fund provided resources under the oil facility to help with the oil shocks of 1973 and 1979, and continues to provide resources under the compensatory financing facility (CFF) to assist with export shortfalls due to circumstances beyond the control of the authorities. In addition, the Fund provides financial resources to assist countries with temporary balance of payments problems; in the context of these programmes, the Fund has continued to play a catalytic role in mobilizing an increased flow of concessional financial assistance from a number of multilateral financial institutions and bilateral donors, while also, in relevant cases, assisting in the rescheduling of the debts of the African countries.

3 "The Fund's Role in Providing Financial Assistance: Some Current Issues" – Remarks by M. Camdessus, Managing Director of the International Monetary Fund to the 23rd Conference of the Governors of SEACEN in Singapore, January 20, 1988.

4 "Economic Outlook for Africa", – Remarks by A.D. Ouattara, Director, African Department, International Monetary Fund at the Seminar on Growth and Structural Adjustment in Africa, Dakar, May 4–5, 1987.

5 "The Prospects for the Flow of Financial Resources to African Countries" – Remarks by Richard D. Erb, Deputy Managing Director of the International Monetary Fund at the Tenth Regular Meeting of the Association of African Central Banks, Libreville, June 22–28, 1987.

6 Richard M. Bird, "Public Finance and Inequality", *Finance and Development,* March 1974, pp.2–5.

7 For details, see "Fund Supported Programmes, Fiscal Policy, and Income Distribution", A Study by the Fiscal Affairs Department of the International Monetary Fund (Occasional Paper No. 46), IMF, Washington D.C., September 1986.

8 An internal fund study showed that for example in some countries, information based on household survey data indicated that relatively open-ended subsidy schemes resulted in perverse distributional effects with, in one case less then 10 percent of the benefits of food subsidies accruing to the poorest 20 percent of the population, while 40 percent of the subsidy went to the richest 27 percent of the urban dwellers. Presumably, in the case of say, petroleum subsidies, which generally benefit more the relatively more affluent, data, if available, would show an even more skewed and regressive pattern of beneficiaries.

9 For purposes of discussion, we ignore the appropriateness of the classification of current and capital expenditures in many countries, as well as questions regarding whether the initial size of the capital budget is realistic, given the limited resources of many of the countries, although these are also important questions.

10 As noted in a recent report of the U.N. Secretary-General: "[The] measures and reforms have so far yielded some positive results in a number of countries, particularly in the mobilization, rationalization and better utilization of resources, and improved agricultural production . . . The heightened performance of the agricultural sector over the past two years had a positive impact on the manufacturing sector because of the improved supply of agricultural raw materials and increased rural demand . . . [but] . . . the lingering external constraints have continued to arrest growth in the region." See Report of the Secretary-General, Critical Economic Situation in Africa: United Nations Programme of Action for African Economic Recovery and Development 1986–1990, U.N. General Assembly Document No. A/42/560, 1 October 1987, pp.10–11.

Monitoring Human and Social Indicators in the Adjustment Process

BEVERLEY A. CARSON (UNICEF)

Monitoring and Statistics for Adjustment

There has been an increasing recognition in the last few years of the devastating effects of economic recession on poor and vulnerable groups, especially children, and of the importance of ensuring that the current structural adjustment policies that governments are obliged to carry out are so designed that these damaging effects are reduced to the minimum. The objective of monitoring human and social indicators in the adjustment process is therefore to protect vulnerable population groups, such as young children, from the negative impact of structural adjustment policies. Such protection involves safeguarding and monitoring children's health and, in particular, their nutritional status.

Given the very limited organizational and statistical capacity of the majority of the countries in which the monitoring will take place it is evident that only simple mechanisms will work in national programmes in Africa to monitor trends on a regular, frequent and disaggregated basis and bring them to the attention of the highest level of responsible officials. The macro-economic indicators normally used for monitoring economic adjustment are unable to capture the changes occurring in child welfare. Reliance on these data not only completely neglects non-economic factors, but they are also inadequate, because of the variables selected and the level of aggregation, to capture those processes which affect children, especially in poor households.

Efficient monitoring of changes in child welfare for the purpose of policy making requires the regular collection and analysis of three sorts of indicators – status, process and output. Status indicators, measuring success or failure in the programme to protect vulnerable groups would consist primarily of the nutritional and health status of children. They would include particularly:

(a) indicators of nutritional status for the under fives and for children entering primary school;
(b) low birth weight;
(c) infant and under-five mortality rates; and
(d) indicators of morbidity.

The indicators of low birth weight and nutritional status are particularly suitable for monitoring adjustment because they will show deterioration in a short time span.

Process indicators would include the prevalence of breast-feeding, access to and use of oral rehydration therapy, immunization coverage, availability of clean water and access to health services. Regular monitoring of these and other variables is needed to assess the long-term development strategy for improving the human condition. However, from an adjustment perspective, information is particularly needed on the items which are likely to change with economic recession, adjustment, and policy interventions. Input indicators would include real incomes of low-income groups, real government expenditures per head on social services, maternal health, etc.

It is essential to disaggregate the indicators particularly if interventions are targeted to the specially needy. Without disaggregation policies may be devised which do not effectively reach the children most at risk. The appropriate disaggregation will vary among countries. However, it should include broad regional and provincial breakdowns with sufficient socio-economic detail to identify the nature of the vulnerable groups, e.g. formal or informal sector wage earners, shanty town dwellers, rural and urban populations, recent migrants, cultural and ethnic minorities, etc.

At present, relevant information on vulnerable groups is usually published randomly if at all and often after considerable delay. An ideal system considerably in advance of that prevailing in most developing countries is described by Frances Stewart in the publication *Adjustment with a Human Face*. In it she suggests the collection, analysis, publication and wide dissemination of a set of leading indicators of social stress. This data set would be published every two or three months and would include the most recent data both on actual development, e.g. levels of malnutrition; and prospects, making use of systems like the FAO system of early warning on food shortfalls.

Each of the indicators that have been mentioned would be suitable for inclusion in this set of leading indicators of social stress and something is possible even in countries with the weakest of statistical bases. Frances Stewart gives the example of what could be possible in a country like Ghana where, although many of these data are not available at all or only after long intervals and with considerable margins of errors and bias, there are still enough data to provide a useful set of indicators. In the case of Ghana, the indicators and sources suggested were:

	Indicator	Source
1.	Measures of second- and third-degree malnutrition	Catholic Relief Services
2.	Cases of kwashiokor and marasmus	Major hospitals
3.	Proportion of low-birth weight	Major hospitals
4.	Deaths from measles	Clinics/hospitals
5.	Standing crop and crop conditions	Farmers' own assessment
6.	Food prices in regional markets throughout the country	Ministry of Agriculture
7.	Rainfall	Ministry of Agriculture

In some countries it might be possible to add infant and child mortality; changes in sales of assets, changes in indebtedness, changes in migration, data from the FAO early warning system for food supplies, nutritional status of school entrants, real incomes in the urban informal sector, the proportion of household expenditure spent on food in low income families, etc.

Developing leading indicators of social stress along these lines would fulfill a number of purposes:

(a) provide early warning and assist in monitoring programmes to protect vulnerable groups;
(b) achieve collection of data on the social situation on a regular basis with the dissemination of a minimal data set in the national press, radio and television and the Government's regular official publications;
(c) give prominence to information on the situation of vulnerable groups equal to that given to economic data; and
(d) provide an incentive to search for and develop better data.

Current Initiatives

1. *Interagency Food and Nutrition Surveillance Programme (FNS)*

Monitoring nutrition, particularly of vulnerable groups, is one of the best methods of assessing how people are being affected and how compensatory measures are working. The growing concern with the human dimension of economic adjustment policies has underlined the urgent need to monitor changes in nutritional status in as many countries as possible. The nutritional status of young children is probably the most sensitive indicator of sudden changes in food security and health status, acting as an early warning signal of distress, ill health, famine and, eventually, death.

These ideas have been receiving increasing support within the UN system, from a meeting of the ACC Sub-Committee on Nutrition (SCN) in Tokyo, in April 1986, to one of the World Food Council in Rome in May 1987. There have been important public statements on these themes by the Presidents of the World Bank and the International Monetary Fund, and by delegations to the governing bodies of UNICEF, FAO and WHO, supporting the use of food and nutrition surveillance to keep watch over the human condition and provide information on a regular and systematic basis that, together with other economic indicators, can be used by national policy makers.

As a consequence, UNICEF's Executive Board, at its 1987 session at the beginning of May, approved a recommendation for a $10 million noted project to support the strengthening of food and nutrition surveillance systems. The interagency Food and Nutrition Surveillance programme (FNS) is a joint initiative by the Food and Agriculture Organization of the United Nations, the World Health Organization and UNICEF, and was formally endorsed by the ACC Sub-Committee on Nutrition. The interagency programme plans to assist a large number of countries and regional institutions to strengthen food and nutrition surveillance programmes over the next five years. The main thrust of the programme is to support appropriate institutions in the development of country capability for food and nutrition surveillance. The essential feature of this development is not only the ability to collect and analyze information but also its subsequent linkage to decision-making.

The special focus of the FNS programme is to encourage the regular and frequent reporting of a few common indicators in a standardized fashion in order to alert decision makers to the presence of a problem, and to stimulate them to make use of further information in order to take appropriate action. The programme will also support surveillance systems in the broader context, appropriate to the country situation. The specific objectives of the FNS programme are:

In the short term:

(a) to produce and analyze existing information on trends in a limited number of specified indicators of food and nutrition at national and sub-national levels for 20 to 40 countries;
(b) to promote the prompt use of this information for national and international advocacy, stressing that the identified trends in food availability and nutritional status merit immediate recognition and innovative consideration in development strategies, and national planning with particular reference to structural adjustment programmes.

In the long term:

(c) to strengthen the institutional capacity of 40 to 60 developing countries to produce, analyze and use these food and nutrition data by providing appropriate training and other support; and
(d) to promote recognition and use of this information at country and regional levels by advocating that considerations of human nutrition are essential for the proper development of policies and programmes.

Core indicators

A small international working group met in UNICEF headquarters in October 1987 to discuss the common indicators that the interagency FNS programme should encourage countries to collect and use in their food and nutrition surveillance programmes. The objective of these discussions was to move toward a greater consensus and more standardization in the collection, analysis, presentation and use of a minimum list of common indicators that could measure changes over time in food and nutritional status. These common indicators should be feasible for developing countries with limited statistical and information infrastructures and analytical capabilities to obtain on a regular and frequent basis and use for advocacy, policy, planning and programme monitoring. As far as possible these indicators should be consistent with those already being used by national governments and by the concerned international agencies. It was understood that these basic indicators would be set into national food and nutrition contexts which would vary from country-to-country depending upon their national circumstances and the requirements of the users. Nutritional status indicators by themselves cannot identify the determinants which would require a much broader range of indicators but, allied with the local knowledge of the economic and social situation in the country and through existing information systems, they can be powerful instruments for identifying contributory factors and suggesting appropriate courses of action. The working group agreed that the FNS programme should recommend to countries the use of a few common indicators that would monitor changes over time on a regular, frequent and standardized basis. These common indicators would include three anthropometric indicators plus one or two food indicators.

The three nutritional status indicators that were recommended as common indicators for the FNS programme are as follows:

(a) birth weight: as the measure of the nutritional status of the child at birth, as a predictor of the child's likelihood to grow and develop, as an indirect measure of health and nutritional status of the mother of the child and, in aggregate terms, of pregnant women and mothers as a vulnerable group;

(b) weight-for-age of children under five: for monitoring growth and development of this vulnerable group, preferably disaggregated by more specific age groups and, where possible, as in household surveys, supplemented by weight-for-height and height-for-age which are more specific measures: and

(c) height-for-age of primary school entrants: a measure taken at the end of the early period of growth and development which then becomes a cumulative indicator of the overall nutritional and health status of the child at the beginning of its school-going years and as an overall indicator of social and economic development.

The common indicators would be collected through a broad range of statistical instruments depending upon the nature of the indicators, the capacity of the country to produce them, the frequency with which they would be collected and, above all, the uses to which they would be put. All the collection instruments i.e. clinics, household sample surveys, sentinel sites, schools, etc., will have to be used on various occasions by countries taking into account the advantages and disadvantages in using different collection systems. A major objective of the programme will therefore be to promote the appropriate use of these various collection instruments, to provide the recommended common indicators on a regular and frequent basis and to assist countries in strengthening the capacity of their institutions to undertake this work. It was agreed that, wherever possible, countries should be encouraged to aim for at least quarterly reporting.

The working group meeting recognized that, in practice, a country's choice of specific indicators and collection instruments would be very much dictated by what is already being done or has already been planned. For example if weight-for-age is the common practice it will be impractical to switch to weight-for-height. It will also be necessary to piggy-back food and nutrition surveillance onto existing data gathering operations so as to minimize the additional marginal costs and to take advantage of what is already available, e.g. introducing more frequent reporting in an under five health clinic system, adding a nutritional status module to a forthcoming household survey or presenting nutritional status trends in a regular publication of economic indicators.

Levels of support

Support will be provided at three levels:

(a) Country: The aim of the programme is to help some 40 to 60 countries to produce food and nutrition data on a regular and frequent basis and to use these data to guide their own policies and programmes. The programme recognizes that many countries are already producing food and nutrition data though these are often not adequately collected, analyzed or used. The immediate objective therefore is to make better use of what is or could easily be made available, rather than to initiate new systems.

(b) Regional: The programme calls for regional support to obtain and analyze country data that are immediately available, to hold country workshops and to develop regional cooperative agreements for training and support to countries in the region.

(c) Interregional and global: Overall support to the programme will include the provision of technical documentation, software and hardware support systems, technical studies and training, and consultants in special areas.

Assessment of Social Dimensions of Structural Adjustment in Sub-Saharan Africa (SDA) and the African Household Survey Programme

The World Bank has launched, in collaboration with the UNDP/Africa and the African Development Bank, a regional project to integrate social dimensions in the design of structural adjustment and development programmes in 16 countries in sub-Saharan Africa. These are: Central African Republic, Chad, Congo, Cote d'Ivoire, The Gambia, Ghana, Guinea-Bissau, Madagascar, Malawi, Mauritiania, Sao Tome, Senegal, Togo, Zaire and Zambia.

The project includes three sub-components: 1) the design and monitoring of poverty alleviation programmes through projects to increase the access of the poor to employment and income and programmes to mitigate the transitional impact of adjustment on vulnerable groups; 2) assessing the impact of structural adjustment policies on population groups; and 3) the strengthening of institutional statistical capacity through the execution of permanent household surveys and the use of social accounting matrices for integrating social and economic data.

The challenge for this ambitious programme will be to undertake it in such a way as to provide information on a regular and frequent basis for assessing the dimensions and magnitudes of change and differentiating between those changes brought on by adjustment and other factors and influences. The further question arises as to how this can be accomplished in a sustainable way and most importantly how the quantifications of the problems can be used to stimulate and support effective action in developing compensatory measures and monitoring their effects. A rather serious concern is the extent to which these special purpose national statistical operations will compete with and possibly overwhelm the ongoing business of national statistical authorities to provide basic bread and butter economic, social and demographic data.

An issue yet to be clarified is how the programme to assess the social dimensions of adjustment, which is to a great extent a large scale household survey programme, will link up with the ongoing activities in the African countries that are implementing permanent national household survey programmes. Within this context the African Household Survey Programme and the regional National Household Survey Capability Programme (NHSCP) have helped interested developing countries since the late 70's to obtain through systematic programmes of household surveys and in conjunction with data from other sources, a continuing flow of integrated statistics that they need for their development plans, policies and administration in line with national priorities while at the same time strengthening their survey-taking capabilities.

At the present time twenty eight countries are participating in the NHSCP which means that they are implementing integrated household survey programmes which on average include 70 percent national financing and 30 percent external project support. These include twelve African countries, some of which have since also signed up with the SDA project. The question is: how can countries do both? And, if not, which activity will take precedence with scarce financial, professional and – infrastructural resources? Positively put, how can African countries make the best use of the interest of international institutions to support the strengthening of the social analysis capabilities for monitoring the human condition?

UNICEF and Other International Progammes for Monitoring Human Indicators

UNICEF has a permanent programme of monitoring human indicators in developing countries. In the spring of 1986 UNICEF issued a set of recommendations to its field offices on the monitoring and evaluation of child survival and development activities. The three priority indicator areas it recommended for monitoring were infant and child mortality rates, nutritional status of young children and low birth weight. In addition it recommended monitoring immunization coverage, breast-feeding, access to and use of oral rehydration therapy, primary school completion, female literacy, maternal mortality and children living below the absolute poverty line. It strongly emphasized the importance of disaggregation particularly for disadvantaged groups:

> Data generated and collected through all these mechanisms should be compiled and analyzed to show levels, trends and differentials with particular attention to disadvantaged groups. For effective advocacy these outputs of child monitoring programmes should be presented and disseminated in such a way as to have the greatest impact on decision-makers in public opinion. In this regard, it is important to emphasize the timely publication of the data collected in all statistical digests and yearbooks of frequent and common consultation. It is also important to establish a formal feedback system to planners and policy-makers, so that they take into account the changing situation of children in future development programmes and budget allocations.

As part of the regular programme of UNICEF, there is also an extensive country exercise in preparing a situation analysis about the human conditions in each country in the process of establishing, in close dialogue with the national authorities, a five-year programme of co-operation. There are also detailed annual reports about each country. At UNICEF Headquarters, global, country and regional overviews are issued in the form of the annual State of the World's Children Report, in the annual publication Statistics on Children in UNICEF Assisted Countries, and the six-monthly Statistical Review of the Situation of Children in the World. Annex 1 gives an example of a summary of basic human indicators made in 1986 for continental Africa.

Other current international initiatives include the first World Nutrition Survey with regional analyses prepared by the ACC/SCN and the Demographic and Health Survey Programme in 12 sub-Saharan and three North African countries to include health and nutritional status elements. Other international programmes that monitor human indicators include the WHO Health for All by the Year 2000, ILO's World Employment Programme, FAO's

World Programme of Rural Development (WACCARD) and the United Nations system as a whole in its decennial targets for the various Development Decades.

References

1 ACC/SCN, *First Report on the World Nutrition Situation*. Washington, 1987.

2 Carson, Beverley A. "The potential of national household survey programmes for monitoring and evaluating primary health care in developing countries", *World Health Statistics Quarterly*, 38 (1), 1985.

3 Carson, Beverley A. "Core indicators for the interagency food and nutrition surveillance programme (FNS)", UNICEF, New York, 1987. (Unpublished).

4 Catholic Relief Services, "C.R.S. Food and Nutrition Programme in sub-Saharan Africa", (Unpublished country and overview reports).

5 Cornia, G.A., Jolly, R. and Stewart F. eds., *Adjustment with a Human Face*. UNICEF, Oxford, 1987.

6 FAO, WHO, UNICEF and ACC/SCN. "Information note on the interagency Food and Nutrition Surveillance programme: (FNS)," (Unpublished).

7 Jolly, Richard. Recession, adjustment and nutrition: an overview. *Food and Nutrition Bulletin*, U.N. University 9 (1). 1987.

8 Kenya Central Bureau of Statistics, "The Rural Kenya Nutrition Survey 1977," *Social Perspectives* 2 (4), Nairobi, 1977.

9 Kenya Central Bureau of Statistics, "Report of the Child Nutrition Survey 1978/79," UNICEF, Nairobi, 1979.

10 Kenya Central Bureau of Statistics, "Third Rural Child Nutrition Survey 1982". UNICEF, Nairobi, 1983.

11 Mason J.B. *et al.*, *Nutritional Surveillance*. World Health Organization. Geneva, 1984.

12 Nigeria Federal Office of Statistics. "National integrated survey of households: Health and nutrition module". Lagos, 1982.

13 Pinstrup-Anderson, P. "Macroeconomic adjustment policies and human nutrition". *Food and Nutrition Bulletin*, U.N. University 9 (1), 1987.

14 Test K., Mason J. and C.R.S. Trends in prevalences of malnutrition in five African countries from clinic data 1982–1985. *Ecology of Food and Nutrition*. (Forthcoming).

15 UNICEF *Child Malnutrition in Six African countries*: Press Kit for Within Human Reach, New York, 1985.

16 UNICEF, "Framework for improving the monitoring and evaluation of child survival and development activities". New York, 1986.

17 UNICEF, *Statistical Review of the Situation of Children in the World*. New York, 1987.

18 UNICEF, *Statistics on Children in UNICEF assisted countries*, New York, 1987.

19 UNICEF, *Strengthening Food and Nutrition Surveillance Systems*. UNICEF Executive Board, New York, 1987.

20 UNICEF, *State of the World's Children 1988*. Oxford, 1987.

21 United Nations. "Annual reports of the National Household Survey Capability Programme (NHSCP) to the Programme Review" Committee, United Nations Statistical Office (Unpublished), New York, 1985, 1986 and 1987.

22 United Nations, "How to Weigh and Measure Children" U.N. Statistical Office, NHSCP, New York, 1986.

23 United Nations, "Assessing the nutritional status of young children in household surveys", Statistical Office, NHSCP, (forthcoming).

24 World Bank/UNDP. Assessment of social dimension of Structural adjustment in sub-Saharan Africa. (Project document).

25 World Health Organization, "Development of indicators for monitoring progress towards Health for All by the Year 2000", Geneva, 1981.

26 World Health Organization, "Measuring change in nutritional status", Geneva, 1983.

27 World Health Organization, "Global nutritional status: Anthropometric indicators". Geneva, 1987.

Structural Adjustment, Food Production and Rural Poverty

E.K. TAPSOBA (FAO)

Recently, the efficacy of orthodox structural adjustment programmes in rectifying structural adjustment disequilibria in developing countries has been questioned. Given the magnitude of the external and internal imbalances on financial accounts and the rigid socio-economic structures in many countries, implementation of structural adjustment programmes may incur considerable social costs and can even be counterproductive. While the need for macro-economic adjustment to stimulate economic growth in the long run has not been disputed, the short-run economic and social impacts have increasingly become a source of concern.

Agriculture's Contribution to Economic Imbalances in Africa

In Africa, the agricultural sector, and the food sector in particular, are recognized as a crucial element in any strategy towards growth-oriented structural adjustment. The gravity of the poor performance of the agricultural sector over the past 10–20 years or more, with serious food shortages and famine in half of the African continent during the 1983–1984 drought, has increased awareness and concern in international fora and induced individual governments to search for an "African strategy" for development, with food and agriculture as core elements. *The United Nations Programme of Action for African Economic Recovery and Development, 1986–1990* (UN-PAAERD) explicitly, recognizes that agriculture and agro-based sectors are the main engine for Africa's recovery and the foundation of its long-term development. FAO's strategy for Africa's agricultural development, which was introduced by the Director-General of FAO at the fourteenth FAO Regional Conference for Africa, is based on a Programme of Action which advocates the need for far-reaching internal reforms as symbolized by the four "i"s: incentives to producers, increased use of essential inputs, reform of agricultural institutions and development of infrastructure. The programme of Action is drawn from FAO's recent in-depth study of agriculture and food problems in Africa (i.e. African Agriculture: The next 25 years).

The economic crisis in Africa is associated with the stagnation in agriculture. For the continent as a whole (excluding South Africa) agricultural production growth rates were very slow or even declining and were outpaced by population growth during 1975–1986. Agricultural production per capita fell by an average annual rate of 1.1 per cent. Per capita food production followed a similar trend and on the whole has not kept up with demand. Of the 44 African countries for which data were available, 31 had a lower average self-sufficiency ratio in 1983–1985 than in the 1979/81 period, and for about a quarter of them the decline was more than 10 per cent. These lower ratios were not simply the consequence of the 1983–1984 drought. Only in three years since 1975 (1980, 1985, 1986) were annual percentage changes in per capita (gross) agricultural and food production (net) positive; 1985 was a year with a spectacularly good harvest, the best since 1975. Progress has continued in 1986 but at a much slower rate.

Table 1: Per capita agricultural and food production in Africa: Average annual percentage changes, 1975–1986

	1975–1980	1980–1984	1984–1986
Agricultural production per capita	−1.7	−2.0	3.2
Food production per capita	−1.6	−2.1	3.2

Poor performance of agricultural and food production implies higher dependence on imports. In each year since 1980, the sector was a net foreign exchange user, as agricultural import bills exceeded agricultural export earnings. A peak was reached in 1981 when agricultural import costs were higher by 63 per cent than agricultural export earnings. Food imports increased their share in agricultural imports only slightly between 1975 and 1985 (from 80 per cent in 1975–1980 to 83 per cent in 1981–1985). Agricultural import values accounted for 23 per cent and food imports about 19 per cent of merchandise exports in the 1980s.

Table 2: African trade indicators: Average annual ratios, 1975–1985

	1975–1980	1981–1985
	Percentage	
Agricultural imports/Agricultural exports	92.7	152.6
Agricultural imports/Total exports	17.7	22.7
Food imports/Total exports	14.1	18.9
Food imports/Agricultural imports	79.7	83.0
Agricultural exports/Total exports on which:		
Agricultural exporters[a]	75.1	65.2
Total imports/Total exports	95.9	113.2

[a] Agricultural exporters are defined by IMF as those countries whose exports of agriculture products accounted for over 50 per cent of their total exports in 1980.

Agricultural imports, as a proportion of agricultural exports, have increased whereas the share of agricultural exports in total exports decreased between 1981 and 1985 in comparison to 1975–1980. At the same time imbalances in the total trade accounts accumulated as total imports were 16 per cent higher than total exports in 1981–1985, compared to 1975–1980. The agricultural sector has therefore, contributed to the balance-of-payments deficits during the 1980s, a reversal of its role in the last half of the 1970s.

Heavy dependence on imports places acute strains on the balance-of-payments in the face of severe foreign exchange constraints present in many African countries. It is difficult, if not impossible, to import the food needed to stabilize consumption and offset domestic production shortfalls. Over the period 1975–1985, per capita calorie intake has fluctuated quite widely. It has been estimated that in 14 African countries a shortfall of more than 2.5 per cent in food consumption occurs with a 25 per cent probability, that is once every four years.

Agriculture has also contributed to foreign indebtedness. In recent years the agricultural sector has relied more on debt-creating financial flows. Since 1982, for the entire African continent, agriculture's share in concessional commitments has been declining. More specifically, in sub-Saharan Africa the share of agriculture in total concessional commitments has fallen by almost a quarter, even though agriculture's share of total (concessional and non-concessional) commitments has been maintained at around 22 per cent during 1982–1984. In addition, over the 1975–1985 period, on average, more then 40 per cent of total borrowing from private sources to agriculture was made by African countries. The agricultural sector's contribution to the acute debt burden, therefore, has been significant.

However, scanty available evidence suggests that agriculture has not contributed much to fiscal deficits. A rigorous investigation requires data on agricultural expenditures and agricultural tax revenues but unfortunately comparable data on agricultural taxation are not available and those on expenditures are of dubious quality. In a sample of 21 countries over the 1978–1984 period, the average share of central government expenditure to agriculture in total central government expenditure was lower than 10 per cent in 15 countries and no country had a share greater than 20 per cent (table A.1). These shares are well below agriculture's contribution to GDP (33 per cent in 1981–1983). For half of the countries there was tendency to decrease the agricultural expenditure share in the 1980s.

Impacts of Structural Adjustment Polices on Agriculture

The task of assessing the impact of structural adjustment policies is a complex one and only tentative conclusions can be drawn. The scope and specific components of the package varies from country to country. The policy measures have been adopted only relatively recently; yet some of their effects will be long lasting. Hence to gauge the full impact of these policies longer time series are needed. Even if more data were available, additional issues would have to be confronted. These include the possible conflict between targets and instruments, the difficulty of establishing the timing and the degree to which a single policy instrument affects a particular target, and the need to distinguish the effects of previous policy measures and of exogenous factors such as natural disasters.

Having noted these caveats, preliminary evidence on the experience of the 26 African countries which undertook structural adjustment programmes (SA) between mid-1979 and mid-1984 is presented. Those involved in SA programmes after mid-1984 are excluded because it is judged to be too soon to realize measurable results. The performance of SA countries, with respect to agricultural and food production, trade and nutrition, is compared with the African countries that have not implemented such policies. The main focus will be on the post-1984 period, although, to complete the time series, the results for 1980–1985 are also incorporated in the tables which follow. The SA countries accounted for about 50 per cent of both agricultural and food production in the region, 68 per cent of agricultural exports and 27 per cent of both agricultural and food imports during 1975–1980.

Agricultural terms of trade

Domestic price policies were more favourable, or less unfavourable, in the early 1980s than in the 1970s. According to the FAO Price Study (1985), nominal protection coefficients (NPCs) were increasing and real price biases decreasing. Overall, cereals were protected more than cash crops. However, in the 25 SA countries for which data were available, real cereal producer prices were higher in the early 1980s than in the second half of the 1970s for only 11 (Cote d'Ivoire, Ghana, Malawi, Mali, Mauritania, Mauritius, the Niger, Somalia, the United Republic of Tanzania, Zambia and Zimbabwe). Country reports for 1985–1987 indicate that the move towards higher relative prices for agricultural products in domestic markets became more widespread since the early 1980s, although there have been difficulties in maintaining these in real terms.

Agricultural trade

Countries with SA have reduced their agricultural import bills relative to those without. Agricultural and food import costs were rising rapidly in both groups of countries in the second half of the 1970s (table 3). However, in the 1980s the SA countries reduced import costs significantly whereas those without SA continued to expend more for imports, albeit at a much slower rate.

Table 3: Agricultural trade in Africa: Average annual percentage changes, 1975–1985

	1975–1980	1984–1985	1980–1985
Agricultural imports (Value)			
With SA	12.1	− 6.2	− 3.0
Without SA	16.3	2.6	2.1
Food imports (Value)			
With SA	12.5	− 6.5	− 2.8
Without SA	16.6	3.1	2.0
Agricultural exports (Value)			
With SA	11.8	− 2.1	− 2.0
Without SA	4.6	− 4.1	− 3.8
Agricultural exports (Volume)			
With SA	− 1.4	3.2	1.2
Without SA	− 2.7	− 4.8	− 1.2
Food imports (Volume)			
With SA	8.2	2.2	4.2
Without SA	16.7	11.7	5.8

Countries with SA have a better record in agricultural exports growth. For both sets of countries, the value of agricultural exports fell throughout the 1980s, but in those countries with SA the loss in export earnings was less sharp (table 3). Moreover, in terms of volumes, after slowly declining during 1975–1980 exports in SA countries increased during 1980–1985, with the 3.2 per cent rise in 1984–85 indicating a sustained recovery from the marked fall in the drought year of 1983. On the other hand, export volumes in those countries without SA continued to decline throughout the period. Hence, countries with SA increased exports and reduced imports relative to non-SA countries during 1980–1985, and especially during 1984–1985, when SA measures should have become increasingly effective. Nevertheless, it should be stressed that the improvements during 1980–1985 in the agricultural trade balance were mainly due to curtailments in imports rather than to spectacular acceleration of exports.

Along with the decline in the rate of change in expenditures on total imports in SA countries, food import expenditures have also fallen. Although a similar pattern was noted for both groups in 1975–1980, thereafter food import expenditures were reduced for SA countries. For those without SA, food import costs continued to increase but at a substantially slower rate. A similar pattern in terms of food import volumes is discernible. Although in both groups the rate of growth slowed markedly from 1975–1980 to 1980–1985, the rate of growth during 1984–1985 was much lower for the SA countries. The nutritional consequences of these developments in trade and production will be discussed subsequently.

Agricultural production

Agricultural production growth in SA countries was slower during 1975–1980, mainly due to the decline in non-food production (table 4). However, during 1980–1986 production growth rates have been higher in these countries, although the results are influenced by the extraordinary good harvest in 1985 (11 per cent over 1984). The results for 1984–1986 are most impressive with respect to gains in food production in SA countries, but the increase in non-food production also was substantial, again with the largest gains registered in 1985, a highly favourable weather year.

Table 4: Agricultural production in Africa: Average annual percentage changes, 1975–1986

	1975–1980	1984–1986	1980–1986
Agricultural production			
With SA	0.8	7.4	3.1
Without SA	1.7	5.2	2.4
Non-food production			
With SA	− 0.6	4.8	3.3
Without SA	0.4	2.9	0.9
Food production per capita			
With SA	− 1.8	4.2	− 0.1
Without SA	− 1.4	2.4	− 0.6

Per capita food production changes were similar in both groups of countries between 1975 and 1980, and remained negative over the whole 1980–1986 period. However, during 1984–1986 those with SA managed to register substantially larger increases in per capita for those without SA.

Dietary energy supplies (DES)

The nutritional gap between the African countries with high levels of per capita calorie consumption and those with low has been widening. Countries with already relatively high levels of DES were those which achieved the most significant improvement in the 1980s. Nine out of the 16 countries which had experienced declining DES in 1984–1985 were least developed countries. These findings have serious implications on the welfare, health, and nutritional status of the population.

Nutritional status depends on domestic availability of food which in turn comprises domestic food production and net trade in food products. The preceding analysis suggests that in the 1980s and especially over the last three years, the SA countries experienced a slower growth in food imports but a somewhat faster growth in domestic food production than the non-SA countries. Hence, after rising at a much slower rate during 1975–1980 in SA countries, the annual changes in DES were much the same in both groups of countries during 1980–1985, with both experiencing a reduction in per capita calorie intake, but with stronger gains during 1984–1985 in the SA countries. In terms of the level of DES, the countries without SA managed a slightly better recovery; in 1985 it was close to the previous peak (1981).

Table 5: Per capita dietary energy supply in Africa, 1975–1985

	1975–1980	1984–1985	1980–1985
		Percent	
With SA	0.4	3.3	−0.2
Without SA	1.8	2.2	−0.2
	1975	1980	1985
		kcal/capita/day	
With SA	2,226	2,265	2,237
Without SA	2,128	2,324	2,298

Structural Adjustment Policies and Rural Poverty

It is now widely accepted that the agricultural sector in developing countries has been undervalued in the past and that, because of inappropriate policies, a disproportionate share of resources has been allocated to urban areas and industrialization programmes. The case for policy reform is well established and most SA programmes have been formulated with this necessity firmly in mind. This section focuses specifically on one segment of the population, the rural poor, and examines some of the possible consequences of SA policies on this group. In doing so, however, it is recognized that the adverse impact of SA programmes will be greater on the urban than rural poor.

Using World Bank estimates of the number of people below country-specific poverty lines, rural poverty has been computed to be as high as 65 per cent of the rural population in a sample of 21 sub-Saharan African countries. The rural poor are a heterogeneous group but share common disabilities. These include limited assets, vulnerability to adverse environmental conditions and limited access to public services, particularly education and medical facilities. In Africa, poverty is associated with poor quality soils, low, erratic rainfall and limited access to means of production.

In attempting to assess the impact of SA programmes on the poor, the prosperity of those who rely on wage earnings in agriculture or those who produce for local or export agricultural markets is most directly affected. Many in the latter group are smallholders producing a major share of national marketed surplus (e.g in 1980 smallholders with less than 2 hectares accounted for 73 per cent of the total number of holdings in Ethiopia, 84 per cent in Cote d'Ivoire and 61 per cent in Malawi). On the other hand, there are those in rural areas that will not be significantly affected by SA programmes, at least in the short run. This group comprises those producers who are only able to meet subsistence needs, with little or no marketed surplus. For them, changes in climatic conditions may be more important than changes in macroeconomic policies.

The combination of limited improvements in agricultural technologies, rapid population growth and a rigid institutional structure only serves to worsen the position of the poor in Africa. Where structural adjustment programmes succeed in accelerating agricultural growth they can make a significant contribution to poverty alleviation. But for agricultural growth to benefit the poor, it should take a particular form, namely, improved agricultural technologies, adequate producer prices, marketing services and related infrastructure that should be spread widely throughout the rural sector. Particular attention should be given to effective use of labour, and to increases in domestic availability of food products. Under these circumstances, the rural poor gain as landless labourers employed for longer periods, as producers with a larger marketed surplus and enhanced returns, and as consumers enjoying a more nutritious diet. Absolute poverty is thus reduced, although it may well be the case that a dynamic agricultural sector is yet more advantageous to other income groups (including the urban poor). The question which arises is: will SA policies promote agricultural growth which is "pro-poor" – or, at least, is not "anti-poor"?

Input subsidies – notably on credit, mechanization and fertilizer – can promote the wider use, and quicker adoption of modern technologies, and result in lower production costs. But input subsidies also can encourage inappropriate use of natural resources and, together with input market imperfections, may lead to differential access in favour of the larger producers with regressive effects on income distribution. The essential task of policy reform, therefore, under SA programmes or otherwise, is to maximize the benefits and minimize the adverse impacts, keeping in mind that the poor will be less able to manage the removal of input subsidies than the rich.

Devaluation can adversely affect the ability to import agricultural machinery. This, in turn, has a negative influence on crop production in areas of Africa where there is a serious shortage of farm labour at peak seasons. Mechanical power is appropriate for introduction in areas where animal power cannot be used and the needed timeliness for crop production operations cannot be achieved with only human power. Moreover the realignment of exchange rates discourages the importation of other farm inputs, notably fertilizer, and this may impede, not promote, agricultural growth.

When agricultural growth increases domestic availability of food (rather than merely replacing imports or increasing exports) the rural poor as consumers benefit from lower food prices. With structural adjustment policies, however, in the short term the price of agricultural products will rise if artificial price constraints are dismantled. Though sharp rises in food prices can be a major boost to the agricultural producer, they can have severe implications for the poor net food buyer and in particular they can increase the incidence of malnutrition. This impact is exacerbated when there is a marked reduction or complete removal of food subsidies.

Increased malnutrition in rural areas is also associated with greater health problems. Reduced food intake, increased illness and hunger can reduce productivity as well as increase the burden on households with already limited resources. Furthermore, the substitution of more costly energy foods for cheaper, possibly less nutritious foods can increase the nutritional burden especially for the more vulnerable members of the household. Increased food prices can also reduce incomes for women whose responsibility covers food purchases.

Structural adjustment policies, by altering the terms of trade between tradable and non-tradable goods, will change the product mix of the agricultural sector since both domestic resource costs and producer returns will alter. Concern has been expressed that this shift in production will have unwelcome implications for domestic food availability. Specifically with currency realignment there will be an incentive to increase the production of export crops and reduce production of staples for the home market, for those countries such as the current SA countries which have a larger share in agricultural exports than in food imports. (However, in those cases where food imports are more important, the incentive from devaluation would be to increase imports to substitute for domestic production.). For countries which are foreign exchange-constrained and have a poorly developed marketing infrastructure, the consequences for food security can be serious if domestic food supply is reduced. Imports of food are likely to be curtailed or food prices will increase. Whatever may be the case in an ideal world, in practice less domestic output of food tends to mean less food for the poor.

However, when judged solely on the evidence to date, these fears are not entirely warranted. Devaluation has often been accompanied by increases in producer prices over a wide range of agricultural products, world export prices have been depressed and the scope for expansion in export volumes limited by international agreements. Hence, as noted in the previous section, food availability in SA countries has not been out of line with those without SA programmes, mainly due to better performance by the former during 1984–1985. Whether this continues to be the case as the full efforts of the SA programmes work through, remains to be seen. The implications of these programmes for food security will require further study and monitoring.

Other issues which have emerged concerning the reallocation of resources towards export crops include the reduced control of women over household income, if income generation by men involved in export cash crops is encouraged, and, in the longer term, the dominance of large commercial farms which have a particular advantage in meeting quality standards for export products. Again a judgement as to whether these concerns are justified cannot be made on the evidence currently available.

In the long term the prosperity of the rural poor will also depend on the growth of the non-farm sector, since in the course of economic growth an increasing proportion of the agricultural population must seek employment there. Two points concerning rural poverty may be stressed here. First, many poor households already derive a significant proportion of their income from non-farm activities (In particular an inverse relationship between non-farm employment and farm size has been noted in surveys of Northern Nigeria and Sierra Leone). Second, the counter-cyclical nature of non-farm employment can perform a positive role in smoothing the seasonal pattern of earnings. Specific developments in the non-food sector which can alleviate rural poverty are rural public works and rural industrialization.

Rural public works programmes, which have a broad spatial focus but yet within each region are targeted on the most needy, are an important means by which the poor may be compensated for the adverse effects of SA policies. In addition, there is a primary need for industrialization which has strong links with the rural sector, mainly through the supply of raw materials and labour. Policies designed to increase the flow of information on market opportunities, maintain quality control, develop extension and training services on new technologies and improve the infrastructure, will all enhance the flexibility of the industrial sector to changing market conditions but will also serve to alleviate rural poverty.

Conclusions and Further Policy Considerations

The preliminary evidence presented in the preceding sections indicates that SA programmes so far adopted by African countries may already have had some success in reversing long-term negative trends and stimulating sustainable economic growth. Although SA programmes have not been in force long enough to relax binding structural constraints and low productivity, their overall outcome is contingent upon many factors. These include, inter alia, timeliness, implementation, composition of the policy package and the politico-socio economic structures of countries. Structural adjustment programmes, to be effective, must be tailored to accommodate the particular circumstances of each country. By the same token, given the high degree of interdependence in the world economy the outcome of any single country's SA programme would depend to some extent on similar policies of other countries. In the face of low demand elasticities for developing country exports, in particular African exports, and protectionist policies in the developed economies, competitive devaluations and generalized attempts to boost traditional exports may produce results contrary to those expected. In spite of the lack of strong evidence of short-term effects of SA, sub-Saharan countries are facing increasing population pressures and an extremely unfavourable international market for their goods. While SA policies are not the underlying cause of these problems, so far they have not sufficiently alleviated the negative impacts on food security and nutrition. Furthermore, a genuine concern exists that income distribution, food security, and welfare may be adversely affected in the long run.

As has been emphasized by FAO's study, African Agriculture: The Next 25 Years, in order to increase productivity in agriculture and enhance food production it is not sufficient only to provide incentives in the form of improved relative prices. Other important incentives are those that arise from adequate public investment in infrastructure, marketing, human resources and from improved availability of essential production inputs. As the recent FAO Price Study (1985) amply demonstrates, producers respond significantly to changes in relative prices when other non-price factors are favourable. Growth of the food and agricultural sector depends on an appropriate combination of incentives, inputs, institutions and infrastructure.

The process of SA implies more exposure to market forces and greater reliance on the private sector. The government's role is to shrink while private sector initiatives and institutions develop. However, it may be several years before the private sector will be able to take over certain functions. Therefore, provisions have to be made to protect the most exposed social groups, alleviate hardship, and overcome marketing and related problems, which in the short run may grow more acute. Reductions in consumer and producer subsidies would hurt real incomes and especially the nutritional status and incomes of the economically weak. In order to protect the poor and avoid social unrest, while at the same time reducing public expenditure, food subsidies should be targeted to those in need. Considering that nutritional status is related to poverty and poverty to unemployment, this approach could be complemented with food-for-work options. A similar approach to input subsidies, provided only for means of production and in amounts appropriate to the rural poor, should be considered.

An issue of major policy concern is the exposure of both producers and consumers to wide fluctuations in prices. FAO sees the objective of price stabilization as worth pursuing, despite its costs, mainly for reasons of protection of needier consumer and producer groups. However, price stability should not be synonymous with price rigidity; some price flexibility is advised to reflect actual demand-supply conditions. Excessive, ambitious attempts to stabilize food prices are generally unsuccessful and conducive to undesirable economic and political side effects. A correct policy package would consist of a government backed minimum price to producers of basic foods through public purchases and stockholding sufficient to meet the price target range.

Of major policy concern is how smallholder agriculture which is a source of employment and nutritional safety for large segments of the population in Africa would fare during the adjustment period. Although marketed output from smallholder agriculture is limited, its rapid decline can accentuate income distribution inequalities, endangering nutritional standards and increasing the pace and cost of urbanization. Therefore, institutions should be developed to assist smallholders in introducing appropriate innovations and production systems along with research, extension, marketing and credit schemes. In the production of export cash crops where high-quality control is essential, or capital-intensive processing methods required, the balance of advantage may lie with large-scale commercial farming. However, economies of scale in export-oriented agro-enterprises have definite limits in terms of agricultural production. The scope for both small and large production units is exemplified by the balance struck in countries such as Kenya and Zimbabwe.

For sustained agricultural growth the UN-PAAERD has called for the mobilization of $US 55.2 billion, 72.8 per cent of which must come from domestic resources and 27.2 per cent from external resources. The difficulty which many national governments will face in generating these resources should not be underestimated. Furthermore, given the debt overhang in many of these countries their external resources requirements should be met on highly concessional terms. Recent evidence, however, in this respect is not very encouraging.

This gives an urgency to the efforts of FAO and other international agencies to identify and analyze links between adjustment and stabilization policies and the performance of the agricultural sector on a continuing basis. Only with well considered policy initiatives and an improving understanding of the links can the negative effects be reduced and positive effects enhanced. In addition to delineating short-term initiatives, it is also necessary to examine the implications of long-term effects of structural adjustment programmes. An examination of implications of increased producer prices on rural income, income distribution, savings and use of inputs should be undertaken, with particular attention being given to the effects of price and real income changes on household food security and welfare.

Table Annex 1: Agricultural share of total government expenditure in Africa (percentage)

	1978	1979	1980	1981	1982	1983	1984	1985	1978–80	1981–84
									Average	
Botswana	10.53	9.24	9.71	8.71	8.65	7.90	9.27	–	9.83	8.63
Burkina Faso	4.22	3.88	5.47	5.20	4.53	5.03	4.31	–	4.52	4.77
Cameroon	4.42	4.32	2.22	1.35	–	8.33	6.79	8.02	3.55	6.12
Gambia	22.01	17.27	17.97	13.79	10.92	–	–	–	19.08	12.35
Ghana	12.20	10.38	12.23	12.20	10.70	–	4.95	6.19	11.60	8.51
Kenya	8.46	8.43	8.28	11.16	8.99	10.14	7.63	–	8.39	9.48
Liberia	8.98	5.58	5.02	5.01	7.33	5.76	5.63	6.12	6.53	5.93
Malawi	11.50	11.44	10.15	13.55	15.08	16.05	11.91	–	11.03	14.14
Mauritius	9.35	7.19	6.87	6.57	6.47	5.82	6.15	7.03	7.80	6.25
Morocco	6.57	7.20	6.46	7.00	5.66	5.42	5.62	–	6.74	5.92
Senegal	–	–	4.35	5.09	7.94	7.45	–	–	4.35	6.83
Sierra Leone	3.82	3.50	–	–	–	10.08	6.03	–	3.66	8.06
Sudan	9.00	11.31	9.44	–	8.50	–	–	–	9.92	8.50
Swaziland	8.59	13.06	12.98	10.67	12.32	9.70	7.96	6.22	11.54	10.16
Tanzania	9.33	7.40	10.90	11.07	6.96	6.39	7.36	6.17	9.21	7.95
Togo	6.48	8.90	–	5.07	7.52	5.95	9.14	8.09	7.69	6.92
Tunisia	9.76	12.68	14.52	17.03	16.45	14.24	18.10	–	12.32	16.45
Uganda	10.62	8.40	6.99	10.41	5.75	3.87	3.10	4.31	8.67	5.78
Zaire	2.12	0.78	1.06	1.92	3.00	–	0.92	–	1.32	1.95
Zambia	12.19	17.84	22.97	12.51	16.49	–	–	–	17.67	14.50
Zimbabwe	11.40	6.97	7.03	8.46	10.37	6.09	10.91	–	8.47	8.96

Source: Government Finance Statistics Yearbook 1986, the International Monetary Fund.

Structural Adjustment, Health, Nutrition and Food Aid in Africa

WORLD HEALTH ORGANIZATION (WHO) AND WORLD FOOD PROGRAMME (WFP)

This paper is built on the premise, that without "health for all", true development will elude us. We may have economic and agricultural success but if the health of each family member is fragile, we cannot claim that adequate welfare has been attained. Moreover, poor health negates the attainment of family welfare and therefore of national development goals. A healthy labour force is a necessary condition for sustained socioeconomic development.

There is a need therefore to strengthen preventive and promotive health action at all levels. WHO member States have all adopted national strategies for primary health care and "health for all by the year 2000" (HFA/2000) and recently it was decided to focus WHO's support to primary health care at the local level, i.e., in the districts, and the communities which make up the districts. This approach to attain HFA/2000 through district-level support is outlined in a document which has been unanimously adopted by member States and is serving as a guideline for accelerated efforts for health, not only within the health sector itself, but also involving other sectors whose contribution is essential such as agriculture, education, information, local government, etc.

Health Effects of Structural Readjustment Measures

Although the evidence is incomplete, the following may be cited as examples of health effects associated with structural adjustment measures (keeping in mind that it cannot be deduced that they are directly caused by them):

(a) Analyses have shown that in the African continent (as distinct from other regions), when governments have been obliged to make cut-backs the health sector has been the first to suffer – in more than half the cases. Under such constraints, the first economies are made in the provision of equipment and supplies (especially pharmaceutical), and in maintenance. Nearly all countries are experiencing a severe decline in the quality of the health infrastructures (both hospitals and clinics). Financial contracts have also necessitated the introduction in some cases of systems of fee-for-service or fee-for-drugs. Decline in resources has also resulted in the concentration of health personnel in urban rather than rural centres.

(b) Restriction of certain services, e.g., mobile (MCH) services have had to be radically curtailed or abandoned, resulting in reduced coverage of rural areas in many countries. They have not been adequately replaced by equivalent village-based activities;

(c) Breakdown of certain disease-control services: Due to lack of resources there has sometimes been contraction of control measures such as for trypanosomiasis and schistosomiasis. Even priority measures such as immunization for children have sometimes been severely restricted because of financial constraints, and malaria control is severely hampered by lack of funds for both treatment and prevention;

(d) Impaired nutrition: Structural adjustment has often been associated with increased food prices and reduced food availability, and the removal of subsidies on food, especially staple foods. In some cases, this is worsened by natural causes like drought. Such changes may be beneficial to farmers but cause hardship to low-income periurban households. The discontinuation of subsidized food or food rations for government employees can bring serious consequences (such as malnutrition) to their children, as well as low output because of chronic hunger. The low-income periurban households are in fact believed to be the most hard hit by such structural adjustment measures;

(e) Health manpower: Because of inadequate remuneration, there is a catastrophic outflow of all levels of health manpower and serious morale problems among remaining personnel who have to struggle for other ways to survive in view of hopelessly inadequate salaries.

Approaches to Health Protection and Promotion

To combat the situation, general policies have been defined by most Member States – in the form of "National strategies for HFA/2000" with a regional strategy for HFA also having been defined by WHO.

The approach emphasizes the need to establish at the "local level" (the district) a health subcommittee of the district development committee, chaired by the district commissioner (or equivalent), and a district health management cycle (planning, implementation, monitoring/evaluation) in support of community health activities in villages, communes, locations, suburbs, etc., that make up a district. At the same time, the system would provide information to intermediate and central levels and would require technical and strategic assistance (respectively) from those levels. Community involvement, intersectoral collaboration and appropriate technologies are the essential features of this primary health care system. Principally, WHO is endeavouring to face this challenge by mobilizing resources for support to district health development, through its own programmes and by appealing to the international community: sister United Nations agencies (like UNDP, UNICEF, UNFPA, UNECA) and bilateral agencies. The sad fact is that in spite of tremendous efforts to date, the resources are pitifully small. Almost all agencies are faced with declining resources and escalating costs. What is heartening, however, is that many of the United Nations family agencies are following the call for a district-development focus in their inputs, and the need for intersectoral action at all levels (national, intermediate and local) is agreed by all. What remains is to work out international partnership mechanisms so that we may give more effective joint interagency support, to such intersectoral action.

Food Aid, Health and Nutrition in Adjustment Programmes

As more and more developing countries (especially in Africa) move to adjust their economies to current internal and international circumstances, concern has inevitably grown that food aid – a significant external resource in many developing countries – should also be used more purposefully on a larger scale, to support the adjustment process. This concern becomes even more heightened by the deteriorating health and nutritional status of vulnerable groups which is very often associated with periods of recession and adjustment.

One major purpose of this paper is to examine more closely the role of food aid in the adjustment process especially as it impinges on the health sector.

(a) General support

Food aid as a general support for adjustment most commonly takes the form of programme aid in which the food is provided to a government, all of which is then sold or monetized in the country concerned, and the proceeds from the sale are made available to the national treasury. This form of food aid generally provides substantial balance-of-payments savings, as it releases foreign exchange that would otherwise have been used to import food commercially. Normally it would be part of a total agreement in which the foreign assistance package would be provided conditional upon undertaking agreed, specific adjustment measures.

(b) Sector reform

A second role for food aid in support of policy reform and economic adjustment programmes is its use within a particular sector or sectors. In these cases, food aid is directly tied to reform measures within a particular sector, may involve partial or full monetization of the food, and often involves a commitment extending over a relatively long period of adjustment measures, such as five years. In most cases, agriculture has been the focus of such sectoral adjustment schemes although this emphasis need not be exclusive. In fact, food aid used in this manner could contribute effectively in a health sector reform programme by providing the classical nutrition support to health institutions, by aiding in a general shift of resources to locally oriented community-based health programmes and activities through the generation of funds from food sales and by supporting long-term reforms in health policy with reinforcing budgetary resources.

(c) Specific development investments

Food aid has been deployed in support of a wide range of investment activities which, in the context of adjustment, can become especially effective. Examples include:

- (a) labour-intensive food-for-work schemes;
- (b) agricultural settlement schemes;
- (c) training programmes for the enhancement of skills to increase labour productivity and versatility;
- (d) assistance to women in development;
- (e) investments that address the problems of the urban poor through

support for activities that contribute, for example, to urban employment; and

(f) support for agricultural research, credit and extension programmes.

(d) Compensatory measures

Adjustment, by virtue of the wide-ranging retrenchment it often dictates, inevitably produces "losers". Where the poor are the losers, the ensuing combination of high food prices, widespread shortages (sometimes aggravated by drought), malnutrition and seriously deficient health services makes the margin between life and death precariously thin. In order to arrest the decline in the health and nutritional status of the poor, some form of targeted compensatory programme may be feasible. Such programmes may consist of compensatory employment or nutrition-oriented schemes. Food aid has a special comparative advantage in supporting such programmes. However, it is worth noting that such schemes are best conducted in countries that have a sound administrative structure and can use ongoing food-aided projects as vehicles to expand outreach to those requiring compensation.

Two groups that tend to be hurt by adjustment measures and that may be appropriate beneficiaries of compensatory programmes supported by food aid are those who lose their jobs and those who cannot afford price increases in basic food commodities. For each of these two groups, the most appropriate compensatory measures would be to provide income-earning, productive employment, whether in urban or rural areas. In the short run, however, it may be necessary in some cases to provide food directly to those most adversely affected by the adjustment process.

Regrettably, up to now, efforts to harness food aid in support of health development have not been as extensive and effective as they could be. Resources have traditionally been concentrated on the classical types of food-aided health projects such as institution feeding and the support to health infrastructure construction. Other issues which open up broader avenues for co-operation would include the monitoring of health hazards in other development projects. It is known, for example, that irrigation projects can increase the risk of such parasitic diseases as schistosomiasis and malaria if adequate precautionary measures are not taken. WHO and WFP have, in many cases, collaborated in addressing such issues. At the moment, 99 ongoing projects of various kinds in the African region are being jointly assisted by both agencies. There are broadly four kinds of such projects with a health dimension or component. These are:

(a) support for rural water and sanitation works at the village level, in the context of rural development programmes: i.e., food-for-work for community development;
(b) vulnerable group feeding projects mainly targeted at mothers and children;
(c) institutional feeding including hospitals; health training institutions; secondary, vocational and primary schools; and
(d) emergency relief, especially during drought.

Classical food-aided health activities of this sort certainly merit more attention especially when budgetary retrenchment puts pressure on health services and facilities as countries undergo adjustment. But, in addition to these, greater attention needs to be paid to the potential for using food aid in support of health sector reform. Reform in favour of greater allocation to rural areas of health resources would be a key component of such programmes and would complement the initiatives taken by countries and WHO to implement district-focus health development activities. Sub-components of such sectoral reform programmes which could receive food aid either directly or indirectly through monetization would include:

(a) training programmes for district health and other personnel on the concept of health-for-all and the modalities of intersectoral action for health at district level;
(b) training programmes for village leaders and development committees, village health workers, traditional birth attendants and healers, water-pump maintainers, etc.; and
(c) support for labour-intensive activities such as village health post construction and, especially, improvement of community water supplies (protection of springs; hand dug wells, cisterns, etc.) and sanitation (community, school and household latrines, markets).

Activities listed in category (c) above usually require considerable inputs in terms of supplies and sometimes equipment, e.g., cement and pumps for shallow wells. These components may be expensive and beyond the means of village communities. However, other donors are sometimes able to support such costs. There are many overall costs in developing an effective district health programme (e.g., baseline health situation analysis; costs of supervisory visits, and monitoring/evaluation, as well as initial training in health planning and management as applied to PHC at district level).

In addition to direct distribution to beneficiaries, an appropriate degree of monetization could be introduced in such projects to generate cash resources for meeting at least some of these costs. Most countries have already selected a number of districts for intensified district health activity. This process can be further bolstered if governments gave serious consideration to developing comprehensive sectoral reform programmes (eventually covering all districts) which could be supported with external assistance. In addition, it would be more advantageous if the district-focus health development programmes, now undergoing intensification, could be launched in those districts where WFP and other agencies are already providing substantial assistance and more general support to rural development. In such cases, the health project(s) could constitute a component within a broader multipurpose programme. Guidance along these lines has already been provided to WHO country representatives in the region for further discussion with government and WFP.

While food aid provides enormous opportunities for both mitigating the effects of adjustment and promoting long-term recovery, it does not in any way provide a total solution. In fact, food aid activities are most successful when they are combined with other reinforcing technical, financial, managerial and policy measures.

Conclusion

To regard nutrition, health services and education as the fruits of development to be deferred until high production and growth is achieved is self-defeating. Only the well nourished, healthy and literate can consistently and increasingly be efficient and productive workers.

With effective design and management, food aid projects and programmes can bring real benefits to the poor – especially the vulnerable groups negatively affected by structural adjustment programmes. In addition to avoiding disincentive effects by building on the income transfer potential of food aid and participatory planning of projects, there is scope for using food aid directly and constructively to provide incentives for desirable economic and social action. In the health sector, attention should increasingly turn to the provision of manageable rural health facilities. In addition, food aid projects should be tailored towards new initiatives such as support for health policy reform and for accelerated programmes in immunization in rural areas. There is a need to broaden the basis of raising incomes of the poor from the simple and traditional "only nutrition" (food) input into more comprehensive "health entitlement" and "improved living environment" approaches.

References

1 G.A. Gornia, R. Jolly and F. Steart, *Adjustment with a Human Face*, Economics, UNICEF, New York, 1987.
2 WHO Regional Office for Africa, *Health a Foundation for Development*, Brazzaville, 1987.
3 WHO Regional Office for Africa, *Accelerating the Achievement of Health For All by Action at the Local Level*, document RPM9/WP/03, Brazzaville, 1986.
4 World Food Programme, *Roles of Food Aid in Structural and Sector Adjustment*, WFP/CFA: 23/5 Add.1, Rome, 1987.
5 UNICEF, *Within Human Reach – A Future for Africa's Children*, New York, 1985.
6 UNECA, *The Abuja Statement on Economic Recovery And Long-Term Development in Africa*, 1987.

An Enabling Environment to Retain Africa's High-Level Manpower

CRISPIN GREY-JOHNSON (ECA)

Introduction

Conditions of living in Africa have become so oppressive that those who can, have fled the continent in search of more comfortable environments where they can work, live decently and feel professionally fulfilled. Over the last eight years, as Africa suffered through a devastating socio-economic crisis, the widespread deterioration in human welfare has propelled the drift of all types of Africans – men and women, unskilled, semi-skilled and highly skilled alike – to countries where they hope to find a better life.

The ILO reports that about 2 million Egyptians live abroad and some 500,000 Sudanese work outside Africa.[1] "In Egypt, the loss of skilled workers in the construction industry as a result of emigration to oil-rich Arab States has caused delays and bottlenecks in implementing development projects."[2] The same source estimates that about two-thirds of Sudan's professional and technical workers had left the country by 1985. In that year Guinean, Algerian, Malagache and Beninese doctors and teachers working in France outnumbered the total of technical assistance personnel in the same fields in these countries, and in the Congo, only 38 per cent of Congolese doctors were practicing at home.[3] Uganda lost more than half its high-level professional and technical manpower during the difficult years of the Idi Amin regime, and is still suffering the consequences today. Ethiopia and Ghana were obliged to mount recruitment campaigns in a bid to bring back their skilled nationals working in Western Europe and North America because the substantial loss of these vital development resources had placed strains on the running of the economy. In Southern Africa, the distortion of the wage and salary structure by South Africa, as part of its destabilization policy against the Front Line States has unleashed a new form of brain drain entailing the massive flow of skilled manpower from these States to the Bantustans and to South Africa itself.

Throughout Africa, rates of out migration of the highly skilled have been rising in proportion to the increased level of hardship within African economies. Between 1960 and 1975, some 27,000 highly educated Africans left the continent for the West.[4] Between 1975 and 1984 this number increased to about 40,000 then almost doubled to approximately 70,000 Africans by 1987. This represents almost 30 percent of the total high-level manpower available within the continent today.

Migration flows from Africa are directed towards the free market economies of Western Europe, the USA and Canada. France and Belgium are favorite points of migration for franco-phone Africans,whereas Britain, the USA and Canada attract more of the nationals of English-speaking countries. Countries in the Middle East are also a favorite destination for migrants from the Arab-speaking countries of North Africa, although increasingly, scientific, medical and technical manpower from sub-Saharan African countries such as Ghana, are also being attracted in ever-growing numbers by the tremendous income prospects being of feared in these countries.

Many attempts have been made to quantify the loss, in dollar terms, of the brain drain from developing countries. Some estimates put it at about $US 50 billion between 1961 and 1972.[5] A 1974 USA Government study estimates that in 1972 by importing skilled manpower, the USA saved $US 883 million in direct education expenditures that would have produced that manpower locally, while the countries of origin lost some $US 320 million representing amounts they had invested in educating these migrants.[6]

UNCTAD uses the "imputed capital value of skill flows" approach to estimate the cost of the brain drain. "The human capital embodied in a migrant measures the present value of his productive capacity over the rest of his life. It is calculated by discounting, with regard to time, his expected future earnings year by year. The essence of the approach is that anything that yields a stream of real income over time is capital; and that the value of a migrant's worth as a productive asset, per period, is the marginal product in that period."[7] Using this approach, UNCTAD estimates that the value of one highly skilled migrant aged 25–35 would be in the region of $US 184,000. Most African migrants are within the prime age of 25 to 35 years. Assuming that conditions in the continent keep them away until they retire, and that their number today remains constant, if one applied UNCTAD's "imputed capital value" approach to estimate the cost of the brain drain to Africa over the next 25–35 years, one would arrive at a staggering 12.6 billion 1979 US dollars.

The implications for Africa's development of the loss of skilled manpower are obviously serious. The brain drain will most likely emerge as a major constraint on Africa's chances of achieving full economic recovery and self-reliant and self-sustained development, unless measures are taken now to arrest and if possible, reverse the trend. Barring the application of repressive measures, it is conceivable that more skilled Africans will choose to leave the continent unless an enabling environment is created for them to feel sufficiently comfortable, socially, economically, politically and professionally, to want to stay on.

Some Causes of the Brain Drain

There is a general consensus that the major causes of the brain drain are economic and social in nature, although a strong and growing political dimension to the phenomenon is emerging. The performance of the African economy over the years has been so poor that the ensuing deterioration of social and economic conditions has rendered living conditions unbearable for many. The recent socio-economic crisis underscored Africa's underdevelopment, its deep dependence on the developed world for sustenance and its chronic economic fragility.

These conditions of underdevelopment, which were bearable some time ago, have worsened considerably in the last eight years in African countries. Those who have the credentials to do so opt out of accepting the harsh conditions of living in their countries for more pleasant conditions elsewhere. These are the middle and high-level skilled African men and women who have internationally negotiable skills which can compete in the international skills market. Typically, they are scientific, technical and professional workers with at least seventeen years of formal education and with skills in areas such as medicine, scientific research, engineering and technology, management and education.

(i) *The Stressful Socio-Economic Environment*

Certain elements of the African socio-economic crisis have compounded the problems of living for the African. Real per capita incomes fell by about 16 percent between 1980 and 1985; there were widespread shortages of essential consumer goods, energy supplies, raw materials, spares and equipment for industrial establishments; inputs for agricultural production, such as fertilizers, pesticides, and seeds ran short; supplies to the social sectors, especially education and health, became inadequate to meet the need; hospitals, health centres, maternal and child health clinics were severely deprived and educational establishments almost ground to a halt.

To make matters worse, unemployment and overall levels of poverty increased so dramatically that the dependency burden on heads of household and income earners in the extended family system became crushing. Malnutrition and levels of morbidity shot up as more and more people found it increasingly difficult to meet their daily subsistence needs, and health facilities became more inaccessible, especially to the poor. As the employment market contracted new university graduates experienced difficulties in securing jobs. A few hundred thousand such people exist in Africa today.

Such realities constitute the beginning of a situation in Africa which was described as the "degradation of the very essence of human dignity".[8] It is this human situation that has forced many of Africa's highly skilled men and women to pack up and leave the continent or to stay on in other regions of the world after acquiring skills that could be put to use in their countries' development endeavours.

(ii) *Higher Education and the International High-Level Skills Market*

African higher education institutions developed in the image of western European educational institutions. In the last 20 years, North American higher education systems have also been exerting an influence on the character of African higher education. Course content, syllabi, duration of study and degrees awarded in African higher educational institutions are not significantly different from those of Euro-American institutions. This means that the qualifications received by graduates of African third level educational institutions are similar to those of their North American and European counterparts. Moreover, African higher education systems are very weak on post-graduate programmes, and rely for the delivery of much of these on institutions of the North. Most of Africa's high-level manpower is trained in institutions in North American and European countries, and therefore possess skills that are no different from those turned out in, and required by, developed market economies. Higher education and the qualifications system in Africa are thus very much integrated into the world system.

With the growth of the importance of multinational enterprises in the world economy, and as production enterprises assume an increasingly multinational character, the "nationality" criteria for selecting middle and high-level manpower for industry, banking, telecommunications, mining, etc., has become less important to employers than the "qualifications" and "experience" criteria. In fact, most transnational corporations are beginning to "internationalize" job classifications, salary structures, etc.[9] in recognition of the internationalized market for high-level skilled manpower. In this international skills market, employers compete among themselves for the best skilled people available by outbidding each other in terms of remuneration, fringe benefits, working conditions, pension schemes, insurance and housing. As these same conditions of work deteriorate in African employment markets, more and more Africans who possess the skills being sought in this widening international employment market are coming forward to compete and compete successfully for jobs in the international market place where conditions are much better.

(iii) *Declining Real Incomes of High-Level Manpower in Africa*

Governments in the early post-independence period in Africa were at least conscious of the need to retain high-level manpower within African economies and were also aware of the competition that they faced with the international skills market. Policies, therefore, sought to establish salary structures that would be competitive in attracting and retaining skilled nationals. In 1967, the Mills-Odoi Commission in Ghana argued for high salary levels for public sector high-level manpower because of their "international market and scarcity values".[10] In Kenya, the Ndegwa Commission, arguing for an increase of senior civil service salaries, stated:

> "these are the people upon whom successful Government and development depends; it is their skill, resourcefulness and dedication which will shape the future of the country. There is a need for rededication to the tasks ahead – while this is obviously not just a question of money, it is difficult for even the most dedicated man to meet his commitments without it. If he is to give of his best, he must feel that he is being fairly treated and that his worth is recognized."[11]

Similar views were expressed by the Mohammed Taha Commission of the Sudan in 1979, Nigeria's Undoji Commission and the Elwood Report which, in 1966, argued for a substantial increase in salaries for professional and technical staff to bring Nigeria's salary scales "in line with world market values" . . . and Nigeria, "into competition with wealthier countries in order to secure and retain the services of its own people."[12]

This concern for attracting high quality manpower has, however, diminished markedly with the worsening of the economic crisis, and is clearly not a consideration in the various structural adjustment measures being implemented by many African countries. In fact, some countries have had to reduce nominal salaries and fringe benefits (Cameroon and Nigeria), while others have imposed a freeze on salaries and wages. Real income levels have been so dramatically reduced that it is difficult for the most frugal public servant to meet his/her family's basic needs. The World Bank reports that the situation in many African countries is so bad that "many public sector employees could not afford a balanced diet regardless of whether they spent their entire income on food."[13] A Vice-Chancellor of an African University complains that the low salaries prevailing are "generating serious pressures (on his lecturers) to leave the university."[14] The WHO talks of a "catastrophic outflow of health manpower from African countries" caused by the "hopelessly inadequate" salaries, the general "inertia" and "demoralization" and the constant "struggle for other ways to survive."[15] This describes what not only health personnel, but also all other public sector workers are experiencing with the stringent recovery and adjustment measures being implemented at the behest of the World Bank and the IMF.

The situation is ushering in another, odious form of social decay – namely, corruption. Those who cannot yet find their way out are being reduced to crass immorality, just in order to stay alive. Corruption has begun creeping into the university itself, infecting those left behind. Research funds disappear into private accounts; in the rat race for promotion, curriculum vitae are being forged, and the "line between good and bad has become blurred"[16] in the eyes of those who are supposed to lead the search for truth in African societies.

Moral decay follows closely on the heels of economic decline. When the cake becomes too small, those who are to feed on it become desperate, are driven only by their instinct for survival and will trample on anything or anyone in their way just to get a piece, if not all of the cake. This is how the economic hardships in African countries are transforming the behaviour of the African peoples. Criminal behaviour, corruption, nepotism, armed robberies, bribery, and prostitution, are on the increase in most African countries. Such a social environment becomes overbearing for anyone, not least of which are those professionally qualified people who have the option to choose between this and more socially balanced environments elsewhere.

Political Origins of the Problem

The social and economic decline are nothing but the ultimate manifestations of serious political disequilibria in African countries. To begin with, the type of (and in some cases, the conditions attached to) political "independence" in African countries brings into question the very sovereignty of African governments. Some political scientists argue that "statehood", in its real politico-philosophical sense is still being forged in many African countries. The vulnerability of African economies, and their deep dependence on outside forces and mechanisms also define the limits of independence that can be expected in Africa. Traditional ethnic allegiances will take time to be remolded into allegiance to a nation. Until that happens, clan, ethnic and regional interests will prevail over the interests of the nation, thus fostering ambivalence towards the national interest and promoting anti-national inclinations such as nepotism, tribalism and religious bigotry.

Political theory posits the concept of the "soft state" to describe political systems in Africa.[17] The "soft state" is characterized by "high dependence on outside sources; social undiscipline and disobedience to outside authority; weakened indigenous systems of rights and obligations, laws and standards, resulting in ambivalence towards modern norms; over reliance on government to change social ethics and behaviour, while bypassing traditional arrangements; over-centralized government which undermines local initiatives; rigid bureaucracies unable to adjust to changing circumstances, persisting with outmoded attitudes and administrative arrangements, and relying on heavy-handed enforcement; and endemic corruption that hinders innovation, prevents change and inhibits eradication of corrupt attitudes and behaviour".[18]

This "softness of state" thesis describes the political foundations of underdevelopment. Socio-economic development will occur only with the greatest difficulty, unless African countries emerge into real statehood and African governments become truly sovereign. But if the "softness of state" is allowed to persist or be perpetuated by internal and external forces, the socio-economic decay that has emerged on the continent will remain for a very long time.

Furthermore, the prevailing political fragility in African countries constrains development by undermining the stability necessary to conceive and implement development strategy. It engenders frequent and, at times, violent changes of the guard, a divergence of interest between the leader and the led and diffidence towards the protection of human rights.

The "softness of state" also militates against the full participation of people in development. This negatively affects the type of intellectual enquiry that promotes development and positive forms of social transformation. The Vice-Chancellors, Presidents and Rectors of institutions of higher learning in Africa clearly articulated their concern over this state of affairs when they declared:

> "It is our belief that intellectual communities constituted by institutions of higher learning, serve their societies best when they are allowed the space to develop and test their ideas in an atmosphere of critical discourse. This essential condition may sometimes appear to pit those communities, or some of their members against established or official ideas and policies. Unfortunately some African governments have reacted to such situations in ways that have proved dysfunctional to the development and maintenance of a thriving intellectual atmosphere, without which, institutions of higher learning could not make their due and special contribution to national development. We therefore ask for understanding and tolerance to enable us to discharge our grave responsibilities in an atmosphere of productivity, creativity and increased relevance".[19]

With the deepening of the socio-economic crisis, the African university has had to suffer serious deprivations as already meagre resources are diverted from it. A spokesperson of one university, in lamenting the growing neglect of higher education in Africa, described the problem thus: "For several months now, we have been expected to run a physics laboratory without electricity, perform biology and zoology experiments without water and get accurate readings from microscopes blinded by use and age. Chemicals are unimaginably short. The result of all this is a chemistry laboratory that cannot produce distilled water and hundreds of 'science graduates' lacking the benefits of practical demonstrations".[20]

And this neglect goes further than higher education institutions. Medical doctors and health workers are deprived of the resources they need to save lives. Engineers spend half their time supervising repairs rather than managing production. In all sectors, conditions of work are made extremely stressful for Africa's high-level manpower. This in turn depresses productivity, slows down the pace of economic growth, and tightens the vicious circle in which Africa's political systems are locked.

At the first congress of African scientists in Brazzaville, Africa's top scientific minds bemoaned the inadequate support they receive from their governments: "The plight of the African scientist is a sorry one. Unlike his European counterpart, he is expected to be more than a specialist in his chosen field, because in most cases he must be prepared to make do without back-up teams of technicians and scientific equipment. He must also be content with comparatively low pay and low status in the community."[21] In addition, as one scientist put it, he has to "keep one eye on the microscope and the other at the door in readiness for the unannounced visitor from the state's secret police".[22] If such an atmosphere exists, it would prove stifling for most African scientists and would naturally encourage them to migrate to places where they can work in harmony and peace.

In 1983, the Economic Commission for Africa had this to say:

> "an improved political and social climate is not merely a guarantee for political stability, but a sine qua non for the blooming of the genius of the African people who, in the pre-colonial period, proved themselves highly resourceful in many activities . . . the creation of a peaceful and serene political and social climate is a must if the ultimate goal of development is to be achieved."[23]

Until that climate materializes, more and more of Africa's high-level manpower will continue to leave.

Creating the Environment for Self-Fulfillment

The African people are locked into a precarious and miserable political and socioeconomic environment, and Africa's high-level human resources are faced with conditions of work and day-to-day living that make their contributions to development minimal. These realities of life in Africa fetter the genius of the African people making it impossible for them to do for their societies what the Japanese, the Swiss, the French and the Britons of the immediate pre-industrial revolution era did for theirs. Underdevelopment in Africa accounts for this state of things, but as has occurred elsewhere, the process of change from underdevelopment to development should bring along with it those conditions and opportunities that would unleash the potential of Africa's human resources to be innovative and to spur the process of socio-economic transformation.

Alas, the experience in Africa over the last decade has confirmed that development is, in fact, not occurring. What the crisis has done for Africa is to make the continent even more exposed, more dependent and more susceptible to external controls. In 1985, Africa's intellectuals, deliberating on the socio-economic crisis, warned: "by appealing to the conscience of the international community, the continent might be inviting a new colonialism as had happened in the nineteenth century when Europe had been called upon to save Africa from slavery."[24] Only time will tell whether this new colonialism has indeed arrived in the guise of the several action measures that are being directed towards African countries, purportedly to redress Africa's economic difficulties. What is certain is that underdevelopment has deepened, further dissipating the chances for the African to master his/her environment, chart out his/her own future and be truly self-reliant. African governments should be keenly aware of this situation and embark upon measures that will not only guarantee that their people are provided the environment conducive to efficiency and high productivity, but also serve as a springboard for an escape from underdevelopment and dependency.

The international economic environment also dramatically affects the internal socioeconomic environment in Africa. Therefore, given the present economic relations between Africa and the rest of the world, unless the international economic system improves in favour of Africa's economic growth, the socio-economic conditions within African countries will remain unfavourable to any attempts to retain more of the continent's skilled manpower within African economies.

(i) *A Political Environment for Self-Reliant Development*

There are 50 governments in Africa, one fifth of which govern less than a million people. Twelve other countries have a population below 5 million people, and 14 have below 10 million inhabitants. Such small populations impose constraints on economic expansion and limitations on sovereignty. Since real sovereignty is a precondition of development, one can easily conclude that the prospects for development of at least two thirds of the continent are indeed quite bleak if the present balkanization persists. The other conclusion is that some measure of integration is called for to provide the political preconditions for the development of the African people. Integration will also serve as a buffer against political destabilization which has occurred far too often in the last 25 years to allow any time for development to take root. In addition, it will encourage real economic integration, to which all African governments are committed, by facilitating the opening up of internal markets and removing the barriers on the free movement of goods and people and the sharing of ideas. Africa's human resources will in this way be provided a much bigger space to make their rightful contributions to socio-economic development within the continent.

(ii) *A Socio-economic Environment to Retain Skilled Manpower*

African governments must endeavour urgently to provide more realistic incentives to their high-level manpower. Presently, a Ghanaian doctor earns the equivalent of $US 80 per month. In Sierra Leone, a senior civil engineer's take-home pay amounts to about $US 25. Although these examples may seem extreme, the general situation throughout the continent is, in varying degrees, one of gross under-remuneration of skilled manpower. Those who advocate salary cuts and freezes have argued that high public sector salaries are harmful to the African economy in that they distort wage structures, promote inequalities and cause socio-economic imbalances. But the harm done to African economies by creating conditions that favour the brain drain, such as deliberately underpaying skilled people, is far greater than all the economistic excuses given for not raising salaries to realistic levels. To add insult to injury, public sector workers are made to wait for months before receiving their salary back-pays in installments. This is now almost standard practice in countries such as Sierra Leone, Benin, Mali and the Comoros Islands. The debt-servicing obligations of African governments are placing too heavy a demand on their meagre resources, to the extent that the welfare of their nationals is being sacrificed to honour their external financial obligations. The international community can help African Governments ease this difficult situation by instituting measures such as debt relief, rescheduling or cancellation so that substantially more resources can be directed towards rebuilding and sustaining the domestic economy, and to meeting the subsistence and welfare needs of the African.

The working environment should also be improved to promote efficiency and high levels of productivity. Tools, equipment, books, etc., should be made available to scientific, professional and technical workers to enable them to perform their duties with ease, while striving to make them more actively involved in the search for solutions to problems of national development. The Vice-Chancellors made this plea to their governments when they said:

> "while we undertake to assist our Governments in areas requiring advice, research, analysis and evaluation, we call upon them to recognize this potential in us and to strive, on their part, to make maximum use of it, while lessening their dependence on foreign institutions and consultants to provide these services. In this regard, we strongly urge our governments to establish mechanisms for receiving development ideas and research findings originating from our institutions with a view to utilizing them towards development ends."[25]

Developing these mechanisms would not only have a positive effect on socio-economic development, but would make the African intellectual, scientist, technologist and researcher feel more involved in the effort to chart out a development path for his people, as well as feel that he is being appreciated by the community which he strives to serve. Obviously, such a psychological boost is good for promoting hard work and good results. Professor Adebayo Adedeji summed it thus: "the development of man and the realization and unfolding of his creative potential through improvement not only in his material conditions of living which enable him to satisfy his psychological needs, but also through the satisfaction of his psychic need,"[26] is the ultimate purpose of development.

(iii) *Policies and Mechanisms for the Internal Sharing of Expertise*

The limited number of high-level skilled manpower available to the region is unevenly distributed among African countries. While one country may be oversupplied in one skill area, another may be experiencing acute shortages in that same area of skill. If employment markets were more open, it would be easier for the surplus skilled manpower in one country to move to other employment markets, within the region, and to be provided the opportunity to contribute to the development of the region. Existing labour and immigration laws in many African countries make such movements very difficult for African nationals. In fact, it has been shown that many Africans who seek employment in other regions of the world, do so as a last resort either because their search for employment within Africa has failed or because they anticipated or actually experienced negative responses from immigration or labour authorities in other African countries.

One way of reducing the outflow of skilled Africans from the continent would be to create the appropriate mechanisms at the regional level to make it easy for surplus skilled manpower and vacancies which they could fill in African countries to be easily identified, and for these skilled Africans to be placed in these jobs. This could be done through a regional programme of exchange of experts which African governments could formally establish and to which they could contribute, in order to provide supplementary incentives to induce skilled manpower to remain within the continent.

This programme could also be used as a recruitment agency for technical assistance personnel for development projects within the region. On many occasions, African governments have expressed their desire to see more Africans being recruited into technical assistance positions because of their better knowledge of African development and working conditions and their greater empathy with African problems. Bi-lateral and multi-lateral donor agencies could contribute to seeing this need fulfilled by identifying and recruiting qualified Africans into their project posts in African countries.

Greater support for the reversal of the brain drain could be provided through a more active involvement of African governments in the Return of Skills Programme for Africa which is being implemented by the ECA. This programme identifies qualified Africans living in Western Europe and North America and vacant posts which they could fill in African countries. It then arranges the return to African countries, of those Africans who have been selected by employers and who have accepted their offers of employment. A set of incentives is then provided by the programme including salary topping, insurance, the purchase of working tools and equipment, etc. Several hundred highly qualified Africans have been returned to Africa through this programme, and to date, there has been no case of re-migration to the North. The institutions of higher learning and the private sector have been the most active participants in this programme so far. But perhaps the public sector should begin showing greater support for it by making appropriate provisions to facilitate recruitment within each country's employment policies and priorities. The international community should also cooperate with African governments by providing financial support to the programme and by assisting in the identification of highly-skilled African manpower in Western countries.

(iv) *Increasing Self-reliance in Education and Training*

The inadequacies of facilities for education and training within the region account for the large number of African students who seek higher education opportunities in the countries of the North. Programmes for post-graduate studies and research, especially in medicine, science, engineering and management, are so poorly developed, if at all, that Africans who wish to pursue their study in these fields must do so outside Africa in environments much different from the ones in which they would have to work should they decide to return to Africa. Moreover, with the inadequacy of places to meet the demand for higher education, only exceptional students are admitted into institutions of higher learning within the continent. The rest, with good potential and high aptitudes, must seek their education elsewhere.

It is well known that study abroad is one cause of the brain drain. Many Africans who have pursued higher education in the countries of the North tend not to return to Africa. The government of Mali estimates that at least 15 percent of its students in France will remain there after graduation.[27] Towards the end of the 1970s there were some 104,500 African students registered in educational institutions in six Western European countries.[28] Assuming that 20 percent of these did not return to work in Africa after graduation, the continent lost about 21,000 skills.

It is important for African countries to reduce their dependence on other regions to educate and train their skilled people. This is essential for another very important reason. Zahlan puts it thus: "only when knowledge is internalized can a community hope to transform creatively its cultural heritage into modes and lifestyles unmistakably related to its past, at the same time making full use of all available knowledge. The scholar, scientist or engineer rooted in his culture and institutions is the natural and only instrument for effecting this role. A nation that imports 'modernity' pays a high price: it is cultural suicide."[29] No more needs be said.

African governments should therefore come together to decide how, collectively, they could strengthen their capacities to provide greater educational opportunities especially at the middle and higher levels to their nationals within the framework of regional cooperation. They may wish to designate certain national institutions where resources could be concentrated to provide educational and research facilities in one area of study at both the undergraduate and post graduate levels or contribute resources towards establishing regional institutions with specialization in critical areas of knowledge for use by all. The international community may be requested, in its offer of assistance to African countries in the area of education and training, to provide such assistance, not in the form of fellowships and scholarships, but in building up internal capacities and capabilities along these directions.

Conclusion

Africa's human resources, it must be repeated, are its only hope for survival. Unless they are developed, nurtured and properly utilized they will be ineffective in the production and transformation of physical and natural resources to sustain life on this continent. Present government attitudes towards human resources need to be more positive so as to enable Africa's human resources to operate effectively as the true catalysts of socioeconomic development. A new trend, however, is setting in, creating a hostile environment in which Africans must live and work. The decline in real earnings, the removal of subsidies on consumer goods, the increases in the cost of medical, education and other services, the freeze on salaries and wages, the massive retrenchments from the public services, etc., are all policies being implemented in varying degrees by most African governments. They have rendered life difficult for many and have induced a greater number of highly skilled Africans to leave the continent. These policies are self-defeating and counter-productive in that they shackle the very resources that have to be unleashed to do the job required for recovery and development to come to pass.

African governments should urgently review these adjustment measures from the perspectives of the long-term development of their societies and pursue those policies that would cultivate the resourcefulness and ingenuity of their peoples. In this, they should more consciously strive to create a socio-economic environment to provide the incentives and rewards that would ensure that Africa's skilled men and women are motivated towards hard work, dedication and a relentless search for solutions to problems of society's development. In the process, African governments should also re-examine the political factors that make them weak and render their societies ineffectual in their development endeavours and more and more dependent on others. They should also begin to protect themselves against political, military and economic destabilization and strengthen their sovereignty through measures such as political integration and the development of intra-African cooperation in trade, industry, education and exchange of expertise.

Only by creating these social, economic and, above all, political environments can Africans hope to exert any form of real control over their own destiny, their survival and their future. But until these environments materialize, Africa's human resources, like its natural and financial resources will continue to be drained away from the continent.

Notes

1 ILO, *Africa Supplement Information Bulletin*, No. 1, 1984, p.1.

2 Ibid.

3 *Jeune Afrique* No. 65/20, June 1985 p.55.

4 UNCTAD "The Reverse Transfer of Technology. A survey of its main features, causes and policy implications." TD/B/C/6/47, New York, 1979.

5 See UNDP, "Effects of the Brain Drain on Human Resources Development in Africa; Perspectives for TCDC"; TCDC/AF/5, New York 1982. Also UNCTAD, op. cit.

6 USA House of Representatives, Foreign Affairs Division of the Congressional Research Service, Library of Congress, "Brain Drain: a Study of the Persistent Issue of International Scientific Mobility", Washington, D.C. USGPO, 1974.

7 UNCTAD: "The Feasibility of Measuring International Flows of Human Resources: TD/B/C./6/AC.8/2 p.29.

8 ECA, *ECA and Africa's Development 1983–2008: A Preliminary Perspective Study*, Addis Ababa, 1983.

9 See Rajah Abdin *et al.*, *A World of Differentials*, IDRC, Ottawa, Canada, pp.85–95.

10 Republic of Ghana, Mills-Odoi Commission on a Review of the Ghana Civil Service, Accra 1969, p.28.

11 Republic of Kenya, *Ndegwa Commission Report*, Nairobi, 1972, p.49.

12 Federal Government of Nigeria, *Elwood Commission Report*, 1966, p.9.

13 World Bank "The Effects of Corruption on Administrative Performance. Illustrations from Developing Countries" Staff Working Papers No. 580, 1983, p.25.

14 Akilagpa Sawyerr, "Changing Development Objectives and Strategies for Self-Reliant Economies in Africa: University Responses" Paper presented to the Third ECA/AAU Conference of Vice-Chancellors, Harare, Zimbabwe, 1987.

15 WHO, "Structural Adjustment, Health, Nutrition and Food aid", ECA/ICHD/88/27.

16 *West Africa*, 14 September, 1987, p.1787.

17 Weinstein and Wienstein, "Dependency, Softness of State and National Development: towards an Integrated theory"; Georgia Institute of Technology. USA. quoted in World Bank, op. cit.

18 World Bank, op. cit. pp.18–19.

19 ECA: "The Mbabane Programme of Action: The Response of the African Institutions of Higher Learning to Africa's rapidly deteriorating Economic and Social Conditions", Addis Ababa, 1985.

20 *West Africa*, 12 September 1983.

21 T. Agbiake, "Scientists' Lot not a Happy One" *African Concord* No. 150 July 1987, p.6.

22 Ibid., p.7.

23 "ECA and Africa's Development" op. cit. Paras 254 and 255.

24 ECA: "Report of the Second Conference of Vice Chancellors, Presidents and Rectors of Institutions of Higher Learning in Africa" E/ECA/CM/11/47. Addis Ababa, p.12.

25 Mbabane Programme of Action, op. cit.

26 Adebayo Adedeji, "Perspectives of Development and Economic Growth in Africa up to the year 2008." Statement delivered to the Monrovia Symposium on "Africa: What kind of Development by the Year 2000?"

27 Jeune Afrique No. 65/20, June 1985, p.55.

28 UNESCO, Statistical Year Bood 1980.

29 A.B. Zahlan: "The Problematic of the Arab Brain Drain" in Zahlan ed. *The Arab Brain Drain*, Ithaca Press, London, 1981, pp.9–10.

Management Development and On-The-Job Training

F. FLUITMAN (INTERNATIONAL LABOUR ORGANIZATION)

A. Management Development

No country – developed or developing – ever seems to have enough effective managers. To help African countries fill this gap, ways must be found to improve existing management development institutions so that they are better able to help managers to improve organizational performance in both private and public sectors. Such institutions must adopt approaches that are results-oriented in close collaboration with associations of employers and sectoral enterprise groups. They should concentrate on vital but often neglected and hard-to-reach sectors such a small enterprises and on difficult problems such as public enterprises and rural development. Such programmes must concentrate on improving productivity and competitiveness, and creating backward linkages to agriculture and forward linkages to generate export earnings.

Any strategy for investing in human capital must necessarily focus on doing more with less. In Africa, with its abundant manpower and scarcity of financial and physical capital, the problem is where to start. Both casual observation and an abundance of research indicate that maintenance management is the key to productivity improvement in Africa.

(a) Maintenance management

The need to transfer resources from North to South to sustain Africa's economic recovery should not ignore the need to maintain and build upon what exists. Many African officials today argue – rightly in the present situation – that it makes little sense to allocate scarce local resources to maintain what exists because donors often prefer to build something new or to rehabilitate that which has been allowed to deteriorate.

Donors and recipients alike seem to ignore the fact that wealthy countries are often wealthy because they maintain their patrimony. Present policies of donors and recipients that ignore maintenance of infrastructure doom the recipients to tred water – the transfer of resources leaves them no better off because so much financial capital is used to replace or rehabilitate deteriorated physical assets. Several studies have found that the life-span of equipment in much of Africa is reduced by about 30 per cent for lack of proper maintenance, and that the availability of equipment is often as low as 25 to 50 per cent for the same reasons. It has been reliably estimated that proper maintenance could easily double Africa's productive capacity because so much of it is constrained by unscheduled breakdowns.

So productivity improvement must start with building a new relationship between donors and recipients to strengthen a "maintenance culture". One promising approach is to create and strengthen small-scale enterprises run by artisans and technicians who can provide after sales service on machinery and equipment, who can recondition spare parts and who can maintain buildings and roads. However, such enterprises can survive and prosper only if the owners of such physical assets – often government agencies – see the long-term benefit of budgeting adequately for maintenance.

In Ethiopia and Morocco, for example, ILO has helped several management institutions set up programmes in the transport, agriculture and industrial sectors to switch from wasteful breakdown-and-repair maintenance systems to increase productivity at the same time as they reduce the need to spend scarce foreign exchange on spare parts and new machines. The quantifiable benefits of programmes in maintenance management usually outweighs their costs many times over, especially in saving scarce foreign exchange.

(b) Energy conservation

A closely allied area for productivity improvement is energy conservation. This is vital, since with the increase in energy prices in the 1970s, the energy bill in many parts of Africa soaks up 60 per cent of a country's foreign exchange earnings. Management development and productivity schemes in countries such as Nigeria and Ethiopia have helped energy-intensive enterprises such as cement and transport save millions of dollars – often through improved maintenance and through adoption of improved technologies.

(c) Financial management

While improving the productivity of physical capital can release tied up financial capital, the major constraint is that more African managers need to appreciate how to use financial accounting information to direct the efforts of their enterprises. Public utility managers, for example, who must manage very costly physical infrastructures often understand the technical engineering side of their enterprises, but not the financial side. Consequently, customer service is poor and the physical plant is poorly utilized because the working capital they need is not collected from their customers and not allocated properly to the purchase of materials and services to keep the systems running properly.

Recent ILO research indicates that accounting is unpopular in Africa largely because it is seen primarily as a tool for "catching people out". Financial control is a proper but negative function of accounting. Governments, banks and donors and others who provide assets have a legitimate interest in seeing that the money they provide is not misappropriated. However, almost all accounting in Africa is for financial control. Only a handful of the more than 3,000 public enterprises in Africa have analytical accounting systems that show management how to allocate resources, where to look for energy savings, how much is poor maintenance costing, and so forth.

More management development programmes need to be directed to installing proper accounting systems, showing managers how to use them to improve performance and providing the financial autonomy and accountability for them to do their jobs. Such systems would go a long way to avoiding future financial crises.

(d) Programme design and delivery

Programmes to improve productivity – through maintenance management, energy conservation, financial management and so forth – must be well designed and properly executed. Programmes that consist only of courses where the participants are left on their own to apply what they learned are rarely effective. In fact, the lack of proper needs analysis and follow-up confuses many people – they think that management development is merely another form of education.

Because effective managers are expensive to develop, emphasis needs to be placed on methods of reducing the cost and improving the quality of management development programmes. Training materials that are cheap to produce and easy to use are needed. The ILO's Modular Programme for Supervisory Development, for example, is designed to reduce the cost of customizing large-volume training courses for supervisors. This highly flexible programme trains supervisory trainers in the belief that good supervisors who can motivate and mobilize people's efforts are vital in countries where unemployment is high and capital scarce.

(e) Sectoral approaches

Management development programmes need to be directed towards analyzing sectoral performance and proceed through the design and delivery of programmes to improve sectoral productivity. Since improvements come fastest when chief executives are personally involved, sectoral management development programmes must ensure that all levels of society participate in implementing improvements and sharing recognition and financial gains. In Botswana and Kenya, for example, the heads of contractors' associations are involved in giving awards for productivity improvements. Needs analyses are carried out to find out why construction projects are delayed, costs are over budget or quality unacceptable. Video has been used to help contractors improve site productivity. Participative, flexible training packages are designed to help managers exchange experience. Campaigns are employed to give teams and work groups time and support to implement improvements and make presentations about their achievements.

(f) Improving public enterprise performance

Many of the over 3,000 public enterprises in Africa were established for ideological reasons, some as mechanisms for political patronage; and others were failing private enterprises taken over by governments to forestall increases in unemployment.

Accumulated financial losses, overmanning and poor response to customers' needs has led to a growing loss of public confidence in African public enterprises. Managers of these enterprises usually face more challenges and difficulties than private sector managers. Objectives and targets are often confused and conflicting and career paths vague. Public enterprise managers rarely enjoy sufficient autonomy in financial and personnel decisions and measurement systems are often lacking or out-of-date. Many public enterprises are linked together in a manner that threatens the survival of some if others are ineffective.

To help public enterprise managers overcome such barriers and bring performance up to expectations, innovative approaches are needed. Enterprises that operate too much like government departments need programmes that start with strategic planning and take managers through step-by-step processes of developing and implementing new improvement plans. Ways must also be found to design, test and distribute low-cost training packages to help managers solve functional problems in finance, budgetary control, marketing, technology choice, computer systems and maintenance management, to name a few. In some cases this could be done through associations of managers of public utilities such as the Association of African Water and Sanitation Utilities.

Programmes are also needed to help groups of similar public enterprises such as water utilities or transport companies reduce costs, collect revenues and improve performance so as to break out of vicious circles of high debt, lack of working capital, poor service, low morale and low productivity. Some countries have combined vocational and management training with long-term consulting assistance to implement improvements that add up to better financial viability and improved customer service.

(g) Small enterprises and entrepreneurship

In contrast to public enterprises, small private enterprises account for most of the employment, most of the wealth creation and most of the innovation in African economies. However, because most Africans make their living in agriculture there is as yet no long tradition of industrial entrepreneurship.

More programmes are needed to strengthen existing small and medium enterprises and to create conditions where local entrepreneurs can flourish. This is especially important as a response to problems of structural adjustment, where government employees need to be helped to find jobs in the private sector, especially by setting up their own businesses.

There are two broad types of programmes: those that help existing enterprises and those that help entrepreneurs start new ventures. The key to the first type is to find effective ways to reach the millions of widely scattered entrepreneurs who need help. This can be done by helping businesses form associations through which information and resources can be channelled. Training concentrates on occupational, managerial and entrepreneurial skills and is embodied in training materials such as the ILO "Improve Your Business" programme which operates in a score of African countries. Concrete results range from projects carried out by groups of businesses to improve water supply, roads and bridges in their communities to the adoption of better technologies, cost savings from improved production layouts and improved quality of products and services. Training is coupled with consultancy and advisory services, with establishing links to lines of credit from sources such as development banks and by emphasizing links with other supporting efforts such as industrial estates, free zones and technology information centres.

Projects that help entrepreneurs – especially young people and refugees start new enterprises are vital where unemployment is high. Existing projects (in Malawi and Uganda, for example) need to be studied, and perhaps used as models in other countries. They aim at helping school leavers with technical skills start their own businesses rather than fruitlessly seeking jobs in the already overcrowded job market. These projects also concentrate on improving the enterprise environment so that businesses can survive. These include the use of small-scale credit schemes, appropriate technology and improved government services.

Even with excellent assistance most small entrepreneurs fail in business several times before they finally succeed. To reduce this waste, experiments are needed (such as those in Malawi) to provide selected entrepreneurs in trades such as tile-making, carpentry and auto-repair, with "complete business packages". ILO is also studying how to provide such packages to entrepreneurs in critical fields such as the maintenance of village water supply and sanitation facilities.

(h) Managing rural development

Until recently the policies of most African Governments have been biased against agriculture, even though it generates up to 50 per cent of the gross domestic product, 80 per cent of employment and 90 per cent of export earnings. What has been said above about the management of public enterprises and small private enterprises applies with special force when we speak of rural development. The management of rural development is vital, yet extremely difficult to improve. This is largely so because such managers are difficult to communicate with, travel is difficult, and linguistic differences are great.

People who design management development programmes almost always overlook the fact that most African farmers are women who have very little schooling. Several small ILO projects have demonstrated – experimentally – that such women are excellent managers of what few resources they command and are desperately eager to learn better methods of financial management and marketing. Since this vast audience cannot be reached by conventional management development programmes, ILO is studying how to use distance learning approaches and working through non governmental organizations such as women's associations and church groups.

When it comes to the distribution channels that provide farmers with inputs and innovations and market their outputs, a great deal of effort has been expended trying to improve the performance of parastatals. But such services can usually be provided more efficiently by the private sector, while government can take on the role of monitoring input prices of farm supplies, ensuring that key inputs receive priority in transportation and on helping to formulate technological packages.

Management development services for transporters and distributors are then often best delivered through enterprise associations. Transport associations in several African countries would make ideal channels through which to run management development programmes to reduce operating costs and improve vehicle life, thereby improving quality of service at reduced costs to the consumer. Such efforts could of course, be combined with campaigns to reduce post-harvest losses.

Much of the investment in agricultural development in Africa is done through projects funded by banks and donors and executed through government agencies. Very few such projects have lived up to expectations: the Green Revolution that has helped Asia become self-sufficient in food has not yet started working in Africa. Various needs analyses indicate that the main "management" problems of these projects are poor supervision of extension staff, unbalanced project budgets (e.g., lack of vehicles, spares, and fuel) which makes it difficult to reach farmers, and untimely disbursements (e.g., funds released too late in the crop cycle). Another set of management problems that plague these projects is poor coordination across agencies; this results in things like the wrong fertilizer being delivered to the wrong project at the wrong time or the lack of equipment for plowing, harvesting or transport at critical times.

Since 1985, IFAD, the African Development Bank and the World Bank have collaborated on an innovative programme called AMTA (Agricultural Management Training for Africa). After assessing the needs of agricultural project managers and their teams, training courses are being mounted, eventually for the managers of 72 projects in 24 countries. So far however, very little of this training has been applied back on-the-job, largely because so many management trainers in Africa are skilled as educators and lack the incentive to take on the research and consultancy roles necessary to help managers improve project performance.

(i) Strengthening management development institutions

Existing institutions need to be helped to become: more responsive to specific local needs; more capable of finding practical solutions to problems; and staffed by well-qualified professionals backed by adequate training materials. However, most management institutions in Africa today struggle against great difficulties. Their staff rarely have the status and confidence to organize programmes that attract senior managers, who are often the ones who can contribute most to, and benefit most from management development. Participants are often poorly selected, from the ranks of the expendable "professional training participants". The courses are often merely a series of lectures based on little needs analysis and even less follow-up. Consequently, most of the resources invested in training are lost, and the activities end up being merely entertaining diversions.

(j) A strategy to break the vicious cycle

A strategy to break out of this vicious cycle would be a start with a series of demonstrations based on critical problems faced by African countries. Each step of the management development process must be managed carefully. First, commitment must be obtained from senior officials. Problems must be chosen that are solvable; training needs must be distinguished from non-training needs; and the proper participants must be selected, and properly briefed beforehand as to what they are expected to learn and what they will be expected to do when they return to work. Resources must then be allocated to supporting the participants while they carry out plans to improve organizational performance. They must have the opportunity to describe what they have accomplished, get recognition for it and be able to give credit to the management development programmes for helping them. These efforts must then be publicized and used as models for making African management development more effective.

B. On-The-Job Training in Africa

On-the-job training takes place at an ordinary workplace and makes the task itself a part of the instruction given and a means for the acquisition of practical skill. The traditional apprenticeship system obtaining in all African countries, whether in rural areas or the informal urban sector, is a good example of almost pure on-the-job training free of any addition of organized, planned theoretical courses involving sequences, stages, grades and approval. Certain shortcomings of traditional apprenticeship, however, have led, nearly everywhere in Africa, to the proliferation of laws for the "adaptation" or "renovation" of the apprenticeship system, all of them seeking to improve the theoretical part of training and organize co-ordinated alternation between the handicraft workshop and the classroom.

The key question is how to enrich on-the-job training and in particular the traditional apprenticeship system without laying such heavy burdens and constraints on employers that they will be discouraged, or smothering a system that with all its deficiencies none the less, taking the good years with the bad, provides the basic requirements for the transmission of knowledge and skills in Africa.

An example of pure on-the-job training traditional apprenticeship in Africa

The scope of the phenomena

The traditional handicraft workshop is an excellent place in which to learn a trade in Africa. It is an on-the-job training school which brings young persons into contact with real life working and professional conditions. The apprentice learns with the same material that is used in the trade and is steeped in the social environment where he gets to know, for example, the art of bargaining. Although the training is often sketchy and to be taught using material slightly better than is used in the trade might beget progress, it is nevertheless true that the traditional handicraft workshop is a vast and irreplaceable means for the acquisition of skills at minimal cost. According to a study of the urban informal sector in French-speaking Africa, 84 per cent of small employers learnt their trade through traditional apprenticeship and the same figure holds for Ghana. In Zambia, the level is lower but still stands at 58 per cent.

As far as the apprentice and the different stages of his training are concerned, it must first of all be stressed that the apprenticeship system is firmly rooted in the native culture and is particularly well suited to the conditions of African life. The articling of the apprentice is negotiated by the master craftsman and the parents. The small entrepreneur assumes a big responsibility towards the parents for over and above the purely professional training of the young person He has to attend closely to his education in the broadest sense of the term. All parents benefit from the system: the State has nothing to pay (the parents usually pay a sum amounting to about 150 dollars) and can at the same time use it as a barrier to unemployment and juvenile delinquency. The parents "place" their child in good hands. The young apprentice can hope one day to emulate the success of his master and the master craftsmen at the cost of one or two small sacrifices and a little of his time, (a little more in kind, board and lodging, and sometimes a little pocket money) obtains cheap labour and a certain standing.

The course of the operation

The period of apprenticeship varies in length and is roughly fixed at the start. For the manufacture of rattan furniture, it is only two years. It is over five years on an average in carpentry and six in jewellery. It is generally considered that it tends to be too long, particularly in West Africa, and the responsibility for this is usually laid at the door of the master-craftsmen who are disinclined to carry out systematic intensive training and none too anxious to deprive themselves too soon of cheap labour or create potential competition. The traditional cultural models also include a long period of social training during which the apprentice wins his adoption by the master craftsman and his family by his respect and loyalty, progressively meriting thereby the right to learn. Finally, the termination of the apprenticeship is often delayed quite simply because the apprentice cannot raise the funds he needs to set up on his own.

Evaluation of traditional apprenticeship

Despite its shortcomings, traditional apprenticeship seems to compare favourably with formal technical education institutions not only in cost but also quality and in ensuring subsequent employment. In 1985, a round table was held at Abidjan by young jewelers trained entirely in the informal sector and their vocational school graduate (CAP) colleagues from the jewellery vocational training centre. The conclusions were as follows:

(a) training is more complete in informal sector workshops where apprenticeship includes all aspects of the profession;
(b) the jeweller trained in the informal sector has a better chance of getting work on the labour market. There are many vocational school graduates among the registered unemployed;
(c) the jeweller trained in the informal sector has had contracts with customers and management; and
(d) the cost at the centre is disproportionate to the results.

The principal defect of the traditional apprenticeship system is insufficient theoretical training. This is due to the low level of knowledge of the master craftsmen themselves and also to the fact that the number of apprentices in relation to the number of the skilled workers if often excessive (for example, at Kumasi, Ghana, the proportion was nine to one, according to a study made by G. Aryee). A welcome trend, however, is becoming apparent in the level of the artisans with the arrival of large numbers of redundancies from the modern sector. Indeed these new employers sometimes bring with them technological know-how, personal relations giving them access to subcontracting and a more open-minded outlook. Mechanised work, the reading of plans, the use of new products compose some of the knowledge they can pass on to their apprentices. Young persons and their parents are not mistaken in addressing so many of their demands for apprenticeship to these newcomers.

Before this trend had been accelerated by economic restructuring and adjustments following on large scale transfers of personnel from the modern sector to the informal sector with the consequent transformation of its management and production methods, studies had already shown that the best economic performance in terms of such variables as individual profit and value added were obtained by employers who had benefitted from a combination of technical schooling and traditional handicraft apprenticeship. It seems therefore that turning the complementary nature of the two systems to account gives good results.

On-The-Job Training in Association with Other Types of Training

There have been attempts by governments to legislate on apprenticeship. Totally unadapted to local conditions, however, such legislation has lapsed into well deserved disuse. In Cote d'Ivoire for example, according to the National Vocational Training Bureau survey, in 1984 apprentices articled in accordance with the formal requirements of the law represented only .128 per cent of manpower in the modern sector. In Burkina Faso, only 61 apprenticeship contracts were registered between 1978 and 1980, and 1983.

The laudable desire to ensure minimum protection for young persons liable to become victims of abusive exploitation should not blind us to facts. Many small artisans are put off by the mere idea of having to draft a contract in French or English. Besides, some of the legal provisions are irritatingly trivial and unrealistic. Fear of the financial and fiscal implications is, of course, the main cause of artisan reluctance to sign contracts observing the legal requirements in every respect. Unfortunately, if the apprenticeship laws were strictly applied, the results would be the opposite of those desired; artisans would be unable, and would no longer wish, to take on apprentices and would flood the streets with thousands of young persons. Despite its many defects, traditional apprenticeship is a key factor in vocational training in Africa. It should only be modified with caution and to a limited extent, starting from what exists and trying to improve it little by little.

More recent laws for the "adaptation and renovation" of apprenticeship seek to provide for alternate periods of theoretical training by giving entrepreneurs themselves proficiency courses and pedagogical support in their training function. The chief beneficiary of these new measures has, however, been the structured sector. In Cote d'Ivoire the number of modern enterprises accepting apprenticeship counsellors rose from 12 in 1978 to 165 in 1985, corresponding to 284 apprentices. This is, therefore, an interesting but still very marginal phenomenon, even in the structured sector.

Modern sector enterprises, particularly those concerned with complicated technology calling for a minimum of theoretical training have gone as far as to combine practical and theoretical instruction through alternate periods of on-the-job training and training away from the work station. The training, simpler and paying more attention to know-how than that of the formal educational system, is of various kinds, ranging from basic technological initiation, elementary training, supplementary training, retraining and proficiency training. The courses are generally given at in-plant centres and combined with on-the-job training. The courses include, among other activities, training in methodology for managerial personnel,foremen and gang leaders, who are the main pillars of on-the-job training. Cote d'Ivoire has today twenty enterprises with their own training centre. Most of the African countries have a corresponding number. In many of them, training in enterprises is encouraged by legislation providing for tax relief.

Towards a Better Cost/Efficiency Ratio for Training Through Improved On-The-Job Training

Most apprenticeship laws leave out of account the very obvious fact that artisans cannot be expected to look kindly on, or co-operate in, schemes that are liable to threaten their means of livelihood. If the apprenticeship system is to be strengthened, it will have to be financed, artisans will have to be compensated for the extra burdens to be laid on them. If the costs are greater than the benefits, artisans will refrain from hiring apprentices. Considering the extent to which the formal system of education is subsidized, it can be said that it is unfair to leave the informal sector to bear the cost of its vocational training unaided. For example, the National Vocational Training Office at Abidjan gives the following figures for the two-year CAP (proficiency certificate) course at the Touva Motor Car Training Centre: 3,300 dollars a year per pupil operational costs and 1,500 dollars in fixed assets, or 4,000 dollars, to which should be added 700 dollars a year in fellowships granted the pupils who are all boarders. In other words, 5,500 dollars a year, or 11,000 dollars for the two years. Compared with these enormous sums, a few hundred dollars a head paid for apprenticeship would certainly have a spectacular impact.

Subsidies to master craftsmen should be highly selective and warranted by verifiable improvement in their services as trainers. They should be made conditional on the readiness of the master craftsmen to undergo proficiency training themselves in their professional techniques and training methodology as well as minimum control of the quality of the training methodology as well as minimum control of the quality of the training they give their apprentices. Artisans recently transferred from the modern sector would probably provide a by no means negligible part of this contingent of selected master craftsmen. Parents would quickly seek out these approved and subsidized master craftsmen and leave the others who would inspire less confidence for their children. The subsidy could take the form of money or raw materials at favourable prices; it might also cover the apprentices' pocket money.

The social approach treatment of unemployment

In the industrialized countries in-plant training has undergone a profound change. From an economic tool in the hands of employers, it has become a social tool in the hands of governments and a means of dealing with unemployment among the young.

Lack of modern industrial infrastructures has made it impossible to promote the same kind of measures in Africa, or in any case not on the same scale. The "social treatment" of unemployment has, however, taken other forms there such as the creation of building sites for "production-training", or special programmes of labour intensive public works. In all cases, the aim has been to give the beneficiaries both vocational training and practical experience, at low cost, their saleable production being turned to account to reduce the cost of the training. Unfortunately, these projects generally stress production rather than training. The training given is only a by-product of production and the project is all too often treated solely as a short term palliative for a grave and urgent unemployment situation.

Better training of the promoters and framers of programmes would make it possible to transform these projects into authentic "enterprise schools of production", in which theory would go hand in hand with on-the-job training and participants would have a chance of finding permanent work on leaving.

Conclusion

In the area of in-plant training, Africa seems to be following a development model not far removed from that known in Europe in olden times with its corporations and master-apprentice association. The progress of technology in due course called for more formal organization of vocational training; the blackboard had to be brought in, for example, in teaching elementary mathematics, physics, technical English, as these and other disciplines became necessary for the understanding of sophisticated technology. The evolution is the same, but in Africa the system is not always ready to bear the burden of the costs. Hence the need to renovate also more traditional and less costly approaches such as on-the-job training by improving the skills of "transmitters", those charged with implementing it (inplant trainers, master-craftsmen, foremen and gang leaders, and skilled workers), and by ensuring better co-ordination of the efforts of the enterprise and the school. This is, besides, in keeping with the trend of recommendation 150 of the International Labour Conference which "encourages enterprises to accept the responsibility for the training of the workers they employ" . . . and seeks to promote "open, flexible and complementary systems of instruction . . . whether these activities take place within or outside the school system".

Population Polices and Manpower Development

LAMINE N'DIAYE, UNITED NATIONS POPULATION FUND (UNFPA)

This paper addresses the importance of population factors in the development process of the continent particularly focussing on the crucial role of policies in the population and development field as part of an integrated strategy for the African Economic Recovery Programme. The upsurge in population growth has been the most important social and economic change in recent decades in the third world, including Africa; far more important, as claimed by renowned scholars like Gunnar Myrdal, than any policies or planning up to now. Unfortunately, one still comes across the erroneous argument that the African countries with vast empty lands and low labour and ratios have no population problems and are in need of even higher birth rates to exploit more fully their economic potential, ignoring the very simple fact of substantial and long term cost implications involved in terms of education, health, housing, finding productive employment, etc., for additional people. The dimensions of what has been called "the population problem", however, include not only rapid population growth/high birth rates but also high infant and child mortality rates, rapid rural-urban migration and urbanization, and the roles of women. All these are vital since they touch the basic core of the quality of life of the population and interact directly and indirectly with social and economic factors.

The Population Situation in Africa

The current position of Africa in the evolution of the world's population is striking. Relative to the historical scenario, growth rates on the continent, especially since 1950, are unprecedented in the world. The prevailing population growth rate of 3.0 per cent per annum represents a marked acceleration from the past and is projected to continue for the next couple of decades. This growth level contrasts sharply with the situation in the other developing regions where population growth rates are much lower and are declining. The total population of Africa at the turn of this century stood at about 103 million, took 50 years to double to 206 million in 1950, but then took only another 25 years to more than double to 515 million in 1975. The projected population for Africa in the year 2000 is approximately 900 million, indicating a continuing trend of reductions in the doubling time. This itself raises a number of critical issues pertaining not only to sheer numbers of people in a situation of limited availability of economic resources, but also to the accompanying changes in the population structure, which is expected to become even more youthful than it is today.

Very high birth rates, even by the developing countries' standard, have been responsible for this situation in the wake of rapidly declining mortality rates since the 1960s. Although there are variations in birth rates within the continent, most notably there are some areas which have relatively low rates due to sub-fecundity problems, high rates are expected to continue throughout Africa for some time into the future. Crude birth rates of over 45 per thousand population and total fertility rates of seven to eight births per woman are the generally established figures for the continent. The natural increase rates are consequently very high, ranging from 2.3 per cent to 4.0 per cent or more per annum. There are no clear signs yet that these rates will fall substantially in the foreseeable future, and even if the birth rates fall there is already a growth momentum built into the demographic structure of Africa, so that the increase in population numbers would continue unabated well into the next century.

With regard to the mortality situation, improvements have occurred over the recent decades, and further progress is expected. Nevertheless, there are still pockets of high mortality especially among the more vulnerable groups. Crude death rates of over 15 per thousand population, infant mortality rates of over 120 per thousand births, reaching over 250 to 300 in certain countries, are unacceptable figures in this modern era of medical and health progress. Although expectation of life has risen from less than 40 years about two decades ago to the current figures of 50 to 55 years or more, it remains low as compared to countries in the other development regions. Perhaps it goes without saying that the current declining trends of the economies of African countries will adversely affect the mortality situation through poor nutrition and re-surfacing of preventive diseases which can no longer be contained within the existing health infrastructure.

The third component of the African demographic scenario is migration and associated urban growth. Large movements of the population within countries and across international boundaries in the recent past, both voluntary and forced, and the inability of the receiving areas to adequately house and employ this influx of people has resulted in social and economic conditions which are quite deplorable. The deteriorating situation in the agricultural sector has induced an increasing exodus, especially of the youth, to urban areas. Although still quite low on the world urbanization scale – Africa's current population is 30 to 40 per cent urban – the urban population is doubling every 10 to 14 years. At this rate, and given the prevailing economic conditions in Africa, the economic and social conditions in the cities of Africa are likely to further deteriorate unless the African Economic Recovery Programme and long-term national development programmes are made to work.

A further problem is the unprecedented growth in the refugee population in Africa, increasing from two million in 1979 to over five million today. That is accounting for more than half of the world's total refugee population. Although political upheavals have been largely responsible for this, the demographic impact and associated social and economic hardships are severe and require more than a political solution.

The demographic scenario of the continent as briefly outlined above should be seen against the socio-economic development scenario. The two scenarios, if fairly assessed, indicate a severe mismatch. Both are leading to a drain on the human conditions – the widespread deaths among infants, children and mothers; a labour force with little hope of meaningful productive employment, adequate income, housing, education and health; poor nutrition and food supplies which are growing at a slower rate than the consuming population; unplanned and unorganized population movements; and the associated psychological and mental stresses which accompany such deplorable living conditions. In short, the vast majority of countries in Africa, under current economic conditions, are not even capable of maintaining the present standard of living of their growing populations let alone improving it. Thus it is crucial that the steps taken towards African recovery and development be cognizant of and adequately incorporate population dimensions.

Population Issues Within the Context of Structural Adjustment and Long-Term Development

The structural adjustment programmes adopted by a number of African countries have resulted in budgetary cuts, particularly affecting allocations in the social services sector and opportunities for employment. Given the current and prospective demographic situation, combined with this reduction in resources, it is anticipated that deterioration will occur in the social sectors and in the employment situation in the sense that there will be ever greater demands placed on this lower level of public support. Furthermore, it is unlikely that the private sector will be sufficiently viable to provide the services and jobs required. Within this context, there are several population and development issues which must be accorded high priority in order to minimize the potential negative short-run consequences of structural adjustment and to promote long run development objectives.

(i) *Population, labour force growth and manpower*

Structural adjustment programmes in Africa have led to large-scale retrenchment of the skilled, as well as the unskilled, employed labour force in the various public sectors of the economy, thus aggravating the already high unemployment situation without always providing alternative opportunities for employment in other formal or informal economic activities. The high rate of growth in the labour force is also a contributing factor, aggravating the existing problems of high economic dependency in the overall population. The figures, according to ILO projections, on the growth of the African labour force supply are dramatic – increasing from the current rate of 2.5 percent per annum to approximately 2.75 percent per annum in the year 2000 and 2.9 percent in the year 2020. In terms of absolute numbers, the labour force of Africa is estimated to be increasing by about 53 million between 1980 and 1990, and, in contrast, is projected to increase by 140 million between 2010 and 2020. Thus, the demand for job creation in the long-run is of a staggering magnitude. Meanwhile, education programmes, oriented towards modern-formal employment, have not yet adjusted in order to meet the needs of a newly emerging economic environment. Furthermore, the prospect of creating viable self-employment on the part of the workers is difficult due to the inability of the banking system to provide the needed investment capital.

(ii) *Population growth, education and human resource development*

Throughout the 1970s, Africa experienced the fastest growth rate in education; the allocation of one-third to two-fifths of national recurrent expenditures on education led to a near eradication of illiteracy in some countries, substantially raised the proportion of children attending school, and generally prepared students for modern employment. With the recent and continuing cuts in education budgets, and faced with a rapidly growing population, the quantity as well as the quality of education undoubtedly have suffered. This, in turn, jeopardizes the very foundations of long-run economic development efforts by reducing the productive capacity of the population and generally under-utilizing the country's human resource potential.

(iii) *Population and health development*

Before the implementation of structural adjustment programmes, the average national budget allocated to the modern health sector in African countries was low, around 7 per cent annually. Under the structural adjustment programmes, further cuts in allocations have either already resulted or are envisaged in the future. The results are low and declining per capita expenditures in the various aspects of health care. Areas affected include health personnel, equipment, drugs, vehicles to support health extension work, etc. In a drive to reduce the financial expenditures on health, governments have initiated efforts to involve the community in health care through the introduction of primary health care programmes. These programmes, however, cannot provide adequate health care in the short-run, and there exist several obstacles to their development as viable alternatives in the long-run. The main obstacles are the impoverished conditions of local communities and the lack of political commitment to this ideal. Meanwhile, as health conditions deteriorate, recent evidence indicates that in several African countries, a number of preventable and once eradicated diseases are resurfacing. These phenomena, combined with rapid population growth in these communities, results in an escalating cycle of inadequate health care and deteriorating health conditions, thereby adversely affecting human resource development and productivity.

(iv) *Rapid urban/city growth*

The rapid growth of towns and cities of Africa will continue for years to come until the conditions in the rural areas are improved, and rural communities become sufficiently attractive for people to live in and work. This is a difficult task; it is certainly beyond the current budgetary capacities of African governments to bring about a meaningful relationship between urban and rural development. Rural-urban migration will therefore continue, even though there are still vast unexploited opportunities in the rural areas to increase food and agricultural production. The resulting urban population growth rates of five to ten per cent per annum and urban labour force growth rates of at least three to five per cent per annum, must be viewed within the context of annual economic growth rates of less than two percent on average, and the added stress on the formal employment sector of structural adjustment measures. Thus, it must be stressed that the prospects for the long-run development of Africa are dependent upon the implementation of a strategy that allocates adequate resources to agricultural and rural development.

(v) *Population and food*

The continuing decline in per capita food supply for the people of Africa is one of the greatest tragedies of the current economic crisis. Unfavourable climatic changes through drought and desertification have led to large-scale famine in some countries. Millions have been and are still being affected. The drought-affected children and youth suffer both in terms of their physical and mental development, with the likely result that these children grow up to be far less productive than their potential. The demographic phenomena associated with these droughts include large-scale malnutrition and deaths; scattered refugee settlements without adequate nutrition; an under-utilized labour force with no hope of contributing to and benefitting from meaningful production.

A structural adjustment programme, devoid of human consideration and based on pure short-run economic factors, within the current demographic and agricultural context of Africa, may serve to exacerbate the present food crisis by placing further pressure on a low-productivity agricultural system without providing the necessary inputs to raise productivity and meet food demands.

(vi) *Women, population and development*

The structural adjustment programmes for Africa, as they have been proposed and are currently being implemented, could very well have a negative impact on one of the most vulnerable groups, namely women. With reduced allocations for health care and education, and the shifting of these financial responsibilities to parents and the private sector, girls will be among the first to be affected, as African society still holds to the cultural norm that boys should be accorded priority when it comes to schooling and health. Furthermore, the displacement of predominantly male workers from formal sector employment is likely to induce an influx of these workers into the informal sector, which has traditionally served as a viable source of employment for the female labour force. Thus, men will substitute for women in the informal sector unless efforts are directed towards augmenting job opportunities in this sector and elsewhere. Under this scenario, the costs of structural adjustment will fall disproportionately on women. Furthermore, since it is well established that education and employment opportunities for women promote lower fertility and infant and child mortality, these trends are likely to reinforce high mortality and high fertility, thus exerting greater demographic pressure on the socio-economic system.

In summary, it must be recognized that there exist key population and development issues which are crucial to the prospects for economic recovery and long-run development. A structural adjustment programme should therefore incorporate policy elements and measures to address these issues and prevent a further deterioration of the standard of living of the African people. One such policy area which African countries should seriously consider is population policy within a comprehensive population and development planning framework. It is only through an integrated population and development approach, set up within the context of long-term development considerations, that African governments can hope to achieve a workable balance between population and available resources.

Formulation and Implementation of Population Policies in the Context of Development Planning

A recent assessment by UNFPA of national experiences in selected African countries in integrated population and development planning suggests that most of these countries appreciate the importance of integrated planning. In total, about three-fifths of the African countries have reported, in response to global enquiries on population and development, as explicitly or implicitly taking into account population factors in design of national development plans. Approximately one quarter of the national development plans, designed after the ICP in Mexico used prevailing demographic trends to define development objectives and targets; and another two-fifths have demographic goals defined implicitly. Hence, less than one third of the plans did not take population variables into account explicitly or implicitly.

It appears that a good number of African countries are making a deliberate effort to transform economic, social and demographic policy into a workable design with quantifiable targets and instruments for achieving those targets. Changes are particularly noticeable in the increasing awareness currently displayed by African governments regarding an understanding of population issues, the refinement of population concepts and the consequent attempts to develop explicit policies, either in context – specific population policy areas – such as fertility, mortality, morbidity, migration, urbanization – or through comprehensive population policies. These efforts by governments to come out with explicit population policies are laudable. However, the implementation of such policies continues to present immense problems, including a lack of clear guidelines, political and bureaucratic resistance, a lack of appropriate resources, particularly trained personnel, low levels of public support associated with inadequate popular education/information campaigns as to the objectives of the policy, and poor communication and collaboration among the various ministries and institutions involved. Efforts must focus on overcoming these obstacles.

Nigeria: A case of comprehensive population policy and development planning

Perhaps one of the most important developments in the population field in sub-Saharan Africa in recent years is the formulation of an explicit comprehensive population policy by the Republic of Nigeria, the largest country on the continent. After many years of debate on the issue, this country has now joined the few others in the forefront of finding appropriate solutions to its population problems within the context of long-run development, as defined by its recent policy document. A brief look at the process and content of this policy, and the action plans proposed, may well serve as a contemporary example for the African continent.

The Nigerian population policy represents a dramatic change in attitudes and policy in a country, which although it had long recognized its demographic dynamics as a potential problem in nation-building, nevertheless could not take action earlier due to unfavourable political and socio-cultural circumstances. The country's population currently estimated at over 100 million inhabitants, is growing at an annual rate of over three percent and is projected to double within 20 to 22 years. The population policy declaration recognizes this demographic fact as one of the basic issues affecting development. The declaration also recognizes that the past efforts to improve the standard of living were jeopardized by the laissez-faire approach to population issues which favoured rapid population growth and thereby diminished the gains at the individual level of other social and economic development policies and programmes. Given the population situation, the available resources, and the responsibility of the Government to enhance and sustain the nation's welfare, it became clear that there was a need to re-examine the nation's population trends and their consequences, and to formulate a national policy on population for development. In doing so, it was recognized that population growth and development are inter-related, and that national development policies, plans and programmes should be based on an integrated approach that takes into account the inter-relationships among population factors, resources and the environment (see "Nigerian National Policy on Population for Development, Unity, Progress and Self-Reliance", November 1985). The population policy goals and policy objectives have been based on these declared principles, and are intended to improve the standard of living and the quality of life of the people, promote their health and welfare, achieve lower population growth rates and a more even distribution of population between the urban and rural areas.

An important aspect of the policy formulation process is the recognition given to the development of appropriate strategies to guide the implementation of the policy. The Nigerian policy identifies its strategies as follows:

(a) family planning and fertility regulation;
(b) maternal and child health;
(c) role and status of women in development;
(d) role and responsibilities of men in family life;
(e) population education and information;
(f) spatial distribution of the population;
(g) population data collection, training and research;
(h) institutional and organizational structure;
(i) monitoring and evaluation; and
(j) leadership

Notable in the policy formulation process in Nigeria is the fact that the linkages between the population policy and other sectoral development policies and programmes are well established. Within an integrated population and development planning framework, sectoral plans of action and programmes have either been prepared or are currently underway which will provide support for the realization of the population policy objectives. Thus, sectoral plans which are consistent with the population situation have been prepared for the key Ministries, including Health, Education, Agriculture, Labour and Employment, and Social Welfare, and multi-dimensional programmes have similarly been drafted dealing with issues such as women and development.

Some key lessons from the Nigerian population policy may be noted as follows:

(i) the policy was formulated with the support of adequate knowledge of the population dynamics of the country vis-à-vis the trends of the economy;
(ii) the government machinery was restructured in the process to enable

the system to accommodate new issues arising from the population policy and to take the necessary action to implement the policy;

(iii) the exercise was by and large a local effort, with the provision of technical advice by local and international bodies. The effective leadership role played by the National Government is a key factor in the success of the exercise. This will be even more crucial for the successful implementation of the policy; and

(iv) the public was involved – especially opinion leaders, political organizations, professionals, community leaders, men as well as women – in the formulation of the policy through public debates at local and community centres. There remain pockets of resistance to the policy which will require special handling if the overall support for the policy is not to be jeopardized.

The gain from this effort has been the successful articulation of a set of coherent policies and action programmes aimed towards addressing complex and sensitive population and development issues. The challenges which lie ahead are those which involve the management and implementation of the programmes, ensuring the mobilization of resources to support them, both short- and long-term and the ability to surmount the inevitable obstacles that will arise throughout the course of implementation.

The Tasks ahead

The need for population policy as discussed above stems from the established fact that there are dynamic interactions between the elements of the demographic, social and economic systems; it is thus imperative that population issues be addressed explicitly as a matter of public policy. As Alva Myrdal has stated, "a population policy is the social policy at large". A policy of this type touches on the basic concerns of the life of the people – food, education, housing, health, social welfare, etc. Given this dictum, population policies must be formulated within an integrated development planning framework, which ensures that the aforementioned linkages are taken into account.

African governments should therefore formulate explicit population policies and plans of action as a priority component of development planning. Given the diversity of African countries in terms of socio-cultural, political and economic conditions, each country's experience in the population and development planning field should be treated uniquely. However, while there can be no true replica of any country's policy and programmes in another, there is nevertheless the need to establish an overall strategy for African countries in this field, drawing on the experiences to date, to serve as a guide for the development of policies and programmes at the national level. The key considerations in the population policy formulation process include, inter alia:

(a) the goals and objectives of the policy should promote the overall development objectives of the nation. This implies that sufficient consistency must exist between population policy objectives and other development objectives, and between the means for achieving these objectives;

(b) the policy should meet the socio-cultural and political realities of the nation. For example, in many African cultures, equity is a priority consideration and this should therefore be reflected in the population policy;

(c) irrespective of the direction and content of the policy, greater importance ought to be attached to the quality of life of the population, in both the production and consumption of goods and services; and

(d) within the formulation process it should be recognized that the possible points of intervention of a population policy should not only include population-influencing areas, such as family planning programmes and programmes to affect age at marriage, mortality, population distribution, etc., but also population-responsive areas such as food, housing, education, employment, etc.

The population policy formulation process should proceed in a systematic manner, starting from a thorough and careful identification of the specific problems of the nation, within a long-run perspective, and move towards a plan of implementation. The associated operational implications must be clearly identified and acted upon. The requirements in this process would include the following:

(a) studying the country's population-development linkages, and identifying the priority population issues in specific terms;

(b) from (a), determining and establishing the demographic objectives of the nation;

(c) selecting policy instruments which can realistically be implemented given their cost implications, resource constraints and prevailing bureaucratic procedures;

(d) establishing appropriate institutions or restructuring and strengthening existing ones so as to provide the necessary support for the implementation, monitoring and evaluation of the Programme of Action;

(e) ensuring that the resource allocation necessary to implement the policy measures are made available, particularly in terms of building the national technical capacity required to execute the programme of action;

(f) recognizing and actively supporting at the highest political levels the importance of population issues in development planning;

(g) promoting the inter-sectoral co-ordination and collaboration required to meet targets and objectives; and

(h) identifying specific target groups to be studied with a view to developing measures to address their particular needs.

The above list, although not exhaustive, incorporates the principal elements that are required in order to identify and achieve a country's population objectives in a way that is cognizant of and harmonious with other development objectives and activities. The associated action programmes should contain, at minimum, components pertaining to integrated population and development planning; maternal and child health and family planning population and family welfare information, education and communication; and women, population and development issues. Additional components would be identified given the circumstances in any given country.

Short-, Medium- and Long-Term Support for the Human Dimension: The Role of International Organizations

KENNETH KING (UNDP)

Introduction

Despite the high returns to investment in human resource development demonstrated by research on the subject, there is general agreement that HRD has suffered a marked decline in Africa in the 1980's. Even more distressing is the fact that components of HRD which have a particular bearing on low-income groups such as health care, basic nutritional levels, employment opportunities and education and training have suffered disproportionately.

The major issues in the debate around structural adjustment programmes namely, speed of adjustment and the income groups who will bear the major economic burden of restructuring have relevance to policies governing human resource development.

The human costs of structural adjustment arise from the anticipated fall in both the real income and the employment levels in the period before the beneficial effects of the programme begin to be felt. Real incomes for the urban sector fall because of rising food prices, as the terms of trade are shifted in favour of agriculture, and because of the inflationary impact of the devaluation which raises the price of imports. In addition, the social wage falls as public services are curtailed in an attempt to reduce public sector borrowing and to balance the budget. The reduction of public services especially effects the most vulnerable – urban slum dwellers and rural poor – as outreach clinics, schools, and public works are shut down under mounting pressure on resources.

It is unlikely that the human costs of structural adjustment can be lowered by piecemeal efforts to raise cost-effectiveness or improve resource management. A more satisfactory alternative is a comprehensive strategy on HRD, which recognizes the complementarities among education, employment, nutrition and health, and integrates them into a viable development strategy. The decline in HRD in Africa may well continue into the 1990's unless national governments and international organizations take such an approach to reverse it. This paper suggests a number of possible actions which could be included in a special programme of action for HRD in Africa and the immediate steps which should be taken in organizing it.

There are two considerations which should be taken into account in drawing up an agenda for action on HRD. The first is to decide on the time distribution of various tasks over the short, medium and long run. The second is to arrive at a broad consensus on the comparative advantage of different agencies, so that the programme receives the most effective support.

Although a precise demarcation of tasks over the short, medium and long term is difficult, it is still possible to think in terms of a broad set of priorities within each period. The short period – usually taken as three years in the adjustment packages – is one where production is expected to increase, not through increases in productive capacity but by a more efficient use of existing resources. In an HRD action plan, the short term can be taken as the time to consolidate efforts on the rationalization of the public sector already under way, and to improve the use of scarce technical assistance. It could also be a period of a more detailed assessment of financial and physical requirements of some desired level of population coverage under a package of HRD policies.

The medium term is essentially the period, usually five to seven years, when production structures are being changed. HRD activities, in the medium term, can assist economic adjustment through production-oriented training as well as through employment policies designed to protect the poor. Long-term measures in HRD are those with substantial gestation lags but many of which are essential to maintain tolerable nutritional levels; to promote the choice of appropriate technologies, including agriculture; and to protect real incomes from falling due to sustained environmental degradation.

Assessment of the relative comparative advantage of international organizations is rather problematic because of the considerable overlap between project-related activities, an approach favoured by some agencies, and sectoral or country programming – which form the primary focus of yet others. The picture is also rapidly changing with formerly project oriented agencies such as the World Bank, giving more attention to sectoral and structural adjustment lending. Nevertheless, this remains an important area for further exploration, possibly by a task force which could be set up to draw up a special action programme.

International Organizations and Human Resources Development: Short Run Priorities

(a) Consolidation of existing initiatives in public sector management and the provision of technical assistance

(i) *Improving the delivery of technical co-operation*

Technical co-operation occupies between 25 and 35 per cent of total aid to Africa, and for some countries can constitute as much as 50 per cent of total aid. It is imperative, therefore, that it be used effectively.

Steps in this direction have been made by the UNDP's NATCAPs (National Technical Cooperation Assessment Programmes) missions which have attempted to determine technical cooperation priorities within national development objectives. But their results could be made more operational. First, the NATCAP should assess technical co-operation jointly for the HRD sector, including planning and support for innovative employment programmes. Second, it should attempt a quantitative estimation of the technical assistance requirements, both key quantity and type, and by cost in local currency and foreign exchange. These provide a more tangible basis for discussion between government and donors. Third, it should explore cost-saving mechanisms in the recruitment of technical assistance, indicating the extent of possible savings by such arrangements as institutional training, recruitment of individuals as compared to consultancy firms, and the use of technical co-operation between developing countries. Fourth, NATCAPs could also explore the desirability of establishing technical assistance co-ordinators within relevant sectoral ministries or within a central planning or finance ministry.

An important success story which deserves closer analysis and perhaps emulation is the case of Botswana. There are several features of the Botswana experience which may be relevant to other African countries. Technical assistance in Botswana was managed and co-ordinated between the Ministries of Finance and Development Planning, the former being responsible for overall co-ordination, and the latter for its administration with a focus on localizing technical assistance held positions. Moreover, the assessment of technical assistance is part of the planning/budgeting process and begins with the preparation of a national development plan, which becomes more detailed with an annually updated manpower plan. Hence, "most technical assistance positions are thus budgeted regular civil service positions that are expected to be sustained permanently by government after technical assistance becomes unnecessary". (World Bank, 1984 c. pp.37–52)

(ii) *Public sector resource management*

This issue has already been the subject of attention in SAPAM and in the institution building components of World Bank and UNDP programmes. In the short run, a number of points may need more detailed attention. First, a retraining and redeployment scheme for government officials made redundant by the control on public expenditure is urgently required if this trained manpower is not to be wasted. Second, short-run manpower plans supported by a fund to cover transitional costs may facilitate a phased, withdrawal of skilled manpower from the public sector. Third, core ministries such as Planning and Finance are likely to need additional technical assistance to cope with the increasing responsibilities for policy analysis under structural adjustment. In the longer run, however, localization of technical assistance should be progressively introduced as national and/or regional training centres become effective.

(iii) *Making more efficient use of limited resources in the HRD sector*

In the short run, real resources for HRD are likely to decline as public expenditure is reduced absolutely or is eroded under inflationary pressures generated by large devaluations. In these circumstances, references to the longer term beneficial effects of investment in HRD on economic growth are unlikely to sound convincing unless they are accompanied by a very vigorous effort by international agencies to assist in the design and implementation of more cost-effective delivery systems in health, education and employment generation. Such alternative strategies would typically include:

(a) closure or consolidation of small or low-priority programmes in health and education – expensive, specialized hospitals in urban areas, and narrowly focused university courses are good examples;
(b) promotion of primary health care methods which have the widest

impact in terms of disease prevention or cure – for instance, immunization and oral re-hydration therapy as against the construction of large clinics and hospitals;

(c) changes in the wage to non-wage costs of health and education to ensure that capacity utilization does not diminish because of excessive shortfall in essential materials; and

(d) analyzing the scope for non-governmental sources of finance (NGOs, community based schemes and cost-recovery possibilities) for the HRD sector.

As it happens, several international agencies such as WHO, UNICEF, UNESCO, ILO, UNIDO and the World Bank, have gained considerable experience in devising mechanisms to raise the cost effectiveness of different elements in the HRD package. WHO and UNICEF have promoted immunization; UNESCO has pioneered literacy drives; ILO and UNIDO have stressed vocational training and non-formal education, and the World Bank has paid special attention to possibilities for cost recovery in health and education schemes. In the short run, this pool of international agency experience can be used to assist individual governments in making more efficient use of increasingly scarce resources.

(b) Creation of an information system for human resources development

The problem of a weak data base, in low-income countries, is not peculiar to the human resources development sector but the likely adverse impact of structural adjustment on the poor lends an added urgency to creating an information system designed to monitor, plan and provide financial projections for key human resources development programmes. Besides continued support for special food-aid assisted poverty alleviation programmes, international agencies could collaborate in the following short-run tasks:

(a) the establishment of an in-country monitoring capability to track principal physical and financial indicators of HRD;

(b) the creation of an integrated, inter-ministerial data base as an input into effective HRD planning; and

(c) the generation of budgetary estimates, including foreign and local currency costs, according to differing assumptions regarding the desired coverage and methods of delivery of individual components of the HRD sector.

To place special emphasis on the creation of an effective information system for HRD is not to deny the desirability of organizing a better data collection machinery for the "productive" sectors such as agriculture and industry. Indeed, monitoring indicators in HRD generally use proxy indicators derived from other sectors: food availability per capita to provide early warning on possible shortfalls in nutritional levels; energy consumption statistics in industry to predict the level of output and employment in small-scale industrial production, and so on. However, greater attention must be given to HRD data because few countries monitor HRD indicators and even when they do, the data are often unreliable. Nutritional surveys are rare, and earnings and expenditures surveys of low-income groups are infrequent.

The importance of a reliable data base is well understood by international agencies, NGOs and governments alike. Most of these have made attempts at improving the data base in their own areas of concern. WHO, UNICEF and UNESCO regularly collect data on health, child nutrition and education. The World Bank has produced a number of Living Standard Measurement Studies which encompass household surveys including health and employment data collection. ILO's household capability surveys are another step in supplementing the national income statistical grid in difficult or neglected sectors. The time has now come to launch a major international agency collaboration in providing the information needs of HRD. This should be the first step in determining the relative human cost of alternative strategies for economic recovery.

(i) *Establishment of an in-country monitoring system*

An in-country monitoring system for HRD is necessary for at least three reasons. First, macro-economic and financial indicators used in structural adjustment programmes do not cover HRD. Second, inter-sectoral linkages, a special feature of the HRD sector, are not reflected in data collected by individual ministries. Third, traditional, survey-based information sources are too slow for managerial decision making, often experiencing as they do long delays in data processing.

At present, monitoring indicators often concentrate on physical indicators such as nursing persons per capital, or the school drop-out rate, to the neglect of financial ones. The latter are usually left to individual project monitoring and evaluation systems which are very uneven in quality and field coverage. Yet, if proposals for raising HRD cost-effectiveness – by reducing the high cost and/or low population coverage elements, by maintaining a balance between wage and non-wage costs, and by introducing payment and insurance schemes – are to be tested, financial monitoring of innovative HRD schemes is a high priority.

What is needed is the careful selection of a small number of HRD monitoring indicators which can then be tracked using a specialized, highly mobile and trained field staff. The lessons of organizing early warning systems for famine learnt by United Nations field offices within the last five years – the use of proxy and often qualitative indicators, avoidance of cumbersome survey techniques, rapid data processing and, at the provincial level, using micro-computers and regular dissemination of information gathered to relevant planning, finance and mainline ministries to assist policy choices – are clearly relevant to HRD monitoring. Given the strong inter-ministerial linkages in the HRD sector, the monitoring unit could be attached to a strengthened planning ministry, and the data generated could be scrutinized by a high-level inter-ministerial steering committee meeting at regular intervals.

(ii) *Integrated data base for human resources management*

Information generated by a small but efficient monitoring unit has the advantage of speed and flexibility, important in guiding corrective management decisions, but by itself is unsuitable for long-range planning. Speed and simplicity are often achieved at the cost of statistical comparability, across regions and time, and population coverage. The relation between monitoring data and routine statistical reporting is essentially complementary, since greater effectiveness of the latter opens up wider choices of monitoring indicators, and reduces the weight of qualitative and more subjective methods of information gathering.

Several reasons are given for the low quality of data on HRD. The most frequent is that the composition of HRD "output" and resources are subject to continuous shifts due to migration, changes in technology, and externally imposed resource constraints. A second explanation is that HRD indicators do not fit neatly into the organization of national accounts which were developed to facilitate Keynesian macro-economic demand management. For example, the measurement of "services" has always been a problematic area as the debate over the classification of services, as "productive" or "unproductive" activities, shows. In many developing countries, the value added from services or small industry has been severely underestimated, due to the use of partial variables such as employment as a measure of output, or because it is treated as a "residual" to be somehow adjusted with the income estimates of the "productive sector".

Setting up a country-wide data base for HRD is both a complex and expensive exercise. Unless planned carefully, starting from the retrieval and analysis of existing data, it may produce mountains of unutilizable data, often considerably out of date. There is obvious scope for assisting regional statistical institutions to design good sample surveys balancing statistical reliability with cost of data collection since not all information is needed at a high level of precision.

(iii) *Budgeting for human resources development in the plan for economic reconstruction*

Budgeting for HRD must not simply be an ex-post accounting exercise totalling up existing expenditure on recurrent and capital costs. It should also contain a sensitivity analysis of the budgetary implications of alternative delivery systems. For example, budgets could be prepared for individual ministry expenditures on education, health and employment programmes on the assumption that:

(a) the existing coverage and mix of HRD is about correct but real expenditure must keep pace with the shifts in population levels and composition;
(b) the existing level of public expenditure is correct, but coverage needs to be extended;
(c) both expenditure level and coverage are adequate in the context of competing claims on public expenditure, but the ratio of wage to non-wage costs needs to be altered. The World Bank particularly has argued in favour of reducing the wage bill in favour of safeguarding the supply of essential supplies; and
(d) both the coverage and expenditure on HRD are deficient, but resources should be raised from the non-government sector.

Such an undertaking involves both questions of definition (what is adequate coverage, for instance), and the translation of physical indicators into monetary estimates. In some cases – notably nutrition – the calculation of desirable or even adequate levels by age groups has proved to be a difficult task, due to disagreements over minimum calorie requirements by population age groups or occupation.

A final point which deserves emphasis is the crucial link between the quality of physical data and the reliability of budgetary estimates. Targets for expanding education or health programmes cannot be set unless the existing coverage is known. Changes in budgetary composition of wage and non-wage costs need to be made consequent upon an evaluation of the shortfall in material supplies and its attendant effects. Strengthening the information base for HRD therefore involves the dovetailing of physical and financial parameters. This should be kept in mind when examining the design and relative costs of alternative methods of organizing a data base.

What International Agencies can do in the Medium Term about Human Resources Development

Given the likelihood of some form of structural adjustment, whether linked to IMF/World Bank credit, or along some alternative lines, a diversification of the production structure and improvement in the utilization of public expenditure will remain the major plank of the reform strategy. Moreover, much of the adjustment will have to be implemented over the coming five to seven years, unless debt rescheduling and increased bilateral aid are forthcoming. Policies designed to alter the production structure and improve public sector management will not only affect the resources available for HRD, but determine the key objectives in the domain of education and skill formation, planning and management. In the medium term, HRD has to become not simply the outcome but also the instrument of a refined development strategy.

The principal tasks of the medium run can be grouped as follows:

(a) to complement the information base and public resource management activities of the short run by an integration of HRD planning into national indicative plans;
(b) to continue institution building in public sector management;
(c) to assist production restructuring by appropriate education, vocational training and employment policies; and
(d) to alleviate poverty by extending primary health care and safeguarding minimum nutritional levels.

(a) Integration of human resources development planning into national indicative plans

The intellectual justification for integrating equity objectives and instruments into standard Harred-Domar growth models was expressed most forcefully in the 1960s when many observers noticed high economic growth to be concomitant with a constant if not worsening distribution of income. Added ammunition for this view was provided by Kuznetz's work which showed that economic development was characterized by first a worsening and then an improving income distribution. The principle of "redistribution with growth" attempted to build in the welfare objective of basic needs provision into the growth model itself. A similar case can be made for an integration of relevant HRD parameters – manpower, education, basic health and nutrition – into the development plan.

Integration of HRD variables into the development plan also enhances the internal consistency of the plan since growth models often treat labour as a "homogenous" commodity when in fact the correct skill mix has to be created by manpower and educational planning. Moreover, by making HRD a component of the growth model, trade-offs between growth and current consumption can be more easily detected. This in turn allows policy makers to decide on whether other objectives such as employment or consumption of the very poor or the physical welfare of the population through improved health care should be weighted more highly against economic growth or a favourable balance-of-payments than has been done previously.

(b) Institution building in public sector management

Institution building efforts in the past have taken the form of project-funded institution building components in mainline ministries. The experience has not, however, been very encouraging in most cases. The major problem is the proliferation of project-related management structures which "become self perpetuating;" and remain uncoordinated (UNDP/IBRD, 1985). The second is the weak planning base of institution building components funded by the project. It has been commonly discovered, for instance, that while the technical components for IDA-funded projects were prepared under close supervision of World Bank staff, the institution building components remained external, often farmed out to a consultant – who usually gave insufficient attention to the overall structure within which such technical co-operation was to function (World bank, 1984 b).

Donor assistance for public administration/management institutes has increased in recent years, but lacks the sustained follow-up and support that institution building ventures require. Following the example of ESAMI in Arusha, many African countries have established management institutes but the quality of the instruction offered is often deficient. Most institutions cannot provide all-round instruction in the range of skills needed. Typically, these include not only knowledge of civil services organization and regulations but also techniques of staff motivation and work delegation; understanding of economic policy issues and a more than passing familiarity with accounting and financial management. Besides, there is the generic problem of low salary levels which not only prevent the retention of high calibre staff but also militate against the participation of senior government officials in the training programmes. The situation is aggravated by the fact that in many countries civil servants have focused on the "law and order" aspects of government and have not realized that often development administration is their principal responsibility.

The need to strengthen institutions of public sector management is likely to become even greater if the desire of many governments to promote the privatization of industry is translated into effective programmes. Given Africa's weak industrial base, promoting private investment is not simply a matter of removing licensing controls and liberalizing imports but of actively responding to a wide spectrum of needs, from developing a capital market to the provision of training, technical assistance, and trade information. Techniques to encourage private industry, although commonly known, must be adapted to local situations, and relevant training provided to government officials. Moreover, while willing to support an expansion of the "private sector," most international organizations are unlikely to be able to channel this assistance directly at the enterprise level. To a large extent, agencies will continue to respond to requests by governments to formulate industrial strategies including where appropriate the possible privatization of loss-making enterprises.

(c) Production-related training and employment schemes

(i) *Developing programmes for employment creation*

Although price shifts in favour of tradeables and the agricultural sector, envisaged in structural adjustment programmes, might give an incentive to employment expansion in export-oriented and agricultural processing industries, relative prices are not the only determinants of the choice of technology or scale of production. It is now generally realized that even within a given set of relative factor prices, alternative employment strategies can be chosen. Research sponsored by ILO shows that non-factor-price elements such as: the nature of the product; the weight of labour to total cost; the impact of technology choice on the composition of new materials; and the link between large and small firms are some of the important considerations behind the choice of technology.

There is thus much room for innovation, but few generalizations are possible. In African economic recovery, the industrial and non-agricultural employment base must be oriented towards greater labour absorption in the future. This can be done in many ways. First, existing capacity should be fully used by giving priority to maintenance and raw material imports. Second, capacity utilization can be improved by using such devices as multiple shifts and better transport planning. Third, a greater weight to basic needs oriented-consumption would assist the use of labour-intensive technologies. Fourth, there is a need to foster the informal sector by credit and technical assistance. Fifth, the public works and employment guarantee schemes in rural areas should receive continued support, if necessary, through the WFP-type of food aid. Sixth, vocational and other training should be linked to employment-creation programmes by labour-market monitoring.

(ii) *Support for production-oriented training for structural adjustment*

In the medium term, production-oriented training must support the economic restructuring process. In the case of agriculture, the major thrust is likely to be in the training of farmers and extension workers. Much of this training is likely to be funded by sectoral projects, which provides for necessary equipment, transport and technical cooperation. Many United Nations agencies have increasingly tended to support the idea of "training the trainers" an activity which could draw upon other developing country personnel through the TCDC programme.

Industrial training is more difficult to organize because the educational background of trainees is more divergent, and because centres are unable to provide on-hands practice due to the non-availability of industrial machinery or provide the wrong type of training because the machinery used in training centres is out of date. Both UNIDO and ILO have done much research in this area, and have attempted to develop shorter duration vocational training systems using modular packages. They have also experimented with cheaper forms of training such as mobile units, and using public buildings as skill centres. These are important aspects of increasing cost effectiveness and flexibility and require strong support.

(iii) *Organizing a national umbrella of basic education*

One of the most significant contributions which international agencies could make in the medium term is to encourage the provision of a national umbrella of basic education in most African economies. Besides being equitable, the creation of a national basic education umbrella in sub-Saharan Africa is likely to improve the position of women especially in the rural areas, and promote the effectiveness of extension projects or of vocational training to provide off-farm employment. The expansion of basic education will in part meet the objections of many agencies (see Report of the Joint consultative Group on Policy, 1986) that the target approach to women's development misses the fact that disadvantages for women are built into the structure of skills and production itself. Hence what is required is not just supplemental programmes targeted to women as a disadvantaged group but also a change in the entire skill structure so that the bias against women is eradicated at source.

The real question is whether a basic education umbrella is feasible in the medium term or whether a longer horizon is more appropriate. Ethiopia's literacy campaign is of obvious relevance here, since it is an outstanding example of how illiteracy can be reduced in a very short period. International agencies could do much to publicize the Ethiopian experiment, in the same way as is done for primary health care expansion in China, and to assist national agencies in planning similar campaigns in other countries. They can also seek bilateral assistance for teaching materials and supplies to finance literacy campaigns.

(d) Health-related activities

(i) *Action on primary health care*

The equity effects of extending primary health care are similar to that of education, and especially help the more vulnerable sections such as infants and pregnant women. Two issues are especially relevant in the medium term. The first is to improve the utilization of outreach primary health-care centres by improving supplies, equipment and staff training. The second is to develop a national policy and subsequent production of essential pharmaceuticals. International agencies can assist on both fronts by giving special attention to health-related supplies by technical co-operation in the preparation of essential drugs. Much work on this front has already been done by United Nations Conference on Trade and Development (UNCTAD) and by developing countries themselves as shown by the initiative taken by non-aligned countries (Patel, 1986). The experience of many developing countries, e.g., Turkey and India, suggests that drug assembly is possible in small-scale units while cost of raw materials can be reduced drastically by shopping prudently in the world market. Moreover, efforts to extend basic health care must be accompanied by continuing emphasis on the supply of safe water. The vital significance of the availability of safe drinking water has been stressed by UNICEF and WHO as long ago as 1953. As USAID estimated in 1982, a sanitary water supply could eliminate half the diarrhoea, 90 per cent of all cholera and 80 per cent of all sleeping sickness.

(ii) *Protection of basic nutrition levels*

Programmes to increase the coverage of primary health care are unlikely to amount to much unless they are supplemented by others designed to protect basic nutritional levels among the least poor. Evidence that currently used standards of minimum nutritional requirements may be overstated, and that even prolonged mild to moderate undernutrition in children below the age of five years may cause no lasting damage should not be seen as support for dismantling nutrition-oriented programmes. Research is conclusive on the need to provide nutritional assistance to the poorest 10–15 per cent of the population. This may well resolve the dilemma often faced in target-oriented projects of whether to assist relatively well-off beneficiaries to overcome some threshold or to help the very poor who even after project assistance would be only marginally better off. The latter approach, and with it a recognition of the right of the poorest to survive, is illustrated by the WFP programmes for food aid and the EEC-backed food security strategy for Africa. It also reflects a realization that even the best conceived rural development project may fail to reach the poorest sections. In the drive for economic recovery in Africa, agencies such as IFAD, WFP and EEC should work for an integrated approach to meeting minimum nutritional needs, and ensuring that a special recognition of the requirements of both urban and rural very poor is given in development plans. It should also be realized that agricultural growth is a very location-specific process, and may actually sharpen interregional disparities in per capita food consumption. Nutrition-based programmes can play an important role in redressing this balance.

The Long Term: Actions to Sustain Economic Recovery

The choice of long-term measures to sustain economic recovery, in the field of HRD, is made difficult because of an overlapping of production and equity-related factors. Population policies have a bearing not only on the demand for health and education but also on the available stock of savings with which to generate future growth. Measures to control environmental degradation on land have a direct impact on the poor peasantry if they result in limiting resettlement and raising land productivity. If technical co-operation is treated as a component of HRD, research on science and technology as well as agriculture and industry can be placed on the agenda for long-term action. The list of factors included under long-term actions here is therefore of necessity somewhat arbitrary and covers three major areas:

(a) population policies;
(b) prevention of environmental degradation; and
(c) research in priority areas especially HRD delivery mechanisms, and science and technology.

(a) Population policies

Africa now presents to governments and international organizations some of the most serious issues of population in relation to development. Traditionally the growth of population was identified with national strength, but as the numbers have grown, it is now understood that demographic growth contributes to strength only as long as numbers are matched by the development of agricultural, industrial and social systems which support them. Governments tackling the complicated developmental causes involved in bringing about fertility decline have discovered that it is dependent on a host of social, economic and cultural factors which influence a couple's decisions about ideal family size. Reduction of disparities in income and wealth, opportunities for women to move from traditional to newer occupations, female literacy, access to public health care, population education – all of these contribute to a decline in birth rates. Investment in HRD has therefore a direct impact on fertility ratios, a fact that should be clearly borne in mind when designing population policies in low-income countries. Besides the opening of family-planning clinics, which concentrate on the transfer of birth-control techniques, it is equally necessary to influence the demand for family-planning services. The latter is sometimes underemphasized with the result that discussions of population pressures and appropriate policies frequently exhibit a strong, and somewhat unhelpful, neo-Malthusian position on the subject.

(b) Preventing environmental degradation

Most international agencies as well as Governments within Africa agree on the severity of the crisis caused by soil degradation, deforestation and desertification. The severity of the problem is brought out by the ECA Survey (1987) which reports a depletion rate of 1.3 million hectares per year of closed humid forest. This is reaching alarming proportions in such countries as Cote d'Ivoire, Ethiopia and Nigeria. An area which deserves greater support is that of monitoring existing soil conservation programmes and evolving land-use planning mechanisms which encourage community participation. Although tree planting and construction of terraces, etc., have proceeded at a reasonable pace, monitoring in this important activity is still rudimentary. Crucial aspects of the forestry programme, such as the survival rates for seedlings, or farmers' attitudes towards tree planting under prevailing land tenure patterns for example, have still to be studied. A start has been made both by the World Bank and FAO, as well as bilateral technical co-operation but no effective machinery has been developed.

Land-use planning should be supported because the integrated approach to soil conservation is found to work as seen by the experience in Kenya and Ethiopia. The pressures of fuel, uncontrolled grazing of livestock and falling incomes of farmers have together contributed to declining soil fertility and poor management. Besides supporting the land-use planning activities of line ministries, a farming systems approach to develop land-use plans at the village level is also being attempted in many African countries. This is obviously complementary to other HRD activities which benefit from community participation, and is an area where the United Nations in particular can provide continued long-term support.

Moreover, it is also necessary to prepare viable projects for donor support in the field of afforestation or soil conservation or irrigation. This is a high skill activity, and United Nations agencies such as FAO and UNDP (via UNSO) have taken a lead in the preparation of projects or major studies. One of the most recent has been the Highlands Reclamation Study in Ethiopia executed by FAO. Provision of such technical co-operation is clearly in line with the objective, expressed by several United Nations organizations, in acting as a catalyst for future aid.

(c) Encouraging research in priority areas

Research covers a wide ground but in Africa some activities are especially crucial. These include agricultural research; research on improving the cost-effectiveness of HRD interventions such as education and health, and employment generating appropriate technologies; and research on saving energy, especially fuel.

(i) *Agricultural research*

Agricultural research is a principal component of the restructuring strategy, since price incentives will work only when new technologies exist. In much of Africa, there are no conspicuous success stories in the discovery of new technologies, with the possible exception of hybrid maize 20 years ago. In the case of sorghum and pearl millet, the indigenous cereals in Africa, research achievements have been rather mixed. Improvement in land-race varieties through re-selection has produced improved varieties such as Souna III millet from Senegal, Farafara BL-3-1-6 and SK 5912 sorghum in Nigeria. However, these improved cultivars have yielded only 15 per cent more than traditional varieties, an insufficient margin for large-scale adaptation. The development of new hybrid cultivars, which may raise yields by over 50 per cent above the traditional varieties, have shown yield instability and are still in the process of being adapted to specific individual agroclimatic conditions. Some success has been shown, however, in CE9O (Niger) and 189 (Nigeria) sorghums which under experimental conditions have produced 40 per cent more than traditional varieties (Andrews et al., 1984).

The problem in Africa is not so much a lack of awareness of the need to devote resources to agricultural research. Indeed, expenditure on agricultural research as a proportion of GDP has been significantly higher than in Asia and Latin america, but the results are nowhere as comparable. The higher cost of research in Africa is partly due to the extensive use of expatriate staff; high depletion rates of national staff, and the proliferation of research personnel over a large number of stations thus making it difficult to attain a critical mass. A further problem relates to the nature of the research itself which has shown a bias towards export crops and the staples consumed by the better-off sections of society. What is needed is organization; improved career structures of local staff, the increasing localization of expatriate staff, and a redirection of research to a bias to provide basic food security (Lipton, 1985, Pinstrup Anderson, 1982).

At the same time, in continuing support for research activities, including those in CGIAR, there is much room for a rationalization of aid in this area, since there is much duplication of effort, and many donors have expected results too quickly; often during the course of a single three or five-year project.

(ii) *Research and human resources development*

For United Nations agencies which have been closely identified with HRD, research on cost-effective methods of promoting literacy, water and sanitation, and primary health care, etc., is an obvious area of continued priority.

WHO has encouraged research in immunization technology for several years in the context of the Expanded Programme on Immunization which began in 1974. New vaccines for malaria, viral hepatitis and leprosy are in the research stage and require long-term support. The National Research Council in 1982 identified a number of important diseases including bacterial enteric diseases, tuberculosis, rabies, and respiratory diseases against which effective immunization could be developed over the next five to twenty years. In addition to immunization, new primary health care techniques such as oral re-hydration therapy have been shown to have significant impact on reducing infant mortality and morbidity at very low unit cost.

Applied research on health care, with greater emphasis on cost effectiveness, is likely to become more critical against a background of shrinking financial resources. Adaptive, in-country, research on such aspects of health care as methods of safe drug and vaccine storage under humid conditions, cost comparisons of different systems of oral re-hydration therapy, and the possible integration between modern and traditional medicine are some instances of efforts to reduce the cost of primary health care. These research initiatives could be further supported by international exchange of information organized by international agencies as well as by private, voluntary groups. Examples of the latter are the Programme for Appropriate Technology in Health (PATH) and the Programme for the Introduction of Adaptation of Contraceptive Technology (PIACT).

In the field of education also there is much scope for continuing research. The potential of new information technologies on not only students but as a means of training teachers, community leaders and health workers has yet to be fully explored. School curricula need to be constantly updated in light of changing demands of the labour market. The cost effectiveness, and the educational impact, of alternative pupil-teacher ratios, under such schemes as multiple shift, need to be closely studied before they are adapted on a large scale. International agencies can again contribute to such efforts by financial assistance, information exchange and by in-house research.

(iii) *Research on science and technology*

Economic recovery is not only about creating employment and boosting production in an existing production structure but also promoting the creation of new technologies which will improve resource utilization. Much needs to be done in the field of information technologies and telecommunications; research and health care delivery systems; and especially in new energy technologies. The use of information technologies such as computers in the creation of data banks for policy formulation and research is increasingly being supported by national governments. Audio-visual techniques play an important part in a number of extension and literacy programmes. Research on energy-saving appropriate technologies such as biogas plants or improved stoves is a critical need for most African countries today.

Because existing infrastructure for sustained research and development in science and technology is currently deficient in most African countries, international organizations should support science and technology research and technology transfer by promoting both in-house research in these fields as well as by increasing the flow of information from developed countries to the developing ones. The latter can be done in a variety of ways from organizing symposia, "twinning" arrangements between institutions in developing countries and outside, and inter developing country technical co-operation.

Conclusions and Suggestions for Follow-Up

To be operational the short-, medium- and long-term activities suggested in this paper must be cemented into an action plan. One sequence of steps in this direction is outlined below:

(a) The formation of an international task force comprising representatives from the United Nations and other international organizations. The task force, in detailed consultations with national governments, should formulate a detailed HRD action plan;
(b) The findings of the task force should be presented to a joint round table/consultative group meeting for further refinement;
(c) The revised document should be discussed by a special meeting of ministers at ECA;
(d) If adopted by the meeting of ministers, it should then be discussed by an inter-ministerial task force, within each participating country, which would work out implementation details. Technical co-operation should be offered to assist the process; and
(e) ECA should be responsible for regional monitoring and information exchange of HRD indicators. The findings of this unit should be communicated on a regular basis to national governments to permit a continual sharing of experience.

References

1 Akin, J. and Birdsall, N.,"Financing health in LDCs", *Finance and Development*, June, 1987 pp.40–43.
2 Andrews, D.J., Mughogho, L.K. and Ball S.L., "Sorghum and pearl millet production in Africa: Problems and prospects with new varieties," in D.L. Hawkworth (ed.), *Advancing Agricultural Production in Africa*, Commonwealth Agricultural bureau, 1984.
3 Bates, R.H., *Markets and States in Tropical Africa*, Beverley Hills; Sage, 1984.
4 Berg, R.J. and Whitaker, J.S., *Strategies for African Development*, Berkeley, University of California Press, (1985).
5 Health society and politics, *Bulletin*, Institute of Development Studies, Sussex, (1985).
6 Cochrans, S.H., Leslie, J. and O'Hara, D.J., "Parental education and child health: Intra-country evidence", in *The Effects of Education on Health*, World Bank, Staff Working Paper No. 405, (1980).
7 FAO, *National Agricultural Research – Report of an evaluation study in selected countries*, Joint Study by UNDP and FAO, (1984).
8 Feinberg, R.E. and Kallab, V. (eds.), *Adjustment Crisis in the Third World*, Washington, Overseas Development Council, 1984.
9 Ghosh, J., "Foreign debt and economic development: The case of Zaire", *Development and Change*, vol. 17, No. 3, July, 1986.
10 Godfrey, M., "Trade and exchange rate policy in sub-Saharan Africa", Bulletin, of the Institute of Development Studies, Sussex, Brighton, UK., Vol. 16, No. 3, (1985) pp.31–38.
11 Green, R.H., *The IMF and Stabilization in sub-Saharan Africa: a Critical Review*, Institute of Development Studies, Sussex, Brighton, discussion Paper No. 216, June 1986.
12 Haq, K. and Kirdar, U., *Human Development, the Neglected Dimension*, North-South Roundtable, Islamabad, Pakistan, 1986.
13 Hopkins, A.G., "The World Bank in Africa: Historical reflections on the African present", *World Development*, 1986, pp.1477–1487.
14 Hyden, G., *African Social Structure and Economic Development*, in Berg and Whitaker (eds.) (1986), pp.52–80.
15 ILO, *Technology and Employment in Industry*, A.S. Bhalla (ed.), Geneva, 1985
16 Jamison, D. and Lau, L., *Farmer Education and Farm Efficiency*, Baltimore; Johns Hopkins Press, 1982.
17 Johnston, A. and Sasson, A., *New Technologies and Development*, UNESCO, 1986.
18 Jolly, R., *Adjustment with a Human Face*, in Haq, F. and Kirdar, U. (1986), pp.386–400.

19 Leibenstein, H., *Economic Backwardness and Economic Growth*, New York, John Wiley and Sons, 1957.
20 Leibenstein, H., "The theory of underemployment in backward economics", *Journal of Political Economy*, April, 1957.
21 Lipton, M., "African agricultural development: The EEC's new role", *Bulletin*, vol. 14, No. 3, 1983 Institute of Development Studies, Sussex, Brighton, UK.
22 Lipton, M., *Poverty, Undernutrition and Hunger*, World Bank, Staff Working Paper, 1983.
23 Lipton, M., *The Place of Agricultural Research in the Development of sub-Saharan Africa*, Discussion Paper No. 202, Institute of Development Studies, Sussex, Brighton, UK. 1985.
24 Marin, A. and Psachoropoulos, G., "Schooling and income distribution", *Review of Economics and Statistics*, vol. 58, No. 3, August, 1976 pp.332–338.
25 Michalopoulos, C., "World Bank lending for structural adjustment, finance and Development", June, 1987.
26 Mushkin, S., "Health as an investment", *Journal of Political Economy*, vol. 70, No. 5, Part 2, Supplement, October, 1962.
27 OAU, *Lagos Plan of Action for the Economic Development of Africa, 1980–2000*, 1981.
28 Pinstrum-Anderson, P., *Agricultural Research and Technology in Economic Development*, Harlow; Longmans, 1982.
29 Please, S., "The World Bank: Lending for Structural Adjustment," in Feinberg and Kallab (1984), pp.83–98.
30 Psachropoulos, G., "Returns to education: A further international update and implications", *Journal of Human Resources*, 1986.
31 Schultz, T.W., "Investment in human capital", *American Economic Review*, March, 1981.
32 Sender, J. and Smith, S., What's Right with the Berg Report and what is Left of its Critics, Institute of Development Studies, Sussex, Discussion Paper, No. 192, 1984.
33 Singh, A., "Tanzania and the IMF: The analysis of alternative adjustment programmes", *Development and change*, vol. 17, No. 3, July, 1986.
34 Squire, L., Employment Policy in Developing Countries, Washington, World Bank, 1981.
35 Swedish International Development Authority, *Education in Ethiopia, 1974–82*, June, 1983.
36 United Nations Administrative Committee on Co-ordination, *Co-ordination of the Activities of the United Nations System in Human Resources Development and its Contribution to Meeting the Economic and Social Objectives of the Developing Countries*, Thirty-second series, Geneva, 22–23 June, 1987.
37 UNDP 1983, *Human Resource Development for Primary Health Care*, Evaluation study No. 9, December.
38 UNDP (1986 b), *Human Resource Development: Issues and Implications*, Report of the Administrator, Thirty-third session of the Governing Council, 2–27 June 1986, Geneva.
39 UNDP (1987 a), *Annual Report of the Administrator for 1986*, Thirty-fourth session of the Governing Council, 26 May 1987 – 19 June 1987, New York.
40 UNDP (1987 d), *Special Action Programme for Administration and Management in Africa – (SAPAM)*, New York, May, 1987.
41 UNDP/IBRD (1985 a), *Somalia: Report of a Joint Technical Co-operation Assessment Mission*, October, 1985.
42 UNDP/ILO, *Industrial Training*, Evaluation study No. 11.
43 UNESCO, *New Technologies and Development*, A. Johnston and A. Sasson (eds.), Paris, 1986.
44 UNICEF, *Educational Innovation and Reform*, Evaluation study No. 7., 1984.
45 Wai Tun, U. and Acquah, P.A., *IMF Experiences with Exchange Rate Adjustments in African Countries*, Washington, IMF, 1982.
46 World Bank, *World Development Report 1980, part II, Poverty and Human Development*, Washington.
47 World Bank, *Accelerated Development in sub-Saharan Africa: an Agenda for Action*, Washington, 1981.
48 World Bank (1984 b), *Institutional Development in Africa: A Review of World Bank Project Experience*, Washington, May 17, 1984.
49 World Bank (1984 c), Public Sector Management in Botswana: Lessons in Pragmatism, Staff Working Paper, No. 709, 1984.
50 World Bank (1986 a), *Financing Adjustment with Growth in sub-Saharan Africa – 1986–90*, Washington, 1986.
51 WHO (1981 b), *Development of Indicators for Monitoring progress towards Health for all by the Year 2000*, Geneva.
52 WHO, *Evaluation of the strategy of Health for All by the Year 2000*, Geneva, 1987.
53 Zulu, J.B. and Nsouli, *Adjustment Programmes in Africa: the Recent Experience*, IMF Occasional Paper No. 34, IMF, Washington, April, 1985.

The Role of Bilateral Donor Organizations

ROBERT J. BERG AND ALAN K.L. YU

Why are the bilateral aid agencies relevant to the questions of the causes of Africa's human resources development problems and their solution? First, because the new basis for proceeding with development in Africa, the *United Nations Programme of Action for African Economic Recovery and Development, 1986–1990*, is a partnership between African States and the donors in two ways: it calls for more resources from each side for key development tasks, and it calls for mutual reforms to create a more efficient and effective development.

Second, to the extent that past policies and programmes have caused the current problems, the donors are implicated along with national States. It does little good to apportion blame, but it is worthwhile to review the effects of past donor actions so that the general call for donor reform can be sharpened and given specificity as regards each sector of their activities, in this case, human resources development.

Third, the donors are a large factor in Africa's development. Prior to the recent slump, ODA accounted for about 44 per cent of the gross domestic investment of non-oil exporting countries to Africa (Berg, 1986, p.506) and that figure has undoubtedly increased in recent years. Of that flow, the bilateral donors collectively play the dominant role, providing about 70 per cent of the official aid to Africa. The latest available figures are as follows: sub-Saharan Africa receives 30 per cent of all OECD bilateral aid, but several OECD countries devote the bulk of their aid to the region.

Moreover, the bilaterals dominate the African aid picture as the most important source of finance to the largest aid recipients in sub-Saharan Africa. Finally,some would say that besides being large, the bilateral donors have the power to act for the good. They can sometimes muster the political force necessary to fund social sector and education programmes and historically have done so in advance of other sources of finance. They can muster expertise and even help shape the quality of that expertise through influencing the development of donor country institutions. In addition, they can be important allies to those within African countries who need great legitimation for the reforms or innovations they wish to carry out. On the other hand, since they are large, donors also have the ability to influence actions negatively if they make the wrong choices. These factors, then, make the bilateral donors of more than usual interest in thinking through the future of Africa's education and human resources development.

Current Donor Activity in African Human Resources Development

All donors wish their aid to have significant impact and they look for their monies to bring a cumulative and growing flow of positive events into being. Of course this is unrealistic, but this has been part of the way donor agencies have secured their funding. Promises, often of extravagant nature, have been made to parliaments about the great things which would result from small amounts of money. True, they said a small amount of money spent in our home countries to repair roads or build schools would be subject to normal risks and abuse, but put that same money into sub-Saharan Africa and you have magnificent impact — a continuing fairy tale, and it is wearing thin.

The bad side of this is that in order to keep the interest of parliaments (and of revolving donor staffs), development fads have had to be invented. To the extent that the fads came about because of critical analysis of past programmes leading to new ideas for the future, well and good. Too often, however, a new fad was introduced for less than professional reasons. Education is a case in point. Many donors have become bored with education. It is not new. The results are hard to see. It is never ending.

As a result, most donors have decreased their financial commitment to education aid slightly from their funding levels in the early 1970s, and in effect, education has received a somewhat smaller percentage of overall development assistance. Given tighter budgets and competing demands from other sectors, education's share has not suffered as much as one might expect, but it certainly has not gone up. (Coombs, 1985, p.294)

The World Bank estimates that total bilateral assistance to African education and training (including assistance within the education sector and in other sectors), averaged about $US 994 million annually between 1981 and 1983. Of that total, three former colonial powers (France, Belgium and Britain) accounted for over 48 per cent of that; France's contribution was over 25 percent of the total. (World Bank, 1987, p.108). Besides the three major donors, the other major bilateral contributors belong to one of three sets of actors; the OECD/DAC countries (most notably the United States, Canada, Federal Republic of Germany, the Scandinavian countries, Italy), the OPEC countries and the Eastern bloc countries (most notably the Soviet Union).

Donors assistance by education sector

An increasing number of development experts have called for greater donor flexibility in giving recipient countries increased autonomy in assistance spending. In its recent report "Education policies for sub-Saharan Africa", the World Bank also calls for greater sector assistance, both as a tool to encourage sectoral reform and as a means to lend support to those countries which have already undertaken sectoral changes. (See World Bank, 1987). The bilateral donors seem to be moving towards this approach, some significantly. USAID recently completed education sector studies in both Botswana and Somalia, and has agreed to commit to 10-year sector support programmes in both countries.

(a) Primary education

Experts have argued for many years now that the goal of universal primary education has both strong economic as well as socio-political importance in

African countries. By focusing on primary education, Africa targets the education sub-sector that has the greatest equity implications to the rural/urban issue, the imbalance between opportunities for the rich and poor, and the male/female equity concern. But the conflict between the argument for universal primary education forwarded by many education experts, and the actuality of donor and African budgetary allocations, has made for an interesting, but to us a disturbing picture.

Read at its best, there is a definite slant to secondary and higher education. Obviously there are continuing human development needs, and no one argues against having vigorous secondary and tertiary systems but the degree of bias towards these systems in the face of analyses on the higher rates of return from investments in primary education (Long, 1987, p.8) makes one wonder whether there is an elite bias towards secondary and tertiary systems similar to the urban versus rural bias in social services present in some countries, and similar biases in health programmes wherein policy-makers give greater support to high-cost treatment facilities over lower cost and more broadly based preventative programmes.

In fact, most donors have been more biased than African policy-makers, contributing less than 4 per cent of their educational assistance to primary education. Sweden and Italy are the exceptions; primary education programmes made up 6.9 per cent of USAID assistance, 0.3 per cent of British assistance, 0.4 per cent of Belgium's aid, and 0.9 per cent of French aid. The picture on Africa's side was much better. In 1983, average recurrent budget spending by African countries on primary education was 44 per cent, compared to 31 per cent for secondary education and 18 per cent for higher education.

(b) Secondary education

Secondary education programmes get funded by donors at a much higher level than primary education programmes, with some donors even funding secondary education at similar levels as their higher education programmes. Though most secondary schools are fully staffed by African nationals, there are still some cases of technical assistance at the secondary level, most notably as administrators in urban schools and teachers in the maths and sciences. Secondary education also receives greater funding because of its greater visibility in comparison to the numerous primary schools. Improvements to these secondary schools are more publicized, and usually a higher priority to regional administrators than improvements to primary schools.

Among all donors, the French contribution to secondary education was the largest relative to their overall education assistance budget. In 1983, the percentage of French aid was over 34 per cent, the next highest contribution was Belgium which contributed over 30 per cent of its budget to secondary education. The British contributed almost 20 per cent and the United States contributed over 10 per cent. French Swedish and Belgian assistance to secondary education focused heavily on the vocational training component within that sub-sector.

In the past, most experts agreed that vocational training was an important component of all education systems since such programmes would adequately train people for future technical occupations. More recently, there has been a change of heart among most education experts. Frequently, vocational students were unable to obtain employment in the fields for which they had been trained. In addition, after graduation many vocational students sought higher paying clerical positions and competed with graduates of general education programmes. (Psacharopoulos, 1987, p.202). Many educational development experts now believe that it is better to provide students with generalized skills which allow them the flexibility to adapt to diverse occupational opportunities. Others object to vocational tracking in secondary schools, arguing that the later a system specializes, the later it fosters inequalities in that system.

Higher education and participant training

While bilaterals contributed less than 4 per cent of their assistance to primary education, the most equitable education sub-sector, they targeted over 42 per cent of their assistance to higher education, the most regressive of all educational programmes. On a per student basis the bilaterals spent about $1.10 per student at the primary level and about $575 per higher education student. (World Bank, 1987, p.108).

Among all bilateral donors, Sweden was the only country whose education assistance portfolio did not have higher education assistance as the largest portion of its aid.[1] All other donors, with the exception of Denmark (26 per cent), the Soviet Union (75 per cent) and Canada (76 per cent), devoted between 30 and 60 per cent of their educational assistance to higher education.

Though overall recurrent education budgets show an average of 18 per cent spent on higher education, the impact of donor assistance on higher education is remarkable for a number of African countries. With the notable exceptions of Angola (8 per cent) and Zimbabwe (1.7 per cent) almost all other African countries spent at least 30 per cent of their bilateral educational assistance as aid to higher education. Generally, the largest part of education assistance goes to higher education, though there were several cases in which secondary education spending was commensurate or even more than higher education spending.

In general, participant training is still an integral part of most donor education assistance, with some country programmes, such as the United States growing markedly in recent years.

Analysis: The Old Goals, the New Problems and the Donors

The shape of the systems before the crisis

For clarity of analysis it is useful to determine whether problems which appear so clear today because of the crisis were caused by the crisis of the 1980s or pre-date it. For if this is a time to deal with current problems due to budgetary necessities an analysis of this type may help policy-makers better appreciate just how deep-seated problems are and whether temporary bargains with donors (in structural adjustment and sector agreements) are likely to succeed.

First, it is worth stating that we perceive no serious concern with the stated goals of African educational systems. In general, third world education plans have emphasized: manpower development to enable economies to expand;

increased social equity closely related to the view that education, at least in the lower levels, is a right; education as a means to achieve nation-building and therefore a stress on creating shared values; increased educational quality; and improved efficiency. (Lewin, Little and Colclough quoted in Psacharopoulos, Hinchliffe et al., 1983, p.5). These goals are all laudable, but there have been problems in the implementation. Most of these problems are well known, but we shall mention a few.

The well-known urban bias of systems has, in reality, been a partnership with the donors. Urban systems were established first with an imported curriculum to meet the writing and bookkeeping needs of colonial systems and an urban environment. As urban needs were met, systems spread to rural areas with less relevance along the way. Now the cycle is being repeated at higher levels. (See Coombs, p.18 and p.214). Perhaps this crisis of relevance has something to do with the high dropout rates suffered by a large number of systems. Even universal primary education in the usually defined statistical sense is not the same as measuring educational attainment. Given the high dropout rates (to which one must now add the factor of lowered quality), the number of students graduating with intended skills is a worrisomely small proportion. Furthermore, given the high number of primary school students who will never see a secondary school institution from the inside, more concern is needed to develop a primary curriculum that is an end unto itself. In addition, there needs to be ways of better ensuring that skills acquired in primary school will be kept alive thereafter, even if the student does not go on to further formal education.

Focusing more on actual educational attainments and less on years in place or on formal certifications may be a healthy development. Indeed, one can only applaud the United Kingdom, where efforts are finally being made to ensure that those who do not achieve a certificate for university entrance are given far more educational options than previously.

These problems have been long standing, but the bilateral donors are just beginning to be concerned about them, largely following the lead of the World Bank. The relative bilateral neglect towards basic policy analysis and primary level education does not position them well to contribute significantly to the kind of rethinking which the current crisis now forces. The bilaterals, however, should make every effort to support those African leaders who do see the moment to truly take over old systems to meet current and future needs.

Issues which come closer to home for the bilaterals concern practices at higher levels, especially those at the nexus of donor-supplied help and the increasing ability of African States to supply their own educators and researchers. Some have noted a reluctance among some donors to train trainers. (Njeuma, 1986, p.142). There are also cases where support for foreign-supplied teachers takes place when local talent is available. Clearly, the area of participant training and employment of foreign experts needs better thinking than has been possible to date.

Finally, a long-standing issue is the donor preference for regional institutions over national ones, when a choice was thought possible. Such institutions have had their longstanding opportunities, as well as their long-standing problems. Some education experts, such as the esteemed Dr. Aklilu Habte, feel that the history of such institutions is nothing short of disastrous and that selected national institutions should be imbued with a regional perspective to serve specific tasks. (Habte, 1982, p.2). We tend to believe that this is a time to select regional tasks carefully and that the funds saved from ending some regional efforts could be well used in bolstering the institutions selected for emphasis and continued growth. Perhaps it is time for a group of eminent ex-heads of State in Africa to review the status and future of regional linkages in Africa.

Should donors change their strategies, and if so, how?

In addition to these long-standing issues, the financial crisis of the 1980s has brought with it compelling new issues for donors and those they are trying to help in Africa. One senior donor expert believes that ministers of education in Africa see the crisis mainly as one of needing to pay bills and satisfy teachers' unions in ways which do not provoke rioting either by parents or teachers; working educators try to meet recurrent expenditures while still trying to expand staff and facilities; and donors try to push for structural adjustment to meet long-standing needs for greater equity. The specifics of this are less important than the common perception that all too often now donors and local authorities are pursuing slightly, or greatly, different agendas. Obviously, this is compounded by the proclivity of donors to talk over agenda issues in a bilateral context, rather than in larger groupings of donors.

Perhaps the issues noted below, arising out of the current crisis, are ones about which the donors believe they care the most; we think, however, that this represents poor communication since there is a more widespread interest in these questions.

(i) *The response to the slide in quality*

The most obvious step for donors, in responding to the ministries' difficulties in keeping alive existing systems, is to help explore efficiency steps in what they finance. This is consistent with the call of many African leaders for management reforms and aggressive efficiency steps. (Adedeji, 1987, p.14). Of course, donors will need to search for ways of increasing their own efficiency. They can recognize that generalized systems are less costly than the kinds of specialized systems donors often like to introduce. They can worry about the high unit cost of higher education in Africa to which they have made healthy contributions and they can work towards lowering those costs.[2] In addition, donors can think far more seriously about helping to revitalize existing systems rather than working to build new systems. In this regard, there are two urgent tasks: to provide non-salary support and to provide it in ways in which it counts towards recurrent costs.

(ii) *The challenge of expanding equity in the midst of low or no growth economies*

Though all equity questions concern us deeply, the issue that drives our interest the most is the role of females in African human resources development. Helping women to become more healthy, more educated, and more productive are not unreachable goals; they are goals that can be achieved if both donors and African Governments combine forces to meet the challenge. We are cognizant of a whole literature detailing why equity has been difficult to achieve; the problems of distance, questions of culture, lack of funds as well as a view that education systems can only improve equity when the society, at large, is moving to achieve equity (see Coombs, 1985; Windham,

1987; and Weiler, 1978). We are also aware that there is a whole range of arguments that equity steps have a higher rate of return, a less persuasive approach, since one would be forced to reject education expenditures if higher rate of returns were promised by perhaps less socially useful options. But the most persuasive reasons, to us, in espousing the cause of equity is that many countries have been able to do it regardless of income level.

This seems, to us, to mean that equity steps are a matter more of social and political choice than of any other consideration. Donors, however, would be wrong to merely espouse equity without taking concrete steps to help make more equitable systems a reality. The costs are relatively low, especially when one realizes that unlike the rural/urban equity issue, improving the female equity question brings relatively low extra financial burden to the revitalization of existing systems. Since, generally, girls and boys are distributed equally throughout most regions, the improvement of an existing school can benefit both school-going populations. Yet, national commitments clearly will be needed if growth of systems is to be possible while enhancing equity. Here the financial and moral support of the donors may be particularly constructive, if the aid relationship is right.

The financial crisis of the 1980s has proven how costly the donor proclivity of project finance is. Non-project funding is necessary not only for the policy changes sought by donors and African States, and not only for the revitalization steps so urgently required, but for the long haul as well. But more creativity in the non-project relationships is also needed.

As donors seek to bring about change in the current situation they ought to review all the tools at their disposal. One important tool is the amount of human resources development which goes on as part of technical and capital assistance programmes in other sectors . . . commonly exempt from consideration in terms of educational policies and effects. At USAID this investment in education is equal to about 50 per cent of the officially counted education commitments. (See Method and Shaw, 1981). Donors could greatly increase the effectiveness of their education investments if these activities were considered and implemented as if they had to also help meet human resources development goals.

(iii) *Improving the process of bilateral aid: time for specificity*

There are a large number of technical points which can be made about improving the quality of the performance of the donors, particularly the bilateral donors (see Berg, 1986). Most of the issues raised however boil down to a call for better co-ordination.

> ". . . the different styles and information requirements of various donors pose an immense burden on recipient ministries. Servicing these diverse needs frequently absorbs most of the time of scarce ministry talent. Common to many donors is the desire to make a quick and distinctive impact. This dissuades support for the simple, routine, and the proven, and encourages buildings and bounded projects rather than long-term measures involving recurrent costs. Africa has been host to innumerable projects, experiments, and models which in some cases reflect the wholesale transplant of established foreign models – Swedish folk development colleges, Cuban agricultural schools, British libraries, Canadian technical colleges – and, in others, reflect the powerful and often passing fashion of donor conviction. Consequently, in many African countries, the national system of education is a patch-work quilt of semi-autonomous projects of diverse national hue." (Court and Kinynajui, 1986, p.371).

To have these patterns continue at a time of particularly scarce resources borders on the irresponsible. Large amounts of donor and African money and executive time are wasted. Whole programmes are jeopardized and some major initiatives have failed due to poor co-ordination.

The only answer is for African countries to take charge. One can do this with a heavy hand, as India has historically done with its donors. Another approach is to view donors as an asset and to market needs to donors before they come in with their own ideas, as Cape Verde has done. A third approach is to be sure that a single ministry effectively co-ordinates donors, as the Planning and Regional Management Ministry does in Cameroon. (Njeuma, 1986, p.141).

Donors should never be asked to co-ordinate among themselves. They have not made highly significant progress in this in 25 years of trying and cannot be expected to do much better in the future. The only valid co-ordination is that done by the individual country. In some cases, this might be done in connection with a lead donor (such as is done in the Consultative Group and Round-table process at the macro level), but at the sectoral level it is imperative to the long-term health of good public administration that Africans take over the co-ordination as soon as they feel ready. With this as a general viewpoint, we end with a few added recommendations.

Conclusions and Recommendations

In this short paper we have outlined a major historic and continuing role of an often productive, yet often uneasy, partnership between the bilateral donors and African States. We offer five final points.

First, the history of assistance to human resources development is there for the learning. Donors and their African partners can gain a great deal by a closer study of the successes and failures of their partnerships in human resources development. The very crisis in education in Africa is sufficient reason enough to be sure that worthy initiatives are being supported and that problematic initiatives are ended or altered.

Initiatives to help educate Africa's youth should not be subject to repeated gimmickry, technological quick-fix syndromes, efforts at non-formal education to substitute for core curricula, and attempts to promote regional education centres over national efforts, all of which a study of past history would seriously question. Similarly, successes need to be highlighted and shared.

It is not only the lesson learning which is needed by individual donors and their partners; also needed is a sharing of those lessons across countries (both within Africa and within the donor community). Such comparative work will help African States select better strategies and better understand the comparative strengths and weaknesses of individual donors.

Second, the crisis of the 1980s requires special steps by the donors. Although the donor role in supporting human resources development in sub-Saharan Africa varies within Africa, overall this role is significant and has rarely been more needed. But the potential for donors to help Africa's youth to be better educated far exceeds that which can be done for the sector alone. For as the North-South Round-table concluded in its Istanbul meetings, "Unless substantial increases in net inflows of foreign exchange become available, the human situation in most countries in Africa will remain desperately constrained to a degree which no amount of national or regional effort can overcome". (Ha and Kirdar, 1986, pp.9–10). Even those donors without substantial involvement in education can help Africa by assiduously carrying out the recommendations on African finance agreed to in such fora as the recent UNCTAD meetings in Geneva, the Venice summit of western industrial Powers, and the Abuja meeting of ECA, not to mention the United Nations Special Session.

For those donors assisting the education sector, there must be full regard for the need to revitalize current systems. This calls for its share of changed policies, both by recipients, which is all too well known, and by donors. Non-project sectoral assistance is the appropriate mode now. The principle of not helping with recurrent finance must be tossed aside for the next years. Supplies and support to make existing systems work are vitally needed. New projects should be the exception, not the rule.

Third, the financial and human crisis of the 1980s should not completely keep us from maintaining a long-term vision. Africa's long-term educational goals still remain, and are a sound basis for planning. True, educational systems need revitalization; true, there is a need for greater equity in the services these systems provide; but this should not overshadow the basic requirement for the growth of these systems at the same time. The numbers are persuasive on that count.

Population growth will place tremendous demands on education systems, but the real aim must be to enable systems to grow while improving quality in the systems. Thus the donor role regarding this sector should be on two tracks: to work towards helping Africa to resume its growth, and to work to improve the quality and resource base of its programmes of human resources development.

In so doing, the goal of universal primary education (UPE) ought not be postponed until well into the next century. The record of the poorest countries, presented earlier, clearly shows that even the very poor nations can achieve UPE, if the political will is there. Donors should be supportive of such commitments. The costs are relatively low. (see Faaland, 1986). At the same time, even though past donor efforts have been quite skewed towards assisting tertiary systems, based on African needs there is continuing validity in the goal of maintaining significant donor involvements in support of higher education in Africa.

Fourth, the *United Nations Programme of Action for African Economic Recovery and Development, 1986–1990* is right: reform is needed both by Africans and by donors. Since the donors have the money and the African States are the recipients, reform steps have naturally focused on the reforms the African States need to take. By and large, African States have been deeply involved in carrying out the reforms which they committed themselves to do. The donors, however, have been less accountable.

The donor reforms necessary to better help Africa's education sector should be based on fostering more growth of local institutions and on fostering more mature relationships. Non-project assistance is one hallmark of more mature relationships in which the investment is one of fostering a system rather than fostering ad hoc projects.

The process of technical assistance to education needs updating. Patterns of technical assistance still look like those of the early 1960s when indigenous capabilities were far less than they are now. Two-year technical teams are still too often the norm rather than the exception. Training programmes abroad are still offered more quickly than offers to build up capabilities in-country. We would urge the following:

(a) Finance block grants to higher education institutions to enable them to buy resources (equipment and skills) from the donor's market. If the aided institution chooses to employ foreigners for two-year stints, fine, but we would guess that much more creative and intellectually interactive relationships would develop;

(b) Support joint degree programmes under which only specialized courses unavailable in the home African institution will be taken abroad, and that in the great majority of cases graduate degree research will be done in the home country. There will be new types of costs associated with such programmes (e.g., the costs of faculty travel). We believe, however, that the overall costs of such graduate degree work will be much cheaper, that western faculties will themselves be more attuned to what Africa's needs are; that there will be greater relevance and use put to graduate research; and that the brain drain will be significantly decreased;

(c) Third-country training in Africa can be encouraged. Multilateral donors are more apt to encourage this than bilateral donors. Yet many bilaterals are authorized to "procure services" widely within the third world in the furtherance of specific projects. When it comes to training, however, bilaterals have a poor record of searching for more local options. Financing can be done either on a scholarship basis or through block grants to specific national institutions to enable them to serve demands from their neighbours;

(d) Donors should make efforts to encourage the return of those Africans who have completed their overseas training, but who have not returned home. This is a very tricky issue. After all, one does not want to give incentives to those who have not returned when no incentives are needed for the far larger number who do return. It does seem, however, that the costs of helping highly trained Africans living in donor countries to find opportunities to work at home is a very small fraction of the cost of another MBA or Ph.D. Based on some experience in the United States, sometimes all it takes is better advertisement of job opportunities and more efficient handling of applications and job confirmations from Africa. Donors can help expedite such communications;

(e) Block grants should also be made to regional professional associations so that these groups can foster better intellectual interchange within Africa. While we think there can be some sorting out among regional associations, some have potentially vital roles in leading to the kind of co-operation within Africa which almost all far-sighted African leaders call for.

African States can help in the process of donor reform by being more selective in the donors they use. They can market their needs more clearly and can base more of their choices of donor support on the quality of the particular donor's work, rather than merely on the availability of the donor's offers. Mutual reform means expecting a higher quality of performance from both sides and taking steps to ensure that this takes place.

Fifth, there is a need for long-term commitments to the more fundamental problems facing the development of human resources in Africa. On the presumption that a well coordinated effort, as suggested earlier in this paper, can lead to basic agreements on priorities, donors ought to be invited to enter into longer-term partnerships to develop human resources. This might entail assisting in fostering, where needed, further capabilities in policy analysis and research on basic educational strategy and planning; committing to help close long-term gaps in educational coverage; addressing major institutional development questions and providing some better sense of longer-term financing so that financial planning can take place with more confidence. Obviously, when partnerships can develop, African educational leaders' own abilities to seek commitments from their Governments will be enhanced.

The nature of currently needed commitments requires an artistic blend of revitalization steps leading to new growth of systems in areas poorly covered previously. One such area in which there is wide spread interest in donor constituencies is the extension of educational opportunities to women. African planners ought to be able to tap that interest as they pursue their own plans to extend the equity within their educational systems.

It is interesting how much donors have discussed the need for building recipient country commitments to sound development strategies. (Heaver and Israel, 1986). Yet a comparable literature does not exist on how to build donor commitment. It is needed. Indeed, African States would be wise to read the donor literature on recipient commitment to see if it would help them learn better tactics to cement the donors into long-range commitments.

It will not be enough to merely reform education systems. There must be growth in economies and there must also be bolder attacks on the needs for better quantity and quality of education in Africa. However, as donors embrace these goals, as we hope they would, they also need to improve their own performance . . . in exactly they ways called upon by and for Africans themselves: better policy analysis and changed policies, more effective performance, and longer-term commitments to the fundamentals.

Notes

1 The World Bank data on higher education assistance did not differentiate between in-country higher education and participant training.

2 The annual cost per university student in Africa is around $3,000, eight times that in Asia and double that in Latin America. African university student-faculty ratios are 7:1 versus 12 to 15:1 in Europe and the United States. (Jennifer Seymour Whitaker, manuscript in preparation, 1987).

References

1 Adedeji, Adebayo, " A preliminary assessment of the performance of the African economy in 1986 and prospects for 1987", an address given before the diplomatic corps and the international community in Addis Ababa on 2 January 1987.

2 Berg, Robert J., "Foreign aid in Africa: Here's the answer – is it relevant to the question?", in Robert J. Berg and Jennifer Seymour Whitaker, eds., *Strategies for African Development*, Berkeley, California, University of California Press, 1986.

3 Berg, Robert J., "What is and what could be", in Douglas Daniels, ed., *Evaluation in National Agricultural Research*, Ottawa, International Development Research Centre, 1987.

4 Colclough, Christopher, "Primary schooling and economic development: A review of the evidence", World Bank staff working paper no. 399, Washington, D.C., The World Bank, 1980.

5 Coombs, Philip H., *The World Crisis in Education: The View from the Eighties*, New York, Oxford University Press, 1985.
6 Court, David and Kinyanjui, Kabiru, "African education: Problems in a high-growth sector", in Robert J.Berg and Jennifer Seymour Whitaker, eds., *Strategies for African Development*, Berkeley, California, University of California Press, 1986.
7 Faaland, Just, "The role of primary education", in Haq, Khadija and Kirdar, Uner, eds., *Human Development: The Neglected Dimension*. Islamabad, North-South Roundtable, 1986.
8 Grant, James P., *The State of the World's Children, 1985*, New York, UNICEF,1984.
9 Habte, Aklilu, "Manpower needs in Africa: The role of third country training", notes from a speech given at a USAID-sponsored workshop entitled "Third Country Training in Africa", Washington, D.C., 9 December 1982.
10 Haq, Khadija and Kirdar, Uner, eds., *Human Development: The Neglected Dimension*, Islamabad, North-South Roundtable, 1986.
11 Hawes, Hugh, Coombe, Trevor, *et al.*, *Education Priorities and Aid Responses in sub-Saharan Africa*, London, Overseas Development Administration, 1986.
12 Hay, Roger J. and Clay, E.J., "Food aid and the development of human resources", a paper presented to the World Food Programme/African Development Bank Seminar on Food Aid for Development in sub-Saharan Africa, 8–11 September 1986.
13 Heaver, Richard and Israel, Arturo, "Country commitments to development projects", World Bank discussion papers; 4, 1986.
14 Heyeman, Stephen P., "Improving the quality of education in developing countries", *Finance and Development*, March 1983.
15 Hurley, John, "Institutional development and training policy in Africa: Implications for African Governments and donor organizations", notes from a panel presentation given at a USAID-sponsored workshop entitled "Third Country Training in Africa", Washington, D.C., 9 December 1982.
16 King, Kenneth, "Problems and prospects of aid to education in sub-Saharan Africa", in Hugh Hawes, Trevor Coombe, *et al.*, *Education Priorities and Aid Responses in sub-Saharan Africa*, London, Overseas Development Administration, 1986.
17 Lamb, David, *The Africans*, New York, Vintage, 1984.
18 Lee, Kiong Hock, "Universal primary education: An African dilemma", draft report, Washington, D.C., The World Bank, 1984.
19 Long, Nancy, "Accent on education and training : Transforming human potential into national wealth", *Horizons*, 6, Spring 1987.
20 Method, Francis J. and Shaw, Saundria Kay, "AID assistance to education: A retrospective study", Office of Education-USAID working paper, Washington, D.C., USAID, 1981/?
21 Millot, Benoit, Orivel, Francois, *et al.*, "L'aide externale d'education en Afrique sub-saharienne", draft of forthcoming World Bank report.
22 Moock, Joyce L., "Overseas training and national development: Objectives in sub-Saharan Africa", *Comparative Education Review*, 28, May 1984.
23 Njeuma, Dorothy L., "Aid to education", in Hugh Hawes, Trevor Coombe *et al.*, *Education Priorities and Aid Responses in sub-Saharan Africa*, London, Overseas Development Administration, 1986.
24 OECD, *1985 Report: Development Co-operation*, Paris, OECD, 1986.
25 OECD, *1986 Report: Development Co-operation*, Paris, OECD, 1987.
26 Psacharopoulos, George; Hinchliffe, Keith, *et al.*, "Manpower issues in educational investment: A consideration of planning processes and techniques", World Bank staff working paper no 624, Washington, D.C., The World Bank, 1983.
27 Pscharapoulos, George, "Curriculum diversification, cognitive achievement and economic performance: Evidence from Colombia and Tanzania", Washington, D.C., The World Bank, 1984.
28 Psacharopoulos, George, "To vocationalize or not to vocationalize? this is the curriculum question", *International Review of Education*, 33(2), 1987.
29 Salamone, Frank A., "Relevant education in northern Nigeria", *Anthropology and Appropriate Education*, 31, March 1985.
30 UNESCO, "Manpower requirements forecasting as a tool of educational planning in Tanzania", from *United Republic of Tanzania – Development of Education: Opportunities for External Financing*, UNESCO, 1981/?
31 UNESCO, *Statistical Yearbook*, Paris, UNESCO, 1982.
32 US Agency for International Development, "Third country training in Africa", notes from a conference in Washington, D.C., on 9 December 1982.
33 Weiler, Hans, "Education and development: From the age of innocence to the age of

scepticism, *Comparative Education*, October 1978.
34 Weiler, Hans N., "The political economy of international co-operation in educational development", in Roger M. Garrett, ed., *Education and Development*, New York, St. Martin's Press, 1984.
35 Whitaker, Jennifer Seymour, untitled manuscript, 1987.
36 Williams, Peter, "African education under siege", in Hugh Hawes, Trevor Coombe *et al.*, *Education Priorities and Aid Responses in sub-Saharan Africa*, London, Overseas Development Administration, 1986.
37 Windham, Douglas M., Testimony to the Select Committee on Hunger, United States House of Representatives, 5 March 1987.
38 World Bank, "Education policies for sub-Saharan Africa: Adjustment, revitalization and expansion", draft of forthcoming World Bank report.
39 World Food Programme, "Information paper by the Executive Director" from WFP/ADB Seminar on food aid for development in sub-Saharan Africa, Rome, 20–31 October 1986.
40 Zagorin, Ruth K., Testimony to the Select Committee on Hunger, United States House of Representatives, 5 March 1987.

From Aid to Solidarity: The Past and the Future Role of Non-African NGOs in Promoting the Development of Human Resources in Africa

ANTHONY KOZLOWSKI

Introduction

The year 1960, marking the watershed of political independence for much of Africa, was also a turning-point in the Northern countries' perception of Africa's development needs. It brought the start of the United Nations first Development Decade and of the hugely influential Freedom From Hunger Campaign (FFHC) and of the Food and Agriculture Organization of the United Nations. Several national committees of the FFHC in due course became full-fledged non-governmental organizations (NGO), and the Campaign was important in establishing a basis for collaboration between governments and independent aid agencies.

Recognition of the development needs of the new nations, especially in Africa, provided an impetus for the formation of many new NGOs over the next 20 years. In Canada, for example, the number of such organizations rose from 26 to 127 over this period.

As remarkable as the proliferation of development NGOs since 1960 has been, in many cases, so was the rapid evolution in their thinking about the purposes of development assistance (now called co-operation) and the appropriate means of achieving them. From an early focus on relief and welfare – assisting the victims of conflict and natural disasters with food aid, medicines and blankets – the emphasis shifted to longer-term but 'directed' development . . . and then, more recently, to new forms of partnership with indigenous groups stressing endogenous growth and sustainability. In the same period, as development indicators have shown the sub-Saharan countries facing the most serious spiral of decline, non-governmental agencies have transferred the main thrust of their aid programmes from Asia to the countries of Africa.

The special skills of NGOs – to mobilize people and resources quickly, to take risks with innovative schemes, and above all to reach directly to those most in need – were demonstrated in full measure during the African drought emergency of 1984–1986. Capturing the concern of millions of people in the North and converting it into life-support programmes for the most seriously affected countries, the NGOs' operation was on an unprecedented scale. Though not concealing their limitations and some notable defects, it highlighted many of their real strengths as partners in promoting human welfare in Africa.

As the immediate crisis receded in 1986, this experience contributed to a new debate between African and overseas NGOs on the realignment of their respective roles and future development needs. While generalizations are risky, given the diversity of non-governmental institutions involved and widely varying country situations, there are signs of a recognition on both sides that African NGOs must progressively become the prime movers of grassroots development in their own countries and that, in order to make room for them, their Northern counterparts will need to reappraise several aspects of the role they now play.

Working out the modalities of such a new relationship will require tolerance and vision. No one should expect it to be easy. But NGOs today are at the leading edge of the development debate: they are aware that structures and systems must continue to change and that the challenge is to manage this change creatively in ways that will be of most benefit to human development and well-being.

Origins and Evolution

The diversity of the organizations

Even limiting the term "non-governmental organization" to groups active in development, there is no such thing as a typical NGO. Independent overseas groups promoting development in Africa come in every imaginable shape and size, and with just as wide a variety of intellectual or ideological baggage.

In the first generation of African statehood they have multiplied from a handful to a force of hundreds. At the present time, they are pumping something like $US one billion a year into thousands of individual projects and providing most of the resources to sustain Africa's own development NGOs. There are parts of the continent where one cannot travel any distance without passing vehicles painted with the names or insignia of foreign NGOs. In communities where they are active, Africans will speak of "the project" as a taken-for-granted part of life.

Private North American agencies with programmes or projects in Africa are estimated to number between 300 and 400, while Europe probably has somewhat more. The longest established, in most cases, are missionary organizations and other church-related groups, which today make up about 40 per cent of the largest NGOs on both sides of the Atlantic. The most recent of them tend to be those serving specific sectors or population groups: the needs of women, environmental protection, the promotion of small enterprises or appropriate technology. In between, there is a stratum of broadly based agencies committed to an integrated approach and able to respond, at the level of community needs, to most requirements.

From relief to development

During the first United Nations Development Decade, coinciding with the first decade of freedom from colonial rule in much of Africa, the exposure of Northern project staff to the realities of life in rural Africa brought about a rapid evolution in their perception of their own role. Analyses such as Rene Dumont's *False Start in Africa*[1] also had a seminal influence. The more perceptive NGOs were quick to realize that emergency relief for refugees or famine victims was alleviating only the symptoms, not the causes of poverty. A serious response to Africa's needs required longer-term programmes to help people become self-supporting.

While funding for short-term relief remained almost static in some agency budgets, support for development projects rose dramatically through the 1960s. This trend, in fact, was emphasizing 'help for the poorest of the poor' long before governments and international agencies chimed in with 'poverty-focused strategies' after Robert McNamara's 1973 report to the World Bank meeting in Nairobi.

The NGO development community had come a long way by the early years of the second Development Decade; but there were bigger changes ahead. When the first Lome Convention was being negotiated in 1973 to bring the whole of sub-Saharan Africa into association with the enlarged European Community, European NGOs still saw their role as essentially apolitical. Few took a critical interest in the issues at stake. Soon afterwards, however, a number of factors combined to move them into the area of research and campaigning on official development policies. Among these were:

(a) a recognition that the potential benefits of their programmes in Africa and other parts of the South were frequently being negated by their own governments' restrictive policies on aid and trade;
(b) a broader realization that the combined policies of OECD countries, if not directly impoverishing the third world, were a principal constraint on the South's efforts to break out of the poverty trap;
(c) disillusionment with the DD2 strategy and with its criteria for development based on GNP and sectoral growth targets. At this point it became clear to many that the aims of the NGO community and those of their governments, while compatible in specific cases, were most often asymmetrical and in some instances mutually antagonistic.

New alliances, new values

For some of the same reasons, development researchers who had previously tended to see their work exclusively as an input to official policy-making began to look for new alliances. Thus there emerged in the mid-70s a 'development alternatives' movement exploring a radically different paradigm – one founded on principles of self-reliant, autocentric and ecologically sound development, directed first and foremost to meeting human needs.

Development, still defined by many official bilateral and multilateral agencies as the linear growth of GNP, was coming to be defined by the best NGOs in terms of human/community development and solidarity. On the ground in Africa, some groups were by now providing humanitarian aid – medical supplies and the like – to areas held by liberation movements. In Europe, they formed the International Coalition for Development Action (ICDA) as a fighting front on third world trade issues, and they were somewhat better prepared for the 1977 renegotiation of the Lome Convention.

Euro Action-ACORD, a consortium of 18 European and Canadian NGOs working in Africa, commissioned a detailed critique of the terms proposed by the European Community for renewing the treaty, as a guide for its member agencies and others in lobbying their governments and the Brussels Commission.[2] This and other NGO initiatives urging Europe to concede a more equal partnership with the ACP States may have had little perceptible impact on the treaty terms. They nevertheless served notice on Commission officials that there was now an articulate lobby – representing a sizeable bloc of public opinion in the member States – ready to speak up for the interests of the African, Caribbean and Pacific countries.

Education and advocacy

The importance of informing and educating the Northern public about the economic and human realities of underdevelopment in Africa has been increasingly recognized over the past 15 years by NGOs in Europe and North America. Course material for schools is now produced by many NGOs, and in some countries efforts to stimulate debate on development issues in the news media have had notable success. In Britain, having extracted a government commitment to air time for development education on the fourth television channel, a consortium of 70 NGOs formed and funded a television company – the International Broadcasting Trust – to make it happen.

In the related area of advocacy and public campaigning for international economic reforms, there are wide differences between the United States and European groups. The Public Policy Committee of Inter-Action, a co-ordinating body of over 100 United States NGOs, has stepped up the tempo of its advocacy work with member agencies, arranging briefings on policy issues and testimony before congressional committees. But as one commentator has observed, "much of the existing NGO public policy activity tends to be directed toward assuring more government resources for NGO programmes"[3] – wherefore it lacks the confrontational sting of some of the more effective European campaigns.

Methods, Money and Merits

Operational strategies

To many African governments, outside observers and, not infrequently, their own supporters, the way that foreign NGOs go about their appointed tasks at country level can be a source of bewilderment. True, most now work through counterpart organizations in Africa: village associations, indigenous NGOs, church groups or government departments. The formation of national co-ordinating bodies of NGOs in several African countries has also helped to bring some sense of order and better information exchange. But individual styles of operation remain as different as night and day.

There are those NGOs which can follow a project step by step, having locally engaged staff available as trouble-shooters if problems arise. At the other end of the scale are those who rely principally on written reports and annual project accounts. Equally, some agencies see it as their basic task to elicit the people's own ideas about their problems and help them to formulate an appropriate response; but others still arrive with something that looks like a ready-made, do-it-yourself development kit. For complete self-reliance, it says, all you have to do is follow the instructions.

For the donor, the project formula is neat and efficient: it presupposes a well-defined target (immunize X babies, dig X wells, plant X acres), and a number of prescribed steps, over two or three years, to reach it. The formula works less well, and can often be counterproductive, when applied to social processes where neither the donor nor the implementing agency can predict the speed of assimilation or change. Partly for this reason, African NGOs have set their sights on breaking down the project model, which they increasingly regard as a strait-jacket inhibiting the kind of development they want and the kind of equal, two-way relationship with NGO donors that is a prerequisite for it.

Where the money goes

A graphic summary of the breadth of development co-operation offered by voluntary agencies is given by Joseph Short in his narrative account of the United States NGO survey:

> "Some provide grants and loans to local groups; others provide food, medical supplies, clothes, vehicles, solar water pumps or other material aid. Some provide technical assistance by deploying water engineers or agronomists; others send volunteer professionals. Some send teachers; others train them. Some direct and operate projects primarily with United States or other expatriate personnel; many work with or support counterpart groups; some work in close collaboration with governments; others prefer to work with non-governmental organizations. Some work from the capital out to the villages; others from the villages towards the capital; and so on."[4]

The means by which NGOs fulfil their mission, Short concludes, are every bit as diverse as their ends.

The funding issue has become complicated by the recent major shift of Northern governments' aid funds to their NGOs through co-financing schemes – and the awareness of African NGO leaders that this has changed the terms of engagement. The NGOs who have chosen to become, to a significant degree, handling agents for official funds suddenly find themselves at risk – their independent status mortgaged, their probity a little in doubt, and their money in some cases probably obtainable from the official source direct.

Impact and effectiveness

Serious evaluation of the long-term impact and effectiveness of Northern NGO programmes in Africa are still wanting. The agencies themselves have had neither the resources nor the incentive to attempt any broad assessment of the net social costs and benefits of their programmes.

Allowing that merits and defects are not quantifiable, it is nonetheless possible to identify, from the intense debate of recent times, some of the main entries on each side of the balance sheet. Among the plus-factors, the following stand out:

A holistic world-view

Underpinning their work in Africa, as in other regions, is a concept of the human condition which embraces its cultural and spiritual dimensions as well as the social and economic. The best NGO ethos keeps in mind the wholeness of people and their living environment, recognizing that the materially poor may be rich in ways lost to the wealthy. This world-view yields a markedly different set of criteria for action from those of national or foreign governments – criteria in which economic measures are only one element and will only work as part of a wider process of change.

One African commentator puts it in these words: "Although what is generally termed as Africa's crisis is often considered mainly in terms of Africa's deteriorating economic condition, it needs to be recognized that the crisis is multi-dimensional, and that economic decline and poverty are only an aspect.[5]

The human dimension

Perceiving themselves as intermediaries in an essentially people-to-people relationship, NGOs have always given primacy to meeting human needs at family and community levels, with particular emphasis on the non-material dimension of development. European NGOs believe that in their dialogue with the European Community during negotiations for the third Lome Convention they exerted a positive influence on the previously narrow official view of relations with Africa and the other ACP countries. "Increased contacts and co-operation with NGOs during this period have certainly changed the perceptions of development issues in the European Community", asserts the Liaison Committee of Development NGOs to the European Communities. "Where it used to be conceived in purely economic terms, there is now a greater emphasis on the individual human being as the central point in the development process".[6]

Innovation and the spread of ideas

Progressive NGOs recognize that in addressing the needs of the poorest and most vulnerable people a shared learning process will draw out their perception of the changes needed to improve their own well-being. Working in this way, NGOs are uniquely placed to contribute to innovative thinking by the people themselves and then to help translate it into techniques that yield more sustainable livelihoods. With many countries of sub-Saharan Africa seemingly trapped in a spiral of decline, self-help strategies are the only ones likely to bring hope to the poorest. In this context, new approaches and methods which people can adopt and spread spontaneously, whether in rural or urban areas, are among the most valuable contributions that African and Northern NGOs working together can offer.[7]

Lobbying for reform of international economic relations

Overseas NGOs have become forceful campaigners for the rights and interests of African and other third world people, whose efforts to break out of the poverty trap are seen to be vitiated by external forces. They have formed networks and coalitions, national and international, to press for more equitable policies in many areas of aid and trade – a role which becomes more vital as it becomes more difficult to sustain in the harsh economic climate of the late 1980s.

Turning now to the minus-factors, it can be observed that several of the negative features ascribed to NGO interventions in Africa are the counter-face of their virtues. In some cases it may be difficult to have one without the other, but in many there is substantial scope to offset or eliminate the worst deficiencies.

Disorder and dependency

If diversity is one of the collective merits of the non-African NGOs, the other side of the coin is disorder, duplication and interagency rivalry. Lack of consultation among the myriad foreign NGOs is frequently cited as a major headache for governments and voluntary groups in Africa, and although the creation of national NGO councils has helped in some countries, much more needs to be done to relieve it. This fragmentation, together with the donor groups' sole control of funding, is blamed for keeping their indigenous partners in a dependency relationship.

Narrow project focus

By confining their support to a limited range of project tasks over a relatively brief period, aid-giving NGOs keep their partners on a tight rein. As well as stunting their institutional growth, African NGOs maintain, this prevents them from relating to community level groups in an integrated way.

Religio-political tensions

A small number of NGOs act as covers for undeclared political or religious interests. A report to the United Nations Office for Emergency Operations in Africa highlighted this.[8] Christian NGOs can encounter – and cause – problems in Islamic countries, especially if they have a conservative/ evangelical optic. Wealthy NGOs operating aircraft and radio transmitters in politically sensitive areas during emergencies can be an embarrassment and a danger to the whole NGO community.

A lack of transparency

The motivation of Northern NGOs as a group has come under question as more of them begin to derive a significant part of their finance from Northern government budgets. Without some standard procedure for the disclosure of income sources, institutional background and affiliations, mounting resentment must be anticipated among African NGOs and their colleagues elsewhere in the South that they are regularly required to reveal every detail of their work and yet are seldom accorded the same openness in return.

Geographical and sectoral imbalance

An optimal distribution of resources according to need would be too much to expect, with several hundred Northern NGOs in Africa firing off their project guns in all directions. United States agencies, for example, have more than three times as many projects in comfortable Kenya as they do in Zaire, which is twice as poor and has 50 per cent more people (The European agencies may or may not be any better in this regard, but they have not produced an equivalent survey which would permit such comparisons).

Sectoral distortions, however, may be of equal or greater concern. NGO programmes have, for example, given minimal attention to the problems of the urban poor, relatively little to projects for women and not much to the vital issues of natural resource management. Forty-five African and other third world NGOs, meeting recently in Limuru, Kenya, with their international counterparts, deplored the 'insignificant' proportion of total aid flows devoted to improving shelter and tackling homelessness, only a tiny share of which was made available to NGOs.

"Governments should recognize", they declared, "that appropriate support for individual households and the community-based organizations that they form, and the NGOs with whom they choose to work in their efforts to improve shelter and environmental conditions, represents the most innovative and effective strategy to reverse existing trends".[9]

Towards Something New

The search for solidarity

The ways in which overseas NGOs can in future best contribute to the development of human resources in Africa will depend to a large extent on the designing of new relationships with African NGOs and new structures to match. Exactly what these relationships should be, and how to nurture them, are questions which have come to the forefront of discussion in several recent north-south encounters. If positive answers emerge, the current dialogue could go a long way to selling the parameters for a more constructive and creative north-south alliance.

New relationships are critical, for two fairly evident reasons: first, because our small world will not long survive the stresses imposed on it today by a heedless exploitation of people and resources and by extreme manifestations of power and powerlessness; and second, because many aspects of the present 'partnership' are inherently unequal and in the long run unsustainable.

Specifically in terms of relationships, the search for a new solidarity between African and Northern NGOs is seen to call for:

(a) a new compact between the two sides, detached as much as possible from project funding and based on a complementarity of skills to address the whole panorama of development obstacles, North and South. This sharing of responsibilities should find expression in new national, regional and north-south networks, and the strengthening of those already operational to enable them to extend their work in Africa;

(b) a review of the whole aid process and relations between Northern NGOs and their governments. There is good reason to underline a warning issued several years ago by the former Dutch Minister of Development Co-operation, Jan Pronk, when he said: "The corruption of NGOs will be the political game of the years ahead – and it is already being played today."[10]

(c) a departure from the 2–5 year project framework and from the physical input approach (dams, wells, hardware, seeds, etc.) to straight grants for African groups to use as they see fit.

Beyond the United Nations Special Session

The special session of the United Nations General Assembly in May 1986 provided an opportune moment to review NGO contributions to African development in the wake of the drought emergency. Most observers felt that the NGO community, both indigenous and foreign, had acquitted itself well, carrying a large share of the burden for aid distribution and having to make big adjustments. But with the immediate crisis over, there were longer-term questions about the Northern NGOs' role in Africa, waiting to be asked.

Many of the issues were explored at a 'strategy workshop' organized by the United Nations Non-governmental Liaison Service and co-sponsored by the International Council of Voluntary Agencies (ICVA) and the International Coalition for Development Action (ICDA) in Geneva in November 1985. Bringing together leading representatives of African and international NGOs, the workshop was designed to prepare for their participation in the special session and for this purpose to conduct a wide-ranging and critical analysis of NGO achievements, with a view to identifying future priorities.

Recommendations from the Conference's working groups highlighted, inter alia, the importance of strengthening the information and communications capacity of Southern NGOs, the need to support independent African research and bridge-building information activities between North and South. One group suggested drawing up a code of ethics on NGO fund-raising and setting a target of 10 per cent of individual NGO resources to be devoted to development education.[11]

At the special session itself, African and international NGOs held their own forum in parallel with the official conference, and drafted their own Declaration.[12] Their spokesman also addressed the General Assembly. In its recommendations directed specifically to Northern and international NGOs, the Declaration encouraged them to continue influencing their governments to adopt more democratic, humane and egalitarian policies in Africa; to recognize the linkages between the policies of their governments and other institutions which adversely affect the quality of life and the political and economic independence of African countries; to adopt a more consistent approach in influencing their governments' monetary, trade and fiscal policies, and to resist being used by Northern governments in the furtherance of narrow, short-term interests.

The Declaration also urged Northern and International NGOs to make long-term commitments to sustainable development in Africa, to ensure that their own internal structures were democratic, and to support the institutional growth of autonomous NGOs at the national level in the third world, reorienting their own activities to concentrate increasingly on development education, advocacy, fund-raising and facilitating information flows. Northern and International NGOs, it went on, should not compete with their African counterparts in the implementation of projects but play a supportive role; and they should avoid sending in overseas project staff when appropriate personnel were locally available.

Among issues raised in the plenary sessions of the NGO Forum, one widely recognized, was the importance of strengthening both African NGO networks and the participation of African groups in international networks.

Overcoming the obstacles

The range of problems adduced by both African and Northern NGO representatives in those meetings and others major NGO forums which followed the Special Session can be seen as falling into two broad categories.

At one level there are practical, organizational issues: needs for better information exchange, programme versus project funding, and clearer and more reciprocal accountability. At another, the problems are less definable ones of anxiety (What do they expect of us?), mistrust (What are their real motives?) and resentment (They want it all their own way!).

But in a sense all these obstacles are symptoms of one underlying problem: a basic dysfunction of the development paradigm within which NGOs have to work. Whether indigenous or from overseas, they find themselves trying to evolve a co-operative partnership within what is fundamentally an assistential model of north-south relations.

A first question, therefore, is whether NGOs can apply any of the leverage they have acquired in recent times to begin to transform the aspects of that model that affect them. The best would be to find a level which holds out the possibility of accomplishing several related changes: to create automatic transfers to Southern NGOs, to build new co-ordinating bodies at the national level in Africa, to reduce the overall level of Northern NGOs' dependency on government funding, and to allocate a larger proportion of official co-financing budgets to development education and public information in the North.

In the 10 years to 1983, aid funds channelled to Northern NGOs from governments and other official sources tripled to more than $1 billion. They now account for over one-third of the total NGO resources. In 1984, no less than 60 per cent of assistance to Africa by United States NGOs was provided from official sources, in the form of food aid ($220 million) and grants ($50 million).[13]

In the rush to take advantage of these budget lines, however, some Northern NGOs may have given inadequate attention to two factors – one immediate and one long-term – which stand to diminish their credibility as partners for development in Africa. Whereas in the past recipients of NGO aid were usually too polite or too trusting to ask questions about the source of donor agency funds, the new African agencies, with a highly educated leadership often trained in the North, have such scruples. Indeed, they are well aware of the geo-political designs underpinning the foreign policies of industrialized nations, east and west; and they are familiar with the well documented cases of foreign aid being used to serve those designs.The result is an aura of mistrust which permeates not just the officially-funded segment of an agency's programme but everything else as well.

Agenda for the Future

From the foregoing survey and, more particularly, from the numerous recent analyses of the role of NGOs in Africa, it is possible to compile a check-list of key areas of future action for overseas NGOs in contributing to human development in Africa. Among the most important items on the agenda should be:

(a) activities designed to relieve the external constraints on the self-development of the African people, in order to give them the economic, social and cultural space to design their own futures. In practice, this means giving primacy to efforts for the reform of international trade and development finance. It calls for more concerted development education, advocacy and media work by Northern NGOs, using their collective strength to change the terms of north-south engagement on issues such as trade protectionism and international debt. It also entails monitoring international commitments to African development, in order to access and publicize the performance of both multilateral and bilateral agencies;

(b) combined efforts by Northern, African and other Southern NGOs to alert world opinion to macro-policy issues affecting all countries, e.g. natural resource depletion, energy futures, north-south employment trade-offs, environmental pollution. In this context, Northern NGOs should be expected to forge alliances with wider social movements campaigning on global security, human rights, consumer issues and the role of women, in order to address as broadly as possible the issues of sustainable development, as posed in the report of the World Commission on Environment and Development.[15]

(c) promoting closer ties between development research and NGO action, both within Africa and internationally. Stronger working relationships need to be established, between Northern and African research institutes and between the latter and the indigenous NGOs. This is needed to ensure three things: (i) that research on Africa undertaken by Northern agencies is freely available to their African counterparts and not merely harvested and sold as an export crop; (ii) that African researchers are enabled to contribute in practical ways to community level development work in their own country/region; and (iii) that the experience of NGO development workers is transmitted to the research community as guidance for future planning. In this area also, Northern NGOs should be supporting their African counterparts in acquiring their own skills in research and information-gathering, to be able to evaluate more effectively their interventions and to enhance their status and influence as interlocutors with their own government or foreign agencies;

(d) networking and information exchange at various levels. Overseas NGOs can have an important role in providing conduits for information flows to, from and among African groups. Whereas bilateral information flows can be divisive, horizontal networking can provide a common knowledge-base on which to build regional co-operation among NGOs. Sectoral NGO networks, which have had considerable impact at international levels (e.g. Pesticides Action Network, Health Action International) should be seriously considered as a model for regional collaboration among African NGOs which Northern agencies could support. One such network already operational is the African NGOs Environment Network (ANEN), based in Nairobi. Others could be valuable, perhaps initially at subregional level, in such fields as food security, rural energy and drought survival strategies. One primary purpose of Northern NGOs'involvement in African networking must be to help strengthen the institutional capacity of indigenous NGOs and to define and carry through their own policies and programmes, thus reducing their dependence on foreign technical and tied financial resources.

(e) training as part of a two-way learning process. On one side, Northern groups need to take advantage of the human resources that African

> NGOs can offer to authenticate and enrich their educational and advocacy work in their own constituencies. Through south-to-north visits and consultative arrangements, African NGO personnel can add an important dimension to NGO policy planning, public information work and contact with official aid agencies.

In terms of sectoral programming and information work, there is a recognized need for Northern NGOs to focus a greater proportion of their efforts on the environmental aspects of sustainable development,[16] as well as on the advancement of women and the relatively neglected problems of rapid urbanization. As African groups acquire a greater say in the allocation of total NGO resources in their own countries,it will be increasingly important for them to ensure that due weight is given to these and other concerns.

Conclusion

Non African NGOs have made a significant contribution to human well-being and development in Africa in the first generation of the continent's political independence. But the second generation, now under way, poses a new challenge. Among the most positive aspects of the role played by Northern NGOs has been their encouragement and support for the growth of indigenous non-governmental groups, now increasingly able and determined to take over the lead role in promoting their people's development. An intense debate is therefore now in progress to define the appropriate objectives, organizational structures and working methods for foreign NGOs in a supporting role – and, going beyond this, to find a solid base for partnership between NGOs of all regions, in order that they may pursue together the changes required for justice in a sustainable world.

The outcome of this debate will have a determining influence on both the form and the substance of the overseas NGOs' work in the future. It may result in their presence in Africa becoming less visible. If, however, their technical, organizational and communication skills can be brought to bear in support of Africa's own NGO movement, their contribution will be no less and perhaps more valuable than hitherto. The transfer of power to African NGOs is the first critical step. It is now incumbent on their Northern partners to see that before the process is much more advanced, arrangements are in place to secure them adequate resources and infrastructural support. If governments, particularly in the North, are now looking to the NGO sector for answers to the development puzzle which have eluded them, it is perhaps in this domain of new relationships, more than any other, that the NGOs may hope to contribute to a reorientation of development strategies in the 1990s.

Notes

1 René Dumont, *L'Afrique noire est mal partie*, Paris, 1962.

2 Robin Sharp, 'A Critical Guide to Renegotiation of the Lome Convention', Euro Action-Acord, Amsterdam, 1977.

3 Larry Minear, 'The Other Missions of NGOs: Education and Advocacy', paper presented to the WD/ODI Seminar, London, March 1987.

4 Inter-Action, Diversity in Development: Unites States Voluntary Assistance to Africa, New York 1985

5 Tade Akin Aine, 'Africa's Current Crisis and the Urban Condition', background paper for the Only-One-Earth Forum, New York, May 1987.

[6] EEC/NGO Liaison Committee, Information Note, November 1986.

[7] See Robert Chambers, 'Thinking about NGO Priorities', background paper for an Oxfam workshop on Arid Lands Management, Cotonou, Benin, March 1987.

[8] Report on the African Emergency Relief Operation 1984–1986, with particular reference to the contribution of non-governmental organizations: Report to OEOA by the International Institute for Environment and Development, London, 1986.

[9] Declaration of the International Seminar of NGOs: Their Role in Shelter, services and Community Development, Limuru, Kenya, April 1987.

[10] Jan Pronk, Speech to a United Nations NGO workshop, Geneva, December 1982, quoted in Doug Hellinger's 'NGOs and the Large Aid Donors: Changing the Terms of Engagement', WD/ODI Seminar, London, 1987.

[11] UN-NGLS, "NGOs and Africa: A strategy Workshop", Final Report, Geneva, 1986.

[12] Declaration of Non-Governmental Organizations on the African Economic and Social Crisis, New York, May 1986.

[13] Development Assistance Committee, Development Co-operation: 1986 Report, OECD, Paris, 1986.

[14] Inter-Action, op. cit.

[15] *Our Common Future, report of the World Commission on Environment and Development,* Oxford University Press, 1987.

[16] See NGLS, op. cit., p.98.

References

1 Harrison, Paul, *The Greening of Africa: Breaking Through in the Battle for Land and Food,* International Institute for environment and Development – Earthscan, Paladin Books, London, 1987.

2 International Council of Voluntary Agencies, "Development in an age of economic and social crisis: the challenge to voluntary agencies", Report of the ICVA General Conference, Dakar, May 1987.

3 Reij Chris, with Adrian Cullis and Yacob Aklilu, "Soil and water conservation in sub-Saharan Africa: The need for a bottom-up approach", Oxfam-UK, 1987.

4 Miller, Harold, "Networking African food issues", Mennonite Central Committee, Nairobi, 1986 (mimeo).

5 Padron, Mario: "NGDOs and grassroots development: Limits and possibilities", final report of a workshop of third world NGDOs, Lima, 1982.

6 UNICEF, *Within Human Reach – a Future for Africa's Children,* New York, 1985.

7 Gill, Peter, *Drops in the Ocean: the work of Oxfam 1960–1970,* Macdonald, London, 1970.

8 Arnaud, Gabriel, "Forces et faiblesses des ONG", *Politique Aujourd'hui,* mars-avril, 1985.

9 Hardoy, Jorge and David Satterthwaite, "Some thought on the present and potential role of NGOs in shelter, services and community development", background paper for the International Seminar of NGOs, Limuru, Kenya, April 1987.

10 Mahaniah, Kimpianga, "Promotion of self-reliance programmes among churches, Christian councils and peoples' movement structures in Africa", World Council of Churches, Geneva, 1986 (mimeo).

11 *The Nairobi Forward-Looking Strategies for the Advancement of Women,* World Conference on the United Nations Decade for Women, United Nations, Nairobi, 1985.

12 *Africa Emergency Aid,* Final report of the activities of Canadian NGOs responding to the famine, CCIC, Ottawa, 1986.

13 *What Americans Think: Views on development and US-Third World Relations,* InterAction/Overseas Development Council, Washington, 1987.

Short-, Medium-, and Long-Term Support for the Human Dimension: The Role of the Private Sector

OLADAPO FAFOWORA

Introduction

It has become increasingly apparent in recent years that new economic strategies will have to be adopted in Africa, if the human dimension of Africa's economic crisis is to be fully addressed. To eliminate the mass poverty which now prevails in Africa, major internal economic reforms, which make man the centre of economic planning will have to be undertaken swiftly. Such reforms will have to be comprehensive, involving both the public and private sectors of the economy. This chapter will attempt to focus on what the private sector can contribute to such a recovery.

The Growth and Performance of the Private Sector in African Economies

The private sector has, in general, not contributed significantly to the growth and performance of African economies. There are historical reasons for this. In the first place, even before independence, all the colonial governments ascribed very little importance to the private sector. The logic of colonialism was that the state, the metropolitan power, assumed a dominant role in the economy of the colony, concentrating mainly on the provision of such basic infrastructure as facilitated the exercise of colonial power.

Second, having just emerged from two World Wars which devastated their economies, the major European colonial powers had little or no financial resources left to transfer to the colonies, from which, in fact, substantial resources had been transferred to the metropolitan powers in support of their war efforts. For most of the period 1914–1945, very little attention was paid to the economic development of the colonies, beyond the provision of meagre and totally inadequate social services. Rather, the objective was to make the colonies "pay" their way by ensuring and improving upon the collection of taxes for the maintenance of the colonial administration.

The third historical reason is the almost total absence of the conditions necessary for the development of a private sector that could make any significant contribution to the economic development of the colonies including very poor infrastructural facilities, lack of adequate trained technical and managerial manpower, as well as the poor market prospects in the colonies.

There were, of course, the great trading companies such as UAC, mostly in the then British West Africa, the CFAO, in French West Africa, and Union Miniere in the then Belgian Congo. But these were really trading companies, their activities being confined largely to the export of such agricultural commodities as cocoa, palm oil, cotton, and groundnuts, as well as the exploitation of mineral resources in the colonial territories. They were also responsible for the importation of manufactured goods into the colonies, a trade in which they enjoyed virtual monopolies.

At independence, many of the African countries had little or no industries, beyond light consumer industries in food and beverages, most of which were totally owned and managed by the trading companies. There were no social responsibilities imposed on these trading companies, the state fully accepting responsibility for the provision of basic amenities such as roads, energy, communications, and water. The service industries such as the banks and the insurance companies were also almost wholly-owned in virtually all the new African States by interests based in the metropolitan countries.

In East Africa, a new dimension was added to the situation with the large scale immigration of Asians with the active encouragement of the British colonial power. This was to lead later to problems of ownership of certain business in the private sector which were dominated completely by the Asians, to the almost total exclusion of the Africans. In West Africa too, the Lebanese and Syrians played a similar role in the economic life of the West African States, by taking the lead first in commerce, and then later on, in light manufacturing, mainly in beverages, and other agro-allied industries.

Significantly, those early adventures into manufacturing were based on the use of available raw materials, with only concentrates and some basic chemicals being imported. The consumption of foreign exchange reserves through imports was insignificant; it was well within the financial resources of the colonies. Later on, as industry expanded fairly rapidly, particularly after independence in the 1960s, the utilization of local raw materials which favoured a self sustaining growth in industry, was abandoned in favour of the importation of raw materials, as well as other capital goods. This new element has turned out to be a tragic and costly mistake in the industrial strategy which virtually all the African states adopted in their drive towards industrialization. It created a situation of dependency on the advanced industrial countries for the supply of industrial raw materials, as well as capital goods. This trend was further accentuated with the entry of the state, into the industrial sector through public sector programmes which aimed at rapid industrialization.

The New Industrial Strategy

The new industrial strategy involved the policy of import-substitution. This policy aimed at replacing foreign imports with local manufactures. Initially, the policy, which underlined the thrust of industrial expansion in virtually all the African States, focused attention mainly on light consumer and industrial goods in beverages, textiles, vegetable oils, and tobacco, where the new states had abundant local sources of supply. Partly because of the small size of the private sector, but also as an indication of the commitment of the African states to the objective of rapid industrial expansion, the new African governments began to commit large state resources to the whole programme and process of industrialization. The logic was simple enough. Political independence had to be balanced with economic independence. Essentially, this meant reducing and finally eliminating the dependence of the new states on foreign imports. Little or no thought was given to the export of local manufactures. It was sufficient to meet the local demand for consumer goods.

There were fatal flaws in this new industrial policy which had very serious economic and social implications for the African peasant. The policy was itself based on certain assumptions which proved to be misleading, and these assumptions were, in fact, shared by many foreign economic advisers, who had helped in providing the intellectual prop for the new industrial policy. Starting from the end of the Korean War and well into the 1960s, the new States enjoyed a boom in the price of cash crops and other export commodities such as solid minerals, which enabled them to have balance of payments viability. The terms of trade moved significantly in their favour, thus allowing them to have a balance of payments surplus and a healthy foreign exchange reserve position. It was assumed that this trend would continue, but this was not to be the case. By the 1970s and more significantly in the 1980's the terms of trade moved rapidly against all developing countries. The African economies were particularly vulnerable to this new trend to which the distinguished Argentine economist Raul Prebisch, had first drawn international attention. As a result of this deterioration in their terms of trade which, on the average, had declined by 20% by 1980, all the new states moved into balance of payments disequilibrium. In order to sustain their import-substituting industries, many of them, including the oil-exporting countries, resorted to heavy borrowing abroad – the origin of the African debt problem.

Another development, at the international level, which was not foreseen and which undermined the strategy of import-substitution and the international competitiveness of the new African industries, was the rapidity in changes in technology and new products. Starting from a low technological basis, and lacking in technical manpower, the African economies were not able to keep pace with these changes. This reinforced their dependence on imported technology, with serious adverse implications for their balance of payments viability. In addition, the new industrial strategy was essentially capital rather than labour intensive, thus failing to take advantage of the huge human resources available. As the few jobs created in industry were available mainly in the cities, there was a marked increase in rural-urban migration. Farms were abandoned and the agricultural sector which had been the main stay of the economy was neglected in favour of the expansion of the industrial sector. In 1960, 82% of the labour force in sub-Saharan Africa was engaged in agriculture, but by 1980, this had declined to about 70%. This development was not balanced by a substantial increase in employment in the industrial sector which only increased from 7% in 1960 to 12% in 1980. Similarly, an examination of the distribution of gross domestic product, shows a steady decline in the contribution of agriculture to the GDP. In 1960, agriculture represented on the average 47% of the GDP but by 1982, this had declined to 30%. Again the contribution of manufacturing to the GDP did not increase significantly to compensate for the decline in agriculture. It merely rose from 7% in 1960 to about 9% by 1985.

The structural imbalances inherent in African economies have been fully reflected in its negative impact on the human dimension in the continent, with regard to the provision of employment, education, training, health and other socio-economic factors.

Nature and Impact of the Crisis

Virtually all African countries are now faced with a severe economic crisis. At the domestic level, the agricultural sector, which had been stagnant for two decades through neglect and wrong economic policies, has only just begun to recover. Recovery is taking place in only a few cases, with the vast majority of African countries still unable to reverse the decline in their agricultural sector.

In the prevailing circumstances, African farmers, were left with only two options; to accommodate themselves to a life of penury, or to move into the cities – the origin and cause of the rural-urban migration, now the scourge of most African cities with thousands of urban unemployed cutting across all levels of education. The unemployed university graduate has become a new phenomenon and a major crisis with which virtually all African governments have to contend, with all its social implications of disrupted families, increased urban crime rate, and mass social discontent.

The private sector has not in general, invested much in the agricultural sector, partly for historical but also for economic reasons. With a few exceptions such as in Zaire, Burundi, and Rwanda, (all former Belgian colonies) foreign private investment in the agricultural sector was generally discouraged by the colonial powers. In the case of the British colonial administration, the concept of the mandated territory in which land was held in trust for the "natives" virtually ruled out foreign direct private investment in the agricultural sector. Land was vested in the state which would not allow alienation of land for large-scale private sector farming.

The metropolitan trading houses also did not consider investment in farming profitable in view of its long-gestation character and capital intensity. In the wake of the global economic boom after the Korean war, there existed considerable possibility for private sector investment in the agricultural sector. But the development of farm subsidies in Europe, North America, and Japan made the proposition no longer attractive as it closed these important markets to all but a few cash crops such as cocoa, peanuts, and cotton.

The Private Sector

Most African countries were led to believe, by the prevailing literature on economic development, that rapid development was possible only through industrialization and that the labour force expelled from the agricultural sector could be easily absorbed by the industrial sector. They therefore committed vast public expenditures to programmes of rapid industrialization with the establishment of public sector industrial enterprises. Exchange rate distortions through overvalued local currencies encouraged private sector investments in industrial enterprises too, which African States sought to promote through policies of industrial protection. It is estimated that the net effective protection for modern industries in Africa was over 50%. Other forms of subsidies were also provided to encourage industrialization. But inspite of this massive effort, the results were dismal. In most cases, the contribution of industry to the GDP is less than 10 per cent. Local value added also averages less than 15%. In terms of job-creation, African industries usually capital intensive, have proved to be an unmitigated disaster.

Import-Substitution Strategy

Many African States sought to industrialize through the strategy of import substitution. Basically, this strategy involved the replacement of imported manufactures by local products. But since they lacked the technology, the managerial skills, and capital needed they had to rely on foreign sources for these requirements, a condition which further reinforced their dependence on the industrial countries of Europe, Japan and North America. Today, it is clear that the strategy of import substitution has failed. It has contributed very little to the overall economic development of African States. The few facilities established are long on costs and short on competitiveness and profitability. They can neither satisfy domestic demand for consumer goods nor export. There is both excess installed capacity and a massive underutilization of existing capacity, since they are not able to pay for vital imported raw materials. Heavy foreign exchange burdens have been imposed on these States. At the same time, the rural economy has gone into sharp decline with resources being shifted away from it for an urban-led growth which has not materialized.

In the public sector, costly mistakes were also made by African States in their effort to develop upstream heavy manufacturing industries with high capital intensity, and excess capacity e.g. the steel mills. Heavy industries – the "commanding heights" or so-called strategic sectors of the economy – had a particularly strong hold on the imagination of African politicians and planners. Its development supposedly – symbolized the arrival of a fully developed and self-reliant economy. But in practice such heavy industries drew disproportionately on national savings to create minimal output over a relatively long period and usually at a very high cost. If the prices are subsidized which they normally are, such industries become a permanent drain on public funds. If they are not the high cost is off-loaded on downstream manufacturing, thus increasing their costs. Without competition from imports such industries become technically obsolete.

At the external level, the strategy of import substitution was also subjected to certain constraints. Developments in new technologies in the advanced industrial countries, with an almost limitless capacity to bring new products into the world market, made nonsense of the assumption implicit in the strategy of import substitution that economic growth and industrial development in both the industrial and developing economies were symmetrical. But the growth of monopoly capital had made the industries of the underdeveloped economies increasingly marginal.

The Impact of the Crisis and the Structural Adjustment Programme

Starting roughly from 1980, the economic condition and predicament of the African states and the effect of this condition on the people of Africa has been devastating. The most critical of the economic problems facing the African state is the massive foreign debt crisis.

Under pressure from their international creditors, African states were faced with a twin problem; first, finding the funds to settle their foreign debt and second, finding the foreign exchange to pay for the imports vital for the survival of their industries which were largely import oriented. The efforts of the African states to tackle this problem on a global level were firmly and successfully resisted at the UN by the advanced industrial countries.

Existing international arrangements for coping with this new phenomenon of the massive foreign debt were hardly satisfactory. The IMF loan facility was too little, came too late and its conditionalities were considered generally harsh and inappropriate. Nevertheless, under pressure from their international creditors, many African states accepted the need for adopting a structural adjustment programme.

The cumulative effect of these measures, particularly on the private sector, has been devasting, resulting in massive under capacity utilization, closures, and mass retrenchments. In the case of Nigeria, capacity utilization dropped from an average of 70 per cent to below 30%. About 30 per cent of all manufacturing industries in Nigeria were forced to close with well over 3 million industrial workers losing their jobs. Initially, Nigeria adopted a policy of administrative controls. The way in which this administration of controls was exercised deprived many of the genuine industrial establishments of access to foreign exchange for the importation of vital inputs. Later, when the naira was massively devalued by over 400 per cent, the start up and operational cost of manufacturing increased sharply. When prices were then increased, a sharp decline in sales resulted through domestic consumer resistance.

Quite rightly, African governments tried to ease the pressure on their meager foreign exchange resources by insisting on the utilization of local raw materials. Here again, there were problems as industrial raw materials such as steel and petro chemicals, usually in public sector projects, were either underdeveloped or simply not available. The result was a further depression in the industrial sector with further closures and retrenchments.

The human dimension of the crisis extends beyond the loss of jobs. The curb in public expenditure led to the deterioration and in some cases collapse of such public institutions as energy, transportation, education, and health. In virtually all cases, fees were introduced in health and education. Since many families could not afford the fees, many children were deprived of considerable advance. Family income levels in real terms dropped to the level in 1970. The cumulative effect of all this was to reinforce the instability of the African states with a rash of coups and civil wars.

Whatever merits structural adjustment programmes may have, they have proved to be a perfect prescription for political chaos and economic stagnation in Africa. There is a zero growth scenario at a time when the African population is rising rapidly, and increased resources are needed for rapid economic growth.

Even if the African states had no foreign debt problem to contend with they could only develop their economies rapidly through the sustained transfer of resources from the rich and advanced industrial countries. But with the sharp deterioration in the international economic environment, the limitless possibility for growth of the internal markets of Europe, Japan and North America, the internal conditions of economic and political instability in

Africa, it is, at present, extremely unlikely that such transfer of real financial resources to African states will take place. As a matter of fact, the trend now is for foreign investors in Africa to progressively divest themselves of their investment in Africa, a situation which leads to flight of capital and a further decline in the capability of the African states for further economic growth. This trend should be a cause for major international concern. But it is not, particularly with the relentless pressure on the advanced industrial countries to create their limitless consumer societies. In fact, the dictum of a global and interdependent economy is now being stood on its head with the great divide between the rich North and the poor South getting monstrously wider. The implications of this phenomenon for international peace and stability are usually conveniently ignored.

Recommendations

The basic problem of the African states is one of economic management which involves the adoption of a programme and strategy aimed primarily at restructuring the productive system of their economies for rapid growth. This strategy will place greater emphasis on supply side measures in contrast with measures or approaches that aim at the control of aggregate demand. While structural adjustment is obviously necessary in the economies of the African states, a strategy of adjustment with growth will permit equilibrium to be restored at a higher overall level of economic activity, particularly in the private sector. This strategy will minimize the conflicts between policy objectives of stabilization, growth and social welfare. A wide variety of problems is better tackled in the context of economic growth rather than deep and sustained recession. It is easier to re-align the productive sectors of the economy through growth than through recession.

The pursuit of the strategy of growth is only possible ultimately by involving the masses at both the urban and rural levels of the planning and execution of economic policies. This is not being done now. Planning in Africa remains essentially a bureaucratic affair, the masses not being involved at all. Huge public enterprises are planned without any thought about their relevance to the masses. In essence the "modern" sector of most African economies is not integrated with the rural mass of African peasants. The relationship is still vertical not lateral.

The choice which African States therefore face is between the continuation of present policies which have failed woefully or the adoption of an alternative strategy which would look more closely at the "informal" sector and use it as the main agency for economic growth. The informal sector will ultimately provide greater employment than the modern sector. Its use of foreign exchange for imports is insignificant. It is also important as the training ground for entrepreneurs and will, in future, play a key role in the economic growth of Africa. It deserves greater attention than it is getting now.

Appendix

THE KHARTOUM DECLARATION: TOWARDS A HUMAN-FOCUSED APPROACH TO SOCIO-ECONOMIC RECOVERY AND DEVELOPMENT IN AFRICA

Preamble

1. Under the auspices of the United Nations, an *International Conference on the Human Dimension of Africa's Economic Recovery and Development* took place in Khartoum, Sudan from 5 to 8 March 1988 as part of the follow-up to the implementation of the *United Nations Programme of Action for African Economic Recovery and Development 1986–1990 (UN-PAAERD) and Africa's Priority Programme for Economic Recovery 1986–1990* (APPER) and as a sequel to the International Conference on *Africa: The Challenge of Economic Recovery and Accelerated Development* held in Abuja, Nigeria in June 1987. The Conference brought together a gathering of about 200 policy and decision makers, government officials, professional and technical experts in the field of development and other related fields mostly from various African countries, as well as representatives of governmental and non-governmental organizations, agencies of the United Nations system, including the International Monetary Fund and the World Bank, bilateral and multilateral donor organizations and other resource personnel.

2. The Conference was organized with the whole-hearted support of the government and people of Sudan and participants enjoyed the warm hospitality of the Sudanese people. His Excellency Mr. Al Sadiq Al Mahdi, Prime Minister of the Republic of Sudan, addressed the opening of the Conference. The proceedings were conducted in seven plenary sessions and six working groups. The Conference made a deep and detailed analysis of the African situation, particularly the current economic crisis and all its ramifications on the people of Africa. The Conference is unanimous in its conviction that the crisis that confronts the African continent is one that affects the total human condition of the continent and its people, men and women alike. It is a crisis that challenges the very survival of the African people. It is a crisis of Africa's environment as the desert rapidly overcomes the fertility of the land and the coastlines also recede. It is a crisis of the continent's natural resources exploited more for the benefit of external interests than to meet Africa's dire needs. It is a crisis of the rich cultures of the African people and the cohesion of families broken up by the desperate circumstances of the African people and, *in extremis*, to reduce them to the helpless gaze depicted in the starving faces of Africa's children in the international media. But it is a crisis that can and must be overcome through the concerted and determined action of the African people and their societies and States, as they develop a clearer

understanding of the implications of the current predicament and fashion a decisive and coherent plan of action, with the assistance and understanding of the international community.

3. We are encouraged in this view by the fact that although Africa has been sorely squeezed by the pressures of recent years and million of Africans have suffered severely, no objective observer can fail to be impressed by the vitality and human creativity which strive and flourish in spite of everything. The large cutbacks and constraints of government and urban production have stimulated communities to devise their own solutions to the problem of meeting their own basic human needs. Self-help groups abound in every country; the extended family, though strained, has often provided the means of survival of many of its members; examples of community action can be found in almost every village. It is important to recognize the enormous potential of the human energy and creativity and find ways to harness it rather than ignore it in the total process of national recovery and development. For these and other reasons we repeat that Africa's crisis, though dire, CAN AND MUST BE OVERCOME.

4. As participants in this event, the overwhelming majority of whom come from the African continent, we are moved to place on record our collective voice on the issues we discussed and we accordingly make this KHARTOUM DECLARATION.

A. Overall Assessment of the Human Condition in Africa

5. Since the human being is the centre of all development, the human condition is the only final measure of development. Improving that condition is essential for the poor and vulnerable human beings who comprise the majority of our peoples in Africa. Africa's men and women are the main factors and the ends for whom and by whom any programme and implementation of development must be justified.

6. Regrettably, over the past decade the human condition of most Africans has deteriorated calamitously. Real incomes of almost all households and families declined sharply. Malnutrition has risen massively, food production has fallen relative to population, the quality and quantity of health and education services have deteriorated. Famine and war have made tens of millions of human beings refugees and displaced persons. In many cases, the slow decline of infant mortality and of death from preventable, epidemic diseases has been reversed. Meanwhile the unemployment and underemployment situation has worsened markedly.

7. Acts of destabilization and aggression, being perpetrated against the countries of Southern Africa by the South Africa regime, have also imposed massive human and economic costs, greatly in excess of military budgets or battle casualties. Of the approximately one million human beings dead in southern Africa as a result of South African aggression over 1980–86 about one hundred thousand were war-dead, narrowly defined. Of the approximately thirty billion dollars in lost production, most relates to the creation of chaos and the loss of peasants' crops and national production.

8. Production and other economic aspects of development – especially distribution – are of crucial importance. Production by the poor is vital if they are to become more able to meet at least their basic needs. But it is just as important who produces what. Production of food, of basic consumer goods, of agricultural inputs and construction materials, of basic services such as health, education, and pure water, as well as of exports are central to improving the human condition. Unsustainable imbalances do matter.

9. Nutrition imbalances are as crucial as trade imbalances. High infant mortality requires just as immediate and as serious an attention as high rates of inflation or huge budget deficits. Ultimately the trade, inflation and budget imbalances are serious obstacles to development because they are barriers to enabling the poor to produce more; to the vulnerable to surviving and rehabilitating themselves; and to the state and the society achieving universal access to basic services.

10. Therefore, a basic test for all stabilization, adjustment and development programmes is whether they will improve the human condition from their inception or, on the contrary, worsen it. Social services and human resources development programmes have high short-, medium- and long-term pay-offs on economic as well as on broader development criteria.

11. They are relevant to the reversal of unsustainable imbalances since survival and rehabilitation assistance to the most vulnerable groups – international refugees and displaced persons, disabled persons, youth, women and children – is an important element in reversing production losses. Similarly, the engagement of Africa's most basic resource – its approximately 250 million economically active people – in production, is essential to restoring growth as well as development.

12. The human-centred strategy to the implementing of the Lagos Plan of Action, APPER and UN-PAAERD is vital for reaching out to the aspirations and needs of Africa's people and especially their poor and vulnerable majorities. It is deliverable through the appropriate mobilization, allocation and use of resources. To bring this about it will be essential to restore the strained and torn fabrics of our societies, make popular participation in decision-making processes effective, ensure the preservation of basic human rights and fundamental freedoms and eliminate policies that discriminate against minorities and vulnerable groups.

13. Progress in advancing the human condition in Africa depends on the structure, pattern and political context of socio-economic development. The problems and weakness in these areas must therefore be recognized and attempts must be made to tackle them in order to achieve the objectives of social and human development. This is also necessary because the economic crisis which Africa faced from the late 1970s found fertile ground in the structural and political weaknesses that bred the germs that hastened the intolerable deterioration in the human condition.

14. A fundamental problem is the fast rate of population growth and the uneven and uneconomic distribution of the population in the different age groups. The youthful population makes high demands on educational, medical and other social services while the large number of college graduates and school leavers that enter the labour market each year creates an

imbalance between labour supply and demand.

15. A further structural factor is the urban bias and socially unequal distribution of critical factors and resources for human development such as employment, income, food and nutrition and health and education. As is well known, this distribution is biased against the majority of the population living mainly in the rural areas and in favour of the politically vocal minority in the urban enclaves. Economic issues have overshadowed social concerns and have prevented African countries from according the needed centrality to the human dimension and the human factor.

16. Finally, the political context for promoting healthy human development has been marred, for more than two decades, by instability, war, intolerance, restrictions on the freedom and human rights of individuals and groups as well as overcentralization of power with attendant restrictions on popular participation in decision-making. In such a context, the motivation of many Africans to achieve their best in productivity and the enhancement of their own and society's well-being has been severely constrained. In times of economic crisis, the politically stronger social groups and individuals survive while the weaker ones go under in increasing deprivation, social dislocation, hunger, ill-health or death.

B. The Human Dimension of Structural Adjustment Programmes

17. From the causes mentioned so far flow the consequences of wretched misery, marginalization and – for millions – very literally, premature death. The severity of the African crisis is such that country after country has been putting in place structural adjustment programmes in their effort to halt their economic degradation and achieve a turn-around. Unfortunately, far too many of these programmes – whether nationally conveived or in collaboration with the World Bank, the International Monetary Fund and the donor community – are rending the fabric of the African society. Rather than improve the human condition, some structural adjustment programmes have aggravated it, because they are incomplete, mechanistic and of too short a time perspective.

18. Structural Adjustment Programmes (SAPs) are *incomplete* because they are often implemented as if fiscal, trade and price balances are ends in themselves and are virtually complete sets of means to production increases. Human condition imbalances as related to employment, incomes, nutrition, health and education do not receive equal priority in attention to macro-economic imbalances. Unless and until they make the elimination of these human condition imbalances central targets, stabilization and adjustment programmes cannot provide Africa's growth and development dynamic.

19. They are too *mechanistic* in being inadequately grounded in, or sensitive to specific national economic, human and cultural realities. This is aggravated by an incomplete articulation which allows the gaps between macro models and contextual realities to remain largely unobserved. Nor can we evaluate how rapidly production can be expanded; where, by whom and of what. Thus their human condition impact remains inadequately projected instead of

being at the centre of target setting, policy formulation and programme or project choice.

20. They are in *too short* a time perspective. Africa cannot wait for the attainment of external equilibrium and fiscal balance before seeking to improve the human condition, nor can long-term human investment to strengthen the institutional, scientific, technical and productive capacity operating in environmental balance be postponed. That is essential to attaining the more stable and less vulnerable economic position that we aspire to for the African continent.

21. Further, we must place squarely on record that the external context confronting Africa continues to deteriorate. The terms of trade losses of 1986 vastly exceeded net resource transfers to Africa. APPER is not receiving either the new concessional transfer support or the debt burden relief it projects as essential, or which UN-PAAERD committed the international community to providing. This is not simply an African view – the World Bank has repeatedly said the same thing as has the UN Secretary-General's Advisory Group on Financial Flows for Africa, a majority of whom are practicing bankers.

22. We welcome the increased concern for the human dimension in stabilization and adjustment programmes, broadly expressed within the international community. But this is far from being enough. The gap between the expression of concern and actual programme implementation remains wide. Human dimension elements are additions, often long after programme initiation, rather than integral parts of their overall design. Those poor and vulnerable groups to be served are often narrowed down to those who are the victims of the stabilization programme, rather than addressing the human condition of all the absolutely poor and vulnerable people.

23. In the light of all of the foregoing, we do not hesitate to reiterate the central position that the human dimension should be accorded in the stabilization and structural adjustment programmes, for we are convinced beyond doubt that no nation can be great and prosperous if the majority of its people are poor, malnourished, illiterate, miserable and perpetually vulnerable.

24. Overall, we identify five distinct areas on which greater awareness and action must be focused by the African governments, the international financial institutions and the international community at large. Firstly, all structural adjustment programmes in Africa must be designed, implemented and monitored as part of the long-term framework of Africa's development. These programmes must, therefore, be incontrovertibly compatible with the objectives and aspirations of the African people as outlined in the Lagos Plan of Action and the Final Act of Lagos. Secondly, the human dimension must be the fulcrum of the adjustment programmes. Thirdly, the structural adjustment policies must incorporate the relevant adjustments of the social sector. Fourthly, consideration must be made of the consequences of macro-policies on the poor and vulnerable, not only so as to design temporary and independent compensatory additional programmes, but to make the alleviation of absolute and relative poverty and the elimination of gender biases integral parts and factors of the adjustment programmes. Lastly, the entire process of monitoring the stabilization and structural adjustment pro-

grammes must incorporate the social aspects and criteria.

25. We regard it as the primary responsibility of African Governments to develop a richer articulation of the total macro-framework within which to reorientate these programmes.

26. Structural adjustment programmes must be made to complement the efforts of African Governments to attain their long-term development objectives. Consequently, they should, through their effects on the economy and the African social fabric, contribute to the preservation of basic human rights and fundamental freedoms and help to eliminate policies that discriminate against minority and vulnerable groups. Above all, the application of structural adjustment measures should restore, not corrode the dignity of the African as a human being.

27. It is with these concerns in mind that we set forth in the pages that follow our conclusions and detailed recommendations.

C. Recommendations

28. In the light of the foregoing analysis, the following conclusions and recommendations are proposed for the most careful consideration of African countries and the international community. It is our earnest hope that these recommendations will be taken into account when the mid-term review of UNPAAERD is undertaken by the General Assembly of the United Nations at its 43rd session in 1988. Even before that, we hope that individual governments, international agencies and non-governmental organizations will take them fully into account and implement these recommendations in whatever way they may find appropriate, given their respective mandates.

I. Incorporating the Human Factor in the Recovery and Structural Process

29. Since structural adjustment is intended to improve prospects for longer-term development, the design and context of structural adjustment programmes should incorporate the goals and objectives of long-term development. As the improvement of human condition and welfare is the ultimate objective of development, structural adjustment programmes need to incorporate the human factor into their design and implementation. Towards the achievement of this goal, we call for the following actions at the national, sub-regional, regional and international levels.

Action at the National Level

(i) There is an urgent need to restore the centrality in Africa of long-term development goals and action.

(ii) To this end, there is a need for African countries to design their structural adjustment programmes as part and parcel of their long-term development goals. These indigenous programmes should serve as the basis for discussion with the donor community, multilateral as well as bilateral.

(iii) In this process, the human dimension needs to be brought out both in the definition of the long-term goals and in the priorities and components of the structural adjustment process.

(iv) Each African Government should translate its pronouncements – regarding the centrality of the social sectors in the process of economic recovery and development, as expressed in APPER and UN-PAAERD – into concrete action. In particular, a special appeal is to be made to the governments to speedily carry out their pledge to commit 20–25% of their annual budgets to the agricultural sector.

(v) In designing adjustment programmes, a careful analysis should be made of what categories of the population are most severely affected during the adjustment period, of the magnitude of their needs and of the ways and means that these needs, especially of the poor, can be met during the process of adjustment and beyond.

(vi) In making the protection of the poor an integral part of adjustment, the primary strategy should be that of enhancing their productive capacity through better access to productive resources and assets.

(vii) In the design of adjustment and development programmes, explicit attention must be paid to gender issues so as to accelerate the integration of women in the whole development process. With the clear awareness of women's major contribution to development, there is a new opportunity for making major progress in this direction.

(viii) Special attention should be paid to the vulnerable groups, particularly children, the aged, the disabled and refugees and displaced persons. The design of adjustment programmes should incorporate aspects of support of the retrenched employees to enable them to become viable entrepreneurs. Such support should include provision of loans and extension and advisory services.

(ix) In making policy decisions on the question of subsidies, a thorough analysis of the impact of such decisions on the most affected groups should be made and, if possible, alternative approaches should be found, especially as regards the poor and vulnerable.

(x) Food security and its indispensable adjunct of food self-sufficiency should be treated with the utmost priority in the design of adjustment, recovery and development policies.

(xi) There should be greater openness in the process of designing the adjustment package, both within government and beyond. In particular, employers, trade unions and other relevant groups should be closely associated with the process both to improve the design of the programmes and to ensure their fuller understanding and support.

Action at the Regional and Sub-Regional Levels

(i) National actions will be greatly helped or hindered to the extent that regional and sub-regional environments are conducive. To this end, African countries need to take more positive steps toward peace, stability, human rights and African solidarity.

(ii) Sub-regional and regional data banks, such as PADIS, should strengthen their programmes in order to generate and disseminate current information and data on the social and human conditions in Africa, in order *inter alia* to facilitate the monitoring and implementation of Structural Adjustment Programmes.

(iii) Exchange of experience and in-depth studies should be undertaken by African countries and institutions as well as international organizations about structural adjustment options that would, *inter alia*, take fully into account:
- the human dimension.
- compatibility with long-term development.
- full participation of the people in the design and implementing of the alternative.

(iv) Sub-regional and regional institutions should take appropriate action to strengthen and improve the capabilities and skills of African countries in their negotiations with their development partners, especially on issues related to structural adjustment.

(v) In the long-term, greater sub-regional and regional co-operation is needed to ensure the acceleration and sustainability of long-term African development. In this context, African governments should also try to harmonize the activities of their various institutions in the field of human resources development.

Action at the International Level

(i) Having due regard to the high social costs of structural adjustment programmes, the IMF and the World Bank should endeavour to ensure that adequate and comprehensive safeguards for the protection of vulnerable groups and the human dimension are built into such programmes from the beginning. In this connection, we welcome the recent undertaking by the Bank and IMF to this effect and we urge its rapid implemention.

(ii) International organizations should intensify their efforts in the development and use of appropriate indicators for closely monitoring the human and social dimensions of the adjustment process.

(iii) The world Bank and the UNDP, in their various roles as co-ordinators of Consultative Groups and Round Tables, should pay full attention to the human dimension of adjustment in the preparation and documentation for and the discussion at these Meetings.

II. Paying Special Attention to the Social Sector and the Vulnerable Groups

30. Africa's people are her most valuable asset. Their healthy social development is a *sine qua non* for achieving a productive and sustainable transformation in the continent. Yet, for far too long, the vast majority of the African people, especially women and youth, have been locked into poverty and vulnerability, along with the traditionally disadvantaged, the disabled, refugees and displaced persons. Where the most affected groups inhabit the neglected rural and peri-urban areas, their living conditions have often become intolerable in recent years as a result of the economic crisis and structural adjustment measures. The fundamental problem is that late, official

policies have paid only scant attention and have given very low priority to the social sector and the vulnerable groups in society.

31. Therefore, we strongly recommend the following urgent actions:

Action at the National Level

(i) Measures should be adopted to promote equitable patterns of development based on the democratization and decentralization of the decision-making process.

(ii) Even in times of severe resources constraints, such as experienced during periods of economic adjustment, attempts should be made to ensure acceptable minimum levels of, and access to food and social services, particularly for the vulnerable groups. Furthermore, food aid, being an important portion of ODA to Africa, must be used in direct support of food security, particularly to ensure access to food by the vulnerable groups in times of structural adjustment.

(iii) Investment priorities should be focused on the rural sector so as to raise rural employment, productivity and incomes and to reduce rural poverty.

(iv) Governments that have not already done so, should formulate and implement national population policies as stipulated by the 1984 Kilimanjaro Programme of Action.

(v) To arrest the current drought and desertification, resulting from long-continuing misuse of renewable natural resources and endangering mostly the vulnerable persons in the rural areas, sustainable development and long-term considerations, rather than immediate, quick benefits should be made the over-riding principle governing all development plans, programmes and projects. In each and every socio-economic development plan, programme and project, conservation of nature and natural resources and maintenance of ecosystems and environmental balances should be an in-built primary component.

(vi) Opportunities should be given to women for greater participation in the nation's political and decision making process at all levels, especially at the national centres of power. Where necessary, appropriate training should be given to them to ensure this.

(vii) Accelerated child development and survival strategies (for example, low-cost immunization and oral rehydration therapy) should be implemented so as to reduce the very high levels of infant and child mortality and morbidity.

(viii) Greater efforts should be made to provide the youth with productive employment opportunities and to integrate them more effectively in the development process.

(ix) Concerted efforts should be made to change prevailing attitudes towards the disabled so as to rehabilitate them and bring them into the mainstream of development.

Action at the Sub-regional and Regional Levels

(i) Sub-regional and regional development, research and training and financing institutions should give priority attention in their work programmes to the issues of African women, children, youth and vulnerable groups, particularly the aged, disabled, refugees and displaced persons.

(ii) Governments of each subregion should devise policies and plans for collectively dealing with the root causes of the problems of refugees and displaced persons. Where possible, arrangements should be made to facilitate the voluntary return of refugees to their home countries.

Action at the International Level

32. International organizations should intensify their efforts, in cooperation with African countries, in the development and use of appropriate indicators for closely monitoring and measuring progress in the improvement of conditions of human well-being. Instruments should also be developed to provide early warning on deteriorating human conditions.

III. Manpower Development and Utilization for the Long-Term

33. Africa's long-term development prospects depend on its human resources, and for African countries to achieve the goals of APPER, UN-PAAERD, and the Lagos Plan of Action significant strengthening of their capabilities to develop and adequately utilize their human resources is called for. These efforts should be aimed at reinforcing, expanding and making more relevant, the human resources base, avoiding wastage through under utilization of manpower, or loss through the brain drain, and raising productivity levels, particularly in agriculture, through various support policies and programmes and public sector interventions.

34. In the light of the foregoing observations, the following are recommended:

Action at the National Level

(i) Efforts should be intensified to expand primary and basic education, especially in the urban peripheries and in the rural areas;

(ii) Higher and technical education must, of urgent necessity, be significantly strengthened and reoriented so as to build within them those capabilities that would enable African countries to produce the required middle- and high-level manpower.

(iii) Governments should strive to seek greater relevance in education and training so that the outputs of education and training systems are more readily employable and can function better as job-creators rather than as job-seekers, particularly in the rural areas and the agricultural sector.

(iv) Greater emphasis should be placed on improvements in the teaching of science and technology in African countries, and more effective mechanisms should be evolved for the dissemination of the results of scientific and technological research for purposes of application and development.

(v) Governments should review education expenditure policies with a view to maximizing effectiveness in all areas of education.

35. In view of the seriousness of the unemployment and underemployment problems in African countries and the bleak prognosis for the future in this domain, it is strongly recommended that:

(i) Every development plan should have, as major expressed objectives, the generation of employment and incomes and the reduction of absolute poverty and income inequality among the people and to this end, effective monitoring and implementation mechanisms should be established to ensure the achievement of these objectives.
(ii) Investment priorities should be focused on the rural sector so as to raise rural employment, productivity and incomes and to reduce rural poverty.
(iii) Opportunities should be increased for women to have a greater access to education and training in order to increase their skill levels and enable them to raise their efficiency as a significant group in the African workforce.
(iv) Greater efforts should be made to provide youth with productive employment opportunities and to integrate them more effectively in the development process.
(v) Governments should provide a more congenial environment for the development of the informal sector which has a high potential for employment creation in African countries and is a rich and fertile ground for the development of indigenous entrepreneurship.

Action at the Sub-regional and Regional Levels

36. Governments of the various sub-regions and of the region as a whole are urged to strengthen their bonds of co-operation in the area of manpower development and utilization. Accordingly, they are urged to:

(i) Intensify their efforts to create, maintain and strengthen regional and sub-regional institutions with specialization in specific fields of learning and research for the common use of member States;
(ii) Develop joint research programmes among groups of countries at the sub-regional and regional levels to focus on common problems of development in fields such as science and technology, medicine, engineering, agriculture, management etc.;
(iii) Strive to expand employment markets within a sub-regional context by embarking upon joint employment generation investment programmes accompanied by an opening-up of sub-regional employment markets and the promotion of the free movement of people in order to reduce the unemployment problems facing African countries;
(iv) Enter into agreement among themselves within a sub-regional context to promote the exchange of experts and to make it easier for skilled manpower from countries within their sub-regions to find employment in other countries as a means of reducing the brain drain from Africa;
(v) Participate as fully as possible in ECA's Return of Skills Programme for Africa by exploiting this Programme for the identification and

recruitment of high-level manpower to fill vacancies in their public and private sectors, higher learning institutions as well as technical assistance posts within their countries.

IV. The Role of Regional, International and Non-Governmental Organizations

(a) Bilateral Donors

37. The Conference calls upon the industrialized countries, particularly OECD and CMEA, to report on the reforms and resource allocations they are making and will undertake in support of their commitments under UN-PAAERD.

(b) Role of Regional and Subregional Organizations

38. One cannot overstate the fact that international actions and support are vital to the success of the whole programme of African recovery and development. At the sub-regional and regional levels several actions are vital:

(i) African countries should rationalize the structure of their regional organizations and make better use of key organizations vital to the co-ordination of African development.

(ii) Regional organizations should accord the highest priority to the human dimension in the design and implementation of the recovery and development programmes of the continent, including the resolution of regional conflicts so that scare resources are further saved to protect the human dimension.

(iii) Co-operation at the regional and subregional levels should focus on collective self-reliance to protect the human dimension during the recovery period and beyond.

(iv) African governments are at a disadvantage in international negotiations with the International Monetary Fund and the World Bank. This disadvantage must be overcome. African governments should turn, for assistance, to regional organizations, like the ECA, ADB and OAU, which have the capacity to provide technical and political expertise. In particular, the comparative information provided by the ECA on the nature, details and constraints of structural adjustment programmes should be exploited to the maximum in order to improve the negotiating position of the African governments.

(c) The Role of International Organizations

39. International organizations can and should play a more positive role in Africa's recovery. The major preoccupation of the Conference is the fact that such organizations should be sensitive and more responsive to the realities of the African countries and societies since political, social, and cultural realities condition the dynamics of adjustment, recovery and development. Accordingly, it is proposed that:

(i) International organizations involved in Africa should undertake high priority actions aimed at supporting and enhancing the human dimension in the recovery and development programmes of Africa.

(ii) The Conference endorses the proposal of the UNDP for the establishment of an Inter-Agency Task Force for the assessment of Africa's human resources needs and the development of an appropriate UN System wide programme of Action in the field of human resources development. This task force could *inter alia* establish the modalities and mechanisms for improving coordination in the delivery of programmes in areas related to human resources, public sector resource management, use of resources for human resources development and for the creation of information systems and an integrated data base for human resources development and management. Regional monitoring and information exchange will be conducted by ECA. To this end, the Task Force should in consultation with national governments, draw up a detailed Human Resources Development Plan for submission to, and approval by a Special ECA meeting of ministers.

(iii) The international financial institutions should make prompt and urgent efforts to catalyse the implementation of the recommendations of the Report of the Advisory Group on Financial Flows for Africa; and to bring the attention of the international community to the fact that additional resources and debt reductions are urgently required for Africa's adjustment efforts to succeed.

(iv) International agencies should strengthen their regional and national units by decentralizing power, responsibilities and resources to the regional offices. Increasingly, decision-making on resource allocation should be decentralized to the regional, sub-regional and field offices.

(v) International organizations ought to ensure that their priorities are in line with the aspirations of African countries. In this context, their priorities should be compatible with the stated objectives, priorities and strategies of APPER and UN-PAAERD and the Lagos Plan of Action.

(vi) United Nations organizations should make every effort to collaborate, and coordinate their programmes in order to conserve resources and avoid waste.

(d) The Role of Non-Governmental Organizations

40. There is increasing evidence that non-governmental organizations can make an effective contribution, at the grassroots level, to the process of recovery and development. The NGOs present a number of advantages which must be built upon and strengthened, especially in the context of improving the human condition in Africa. The proposals below are made with the conviction that, if they are adopted, there is a lot to be gained by Africa's poor and vulnerable during the recovery period and by the African people at large during the process of development:

(i) NGOs should always respect Africa's own priorities and sectoral choices as this is the most sure way of contributing to the overall national efforts.
(ii) NGOs based in donor countries should review their technical assistance with a view to using, as much as possible, national expertise and to the extent possible, transferring power to local NGOs.
(iii) African governments should give due recognition to African NGOs and create the legal and fiscal framework for their activities. NGOs should improve their policy analysis so as to incorporate longer-term perspectives and commitments.
(iv) NGOs should have an important role at the international level in monitoring the implementation of internal commitments and improving public awareness among their nationals, of the realities of the African countries and societies. African NGOs should be encouraged, as appropriate, to respond to the human and social needs of the poor, especially in rural areas where structural adjustment programmes have resulted in the reduction of social services.

D. Conclusion and Follow-Up

41. The DECLARATION, then, affirms and asserts that the human dimension is the *sine qua non* of economic recovery. We, the delegates here assembled, will not abide economic rationale, will not tolerate economic formulas, will not apply economic indices, will not legitimize economic policies which fail to assert the primacy of the human condition. That means, quite simply, that no structural adjustment programme or economic recovery programme should be formulated or can be implemented without having, at its heart, detailed social and human priorities. There can be no real structural adjustment or economic recovery in the absence of the human imperative.

42. And how is that imperative defined?

43. Fundamentally, it means that the vulnerable and the impoverished, the uprooted and the ravaged, women, children, youth, disabled, aged, the rural poor and the urban poor, every group and individual in society who is in some way disadvantaged, must be given paramount consideration in the socio-economic development process. That is a sacrosanct principle. And in the service of that principle, health, education, welfare and all related social sectors become indispensable components of every national policy, every national programme, every national plan, and every regional or sub-regional collaboration.

44. So should Africa conduct itself. But Africa cannot do it alone. The centre – piece of UN-PAAERD, 1986–1990 – of which this DECLARATION is an organic part of the follow-up enshrines a shared partnership between Africa and the rest of the international community.

45. The understanding is explicit: Africa acts and the international community commensurately responds through its own donor reforms and increased levels of assistance. Fidelity begets fidelity. It is a mutual pact. Both sides have binding obligations.

46. Alas, the international community has not yet fulfilled its part of the bargain. African economic recovery continues to be threatened on every front by catastrophic debt, collapsed commodity prices, stagnating concessional flows, and crippling terms of trade. Because the front-line of recovery is the human dimension, the human dimension is at greatest risk. If structural adjustment with a human face does not succeed, then the failure, in considerable measure, will be laid at the feet of the international community.

47. It is this sense of urgency which has animated this Conference and suffuses this DECLARATION. We are nearly two years from the UN Special Session. We are on the eve of the Secretary-General's Mid-Term Review. The UN Programme ends in 1990. We are in a desperate race with time. No one pretends that African economic recovery is a short-term proposition, but the prospects for the human dimension of recovery will be writ in the actions of the next two years.

48. It is therefore our collective recommendation that this DECLARATION be endorsed by the Third ECA Conference of African Ministers Responsible for Human Resources Planning, Development and Utilization, which follows immediately. It is then our hope that the Ministers will transmit this DECLARATION to the 3Oth Anniversary Session of the ECA Conference of Ministers scheduled for Niamey, Niger in mid-April of 1988. If, then, as we would wish, the DECLARATION is again embraced, it can be transmitted directly to the General Assembly of the United Nations to be considered by the whole international community of sovereign States, in the highest of forums, as an integral part of the follow-up to the UN Programme.

49. When the Prime Minister of the Sudan opened this Conference to which this DECLARATION stands as an enduring testament, he called for the restoration of the dignity of the African person, for peaceful relations among peoples and States, and for the pursuit of fundamental human rights rooted in the consent of the governed.

50. In so speaking, he mirrors the principles of the United Nations Charter. This DECLARATION, with its total focus on the human dimension, is a challenge to Africa and to the world to turn yearning into reality.

Done at Khartoum,
The Republic of the Sudan,
8 March 1988